ALTERNATIVE DISPUTE RESOLUTION IN THE WORKPLACE

ALTERNATIVE DISPUTE RESOLUTION IN THE WORKPLACE

Concepts and Techniques for Human Resource Executives and Their Counsel

E. Patrick McDermott

with

Arthur Eliot Berkeley

QUORUM BOOKS
Westport, Connecticut • London

Library of Congress Cataloging-in-Publication Data

McDermott, E. Patrick.
Alternative dispute resolution in the workplace : concepts and techniques for human resource executives and their counsel / E. Patrick McDermott with Arthur Eliot Berkeley.
p. cm.
Includes bibliographical references and index.
ISBN 1-56720-055-9 (alk. paper)
1. Arbitration, Industrial—United States. 2. Mediation and conciliation, Industrial—United States. 3. Labor disputes—United States. I. Berkeley, Arthur Eliot. II. Title.
KF3424.M38 1996
344.73'018914—dc20 96-2211
[347.30418914]

British Library Cataloguing in Publication Data is available.

Library of Congress Catalog Card Number: 96-2211
ISBN: 1-56720-055-9

First published in 1996

Quorum Books, 88 Post Road West, Westport, CT 06881
An imprint of Greenwood Publishing Group, Inc.

Printed in the United States of America

The paper used in this book complies with the Permanent Paper Standard issued by the National Information Standards Organization (Z39.48-1984).

10 9 8 7 6 5 4 3 2 1

Copyright Acknowledgments

The authors and publisher gratefully acknowledge permission to reprint the following material.

The Travelers Group Employment Arbitration Policy and Dispute Resolution Procedure. With permission of the Travelers Group.

The Brown & Root Dispute Resolution Program, Dispute Resolution Plan, and Legal Consultation Plan. With permission of Brown & Root Corporation.

Frank and Edna Elkouri dedicated their pioneering book "How Arbitration Works" to "America's arbitrators who labor earnestly and ably."

The authors dedicate this book to those pioneers of alternative dispute resolution at the workplace, the many men and women who realize that no workplace dispute is unimportant and are creating new and inventive techniques to resolve conflict efficiently, quickly, and, most of all, equitably.

Conflict in itself is not a bad thing. What's important is the way in which we deal with conflict.

— Bishop Frey

Contents

Preface

Consider the Family and Medical Leave Act of 1993 that went into effect during the summer of 1993. While most businesspersons are sympathetic to an employee's need for time off to care for a sick family member, the new law presents many questions. Who is covered by this law? Does an employer have to give time off without pay to an employee who wishes to give care to an elderly uncle who raised the employee as a child; a person with whom the employee is living, but not married; or the child of the person the employee plans to marry?

Other thorny issues deal with the nature of covered illnesses and medical conditions, the job rights of an employee returning from leave, and whether an employee has provided appropriate notice to an employer as contemplated by the act.

To be sure, these and other questions will be definitively answered by decisions from the judiciary — but not with finality before the turn of the century. What are managers and employees to do until then? Answers are needed now, not years in the future.

The authors believe that the best way to resolve these and other workplace problems is through an equitable and accessible complaint resolution system. In most cases, this is the most viable alternative to litigation or administrative proceedings.

As we stress repeatedly, there is no one complaint resolution system perfect for all employment settings. However, we address the need in today's workplace to equitably resolve complaints outside of the courtroom. We discuss the changing legal and legislative landscape that has increased the need for and the acceptance of alternative dispute resolution systems in the workplace. We also examine the different methods and techniques of dispute resolution, identify what certain trailblazing organizations have done and are doing, and offer assistance in the development of a dispute resolution procedure, including an annotated listing of model clauses that may be included in a complaint resolution procedure.

MINOR SURGERY

There is an old definition of minor surgery: an operation someone else has. To an employee with a problem in the workplace, it is serious, indeed. To the organization, that employee's problem can quickly become an organizational problem.

Barbara Hoffman has written that in a sound relationship, fights do not end with a winner or a loser, but with solutions. Conversely, in a bad relationship, small problems escalate into larger and more serious ones, often ending with losers on both sides. This book examines ways of resolving workplace disputes quickly, efficiently, and, most of all, equitably. The authors believe that the best resolution of any problem is one the disputants fashion themselves. Further, if the parties can stay out of court, they save time, money, and energy, while avoiding the protracted uncertainty and increasing acrimony of a long and tortuous trial and appeal process. Unlike other disputes, an unresolved workplace confict becomes more bitter with each passing day because the parties are in conflict with each other on a daily basis. For employees who believe they were wrongfully denied a promotion, every day at work may contain episodes of frustration and anger, leading to lower morale and decreased organizational effectiveness. The newly promoted employee may feel insecure, knowing there continue to be active claimants for the job. For employees who believe they were wrongfully terminated, each day may bring increased economic uncertainty and emotional distress. For the organization, there is the residue of bad feelings that protracted litigation can only exacerbate and the organizational time and resources spent to defend the organization in a legal proceeding. There is also the possibility of a jury award for punitive damages that are in addition to a jury's damage award for pain and suffering and actual pecuniary losses, legal fees that must be paid regardless of the outcome, and the potential loss of customer goodwill from the public airing of an employment dispute.

When the authors set out to write this book over four years ago there was little discussion over how ADR and binding arbitration could be used as a win-win approach to resolve employment disputes inexpensively and fairly. As we labored over earlier drafts of this text and the correct way to present our vision of the benefits of ADR, each day brought new legal and corporate developments supporting our heartfelt belief that a corporate ADR program is preferable to litigation.

The most recent development in the trend toward use of ADR to resolve employment law disputes occurred as this book was going to print. On May 31, 1996, the American Arbitration Association introduced, effective June 1, 1996, its "National Rules for the Resolution of Employment Disputes." These arbitration and mediation rules, many similar to existing AAA dispute resolution procedures, are too recent to be included in the body of this text but should be considered when designing a corporate program. Although the clauses included herein address the same issues, we encourage readers to design an ADR model to fit their particular needs and to add these national rules to their library.

Acknowledgments

The authors express their appreciation to Alan Anderson for his administrative support and typing assistance during the first years of work on this text. The authors are also indebted to the law firm of Weinberg and Green for support services, Westlaw for donated legal research services, and friends at the American Arbitration Association and Capital Cities ABC, Inc., a subsidiary of The Walt Disney Company.

The authors also acknowledge the support and assistance that they have received from Dorothy A. Wade, vice president of Corporate Human Resources at Travelers Group and William Bedman, associate general counsel, Brown & Root. Dottie and Bill are two pioneers of the in-house dispute resolution movement and have provided vision and guidance to their organizations and taken the time to do the same for the authors. Their counsel and guidance have been invaluable.

A final thank you to Louie, Hillary, Rachel, and Renae for their love and support.

Introduction

There is a quiet and ongoing revolution in the workplace. This revolution involves the rise of legal disputes between employees protected under employment law and their employers. Several issues — the increasing diversity of the work force, new laws creating new workplace rights enforceable by litigation, the significant strengthening of existing discrimination laws by the Civil Rights Act of 1991, state employment laws and legal remedies, the rise of an employment discrimination plaintiff's bar, and the willingness of employees to sue their employer — have exposed almost all employers to an increasing volume of litigation related to workplace conduct or the human resource decisions made on an almost daily basis.

While many employment practices and human resource decisions are not challenged by even the most litigious employees, workplace-related litigation is exploding. This is evident from a cursory review of statistics on the filing of sexual harassment lawsuits — just one portion of the mosaic of employment law litigation. From 1991 to 1993, the Equal Employment Opportunity Commission (EEOC) experienced a near doubling of the number of charges filed alleging sexual harassment. From 1992 to 1993 awards from judges and juries in these cases increased 98 percent, to a record $25.2 million.[1]

This litigation is not expected to subside in the short run and may become a common occurrence in the future. Given the economic and other costs associated with employment litigation, today's employer is being challenged to find new ways to resolve workplace disputes short of courtroom litigation.

THE EMPLOYER'S PERSPECTIVE

The Cost of Employment Litigation

As employers participate in employment law litigation, they are recognizing that the defense costs of litigation are staggering, regardless of the merits of the lawsuit. Most employers must hire an attorney at hundreds of dollars per hour to defend them. In addition to these costs, which usually cannot be avoided if the lawsuit goes to trial, employers are losing some of these suits. A loss often results in back pay owed the plaintiff, compensatory damages awarded by a jury for pain and suffering, and sometimes even punitive damages, designed to punish the offending employer. Adding insult to injury, the losing employer also is required to pay the winning employee's attorney fees, which can be thousands of additional dollars. Even when the employer is vindicated, there is still a sizable legal bill.

Lawyers who defend employers have recognized that many of their clients are just beginning to feel the impact of this litigation explosion. Employers facing their first employment lawsuit often carry a personal, emotional perspective into the litigation. While initially seeking justice and vindication at all costs, the enormous expense of litigation can become overwhelming after only a few months. These employers recognize that there should be a better way to resolve these disputes which both saves money and time while protecting their legitimate rights to manage their organization and direct their work force.

It Can't Happen To Me

Some employers reading the above scenario may not believe that they will ever have such an experience because "We treat our employees fairly" or "My employees can come to me through my open door policy — they don't need a lawyer." Much of what is discussed appears to be another employer's problem, the result of bad management, or other management mistakes that "couldn't ever happen here." When these litigation issues do become their problem, these employers are often surprised and ill-equipped to deal with them. Attorneys representing management have observed that, due to the present array of employment-related laws, their clients can be divided into two categories: the burned and the yet-to-be-burned. The burned know that their commitment to enforcement of workplace laws and fair treatment of all employees does not guarantee that they will avoid costly employment law litigation, possibly resulting in an adverse finding by a jury. The yet-to-be-burned continue to chant "It can't happen to me, I'm too good to my employees" or similar mantras. Those who have suffered through employment litigation, regardless of the final outcome, know that there must be a better way to resolve such disputes when they do happen, before they end up in court.

TODAY'S EMPLOYMENT LITIGATION SCENARIO

The Employer's Experience

If the above discussion does not raise your concern, let us explore the typical scenario faced by an employer involved in employment litigation. This scenario assumes only that the plaintiff (the employee or ex-employee) refuses to accept a monetary settlement at an early stage of the litigation or presses ahead with a lawsuit that has no merit. We will use a claim of age, gender, or race discrimination as our example.

The employer first faces a charge filed with the EEOC or a related state agency alleging discrimination. This charge is investigated by an agency investigator who typically solicits an employer position statement, as well as other information relating to how other employees in the plaintiff's class are treated. Compliance with this initial information request alone is often burdensome for an employer without previous experience with this process, entailing much time and energy of managers and other employees. Thereafter, the EEOC investigator may visit the employer's worksite to review employer records and to interview witnesses. The investigator will make a written finding as to whether cause exists to believe that the law has been violated. Up to this point, the employer may have spent considerable time and money preparing its position statement and cooperating with the investigation.

Regardless of the determination of probable cause, the plaintiff may file a lawsuit in federal court seeking to litigate the alleged discriminatory conduct. This lawsuit is referred to as *de novo* litigation because the court considers the case to be new, not relying on the findings of the government agency. Thus, this is often the "second bite at the apple" for the employee. If such a lawsuit occurs, the employer — who may have handled the matter through the personnel department or other internal representative — must now hire a lawyer to represent the corporation in court.

After the lawsuit has been filed, witnesses are deposed, interrogatories are served by both parties, documents are requested, and other traditional litigation conduct ensues. This process, known as discovery, usually involves disagreements over who should be deposed and how, what documents are relevant, and many other issues that are hotly contested by the parties. Discovery can result in significant costs for legal research, briefs, hearings before a judge or magistrate, and other activities. The employer must review various records, make employees available for depositions, and otherwise support the company's counsel in preparing a defense. The cost of discovery to the employer is often thousands of dollars in legal fees, as well as the loss of the manager's valuable time and opportunity costs. At this point, no one has been to court yet and it is still not clear whether the employee even has a case.

At this juncture, the employer's lawyer is seeking to amass enough information to file a motion for summary judgment, asking the court to dismiss the lawsuit. In this motion, the employer asks to have the case dismissed or severely reduced, due to lack of evidence. Should the judge agree, the case is dismissed or certain allegations or damage claims are stripped from the suit. When an employer can get out of the lawsuit at this point, without having to participate in a trial, this is considered a major victory.

While the plaintiff can appeal a judge's decision on summary judgment, for the purposes of this hypothetical case, we will assume that no appeal occurs. Thus, even when the employer prevails on summary judgment, he has usually spent $50,000 or more in attorneys' fees, in addition to the organization's time and resources. Again, this is for a lawsuit where a judge has found that no law or fact exists upon which the employee could prevail.

What happens if the judge decides not to grant summary judgment? Where summary judgment is denied, the employer must prepare for a trial before a jury. In addition to the resources that have been spent in discovery and the attempt at summary judgment, the employer now must pay an attorney for the painstaking, costly, and time-consuming process of a jury trial. As a rule of thumb, it is possible to spend another $50,000 on attorneys' fees for preparation and participation at trial. For this reason alone, many defense attorneys recommend that once the employer has failed to prevail at summary judgment, the employer should seek to settle the case to avoid even more substantial legal costs — even where the employer has a better than even chance of prevailing at trial.

One last disconcerting fact from the vantage point of the employer: By surviving summary judgment, the plaintiff's attorney knows that the employer's cost of settlement has increased significantly. This is because the plaintiff's attorney will have a chance to tell the employee's story to a jury. As discussed above, juries are usually sympathetic to an employee's plight. Hopefully, the case can be settled before significant trial preparation occurs. However, many times settlement does not occur until the case reaches the "courthouse steps." At this point, the employer has paid the full costs of the initial investigation of the merits of the lawsuit, the discovery process, various motions and accompanying briefs including the summary judgment motion, and the trial preparation. These costs often exceed $100,000, in addition to what was paid to the employee to settle the lawsuit.

The Plaintiff/Employee's Perspective

For an employee or a former employee who sues an employer, there are also costs, albeit different ones. Many who file suit may be seeking vindication for what they believe is unfair treatment or to have their employee voice heard. Yet, there are significant monetary and emotional costs in seeking such vindication through litigation.

For individuals still employed by the organization, a discrimination lawsuit is often seen as a declaration of war against that employer, usually closing any remaining lines of communication. While former employees do not experience the isolation often felt by employees who sue their employer, they do recognize that the litigation process exacerbates the existing animosity between the parties. This process also makes it difficult for the former employee to move on with life — at least until this issue has been resolved.

While the costs of retaining a lawyer may be less for the employee, because many of these cases are accepted by attorneys on a contingency basis with some minimum retainer (for example, $5,000), there are, nevertheless, significant costs to the individual bringing such a lawsuit. Costs not covered by the contingency arrangement, the inconvenience of taking time off from a new job to attend depositions or trial, the fear that a new employer will look unfavorably on a lawsuit against a prior employer, and the uncertainty and emotional costs associated with litigation cause many plaintiffs to recognize that there should be a better way to resolve these disputes.

ALTERNATIVE DISPUTE RESOLUTION — A BETTER WAY

Many of the statistics cited throughout this book are the result of litigation that occurred before the passage of the Civil Rights Act of 1991. Now, sexual harassment, gender, race, religious, and ethnic origin discrimination claims will be tried before a jury, not a judge. The relatively new Americans With Disabilities Act, which prohibits discrimination against a person because of a disability, also contemplates jury trials. This shift to the jury trial system will open a floodgate of litigation with increasing jury awards.

A better way for employers and employees to resolve their differences is needed. The use of alternative dispute resolution (ADR) techniques can simplify the resolution of these disputes at significant cost savings to all parties involved. These techniques, in particular mediation, fact finding, and arbitration, should be considered as a part of an employer's overall employment relations — legal structure.

The use of ADR can reduce an employer's exposure to the costs of employment litigation, while providing for the equitable and prompt resolution of various disputes. Various types of ADR techniques provide different benefits to the parties to the dispute. These techniques and their advantages and disadvantages will be discussed at length. The reader will learn how to select and design workplace dispute resolution procedures that will fairly and economically resolve many workplace disputes encountered today. These models do not impair an employee's statutory rights. Rather, a win-win model will be set forth, where disputes can be resolved before they become "a federal case."

If the use of ADR techniques is to be expanded, it is critical that those who preside over these cases be neutral to the case and knowledgeable about the law involved. More fundamentally, all employees who participate in the ADR process must be assured that they are not losing their right to justice but rather gaining the benefits of speed and economy. A practical and efficient model to guide both employees and employers through this dynamic field will be provided.

Nonjudicial dispute resolution has a long and honorable history. In the Bible, references are made to negotiation, mediation, and arbitration. In the modern era, ADR has become a catchphrase to describe any nonjudicial form of dispute resolution.

There are many cogent reasons to seek resolution of a dispute, particularly one involving employment, out of court. Court dockets are overcrowded at the federal and state trial levels and appellate courts can be one year behind in issuing their decisions. Obviously, time is money and protracted uncertainty makes business and career planning speculative at best. Using nonjudicial techniques to settle a dispute ensures privacy and allows the parties to control much of the process. For example, a court case is assigned to a judge; in ADR, the disputants may select a neutral decision maker themselves. Further, court litigation must conform to civil procedure guidelines and rules; using a nonjudicial technique permits the parties to select the degree of formality to be used. This flexibility allows the parties to select a neutral individual with expertise in resolving employment disputes in a style with which they are comfortable. This almost always results in a more expedient, less expensive, final resolution of the dispute.[2]

In Section II, the benefits and drawbacks of a number of ADR approaches are considered. The authors believe no one system is perfect for every employment setting; we encourage creativity. For example, we examine mediation-arbitration, a hybrid of mediation and arbitration. This technique gives the disputants both the benefits of the voluntary nature of mediation and the binding finality of arbitration. This is only one example of the flexibility of ADR to facilitate dispute resolution.

Indeed, the specific technique adopted is less important than the result — final resolution of a dispute that provides for substantive due process quickly and with lower costs. In court, one faces not only higher cost and delay but also the lack of final results. Often, protracted litigation and appeal lead to years of uncertainty and such enormous expense that there is ultimately no winner.

WHEN TO SELECT A PROCEDURE

The best time to select a dispute resolution procedure is before a dispute arises. Once the parties are enmeshed in a disagreement, their lines of communication and level of trust are low, as each side seeks an advantage at every turn. In essence, if no pre-dispute procedure has been established, the parties must deal with procedural and substantive issues simultaneously — and at the time least likely to yield successful communication and agreement.

Establishing a process for resolving disputes before a disagreement occurs usually ensures that the dispute can be concluded quickly. If the parties have the opportunity to fashion their own settlement, it will usually meet both sides' needs. If unassisted, voluntary agreement is not possible, the parties who can resort to a streamlined, workable dispute resolution system are more likely to reach a satisfactory settlement.

Sometimes the parties, through oversight or intention, do not create a pre-dispute resolution procedure. They are free to do so, by mutual consent, at any point after the dispute has arisen. For example, the disputants may choose to bring in a mediator or agree to binding or advisory arbitration, a mini-trial before a retired judge, or any other ADR technique with which they feel comfortable.

An employer may create a pre-dispute resolution procedure and make mandatory participation in it a condition of employment. Another employer may decide to offer the employee the choice of agreeing to a dispute resolution procedure. Still another employer may wait until a dispute arises and then offer the employee a choice of seeking internal remedies before litigating.

The purpose of this book is to examine and analyze the why, the what, and the how of nonjudicial dispute resolution in the workplace. Section I examines the changing legal environment that has made ADR such an attractive approach for resolving employment disputes. Section II looks at the various forms of ADR, how each works, and the advantages and disadvantages of different techniques. Section III considers current trends and suggests language to implement a successful ADR procedure incorporating mediation and arbitration.

NOTES

1. K. Bruce Stickler, "For Job-Bias Suits, Ballooning Costs," *New York Times*, Sunday, July 17, 1994, p. F11.

2. In 1992 the *Daily Labor Report* stated that an average arbitration costs from $1,000 to $5,000 while it usually costs approximately $5,000 to $10,000 merely to begin the litigation process. Costs have increased since then. *Daily Labor Report*, January 2, 1992, p. A5.

ALTERNATIVE DISPUTE RESOLUTION IN THE WORKPLACE

I

The Changing Legal and Legislative Landscape

While this text will address all types of alternative dispute resolution (ADR), we begin by discussing the hottest topic faced by executives, human resource professionals, and their attorneys today: a complaint resolution procedure that results in binding arbitration in lieu of courtroom litigation. The use of binding arbitration as an alternative to courtroom litigation has recently gained increasing acceptance by the courts, Congress, attorneys, employees, and employers. This was not always the case. In the first half of the twentieth century, the courts were generally suspicious of binding arbitration to resolve any type of legal dispute. The first acceptance of workplace arbitration occurred in the labor-management context.

During World War II, the War Labor Board, a federal agency charged with promoting industrial peace, aggressively promoted the use of mediation and binding arbitration to resolve labor-management disputes peacefully and without the use of the strike or lockout. As R. W. Fleming, an academician who also served as an arbitrator, wrote in 1965:

> In retrospect it is clear that World War II did three things insofar as voluntary arbitration is concerned. First of all, it encouraged widespread adoption of arbitration techniques. Second, it sharpened the distinction between arbitration over "rights" and interests. Henceforth, it would be clear that the commitment of the parties was to grievance arbitration, not to arbitration of the terms of a new agreement or to substantive issues not covered by the contract. Finally, the War Labor

Board served as a training ground for the men who subsequently served as arbitrators. This cadre has ever since constituted the hard core of the arbitration profession. Without the understanding which they brought to the job it is possible that grievance arbitration would have been less readily accepted.[1]

During World War II, the federal government had a staff of full-time, paid arbitrators. After the war ended, this procedure was discontinued. Since that time, the parties to arbitration have been required to assume the cost of compensating the arbitrator for fees and expenses.

Thus, not only does labor-management arbitration function in a well-developed system, but because arbitrators are paid, there is a group of individuals who spend some, much, or all of their time arbitrating labor-management disputes. This labor-management arbitration model has recently been adapted and adopted by nonunion companies to resolve employment disputes. As a result, new arbitrators and processes are developing to serve this new dispute resolution market.

As arbitration has grown more professional and become an integral part of employment relations, the judiciary has begun to take a more positive view of the process. In employment law, the U.S. Supreme Court first and most famously supported the use of binding arbitration for the resolution of union-management disputes in 1960 in three decisions, commonly referred to as the Steelworkers Trilogy. In the *American Manufacturing* decision, the Court held that, where an agreement to arbitrate all disputes existed, the courts had no role in deciding whether a grievance was meritorious. Rather, the grievance must be decided by arbitration. In the *Warrior and Gulf Navigation* case, the Court applied a broad definition of what constitutes a grievance arising from a contract dispute. In the *Enterprise Wheel and Car Corp.* decision, the Court held that the courts should not consider the merits of a particular grievance but only whether the grievance was arbitrable under the contractual agreement to arbitrate.[2] These three decisions established binding arbitration as the preeminent method for resolution of employment disputes arising under collective bargaining agreements. These decisions also contributed to the development of a group of dispute resolution professionals who could hear and resolve employee grievances arising under a collective bargaining agreement.

FEDERAL CASE LAW: *ALEXANDER V. GARDNER-DENVER CO.*

While binding arbitration became the accepted procedure for resolving employee grievances under collective bargaining agreements, the Supreme Court later limited the scope of the legal issues that could be decided under binding arbitration. In *Alexander v. Gardner-Denver Co.*, 415 U.S. 36 (1974), the Court held that an arbitration decision issued pursuant to binding arbitration of a grievance arising under a collective bargaining agreement could not bar a subsequent lawsuit over the same facts in federal court under Title VII of the Civil Rights Act of 1964. Thus, labor-management arbitrators were without authority to resolve, with finality, federal statutory causes of action. Instead, they were limited, with few exceptions, to interpreting the "four corners of the contract" but not statutory issues.

Alexander involved a discharged, African-American, union-represented employee who had worked under a collective bargaining agreement that contained a nondiscrimination clause and a just-cause termination standard. Pursuant to the agreement, the arbitrator considered the employee's claim of race discrimination, which was specifically prohibited by the nondiscrimination clause in the collective bargaining agreement. The arbitrator found that the employee was discharged for just cause. The employee had separately filed a charge of racial discrimination with the Equal Employment Opportunity Commission (EEOC). After receipt of the arbitrator's decision, the employee filed a suit in federal court challenging his termination, alleging race discrimination in violation of Title VII.

The specific issue presented to the Court in *Alexander* was, "under what circumstances, if any, an employee's statutory right to a trial *de novo* under Title VII may be foreclosed by prior submission of his claim to final arbitration under the nondiscrimination clause of a collective bargaining agreement."[3]

The *Alexander* decision, written by Justice Powell, reasoned that the powers of enforcement under Title VII were provided by Congress to both the federal courts and to individuals. The Court noted that there was no suggestion by Congress in the statutory scheme of Title VII that a binding arbitration decision adjudicating the merits of a Title VII claim would foreclose an individual's right to litigate the same issue *de novo* in federal court. The Court decision stated that "There is no suggestion in a statutory scheme that a prior arbitral decision either forecloses an individual's right to sue or divests federal courts of jurisdiction."[4]

Citing the absence of statutory language approving binding arbitration of an employee's Title VII claim, and noting that legislative enactments under civil rights law have "long evinced a general intent to accord parallel or overlapping remedies against discrimination," the Court concluded that "the legislative history of Title VII manifests a congressional intent to allow an individual to pursue independently his rights under both Title VII and other applicable state and federal statutes (footnote omitted)."[5] Thus, the Supreme Court concluded that an employee was not obligated to choose either arbitration or the pursuit of a Title VII claim in federal court. The employee could elect to use both procedures, obtaining "two bites at the same apple."

The refusal of the Court to recognize the acceptability of binding arbitration in final resolution of claims arising under Title VII foreclosed the use of pre-dispute agreements to arbitrate in nonunion settings. Since any arbitration decision of a claim arising under Title VII could be relitigated *de novo*, arbitration could not guarantee a final resolution for these federal statutory claims. This was true notwithstanding the fact that footnote 21 of the *Alexander* decision indicated that the courts could, if they so chose, give an arbitration decision appropriate weight in making a decision.[6] In that footnote, the Court stated that it adopted no standards as to the particular weight a court could accord an arbitrator's decision. The Court identified relevant criteria in the weighting process, including the procedural fairness of the forum, adequacy of the record regarding the discrimination issue, and the special competence of the arbitrator. Where this criteria was satisfied and the arbitration decision fully considered the employee's rights, the Court indicated that "great weight" could be accorded, particularly where the issue was one of fact, addressed by the parties, and decided on an adequate record.

Notwithstanding identification of circumstances where great weight could be given an arbitration decision by the court, the practical effect of *Alexander* was the encouragement of a bifurcated process. Discharged employees would first proceed to labor-management arbitration under the just-cause standard in the collective bargaining agreement. If unsuccessful, many would then proceed with their narrower claim of race discrimination, or other Title VII claim, in federal court. This was a duplicative and wasteful process for all concerned. For the employer, it meant defending the same or similar action in two different forums. For the employee, it meant bringing the same claim before two different decision makers.

THE RISE OF ALTERNATIVE DISPUTE RESOLUTION

Since *Alexander*, the Supreme Court's view of the efficacy and acceptability of arbitration has changed markedly. A turning point in the federal judiciary's view was a dissenting opinion by Chief Justice Warren E. Burger in *Barrentine v. Arkansas-Best Freight System, Inc.*, 450 U.S. 728, 746-753 (1981).

In *Barrentine*, a union had presented employees' grievances regarding unpaid overtime to a joint labor-management grievance committee, established pursuant to the collective bargaining agreement. The joint committee rejected the grievances. The employees then sued in federal court on the same grievances under the Fair Labor Standards Act (FLSA). The issue before the Court was whether an arbitration decision addressing a wage claim under a collective bargaining agreement precluded the employees from filing a statutory wage claim under the FLSA. The majority decision did not find the prior arbitration decision to bar the FLSA wage claim.

Chief Justice Burger's dissenting opinion in *Barrentine* extolled the benefits of arbitration and criticized the cost and inappropriateness of federal court litigation of employment law disputes. His dissent noted the various public policies in favor of extrajudicial methods of dispute resolution, particularly for employment law issues.

Shortly thereafter, Chief Justice Burger gave a speech entitled "Isn't There A Better Way?" at an American Bar Association meeting in January 1982. He restated his belief that the litigation crisis and resultant court backlog could be partially addressed by the use of ADR techniques, including binding arbitration.[7]

While Chief Justice Burger was imploring the legal community to consider new ways to resolve employment law disputes, the Supreme Court began to expand its acceptance of arbitration in the resolution of other legal disputes. In *Moses H. Cone Memorial Hosp. v. Mercury Construction Corp.*, 460 U.S. 1 (1983), the Court ordered the enforcement of an agreement to arbitrate a hospital construction contract dispute, stating that the Federal Arbitration Act (FAA), 9 U.S.C. § 1, created a body of federal substantive law of arbitrability applicable to any arbitration agreement within the coverage of the FAA. The Court noted that the FAA established a federal policy favoring arbitration.[8]

In *Mitsubishi Motors Corp. v. Soler Chrysler-Plymouth, Inc.*, 473 U.S. 614 (1985), the Supreme Court found subject to arbitration a predispute agreement to arbitrate a legal claim under the Sherman Antitrust Act. The Court's opinion noted the fundamental historical shift in its view of arbitration. The Court recognized that it had previously rejected the argument that arbitration was an alternative forum for trial. The Court also stated that its earlier decisions had found that arbitration lacked the certainty of a suit at law. The *Mitsubishi* opinion rejected these prior views stating that "By agreeing to arbitrate a statutory claim, a party does not forego any substantive rights afforded by the statute; it only submits to their resolution in an arbitral, rather than a judicial, forum."[9]

In *Shearson/American Express, Inc. v. McMahon*, 482 U.S. 220 (1987), the Supreme Court supported the enforceability of pre-dispute agreements to arbitrate under federal securities law and under the Racketeer Influenced and Corrupt Organizations Act. Thereafter in *Rodriguez de Quijas v. Shearson/American Exp., Inc.*, 490 U.S. 477 (1989), the Court further encouraged the use of pre-dispute agreements to arbitrate securities law claims. The Court rejected the "old judicial hostility to arbitration" expressed by it in 1953, noting that this hostile view had been steadily eroding over the years and that "The erosion [was] intensified in our most recent decisions upholding agreements to arbitrate federal claims under the Securities Exchange Act of 1934."[10]

ALEXANDER V. GARDNER-DENVER CO. REVISITED — THE *GILMER* DECISION

It is worth noting that the U.S. Supreme Court has grown increasingly conservative with each appointment by Presidents Reagan and Bush. One of the basic tenets of conservative philosophy is that private decision making is always preferable to government decision making. It is therefore hardly surprising that a majority of justices on the Supreme Court began to look favorably upon arbitration and other forms of nongovernmental dispute resolution.

On the other side of the political spectrum, some employee rights advocates are also supportive of ADR, but for different reasons. Employee rights advocates typically favor any initiative which gives greater power to the traditionally less empowered, and easy access to arbitration for individuals makes vindicating rights quicker and less expensive. Further, many employee rights advocates have become disenchanted with the cumbersome enforcement process of many governmental agencies, which are perceived as slow-moving and excessively bureaucratic.

Thus, while the composition of the Supreme Court and lesser federal courts may change as political trends shift, it seems likely that ADR will continue to enjoy broad support.

This increasing acceptability of arbitration to resolve various types of federal statutory disputes sets the stage for the Supreme Court's revisiting of the *Alexander v. Gardner-Denver Co.* decision. While the Court has not yet directly addressed the validity of the enforcement of a pre-dispute agreement to arbitrate claims under Title VII of the Civil Rights Act of 1964, the Court came as close to overturning *Alexander* as the facts of the lawsuit would allow.

In *Gilmer v. Interstate/Johnson Lane Corp.*, 111 S. Ct. 1647 (1991), the Supreme Court addressed the issue of whether a pre-dispute agreement to arbitrate a statutory claim under the Age Discrimination in Employment Act of 1967 (ADEA) was subject to mandatory arbitration pursuant to an arbitration clause. This pre-dispute arbitration clause was set forth in the employees' stock exchange registration application with the New York Stock Exchange. Thus, the Court was not faced with an employment contract but with a contract between the employee and the regulatory agency (known as a U-4). The *Gilmer* decision enforced this arbitration clause, ordering arbitration of the employee's statute-based age discrimination claim. While the *Gilmer* decision is a narrow legal holding, it has unleashed the pent-up demand by employers, employees, and the judiciary to find a better way to resolve employment law disputes.

The *Gilmer* decision abandoned the *Alexander* holding, but did not directly address the issue of the use of pre-dispute agreements to arbitrate under an employee-employer contract. This occurred because the arbitration clause in *Gilmer* was not contained in a contract between employer and employee but rather in the employee's separate stock exchange securities registration application.

The Court also held that it was not necessary to decide the issue of whether the FAA would bar arbitration of this employment law dispute.[11] Thus, the Court did not squarely provide a decision on the enforceability of pre-dispute agreements to arbitrate employment disputes between employees and employer and the relationship of the FAA to such agreements.

The Supreme Court decision in *Gilmer* appears to signal judicial approval of the use of a pre-dispute agreement to arbitrate an employment law dispute. The Court did this by narrowing its earlier holding in *Alexander*. The Court stated that *Alexander* decided the issue of the enforceability of an employee's Title VII rights pursuant to labor-management arbitration. The Court also noted that *Alexander* involved an arbitration clause in a collective bargaining agreement and a union's waiver of a member's individual federal statutory claim by arbitration. The Court distinguished the facts in *Gilmer*, explaining that the employee's intentional agreement for submission of his own statutory claims to procedures under the arbitration clause in the stock exchange registration application supported arbitration.

The *Gilmer* decision established a new legal environment favoring the use of pre-dispute agreements to arbitrate. First, the Court recognized that federal statutory claims involving employment rights may be the subject of an arbitration agreement enforceable under the FAA. Second, the Court noted that the party opposing arbitration has the burden of establishing that Congress intended to preclude waiver of the judicial forum for the particular statutory claim at issue. Third, the Court found that the compulsory arbitration of an ADEA claim pursuant to an arbitration agreement was not inconsistent with the statutory framework of the ADEA. Fourth, the *Gilmer* Court noted that the mere involvement of an administrative agency (the EEOC) in the enforcement of a statute is not sufficient grounds to preclude the arbitration of a dispute concerning the alleged violation of that statute. Fifth, the Court refused to consider the issue of whether the arbitration panel would be biased where certain safeguards and procedures were evident in the arbitration procedure. Sixth, the Court rejected the argument that the reduced opportunities for discovery found in arbitration would preclude arbitration of an age discrimination claim without a showing that applicable discovery provisions would be insufficient to allow the employee representative a fair opportunity to present a claim. Seventh, the Court rejected the allegation that unequal bargaining power between employers and employees was sufficient to preclude enforcement of such an arbitration agreement. Finally, the Court explained away the *Alexander* decision so as to remove it as a barrier to the finality of a pre-dispute agreement to arbitrate federal statutory claims. The *Gilmer* decision set the stage for judicial decisions and legislation supporting the increased use of ADR techniques in a broad range of employment law disputes.

POST-*GILMER* FEDERAL DECISIONS SUPPORTING ALTERNATIVE DISPUTE RESOLUTION IN THE WORKPLACE

While the *Gilmer* decision involved an ADEA claim, its rationale was soon applied to Title VII claims that arose in the context of a pre-dispute agreement to arbitrate. Various circuit courts of appeals have extended the Supreme Court's holding in *Gilmer* to Title VII cases.[12]

In *Willis v. Dean Witter Reynolds, Inc.*, the plaintiff filed a sexual harassment lawsuit against her employer, Dean Witter. Dean Witter sought to compel arbitration due to the plaintiff's execution of a securities registration form. In this registration, the employee agreed to "arbitrate any dispute, claim or controversy that may arise between me and my firm." The Sixth Circuit Court of Appeals relied on *Gilmer*, finding that nothing in Title VII text or legislative history prohibited the arbitration of employment discrimination claims.[13]

In *Mago v. Shearson Lehman Hutton, Inc.*, an employee's arbitration of sexual harassment was compelled by the Ninth Circuit Court of Appeals. Here the employee had signed an employment application requiring arbitration of employment disputes. The court noted that *Gilmer*, while an ADEA cause of action, also required the arbitration of Title VII disputes.[14]

The Ninth Circuit Court of Appeals has not granted a carte blanche approval to such agreements. In *The Prudential Ins. Co. of America v. Lai*, the court held that a U-4 form agreement to arbitrate is enforceable if both parties knowingly entered into the agreement. In *Lai*, the court noted that even after *Gilmer*, "there [must] be at least a knowing agreement to arbitrate employment disputes before an employee may be deemed to have waived the comprehensive statutory rights, remedies and procedural protection prescribed in Title VII and related state statutes."[15]

On October 2, 1995 the Supreme Court declined to hear the *Lai* appeal.[16] The Eleventh Circuit Court of Appeals has also enforced the identical arbitration clause that the Ninth Circuit did not enforce in *Lai*.[17]

In *Farrand v. Lutheran Brotherhood*, the Seventh Circuit Court of Appeals addressed a lawsuit wherein an employee of the Lutheran Brotherhood, a financial services firm, had signed a U-4 form agreeing to arbitrate any dispute claim or controversy arising from his employment with the Lutheran Brotherhood.[18] The employer sought a court order compelling arbitration. The case was distinguished from *Gilmer*, in that *Gilmer* had registered with the New York Stock Exchange, while Farrand was registered with the National Association of Securities Dealers (NASD). The court stated that it must decide whether the rules of the NASD require arbitration of employment disputes. The court noted that "*Gilmer* did not establish a grand presumption in favor of arbitration; it interpreted and enforced the texts on which the parties had agreed." Finding that the underlying agreement to arbitrate was not clear regarding the extent of the agreement to arbitrate, the court precluded arbitration and remanded the matter to the federal district court. The Seventh Circuit Court of Appeals did not oppose *Gilmer*, but rather required that there must be a contract to arbitrate prior to the court's enforcement of said contract.

In *Bender v. A.G. Edwards & Sons, Inc.*, the Eleventh Circuit Court of Appeals ruled that a female stockbroker cannot pursue a sexual harassment claim under Title VII unless she first submits her dispute to the compulsory arbitration procedures governing the New York Stock Exchange.[19] Thus the Eleventh Circuit joined the Fifth, Sixth, and Ninth Circuits in holding that Title VII claims are similarly subject to compulsory arbitration under the FAA. Here the court stated "We see no reason to distinguish between ADEA claims and Title VII claims."

In *Bender v. Smith Barney, Harris Upham and Company*, a plaintiff sued her employer under Title VII for breach of contract, intentional infliction of emotional distress, and other common-law claims.[20] The employee claimed that she was fraudulently induced into signing the arbitration agreement since her employer failed to affirmatively disclose to her the specific clause and that the enforcement of this arbitration policy would be against public policy. The plaintiff also sought a jury trial on whether there existed an agreement to arbitrate claims arising from her employment, citing part of the FAA, 9 U.S.C. 4. The court denied the jury trial, stating that the plaintiff was challenging the scope of the clause, not the existence of the underlying agreement. The court also rejected the claim of fraudulent inducement since the plaintiff could not show that she had relied on any affirmative false representation or that there was any withholding of truth which should have been disclosed. The court also held that any public policy arguments against enforcement of agreements to arbitrate Title VII claims "were necessarily rejected by *Gilmer*." Therefore, both the common-law claims and the statutory claims were appropriately subject to arbitration.

After federal district courts and circuit courts of appeals expanded on the *Gilmer* decision to include Title VII claims in the securities industry, the Supreme Court had the opportunity to review a decision of the Ninth Circuit regarding whether pregnancy discrimination claims brought under Title VII by an employee of a securities firm must go to arbitration.[21] The justices let stand a lower court's holding that claims under Title VII must be arbitrated, supporting the Ninth Circuit's earlier decision in *Mago v. Shearson Lehman Hutton, Inc.*

The trend continues whereby U-4 agreements to arbitrate all disputes, including those arising under various civil rights laws, are enforced by the federal courts. In *Maye v. Smith Barney Inc.,* the court distinguished its ruling from that of the earlier Ninth Circuit Court in the *Lai* case by noting that the Smith Barney handbook before the court referenced employment disputes, while in *Lai* no such reference to employment disputes was made in the contract to arbitrate or in related documents.[22] Also, in *Lai* the employees were not given a copy of the NASD manual containing the terms of the arbitration agreement, which did not reference the arbitration of employment disputes. Thus, it appears the import of *Lai* is minimal where the contract to arbitrate specifically refers to the arbitration of employment disputes.

The Ninth Circuit Court of Appeals has also extended the *Gilmer* decision to include arbitration of an employee's claim under the federal Employee Polygraph Protection Act (EPPA) of 1988 (29 U.S.C. 2001-2009).[23] The court required arbitration of a dispute between a brokerage firm and a former account executive stemming from the executive's termination for his alleged refusal to take a polygraph test in connection with a theft investigation. While the plaintiff argued that arbitration could not be compelled because the statutory scheme of the federal EPPA differed from the ADEA, the court found that this dispute should be arbitrated because Congress did not evidence any intent that EPPA claims would not be arbitrable where a proper contractual base is found.

The U.S. Court of Appeals for the Third Circuit has extended the presumption in favor of arbitration to include mandatory arbitration of claims arising under the Employee Retirement Income Security Act (ERISA). In *Pritzker v. Merrill Lynch, Pierce, Fenner & Smith, Inc.*, a three-judge panel rejected the court's earlier holding that statutory claims under ERISA are not subject to the mandatory arbitration provisions of brokerage contracts.[24] In rejecting its 1985 decision in *Barrowclough v. Kidder, Peabody & Co., Inc.*, 752 F.2d 923 (3rd Cir. 1985), the Third Circuit panel recognized that many of the concerns about arbitration of ERISA claims set forth in *Barrowclough* were subsequently rejected by the Supreme Court in the *Shearson/American Express, Inc. v. McMahon* decision.[25]

The Tenth Circuit Court of Appeals also held that claims of race, sex, and national origin discrimination must be submitted to arbitration where the plaintiffs signed a U-4. *Armijo v. Prudential Insurance Co. of America*, 10th Cir., No. 94-2131, 12/15/95.

A February 1996 decision by the U.S. District Court for the Southern District of New York continued the legal trend in favor of the use of arbitration to resolve statutory employment discrimination claims.[26] This case is of special note because the plaintiff presented every possible legal argument in opposition to such agreements to arbitrate. It is also important because it represents judicial approval of the Travelers Group arbitration model, which is a leading arbitration model and is provided as an example beginning on page 108 of this book.[27]

In *DiGaetano v. Smith Barney Inc.*, the company's arbitration procedure was fully challenged by a leading plaintiff attorney in the field of employment discrimination litigation. The plaintiff claimed that she did not receive a copy of the arbitration policy before signing the agreement to arbitrate. She also claimed that the arbitration agreement was inconsistent with the purposes of Title VII because it precluded certain remedies such as attorneys' fees, punitive damages, and injunctive relief. The Court rejected this argument, holding that the agreement to arbitrate should be enforced as made.

The plaintiff also argued that her agreement to arbitrate was not a voluntary and knowing waiver of her right to sue in court. Here the plaintiff cited the *Lai* decision. The Court noted that it did not necessarily agree with the *Lai* decision and then proceeded to distinguish that decision from the case before it.

Finally, the plaintiff argued that even if the agreement to arbitrate was enforceable as it related to Smith Barney it did not apply to the plaintiff's individual claim against her supervisor. The court rejected this challenge holding that the language of the Travelers Group/Smith Barney arbitration agreement contemplated that such causes of action be arbitrated pursuant to the arbitration agreement.

Claims under the FLSA have also been held to be arbitrable. In *Hampton v. ITT Corp.*, 829 F. Supp. 202 (S.D. Tex. 1993), the U.S. District Court for the Southern District of Texas held that an agreement to arbitrate all employment-related legal claims includes overtime claims arising under the FLSA. In response to the plaintiffs' claim that the FAA barred such arbitrations, the court found that the plaintiffs — employees engaged in the business of servicing and managing consumer loans — were not included in the narrow category of employees covered by the transportation industry exclusion set forth under Section 1 of the FAA.

The trend away from *Alexander* recently reached a key point with the Fourth Circuit decision in *Austin v. Owens Brockway Glass Container Inc.*[28] Here, a three-judge panel of the Fourth Circuit became the first federal circuit court of appeals to abandon *Alexander* and decide that a union-represented employee must pursue his or her discrimination claim at arbitration under the collective bargaining agreement as the sole remedy — not in federal court under the Americans With Disabilities Act (ADA). The Fourth Circuit held that the language of the Civil Rights Act of 1991 and the ADA encourages the use of arbitration. Given this stated congressional intent, the Court held that statutory claims of employment discrimination under the ADA that arise under a collective bargaining agreement with an arbitration clause must be arbitrated.

The *Austin* case is the only circuit court of appeals decision requiring arbitration of civil rights claims under a collective bargaining agreement. If the *Austin* decision stands in the Fourth Circuit, within the next few years it appears that the Supreme Court will decide whether *Alexander* is still good law or whether all civil rights claims that arise under a collective bargaining agreement prohibiting such conduct must be arbitrated under that agreement.

LEGISLATION

After the *Gilmer* decision, Congress soon elected to encourage the use of ADR for all claims arising under the Civil Rights Act of 1991.[29] This expression of congressional intent, enacted shortly after *Gilmer*, is an additional important development in favor of pre-dispute agreements to arbitrate. This is because all of the case law cited herein requires analysis of congressional intent regarding the appropriateness of arbitration of the specific federal statutory claim at issue. For example, while the *Alexander* decision specifically noted that there did not exist any stated congressional intent in support of ADR, the Court noted in *Gilmer* that, when parties agree to arbitrate, they are obligated to do so unless Congress expressed an intent to preclude such waiver of judicial remedies. The Court also noted that the language of the ADEA supported ADR.[30]

Since *Gilmer*, congressional intent has been set forth in Section 118 of the Civil Rights Act of 1991 (1991 Act). The 1991 Act encompasses all causes of action under Title VII of the Civil Rights Act of 1964, the Age Discrimination in Employment Act of 1967, the Americans With Disabilities Act, and the Civil Rights Act of 1866. Section 118, "Alternative Means of Dispute Resolution," states that "Where appropriate and to the extent authorized by law, the use of alternative means of dispute resolution, including settlement negotiations, conciliation, facilitation, mediation, fact finding, mini-trials, and arbitration, is encouraged to resolve disputes arising under the Acts or provisions of Federal law amended by this title." Senate Minority Leader Robert Dole (R-Kan.), authored the 1991 Act's interpretive statement, adopted by President Bush, which stated, "This provision encourages the use of alternative means of dispute resolution, including binding arbitration, where the parties knowingly and voluntarily elect to use these methods. In light of the litigation crisis facing this country and the increasing sophistication and reliability of alternatives to litigation, there is no reason to disfavor the use of such forums. See *Gilmer v. Interstate/Johnson Lane Corp.*, 111 S. Ct. 1647 (1991)." President Bush stated at the signing ceremony that the Dole analysis will be treated as "authoritative interpretive guidance." Several courts have since interpreted the language of Section 118 of the Civil Rights Act of 1991 to be consistent with the *Gilmer* decision.[31]

The Americans With Disabilities Act was signed by President George Bush on July 26, 1990, and prohibits employment discrimination based upon a physical or mental disability by employers of 15 or more employees.

Title V of this law contains a provision for ADR, stating: "Where appropriate and to the extent authorized by law, the use of alternative means of dispute resolution, including settlement negotiations, facilitation, conciliation, mediation, fact-findings, mini-trials, and arbitration, is encouraged to resolve disputes arising under this Act."

As many observers have noted, this new law explores uncharted waters and will likely lead to many controversies and disputes as it becomes more clear over the next few years. For example, in considering an employee with a disability for a job or promotion, it is crucial that the candidate be able to perform "the essential functions" of the job. A job candidate must be "otherwise qualified" with or without accommodation of the disability by the employer. A job candidate is entitled to "reasonable accommodation" by an employer, as long as it does not cause an "undue hardship" on that employer. Certainly for both the employee and the employer, ADR procedures would appear to be necessary to avoid protracted and costly legal or administrative proceedings which will inevitably emanate from a new and somewhat vague law with society-wide coverage.

The Older Workers Benefit Protection Act (OWBPA) was enacted by Congress in 1990 to protect older employees from deprivation of expected benefits such as retirement pensions. As many corporations have downsized in recent years, there have been numerous reports of older employees encouraged to take early retirement, with a reduced level of benefits from what they would have received a few years later. These employees often chose to take early retirement because the alternative might have been a permanent layoff with no retirement benefits.

The OWBPA was designed to protect older employees from being taken advantage of and ensure that if an employee elects early retirement, that decision is truly made out of free will. Many employers have been concerned that older employees might accept the early retirement benefit package and then sue for both lost future wages and the retirement benefits they would have received had they continued to work. The employer thus often seeks a signed waiver of present and future claims by the employee taking early retirement.

The OWBPA also set forth a standard for what is considered a "knowing and voluntary" waiver of the right to sue by an employee. This standard requires that the employee be advised to consult an attorney prior to executing the agreement, that the employee not be required to waive any future causes of action, that the employee have up to 21 days to sign the agreement, that the employee have up to seven days to revoke the agreement after signature, that the agreement be written in understandable language, and that the employee be paid separate additional consideration for waiver of the age discrimination claim. This congressional expression of the standard for a "knowing and voluntary" waiver of a legal claim could be adopted as the safest possible standard for an employer seeking an employee's consent to a binding arbitration procedure. If the employee knowingly signs a waiver, any future claim could be subject to neutral arbitration, and avoid expensive litigation. By agreeing to arbitrate, the employee would not be surrendering substantive rights to have his claim heard, but would agree to a different procedural forum.

This point bears emphasis and repetition: the arbitration process that replaces the judicial or administrative forum for any employee's claim must be truly neutral, fair, and impartial. An arbitration forum that does not meet the standard of affording the aggrieved employee substantive due process is not only unethical but also probably unlawful; its decisions are unenforceable.

The Family and Medical Leave Act of 1993 (FMLA) provides for employee leave for certain medical conditions that affect the employee or certain members of the employee's family. This law was signed by President Clinton on February 5, 1993, and was effective for employers of 50 or more employees on August 5, 1993. Numerous complex issues and points of disagreement between employer and employee will likely result under this law.

One of the many issues that will initially be subject to dispute under the FMLA is the definitions of "spouse" and "parent." Final Regulations define "spouse" as a husband or wife, as defined or recognized under state law for the purposes of marriage. This includes common-law marriages in states where such marriages are recognized. A "parent" is defined as a biological parent or individual who stands or stood *in loco parentis* to an employee when the employee was a child, but does not include parents of an employee's spouse. Disputes arising from the application of these definitions under the FMLA are anticipated.

Similarly, the FMLA requires that 30 days notice of intended use of FMLA benefits be given "when foreseeable." Where 30 days notice cannot be given, notice must be given as soon "as is practicable." The issue of whether reasonable notice has been given will probably result in numerous lawsuits.

Finally, the FMLA Final Regulations use the phrase "serious health condition." Yet, these provisions leave open many issues surrounding the definition of this "serious health condition."

These are just a few of the issues where statutory guidance is lacking or incomplete. It is anticipated that disputes will arise under the FMLA based on the facts and the interpretation of the law. An ADR process to resolve these disputes is preferable to litigation under this law.

The sole remaining legal roadblock to the use of pre-dispute agreements to arbitrate appears to be the relationship of Section 1 of the FAA to an employment contract containing an agreement to arbitrate.

The FAA was passed by Congress in 1925 and codified in July 1947 in Title 9 of the U.S. Code.[32] The intent of Congress in passing the FAA was to place arbitration agreements "upon the same footing as other contracts."[33] The FAA provides that arbitration agreements "shall be valid, irrevocable, and enforceable, save upon such grounds as exist at law or in equity for the revocation of any contract."[34] This section establishes a legal presumption in favor of arbitration.

The FAA provides that a court must stay all proceedings before it if the court is satisfied that the issue before it is arbitrable under an enforceable agreement.[35] The FAA also authorizes a federal district court to issue an order compelling arbitration where there has been a "failure, neglect, or refusal" to comply with the arbitration agreement.[36]

Any party opposing arbitration must establish that Congress intended to preclude a waiver of the judicial remedies for the statutory rights at issue.[37] Where Congress intended to limit or prohibit waiver of a judicial forum for a particular claim, the Supreme Court noted in *McMahon* that this intent will be ascertainable from the statute's text, from its legislative history, or from an inherent conflict between arbitration and the statute's underlying purposes.[38] Thus, without a well-founded claim that an arbitration agreement resulted from fraud or excessive economic power that would provide grounds for the revocation of any contract, there is no legal basis for the court to disfavor arbitration agreements.[39]

Section 2 of the FAA has been interpreted to allow the court to give relief where the party opposing arbitration presents "well-supported claims that the agreement to arbitrate resulted from the sort of fraud or overwhelming economic power that would provide grounds for 'the revocation of any contract.'"[40]

Section 1 of the FAA expressly excludes "contracts of employment of seaman, railroad employees, or any other class of workers engaged in foreign or interstate commerce."[41]Thus, it can be argued that the FAA should be read to govern all contracts of employment in interstate commerce, including pre-dispute agreements to arbitrate. The alternative argument is that this section should be read to exclude employment disputes from arbitration. The key issue yet to be resolved is whether a pre-dispute agreement between an employee and an employer is barred from enforcement by Section 1.

In prior cases involving Section 1 of the FAA, the Supreme Court has discussed Section 1 but has not provided explicit guidance. In *Bernhardt v. Polygraphic Co. of Am. Inc.*, 350 U.S. 198 (1956), the Court reviewed an action involving the breach of an employment contract brought by a plant manager employed at a Vermont manufacturing plant. The Court, addressing the issue of a stay of arbitration pursuant to the jurisdictional limits set forth in Sections 1 and 2 of the FAA, found that there was no enforceable contract under the FAA because this contract did not evidence "a transaction involving commerce." The Court stated "there is no showing that petitioner while performing his duties under the employment contract was working 'in' commerce, was producing goods for commerce, was engaging in an activity that affected commerce within the meaning of our decision."[42] Without such a link to commerce, the FAA does not apply. The issue of whether this type of contract would be part of the Section 1 exclusion was undecided.

Where federal appellate court decisions have discussed Section 1 of the FAA, the weight of such authority supports a narrow interpretation of Section 1, favoring arbitration of employment law disputes under the FAA. The First, Second, Sixth, and Seventh Circuit Courts of Appeals and several federal district courts have held that the Section 1 exclusion is limited to employees engaged in the transport of goods in interstate commerce.[43]

In contrast to the decisions noted above, the Fourth Circuit Court of Appeals, in 1954, held that the Section 1 exclusion applies to all contracts of employment.[44] Similarly, the Ninth and Tenth Circuit Courts of Appeals have held that the employee and commerce exemption of Section 1 applies to all contracts of employment including collective bargaining agreements.[45] The Eleventh Circuit Court of Appeals has avoided a direct decision on this issue.[46]

Recent federal district court decisions have rejected the exclusionary interpretation of the FAA. The U.S. District Court for Pennsylvania ordered the mandatory arbitration of an ADEA claim and a common-law, wrongful-discharge claim of an accounting firm partner under the FAA.[47]

In this matter, the plaintiff was hired by Coopers & Lybrand as director of a group of management consulting services. After becoming a partner at Coopers and Lybrand, the plaintiff executed a partnership agreement that included a provision requiring arbitration of claims or controversies arising out of the partnership agreement or arising out of the affairs of Coopers and Lybrand. The plaintiff was subsequently asked to withdraw from the partnership. He filed a charge with the EEOC alleging age discrimination and violation of the ADEA. The EEOC declined to review the plaintiff's claim because the plaintiff was a partner and, according to the EEOC, not entitled to ADEA protection. The plaintiff then filed a suit in federal court alleging violations of the ADEA and a common-law, wrongful-discharge claim. Coopers & Lybrand filed a motion to compel arbitration pursuant to the arbitration clause.

The court narrowly construed the FAA's exclusionary clause, holding that this clause did not apply to an accounting firm partnership agreement.[48] Regarding the FAA, the court held that the partnership agreement was not excluded from the scope of this act because the plaintiff engaged in consulting services and thus was not "in any way part of a class of workers actively involved in interstate transportation."[49]

The U.S. District Court for Massachusetts supported an employee's application seeking mandatory arbitration of a wrongful discharge claim pursuant to an agreement to arbitrate contained in the employer's employment manual. There the court ruled that the exclusionary language of the FAA applied only to employees "actually in the transportation industry." Thus, the court reasoned that all other types of employment contracts were not covered by Section 1 of the FAA.[50]

The U.S. District Court for the Northern District of Ohio granted a motion to compel arbitration of a nonunion account executive's employment dispute, pursuant to that executive's agreement to arbitrate "all controversies, claims, disputes and matters in question."[51] In granting the employer's motion to compel arbitration, the court specifically rejected the argument that Section 1 of the FAA covered this agreement to arbitrate, stating that the nonunion account executive was not engaged in interstate commerce or transportation, and did not belong to a class of employees engaged in such activities.[52]

THE *GILMER* DECISION, THE FEDERAL ARBITRATION ACT, AND THEIR RELATIONSHIP TO STATE LAW

The discussion so far has centered on the evolving federal law favoring the use of pre-dispute agreements to arbitrate employment law disputes. Many employment laws are promulgated at the state level, often creating new obligations or supplementing existing obligations under federal law. Thus, when considering the adoption of a dispute resolution procedure it is important to determine whether existing state law claims can also be adjudicated with federal claims. Most courts recognize that the contract to arbitrate employment law disputes is a contract under the FAA. Thus, it "federalizes" any agreements to arbitrate state law claims. It appears that all possible state common-law or administrative claims can be addressed in this federal contract to arbitrate.[53]

State law may also provide for parties to use state law as an alternative to the FAA for the enforcement of arbitration provisions in employment contracts. In *Bolt Information Services, Inc. v. Leland Stanford Junior University*, 350 U.S. 198 (1956), the Supreme Court found that state law arbitration procedures may exist alongside the FAA since there was no clear congressional intent to occupy the entire field of arbitration. Thus, a state law enforcing arbitration provisions in employment contracts is not in conflict with the federal law and would, in all likelihood, be allowed to exist alongside the FAA.[54]

While some states enforce only agreements to arbitrate existing disputes, but not future ones, the majority of states have laws allowing for the enforceability of arbitration agreements without reference or exclusion of employment law contracts.[55] New York and California court decisions have addressed the ability of employment law disputes to be arbitrated; in the area of employment law developments, these two states are considered bellwether states.

The New York Supreme Court ruled that a former securities firm employee, who alleged that Goldman, Sachs and Co. engaged in sex discrimination, must arbitrate the dispute with her former employer rather than proceeding directly to state court.[56] This case involved an $18 million sex bias suit filed by a former Goldman, Sachs vice president. The state supreme court held that the plaintiff was compelled to arbitrate under the FAA because she had signed a New York Stock Exchange registration agreement.

The court specifically rejected the argument that the arbitration clause fit within an exception under the FAA. Rather, in granting a motion to stay judicial proceedings until the arbitration of the discrimination claim, the New York Supreme Court relied on the *Gilmer* decision. The New York Supreme Court noted that the "emphatic national policy favoring arbitration is binding on state courts." The court added that the fact that the plaintiff's discrimination allegation was made under a state law instead of a federal law did not affect the result. The court reasoned that the New York courts are bound to apply the FAA as interpreted by the U.S. Supreme Court.

Thereafter, in *Fletcher v. Kidder, Peabody & Co.*, New York's highest court, the New York Court of Appeals, addressed the issue of the mandatory arbitration of statutory discrimination claims pursuant to the execution of a U-4 agreement.[57] The issue before the court in *Fletcher* was whether subsequent case law (*Gilmer*) rendered prior New York case law obsolete on the enforceability of anticipatory agreements to arbitrate claims of unlawful discrimination. The court noted that in the *Matter of Wertheim & Co. v. Halpert*, 48 N.Y.2d 681, 321 N.Y.S.2d 876, 397 N.E. 2d 386 (1979), it had prohibited enforcement of such arbitration clauses.

The *Fletcher* court noted that the enforceability of arbitration clauses found in U-4 agreements is governed by the FAA. Furthermore, the court noted that the provisions of the FAA are controlling even where the dispute itself may arise under state law.[58]

Referencing the *Gilmer* decision, the court held that the arbitration of all legal causes of action was required. The court noted that the party seeking to avoid arbitration must establish a congressional intent to preclude the waiver of a judicial forum. The court found no such intent.

Finally, regarding the claim that Section 1 of the FAA precluded contracts of employment, the court rejected this argument, noting that the *Gilmer* decision had specifically addressed whether a U-4 was a contract of employment.[59]

Federal courts have also interpreted New York law to require arbitration. In *DiCrisi v. Lyndon Guaranty Bank*, 807 F. Supp. 947 (W.D. N.Y. 1992), the U.S. District Court for the Western District of New York held that a New York State Division of Human Rights charge alleging gender discrimination and a federal Title VII cause of action alleging gender discrimination must be arbitrated pursuant to a pre-dispute agreement to arbitrate executed by the parties to the dispute.

The plaintiff was a bank operations manager who had entered into a written employment contract which called for the binding arbitration of all disputes. The court rejected the claim that the FAA precluded such arbitration and ordered arbitration. Regarding the claim that arbitration was not appropriate because the plaintiff sought punitive damages, which could not be granted by an arbitrator as a matter of law in the state where the plaintiff resided (New York), the court ordered arbitration and stayed further proceedings on the claim for punitive damages. The court stated "If necessary, this court can deal with the punitive damages issue after the conclusion of arbitration."[60]

A California state appeals court ruled that claims of race discrimination in employment must be submitted to arbitration when the employee had previously signed a legal agreement to arbitrate the employment disputes.[61] In that decision, relying on *Gilmer*, the court ruled that the plaintiff must arbitrate a race discrimination claim. The California court reasoned that "in enacting Section 2 of the FAA, Congress declared a national policy favoring arbitration and withdrew the powers of the state to require a judicial form for the resolution of claims which the contracting parties agreed to resolve by arbitration." Regarding the plaintiff's reliance on California's antidiscrimination statutes, the court stated, "Reliance on a state's statutory anti-discrimination scheme, as here, rather than on a federal Title VII claim, does not alter the analysis of enforceability of arbitration agreements under the FAA." The court likewise rejected the plaintiff's attempt to avoid arbitration by reference to the FAA, finding that the securities firm employees were engaged in interstate commerce. Here the court noted that several courts had limited the exceptions of Section 1 of the FAA to employees involved in the actual movement of goods in interstate commerce. The court stated that it favored this narrow construction of Section 1 of the FAA since it supports the strong national policy favoring arbitration as a means of settling private disputes.

In *Sacks v. Richardson Greenshield Securities, Inc.*, 781 F. 2d 1475 (E.D. Cal. 1991), the U.S. District Court for the Eastern District of California considered the issue of whether a plaintiff could arbitrate a state law gender discrimination claim and, after losing this issue at arbitration, seek *de novo* judicial review of this cause of action maintained under the California Fair Employment & Housing Act.

The court held that this state law claim was subject to arbitration under *Gilmer*. The court noted that the parties did not expressly reserve this issue for the court or exclude the issue from any agreement to arbitrate. Thus, the court found that the "two bites at the apple" contemplated by *Alexander v. Gardner-Denver Co.* were eliminated by the *Gilmer* decision. Since the plaintiff had entered into an unconditional agreement to arbitrate and since such arbitration of any and all issues (including state law issues) had occurred, the court upheld the arbitration award and declined to hear the claim.

In *Scott v. Farm Family Life Insurance*, DC MASS, 92-12774-T, 727 (1993), the U.S. District Court for Massachusetts found that an employee who signed a contract with an insurance company providing that "all disputes arising under this agreement . . . shall be resolved by binding arbitration pursuant to the rules of the American Arbitration Association," must arbitrate her claim of wrongful discharge and sex discrimination.

The court rejected the argument of the plaintiff that a narrow exemption under the FAA should be applied to all employment contracts and that the *Gilmer* decision should not be applied retroactively. The court noted that "Current public policy suggests that the FAA should be read to further, rather than discourage, the use of arbitration."[62]

In addition to the causes of action cited above, state courts are ordering that a wide range of employment law claims be arbitrated pursuant to anticipatory agreements to arbitrate. In the District of Columbia and Pennsylvania, the courts have determined that such agreements apply to the arbitration of state human rights law charges.[63]

State common-law claims have also been found to be subject to arbitration as follows:

California: state law claims of breach of implied contract, breach of good faith covenant of fair dealing, and fraud — *Delaney v. Continental Airlines Corp.*, 1993 U.S. Dist. LEXIS 9868 (C.D. Cal. June 22, 1993);

Tennessee: state law claims of defamation, emotional distress, and invasion of privacy claims — *Aspero v. Shearson/American Express, Inc.*, 768 F. 2d 106 (6th Cir. 1995) *cert. denied*, 474 U.S. 1026 (1985);

New York: state law claim of defamation — *Singer v. Jeffries & Co.*, 78 N.Y.2d 76, 571 N.Y.S.2d 680 (1991);

Florida: state law sexual harassment claim, invasion of privacy, and intentional infliction of emotional distress — *Nazon v. Shearson Lehman Bros., Inc.*, 1993 WL 387358 (S. D. Fla. 1993).

Finally, a Prudential securities industry registration agreement (U-4) signed in 1982 was recently found to require arbitration of an ex-employee's claims under the New Jersey Conscientious Employee Protection Act and the New Jersey Law Against Discrimination. Here the New Jersey superior court decision stated that "Arbitration is a highly favored remedy in our legal system."[64]

THE RISE OF EMPLOYMENT LITIGATION

Over the past two decades, employment litigation in state and federal courts has continued to increase. Anecdotal evidence supports the conclusion that this rapid rise in employment litigation will be exacerbated by the recent passage of the Civil Rights Act of 1991, the Americans With Disabilities Act, the Family and Medical Leave Act of 1993, and other possible state and federal laws governing the workplace.[65]

The rise in employment litigation can be documented by statistics provided by an American Bar Foundation study published in the *Stanford Law Review*.[66] These statistics show that the number of employment discrimination lawsuits in the federal courts rose almost 2,200 percent in the past two decades. This is almost ten times the rate of all other civil litigation combined. Furthermore, these increases do not include the parallel rise of state contract and tort litigation of employment disputes.

The federal courts have also recognized that employment discrimination lawsuits now impose a significant burden on federal judges. This was explicitly discussed in the Federal Courts Study Committee report.[67] From fiscal years 1970 through 1989, the general federal civil caseload increased 125 percent. Employment discrimination case filings for the same time period registered a 2,166 percent growth.

The most recent government statistics on federal district litigation underscore the continuing rise in employment litigation. When a federal lawsuit is filed, the plaintiff is required to identify the type of litigation on the civil case cover sheet. While counsel often overlooks or mistates the subject matter of the litigation, the civil cover sheet notations provide the basis for statistics on federal litigation trends. For the period ending September 30, 1992, the following statistics illustrate the rise in employment litigation.

In 1991, 8,370 lawsuits were filed in federal court alleging civil rights violations in employment. In 1992, 10,771 lawsuits were filed. This represents a one-year increase of 28.7 percent in employment-related civil rights lawsuits. These statistics do not take into account almost any of the increase in litigation attributed to the Civil Rights Act of 1991 or the Americans With Disabilities Act, since these types of lawsuits, for the most part, were not procedurally ready for federal court filing by the fall of 1992. In sum, without consideration of recent laws which have revolutionized federal employment law litigation, employment law litigation under federal civil rights law rose almost 30 percent from 1991 to 1992.

Public opinion polls support the conclusion that employment litigation will continue to rise. A 1990 survey by the *National Law Journal* found that 62 percent of respondents stated that they would be more willing to take legal action regarding employment discrimination than they were five years ago. Furthermore, one of four respondents stated they had experienced job bias.[68]

Numerous factors have been identified as possible causes of the rise in employment related litigation. They include but are not limited to:

the rise in unemployment;

the demographic growth in the legally protected work force (i.e., the entry of females into the work force, the aging of the work force, and the increasing participation of minorities);

a possible cohort effect wherein younger females and minorities refuse to tolerate discriminatory treatment experienced by their predecessors and have a readily accessible white male coworker against whom they can compare their treatment in the labor market;[69]

increased aggressiveness by federal agencies responsible for enforcing employment discrimination law;

passage of new legislation expanding the scope of persons and rights protected and the economic rewards from prevailing in litigation;

litigation promoted by lawyers;

the increased litigiousness of employees due to lack of employee loyalty;

the decline of employer loyalty to employees;

the introduction of new legal theories of recovery (i.e., reverse discrimination, the expansion of Section 1981 [of the Civil Rights Act of 1866] to include employment contracts); and

clumsy downsizing by many employers with resultant exposure to employment law litigation, compounded by the decline of promotional opportunities and economic security among those employees remaining after the downsizing.

The average growth rate of 16.8 percent per year between 1969 and 1989 occurred from lawsuits for the most part devoid of the potential for obtaining high damages through award of compensatory or punitive damages. Most of this litigation, except causes of action seeking recovery of liquidated damages under the ADEA or punitive damages under Section 1981, occurred under a "make whole" remedy provision.

In addition to the spectacular rise of federal employment discrimination lawsuits under a restitution model, the 1991 Act's shift to a tort damages model may include a new class of employee litigant that has traditionally not resorted to litigation — low-paid employees.[70] Numerous studies suggest that discrimination suits are disproportionately concentrated among the more affluent and better educated. It has been postulated that since the potential back pay award to a person holding a low-paying job was less, and that person often could mitigate economic loss by obtaining another, readily available, low-paying job, from an economic, cost-benefit analysis approach it did not pay to litigate. With the inclusion of compensatory and punitive damages in the 1991 Act, the increased expected reward may induce an entire class of protected persons (the lower-paid) to seek redress through litigation. Thus, it is reasonable to conclude that the economic benefits of litigating have been significantly expanded for low-wage employees.

THE COST OF EMPLOYMENT LITIGATION

The increasing cost of defending an employment discrimination lawsuit is caused by many different factors. Claims arising under the Civil Rights Act of 1991 now include compensatory damages (pain and suffering, loss of consortium, embarrassment, loss of dignity), punitive damages, and payment of the opposing party's expert witness and attorneys' fees.[71] In addition, a company expends considerable money, staff time, and corporate energy defending such a lawsuit.

Prior to the Civil Rights Act of 1991, a plaintiff could not receive compensatory or punitive damages under Title VII of the Civil Rights Act of 1964. Because of the federal civil rights employment litigation shift from a restitution model to a tort model, when a plaintiff prevails under the 1991 Act, the average damages awarded will probably be much greater than the amount awarded before the passage of the 1991 Act.

In addition to the expansion of damages that can be claimed, the 1991 Act provides for a jury trial of a claim of willful violation of the act. The substitution of a jury for a judge will add to an employer's potential economic exposure by decreasing the opportunity to obtain summary judgment prior to trial, increasing the amount of plaintiff jury awards, and increasing the compensatory and punitive damages that a jury awards. Prior to the 1991 Act, employers feared federal age discrimination lawsuits under the ADEA because these were among the few that could be tried before a jury and because the jury was empowered to award liquidated (or double) damages for willful violations of the ADEA. This fear appears well-founded when one credits the results of public opinion polls. A poll conducted by the *National Law Journal* found that one of four persons believe they have personally experienced job bias. This poll also revealed that 78 percent of adult Americans believe some, most, or all employers engage in some type of discrimination in hiring or promotion. Fifty-one percent stated that all or most employers are guilty of discriminating practices.[72] This confirms most employer's fears of a trial by jury of an employment discrimination claim.

The rise in the costs associated with litigating under the 1991 Act is so recent that there is not sufficient data with which to measure its impact. The authors have relied on extensive pre-1991 Act data to extrapolate. Also, the cost of litigation of wrongful discharge matters under state law providing for compensatory and punitive damages has pre-dated the increase in the remedies available under federal litigation. In particular, California laws have encouraged employment law litigation. The California experience provides some insight into employment litigation where significant damages can be awarded through jury trials.

The theories of retaliatory discharge in violation of an important state public policy, breach of contract, and bad faith discharge by breach of implied covenant of good faith and fair dealing, have been extensively litigated in California. Prior to 1988, an employee in California could obtain contract, tort, and punitive damages for a bad faith discharge. The tort-based cause of action and resultant punitive damages were eliminated in 1988.[73] Before the California Supreme Court decision in *Foley v. Interactive Data Corporation*, where potential damages were similar to the current Civil Rights Act of 1991 damage model, total awards in California discharge cases between 1979 and 1988 are shown in Table I.1.

TABLE I.1
Total Awards in California Wrongful Discharge Cases, 1979–88

	Average Award	Median Award[1]	Expected Award[2]
All wrongful discharge cases	$452,570	$133,700	$317,686
Retaliation	579,974	215,000	434,980
Breach of contract	193,898	100,000	109,594
Bad faith	426,929	150,000	333,304

[1]The median award is, simply, the middle award: half of the jury awards in the sample are larger than the median, half are smaller.

[2]The expected award is an average of the awards in all of the cases in the sample, including defense verdicts.

Source: David J. Jung and Richard Harkness, "Life After Foley: The Future of Wrongful Discharge Litigation," *Hastings Law Journal*, 41 (November 1989): 131.

While many experts predicted that the *Foley* decision and its elimination of tort and punitive damages would result in lower wrongful discharge jury verdicts in California, studies have indicated that *Foley* has had a very limited effect on the size of jury awards, which have continued to rise.

The *California Labor & Employment Law Quarterly* reported that the average verdict awarded to an individual plaintiff in California was $1,417,000.[74] Furthermore, while the two most comprehensive studies of pre-*Foley* verdicts reported average jury verdicts in the range of $450,000 to $650,000, these recent figures establish that the average plaintiff's verdict in California has approximately tripled in the three years immediately following the *Foley* decision's limitation on tort damages (Table I.2). The trend of increasing jury verdict award amounts in California has continued, compared to the pre-*Foley* median of $135,000 to $175,000. During these three years, the average verdict shows a sharp climb followed by a leveling off. This compares to the pre-*Foley* average of $450,000 to $650,000. This pattern has continued with high verdicts awarded to a single plaintiff.

TABLE I.2
Total Awards in California Wrongful Discharge Cases, 1989–91

Year	Median Verdict	Average Verdict	Highest Single Employee Verdict
1989	$325,000	$ 519,000	$ 2,275,000
1990	442,000	1,888,000	17,522,000
1991	500,000	1,541,000	20,300,000

Source: *California Labor & Employment Law Quarterly*, 8(8) (Spring 1992): 3.

The last set of data, the most recent for California employment law jury verdicts, represents a trend line from January 1981 to September 1995. This data establishes that the total amount of jury awards has increased substantially; the total awards where the plaintiff has prevailed have increased to over 50 percent. Finally, the median amount of these awards continues to increase at a dramatic rate.

These large jury verdicts are not limited to termination cases. Cases of non-termination also result in hefty jury awards.

It is important to note that the reporting of jury awards is often the most publicized portion of a highly visible employment litigation matter; many of these awards are eventually reduced. According to a study by the Rand Corporation, while initial jury awards for wrongful termination in California average almost $700,000, post-trial adjustments, settlements, and rulings decrease most awards by more than half. This study also noted

TABLE I.3
California Jury Verdicts for Total Awards in Employment Cases, January 1981 through September 1995

Year	Median Jury Award	Average Jury Award	Total Verdicts	Plaintiff Prevailed Number	Percent
1981	$300,000	$ 490,091	17	11	65
1982	136,660	472,946	35	22	63
1983	76,000	238,221	24	13	54
1984	230,000	766,152	29	17	59
1985	252,743	795,343	64	50	78
1986	109,000	268,395	72	42	58
1987	260,500	866,074	80	42	53
1988	120,742	610,613	63	42	67
1989	162,500	341,430	42	28	67
1990	275,000	1,684,487	72	52	72
1991	251,752	445,844	81	37	46
1992	330,000	816,857	84	37	44
1993	242,500	432,628	95	52	55
1994	250,000	460,745	147	79	54
1995	491,500	605,755	44	23	52

Source: *Daily Labor Report*, No. 210, Special Report, October 31, 1995, pp. C3–C4. Data compiled by the law firm of Orrick, Herrington & Sutcliffe and reprinted by the Bureau of National Affairs in the *Daily Labor Report* with the permission of the firm.

that 95 percent of all wrongful termination suits in California settle at an average total cost of $40,000.[75]

In addition to anecdotal evidence and California state court statistics that support employer concern over potential jury awards, the jury awards themselves reinforce this concern. For example, in *Cancellier v. Federated Dept. Stores*, an employee obtained a $2.3 million jury award in a lawsuit involving a federal age discrimination claim and pendant state contract and tort claims.[76] Similarly, under federal and Texas state law, an employee obtained a $3.4 million jury award on federal claims of age discrimination and retaliation and a state claim of intentional infliction of emotional distress.[77]

The most recent jury decisions confirm that an employer can face significant exposure when an employment discrimination case is heard. For example a female Wal-Mart employee maintained a sexual harassment lawsuit claiming a hostile work environment due to supervisors'

TABLE I.4
California Jury Verdicts for Non-termination in Employment Cases, January 1989 through September 1995

Issues	Median Jury Award	Average Jury Award	Total Verdicts	Plaintiff Prevailed Number	Plaintiff Prevailed Percent
Discrimination					
Sex	$326,750	$959,496	44	20	45
Race	112,855	409,252	33	12	36
Age	164,048	385,688	9	5	56
Disability	416,059	416,059	5	1	20
Total			91	38	42
Non-Discrimination					
Violation of Public Policy	571,000	679,200	12	6	50
Breach of Contract/ Covenant	99,420	99,420	4	2	50
Total			16	8	50

Non-termination includes such issues as harassment, failure to hire, failure to promote, and demotion.

Source: *Daily Labor Report*, No. 215, December 1, 1995, p. C3.

jokes, comments about her anatomy, and abusive remarks against women in general. The plaintiff alleged that her complaints about this conduct fell on deaf ears at Wal-Mart. The jury awarded $1 in lost wages, $35,000 in pain and suffering, and $50 million in punitive damages.[78]

In a disability discrimination case filed under the ADA, a former Coca-Cola executive, who was fired while being treated for alcoholism, received over $1 million in compensatory damages and front and back pay and an additional $6 million in punitive damages from a federal district court jury in Dallas. While this award will be reduced to the maximum of $300,000 that is permitted under the ADA and Title VII, it indicates the exposure that an employer may face in litigation before a jury.[79]

In February 1996 a Hawaii state jury awarded a plaintiff $1,812,000 in an age and sex discrimination lawsuit; this award is the highest jury verdict in Hawaii for an employment discrimination lawsuit.[80] In this case a former general sales manager of several car dealerships claimed that she was fired in 1994 at the age of 49 because of her age and sex. The jury awarded the woman $150,000 in back pay, $800,000 for future pay, $362,000 in general damages, and $500,000 in punitive damages. In addition, the plaintiff's attorney has a pending request for the court to award him an additional $271,000 in fees, which are recoverable from the defendant by a prevailing party.

In April 1996 a California superior court jury awarded $1.5 million in damages to a former K-mart employee after finding that she was sexually harassed by her supervisor.[81] The plaintiff was awarded $200,000 in compensatory damages and $1.3 million in punitive damages.

In addition, the cost of an employer's defense of an employment discrimination claim may be paid entirely by the employer, since intentional discrimination claims are not covered by an insurance policy. The cost of one attorney for such defense approximates $200 per hour.[82] Since most employment discrimination lawsuits involve claims of intentional conduct, it is unlikely that future insurance policies will be designed to provide an employer protection from this type of litigation.

STATE LAW AND BREACH OF CONTRACT CLAIMS

While many may believe that employment-at-will is a well-established historical practice, it is a relatively recent state common-law legal theory that is contrary to most employment law systems today. In 1877, Harris Gay Wood, an Albany, New York, attorney, proposed the thesis that a general or indefinite hiring is prima facie evidence of hiring at will, with the burden on the party seeking to show a term of hire.[83] The at-will theory was a radical departure from the prevailing view of that era, articulated by the legal scholar Blackstone, that, "If the hiring be general, without any particular time limited, the law construes to be a hiring for a year; upon a principle of natural equity, that the servant shall serve, and the master maintain him, throughout all the revolutions of the respective seasons, as well when there is work to be done as when there is not."[84]

The employment-at-will doctrine views the employment relationship as voluntary and bilateral. That is, either the employee or the employer is free to terminate the employment relationship at any time, for any reason, or for no reason. Under this doctrine, there is no cause of action for wrongful discharge. Implicit in this doctrine is the assumption that both parties in the employment relationship possess equal bargaining power. In fact, most observers have concluded that the employer usually possesses far greater economic power than the employee and consequently, particularly in the past two decades, state courts have sought to provide legal protection to employees in an effort to equalize the disparity in their economic resources.

In the past twenty years, state law has played an increasingly important role in the resolution of employment disputes. The traditional employment-at-will doctrine has been eroded by these state court decisions, which have recognized contract and tort causes of action and public policy exceptions to at-will employment.

State courts have also been flooded with employee claims of implied and oral contracts. These implied contract claims are frequently characterized as claims of employee reliance on employer promises (estoppel), and claims that an employer has made implied promises through company policies, handbooks, procedures, or oral representations.

STATE TORT CLAIMS

In addition to an increase in contract litigation, there has been a similar increase in employment-related tort lawsuits filed in state courts. These are typically claims of defamation, intentional infliction of emotional distress, or battery. The latter is often appended to a federal Title VII sexual harassment lawsuit. Thus, today's employers are increasingly defending their practices under both state and federal law.

In *Leikvold v. Valley View Community Hosp.*, 688 P.2d 170 (Ariz. 1984), a breach of contract action was brought after a hospital administrator was fired, allegedly for requesting reassignment to her former position in the operating room. Although the employee asked for a grievance hearing as provided in the hospital policies manual, her request was denied.

The pertinent issue in the case was whether a representation in a personnel manual may limit an employer's power to terminate an employment relationship. The court found that such a manual can limit an employer's ability to discharge employees and explicitly limited its holding to a breach of contract action. Additionally, it made it clear that the provisions of a personnel manual are incorporated into an employment contract and what these provisions mean is a question of fact.

In *Whitlock v. Haney Seed Co.*, 715 P.2d 1017 (Idaho App. 1986), a wrongful discharge action was brought by a plant manager who was fired, allegedly in breach of his oral employment contract. Although the parties disagreed as to the exact terms of the verbal agreement, they agreed that if the manager performed satisfactorily, they had agreed that he would keep his job until some extrinsic event, such as a change in company ownership, occurred.

The court held that this agreement meant the manager was not an employee at will. Additionally, because the contract was conditioned on an event that could possibly have occurred within one year of its formation, the statute of fraud did not invalidate the agreement.

In *Houston Belt & Terminal Ry. Co. v. Wherry*, 548 S.W.2d 743 (Tx. App. 1977), an action for libel was brought by a terminated employee after the defendant railroad wrote, published, and caused to be delivered, a report that methadone, a synthetic drug commonly used in the withdrawal treatment of heroin addicts, had been found in the plaintiff's system. The statements appeared in various documents used in the company's investigative and dismissal process. The court affirmed a jury verdict of $150,000 in favor of the plaintiff.

In *Schmidt v. Yardney Elec. Corp.*, 492 A.2d 512 (Conn. App. 1985), an action for breach of contract and wrongful and negligent discharge was brought after a vice president was discharged, allegedly for cooperating with auditors and disclosing that he had committed insurance fraud at the direction of his superiors.

Although it held that several other claims did not state a cause of action, the court held that these facts did support a cause of action. In particular, it noted that the plaintiff's dismissal contravened the public policy of encouraging citizens to come forward with the illegal activities of their employers. The court remanded the case for trial.

In *Rulon-Miller v. Intn'l Bus. Machines Corp.*, 208 Cal. Rptr. 524 (1984), an action for wrongful discharge and intentional infliction of emotional distress was brought after a female, low-level manager was fired for allegedly having a romantic relationship with the manager of a rival firm.

The question before the court was whether there was substantial evidence supporting a jury judgment of $100,000 in compensatory and $200,000 in punitive damages. The court found that the company breached its duty of good faith and fair dealing when it failed to follow its own rules and regulations, and affirmed the jury verdict.[85]

In New Jersey, an ex-employee sued under that state's whistleblower law and was awarded $1.37 million by a U.S. district court jury in *Bowman v. Mobil*, No. 87-4093 (D. N.J. 1990). A California jury awarded $17.657 million on a sex discrimination claim in *Martin v. Texaco Refining & Marketing, Inc.*, C 613044 (Cal. Super. Ct. 1991). This verdict was later voided by the judge, who found that the amount of the award was so disproportionate to the injuries that it "shocks the conscience of this court."[86] An Oregon wrongful termination claim resulted in a state court jury verdict of $6.2 million in *Banaitas v. Mitsubishi Bank Ltd.*, No. 89-12-07357 (Or. Cir. Ct. 1991).

WHISTLEBLOWER LAWS

In addition to expanding federal employment discrimination law and the rising tide of state contract and tort litigation, an employer now faces state and federal whistleblower causes of action, a new area of law that has become the source of tension and legal disputes. These laws emanate from the widely held perception that if an employer is acting contrary to the public interest, protection must be afforded to an employee who "blows the whistle," informing society of the harmful employer action. When the employee's allegations come to light, the employee is sometimes terminated, demoted, or penalized in some manner. The employer customarily denies allegations of retaliation and puts forth a rationale for the action taken against the employee, usually citing disloyalty, divulging proprietary information, poor job performance, or violation of corporate policies.

When the employee brings a lawsuit, the jury must evaluate both the conduct of the corporation and the employee. Not surprisingly, juries often find for the whistleblower and award not only compensatory damages but also large punitive damages.

The whistleblowing law is a complex overlay of both federal and state statutes. In July 1992 the *New York Times* reported that an employee of a Binghamton, New York, defense contractor obtained an award of $7.5 million in a whistleblower case.[87] As these large awards are publicized, an employer should expect additional exposure to whistleblower suits. For example, a former vice president of General Electric Co. filed a suit in U.S. District Court for the Southern District of Ohio claiming that he was fired because he blew the whistle on a diamond price-fixing scheme. He stated that GE allegedly conspired with South Africa's DeBeers Consolidated Mines Ltd. to fix the prices of diamonds used in saw blades. It was also alleged that GE parked stock in the Asahi Diamond Industrial Co. with Mitsui & Co. to inflate GE's balance sheet by $41 million in 1989. The U.S. government intervened in the lawsuit and prompted the U.S. Attorney to open a criminal investigation of GE for alleged violations of antitrust, securities, and tax laws.[88]

Each whistleblowing statute is unique and the parameters of protected whistleblowing activity are dictated by that particular statute's language. For today's employer, the complexity of these laws presents another source of concern. Whistleblowing laws often protect "mistaken" whistleblowing conduct, which has caused serious damage to an employer's business and reputation. Furthermore, where an employer is forced to litigate a whistleblowing matter, the publicity over the litigation and the public nature of court records often impose an additional burden on the employer.

SEXUAL HARASSMENT

Sexual harassment is an area of employment law that deserves separate discussion because society has recently become increasingly sensitive to this subject. The Anita Hill–Clarence Thomas hearings caused many people to discuss and reassess their attitude toward sexual harassment in the workplace. This change in the treatment of sexual harassment, from both an employee and employer standpoint, has resulted in a landslide of additional sexual harassment complaints (Figure I.1).

There are two categories of sexual harassment: the "quid pro quo" type and the newer, "hostile environment" type. In quid pro quo sexual harassment, the victim is pressured to provide sexual favors to someone who exercises power in making employment decisions such as hiring, firing, and promoting. In the hostile environment cases, the victim argues that because of an inappropriate atmosphere, she (or he) cannot perform job tasks. Typical inappropriate environmental factors cited by female plaintiffs are posting of photographs of nude women, sexually charged verbal comments, and sexually oriented notes or letters from coworkers. Harassment claims by male plaintiffs and same-sex claims are the newest twists in this area of litigation.

In addition to the employer embarrassment that usually occurs in a sexual harassment claim, the lawsuits can be expensive. Juries that hear these lawsuits are increasingly being instructed to consider whether a "reasonable woman" would feel harassed by comments, innuendoes, or other conduct. This increasingly accepted standard will provide female plaintiffs with a less difficult legal standard under which to successfully litigate.

THE INCREASING ATTRACTIVENESS OF ALTERNATIVE DISPUTE RESOLUTION TO COUNSEL, EMPLOYERS, AND EMPLOYEES

In addition to the legal and legislative developments in favor of it, and the increasing cost of litigating employment law disputes, many employment law attorneys are beginning to support the rise of ADR. At the 1992 mid-winter meeting of the Equal Employment Opportunity Committee of the American Bar Association, Paul Grossman, author of *Employment Discrimination Law*, the leading treatise on equal

FIGURE I.1
Sexual Harassment and Alternative Dispute Resolution

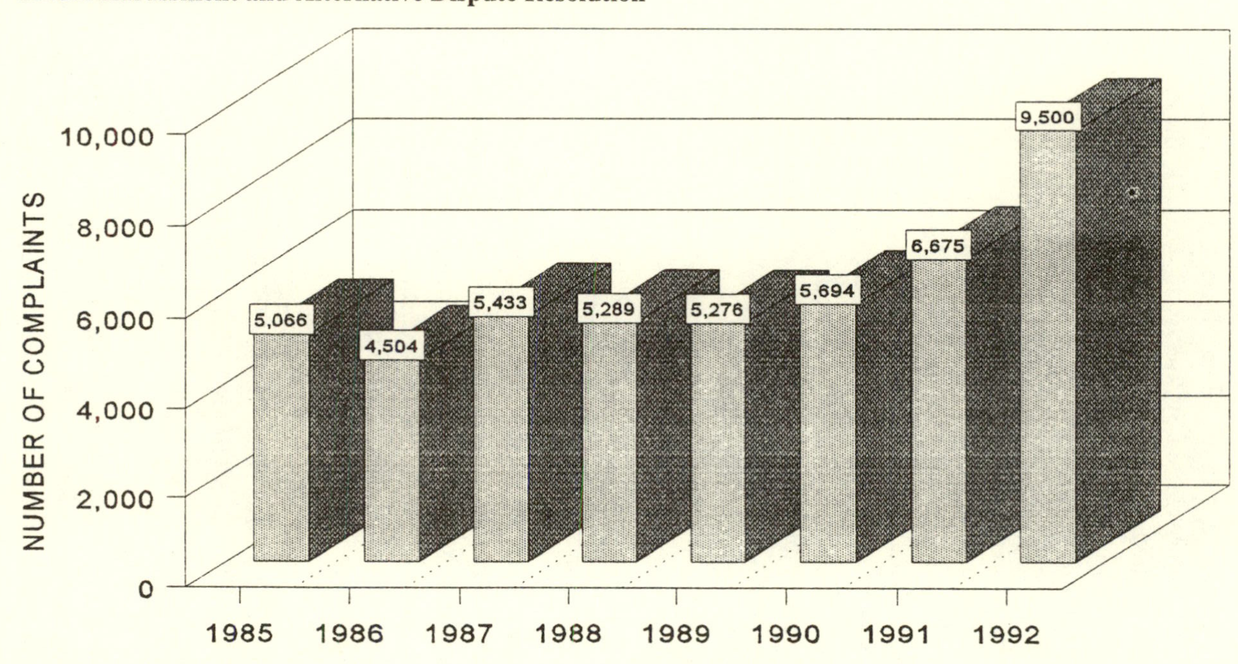

Source: Jane Gross, "Suffering In Silence No More: Fighting Sexual Harassment," *New York Times*, July 13, 1992.

employment opportunity law, stated that "Arbitration is an idea whose time has come."[89] Grossman said that his law firm was already counselling major clients to enter into formal arbitration agreements. Similarly, Vincent J. Apruzzese, past president of the American Bar Association and its Labor & Employment Law Section, stated at the Seventh Annual National Conference on Labor and Employment Law at Stetson University College of Law that "A well conceived, well drafted, and fair alternate dispute resolution procedure is very much in order and can save much anxiety and expense for all concerned. The time for ADR has come."[90] Frank C. Morris, Jr., senior partner of labor employment law at Epstein, Becker and Green, noted that with multi-million dollar judgments becoming more common, the increasing cost of litigation, and the fact that a simple case is difficult to defend for less than $100,000, employment arbitration is becoming more attractive to employers.[91]

The continuing popularity of this trend is evident when the topics that are covered at employment law seminars across the country are considered. For example, the theme of the Eleventh Annual National Conference on Labor and Employment Law, sponsored by the Center for Dispute Resolution of Stetson Law School, was "Critical Issues for 1996."

EMPLOYEE FEEDBACK ON ARBITRATION OF EMPLOYMENT LAW DISPUTES

It is difficult to determine employee sentiment toward pre-dispute agreements to arbitrate. Anecdotal evidence to date establishes that major corporations that have introduced such programs have met with minimal employee opposition. A poll found that over half of all employees surveyed indicated that they be willing to give up their right to a court trial in favor of submitting a grievance to arbitration.[92]

THE ADVANTAGES OF PRE-DISPUTE AGREEMENTS TO ARBITRATE

Any discussion of pre-dispute agreements to arbitrate must be tempered with the caution that these agreements do not vitiate or subordinate federal civil rights law.[93] It is neither a pro-employer nor pro-employee process but should benefit both sides. Furthermore, while an employee surrenders certain rights by agreeing to pre-dispute arbitration, so does an employer. In any dispute that reaches litigation, a party to a pre-dispute agreement may regret signing that agreement. For example, an employee may prefer to present his case to a jury instead of to an arbitrator. Similarly, an employer may be forced to arbitrate on a matter that may have been terminated early in the litigation process. Thus, the fairness of this process should not be determined by an *ex post facto* review.

The fact that a particular party may oppose arbitration after a dispute has arisen is a by-product of any arbitration agreement. Such opposition simply establishes that both parties give up certain rights when they waive their access to a judicial forum.

Nevertheless, there are many benefits to the employer and employee in a pre-dispute agreement to arbitrate. First, arbitration has generally proved to be faster than courtroom litigation. Crowded federal and state court dockets, which give priority to criminal matters, can result in a final trial years after the filing of a civil complaint; arbitration can usually be scheduled within a few months.

Second, arbitration is usually less procedurally cumbersome. Prior to a hearing, the parties usually do not engage in drawn-out discovery disputes and the filing of motions. In an arbitration hearing, the proceedings are generally less rigid than the courtroom because the arbitrator enjoys wide latitude in conducting the hearing. For example, most arbitrators do not strictly adhere to the Federal Rules of Evidence. Also, an arbitrator is not a jury. Thus the additional costs associated with a jury — jury research, motions resultant from a jury trial, and slower trial presentation due to a jury — are avoided.

A third benefit of arbitration flows directly from its informality and flexibility: each side does not require representation by a lawyer. In labor-management arbitration, for example, often neither party will use legal counsel, preferring to represent their interests through nonlawyers. This results in significant savings of time and money.

Arbitration also provides the parties with the opportunity to select an arbitrator with significant expertise in a particular industry or issue in dispute. Thus, from the inception of the hearing both parties are before an expert fact-finder in their particular industry and area of law.

Arbitrator's decisions are usually issued soon after the hearing. Court decisions can take several months. Furthermore, the parties to arbitration can require that a decision be issued within a certain number of days of the close of hearing. For minor disputes, parties can elect to waive the issuance of written opinions and require only a written award. Further, the parties may, in some circumstances, waive a written award in favor of a binding oral award.

Arbitration is more final than courtroom litigation. Because arbitration decisions are reviewed on narrow grounds by the courts, the grounds for appeal are quite narrow. Thus, parties to arbitration usually obtain a final resolution of the dispute within a few months, unlike judicial appeals that can take years.

This finality affords another benefit to disputants: less bitterness and hostility. An unresolved dispute can undercut workplace morale and interpersonal relationships. In arbitration, when the arbitrator issues the binding award, the dispute is over.

Arbitration is a flexible process that belongs to the parties who usually agree to shape it to fit their needs. Hearings and other procedural matters can be scheduled at the parties' convenience. In contrast, parties in a federal or state court sacrifice all flexibility to the scheduling decisions of the judge and docket clerk. Courts are seldom as cooperative or flexible as an arbitrator. As the Supreme Court noted, "By agreeing to arbitrate, a party trades the procedures and opportunity for review of the courtroom for the simplicity, informality, and expedition of arbitration."[94]

Arbitration results in obtaining a faster decision. The benefit to an employer is that there is less back pay exposure due to the swift scheduling of the proceeding and issuance of a decision. Both parties' legal fees should also be significantly less. This benefits the employer when the plaintiff is awarded attorneys' fees, because significant fees should not accrue when the matter is resolved expediently.

The plaintiff also benefits from an expedient, less expensive process. Attorneys can represent employees in many arbitration matters; this includes cases where counsel could not afford to take the matter to courtroom litigation on a contingency basis.

Another benefit of arbitration is that it is a private dispute resolution process that can be made as confidential as the parties choose. For whistleblower cases, cases involving employer trade secrets or other proprietary information, or allegations of employer misconduct, such as sexual harassment, confidentiality is a valuable advantage.

There are other benefits to arbitration. In addition to the costs associated with a jury trial, many employers believe that juries unfairly favor employees against employers. Juries may evaluate an employment decision or dispute based on fairness and not on whether a specific law was violated. An unfair employment decision may not be illegal; arbitrators may more readily grasp this distinction, viewing the matter in a less emotional, more dispassionate light.

Another advantage of arbitration is that employees and employers can structure the proceeding to their particular needs. For example, the parties may agree that the employer will assume all the costs of arbitration. The parties may agree on a particular location for arbitration, reducing possible inconvenience and attendant expense. The parties may agree that certain evidence, possibly inadmissible in a courtroom, should be admitted. The parties may wish to arbitrate with a three-person panel, rather than a single arbitrator. This panel typically includes a professional, outside, neutral panel member with two neutral panel members selected from within the organization, one by management and one by the nonmanagement work force. These panels are particularly helpful when the outside arbitrator faces certain technical issues that can be explained informally in caucus by the other panel members.

A final advantage of a pre-dispute arbitration model is often overlooked by the legal profession. That advantage is the productivity and human gains arising from the institutionalization of a process providing for fair treatment of employees in the workplace and a fair hearing of employment disputes. Where employees are empowered to raise workplace grievances or other issues, management will be better informed of the issues that affect workplace productivity and morale. The resolution of such issues should raise both productivity and morale and lead to less employee turnover.

Very simply, when an employee can use an established procedure to pursue a claim, it requires less time and energy. Thus, the procedure is more likely to be used than if the employee must blaze a new trail within the organization with a complaint. While some may see this increased accessibility to a dispute resolution procedure as a negative factor, most observers agree that, in many cases, the one complaint management does not know about can be far more harmful than the ten it does know about.

THE DISADVANTAGES OF PRE-DISPUTE AGREEMENTS

To some, many of the advantages of pre-dispute agreements could be expressed as disadvantages. As discussed, both employer and employee surrender certain rights and possible tactical advantages by entering into a pre-dispute agreement to arbitrate.

First, many corporate and employee counsel, while in favor of various ADR techniques, oppose locking into a pre-dispute procedure. They would prefer to evaluate cases as they arise, possibly agreeing to a post-dispute arbitration procedure.

Second, some employers may not prefer the increased accessibility of this dispute resolution forum. The strategy of burying the plaintiff in litigation costs is not available under the pre-dispute arbitration model.

Third, many counsel are not comfortable or even familiar with the arbitration process. They may prefer to be in a federal or state court before a judge. They may also prefer the rigidity of courtroom litigation, including the strict application of the Federal Rules of Civil Procedure and Evidence.

A related concern is the finality of an arbitration decision. Many cautious attorneys do not want to give up the right to appeal a judge or jury's decision to a higher court. While such appeal is an expensive proposition, many counsel prefer to keep this option open. Since an arbitrator's award can be appealed only on narrow grounds, a pre-dispute agreement could be considered disadvantageous if one wishes to maximize appeal rights.

Another possible disadvantage of a pre-dispute agreement to arbitrate is the arbitrator selection process. At present, arbitrators are available from various dispute resolution organizations. The most well-established, the American Arbitration Association, offers both commercial and labor arbitration panels from which to select an arbitrator. Some labor lawyers may prefer not to select arbitrators from a commercial panel, because they may be unknown to counsel or unskilled in employment relations issues. Other lawyers may not be comfortable with traditional labor-management arbitrators, since they may be perceived to have an inherent bias developed from their years of arbitrating in the culture of the union-management model. For example, in the nonunion sector, there is no "just cause" requirement. This requirement is so entrenched in the union-management setting that these labor-management arbitrators may view nonunion arbitration issues from "just-cause-colored glasses."[95] Many employers do not want to introduce a just-cause standard into their workplace.

Another possible disadvantage of pre-dispute arbitration is the selection of arbitrators to resolve statutory issues. Arbitrators in traditional labor-management matters usually interpret the "four corners" of the collective bargaining agreement. While the National Labor Relations Act deferral policy requires arbitrators to decide many statutory issues, there is a continuing debate among arbitrators, academics, and practitioners regarding the ability or desirability of an arbitrator interpreting and applying statutes outside of these four corners. Interestingly, this debate has already been resolved by the U.S. Supreme Court, which has recognized that arbitrators are capable of deciding complex statutory issues.[96]

Finally, there are open legal issues regarding the federal and state courts' acceptance and willingness to enforce pre-dispute agreements to arbitrate and the possible intervention of Congress to bar such models. To date, it is clear that the courts, for the most part, have supported the use of binding arbitration procedures. Similarly, Congress has had the opportunity but has declined to intervene through legislation.[97]

NOTES

1. R. W. Fleming, *The Labor Arbitration Process* (Urbana: University of Illinois Press, 1965), 19.

2. *United Steelworkers of America v. American Manufacturing Co.*, 363 U.S. 564 (1960); *United Steelworkers of America v. Warrior and Gulf Navigation Co.*, 363 U.S. 574 (1960); *United Steelworkers of America v. Enterprise Wheel and Car Corp.*, 363 U.S. 593 (1960).

3. Id. at 38. A trial *de novo* means a full trial on the issues, without any legal obligation to follow the factual or legal conclusions reached in the first hearing.

4. Id. at 47.

5. Id. at 47–48.

6. Footnote 21 states:

> We adopt no standards as to the weight to be accorded an arbitral decision, since this must be determined in the court's discretion with regard to the facts and circumstances of each case. Relevant factors include the existence of provisions in the collective-bargaining agreement that conform substantially with Title VII, the degree of procedural fairness in the arbitral forum, adequacy of the record with respect to the issue of discrimination, and the special competence of particular arbitrators. Where an arbitral determination gives full consideration to an employee's Title VII rights, a court may properly accord it great weight. This is especially true where the issue is solely one of fact, specifically addressed by the parties and decided by the arbitrator on the basis of an adequate record. But courts should ever be mindful that Congress, in enacting Title VII, thought it necessary to provide a judicial forum for the ultimate resolution of discriminatory employment claims. It is the duty of courts to assure the full availability of this forum.

7. Burger, "Isn't There A Better Way?" 68 ABA J 274 (1982).

8. Id. at 24.

9. Id. at 628.

10. Id. at 480.

11. Section 1 states that "contracts of employment of seamen, railroad employees, or any other class of employees engaged in foreign or interstate commerce" are excluded from enforceability under the FAA. 9 U.S.C. § 1.

12. *Alford v. Dean Witter Reynolds, Inc.*, 939 F.2d 229 (5th Cir. 1991); *Willis v. Dean Witter Reynolds, Inc.*, 948 F.2d 305 (6th Cir. 1991); *Mago v. Shearson Lehman Hutton, Inc.*, 956 F.2d 932 (9th Cir. 1992); *Bender v. A.G. Edwards & Sons, Inc.*, 971 F.2d 698 (11th Cir. 1992). The First and Eighth Circuit Courts of Appeals have ruled that Title VII discrimination actions are not subject to arbitration, noting the distinct status of Title VII among federal statutory schemes. *Utley v. Goldman Sachs and Co.*, 883 F.2d 184, 187 (1st Cir.

1989), *cert. denied*, 110 U.S. 842; *Swenson v. Management Recruiters Internat'l, Inc.*, 858 F.2d 1304, 1306-07, n.6 (8th Cir. 1980). These particular First and Eighth Circuit Courts of Appeals decisions were issued prior to *Gilmer*.

13. *Willis v. Dean Witter Reynolds, Inc.*, 948 F.2d 305, 310.

14. 956 F.2d 934, 935.

15. *The Prudential Ins. Co. of America v. Lai*, 42 F.3d 1299, 1304 (9th Cir. 1994), *cert denied*, 133 L. Ed. 2d 24, 116 S. Ct. 61 (1995).

16. *Prudential Insurance Company v. Lai*, 42 F.3d 1299 (9th Cir. 1994), *cert. denied*, 133 L. Ed. 2d 24, 116 S. Ct. 61 (1995).

17. *Prudential Kidd v. Equitable Life Assurance Soc'y of Amn.*, 32 F.2d 516 (11th Cir. 1994); *Accord, Metz v. Merrill Lynch, Pierce, Fenner & Smith, Inc.*, 39 F.3d 1482 (10th Cir. 1994); *Association of Inv. Brokers v. Securities & Exchange Com.*, 676 F.2d 857, 861 (D.C. Cir. 1982); *Scher v. Equitable Life Assurance Soc'y of the United States*, 866 F. Supp. 766 (S.D.N.Y. 1994).

18. *Farrand v. Lutheran Brotherhood*, 993 F.2d 1253 (7th Cir. 1993).

19. *Bender v. A.G. Edwards & Sons, Inc.*, 971 F.2d 698 (11th Cir. 1992).

20. *Bender v. Smith Barney, Harris Upham and Company*, 901 F. Supp. 863 (DC-NJ 1994).

21. *Bierdeman v. Shearson Lehman Hutton, Inc.*, U.S. S. Ct., No. 92-314 (10/13/92).

22. *Maye v. Smith Barney Inc.*, 897 F. Supp. 100 (S.D.N.Y. 1995); see also *Gateson v. ASLK-Bank*, 1995 U.S. Dist. LEXIS 9004 (S.D.N.Y. 1995); *Pitter v. Prudential Life Insurance Company of America*, 906 F. Supp. 130 (E.D.N.Y. 1995).

23. *Saari v. Smith Barney, Harris Upham and Co.*, 968 F.2d 877 (9th Cir. 1992).

24. *Pritzker v. Merrill Lynch, Pierce, Fenner, & Smith, Inc.*, 7 F.3d 110 (3rd Cir. 1993).

25. *Shearson/American Express, Inc. v. McMahon*, 482 U.S. 220 (1987).

26. *DiGaetano v. Smith Barney, Inc.*, 1996 U.S. Dist. LEXIS 1140 (S.D.N.Y. 1996).

27. The Travelers Group policy was previously known as the "Primerica/Smith Barney Dispute Resolution Procedure" until the merger of Primerica into Travelers to create the Travelers Group. This procedure was also upheld in *Maye v. Smith Barney Inc.*, 897 F. Supp. 100 (S.D.N.Y. 1995).

28. *Austin v. Owens-Brockway Glass Container, Inc.*, 1996 U. S. LEXIS 4370, 151 L.R.R.M. 2673 (4th Cir. 1996).

29. This law amends 42 U.S.C. 2000e (Title VII of the Civil Rights Act of 1964), 42 U.S.C. 1981 (Civil Rights Act of 1866), 42 U.S.C. 1988 (Civil Rights Attorneys' Fees), 42 U.S.C. 12101 (Americans With Disabilities Act), 29 U.S.C. 791 (Rehabilitation Act of 1973). Note that the ADEA, while not addressed in the Civil Rights Act of 1991, already contains language encouraging the use of ADR.

30. *Gilmer v. Interstate/Johnson Lane Corp.*, at 1652, 1654.

31. *Nghiem v. NEC Elec.*, 25 F.3d 1437, 1441 (9th Cir. 1994); *Williams v. Katten, Muchin & Zavis*, 837 F. Supp. 1430, 1436 (N.D. Ill. 1993); *Lockhart v. A.G. Edwards & Sons*, 65 Fair Empl. Prac. Cas. (BNA) 5, 7 (D. Kan. Jan. 25, 1994); *Benefits Communications Corp. v. Klieforth*, 642 A.2d 1299 (D.C. 1994); *Fletcher v. Kidder, Peabody*, 81 NY 2d 623, 619 N.E. 2d 998, 601 N.Y.S. 2d 686 (N.Y. 1993), *cert. denied*, 126 L. Ed. 2d 455, 114 S. Ct. 554 (U.S. 1993).

32. 9 U.S.C. § 1, et seq.

33. HR Rep. 96, 68th Cong., 1st Sess. 1, 2 (1924).

34. 9 U.S.C. § 2.

35. 9 U.S.C. § 3.

36. 9 U.S.C. § 4.

37. *Shearson/American Express, Inc. v. McMahon*, 482 U.S. 220, 226 (1987).

38. Id. at 227.

39. Id. at 266; a claim that the contract containing the arbitration clause was induced by fraud cannot defeat a motion to compel arbitration unless it is shown that the arbitration clause itself was fraudulently induced. *Prima Paint Corp. v. Flood & Conklin Mfg. Co.*, 388 U.S. 395 (1967).

40. *Rodriguez de Quijas v. Shearson/American Express*, 490 U.S. 477, 483-484 (1989), citing *Mitsubishi Motors Corp. v. Soler Chrysler-Plymouth, Inc.*, 473 U.S. 614, 627 (1985).

41. 9 U.S.C. § 1.

42. 350 U.S. at 204.

43. *Dickstein v. duPont & Co.*, 443 F.2d 783, 785 (1st Cir. 1971) (the Section 1 exception under the FAA is limited to employees involved in or closely related to the actual movement of goods and interstate commerce, therefore the FAA does not apply to securities industry employee); *Signal-Stat Corp. v. Local 475, United Elec., Radio and Machine Workers of America*, 235 F.2d 298, 301-03 (2d Cir. 1956), *cert. denied*, 354 U.S. 911 (1956); *Erving v. The Virginia Squires Basketball Club*, 468 F.2d 1064, 1069 (2d Cir. 1972) (FAA applies to a professional basketball player's contract because player was not involved in the transportation industry); *Tenney Engineering, Inc. v. United Elec. Radio and Machine Workers*, 207 F.2d 450 (3d Cir. 1953) (Section 1 of the FAA does not exclude all contracts of employment from its scope as the drafters of the FAA intended to exclude only arbitration agreements covering classes of employees actively involved in the transportation industry); *Bacashihua v. United States Postal Service*, 859 F.2d 402, 405 (6th Cir. 1988) (a postal employee was excluded from the FAA because she belonged to a class of employees directly involved in interstate commerce); *Willis v. Dean Witter Reynolds, Inc.*, 948 F.2d 305 (6th Cir. 1991); *Miller Brewing Co. v. Brewery Workers Local Union No. 9*, 739 F.2d 1159, 1162 (7th. Cir. 1984), *cert. denied*, 469 U.S. 1160 (1985); *Legg, Mason & Co., Inc. v. Mackall & Co., Inc.*, 351 F. Supp 1367, 1371 n.4 (D. D.C. 1972); *Malison v. Prudential-Bache Securities, Inc.*, 654 F. Supp 101, 104 (W.D. N.C. 1987); *Hydrick v. Management Recruiters, Int'l, Inc.*, 738 F. Supp 1434, 1435

(N.D. Ga. 1990); *Management Recruiters Int'l v. Nebel*, 765 F. Supp 419, 421-22 (N.D. Ohio 1991) (nonunion account executives are not within the exception from coverage outlined in Section 1 of the FAA since they are not engaged in interstate commerce or transportation).

44. *United Elec., Radio and Machine Workers of Am. v. Miller Metal Prods., Inc.*, 215 F.2d 221, 224 (4th Cir. 1954).

45. *UFCW v. Safeway Stores*, 889 F.2d 940 (10th Cir. 1989); *Herring v. Delta Airlines*, 894 F.2d 1020 (9th Cir. 1990), *cert. denied*, 110 S.Ct 1319 (1990); however, the Ninth Circuit Court of Appeals has subsequently indicated that this is an open issue. In *Mago v. Shearson Lehman Hutton, Inc.*, the Ninth Circuit compelled arbitration of an employee's sexual harassment claim because the employee signed an employment application requiring her to submit to arbitration any employment disputes. However, the court declined to address the FAA because the plaintiff did not raise this issue in the litigation. The court describes this FAA issue as "an unresolved question." *Mago v. Shearson Lehman Hutton, Inc.*, 956 F.2d 932, 934 (9th Cir. 1992).

46. *American Postal Workers Union v. U.S. Postal Serv.*, 823 F.2d 466, 473 (11th Cir. 1987).

47. *Dancu v. Coopers & Lybrand*, 778 F. Supp. 832 (D.C. Pa., 1991).

48. Id. at 833.

49. Id.

50. *Corion Corporation v. Gih-Horng Chen*, 1991 U.S. Dist. LEXIS 18395; 1991 WL 280288 (D. Mass. 1991). This decision was appealed to the First Circuit Court of Appeals on an interlocutory basis. The court denied immediate appeal, holding that this issue of the appropriateness of the order staying court proceedings pending arbitration is not subject to immediate appeal. *Corion Corp. v. Chen*, 956 F.2d 55 (CA-1, 1992).

51. *Management Recruiters International Inc. v. Nebel*, 765 F. Supp. 419, 420 (N.D. Ohio 1991); See also *Hampton v. ITT Corp.*, 829 F. Supp. 202 (S. D. Tex. 1993).

52. Id. at 422. The rise in the attractiveness of ADR is not limited to employment discrimination litigation. The federal court system is moving swiftly toward implementation of mandatory ADR and many states are doing the same. The legal profession is following suit as the ABA has elevated its Standing Committee on Dispute Resolution to Section status.

53. Most of the statutory arbitration envisioned by this book would involve federal statutes and thus would be governed by the FAA, regardless of the location where the alleged illegal conduct occurred. However, causes of action that involve state statutes may be arbitrated under the arbitration law of the particular state. Here most state laws encourage arbitration even though each state statute and related law is unique and should be interpreted by local counsel. See, e.g., Stuart M. Riback, "Are Arbitrations Final?" *New York State Bar Journal* (November 1995), 18-19, 52.

54. The following states have arbitration laws excluding labor contracts: Alaska Stat. Ann. Section 9.43.010 (unless Act is incorporated into agreement); Ariz. Rev. Stat. Ann. Section 12-1501; Ark. Stat. Ann. Section 34-511 (1981); Idaho Code Section 7-901; Iowa Code Ann. Section 679A.1; Ky. Rev. Stat. Section 417.045; La. Rev. Stat. Ann. Section 9:4201; Md. Cts. and Jud. Proc. Code Ann. Section 3-201 (unless Act incorporated into agreement); Mass. Gen. Laws Ann. Ch. 251, Section 1; Mich. Comp. Laws Section 600.5001 (Mich.); N.H. Rev. Stat. Ann. Section 542:1; N.C. Gen. Stat. Section 1-567.1 (unless Act incorporated into agreement); Okla. Stat. Title 15, Section 801; Ore. Rev. Stats. Section 33.210; R.I. Gen. Laws Section 10-3-1; Texas Rev. Civ. Stat. Ann. Art. 224; Wis. Stat. Ann. Section 788.01.

55. Ala. Code Section 6-6-1 (1977); Miss. Code Ann. Section 11-15-1 (1972); W. Va. Code Section 55-10-1 (1981); Cal. Civ. Pro. Code Section 1280; Colo. Rev. Stat. Section 13-22-201; Conn. Gen. Stat. Ann. Section 52-408; D.C. Code Ann. Section 116-4301; Del. Code Ann. Title 10, Section 5701; Fla. Stat. Ann. Section 682.01; Ga. Code Ann. Section 9-9-1 (if the arbitration clause is initialed at time of execution of agreement); Hawaii Rev. Stat. Section 658-1; Ill. Rev. Stat. Ch. 10, Section 101; Ind. Code Ann. Section 34-4-2-1; Kan. Stat. Ann. Section 401; Me. Rev. Stat. Ann. Title 14, Section 5927; Minn. Stat. Ann. Section 572.08; Mo. Rev. Stat. Section 435.350 (only agreements between "commercial persons"); Mont. Rev. Codes Ann. Section 27-5-111; Neb. Rev. Stat. Section 25-2601; Nev. Rev. Stat. Section 38.015 (unless Act is incorporated into agreement); N.J. Rev. Stat. Section 2A:24-1; N.M. Stat. Ann. Section 44-7-1; N.Y. Civ. Prac. Law Section 7501 (New York); N.D. Cent. Code Section 32-29.2-01; Ohio Rev. Code Ann. Section 2711.01; Pa. Stat. Ann. Title 42, Section 7301; P.R. Laws Ann. Title 32, Section 3201; S.D. Codified Laws Ann. Section 21A-1 25; Tenn. Code Ann. Section 29-5-301; Utah Code Ann. Section 78-31a-1; Vt. Stat. Ann. Title 12, Section 5651 (excludes civil rights disputes); Va. Code Section 8.01.581.01; Wash. Rev. Code Section 7.04.010; Wyo. Stat. Section 136-101.

56. *Reid v. Goldman, Sachs & Co.*, 154 N.Y. Misc. 2d 756, 586 N.Y.S. 2d 459 (N.Y. Sup Ct.1992), affirmed 590 N.Y. Supp. 2d 497 (1992).

57. *Fletcher v. Kidder, Peabody & Co.*, 81 N.Y.2d 623, 601 N.Y.S.2d 686 (1993).

58. Id. at 600.

59. Id. at 604.

60. Id. at 954.

61. *Spellman v. Securities, Annuities and Insurance Services*, Cal. Ct. App., No. B05 7549, 7292.

62. *Daily Labor Report* (BNA), A-4 (No. 151) 8/9/93.

63. *Gardner v. Benefits Communications Corp.*, 1991 U.S. Dist. LEXIS 18367 (D.D.C. 1991); *Kaliden v. Shearson Hutton, Inc.*, 789 F. Supp. 179 (W.D. Pa. 1991).

64. *Young v. Prudential Insurance Co.*, NJ SuperCt No. SOM-L-907-95, 10/19/95.

65. Seth Faison, Jr., "Rash Of Suits Seen After Rights Act," *New York Times*, November 30, 1991, p. 1; Michael K. Burns, "Sex Bias Complaints Soar — Added Impetus Seen With U.S. Law," *Baltimore Sun*, November 26, 1991, p. 1. "Study Shows Job Bias Changing — As Judges Wrestle With Pinups And Massages, Litigation Skyrockets," *ABA Journal*, May 1991, pp. 34–35.

66. John J. Donohue III and Peter Siegelman, "The Changing Nature of Employment Discrimination Litigation," *Stanford Law Review*, 43(5) (May 1991): 983–1033. The authors consider the data in this study, obtained from the Administrative Office of the U.S. Courts (1989 Computer File), EEOC annual reports, and the American Bar Foundation Employment Discrimination Litigation Survey Computer File to be the most exhaustive and reliable set of data yet compiled.

67. Federal Courts Study Committee, "Tentative Recommendations for Public Comment," *Proposed Long Range Plans for the Federal Courts* (1989): 49–50.

68. Randall Samborn, "Many Americans Find Bias at Work," *National Law Journal*, July 16, 1990, p. 1.

69. Peter Kuhn, "Sex Discrimination in Labor Markets: The Role of Statistical Evidence," *Am. Econ. Rev.*, 77 (1987): 567, 579.

70. The Rand study found that 54 percent of claimants of wrongful discharge in California were from middle or top management.

71. The Rand study found that defendants as a group spent an average of $293,000 of which the lawyers received $165,000 ($81,000 for the plaintiff's lawyer and $84,000 for the defendant's lawyer) while the employee received on average $128,000 — about 44% of the total.

72. Randall Samborn, "Many Americans Find Bias at Work," *National Law Journal*, July 16, 1990, p. 1.

73. *Foley v. Interactive Data Corporation*, 47 Cal. 3d 654, 765 P.2d 373, 254 Cal. Rptr. 211 (1988).

74. "Employment Litigation Jury Awards," *California Labor & Employment Law Quarterly*, 8(8) (Spring 1992): p. 3.

75. James N. Dertouzas, Elaine Holland, and Patricia Ebener, *The Legal and Economic Consequences of Wrongful Termination* ("The Rand Study"). (Santa Monica: Rand Institute for Civil Justice, 1988).

76. *Cancellier v. Federated Dept. Stores*, 672 F.2d 1312 (9th Cir. 1982) *cert. denied*, 459 U.S. 859 (1982).

77. *Wilson v. Monarch Paper Co.*, 939 F.2d 1138 (5th Cir. 1991).

78. *Kimzey v. Wal-Mart Stores, Inc.*, Cas. No. CV-C-5, 1995 U.S. Dist. LEXIS 9867 (W.D. Mo. June 29, 1995).

79. "Hawaii Jury Awards Over 1.8 Million to Female Managers Fired by Car Dealer," *Daily Labor Report*, April 5, 1996, pp. A4–A5.

80. *Nordlin v. Kmart Corp.*, No. 35243, 4/6/96.

81. *Burch v. Coca-Cola Co.*, 3:93 Civ. 1894 (N.D.Tex. June 28, 1995).

82. As stated earlier, it has been reported that an average arbitration costs from $1,000 to $5,000, while litigation costs $5,000 to $10,000 just to start! *Daily Labor Report*, January 2, 1992, p. A-5.

83. Robert J. Aalberts and Lorne Seidman, "The Employment At Will Doctrine: Nevada's Struggle Demonstrates The Need For Reform," *Labor Law Journal*, October 1992, pp. 651–661.

84. Blackstone Commentaries 425.

85. IBM may consider itself fortunate. The Rand study found that in California wrongful dismissal trials, almost half (40 of 81) of the successful plaintiffs were awarded punitive damages averaging more than $500,000.

86. "$20.3 Million Verdict Overturned in Texaco Sex-Bias Suit," *New York Times*, July 24, 1992, p. 1.

87. Richard W. Stevenson, "A Whistle-Blower To Get $7.5 Million In Big Fraud Case," *New York Times*, July 15, 1992, p. A1.

88. "Deal & Suits," *Legal Times*, August 10, 1992, p. 9.

89. *Daily Labor Report*, March 15, 1992, pp. A7–A8.

90. Vincent J. Apruzzese, "Selected Recent Developments In EEO Law: The Civil Rights Act of 1991, Sexual Harassment, and the Emerging Role of ADR," *Labor Law Journal*, June 22, 1992, p. 334.

91. "Employment Arbitration Becoming More Attractive to Employers," *Daily Labor Report*, December 18, 1991, pp. A8–A9; Arthur Eliot Berkeley and E. Patrick McDermott, "The Second Golden Age of Employment Arbitration," *Labor Law Journal*, December 1992, pp. 774–779; E. Patrick McDermott, "Time Involved In Litigation Makes ADR An Attractive Option," *The Daily Record*, Monday, August 17, 1992; E. Patrick McDermott, "Fleet, Discrete and Complete — The Use Of ADR In Employment Law," *Maryland Bar Journal*, 26(2) (March–April 1993): 6–11.

92. Randall Samborn, "Many Americans Find Bias at Work," *National Law Journal*, July 16, 1990, p. 1.

93. Note that the use of a binding arbitration procedure or other ADR procedure would not prohibit the EEOC from separately investigating a claim of discrimination. *EEOC v. Cosmair, Inc., L'Oreal Hair Care Div.*, 821 F.2d 1085, 1091-92 (5th Cir. 1987). In practice, the arbitration award would bar any other court proceeding. The EEOC would still be able to consider class action issues or in an individual case seek injunctive relief prohibiting future discriminatory conduct by the employer. However, the arbitration decision would determine whether back pay and other relief was appropriate.

94. *Gilmer v. Interstate/Johnson Lane Corp.*, at 1654.

95. Arbitrators have been confused over their new role. At the National Academy of Arbitrators 1992 annual convention in San Francisco, the academy debated whether they should amend their constitution or establish guidelines for arbitration in nonunion arbitration settings. The Academy's constitution currently covers only union-management arbitration. Anthony V. Sinocropi, "The Future Of Labor Arbitration: Problems, Prospects and Opportunities, The Presidential

Address, 1992," presented at the Annual Meeting of the National Academy of Arbitrators, San Francisco, 1992.

96. *Shearson/American Express, Inc. v. McMahon*, 482 U.S. 220 (1987).

97. S. 2405, 103rd Congress, 2nd Sess. (1994), introduced by Senator Feingold (D.Wis.) in August 1994 and H. R. 4981, introduced by Representatives Schroeder (D. Colo.) and Markey (D. Mass.) in August 1994.

II

Varieties of Alternative Dispute Resolution

In this section, we discuss a variety of Alternative Dispute Resolution techniques and approaches. It is worth emphasizing once again that an organization is well-advised to consider which technique or combination of approaches is best for its individual needs, personnel, and organizational culture.

The techniques discussed, in order, are open door policy, peer review, ombudsman, union-management model, employer-run dispute resolution procedures, mediation, mediation-arbitration, and fact finding.

OPEN DOOR POLICY

While many organizations boast of an open door policy, under which workplace issues can be quickly resolved, these systems are often too informal and unstructured to be truly effective for all types of workplace disputes. An employee must take the initiative to "open the door" and meet with a member of upper management to register a complaint against a lower-level manager. Generally, employees are reluctant to engage in confrontation on their own and pessimistic in their expectation of an equitable outcome.

There may well be small, informal organizations in which the open door policy works well, but for most large organizations, it is probably not effective. Such a policy asks too much of the individual employee and too little of management.

In response to these flaws in an open door policy, some organizations have instituted peer review systems to resolve employee problems at the workplace.

PEER REVIEW

Peer review is a process in which certain employee complaints are heard by a panel comprised of the organization's employees and supervisors. Typically, top management may select or train those who serve on the panel.

Each organization that operates a peer review system may create its own process, but fundamentally, it works as follows: An employee with a grievance first seeks to discuss the problem with his or her immediate supervisor.

If this is not successful, the employee may seek a peer review. Peer review committees usually consist of specially trained individuals from all parts of the organization who attempt an objective examination of the dispute and provide a binding decision. Generally, peer review panels are made up of several rank and file employees and a few supervisors.

Typically, these panels are limited in their power and authority. They usually cannot alter any existing organizational policy, work rules, or salary and benefits. What they can do is provide a remedy for unfair treatment of an employee or the inconsistent application of established rules, policies, or procedures. The matters that customarily come before these panels are appeals of discipline, work assignments and schedules, safety and health issues, promotions, transfers, and performance evaluations. A peer review panel is like a jury that decides a case, not a legislature that creates laws.

Supporters of peer review contend that, by using those within the organization to review grievances, better and wiser decisions are made by the people who truly understand the organization, its mission, and its people. They point out that management personnel do not numerically dominate the panel or unduly influence its deliberations and that the employee with a complaint gets a fair hearing and wins a remedy when one is deserved.

Critics of peer review argue that since management creates, selects, trains, and operates the system, the employee with a complaint faces a biased system from every angle. The limited power and authority of the panel is another indicator of its lack of real clout, as is the presence of managers on the panel. Further, many union supporters point out that this technique is often an integral part of a management union-avoidance campaign, and for that reason alone is highly suspect.

In sum, a peer review panel is potentially a valuable employee relations tool, but great care must be exercised to ensure that the aggrieved employee receives an objective hearing by an open-minded panel of employees from all levels.

OMBUDSMAN

This is a Swedish concept that many large corporations, government agencies, and universities have adopted. The ombudsman operates an independent office within the organization to investigate and resolve problems. For example, a first-line supervisor may feel she is being sexually harassed by someone higher up in management. If the organization can resolve this problem fairly and efficiently, it can avoid time-consuming litigation which would be embarrassing, expensive, and disruptive to the organization.

According to *The Wall Street Journal*, the use of ombudsmen at medium- and large-sized companies has more than doubled in the past five years, partly in response to a rise in lawsuits by employees alleging discrimination, wrongful discharge, or sexual harassment. It is estimated that about 500 companies, most with 500 or more employees, now use ombudsmen to resolve workplace problems.

Most ombudsmen use informal investigatory and conciliatory tactics and differ from staff relations or grievance officials because of their neutrality. In large, bureaucratic organizations, situations can develop that negatively affect employee morale and efficiency. For example, if an employee is having difficulty with his health insurance, a creative ombudsman may be able to resolve the problem by gathering information and suggesting ways of getting the employee's medical costs covered, while not violating the policies of the insurance carrier.

Most organizations that use ombudsmen have guidelines providing that all conversations and communications by employees with the ombudsmen are confidential. Further, it is crucial that the ombudsman be truly independent of management. For example, at a university, if the ombudsman is a junior, untenured faculty member, students and other faculty may well question the independence of an individual who will need the support and approval of administrators to achieve promotion or tenure in the future.

Legally, the benefit of having an ombudsman can be significant, even if his efforts at resolving the dispute are unsuccessful. For example, in cases involving issues like sexual harassment, the informal and confidential approach may temper many of the feelings that often accompany such charges. Further, a judge and jury will want to know whether the employer sought to take all reasonable measures against the alleged harasser in considering good faith, a key issue in assessing punitive damages.

Supporters of using ombudsmen note that beyond the legal issues, many workplace problems stem from poor communication and an ombudsman can often assist communication and help people handle themselves more professionally.

Critics question whether ombudsmen are truly independent and note that they lack legal authority to impose a settlement on the disputants. Supporters contend that it is the independence and informality that make this process so successful and efficient.

UNION-MANAGEMENT MODEL

This is the most well-established and familiar system for the resolution of workplace disputes. The labor-management grievance procedure evolved over time, receiving a powerful boost as a dispute resolution tool during World War II when there were concerns about the high inventory of loss when disputes were unresolved or subject to self-help approaches. The strike by the union or the lockout by the employer to pressure the other side to resolve a grievance meant disruption to production and lost income to all. This pragmatic grievance procedure allows the work to continue and income to be earned while no party's rights are lost or compromised.

In many European countries, workplace grievances are often resolved by self-help techniques, resulting in disruption of services or production and financial loss to all concerned. In the United States, both labor and management are willing to forgo a possible short-term tactical advantage in favor of a more pragmatic approach with less loss.

Over time, a "common law of the shop" or concepts of industrial jurisprudence have developed, as well as a group of experienced arbitrators who apply this evolving body of law. A generally accepted interpretation of such concepts as "just cause" and "insubordination" lend greater predictability to a case outcome while providing guidance standards for settlement discussions. It is worth emphasizing that, although arbitration is a form of private, nonjudicial, dispute resolution, there are well-developed and broadly accepted standards which make the process more reliable and predictable.

How then does a typical labor-management grievance procedure work?

Labor-management Grievance Procedure

Each grievance procedure is a creation of the collectively-bargained contract between a union and the employer. Because each employment setting has its own particular needs and dimensions, each grievance procedure can be tailored to fit the parties' requirements. For example, if the employees travel extensively as part of their job or are widely dispersed at remote locations, the parties may agree to lengthen the time for response to the grievance at each step.

Typically, each collective bargaining agreement will define what is and is not grievable. For example, since supervisors are usually excluded from the bargaining unit, a supervisor may not challenge his termination through this procedure.

Although there are considerable variations among contracts, all agreements provide a mechanism to encourage grievance settlement in an orderly, step-by-step fashion. The final step of these procedures is arbitration — a dispute resolution process where an outside party adjudicates the merits of the grievance.

The first step of the grievance procedure usually provides for an informal discussion between an employee with a problem and a member of the lowest level of supervision. Most problems are resolved at this step, but if not, the next step provides for the filing of a written, formal grievance with the first-line supervisor.

To keep the process moving, there are usually short time limits for moving the grievance to the next level. This ensures the parties cannot lose a grievance or leave it in limbo for an undetermined time period. As noted above, the parties are free to establish whatever time limits they choose and to waive noncompliance by the other side.

Most unions and their employers are able to operate a grievance procedure efficiently and equitably. The parties know they must get along if they are to prosper; that is why very few grievances reach arbitration.

The grievance procedure provides multiple opportunities for settlement at meetings with representatives at increasingly higher levels of each organization. Thus, a third step to resolve a grievance might involve an employee and the union steward in a meeting with a second- or third-level supervisor. At the fourth step, the director of human resources might meet with the union's business agent.

It is often said that while those closest to the problem may know the most about their situation, they may be too emotionally involved to be objective. As those with less personal connection with the grievance enter the process, their objectivity and experience in industrial relations may facilitate a speedy and fair resolution.

The final step of almost all union-management grievance procedures is binding arbitration. The parties will have agreed in advance to a procedure for the selection of a neutral arbitrator whose decision will be final and binding.

The parties establish the jurisdiction and authority of the arbitrator. Typically, the arbitrator may interpret the terms of an existing contract, but may not add to, subtract from, alter, or modify the terms of the contract. Similarly, an arbitrator's remedial powers are circumscribed by both contract language and commonly accepted principles of industrial jurisprudence. If an employee was fired and the arbitrator concluded the termination was not for just cause, the employee would be reinstated with lost back pay and benefits, but would not receive punitive damages.

It must be emphasized that the arbitrator draws his or her authority from the parties and enjoys this power due only to this mandate. For example, once a final award is issued, the arbitrator is considered *functus officio*, without any further authority over the case. Thus, after the final award is made, should one party seek to have the arbitrator alter or clarify the award, the arbitrator may not do so unless jointly empowered by both sides.

It is appropriate to reiterate a key point: The arbitration process belongs to the parties. Thus, if the parties want a formal, legal hearing, the arbitrator will usually oblige, although most parties — and arbitrators — prefer an informal process. The rules of evidence are exclusionary in nature, and most arbitrators want to hear more, as opposed to less, about the case at hand. Most, but by no means all, arbitrators have sufficient legal training to conduct a formal hearing if the parties want it. The parties may choose a formal approach for a number of reasons. For example, if there may be subsequent or collateral proceedings — as in the case of a grievance involving allegations of race or sex discrimination — the parties may wish to have a full record developed, including a verbatim transcript and strict adherence to the Federal Rules of Civil Procedure.

The rationale behind a nontechnical approach to arbitration goes deeper than a mere preference for informality. As the late Harry Shulman, perhaps the dean of labor arbitrators, once explained, the nature of labor arbitration is fundamentally different from courtroom litigation. He noted that, unlike litigants in court, the parties in a collective bargaining agreement must continue to live with one another, both during the dispute and after. He urged the parties to view grievance arbitration as a mutual problem that can affect the future relations of the parties and the smooth operation of the enterprise.

This means that the parties' approach must be radically different from that of litigants. Shulman wrote:

> A litigant does not care whether he wins his law suit because the tribunal understood the problem and made a wise judgment, or because the tribunal was actually confused or was influenced by wooden technicality, or irrelevant or emotional considerations. But the parties in a labor dispute submitted to arbitration, seeking an award with which they must both live harmoniously in the future, must seek not merely a victory but a wise and enlightened award based on relevant factors and full understanding of the problem. And they must, therefore, seek to have the arbitrator know as much as possible about their enterprise, their interest in it, and the problem involved.

In sum, grievance arbitration exists to resolve problems arising during the course of the parties' ongoing relationship. It is a valuable tool of dispute resolution, and most parties use it wisely and well. The two recommended dispute resolution procedures for statutory employment discrimination claims, mediation and arbitration, should exist alongside, and in harmony with, an employer's existing labor-management grievance procedure.

About Arbitrators: Selection and Cost

Because great power is given to the arbitrator by the parties, a closer examination of the arbitrator is necessary. Many of the arbitration selection processes currently in effect in the labor-management model may be considered by nonunion employers in the design of a binding dispute resolution model.

First, in our credential-happy society, wherein everyone from beauticians to electricians to realtors is licensed, arbitrators are not. There is no licensing exam, no education requirement, no certifying board, no paper to hang on the wall saying "arbitrator." Put simply, you become an arbitrator when both parties accept you as an arbitrator, and not before.

While there are no formal requirements to become an arbitrator, certain standards have evolved from common practice. The first is neutrality; that is, the arbitrator should not be an advocate one day and seek to be a neutral party the next. A knowledge of industrial relations, the common law of the workplace, is certainly sought, as is the ability to write a comprehensible opinion. While most arbitrators have a legal background, not all are lawyers, and while many teach at law schools and universities, not all are professors. The profession of labor-management arbitration is changing as the original cadre, the War Labor Board members, retire. One can only hope the new generation of arbitrators will maintain the high standards set by these distinguished individuals.

The parties to a collective bargaining agreement look principally to two organizations to provide lists from which they will select an arbitrator. In a sense, these organizations act as preliminary screeners of arbitrators through their admittance procedures. Both organizations require some background investigation and documentation before an arbitrator candidate is admitted, but it is always left to the parties themselves to select the arbitrator who will hear their case, a right the parties guard zealously.

The American Arbitration Association (AAA) is a not-for-profit organization dedicated to the voluntary resolution of a wide range of disputes — not only labor-management controversies, but commercial, construction, international, insurance, and community disputes as well. The AAA, as a nongovernmental entity, can conduct employee representation elections, improper practice hearings, and other dispute resolution proceedings, such as fact-finding, even in jurisdictions or sectors with no law governing employee relations, provided the disputants so agree. The AAA has 35 regional offices and can administer cases anywhere in the country.

For a nominal fee, an AAA regional office will provide the disputants with a list of arbitrators, accompanied by a short biographical sketch of each one. Through a system of alternate striking or preference ranking, both sides select the arbitrator to hear their case. The fee each party pays to the AAA is for case administration, which means that important details, such as scheduling the hearing and requests for postponements, are handled by the AAA, not by the arbitrator. This is not only a convenience for the arbitrator and the parties, but, perhaps more important, it provides a buffer between the arbitrator and disputants that serves to keep the process more neutral. AAA administration avoids the problem of *ex parte* contact between the neutral and one of the advocates.

The Federal Mediation and Conciliation Service (FMCS) is a federal agency that provides mediators free of charge to parties at impasse in contract negotiations. As part of its peacemaking and peacekeeping mission, the agency also provides parties with lists of grievance arbitrators, allowing for a similar selection process. Like the AAA, the FMCS investigates the background of potential arbitrators in an effort to ensure that lists sent to the parties contain only the names of qualified neutrals.

The FMCS does not charge a case administration fee or administer cases. Once the parties select an arbitrator, it is the arbitrator's responsibility to contact the parties directly to make all the necessary arrangements without any further involvement by the agency.

Most acceptable arbitrators are on the panels of both the AAA and FMCS. It is not uncommon for the parties to agree to appoint an individual to serve as an arbitrator without using either organization.

Some state labor relations agencies or boards also have rosters of arbitrators available for dispute resolution. Some parties with a continuing volume of grievance arbitrations will create a permanent position, wherein the same individual (or small group of individuals) will hear all grievances. It is perhaps a misnomer to call these positions permanent, because the arbitrator serves at the pleasure of the parties and can be removed by either or both sides. Nonetheless, some arbitrators have served the same parties for many years and have become an integral part of the relationship.

In ad hoc arbitration, once the parties have received a list of arbitrators and examined the accompanying biographical sketches, they are ready to begin the actual selection of an arbitrator. How do parties make this important decision?

First, many advocates will be familiar with one or more of the names on the list, perhaps from previous cases. Many law firms, employers, and unions maintain, formally or informally, a roster or directory of arbitrators. Those advocates who are unfamiliar with the work of a particular arbitrator will usually inquire among fellow advocates concerning the arbitrator's ability to run an orderly, productive hearing and issue a well-written, well-reasoned opinion and award. Many advocates use reporting services to gather information about a particular arbitrator and read any published awards issued. This provides a sense of the track record of the arbitrator.

Inherent in all of these approaches is the danger of considering an arbitrator's acceptability based solely on his or her "score card": the decisions issued for labor or management. This approach is probably not terribly effective in predicting the performance of a particular arbitrator because there is no way, short of reading all the opinions written by the arbitrator, of determining any bias or predilection. Put simply, arbitrators would enjoy broad and continuing acceptability if they evidenced a pronounced bias toward one side or the other.

Arbitrators are paid for hearing time, travel time, and study time. Per diem rates vary with the arbitrator, but generalizations are still valid. The arbitrator will typically charge for one day to hear the case and two days to study, write, and issue the award. Assuming a per-diem charge of $500, a typical case will cost the parties $1,500 in fees, plus travel, food, and lodging expenses. The arbitrator's bill is usually split evenly by the two parties. Thus, in the illustration above, each party would pay about $800, assuming $100 in arbitrator expenses for travel, food, and lodging.

The real expense of arbitration lies in each side's own case preparation costs. If outside legal counsel is used, if witnesses are called, if preparation time is taken (as it most certainly should be) before the hearing, the cost to each side may well be two or three times the arbitrator's fee. Time spent preparing, investigating, documenting, and presenting the case involves expense and lost work time. But case preparation, the key to successful arbitration practice, is well worth the expense, especially considering the risk of a negative decision. Put simply, if the matter were not of some importance, it would not have been brought to arbitration. Because the matter is at arbitration, it is important enough to warrant the expense and time for thorough preparation.

An additional benefit of comprehensive case preparation is that it enables a party to fully evaluate the merits of its case, which often encourages a prearbitration compromise settlement or even an alteration in position, resulting in a withdrawal of the grievance by the union or a granting of the grievance by management.

Advantages of Arbitration under a Collective Bargaining Agreement

The enormous acceptance of grievance arbitration is because of the advantages of the process. Compared to courtroom litigation, or administrative proceedings, arbitration is faster, less expensive, and more informal. Unlike crowded court dockets and long waits for a case hearing, arbitration allows the hearing to be conducted as quickly as the parties and the arbitrator can schedule it. Money is saved because no attorneys are needed, since the process usually is flexible and informal.

Unlike judges who hear a variety of matters and may not gain expertise in one particular field, labor arbitrators are well versed in what is variously called industrial jurisprudence or the law of the shop. Because both parties empower the arbitrator, his or her decision is final and binding on both sides, and the arbitrator's award is enforceable in a court of law. This finality can be dramatically contrasted with the administrative or judicial appellate system, which can take many years (and many dollars) to achieve finality.

Although it is possible to challenge an arbitrator's award in court, few parties do. Typical grounds for a successful court challenge to an arbitrator's award would be those rare instances in which the arbitrator rendered an award exceeding his or her authority or had an undisclosed partisan interest in one side, such as an arbitrator whose law firm represented a union or employer. The net positive effect of the speedier hearing and the finality of the award is the creation of a better climate of human relations at the workplace. Even if the ultimate resolution of the grievance is not fully to the liking of one of the parties, it is a resolution, and the parties are free to move on with their lives and work relationships.

Fundamentally, the basic advantage of arbitration is that the dispute resolution process belongs to the parties themselves, and they are jointly free to shape it and control it to meet their needs. From the selection of the arbitrator to the level of legality and formality desired, the process belongs to both labor and management. This is, of course, not true of judicial or administrative dispute resolution processes wherein the procedural rules and selection of the judge or hearing officer are totally beyond the control of the disputants.

With this background, we turn to an examination of the nonunion or employer-run grievance procedure.

EMPLOYER-RUN DISPUTE RESOLUTION PROCEDURES

This approach provides the aggrieved, nonunion employee with a number of opportunities within the organization to have his complaint examined by fellow employees and members of management who are not directly involved in the dispute.

Typically, this procedure is mandatory and must be followed by all covered employees before they can use the courts for relief. While there are many variants of the procedure, the one used by Federal Express is a good illustration of how a corporation and its employees can resolve employment disputes. This complaint resolution procedure is considered nonbinding because it does not mandate final and binding arbitration of the complaint. Binding procedures will be discussed in Section III.

Federal Express calls this program the Guaranteed Fair Treatment Procedure. Federal Express also has an open door policy that employees are encouraged to utilize first, but if there is a problem or disagreement between an employee and his or her manager, the employee may utilize the Guaranteed Fair Treatment Procedure.

Like the labor-management grievance procedure, there are a series of steps and prescribed time limits that must be followed. Here is how Federal Express explains the Guaranteed Fair Treatment Procedure to its employees:

Below are the steps which you can take to ensure that the procedure for the resolution of your concern is fair and equitable. Should you feel that at any step of this procedure the response is unsatisfactory or if management fails to respond, you may proceed to the next step. These steps will be followed.

Step 1: Discuss the concern with your manager in an open and frank manner. If you do not receive an answer you feel to be fair and equitable with 7 calendar days, or if your manager fails to respond, you may proceed to Step 2 within 7 calendar days of the decision.

Step 2: Submit a written synopsis of your concern to your senior manager. The senior manager will arrange a meeting with you and your manager to discuss the concern, after which the senior manager will submit a written decision to you within 7 calendar days. When more levels of management exist than indicated in the procedure, each additional level of management will consolidate their joint review and comments. If in good faith, you believe the decision is unfair, you may proceed to Step 3 within 7 calendar days of the decision.

Step 3: Submit a written synopsis of your concern to the Senior Vice President of your division. After investigation, the Senior Vice President of your division will submit a written decision to you within 7 calendar days. The Senior Vice President may elect to: (1) uphold the decision of management, (2) overturn the decision of management, or (3) initiate a Board of Review (in accordance with Step 4). If you believe that your concern still has not been resolved in a fair and equitable manner, you may proceed to Step 5 within 7 calendar days of the decision.

Step 4: When a Board of Review is found necessary, it will consist of a chairman (non-voting) and five voting members. The Senior Vice President of the division where the complaint originates will appoint a chairperson who has no direct or indirect management relationship to you, the complainant.

Step 5: If you were denied a Board of Review in Step 3, or if you believe that your concern still has not been resolved in a fair and equitable manner, you must request in writing a hearing of the complaint by the Appeals Board. Within 14 calendar days of the request, an Appeals Board consisting of the Chief Executive Officer, the Chief Operating Officer and the Senior Vice President of Personnel, will review the facts and circumstances surrounding the complaint. The Appeals Board may elect to (1) uphold the decision of management, (2) overturn the decision of management, or (3) initiate a

Board of Review (in accordance with the procedure in Step 4). The decision of the Appeals Board is final and binding on you and the company.

While the above procedure is quite straightforward, a few points should be noted. First, the employer administers the process and serves as the final and binding decision maker. Second, there are different levels of management involved in advanced steps of the procedure. This is similar to the labor-management arbitration process discussed earlier and seeks to bring different perspectives to the dispute. Finally, an employee in this type of procedure usually has a series of rights, roughly categorized under the heading of due process.

Employee due process rights have evolved from the basic concepts of societal equity and due process. In assessing whether an employee has been treated equitably, courts and administrative agencies often look at the following factors:

Right of Notice

The affected worker has the right to learn, in writing and with appropriate specificity, the nature of the charges against him and the proposed penalty. For example:

You are being given a three-day disciplinary suspension which you will serve on October 18, 19, and 20 for your insubordination on September 21. At approximately 10:45 A.M. on that date, your supervisor, Jane Adams, directed you to immediately take a file of important documents to the accounting supervisor, Peter Davis. You repeatedly refused to obey Ms. Adams' direct order, stating to her that you were starting your morning coffee break and would do it at 11:00 A.M., once your break was over, or that another employee, Ellen Perry, could immediately take the material to accounting. You disobeyed a direct order and it is not your role to assign work to co-workers or tell your supervisor where to assign various tasks. This is a serious offense and if you are again insubordinate you may serve a longer disciplinary suspension or even lose your job. Please be advised that if you wish to dispute this discipline, you may utilize our internal grievance procedure.

Right to Present a Defense

For a system to function fairly, an aggrieved employee is entitled to present his or her side of the story. Generally, this defense is initially presented in writing, within a specified time period, to the management employee who issued the initial disciplinary document.

Most procedures allow an employee to have the assistance of a representative of his or her own choosing. Frequently the person helping to prepare and present the defense is allotted some paid time, perhaps no more than eight hours, to do the work. If the aggrieved employee wishes to hire a lawyer or other outside representative, it is the employee's financial responsibility to pay for it. This is in contrast to due process rights in a criminal case; if an accused person cannot afford a lawyer, one will be provided at no cost to the defendant.

Right to be Heard by a Fair-minded Person or Panel

Inherent in the concept of workplace due process is the right to have your matter heard and decided by a fair-minded person or panel. In most employer-run grievance systems, an informal hearing is held before a supervisor not directly involved in the grievance or a panel of workers and managers who do not work with the aggrieved person. At this hearing, the aggrieved employee can present his or her side of the issue, relevant witnesses and exhibits, and cross-examine opposing witnesses.

Many critics of employer-run grievance systems cite the lack of objectivity by the individual or panel as the most serious flaw in this process. They contend that managers tend to be sympathetic to other managers and are predisposed to find against the workers. Similarly, on peer panels it is argued that not only are the managers ready to support other managers, but also that a supervisor on a panel will dominate the rank and file panel members who, in turn, are selected and trained by management.

Supporters of this process argue that if a worker does not receive a hearing before a fair-minded body, it would serve to defeat the purpose of the system and leave the employer vulnerable to a judicial challenge. Further, if hearing decisions are always for the employer and against the workers, regardless of the facts, no one will have any faith in it and aggrieved employees will seek other avenues of redress.

Right to Learn of the Decision in Writing

After presenting his or her case at a hearing, the aggrieved employee is entitled to promptly learn of the decision, and its reasoning, in writing. The written decision need not be lengthy, but it should give the employee enough information so he or she knows the rationale for the decision.

Rights of Appeal

After receiving the decision of the hearing, an employee who is dissatisfied should have some recourse. In many organizations, he or she may appeal to the chief executive officer, chief operating officer, or their designee. Generally, this appeal must be filed promptly after receipt of the hearing decision with the appropriate official.

If an aggrieved employee omits the appeal step and seeks to proceed directly to court, the employer will argue the suit is not yet ripe for hearing and ask the court to direct the employee to first exhaust the available internal remedies.

If the court is convinced that this internal appellate step offers a bona fide fair review of the case, the employee will be directed to complete this internal process; if the court is convinced that the appeal process offers no real equity to the worker, it will allow the judicial matter to proceed.

In sum, these five workplace due process rights seek to ensure the aggrieved worker receives an objectively-based appraisal of a grievance through a process that provides the essence of equity.

MEDIATION

Mediation is a process that uses a neutral party to serve as an impartial channel of communications between the disputants in an effort to achieve a voluntary compromise agreement. The mediator is a sounding board for the parties; he attempts to convince the parties to reach a voluntary resolution of the dispute.

Because a mediator does not have the power or authority to impose a settlement on the parties, the process offers little risk and is therefore broadly accepted in many disputes. An ombudsman may mediate the settlement of an employee grievance as part of his job. The FMCS has frequently provided mediators to resolve outstanding labor-management grievances as part of its mission.

A mediator may be able to provide a fresh perspective and suggest creative ways to resolve a problem. Some mediators are more forceful than others in urging acceptance of a settlement offer, but the parties are always free to decline the settlement offer.

The mediator's perspective may be valuable in convincing one or both parties that their position is unreasonable and untenable. After all, if an unbiased observer tells you that you are either asking for too much or offering too little, it may compel you to reassess and possibly change your position.

The AAA has developed a set of rules for employment law mediation that are set forth in full at page 117.

MEDIATION-ARBITRATION

Most workplace problems are resolved by the parties themselves through discussion and negotiation. A negotiated settlement, whether achieved through direct bargaining or with the help of a neutral party, is usually preferable to an adjudicated one. When the parties can fashion the settlement, they can usually meet their mutual needs and provide a positive framework for dealing with future problems. An arbitration award, no matter how well-written or enlightened, can only resolve the immediate case and is not always designed to enhance the parties long-term relationship.

Often, when the parties cannot resolve a grievance through negotiation, they seek the assistance of an outside, neutral party. When an arbitrator is brought in to hear and decide a grievance, the parties may encourage the arbitrator to mediate the dispute.

Mediation-arbitration requires delicacy and tact on the part of the neutral party. Indeed, some arbitrators will not even consider mediation, believing their mission is to decide the matter and nothing else. Other arbitrators will not mediate but urge the advocates to discuss settlement while the hearing is in recess. Many experienced arbitrators, especially those familiar to the parties or their advocates, may seek to mediate, reserving the right to issue a binding award.

An advocate may be reluctant to have an arbitrator mediate the dispute for several reasons. In the mediation process, the neutral party often hears information that, as an arbitrator, she or he would not have the opportunity to hear, such as opinions, beliefs, conjecture, and second-hand hearsay testimony. Some advocates are concerned that, if the mediation process fails and the neutral party resumes the arbitral posture, the final and binding decision may be subconsciously influenced by the information heard while mediating.

The dynamics of the mediation-arbitration process are interesting. When the arbitrator-turned-mediator makes a suggestion about a possible compromise settlement, both sides usually take notice, because if mediation fails, the suggested settlement may well become embodied in the final, binding decision.

Some arbitrators who engage in mediation-arbitration may suggest what their final decision might be if mediation were unsuccessful; other arbitrators attempt to keep the two processes separate and distinct by never indicating during mediation what their arbitral decision might be.

Mediation-arbitration can only succeed if both sides authorize the neutral party and cooperate fully with the process. That mediation-arbitration is often successful should come as no surprise, because it occurs only when all participants support it. Finally, the fact that the person mediating has the power to issue a binding decision ensures that the mediator's suggestion will be seriously evaluated.

FACT FINDING

Sometimes called advisory arbitration, the fact-finding process utilizes an outside third party who hears both parties' positions in a grievance, studies the dispute, and then issues an award which is not binding on either side.

Because the fact finder's decision is nonbinding this is a low-risk process for the parties and would seem to be widely acceptable. However, because the decision is advisory, the losing party often chooses not to accept the award. The parties will often proceed to binding arbitration, which results in escalating expenditures of time, money, and effort.

However, if the parties both respect the fact finder's judgment, the advisory decision will be seen as similar to what an arbitrator's decision might be. If, for example, the fact finder concludes that the aggrieved employee was wrongfully terminated due to racial discrimination, the employer, though not legally bound to accept that decision, may well conclude that if the case were to go to binding arbitration, the result would be the same, and may therefore seek to work out a settlement with the employee.

Advocates often contend that their client sees no merit in the other party's case, but when an objective third party tells them directly how they perceive the dispute, they may have a different perspective.

The advisory award is often accepted by both sides, but it is not uncommon to find that the fact finder's nonbinding decision serves as a basis for intense and productive settlement discussions.

THE ROLE OF COUNSEL

The role of counsel is important in any successful dispute resolution procedure. Some of the more informal dispute resolution procedures, such as an open door procedure and peer review, may be designed so outside counsel is not allowed to participate in the process. The participants to any dispute resolution process should, at minimum, be advised by their employer to consider seeking labor and employment law counsel to assist them. While it is up to the designer of the dispute resolution model whether attorneys should be involved, the greater the involvement in outside counsel, the greater the viability and acceptability of the dispute resolution process.

In this regard, outside counsel should be included in employment mediation and binding arbitration, particularly if a statutory right is at issue. This ensures that the dispute resolution process is a full and fair adversary proceeding and not merely a sham. Thus, if employers wish to have their procedures deferred to by the courts and appropriate administrative bodies, they must build in due process. Of course, the first building block in due process is the right of and access to legal counsel.

Later in this book you will see how some companies have practicably addressed the issue of right to counsel. Some base the right to counsel on whether a statutory right has arisen. Others provide for counsel at certain stages of the process. Almost all companies provide some type of reimbursement for employees so that where counsel is necessary, employees are not barred from seeking counsel due to their financial circumstances.

The introduction of counsel will usually reduce the informality of a dispute resolution process. It may also raise the emotional and economic cost of access to a dispute resolution process. Nevertheless, a healthy balance must be struck between informality and accessibility and the preservation of individual employee's legitimate legal rights.

III

The Trend: Corporate Alternative Dispute Resolution Programs

Various alternative dispute resolution (ADR) techniques and the reasons for their increased adoption at the workplace have been discussed. What follows are some examples of what some corporations are doing, as well as a guide with suggested clauses to enable an organization to initiate an ADR program of its own. There is no single dispute resolution system appropriate for every organization and therefore creativity and experimentation are encouraged. This subject is so dynamic that many new developments and inventive approaches are sure to surface in the future.

Many corporations presently use some type of dispute resolution procedure. They include corporate open door policies, nonbinding employee grievance procedures, use of a corporate ombudsman, binding or nonbinding peer review of employee grievances, and similar policies that seek to resolve disputes at the workplace.

For example, Federal Express's Guaranteed Fair Treatment Procedure provides a system for employees to seek to resolve grievances through internal company appeal. Aetna Casualty and Life has a dispute resolution process that encourages the use of mediation prior to litigation. AT&T and United Airlines also use mediation programs. AT&T's mediation program is incorporated into the AT&T-Communication Workers of America contractual grievance procedure.[1] Rockwell International has an arbitration program for its top management where both the employee and company agree to arbitrate all employment-related disputes.[2] Bechtel will engage in discovery in litigation to identify relevant facts. Then, the company usually seeks to use ADR techniques to resolve the dispute.

While many corporations provide dispute resolution procedures, few of them end in binding arbitration. A 1988 study of 78 nonunion companies conducted under the auspices of the National Association of Manufacturers disclosed that while all of the companies surveyed utilized some type of employee grievance procedure, only six companies (7.7 percent) provided for binding arbitration.[3]

After the *Gilmer* decision, the American Bar Association Labor Law Section Subcommittee on Alternate Dispute Resolution surveyed major companies to determine whether *Gilmer* had encouraged the adoption of mandatory dispute resolution procedures. The study found that, while ADR was an attractive alternative to litigation, companies were hesitant to adopt mandatory ADR procedures. Of the 68 companies surveyed, only 2 had adopted mandatory ADR procedures. Many respondents indicated they would wait to determine the impact of *Gilmer*. This study also surveyed public attitudes toward ADR. It was discovered that, once individual respondents understood the process of ADR, they expressed strong support for arbitration, mediation, or other procedures in lieu of litigation. Forty-two percent of the persons surveyed stated that they were "very likely" to use ADR while 40 percent stated they were "somewhat likely" to use ADR.[4]

In January 1995 McDermott published the results of a survey of companies and the attractiveness of ADR procedures to these companies.[5] This survey, conducted in 1993, sought to measure the attractiveness of various ADR techniques among organizations. The survey found that respondents' views of the use of ADR to resolve employment disputes were favorably influenced by the Civil Rights Act of 1991.[6] Regarding arbitration, respondents were asked whether they would allow an "outside professional arbitrator to resolve with finality, through a binding decision, an employment law dispute in return for an employee giving up the right to sue in court." Seventy-eight percent of the respondents replied that they would be willing to allow an arbitrator to resolve such a dispute.

On July 5, 1995, the General Accounting Office (GAO) of the federal government issued a study on the use of ADR methods, particularly arbitration, by employers to resolve discrimination complaints.[7] The study examined the extent to which private-sector employers use ADR and the fairness of employers' arbitration policies.

The GAO mailed the survey to a stratified, random sample of 2,000 businesses with more than 100 employees that had filed the legally required equal employment opportunity reports with the Equal Employment

Opportunity Commission (EEOC) in 1992. The questionnaire included 45 questions on the employer's use of ADR. The ADR techniques identified by the GAO included negotiation, fact finding, peer review, internal mediation, external mediation, and arbitration. The GAO telephoned those employers who said they used arbitration and requested that they send the GAO a copy of their arbitration policy.

The GAO then compared the employer arbitration policies with the key quality standards proposed by the Commission on the Future of Worker-Management Relations (the Dunlop Commission) as standards for private arbitration that ensured employees a fair and full airing of their complaints. These six standards involve the selection of the arbitrator, the procedures for the aggrieved employee to gather information, the payment of the arbitrator, awards and remedies, the final arbitrator ruling, and judicial review. The GAO added the criterion of the right of the complainant to independent representation.[8]

The GAO report concluded that few of the employers surveyed used arbitration as part of their ADR model. The GAO also found that the arbitration policies reviewed varied greatly and that "If expected to conform with all the criteria for fairness recently proposed by the Commission on the Future of Worker-Management Relations, most would not do so."[9]

Other than these surveys, there have been few efforts to identify the attractiveness of ADR in a resolution of employment law disputes to employers, employer efforts to incorporate ADR and predispute agreements to arbitrate in particular after the *Gilmer* decision, and overall employers' opinions regarding alternative dispute resolution.

ALTERNATIVE DISPUTE RESOLUTION MODELS

Major corporations have introduced ADR programs that have binding arbitration as the final step. Some of the more prominent programs are discussed here.

Northrup Corporation

The oldest binding nonunion arbitration model has been in use at the Northrup Corporation since 1945. This procedure provides for a formal grievance process ending with binding arbitration. An employee grievance that cannot be resolved informally is considered at the Administrative Office level. If denied, a Management Appeals Committee hears an appeal of the Administrative Office decision. After this decision, the employee may appeal to an arbitrator selected by both the employee and the company. The arbitrator's decision is binding on both parties.

Rockwell International Corporation Model

Since *Gilmer*, others have moved to implement internal ADR procedures culminating in mandatory arbitration. Rockwell International Corporation introduced a Mutual Agreement to Arbitrate Claims, which provides for mandatory arbitration of "all claims or controversies for which a court otherwise would be authorized by law to grant relief, in any way arising out of, relating to or associated with the Employee's employment with the Company, or its termination." The execution of this agreement is a prerequisite to employee receipt of certain corporate stock options which would otherwise lapse. While this policy is targeted at executives eligible for such options, Rockwell has also implemented predispute agreements to arbitrate for all new hires and on a voluntary basis for existing nonexecutive employees.[10]

The Rockwell agreement contemplates arbitration for all claims held by the employee or employer except claims for workers' compensation benefits, unemployment compensation benefits, company claims for injunctive, or other equitable relief for unfair competition or unauthorized disclosure of trade secrets or confidential information, and employee pension or benefit plan claims where binding arbitration or other nonjudicial dispute resolution procedure is required.

The Rockwell arbitration procedure includes discovery between the parties. Each party has the right to take the deposition of one individual and any expert witness designated by another party. Parties are allowed to request the production of documents by any other party. Additional discovery may be allowed by the arbitrator upon a showing of substantial need. Thirty days before the arbitration hearing, the parties are obligated to exchange lists of witnesses and copies of exhibits intended for use at the hearing.

The arbitrator is selected from a list provided by the American Arbitration Association (AAA). The Rockwell procedure requires that the Model Employment Arbitration Procedures of the AAA apply from the time a notice of claim is given, except as modified by other language in the Mutual Agreement to Arbitrate. The arbitrator must apply the law of the state where the claim arose, as well as any applicable federal law. The Federal Rules of Evidence apply. The arbitrator has the authority to consider pre-hearing motions for dismissal and for summary judgment, pursuant to the standards set forth under the Federal Rules of Civil Procedure.

The Rockwell agreement also contemplates that each party will pay an equal share of the fees and costs of the arbitration. Where a statutory claim provides for payment of the prevailing party's attorneys' fees and costs, the arbitrator may award such reasonable fees and costs. Parties are permitted to file briefs; the arbitrator's award and opinion will be issued in the "form typically rendered in labor arbitrations."

Travelers Group

In September, 1992, the Primerica Corporation, which later merged into the Travelers Group, an organization with divisions offering a wide array of services including consumer financial, investment, and insurance services, implemented a procedure wherein pre-dispute agreements to arbitrate recognize arbitration as the exclusive forum for "the resolution of all employment disputes that may arise . . . under any federal, state or local statute, regulation, or common law doctrine regarding employment discrimination, conditions of employment or termination of employment." The Travelers Group Handbook advises employees that "Arbitration is an essential element of your employment relationship and is a condition of your employment."

The Travelers Group Arbitration Policy incorporates, to a large extent, the Model Employment Arbitration Procedures of the AAA. In addition, the policy permits limited discovery. Each party is entitled to propound one set of interrogatories pursuant to the Federal Rules of Civil Procedure; these interrogatories are limited to the identification of potential witnesses. The procedure also provides for one set of up to 25 Requests for the Production of Documents and allows up to two days of depositions of witnesses subject to the Federal Rules of Civil Procedure.

Under the Travelers Group procedure, the company pays all arbitration administrative fees in excess of $25. Should the arbitration proceed beyond one day, the incremental expenses of the additional days of hearing are borne equally by both parties.

Brown & Root

Brown & Root is an employer in heavy construction and related industries, headquartered in Houston, Texas. In June 1993 Brown & Root introduced a comprehensive employee dispute resolution program. The Brown & Root dispute resolution program provides four options: open door policy, conference, mediation, and arbitration. Option One, the open door policy, "guarantees that all doors are open to you within Brown & Root."[11] It is a voluntary process that allows the employee to talk with his or her immediate supervisor or to a higher level of management without fear of retaliation. The employee is encouraged to resolve the problem at the lowest possible level, but can take the complaint as far up the chain of command as the employee deems necessary. The employee is given guidance in using this open door policy through a toll-free employee telephone hot line.

In addition to the employee hot line, the Brown & Root program also provides a program administrator who will assist an employee in use of the dispute resolution program, including use of all options.

The dispute resolution program also recognizes that where a dispute involves a "legally protected right," an employee is provided the opportunity of obtaining a legal consultation with the attorney of his or her choice. The legal consultation is treated similarly to benefits under the Brown & Root medical plan, with the employee paying a deductible and a co-payment. Brown & Root then pays the balance of the costs. The maximum annual benefit of this program is $2,500 per employee. In the example in the Brown & Root dispute resolution manual, an employee would pay a deductible of $25 and then 10 percent of the balance of the legal bill, with Brown & Root paying the remaining 90 percent of that cost. The program administrator must approve all payments under the legal consultation plan.

Option Two, the conference, is a meeting at Brown & Root where the employee and a company representative meet with a representative from the company's dispute resolution program to discuss the dispute and choose a process for resolution. The goal of the conference is to help the employee and the company agree on a way to settle the dispute and choose a person to help resolve the dispute. The employee's options at this conference include: loop-back to the chain of command; use of an informal process, such as informal mediation; and direct access to an outside process.

The outside processes are Options Three and Four, and involve mediation through the auspices of a professional, neutral, third party selected through the American Arbitration Association. Under Option Three, the employee must pay a $50 processing fee to obtain outside mediation. The company pays any costs in excess of this fee. The employee is provided the number and address of the American Arbitration Association to request mediation.

When a dispute has not been resolved through Options One, Two, or Three, either the employee or the company may seek arbitration under Option Four. The company does not require an employee to proceed through each of the options in sequence to reach Option Four arbitration. However, the company emphasizes that these multiple steps are designed to maximize the possibility of resolution. When Option Four is reached, the outside dispute resolution processes involve use of professional neutrals provided through the AAA. To request arbitration, the employee must pay a $50 processing fee; the company pays all costs that exceed $50. Once again, the employee is provided the phone number and address of the AAA to request arbitration. The employee is allowed to move to Option Four directly from Option Two when the dispute involves a legally protected right. Thus, when the dispute does not involve an identified, legally protected right, arbitration is not provided under the Brown & Root dispute resolution program.

The Brown & Root program also recognizes that employees are allowed to consult a lawyer or other advisor of the employee's choice. Here, Brown & Root will pay the major part of the legal fees pursuant to the legal consultation plan. Employees are not required to hire a lawyer to participate in arbitration. Where an employee elects not to bring a lawyer to arbitration, the company participates without a lawyer.

Effective June 1, 1993, the four-option program has been the exclusive means of resolving workplace disputes for legally protected rights at Brown and Root. The company manual states, "That means, if you expect to continue your job at Brown & Root after that date, you will agree to resolve all legal claims against Brown & Root through this process instead of through the court system. Use of Options One and Two of the program for cases not involving legal rights is voluntary."

Burlington Northern Railroad

The Burlington Northern Railroad work force consists of approximately 3,800 exempt employees and 28,000 scheduled employees covered by a collective bargaining agreement. The company and its employees were familiar with the arbitration process as a result of the Interstate Commerce Commission's regulatory approval of mergers and the arbitration procedures covering scheduled employees under the Railway Labor Act.

As a result of numerous reorganizations in the mid-1980s and the Age Discrimination Employment Act of 1967 lawsuits spawned by these reorganizations by terminated exempt employees, the company recognized that a better way was needed to resolve discrimination disputes. The company's internal complaint procedure was revised to include an arbitration policy that addressed only termination disputes. This policy was implemented by a letter from senior management announcing the new procedure. The letter also advised employees to insert a new page addressing this new procedure into their employee handbooks.

While the company may mediate a termination dispute prior to arbitration, there is no formal written agreement or procedure addressing this process. If mediation is not successful or not used, arbitration is invoked. This procedure provides that the parties will select an arbitrator; if they cannot agree, the AAA will select the arbitrator and administer the arbitration process.

Continental Airlines

The Continental Airlines discipline and appeal process provides an employee appeal procedure for nonmanagement, nonunion employees. The procedure, found in the company's policy and procedures manual, provides that the internal appeal procedure is the "sole remedy for any employee who believes that he/she has been treated unfairly." As opposed to the Brown & Root or Burlington Northern models, which provide for arbitration of only statutory or termination disputes, this procedure provides a binding dispute resolution procedure for any employee complaint.

Where the dispute cannot be resolved at earlier steps of the process, the procedure calls for an initial, informal hearing before a hearing manager appointed by the management employee who received the appeal from the employee. If the employee disagrees with the result, he may appeal to a board comprised of two management employees appointed by the company and two peers selected by the employee from an employee council. This hearing is also informal and no transcript is taken. Nevertheless, the decision of the board is final and binding.

Where the board deadlocks, a list of three outside arbitrators is submitted to the employee by the labor relations department. The employee chooses an arbitrator from among these three persons. This arbitrator's decision is final and binding. The company pays the arbitrator's expenses.

This procedure has been challenged by employees in federal court on two occasions. Both times, the dispute resolution process was upheld and the award of the board was honored by the court. In both cases, the court relied on the plaintiff's voluntary participation in the procedure, through the issuance of a final decision, to preclude later judicial review of any claim.[12]

HOW TO IMPLEMENT A BINDING PRE-DISPUTE AGREEMENT TO ARBITRATE

The appropriate procedures or standards for introduction of a pre-dispute agreement to arbitrate have not been directly addressed by the courts or Congress. In *Gilmer*, the Supreme Court noted that it would consider underlying due process factors when reviewing the appropriateness of arbitration. Footnote three of the *Gilmer* decision suggests that the waiver of the right to a judicial forum may be subject to the waiver requirements of the Older Workers Benefit Protection Act (OWBPA). However, *Gilmer* did not provide any other guidance.

The recent report of the Commission on the Future of Worker-Management Relations (Dunlop Commission) addressed the growing importance of private employer grievance procedures that end in binding arbitration. As part of its original charge, the Dunlop Commission was asked to consider what could or should be done to increase the extent to which workplace conflicts are resolved directly by those involved, rather than by resorting to administrative agencies, such as the National Labor Relations Board, the EEOC, or the courts.[13] The final report noted that there was an explosion of employment related disputes and that at present there was a staggering caseload before the EEOC.[14] The commission recommended "encouraging experimentation and use of private dispute resolution systems that meet high quality standards for fairness, provided these are not imposed unilaterally by employers as a condition of employment."[15] According to the commission, low-wage employees who seek to remain in their jobs do not appear to be able to use the litigation system to resolve their statutory complaints.

The commission then set forth standards under which private arbitration may serve as a legitimate form of private enforcement of public employment law. These standards include a neutral arbitrator with knowledge of the law at issue, fair cost sharing, the right to independent representation if the employee wants it, and remedies equal to those available through litigation.[16]

The OWBPA was passed by Congress and signed by President Bush in 1990. The OWBPA sets forth a threshold standard for ascertaining whether a waiver and release of an age discrimination claim was "knowing and voluntary." The criteria under this law provide guidance as to what Congress believes is a "knowing and voluntary" waiver by an employee.

Those criteria state that a waiver may not be considered knowing and voluntary unless at a minimum:

the waiver is written in a manner calculated to be understood by the individual or average individual eligible to participate;

the waiver specifically refers to rights or claims under the OWBPA;

additional consideration for an age discrimination waiver is provided;

the employee is advised in writing to consult with an attorney;

the employee is allowed 21 days to consider whether to sign; and

the employee is allowed 7 days to revoke the executed agreement.

The OWBPA places the burden of proof on the employer to prove in any subsequent litigation that the waiver was knowing and voluntary. However, the law governing agreements to arbitrate, the Federal Arbitration Act (FAA), places the burden on the person seeking to avoid the arbitration clause. It is unclear which approach will prevail.

In addition to Congress's definition of "knowing and voluntary" under the OWBPA, the interpretive statement for the OWBPA, issued by Senator Dole, also indicates that the alternate dispute resolution contemplated by Section 118 of the 1991 Act must be "knowing and voluntary."

While many of the practices and procedures associated with the implementation and administration of pre-dispute agreements to arbitrate will be influenced by subsequent legislative and court decisions, there are several advantages to immediate introduction of this procedure. A procedure introduced now can be amended after additional legal guidance has been provided. The main advantage of immediate implementation of a binding arbitration procedure is that there is a legal presumption in favor of enforceability under the FAA and *Gilmer*. Thus, with an agreement in hand, should one party later seek to avoid the contemplated arbitration, they may be required to exhaust the internal grievance procedure first through arbitration or spend considerable legal fees seeking to avoid arbitration.

Another advantage to the immediate implementation of a pre-dispute procedure ending in binding arbitration is that when a party seeks to avoid arbitration, the other party can seek to renegotiate the pre-dispute agreement, thus converting the pre-dispute agreement into an enforceable post-dispute agreement to arbitrate. For example, an attorney representing an employee subject to a pre-dispute agreement to arbitrate may be obligated to exhaust the employee's internal remedies before filing suit in federal court. Thus, arbitration will occur, subject to the parties' disagreement as to the finality of the decision. Counsel may recognize the substantial legal costs associated with petitioning a court to obtain a stay of arbitration or with arbitrating and then attacking the arbitration process. Thus, employee counsel may agree to convert the pre-dispute agreement into an acceptable post-dispute agreement, incorporating certain additional terms and conditions of arbitration favored by the employee. Company counsel may agree to the alteration of certain portions of the pre-dispute arbitration agreement in return for consent to a clearly enforceable post-dispute arbitration agreement.

Any agreement to arbitrate should be knowing and voluntary. In adopting a procedure for prospective hires, the employment application should state that the applicant agrees to submit any claim or dispute arising from hire or refusal to hire, actual employment, or termination from employment, to arbitration. Prior to hire, the applicant should also be presented with a pre-dispute agreement to arbitrate that incorporates the OWBPA guidelines. Alternatively, an employer could request an applicant to execute such an agreement and return it prior to making an offer of employment.

One unresolved issue is whether an employer can require a prospective employee to execute a pre-dispute agreement to arbitrate as a condition of employment. The law is not clear. Some would argue that such an agreement is, *a fortiori*, a contract of adhesion.[17] A separate issue is whether employers may implement, as a condition of employment, a pre-dispute procedure for current employees. The issue of whether an employer can require such an agreement as a condition of employment, either for new hires or existing employees, is unresolved. The National Labor Relations Board opposes any arbitration agreement that requires an employee to waive the right to access to the board in favor of arbitration where acquiescence to arbitration in lieu of board procedures is a condition of employment.[18] Another open issue is whether consideration is necessary to support such agreement, and the amount and type of valid consideration.

Regarding the issue of the type of consideration necessary to support the enforcement of an arbitration agreement, the courts have found adequate consideration in various situations. For example, the Eleventh Circuit Court of Appeals has held that "the consideration exchanged for one party's promise to arbitrate must be the other party's promise to arbitrate at least some specified class of claims."[19]

The Michigan Court of Appeals has found that a securities industry agreement to arbitrate is not a contract of adhesion and that the unilateral implementation of an internal arbitration procedure is binding on current employees, because the continued employment of the employee consisted of adequate consideration to support enforcement of the agreement[20] The Michigan Court has also found that an employee is bound by a pre-existing arbitration procedure in an employee handbook where the employee accepted employment.[21] In general, most courts will consider a mutual promise to arbitrate or the hiring of an individual as sufficient consideration.[22]

One author argues that, because the Supreme Court has yet to decide whether arbitration agreements contained in employment contracts are enforceable under the FAA, an agreement to arbitrate should be separate from an employment contract. It is argued that the arbitration agreement should state that the agreement is not an employment contract and that the employee is employed at will. The agreement should state that it is not intended to add to or create any employment rights or to imply that any employment rights exist beyond those otherwise imposed by law. An employer takes a risk when providing for arbitration in an employee personnel manual. This risk is that the manual will not be treated as contractually binding or may be interpreted by a court to create unintended contractual obligations.[23]

Without a handbook provision, other contractual provision, or other enforceable promise to the contrary, an employer should be allowed to introduce a new dispute resolution process. The employer should seek to obtain employee acceptance of the arbitration model through employee communication and education. If the process is properly marketed it should result in a majority of employees accepting the process. Anecdotal evidence to date supports this approach.

For those employees who refuse to agree, the employer is placed in a difficult situation. Since it is not clear that the employer can require the agreement as a condition of employment, the employer may prefer to allow the development of a bifurcated process whereby certain employees agree to arbitrate all disputes, while others may litigate in court. In each dispute, a party may deem a dispute's locus to be preferable in arbitration or court, depending on the facts. Thus a bifurcated process does not necessarily cause greater economic exposure to the employer. A bifurcated process also will allow an employer to measure the experience of the arbitration model vis-à-vis courtroom litigation.

THE DESIGN OF A BINDING ARBITRATION PROCEDURE

The design of particular pre-hearing procedures and rules of conduct at arbitration is as important as the general agreement to resolve a dispute by arbitration.

One of the major benefits of arbitration is that the parties can agree on a particular procedure tailored to the needs of each disputant that covers the inception of a dispute through the arbitration hearing. The process should be carefully crafted, with regard for each party's due process rights. Since most arbitration procedures and written agreements will be drafted and proposed by an employer, it is critical that an employer does not overreach in the agreement.

An appropriately drafted agreement to arbitrate should address many of the particular aspects of the investigation and presentation of each party's case. The agreement should spell out in detail the pre-hearing dispute resolution process and procedure. The agreement should address the following issues:

the scope of disputes subject to binding arbitration, specifically those issues excluded from arbitration, such as, workers' compensation and unemployment;

the time limits for presenting or maintaining an issue within the grievance procedure and at arbitration;

the levels of management afforded an opportunity to resolve the dispute prior to arbitration;

the point at which the final management decision is issued;

the time limits after the final management decision within which one must request arbitration;

whether other procedures such as mediation or peer review can be voluntarily or mandatorily invoked by either party prior to arbitration;

the existence and extent of pre-hearing summary judgment procedures;

the existence and extent of discovery;

sanctions on parties;

apportionment of costs and/or attorneys' fees;

all of the parties who are required to be sued in this forum (all company supervisors, agents, subsidiaries, and so forth); and

all other procedures that seek to resolve or clarify the issue prior to a hearing.

The agreement should also address how the arbitrator will consider prehearing motions to dismiss or for summary judgment and the procedures governing them.

An arbitration agreement should also pay careful attention to how the arbitrator will be selected. The parties should have considered and agreed upon the panel from which to select an arbitrator. Since the arbitrator is obligated to honor the "four corners" of the agreement to arbitrate, careful attention should be placed on all procedures that either party believes are important to govern the arbitration procedure. For example, the parties may wish to address the following issues:

the apportionment or sharing of certain costs;

the award of prevailing party attorneys' fees and costs;

the appropriateness of a transcript and who will pay for it;

the site of the hearing;

the procedure for company release of witnesses;

issues regarding the subpoena power of the arbitrator;

the effect of a witness or party's failure to appear;

the use of telephone testimony or affidavits;

the applicability of federal or state rules of evidence and procedure;

whether an expedited arbitration procedure for claims under a certain dollar amount will be available;

the number of arbitrators;

whether the arbitration is a closed or open proceeding; and

other issues dealt with in the model procedures set forth in Appendix A.

Even where the arbitration agreement clearly identifies all major procedures, the agreement should also state the rules that apply in the absence of specific reference in the agreement. Such a default provision must be provided. The Employment Dispute Resolution Rules of the AAA, the Final Report on Model Rules for the Arbitration of Employment Disputes by the Committee on Labor and Employment Law of the Bar Association of the City of New York, or the employment dispute resolution rules of the Center for Public Resources are recommended in lieu of specific language in the agreement to arbitrate. When these rules are referenced, both parties to the agreement should ensure that the present version of the rules referenced and each model rule in itself is acceptable. These rules should be referenced by date or edition so that a new edition does not automatically supplant the rules selected.

An employer needs to consider how non-meritorious claims will be handled in the arbitration process. In particular, the employer may want to provide for both parties to adjudicate the claim by submission of documents and position statements to the arbitrator in lieu of a hearing. This procedure avoids convening a hearing where there is no basis for the claim in law or fact.

Also, the employer may want to provide a procedure wherein after initial discovery is complete the parties are permitted to petition the arbitrator for summary judgement on the pleadings similar to summary judgment motions under Rule 56 of the Federal Rules of Civil Procedure or under a summary judgment procedure tailored by the employer.

The employer must recognize that the selection of the organization that will administer the procedure is an important decision. Various organizations offer such services and all should be carefully investigated before one is selected. One organization, J.A.M.S./ENDISPUTE, has stated that it will not accept cases where the arbitration agreements do not allow for full remedies, reasonable discovery, the right to counsel, and other safeguards. J.A.M.S./ENDISPUTE also will administer only those agreements that provide the remedies of punitive damages and attorney fees.[24]

The selection of the arbitrator is as important as the design of the process and the selection of the organization that will administer the procedure. Arbitrators are unique and will react differently to certain issues, advocates, organizations, and plaintiffs. It is important for the organization to fully research the arbitrator prior to selection.

The Committee on Labor and Employment Law of the Bar Association of the City of New York recently published a Final Report on Model Rules for the Arbitration of Employment Disputes. These model rules are the most recent issued, and provide excellent guidance for an employer considering the introduction of a binding arbitration procedure. They were developed with reference to existing employment arbitration rules promulgated by the AAA, the Center for Public Resources, and the New York Stock Exchange. Some of the issues that were addressed in these rules, and which must be addressed in any procedure include:

the availability and scope of pre-hearing discovery,

the procedure for selecting the arbitrator,

the costs of the arbitration,

the scope of authority and remedial powers of the arbitrator, including the arbitrator's power to award attorneys' fees, and

whether the proceedings or decisions of arbitrators should be confidential.

Some of the more interesting elements of the model procedure include the requirement of a voluntary exchange of detailed statements of position, a presumptive right to one deposition with application for cause to the arbitrator for additional depositions,[25] disclosure of the employee's personnel file documents and all documents related to the personnel decision at issue, costs to be handled per traditional litigation standards except for the arbitrator's fee, a cap on the payment of the arbitrator's fees by the employee in the amount of two days' gross salary, full remedial powers for the arbitrator identical to the powers of the court including the right to order an attorneys' fees award, and provisions for confidentiality of the proceedings and awards. Furthermore, the model rules require that any and all counterclaims must be maintained at the arbitration.

The model rules do not require a transcript but do require that the hearing be recorded by audio tape so that any procedural irregularities do not escape judicial review. The rules provide that a proceeding must be initiated within 180 days of the time an employee has been notified or otherwise learns of the employer's action that is challenged. The rules allow for representation by nonlawyers and follow the same order of presentation as the courts, with the plaintiff going first. Finally, the rules provide for the use of expert witnesses and the disclosure of the expert's testimony in advance. Where substantial need exists, a party can obtain the right to depose the expert witness.

MODEL CLAUSES

Matters Subject to Arbitration

Many arbitration agreements are simple, one page documents. They set forth that all disputes and controversies arising out of the employment relationship are subject to arbitration, and reference a particular set of rules governing the conduct of arbitration (usually the Model Rules of Arbitration set forth by the AAA or other third-party administrator for the particular type of dispute or industry). For example, the AAA rules recommend the following language to resolve future disputes:

> Any controversy or claim arising out of or relating to this contract, or the breach thereof, shall be settled by arbitration in accordance with the Employment Dispute Resolution Rules of the American Arbitration Association, and judgment upon the award rendered by the arbitrator(s) may be entered in any court having jurisdiction thereof.

The following language can be used to resolve existing disputes:

We, the undersigned parties, hereby agree to submit to arbitration under the Employment Dispute Resolution Rules of the American Arbitration Association the following controversy: [cite briefly]. We further agree that the above controversy be submitted to [one] [three] arbitrator(s) selected from the panels of arbitrators of the American Arbitration Association. We further agree that we will faithfully observe this agreement and the rules, and that we will abide by and perform any award rendered by the arbitrator(s) and that a judgment of the court having jurisdiction may be entered upon the award.

Alternative language can be:

You agree to observe our dispute resolution/arbitration procedures for employee disputes [OPTIONAL: arising under the law]. While we hope that disputes with our employees will not arise, we want them resolved promptly if they do. These procedures include all [OPTIONAL: statutory] employment disputes, including disputes relating to termination of employment, that you might have with [company name] or its affiliates. These include all claims, demands, or actions under Title VII of the Civil Rights Act of 1964, the Civil Rights Act of 1866, the Civil Rights Act of 1991, the Age Discrimination in Employment Act as amended, the Rehabilitation Act of 1973, the Americans With Disabilities Act, The Family and Medical Leave Act of 1993, the Employee Retirement Income Security Act of 1974, and all amendments thereto, and any other federal, state, or local statute or regulation regarding employment discrimination in employment, or the termination of employment, and the common law of any state.

or

Except as otherwise provided in this agreement, the company and the employee hereby consent to the resolution by arbitration of all claims or controversies for which a court otherwise would be authorized by law to grant relief, in any way arising out of, relating to, or associated with, the employee's employment with the company, or its termination (claims), that the company may have against the employee or that the employee may have against the company or against its officers, directors, employees or agents in their capacity as such or otherwise. The claims covered by this agreement include, but are not limited to, claims for wages or other compensation due; claims for breach of any contract or covenant, express or implied; tort claims; claims for discrimination, including but not limited to, discrimination based on race, sex, religion, national origin, age, marital status, handicap, disability, or medical condition; claims for benefits, except as excluded in the following paragraph; and claims for violation of any federal, state, or other governmental constitution, statute, ordinance or regulation.

Exclusion of Matters

The parties may also wish to specifically identify what is excluded:

Except for disputes, claims or grievances concerning [state all excludable matters, i.e., workmens' compensation, unemployment, claims not involving a claim of legal right], any dispute, claim, or grievance arising out of or relating to this agreement shall be submitted to arbitration pursuant to the terms and conditions of this agreement.

The parties may also wish to exclude certain matters, for example:

Claims Not Covered by this Agreement

This agreement to arbitrate does not apply to or cover claims for workers' compensation benefits or compensation; claims for unemployment compensation benefits; claims by the company for injunctive or other equitable relief for unfair competition or the use or unauthorized disclosure of trade secrets or confidential information; and, claims based upon an employee pension or benefit plan the terms of which contain an arbitration or other nonjudicial dispute resolution procedure, in which such case the provisions of such plan shall apply.

In sum, it is imperative that a broad dispute and controversies clause be included as the first part of any agreement to arbitrate. The clause should clearly specify the type of disputes covered and identify those disputes within this definition that are excluded. Employers must pay careful attention to whether they want to provide the right to arbitrate all disputes or only disputes involving a claim of a legal or statutory right. Employers must also make sure that they address whether the arbitration agreement includes an employee cause of action against a supervisor as an individual defendant.

Other Clauses

Once the arbitration clause tailored to the parties' needs has been included, the parties are free to address all arbitration procedures and practices. This is the opportunity to carefully craft the arbitration process to meet particular needs. The following is a suggested list of possible clauses to be included in any arbitration agreement, either pre-dispute or post-dispute.

Initiation of Arbitration

Arbitration under an arbitration provision in a contract shall be initiated in the following manner:

The initiating party (hereinafter claimant) shall, within the time period, if any, specified in the contract(s), give written notice to the other party (hereinafter respondent) of its intention to arbitrate [identify the dispute], which notice shall contain a statement setting forth the nature of the dispute, the amount involved, if any, the remedy sought, and the hearing locale requested, and shall file at any regional office of the AAA three copies of the notice and three copies of the arbitration provisions of the contract, together with the appropriate filing fee unless the parties agree to some other method of fee advancement.

The AAA shall give notice of such filing to the respondent or respondents. A respondent may file an answering statement in duplicate with the AAA within ten days after notice from the AAA, in which event the respondent shall at the same time send a copy of the answering statement to the claimant. If a counterclaim is asserted, it shall contain a statement setting forth the nature of the counterclaim, the amount involved, if any, and the remedy sought. If a counterclaim is made in the answering statement, the appropriate fee provided in the schedule shall be forwarded to the AAA with the answering statement. If no answering statement is filed within the stated time, it will be treated as a denial of the claim. Failure to file an answering statement shall not operate to delay the arbitration.

The AAA Employment Dispute Resolution Rule 3 states:

Cases may be initiated by joint submission in writing or in accordance with provisions in a personnel manual or employment agreement, and filed together with the appropriate filing fee as provided herein.

Time Limitations

It is within the power of the parties to establish their own time limitations for the seeking of relief or other mandated action. This is where the various procedural steps of the dispute resolution process should be carefully and explicitly detailed. For example:

Any dispute or claim arising under this agreement must be presented to [name of in-house program administrator], by [writing or other method], within [number of days] of [the incident giving rise to the claim]. Should the parties be unable to resolve this dispute, either party must file a demand for arbitration with [name of in-house or other administrator of arbitration process] by [writing or other method], within 30 days of [denial of complaint by supervisor or other predetermined final step]. Any proceeding under this procedure must be brought within one year of the act or omission giving rise to the controversy.

Changes of Claim

Regarding the right of parties to amend or change their claims, the AAA model rules recommend:

After filing of a claim, if either party desires to make any new or different claim or counterclaim, it shall be made in writing and filed with the AAA, and a copy shall be mailed to the other party, who shall have a period of ten days from the date of such mailing within which to file an answer with the AAA. After the arbitrator is appointed, however, no new or different claim may be submitted except with the arbitrator's consent.

Discovery

Parties may wish to set forth the parameters of permissible discovery, if any. Parties can set a maximum limit on the number of depositions, length of depositions, maximum number and format of interrogatories, maximum number and format of document product requests, scope of sanctions for failure to cooperate in discovery, the standards for application of sanctions, and all other discovery provisions. For example:

Parties are entitled to take the depositions of up to two persons. These depositions cannot exceed four hours unless permission is obtained from the arbitrator upon showing of good cause. Good cause is defined as [give definition].

Each party is entitled to serve up to 30 interrogatories on the opposing party. Each interrogatory should consist of a single interrogatory. Upon service of interrogatories, the opposing party will have 30 days to respond.

Parties may serve an unlimited number of document production requests.

The above discovery provisions should be interpreted in a reasonable manner, with guidance provided by the Federal Rules of Civil Procedure.

Where a party is deemed by the arbitrator to have failed to cooperate in discovery as required herein, the following sanctions may be imposed by the arbitrator: (select sanctions)

or

Each party shall be entitled to propound and serve upon the other party one set of interrogatories in a form consistent with the Federal Rules of Civil Procedure and which shall be limited to the identification of potential witnesses. Each party shall be entitled to propound and serve upon the other one set of Request for the Production of Documents in a form consistent with the Federal Rules of Civil Procedure and which shall be limited in number to twenty-five (25) requests (including subparts, which shall be counted separately). Additionally, each party shall be entitled to conduct two (2) days of depositions of witnesses or of the parties in accordance with the procedures set forth in the Federal Rules of Civil Procedure.

Each party shall have the right to take the deposition of one individual and any expert witness designated by another party. Each party also shall have the right to propound requests for production of documents to any party. The subpoena right specified below shall be applicable to discovery pursuant to this paragraph. Additional discovery may be had only where the Arbitrator selected pursuant to this document so orders, upon a showing of substantial need.

Federal or State Rules of Civil Procedure

The parties may wish to provide that all discovery or other pre-arbitration proceedings are to be conducted pursuant to the Federal Rules of Civil Procedure as continuously amended and/or current local court rules of the United States District Court or particular state court Rules of Procedure. In particular, the parties may wish to preserve those parts of the Federal Rules of Civil Procedure that address discovery and pre-trial motions. An attractive option to many employers may be the inclusion of the right of a party to file a motion to dismiss or summary judgment with the arbitrator.[26]

Rules of Evidence

The parties may provide that the arbitration hearings will be conducted in accordance with the Federal Rules of Evidence or particular state Rules of Evidence.

The parties may specifically empower the arbitrator to conduct a full and impartial hearing without reference to particular rules of evidence. For example, AAA rules recommend:

The parties may offer such evidence as is relevant and material to the dispute and shall produce such evidence as the arbitrator deems necessary to an understanding and determination of the dispute. An arbitrator or other person authorized by law to subpoena witnesses or documents may do so upon the request of any party or independently.

The arbitrator shall be the judge of the relevance and materiality of the evidence offered, and conformity to legal rules of evidence shall not be necessary. All evidence shall be taken in the presence of all of the arbitrators and all of the parties, except where any of the parties is absent in default or has waived the right to be present.

The arbitrator may receive and consider the evidence of witnesses by affidavit, but shall give it only such weight as the arbitrator deems it entitled to after consideration of any objection made to its admission.

If the parties agree or the arbitrator directs that the documents or other evidence be submitted to the arbitrator after the hearing, the documents or other evidence shall be filed with the AAA for transmission to the arbitrator.

All parties shall be afforded an opportunity to examine such documents or other evidence.

Cost of Arbitration

The parties may wish to allocate the cost of arbitration pursuant to a specific formula. For example, an employer may agree to pay all costs, a certain percent of costs, or a certain amount after an employee payment of a filing fee plus all arbitrator fees and costs up to a certain amount of days of arbitration hearing. Thereafter such costs may be borne equally. Here the AAA Rules recommend:

As a not-for-profit organization, the AAA shall prescribe filing and other administrative fees to compensate it for the cost of providing administrative services. The fees in effect when the demand for arbitration or submission agreement is received shall be applicable.

The filing fee shall be advanced by the initiating party or parties subject to final apportionment by the arbitrator in the award.

The AAA may, in the event of extreme hardship on the part of any party, defer or reduce the administrative fees.

Unless otherwise agreed by the parties, the expenses of witnesses for either side shall be paid by the party producing such witnesses. All expenses of the arbitration, including required travel and other expenses of the arbitrator, AAA representatives, and any witness, and the cost of any proof produced at the direction of the arbitrator, shall be borne equally by the parties, unless they agree otherwise or unless the arbitrator directs otherwise in the award.

An appropriate daily rate and other arrangements will be discussed by the administrator with the parties and the arbitrator. If the parties fail to agree to the terms of compensation, an appropriate rate shall be established by the AAA and communicated in writing to the parties.

Any arrangement for the compensation of a neutral arbitrator shall be made through the AAA and not directly between the parties and the arbitrator.

The AAA may require the parties to deposit in advance of any hearings such sums of money as it deems necessary to cover the expenses of the arbitration, including the arbitrator's fee, if any, and shall render an accounting to the parties and return any unexpended balance at the conclusion of the case.

Duration of the Hearing

Both parties may wish to set a time frame for the arbitration hearing within which all evidence must be heard. For example, parties may agree that each party will have up to one full hearing day for the presentation of their positions, with the arbitrator permitted to determine appropriate hearing time for rebuttal.

Stenographic Costs

The parties should agree to the procedure for stenographic costs in the arbitration agreement. For example:

The parties hereby agree that all costs of stenography will be assumed by the party requesting such record. Should both parties seek a stenographic record, the costs shall be split equally between them. In any event, where one party has obtained a stenographic record, the other party should be allowed to copy the record at the requesting party's cost.

or

There shall be no stenographic record of these proceedings unless either party requests it. In the event a party requests a stenographic record, that party shall bear the cost of such a record. If both parties request a stenographic record, the cost shall be borne equally by the parties.

or

The cost of the stenographic record, if any is made, and all transcripts thereof, shall be prorated equally among all parties ordering copies, unless they shall otherwise agree, and shall be paid for by the responsible parties directly to the reporting agency.

Location of Arbitration Hearing

The parties may wish to identify a particular location where arbitration hearings will be conducted.

The parties may mutually agree on the locale where the arbitration is to be held. If any party requests that the hearing be held in a specific locale and the other party files no objection thereto within ten days after notice of the request has been sent to it by the AAA, the locale shall be the one requested. If a party objects to the locale requested by the other party, the AAA shall have the power to determine the locale and its decision shall be final and binding.

An alternative clause may be:

The parties hereby agree that all disputes arising from this arbitration agreement will be heard in [state, city, or exact location]. The parties should identify how the hearing will be scheduled.

Date, Time, and Place of Hearing

The arbitrator shall set the date, time, and place of the hearing, notice of which must be given to the parties by the AAA at least ten days in advance, unless the parties agree otherwise.

Attorneys' Fees

The parties may wish to waive any attorneys' fees award provisions of a particular law in the agreement to arbitrate. For example:

The parties hereby agree that the arbitrator's award shall not include provision of any attorneys' fees or costs to either party. Such attorneys' fees or costs shall be assumed solely by the respective parties.

Alternatively, the parties may prefer to empower the arbitrator to award prevailing party attorneys' fees as permitted under the statutes at issue. The failure to do so may be evidence of employer overreaching. For example:

The parties shall share equally the fees and costs of the arbitrator. Each party will deposit funds or post other appropriate security for its share of the arbitrator's fee, in an amount and manner determined by the arbitrator, ten days before the first day of hearing. Each party shall pay for its own costs and attorneys' fees, if any. However, if any party prevails on a statutory claim which entitles the prevailing party to attorneys' fees, or if there is a written agreement providing for fees, the arbitrator may award reasonable fees to the prevailing party in accordance with such statute or agreement.

Tripartite Panel

The parties may wish to use a three-person (tripartite) panel in lieu of the selection of a single arbitrator. In this situation, each party is allowed to appoint one arbitrator. The two arbitrators selected then select a third arbitrator. For example:

Any claim or controversy arising under this arbitration agreement shall be referred to three arbitrators. One arbitrator will be appointed by each party and a third will be appointed by the two arbitrators heretofore selected. An award in writing signed by any two of the arbitrators shall be final. If either party shall refuse or neglect to select an arbitrator within 30 days after the other has appointed an arbitrator, and written notice is served upon that party requesting the appointment of an arbitrator, the arbitrator so appointed by the first party shall have power to proceed to arbitrate and determine the matters of disagreement as if that arbitrator were appointed by both parties for that purpose. The award of that arbitrator in writing, signed by the arbitrator, will be final.

A tripartite panel is not recommended because it is more expensive, less procedurally streamlined, and may be more predisposed to encourage a challenge of the award where there is a two-to-one split. For example, AAA rules provide:

If the arbitration agreement does not specify the number of arbitrators, the dispute shall be heard and determined by one arbitrator, unless the AAA, in its discretion, directs that a greater number of arbitrators be appointed. If the parties have not appointed an arbitrator and have not provided any other method of appointment, the arbitrator shall be appointed in the following manner: immediately after the filing of the demand or submission, the AAA shall send simultaneously to each party to the dispute an identical list of names of persons chosen from the panel. Each party to the dispute shall have ten days from the transmittal date in which to strike any names objected to, number the remaining names in order of preference, and return the list to the AAA. If a party does not return the list within the time specified, all persons named therein shall be deemed acceptable. From among the persons who have been approved on both lists, and in accordance with the designated order of mutual preference, the AAA shall invite the acceptance of an arbitrator to serve. If the parties fail to agree on any of the persons named, or if acceptable arbitrators are unable to act, or if for any other reason the appointment cannot be made from the submitted lists, the AAA shall have the power to make the appointment from among other members of the panel without the submission of additional lists.

Successor Arbitrator

Parties may wish to anticipate situations where the initial arbitrator or arbitrators selected cannot complete the hearing. For example:

In the event that any arbitrator dies, or refuses to act, or becomes incapable, incompetent, or unfit to act before hearings have been completed, or before an award has been rendered, a successor arbitrator may be appointed by the party pursuant to the selection procedures set forth in this agreement. A *de novo* hearing is not necessary unless either party, or the new arbitrator requests one.

or

If for any reason an arbitrator is unable to perform the duties of the office, the AAA may, on proof satisfactory to it, declare the office vacant. Vacancies shall be filled in accordance with the applicable provisions of these rules. In the event of a vacancy in a panel of neutral arbitrators after hearings have commenced, the remaining arbitrator(s) may continue with the hearing, and determination of the controversy, unless the parties agree otherwise.

Arbitrator Powers Clause

Parties may wish to set forth a clause specifically identifying and possibly limiting the powers of the arbitrators. In general, these clauses establish that the arbitrators' powers are all inclusive. For example:

The arbitrator shall have full power to give such directions and to make such orders as he shall deem fit and just.

Clause Regarding the Death of a Party

The parties may wish to specifically agree that an arbitration and all underlying claims are terminated by the death of a party. Here it should be noted that the death of a party revokes an arbitration agreement unless the agreement or submission or a statute expressly provides otherwise (Corpus Juris Secundum, Arbitration, Section 54). Thus, if parties intend to ensure that arbitration will continue after death, it should be specifically stated.

Arbitration as a Condition Precedent to Any Court Action

For those employers who wish to ensure that the arbitration process is fully utilized by an employee prior to that employee's resort to court, the following clause may be of assistance:

The parties agree that a condition precedent to the commencement of court proceedings of any nature arising out of any disputes from this agreement shall first be submitted to arbitration as set forth herein.

Provision that Judgment May be Entered on Award

The parties may wish to specifically provide that the arbitrator's award may be entered in the highest court of the particular state or federal jurisdiction. For example:

Both parties agree that the judgment upon the arbitration award issued in this proceeding may be entered in the highest court of the state or federal jurisdiction.

This provision is particularly helpful where one of the parties is a nonresident and subsequent difficulty may arise regarding the power of the court to enter judgment on the award.

Award of Attorneys' Fees for Challenge to the Arbitration Agreement

Since arbitration is designed as an expedient, less expensive process than courtroom litigation, the parties may wish to introduce a cost-shifting provision in the situation where either party unsuccessfully challenges the legality of the arbitration agreement or unsuccessfully appeals an arbitrator's award beyond the arbitrator's jurisdiction. For example:

Both the parties agree that, should either party to this agreement seek to avoid arbitration prior to its inception by resort to federal or state court process or by refusing to arbitrate, should the party seeking to avoid arbitration fail to prevail, the attorneys' fees of the other party spent in defense of this arbitration provision or the compelling of arbitration shall be awarded to that party.

or

The parties agree that should either party appeal the arbitration award and opinion or any part thereof beyond the arbitrator, should that party fail to prevail in their appeal, all attorneys' fees and costs expended by the other party shall be paid for by that appealing party.

Reconsideration by the Arbitrator

Parties may wish to specifically obligate an arbitrator, upon request, to reconsider the award and opinion or request for rehearing within so many days of issuance.

Within 30 days of the date of issuance of an arbitrator's opinion and award, or any part thereof, either party may petition the arbitrator for reconsideration or rehearing of the matter.

Time Limits for Issuance of an Arbitrator's Award and Opinion

Parties may wish to obligate an arbitrator to issue a decision within so many days of the close of the hearing. For example:

Within [number] days of the close of the hearing, the arbitrator shall issue an opinion and award in this matter. Should the arbitrator fail to issue this opinion and award within the time frame set forth above, both parties are released from all costs associated with the arbitration.

or

The Award

(a) The award shall be made promptly by the arbitrator, and, unless otherwise agreed by the parties or specified by law, no later than 30 days from the date of closing of the hearing or, if oral hearings have been waived, from the date of the AAA's transmittal of the final statements and proofs to the arbitrator.

(b) The award shall be in writing and shall be signed by a majority of the arbitrators. Unless the parties agree otherwise, any opinion shall be in summary form. It shall be executed in the manner required by law.

(c) The arbitrator may grant any remedy or relief that the arbitrator deems just, equitable, and within the scope of the agreement of the parties, including, but not limited to, specific performance of a contract. The arbitrator shall, in the award, assess arbitration fees, expenses, and compensation as provided herein in favor of any party and, in the event any administrative fees or expenses are due the AAA, in favor of the AAA.

(d) If the parties settle their dispute during the course of the arbitration, the arbitrator may set forth the terms of the agreed settlement in an award. Such an award is referred to as a consent award.

(e) The parties shall accept as legal delivery of the award the placing of the award or a true copy thereof in the mail, addressed to a party or its representative at the last known address, personal service of the award, or the filing of the award in any manner that is permitted by law.

Release Time for Witnesses

Parties should consider how release of witnesses will be performed. This is especially important where a company anticipates a problem allowing numerous company employees to testify at a hearing. For example:

The parties hereby agree that should any witnesses be under the control of the opposing party that party will release those witnesses for testimony. All costs of said witnesses are to be assumed by the party presenting the witness.

Telephone Testimony

Parties may wish to control the costs of the arbitration by allowing for telephone testimony by a non-party witness, subject to either party's right to veto this testimony in favor of person-to-person confrontation. For example:

Both parties hereby agree that the telephone testimony of a witness may be taken upon consent of the parties. Should either party request to confront the witness in person, no telephone testimony will be permitted. Should either party initially consent to telephone testimony and subsequently revoke this consent, the objecting party must assume all costs of all parties related to the revocation of consent.

Videotape Depositions

Parties may provide for the use of videotaped depositions pursuant to procedures set forth under Federal or State Rules of Procedure.

The parties agree that videotaped depositions of witnesses shall be governed by Local Court Rule __________ of the U.S. District Court for the District __________ of __________ . [Here parties select the Local Court Rule of the Federal District Court]

Postponements

To expedite a hearing and ensure appropriate preparation the parties may wish to penalize postponement requests by use of a fee shifting device. For example:

Should either party request postponement of a hearing, to the extent that any fees or costs are incurred by the opposing party as a direct result of such postponement request, those fees and costs shall be paid by the party requesting postponement.

or

The parties agree that should either party request a postponement that prevents the close of hearing which in the arbitrator's opinion would have otherwise occurred at the time of the postponement request, should the opposing party consent to the postponement request, the party requesting postponement shall be responsible for all attorneys' fees and costs and arbitration fees associated with the postponement or reconvening of the hearing. Should a party oppose said postponement request, the arbitrator may, but is not required to, award similar fees and costs where consent is granted.

The AAA Rules recommend:

The arbitrator, for good cause shown, may postpone any hearing upon the request of a party or upon the arbitrator's own initiative and shall also grant such postponement when all of the parties agree.

Filing of Briefs

Parties should specify whether briefs are permitted. Parties not incorporating state or federal rules of procedure may wish to set time limits for the filing of briefs. For example:

Either party may file a brief at the time of the hearing or any time prior thereto. Either party may file a reply to any brief not later than five days after the close of hearing. In all other situations, either party may file a reply brief within ten days after receipt of an opposing party's brief. Where a brief is filed with the arbitrator, a copy of said brief shall be filed concurrently with the opposing party. The arbitrator may alter the time periods for the filing of any briefs or reply briefs.

Admissibility of Affidavits

The admissibility of affidavits is often a point of contention in arbitrations. The parties may wish to expedite a hearing by anticipating this issue. For example:

The arbitrator may, in his sole discretion, admit as evidence any affidavit or declaration concerning the matters in difference, provided that a copy of any said document has been previously served to all opposing parties at least three days prior to the time at which the affidavit is offered into evidence. The burden is on the party seeking to admit said affidavit to establish appropriate service. The party against whom the affidavit is offered into evidence is permitted to seek to subject that affiant to cross-examination. Should that affiant be unavailable for cross-examination, the affidavit may not be admitted, absent admissibility pursuant to the Federal Rules of Evidence.

AAA Rules recommend:

The arbitrator may receive and consider the evidence of witnesses by affidavit, but shall give it only such weight as the arbitrator deems it entitled to after consideration of any objection made to its admission. If the parties agree or the arbitrator directs that the documents or other evidence be submitted to the arbitrator after the hearing, the documents or other evidence shall be filed with the AAA for transmission to the arbitrator. All parties shall be afforded an opportunity to examine such documents or other evidence.

Failure of a Party to Attend Hearing

Where a party fails to attend the arbitration hearing, the parties may wish to carefully consider how to handle this incident. Parties may provide that a hearing will be held in the absence of any such party. However, this provision may run afoul of due process requirements. In the alternative, parties may wish to provide that if a party fails to attend, that party must pay all fees and costs associated with that day's scheduled hearing and all opposing party's attorneys' fees and costs associated with the failure to attend. Furthermore, one may wish to consider the placement of that demand for arbitration on an inactive roster for 60 days. At the end of the 60 days, if not rescheduled for hearing, the parties may provide that the claim is deemed dismissed with prejudice and barred from relitigation by all applicable limitations. For example:

In the event of either party or his witness failing to attend before the arbitrator, after [number] days' written notice given to such party by the arbitrator, the arbitrator may proceed with the arbitration in the absence and without further notice to such party or witness.

or

In the event of either party or his witness failing to attend before the arbitrator, after [number] days written notice given to such party, the hearing will be placed on an inactive roster for 60 calendar days. Should that party fail to appear or request rehearing in writing to the arbitrator, the arbitration demand is deemed to have been abandoned and the arbitrator is required to dismiss said arbitration claim with prejudice. The limitations period will bar any reprosecution of said arbitration demand.

or

Should either party fail to produce a witness, the party may elect to continue the proceeding absent said witness or the party may request that the arbitrator rule on the record as established to date by that party. In any event, the opposing party shall have the full right to present their witnesses in full testimony and shall not be prejudiced by the opposing party's failure to produce a witness.

AAA Rules recommend:

Unless the law provides to the contrary, the arbitration may proceed in the absence of any party or representative who, after due notice, fails to be present or fails to obtain a postponement. An award shall not be made solely on the default of a party. The arbitrator shall require the party who is present to submit such evidence as the arbitrator may require for the making of the award.

Use of Consultants

Unless expressly authorized by the parties, arbitrators may not consult or employ counsel, accountants, or other experts. Thus, the parties may wish to consider permitting the arbitrator to seek the advice of outside counsel, accountants, or other experts. For example:

The arbitrators may submit to [name of consultant] whom they may select any [identity of submission] arising in the course of the arbitration, and may accept such opinion as conclusive.

For example, AAA Rules recommend:

An arbitrator finding it necessary to make an inspection or investigation in connection with the arbitration shall direct the AAA to so advise the parties. The arbitrator shall set the date and time and the AAA shall notify the parties. Any party who so desires may be present at such an inspection or investigation. In the event that one or all parties are not present at the inspection or investigation, the arbitrator shall make a verbal or written report to the parties and afford them an opportunity to comment.

Procedure for Arbitrator Selection

Under AAA procedures, the AAA may offer prospective parties to arbitration a list of commercial or labor-management arbitrators. The parties may wish to set forth additional procedures for the selection of such arbitrators to include the particular type of panel from which the arbitrators will be selected, the procedure for striking the arbitrators, and whether either party may initially reject an arbitration panel. For example:

The parties agree that a single arbitrator will be selected from a panel of [labor-management] or [commercial] arbitrators supplied by the American Arbitration Association. Either party may reject the full panel within 10 days of receipt by requesting a new panel from the AAA.

or

The parties will select an arbitrator from the panel by mutual agreement or by alternate striking of arbitrators until one arbitrator remains. Where alternate striking is used, a coin flip or any other procedure may be used where the parties can agree on who will make the first strike.

Here, AAA Rules recommend:

If the arbitration agreement does not specify the number of arbitrators, the dispute shall be heard and determined by one arbitrator, unless the AAA, in its discretion, directs that a greater number of arbitrators be appointed. If the parties have not appointed an arbitrator and have not provided any other method of appointment, the arbitrator shall be appointed in the following manner: Immediately after the filing of the demand or submission, the AAA shall send simultaneously to each party to the dispute an identical list of names of persons chosen from the panel. Each party to the dispute shall have ten days from the transmittal date in which to strike any names objected to, number the remaining names in order of preference, and return the list to the AAA. If a party does not return the list within the time specified, all persons named therein shall be deemed acceptable. From among the persons who have been approved on both lists, and in accordance with the designated order of mutual preference, the AAA shall invite the acceptance of an arbitrator to serve. If the parties fail to agree on any of the persons named, or if acceptable arbitrators are unable to act, or if for any other reason the appointment cannot be made from the submitted lists, the AAA shall have the power to make the appointment from among other members of the panel without the submission of additional lists.

Confidentiality

A major advantage of arbitration is that it is a private process. The parties may wish to bind themselves and the arbitrator to strict confidentiality concerning the facts of the matter at issue. This will avoid the possibility that an individual party will seek to influence the outcome of the dispute by outside publicity, or that the arbitrator may later publish the arbitration decision in an arbitration report.

The parties may also wish to agree on who will be allowed to attend the proceeding and whether the proceeding will be considered closed to the public. Finally, if confidentiality is valued, an appropriate sanction should be identified for breach of this provision. For example:

Both parties recognize that any claim, dispute, or arbitration under this agreement is considered confidential. In this regard, the dispute or claim at issue, the arbitration proceedings, and the arbitration award and decision may be disclosed solely to a parties' attorney, potential witnesses, accountant, spouse, and only after each of those persons have executed a confidentiality agreement as set forth at Appendix [an appropriate confidentiality agreement should be attached as the referenced appendix] in this agreement. Both parties agree that any breach of this confidentiality clause will relieve the other party from all payment obligations of any kind due to that party plus a damages award in the amount of [dollar amount to be set by the parties].

AAA Rules recommend:

The arbitrator shall maintain the privacy of the hearings unless the law provides to the contrary. Any person having a direct interest in the arbitration is entitled to attend hearings. The arbitrator shall otherwise have the power to require the exclusion of any witness, other than a party or other essential person, during the testimony of any other witness. The arbitrator shall determine whether any other person may attend the hearing.

Confidentiality — Request of an Award Only

The award shall be in writing and shall be signed by the arbitrator. If either party requests, the arbitrator shall issue an opinion in writing, which shall set forth in summary form the reasons for the arbitrator's determination. All awards shall be executed in the manner required by law.

Both parties are permitted to request that, pursuant to confidentiality considerations, an award without an accompanying opinion be issued. Should either party request that an award only be issued for this reason, the arbitrator is required to honor that confidentiality request unless [parties to determine standards to waive confidentiality].

Default Provision

Even where the parties have a tailored procedure, parties should establish a default set of procedural rules. For example:

To the extent that any procedural issues are not addressed by the parties herein, the parties stipulate that the Employment Dispute Resolution Rules of AAA shall govern.

Requirement of Enumerated Claims and Damages Claims

The parties may wish to require enumeration of all claims and damages sought at the time of filing or amendment. For example:

At the time of filing of a demand for arbitration, the party filing such demand is required to specifically set forth the basis of all statutory claims. A failure to specifically identify a claim by reference to statute, case law, or common denomination, bars that party from raising that claim or claims at hearing. The filing of an arbitration demand does not toll or otherwise suspend the running of time for purposes of compliance with contractual time limitations set forth herein. A party seeking relief must file at the time of a demand for arbitration or relief, whichever is earlier, an itemized statement of claims specifically identifying the amount of relief requested pursuant to each legal claim and the denomination of such claimed relief by punitive, compensatory, back pay, front pay or other.

Waiver of Defects

This clause ensures that the parties have had a full and fair hearing and minimizes the possibility that they may later claim otherwise.

At the close of the arbitration, both parties agree that they will be queried by the arbitrator as to whether they have any objections to the conduct of the arbitrator or the arbitration proceedings. At that time, both parties will be requested to waive any claim of defects or to stipulate that said objections have been cured and that an arbitration opinion and award shall issue without regard to any above-stated objections.

For example, AAA Rules recommend:

Any party who proceeds with the arbitration after knowledge that any provision or requirement of these procedures has not been complied with and who fails to state objections thereto in writing, shall be deemed to have waived the right to object.

Attorneys' Fees

It is further agreed that the arbitrators may, in their sole discretion, award attorneys' fees to the prevailing party.

Waiver of Procedures

Any party who proceeds with the arbitration after knowledge that any provision or requirement of these procedures has not been complied with, and who fails to state objections thereto in writing, shall be deemed to have waived the right to object.

Apportionment of Expenses

The cost and expenses of the arbitration shall be borne and paid as the arbitrators by their award direct (or shall be paid by the parties in equal share).

Deposit for Arbitrators' Fees and Costs

At any time during the proceeding the arbitrator(s) may request that both parties deposit a security amount satisfactory to the arbitrator. Unless both parties are required to make said security deposit, this request may not be made by the arbitrator. For example, AAA Rules recommend:

The AAA may require the parties to deposit in advance of any hearings such sums of money as it deems necessary to cover the expenses of the arbitration, including the arbitrator's fee, if any, and shall render an accounting to the parties and return any unexpended balance at the conclusion of the case.

Representation by Counsel

Any party may be represented by counsel or by any other authorized representative. A party intending to be so represented shall notify the other party and the AAA of the name and address of the representative at least three days prior to the date set for the hearing at which that person is first to appear. When such a representative initiates an arbitration or responds for a party, notice is deemed to have been given.

Interpreter Clause

Both parties, subject to the arbitrator's power to resolve any disagreements, shall make the necessary arrangements for the services of an interpreter upon the request of one or more of the parties, who assume the cost of such service.

Oaths

The arbitrator has the discretion to require witnesses to testify under oath administered by any duly qualified person, or if required by law, or demanded by either party, shall do so. The AAA Rules recommend:

Before proceeding with the first hearing, each arbitrator may take an oath of office and, if required by law, shall do so. The arbitrator may require witnesses to testify under oath administered by any duly qualified person and, if it is required by law or requested by any party, shall do so.

Order of Proceeding

The AAA Rules recommend:

A hearing shall be opened by the filing of the oath of the arbitrator, where required; by the recording of the place, time, and date of the hearing, and the presence of the arbitrator, the parties, and their representatives, if any; and by the receipt by the arbitrator of the statement of the claim and answering statement, if any. The arbitrator may, at the beginning of the hearing, ask for statements clarifying the issues involved. In some cases, part or all of the above will have been accomplished at the preliminary hearing conducted by the arbitrator pursuant to Section 6. The complaining party shall then present evidence to support its claim. The defending party shall then present evidence supporting its defense. Witnesses for each party shall submit to questions or other examination. The arbitrator has the discretion to vary this procedure but shall afford a full and equal opportunity to all parties for the presentation of any material and relevant evidence. Exhibits, when offered by either party, may be received in evidence by the arbitrator. The names and addresses of all witnesses and a description of the exhibits in the order received shall be made a part of the record. There shall be no direct communication between the parties and a neutral arbitrator other than at oral hearing, unless the parties and the arbitrator agree otherwise. Any other oral or written communication from the parties to the neutral arbitrator shall be directed to the AAA for transmittal to the arbitrator.

Expedited Arbitration for Claims Involving Less Than $50,000

The AAA Rules provide for expedited arbitration of claims for less than $50,000. These procedures are set forth below:

Unless the AAA in its discretion determines otherwise, the Expedited Procedures shall apply in any case where no disclosed claim or counterclaim exceeds $50,000, exclusive of interest and arbitration costs. Parties may also agree to use the Expedited Procedures in cases involving claims in excess of $50,000.

Notice by Telephone: The parties shall accept all notices from the AAA by telephone. Such notices by the AAA shall subsequently be confirmed in writing to the parties. Should there be a failure to confirm in writing any notice hereunder, the proceeding shall nonetheless be valid if the notice has, in fact, been given by telephone.

Appointment and Qualifications of Arbitrator: The AAA shall appoint one neutral arbitrator from its Panel of Arbitrators who has familiarity with the employment field, who shall hear and determine the case promptly. The parties will be given notice by telephone by the AAA of the appointment of the arbitrator, who shall be subject to disqualification for the reasons specified in "Cost of Arbitration" (p. 88, this volume). Within seven days, the parties shall notify the AAA, by telephone, of any objection to the arbitrator appointed. Any objection by a party to the arbitrator shall be confirmed in writing to the AAA with a copy to the other party or parties.

Date, Time, and Place of Hearing: The arbitrator shall set the date, time, and place of the hearing. The AAA will notify the parties by telephone at least seven days in advance of the hearing date. A formal notice of hearing will also be sent by the AAA to the parties.

The Hearing: Generally, the hearing shall be completed within one day, unless the dispute is resolved by submission of documents, upon the agreement of all parties. The arbitrator, for good cause shown, may schedule an additional hearing to be held within seven days.

Time of Award: Unless otherwise agreed by the parties, the award shall be rendered not later than 14 days from the date of the closing of the hearing.

Requirement of Mediation Prior to Arbitration

Either party may request as a precondition to arbitration of any claims or dispute that mediation be employed pursuant to Appendix [reference to AAA Mediation Rules] of this agreement. All costs of mediation will be [shared] [paid by one party].

Designation of Witnesses

At least 30 days before the arbitration, the parties must exchange lists of witnesses, including any expert, and copies of all exhibits intended to be used at the arbitration.

Enforcement

The decision of the arbitrator may be enforced under the terms of the Federal Arbitration Act (Title 9 U.S.C.) or under the law of any state. If the decision is not completely enforceable, final, and binding, it shall be enforced and binding on both parties to the extent permitted by law. Even if a party of this procedure is held to be void or unenforceable, the remainder of the procedure will be enforceable and any part may be severed from the remainder, as appropriate.

Administrative Conference, Preliminary Hearing, and Mediation Conference

At the request of any party or at the discretion of the AAA, an administrative conference with the AAA and the parties or their representatives will be scheduled in appropriate cases to expedite the arbitration proceedings. There is no administrative fee for this service.

In large or complex cases, at the request of any party or at the discretion of the arbitrator or the AAA, a preliminary hearing with the parties or their representatives and the arbitrator may be scheduled by the arbitrator to specify the issues to be resolved, to stipulate to uncontested facts, and to consider any other matters that will expedite the arbitration proceedings. Consistent with the expedited nature of arbitration, the arbitrator may, at the preliminary hearing, establish the extent of and schedule for the production of relevant documents and other information, the identification of any witnesses to be called, and a schedule for further hearings to resolve the dispute. There is no administrative fee for the first preliminary hearing.

With the consent of the parties, the AAA at any stage of the proceeding may arrange a mediation conference under its mediation rules, in order to facilitate settlement. The mediator shall not be an arbitrator appointed to the case. Where the parties to a pending arbitration agree to mediate under the AAA's rules, no additional administrative fee is required to initiate the mediation.

Qualifications of Neutral Arbitrator

A. Arbitrators serving under these rules shall have familiarity with the employment field.

B. Any neutral arbitrator appointed shall be subject to disqualification for the reasons stated in paragraph C of this section. If the parties specifically so agree in writing, the arbitrator shall not be subject to disqualification for those reasons.

C. No person shall serve as a neutral arbitrator in any matter in which that person has any financial or personal interest in the result of the proceeding. Prior to accepting appointment, the prospective arbitrator shall disclose any circumstance likely to prevent a prompt hearing or to create a presumption of bias. Upon receipt of such information, the AAA will either replace that person or communicate the information to the parties for comment. Thereafter, the AAA may disqualify that person and its decision shall be conclusive.

D. The term "arbitrator" in these rules refers to the arbitration panel, whether composed of one or more arbitrators.

Majority Decision

All decisions of the arbitrators must be by a majority. The award must also be made by a majority, unless the concurrence of all is expressly required by the arbitration agreement or by law.

Interim Measures

The arbitrator may issue such orders for interim relief as may be deemed necessary to safeguard the subject matter of the arbitration, without prejudice to the rights of the parties or to the final determination of the dispute.

Closing of Hearing

The arbitrator shall specifically inquire of all parties whether they have any further proofs to offer or witnesses to be heard. Upon receiving negative replies or if satisfied that the record is complete, the arbitrator shall declare the hearing closed.

If briefs are to be filed, the hearing shall be declared closed as of the final date set by the arbitrator for the receipt of briefs. If documents are to be filed and the date set for their receipt is later than that set for the receipt of briefs, the later date shall be the date of closing the hearing. The time limit within which the arbitrator is required to make the award shall commence to run, in the absence of other agreements by the parties, upon closing of the hearing.

Reopening of Hearing

The hearing may be reopened on the arbitrator's initiative, or upon application of a party, at any time before the award is made. If reopening the hearing would prevent the making of the award within the specific time agreed on by the parties in the contract(s) out of which the controversy has arisen, the matter may not be reopened unless the parties agree on an extension of time. When no specific date is fixed in the contract, the arbitrator may reopen the hearing and shall have 30 days from the closing of the reopened hearing within which to make an award.

Waiver of Oral Hearing

The parties may provide, by written agreement, for the waiver of oral hearings in any case. If the parties are unable to agree as to the procedure, the AAA shall specify a fair and equitable procedure.

Extensions of Time

The parties may modify any period of time by mutual agreement. The AAA or the arbitrator may for good cause extend any period of time established by these rules, except the time for making the award. The AAA shall notify the parties of any extension.

Serving of Notice

Each party shall be deemed to have consented that any papers, notices, or process necessary or proper for the initiation or continuation of an arbitration under these rules; for any court actions in connection therewith; or for the entry of judgment on an award made under these procedures may be served on a party by mail addressed to the party or its representative at the last known address or by personal service, in or outside the state where the arbitration is to be held, provided that reasonable opportunity to be heard with regard thereto has been granted to the party.

The AAA and the parties may also use facsimile transmission, telex, telegram, or other written forms of electronic communication to give the notices required by these rules.

Release of Documents for Judicial Proceedings

The AAA shall, upon the written request of a party, furnish to the party, at its expense, certified copies of any papers in the AAA's possession that may be required in judicial proceedings relating to the arbitration.

Interpretation and Application of Procedures

The arbitrator shall interpret and apply these procedures as they relate to the arbitrator's powers and duties. When there is more than one arbitrator and a difference arises among them concerning the meaning or application of these rules, it shall be decided by a majority vote. If that is not possible, either an arbitrator or a party may refer the question to the AAA for final decision. All other procedures shall be interpreted and applied by the AAA.

Signature Clause

Employee acknowledges that he or she has carefully read this agreement, that he or she understands its terms, that all understandings between the employee and the company relating to the subjects covered in this agreement are contained in it, and that he or she has entered into this agreement voluntarily and not in reliance on any promises or representations by the company other than those contained in this agreement itself.

Employee further acknowledges that he or she had an opportunity to discuss this agreement with his or her personal legal counsel and has used that opportunity to the extent he or she wishes to do so.

[EMPLOYEE NAME]	[COMPANY NAME]
______________________	______________________
Signature of Employee	Name of Company Official
	______________________
	Title of Company Official

Date: ______________________

Consideration

Each party's promise to resolve claims by arbitration in accordance with the provisions of this agreement, rather than through the courts, is consideration for the other party's like promise.

Not An Employment Agreement

This agreement is not, and shall not be construed to create, any contract of employment, express or implied.

One of the leading in-house ADR programs mandating arbitration as a condition of employment was introduced by the Primerica Corporation in September 1992. This program has been modified since its introduction. For example, when first introduced it provided for a procedure ending in arbitration for all employment disputes. Now, it applies solely to those disputes that involve a legal cause of action.

When this program was introduced, Primerica was far ahead of other organizations in developing a workplace due process model that avoided the courtroom in favor of arbitration. The vision of Primerica's executives and legal counsel has been rewarded with a dispute resolution process that is now one of the model programs in industry.

Primerica merged into the Travelers Corporation; the new organization is called the Travelers Group. The Primerica ADR program has now been introduced throughout the Travelers Group.

TRAVELERS GROUP DISPUTE RESOLUTION PROCEDURE

INTRODUCTION

Travelers Group is committed to fair and equitable employment practices. We recognize that misunderstandings or conflicts can and do arise in the course of daily business relationships. While most situations resolve themselves naturally, there are times when an employee may wish to seek review of an employment-related action or decision. The Dispute Resolution Procedures is an impartial process by which employees may request resolution of any employment-related concern.

PROCESS

Step 1. Employees are encouraged to first discuss informally any concern they have with their immediate manager prior to initiating a formal review. However, if this discussion is not successful from the employee's point of view, the review should be submitted in writing within thirty (30) days of the incident to their manager with a copy to their Human Resources representative. The manager and

Human Resources representative have twenty (20) working days to investigate the claim and respond to the employee.

Step 2. If the employee is not satisfied with the response in Step 1, he/she may submit an appeal to the next level manager within ten (10) working days of receiving an answer from Step 1, with a copy to the Manager, Human Resources within his/her subsidiary. At the conclusion of the discussion relating to the dispute, the parties shall agree that all the facts have been brought forward. A written response is given to the employee within twenty (20) working days after the discussion.

Step 3. If the employee is not satisfied with the response in Step 2, he/she may submit an appeal to the next level manager within ten (10) working days of receiving an answer from Step 2, with a copy to the Vice President, Human Resources within their subsidiary.

The third level of appeal is with the Division/Regional/Department Manager and the Vice President, Human Resources within the subsidiary. The Vice President, Human Resources will consult with the Senior Vice President, Human Resources, Travelers Group. This step is the final level of appeal in the internal Dispute Resolution Procedure. After this meeting, the employee will receive a written response within twenty (20) working days.

If the dispute is still not resolved, the employee is entitled to request aribtration in accordance with the Travelers Group Employment Arbitration Policy.

TERMINATION

An employee may appeal a termination within thirty (30) days. The appeal will automatically progress to Step 2 of the process.

FIELD OPERATIONS

At times it may be impractical to arrange face-to-face meetings within the specified time limits of the program. In these circumstances, the Vice President of Human Resources may make modifications to the process as necessary.

EXCEPTIONS

The existing procedures for reporting alleged incidents of sex discrimination (including sexual harassment), racial discrimination, age discrimination, disability discrimination and other illegal forms of discrimination will remain in place to provide the maximum confidentiality and privacy. Such complaints should be sent directly to the Vice President, Human Resources of each subsidiary.

SUMMARY

The internal Dispute Resolution Procedure is a sequential process which stops wherever the individual bringing forward a perceived problem accepts a decision at one of the interim steps. Decisions concerning terminations, promotions and disciplinary actions are typical types of issues raised. This process ensures prompt confidential resolution of such issues. Employees who wish to avail themselves of the process will not be subject to any retaliatory action by management. No disciplinary action or other management decision will be postponed as a result of the presentation of a dispute by the employee.

TRAVELERS GROUP EMPLOYMENT ARBITRATION POLICY

STATEMENT OF INTENT

Travelers Group and its affiliates (referred to collectively as "Travelers Group") value each of its employees and look forward to good relations with, and among, all employees. Occasionally, however, disagreements may arise between an individual employee and Travelers Group, or between employees in a context that involves Travelers Group. Travelers Group believes that the resolution of such disagreements will be best accomplished by internal dispute review and, where that fails, by arbitration conducted under the auspices of the American Arbitration Association. For these reasons, Travelers Group has adopted this Employment Arbitration Policy ("the Policy"). The Policy applies to all persons employed by Travelers Group on the date of its adoption (September 1, 1992) and all employees joining Travelers Group after that date.

This Policy does not constitute a guarantee that your employment will continue for any specified period of time or end only under certain conditions. Employment at Travelers Group is a voluntary relationship for no definite period of time, and nothing in this Policy or any other company document constitutes an express or implied contract of employment for any definite period of time. This policy does not constitute, nor should be construed to constitute, a waiver by the Travelers Group of its rights under the "Employment-at-will" doctrine; nor does it afford an employee or former employee any rights or remedies that the employee or former employee does not otherwise have under applicable law.

SCOPE OF THE POLICY

The Policy makes arbitration the required, and exclusive, forum for the resolution of all employment disputes based on legally protected rights (i.e., statutory, contractual or common law rights) that may arise between an employee or former employee and the Travelers Group or its affiliates, officers, directors, employees and agents (and which are not resolved by the internal dispute resolution procedure), including claims, demands or actions under Title VII of the Civil Rights Act of 1964, the Civil Rights Act of 1866, the Age Discrimination in Employment Act, the Rehabilitation Act of 1973, the Americans with Disabilities

Act, the Employee Retirement Income Security Act of 1974, and all amendments thereto, and any other federal, state or local statute, regulation or common law doctrine, regarding employment discrimination, conditions of employment or termination of employment. The Policy does not require that Travelers Group institute arbitration nor is it required to follow the steps of the dispute resolution procedure before taking disciplinary action of any kind, including termination; however, if an employee disagrees with any such disciplinary action, and believes that such action violated his or her legally protected rights, he or she may institute proceedings in accordance with the Policy.

ARBITRATION RULES AND PROCEDURES

The following rules and procedures are based on, and largely incorporate, the Employment Dispute Resolution Rules of the American Arbitration Association ("AAA"). Travelers Group has modified and expanded these rules and procedures in certain respects. In particular, provisions regarding fees and costs have been modified to provide that many of the costs typically shared by the parties will be borne by Travelers Group. In addition, provisions permitting limited discovery have been added to insure equal access to relevant information.

1. Initiation of Arbitration Proceeding

Arbitration may be initiated by a written demand for arbitration submitted to the Senior Vice President, Human Resources, Travelers Group together with a check payable to the AAA for the requisite administrative fee as provided in the AAA's fee schedule. The fee schedule is available from the Human Resources Department. Employees, however, whose total compensation for the previous calendar year was $150,000 or less (or former employees whose total compensation for the last calendar year they were a Travelers Group employee was $150,000 or less) need only submit a check for $50 payable to the Travelers Group. The demand shall set forth the claim, including the alleged act or omission at issue and the names of all persons involved in the act or omission. Within ten (10) business days of receiving such demand, Travelers Group shall file the demand with the appropriate office of the AAA, together with the applicable administrative fee as provided in the AAA's fee Schedule. The employee or former employee will be required to sign a submission agreement.

2. Appointment of Neutral Arbitrator

The AAA shall appoint one neutral arbitrator from its Panel of Arbitrators, unless one party requests that a panel of three (3) arbitrators be appointed. In the event a panel of arbitrators is appointed, all decisions of the panel must be by a majority and the use of the word "arbitrator" in these Rules shall refer to the panel.

The arbitrator shall be appointed in the following manner:

(a) immediately after the filing of the demand, the AAA shall submit to each party an identical list of proposed arbitrators;

(b) each party shall then have ten (10) business days from the mailing date of the list to cross off any names to which the party objects, number the remaining names in order of preference and return the list to the AAA;

(c) if the party does not return the list within the time specified, all persons on the list shall be deemed acceptable; and

(d) the AAA shall invite arbitrators remaining on the list in the order of preference, to the extent the order of preference of the parties can be reconciled by the AAA.

In the event the parties fail to agree on any of the persons named, or if an acceptable arbitrator is unwilling to act, the AAA may issue additional lists or, at its option, make the appointment from among other members of its panel of arbitrators without submitting additional lists.

3. Qualifications of Neutral Arbitrator

No person shall serve as a neutral arbitrator in any matter in which that person has any financial or personal interest in the result of the proceeding. Prior to accepting appointment, the prospective arbitrator shall disclose any circumstance likely to prevent a prompt hearing or to create a presumption of bias. Upon receipt of such information, the AAA will either replace that person or communicate the information to the parties for comment. Thereafter, the AAA may disqualify that person and its decision shall be conclusive. Vacancies shall be filled in accordance with Rule number 2.

4. Vacancies

The AAA is authorized to substitute another arbitrator if a vacancy occurs or if an appointed arbitrator is unable to serve promptly.

5. Date, Time and Place of Hearing

The arbitrator shall set the date, time, and place of the hearing, notice of which must be given to the parties by the AAA at least ten days in advance, unless the parties agree otherwise.

6. Representation

Any party may be represented by an attorney, a non-supervisory co-worker or by him or her self. If the employee or former employee chooses not to be represented by an attorney, Travelers Group shall waive its right to be represented by an attorney unless such person is or was licensed to practice law in any jurisdiction in the United States.

7. Attendance at Hearing

The arbitrator shall maintain the privacy of the hearings unless the law provides to the contrary. Any person having a direct interest in the arbitration is entitled to attend hearings. The arbitrator shall otherwise have the power to require the exclusion of any witness, other than a party or other essential person, during the testimony of any other witness. The arbitrator shall determine whether any other person may attend the hearing.

8. Postponement

The arbitrator, for good cause shown, may postpone any hearing upon the request of a party or upon the arbitrator's own initiative, and shall also grant such postponement when all of the parties agree thereto.

9. Oaths

Before proceeding with the first hearing, each arbitrator may take an oath of office and, if required by law, shall do so. The arbitrator may require witnesses to testify under oath administered by any duly qualified person and, if it is required by law or requested by any party, shall do so.

10. Stenographic Record

There shall be no stenographic record of these proceedings unless either party requests it. In the event a party requests a stenographic record, that party shall bear the cost of such a record. If both parties request a stenographic record, the cost shall be borne equally by the parties.

11. Proceedings

The hearings shall be conducted by the arbitrator in whatever manner will most expeditiously permit full presentation of the evidence and arguments of the parties. Normally, the hearing shall be completed within one day. In unusual circumstances and for good cause shown, the arbitrator may schedule an additional hearing to be held within five business days.

12. Arbitration in the Absence of a Party

Unless the law provides to the contrary, the arbitration may proceed in the absence of any party or representative who, after due notice, fails to be present or fails to obtain a postponement. An award shall not be made solely on the default of a party. The arbitrator shall require the party who is present to submit such evidence as the arbitrator may require for the making of the award.

13. Discovery

Each party shall be entitled to propound and serve upon the other party one set of interrogatories in a form consistent with the Federal Rules of Civil Procedure and which shall be limited to the identification of potential witnesses. Each party shall be entitled to propound and serve upon the other one set of Requests for the Production of Documents in a form consistent with the Federal Rules of Civil Procedure and which shall be limited in number to twenty-five (25) Requests (including sub-parts, which shall be counted separately).

14. Evidence

The arbitrator shall be the judge of the relevance and materiality of the evidence offered, and conformity to legal rules of evidence shall not be necessary.

15. Evidence by Affidavit and Filing of Documents

The arbitrator may receive and consider the evidence of witnesses by affidavit, but shall give it only such weight as the arbitrator deems it entitled to after consideration of any objection made to its admission. All documents to be considered by the arbitrator shall be filed at the hearing. There shall be no post-hearing briefs.

16. Closing of Hearing

The arbitrator shall ask whether the parties have any further proofs to offer or witnesses to be heard. Upon receiving negative replies, or if satisfied that the record is complete, the arbitrator shall declare the hearing closed and the minutes thereof shall be recorded.

17. Reopening of Hearing

The hearing may be reopened on the arbitrator's initiative, or upon application of a party, at any time before the award is made. The arbitrator may reopen the hearing and shall have fourteen (14) days from the closing of the reopened hearing within which to make an award.

18. Waiver of Procedures

Any party who proceeds with the arbitration after knowledge that any provision or requirement of these procedures has not been complied with, and who fails to state objections thereto in writing, shall be deemed to have waived the right to object.

19. Time of Award

The award shall be made promptly by the arbitrator unless otherwise agreed by the parties or specified by law. The arbitrator shall be instructed to make the award within thirty (30) days of the hearing or as soon as possible thereafter.

20. Award

A. Form

The award shall be in writing and shall be signed by the arbitrator. If either party requests, the arbitrator shall issue an opinion in writing, which shall set forth in summary form the reasons for the arbitrator's determination. All awards shall be executed in the manner required by law.

B. Scope of Relief

The arbitrator shall be governed by the rule of law of the state where the employee worked as well as taking note of applicable Federal law as submitted by the parties and shall be bound by Travelers Group policies and procedures. Furthermore, the arbitrator shall have no authority to alter or otherwise modify the parties' at will relationship or substitute his or her judgment for the lawful business judgment of the Travelers Group management. The arbitrator shall have the power to award, in appropriate circumstances, money damages in an amount sufficient to compensate the aggrieved party for such direct injury as the arbitrator determines such party has suffered. The arbitrator shall have the authority to order reinstatement of employment to a former employee only if money damages are insufficient as a remedy. Unless expressly provided for by applicable statute, the arbitrator shall not have the authority to award punitive damages, attorney's fees or injunctive relief of any nature. The arbitrator shall not have the authority to make any award that is arbitrary and capricious or to award to Travelers Group the costs of the arbitration that it is otherwise required to bear under this Policy.

21. Delivery of Award to Parties

Parties shall accept as legal delivery of the award the placing of the award or a true copy thereof in the mail, addressed to a party or its representative at the last known address via certified mail, return receipt; personal service of the award; or the filing of the award in any manner that is permitted by law.

22. Enforcement

The decision of the arbitrator may be enforced under the terms of the Federal Arbitration Act (Title 9 U.S.C.) and/or under the law of any state. If the decision is not completely enforceable, final and binding, it shall be enforced and binding on both parties to the extent permitted by law. Even if a part of this procedure is held to be void or unenforceable, the remainder of the procedure will be enforceable and any part may be severed from the remainder, as appropriate.

23. Judicial Proceedings and Exclusion of Liability

A. Neither the AAA nor any arbitrator in a proceeding under these procedures is a necessary party in judicial proceedings relating to the arbitration.

B. Parties to these procedures shall be deemed to have consented that judgment upon the arbitration award may be entered in any federal or state court having jurisdiction thereof.

24. Expenses

In order to make these arbitration procedures available to all employees, Travelers Group or its affiliate shall pay 100 percent in excess of fifty dollars ($50) of any administrative fee required by the AAA for those employees whose total compensation for the previous calendar year was $150,000 or less (or former employees whose total compensation for the last calendar year they were a Travelers Group employee was $150,000 or less.) The expenses of witnesses for either side shall be paid by the party requiring the presence of such witnesses. Each side shall pay its own legal fees and expenses. All other expenses (except Postponement Fees or Additional Hearing Fees) of the arbitration, such as required travel and other expenses of the arbitrator (including any witness produced at the direction of the arbitrator), and the expenses of a representative of AAA, if any, shall be paid completely by Travelers Group and affiliates. If the arbitration proceeding continues more than one day, the incremental expenses of the additional days shall be borne equally by the parties. This allocation of expenses may not be disturbed by the arbitration award.

25. Serving of Notice

Any parties, notices, or process necessary or proper for the initiation or continuation of an arbitration under these procedures; for any court action in connection therewith; or for the entry of judgment on an award made under these procedures may be served on a party by mail addressed to the party or its representative at the last known address or by personal service, in or outside the state where the arbitration is to be held, provided that reasonable opportunity to be heard with regard thereto has been granted to the party. The AAA and the parties may also use facsimile transmission, telex, telegram, or other written forms of electronic communication to give the notices required by these procedures, provided that such notice is confirmed by telephone or subsequent mailing to all affected parties.

26. Time Period for Arbitration

Any proceeding under this procedure must be brought within one year of the act or omission giving rise to the controversy. This time period may be extended, however, by any circumstance that would otherwise toll the applicable statute of limitaitons, but in no event shall the time for initiating an arbitration be extended beyond two years.

27. Amendment or Termination of Arbitration Policy

From time to time the Policy may be amended. Such amendments may be made by publishing them in the Employee Handbook or by a separate release to employees.

28. Interpretation and Application of Procedures

The arbitrator shall interpret and apply these procedures insofar as they relate to the arbitrator's powers and duties. All other procedures shall be interpreted and applied by the AAA.

MEDIATION

The parties may wish to require mediation as a precondition to arbitration. Alternatively, they may wish to identify mediation and offer it, but not require it.

The AAA Rules recommends the following language to cover future disputes:

If a dispute arises out of or relates to this contract, or the breach thereof, and if said dispute cannot be settled through negotiation, the parties agree first to try in good faith to settle the dispute by mediation under the Employment Mediation Rules of the American Arbitration Association before resorting to arbitration, litigation, or some other dispute resolution procedure.

The AAA Rules recommend this language for existing disputes:

The parties hereby submit the following dispute to mediation under the Employment Mediation Rules of the American Arbitration Association.

(The clause may also provide for the qualifications of the mediator(s), method of payment, locale of meetings, and any other item of concern to the parties.)

The AAA's Employment Mediation Rules state:

Employment Mediation Rules

(1) Agreement of Parties — Whenever, by provision in an employment dispute resolution program, or by separate submission, the parties have provided for mediation or conciliation of existing or future disputes under the auspices of the American Arbitration Association (AAA) or under these rules, they shall be deemed to have made these rules, as amended and in effect as of the date of the submission of the dispute, a part of their agreement.

(2) Initiation of Mediation — Any party to an employment dispute may initiate mediation by filing with the AAA a submission to mediation or a written request for mediation pursuant to these rules, together with the appropriate administrative fee contained in the Administrative Fees.

(3) Request for Mediation — A request for mediation shall contain a brief statement of the nature of the dispute and the names, addresses, and telephone numbers of all parties to the dispute and those who will represent them, if any, in the mediation. The initiating party shall simultaneously file two copies of the request with the AAA and one copy with every other party to the dispute.

(4) Appointment of Mediator — Upon receipt of a request for mediation, the AAA will appoint a qualified mediator to serve. Normally, a single mediator will be appointed unless the parties agree otherwise or the AAA determines otherwise. If the agreement of the parties names a mediator or specifies a method of appointing a mediator, that designation or method shall be followed.

(5) Qualifications of Mediator — No person shall serve as a mediator in any dispute in which that person has any financial or personal interest in the result of the mediation, except by interest in the result of the mediation, except by the written consent of all parties. Prior to accepting an appointment, the prospective mediator shall disclose any circumstance likely to create a presumption of bias or prevent a prompt meeting with the parties. Upon receipt of such information, the AAA shall either replace the mediator or immediately communicate the information to the parties for their comments. In the event that the parties disagree as to whether the mediator shall serve, the AAA will appoint another mediator. The AAA is authorized to appoint another mediator if the appointed mediator is unable to serve promptly.

(6) Vacancies — If any mediator shall become unwilling or unable to serve, the AAA will appoint another mediator, unless the parties agree otherwise.

(7) Representation — Any party may be represented by persons of the party's choice. The names and addresses of such persons shall be communicated in writing to all parties and to the AAA.

(8) Date, Time, and Place of Mediation — The mediator shall fix the date and the time of each mediation session. The mediation shall be held at the appropriate regional office of the AAA, or at any other convenient location agreeable to the mediator and the parties, as the mediator shall determine.

(9) Identification of Matters in Dispute — At least 10 days prior to the first scheduled mediation session, each party shall provide the mediator with a brief memorandum setting forth its position with regard to the issues that need to be resolved. At the discretion of the mediator, such memoranda may be mutually exchanged by the parties.

At the first session, the parties will be expected to produce all information reasonably required for the mediator to understand the issues presented.

The mediator may require any party to supplement such information.

(10) Authority of Mediator — The mediator does not have the authority to impose a settlement on the parties but will attempt to help them reach a satisfactory resolution of their dispute. The mediator is authorized to conduct joint and separate meetings with the parties and to make oral and written recommendations for settlement. Whenever necessary, the mediator may also obtain expert advise concerning technical aspects of the dispute, provided that the parties agree and assume the expenses of obtaining such advice. Arrangements for obtaining such advice shall be made by the mediator or the parties, as the mediator shall determine.

The mediator is authorized to end the mediation whenever, in the judgment of the mediator, further efforts at mediation would not contribute to a resolution of the dispute between the parties.

(11) Privacy — Mediation sessions are private.

The parties and their representatives may attend mediation sessions. Other persons may attend only with the permission of the parties and with the consent of the mediator.

(12) Confidentiality — Confidential information disclosed to a mediator by the parties or by witnesses in the course of the mediation shall not be divulged by the mediator. All records, reports, or other documents received by a mediator while serving in that capacity shall be confidential. The mediator shall not be compelled to divulge such records or to testify in regard to the mediation in any adversary proceeding or judicial forum.

The parties shall maintain the confidentiality of the mediation and shall not rely on, or introduce as evidence in any arbitral, judicial, or other proceeding:

a. views expressed or suggestions made by another party with respect to a possible settlement of the dispute;
b. admissions made by another party in the course of the mediation proceedings;
c. proposals made or views expressed by the mediator; or
d. the fact that another party had or had not indicated willingness to accept a proposal for settlement made by the mediator.

(13) No Stenographic Record — There shall be no stenographic record of the mediation process.

(14) Termination of Mediation — The mediation shall be terminated:

a. by the execution of a settlement agreement by the parties;

b. by a written declaration of the mediator to the effect that further efforts at mediation are no longer worthwhile; or

c. by a written declaration of a party or parties to the effect that the mediation proceedings are terminated.

(15) Exclusion of Liability — Neither the AAA nor any mediator is a necessary party in judicial proceedings relating to the mediation.

Neither the AAA nor any mediator shall be liable to any party for any act or omission in connection with any mediation conducted under these rules.

(16) Interpretation and Application of Rules — Mediator shall interpret and apply these rules insofar as they relate to the mediator's duties and responsibilities. All other rules shall be interpreted and applied by the AAA.

(17) Expenses — The expenses of witnesses for either side shall be paid by the party producing such witnesses. All other expenses of the mediation, including required traveling and other expenses of the mediator and representatives of the AAA, and the expenses of any witness and the cost of any proofs or expert advice produced at the direct request of the mediator, shall be borne equally by the parties unless they agree otherwise.

NOTES

1. Nancy C. House, "Grievance Mediation: AT&T's Experience," *Labor Law Journal*, August 1992, pp. 491–495.

2. "ADR Techniques Gaining Favor in Non-Traditional Settings," *Daily Labor Report,* March 15, 1993, p. C1.

3. Douglas M. McCabe, "Corporate Nonunion Grievance Arbitration Systems: A Procedural Analysis," *Labor Law Journal*, 40 (July 1989): 432–437.

4. "Most Support ADR, Survey Says," *Daily Labor Report*, June 30, 1992, p. A18.

5. Edward P. McDermott, "Survey: Using ADR To Settle Employment Disputes," *Dispute Resolution Journal*, 50 (January 1995): 8–13.

6. This survey was not random.

7. *Employment Discrimination — Most Private-Sector Employers Use Alternative Dispute Resolution* (GAO/HEHS-95-150) Washington, D.C.: General Accounting Office, 1995. The GAO had previously issued a study on the use of arbitration to resolve discrimination disputes in the securities industries, where arbitration of all employment related claims is often mandated. In this earlier study, the GAO stated that it did not address the fairness of the arbitration process but rather identified weaknesses and inconsistencies in some NYSE and NASD procedures that could result in inappropriate decisions on

which arbitrators they select for their pools and to serve on panels arbitrating discrimination cases. *Employment Discrimination: How Registered Representatives Fare in Discrimination Disputes* (GAO/HEHS-94-179) Washington, D.C.: General Accounting Office, 1994, p. 9.

8. *Employment Discrimination*, 1-3.

9. Ibid., 15.

10. "Lawyers at ABA Session Discuss Ways to Avoid Costly Employment Litigation," *Daily Labor Report*, August 12, 1992, p. A1.

11. Resolution, Brown & Root Dispute Resolution Program. Houston, Texas: Brown & Root Holdings, Inc., 1993, 3.

12. *Delaney v. Continental Airlines*, 8 IER 1170 (C.D. Cal. 1993); *Bakri v. Continental Airlines*, 8 IER 937 (C.D. Cal. 1993).

13. U.S. Department of Labor, "Report and Recommendations of the Commission on the Future of Worker-Management Relations," (BNA Special Supplement, 1/10/95), p. x.

14. Ibid., 25–26.

15. Ibid., 25.

16. Ibid., 32.

17. See Walter C. Bravet III, "Public Law and Arbitration," *Labor Law Journal*, 43 (August 1992): 547, 548–49.

18. "NLRB General Counsel Report, January to September 1995," *The Daily Labor Report*, February 23, 1996, p. E6.

19. *Hull v. Norcom, Inc.*, 750 F.2d 1547, 1550 (11th Cir. 1985).

20. *Carlson v. Hutzel Corp. of Michigan*, 183 Mich. App. 508, 455 N. W.2d 335 (1990); *Ryoti v. Paine, Webber, Jackson & Curtis, Inc.*, 142 Mich. App. 805, 371 N.W.2d 454 (1985).

21. *Zeniuk v. RKA, Inc.*, 189 Mich. App., 472 N.W.2d 23 (1991).

22. *Hellenic Lines Ltd. v. Louis Dreyfus Corp.*, 372 F.2d 753, 758 (2d Cir. 1967; *Curtis v. Amelia-Bouyea*, 137 A.D. 2d 944, 525 N.Y.S.2d 69, 1988 N.Y. App. Div. (3rd Dept. 1988).

23. Thomas, Todd H., "Using Arbitration to Avoid Litigation," *Labor Law Journal*, 44 (January 19, 1993): 3–17.

24. Reuben, Richard, C. "Getting Out of a J.A.M.S.," *A.B.A Journal*, 82 (April 1996): 41.

25. This is different from the AAA rules that do not provide for pre-hearing depositions.

26. The practical implications of providing a summary judgment procedure for arbitration are addressed at pages 79–80.

APPENDIX

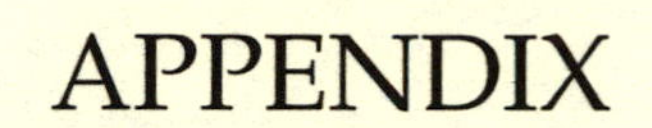

Brown & Root Dispute Resolution Program

BACKGROUND

Brown & Root cares about its people. It knows that even strong and productive employees can have problems at work . . . and that even routine differences with the Company can get bigger when there are no resources to help solve them.

Brown & Root must also care about how the Company is doing financially. Employee disputes can be time-consuming and very costly, particularly when they end up in lawsuits between the employee and the Company. In recent years, legislatures have encouraged employees to go to court by making it easier for them to recover money damages from their employers — especially in cases involving *a legally protected right*, such as protection from race, sex or age discrimination or sexual harassment. Many employees who have brought lawsuits, however, have been disappointed with the results. After long delays, years of worry and interrupted careers, much of what they recover, if anything, has gone to their lawyers. Brown & Root hasn't fared much better in the court system. Although it has paid out very little in actual settlements, it has spent **over a million dollars per year** in legal and court fees for cases involving only a few employees. This money could have been used for other purposes, such as medical and retirement benefits, compensation and investment in the Company's future.

For the Benefit of All

Brown & Root set out to find a more effective way to resolve all workplace disputes — one that would benefit all parties. The Open Door Policy seemed a good place to start. Over the years, the company has had an unwritten policy to help employees handle problems through the chain of Command. To make this Open Door Policy better known and improve its effectiveness, Brown & Root is adding new features, including an Employee Hotline and a Legal Consultation program. The Company is not only communicating the policy to all employees, but will also train management and employees how to use it.

For those situations involving legally protected rights that, for whatever reason, cannot be resolved in-house, Brown & Root has adopted a private, professional way *outside* the Company to settle them. This outside process will involve either mediation and/or arbitration led by the American Arbitration Association (AAA), an objective third party. **Mediation** means presenting your legal dispute to a neutral third party for help in finding a solution; **arbitration** means presenting your dispute to a neutral third party for a final decision.

The American Arbitration Association (AAA) is a public service, nonprofit organization that offers a wide range of dispute resolution services to private individuals, businesses, associations and all levels of government. It handles approximately 60,000 cases each year and has access to over 50,000 neutral experts who can hear and decide cases.

Mediation and arbitration through AAA can:

...provide quick and fair resolution of your legal dispute.
...protect your work relationships instead of disrupting them.
...and, at the same time, prevent excessive spending on lawyers' fees.

The new approach, packaged as a four-option plan, will be called the Brown & Root Dispute Resolution program. The program will take effect June 15, 1993. The following pages explain how it works.

THE PROGRAM IN DETAIL

Option One — Open Door Policy

When difficult situations happen at work, you may feel there is no place to go to resolve them. How can you go to your supervisor if your problem is **with** *your supervisor? Where can you take your problem that will not* *threaten your job? You talk to your friends and family who may offer sympathy and advice but no real answers. Tensions build up at work and the problem gets bigger.*

Working out problems when they're small often prevents the misunderstandings that occur when communication breaks down. When people stop talking to each other, they focus on their anger and what they imagine to be true instead of the facts. You and the Company stand the best chance of resolving problems by tackling them together through the Open Door Policy . . . before they become crises.

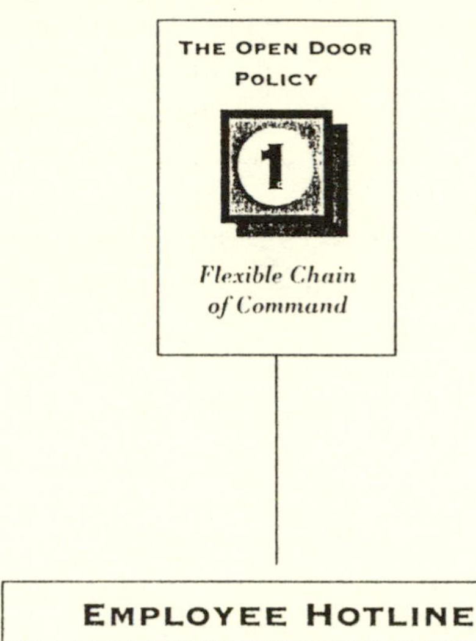

What is the Open Door Policy?

The Open Door Policy guarantees that all *doors are open* to you within Brown & Root. It offers you a variety of ways in which you can solve your problem including a confidential hotline and, under some circumstances, a legal consultation. It is a **voluntary** process that allows you to talk to your immediate supervisor or to a higher level of management . . . **without fear of retaliation**. Although you are encouraged to solve your problem at the lowest possible level, you may take it as far *up* the Chain of Command as needed.

Using the Chain of Command

At Brown & Root, you are free to raise a concern with **any level of management**. That's the Open Door tradition. To make the process work better, all supervisors and managers will receive special training in handling problems and managing conflicts.

That means, no matter who you call, Brown & Root management will understand:

- The four options of the Dispute Resolution Program.
- That it's part of management's job to help you solve your workplace problems through the Open Door Policy.
- That Brown & Root **forbids any retaliation** for trying to solve a workplace dispute within the terms of the Dispute Resolution Program.

Immediate Supervisor — Whenever possible, you should try to resolve any problems at work with your immediate supervisor. Because this person is close to your situation, he or she may already be aware of the problem or be in a position to offer a new perspective or some new facts that may be helpful to you.

Higher Level of Supervision — Unfortunately, sometimes your supervisor is part of the problem. If you are unsatisfied with your immediate supervisor's response **or** need to talk to someone other than your supervisor, you may take your problem to the next higher level of supervision. You are encouraged to follow the specific chain of command in your department or work group, since that is often the most direct way of getting matters resolved.

Business Unit Personnel or Employee Relations— At any time, you may also choose to contact your business Unit Personnel office or the Corporate Employee Relations department for advice or assistance. These departments have many years experience helping employees deal with a variety of workplace problems.

Calling the Employee Hotline

You may call the Employee Hotline at (800) 947-7658. When you call the Hotline, you'll talk to an Adviser who can provide free, expert and confidential advice. The Adviser can tell you about how to solve problems informally within the Company and the external options through AAA.

The Adviser does not need your name in order to help you. You may want to remain anonymous and just ask a few questions. Or, you may wish to discuss all the details of your situation and be coached through the Open Door process. How *or if* you use the Employee Hotline is entirely up to you.

Here are some of the ways the Adviser can help you:

- Answering your questions.
- Acting as a go-between.

- Reviewing your options.
- Getting the facts.
- Helping you "open doors."
- Referring you to other resources.
- Helping you help yourself.

The Program Administrator

The Program Administrator is also available to help you. The Administrator will handle most of the details involved in running the new Dispute Resolution Program, including:

- Arranging conferences (see Option Two) and other internal dispute resolution processes,
- Overseeing the Legal Consultation program,
- Answering employee questions.

If you wish to contact the Program Administrator, please call (713) 676-3771.

Requesting a Legal Consultation

An important feature of the program is a legal consultation with the attorney of your choice. You may apply for this legal consultation if your dispute involves a legally protected right. The consultation can provide you with valuable information about your legal rights.

Legal consultations are paid much like benefits under your medical plan, that is, you pay a deductible and a copayment. Brown & Root pays the balance. In this case:

- You pay a deductible of $25.
- After the deductible, you pay 10% of the balance.
- The Company pays 90% of the balance.
- **Maximum annual benefit of $2,500 per employee**.

For example, if the legal consultation was $1,000, you would pay a deductible of $25 and then 10% of $975 or $97.50. The Company would pay $877.50.

The Program Administrator must approve all payments from the Legal Consultation Plan. If you would like this consultation, contact the Dispute

Resolution Program Administrator directly. Of course, if you choose to hire and pay for your own attorney, you are free to do so at any time.

If you believe that your dispute involves or may involve a legally protected right, you may request a legal consultation under this plan at any time during the resolution process, that means during Options One, Two, Three or Four.

Ten Good Reasons to Use the Open Door Policy

1. Management is committed to it.
2. It makes early on-site problem-solving more likely.
3. It encourages you to give feedback to management.
4. You get your questions answered and learn about your options.
5. You have instant support.
6. It's free.
7. It's flexible.
8. You can contact an Adviser in confidence.
9. Retaliation is forbidden.
10. It helps you help yourself.

Option Two — The Conference

You will be able to resolve most routine problems within the Company through the Chain of Command. If it does not produce results, however, you can sit down at a Conference with a Brown & Root representative to see if you can agree on what to do next.

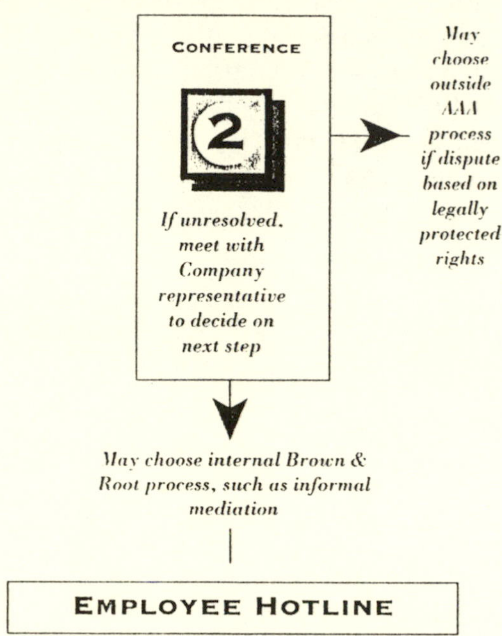

What is a Conference?

A Conference is a meeting at Brown & Root in which you and a Company representative sit down with someone from the Dispute Resolution Program to talk about your dispute and choose a process for resolving it. The goal of the conference is to help you and the Company agree on a way to settle your dispute and to choose someone to help you do it. You may decide to do one of the following:

Loop-back to the Chain of Command — Once at the conference, you may agree that the best way to resolve your differences is by going back to the Chain of Command.

Try an Informal Process within Brown & Root — You and the Company may agree to try an in-house dispute resolution process, such as informal mediation. The mediator in this case would be a well-respected Brown & Root employee who is experienced in employee disputes. This Brown & Root dispute resolution expert would listen objectively while both parties tell their stories and try to help them work out their dispute themselves.

Go Directly to an Outside Process (Options Three or Four) — In some cases involving legally protected rights, you may want to proceed directly from the Conference to an *outside* resolution process through AAA, such as mediation or arbitration. In mediation, you will have the opportunity to discuss your dispute with an outside expert and work out a solution yourself. In arbitration, you present your dispute to the outside expert who will then hand down a **final** decision. If you wish to take a dispute to AAA for resolution through an outside process, you must pay a processing fee of $50. For information on how to request mediation or arbitration, see pages 10 or 12 respectively [Options Three and Four].

Option Three — Mediation

If your dispute is based on legally protected rights, you may feel an outside process, such as mediation, is necessary to resolve it. For many people, just presenting their case to someone outside the Company who is not involved in their problem is all that is needed to break a stalemate.

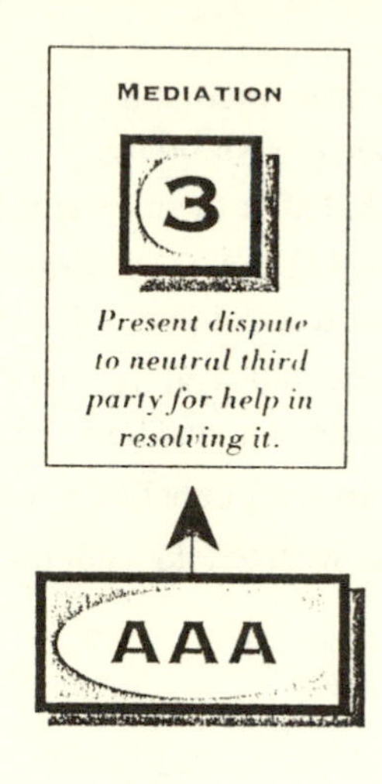

What is Mediation?

Mediation is often the most straightforward and cost-effective method of examining and resolving disputes. It is a meeting in which a neutral third party, called a mediator, helps you and the Company come to an agreement of your own, based on your needs and interests. Mediation helps primarily by opening up communication and by coming up with options. It is a nonbinding process. That means, the mediator can make suggestions, but you and the other party are responsible for resolving your dispute. All mediations in this Program will use a AAA mediator as the neutral party. *In some cases involving legally protected rights, both parties may agree to bypass this option and move directly from the Conference to Option Four for a final decision.*

Requesting Mediation

You must pay a $50 processing fee to take your legal dispute to an outside resolution process, such as mediation. Brown & Root will pay any costs that exceed this $50 fee. To request an outside process, call or write AAA at (713) 739-1302, 1001 Fannin Street, Suite 1005, Houston, TX 77002.

Once you have made this request and paid your fee, Brown & Root will participate with you in the mediation process.

Other resolution processes are also available from AAA upon request. Keep in mind that if a process uses more than one neutral party, there will be additional cost to you.

Typical Mediation Steps

When you or the Company request mediation, AAA will assign a professional mediator who is located close to your home.

The first meeting date is arranged after the mediator is selected.

You and a Company representative will meet with the mediator who will guide your discussion and help you work out your differences.

The mediator may meet privately with you and the Company to try to develop a better understanding of the problem, and help you solve it.

Mediation is almost always successful in helping you reach a settlement.

If not, you or the Company may wish to take your dispute to arbitration for a final and binding decision.

Key Advantages of Mediation

Because mediation has proven highly successful in the majority of cases, it is generally the outside resolution process of choice. It offers the following advantages:

- Provides the opportunity for both sides to tell their story.
- Lets both sides have a third party perspective.
- Helps reduce feelings of hostility.
- Helps separate emotional issues from factual issues.
- Promotes discussion of creative solutions.
- Helps people work things out themselves.
- Offers an opportunity for win-win solutions. (A solution that is good for both you and the Company).

Option Four — Arbitration

If the dispute involves a legally protected right, such as protection against age, race, sex discrimination, or sexual harassment, and has not been resolved in Options One, Two or Three, you or the Company may request arbitration. While you do not have to proceed through each of the options in their exact numerical order, the Program is designed with multiple steps to maximize the possibility of resolution prior to Step 4. All outside dispute resolution processes in this program will use neutral parties provided through the American Arbitration Association.

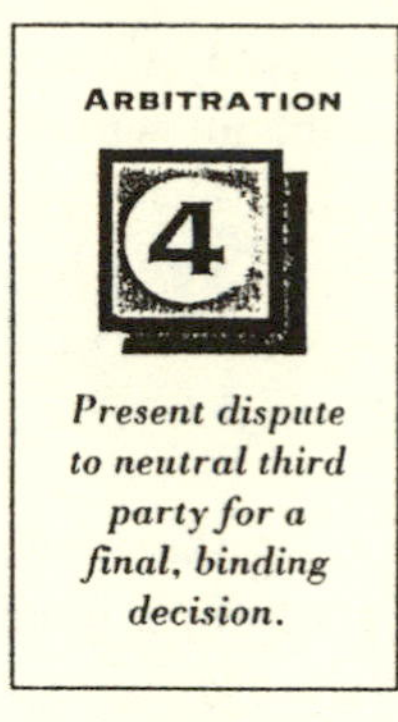

What is Arbitration?

Arbitration is a process in which a dispute is presented to a neutral third party, the arbitrator, for a final and binding decision. The arbitrator makes this decision after both sides present their arguments at the arbitration hearing. There is no jury. If you win, you can be awarded anything you might seek through a court of law.

The neutral party, AAA, runs the proceedings which are held privately. Since 1926, AAA has handled hundreds of thousands of cases. Though arbitration is much less formal than a court trial, it is an orderly proceeding, governed by rules of procedure and legal standards of conduct.

Requesting Arbitration

You must pay a $50 processing fee to take your legal dispute to an outside resolution process, such as arbitration. Brown & Root will pay any costs that exceed this $50 fee. To request an outside process, call or write

AAA at (713) 739-1302, 1001 Fannin Street, Suite 1005, Houston, TX 77002. Once you have made this request and paid your fee, Brown & Root is legally bound to participate with you in arbitration. If you have already participated in mediation through the AAA and have paid a processing fee of $50, you will not have to pay any additional costs to initiate arbitration.

You may move to Option Four directly from the Conference or if mediation through AAA proves unsuccessful — *as long as your dispute involves a legally protected right.*

The Role of Lawyers

The Company has access to legal advice through its law department and outside lawyers. You may consult with a lawyer or any other adviser of your choice. Upon approval of the Program Administrator, Brown & Root will pay the major part of your legal fees through the Legal Consultation Plan, up to a maximum of $2,500. (See page 5. [See "Requesting a Legal Consultation"]) Call the Program Administrator for details of this program.

You are not required, however, to hire a lawyer to participate in arbitration. If you choose not to bring a lawyer to arbitration, the Company will also participate without a lawyer.

Typical Arbitration Steps

1. A party involved in a legal dispute files a demand for arbitration with an AAA office.
2. Any other parties involved are notified.
3. AAA offers a list of qualified candidates.
4. Each party numbers the list in order of preference.
5. An arbitrator is selected based on the parties' preferences.
6. AAA arranges a hearing date at a convenient location.
7. At the hearing, testimony is given and documents exchanged.
8. Witnesses are questioned and cross-examined.
9. The arbitrator issues a final and binding decision.
10. Copies of this decision are sent to both parties.

Arbitration Makes Sense

- **Quick Resolution** — You can expect a quick resolution of your problem. That means weeks or months instead of years in the legal system. This benefits everybody.
- **Keep Your Recovery** — You may be able to obtain any legal advice you need under the Legal Consultation Plan, saving you expensive legal fees. Except for

a $50 processing fee, the Company pays the cost of mediation and arbitration. If you operate within the terms of the Program and the Legal Consultation Plan, you may not have to share an arbitrator's award with a lawyer.

- **Independent Third Party** — You can benefit from the objectivity and experience of an outside, neutral arbitrator.
- **Get Back What You Lost** — Arbitration can restore to you what you had lost. Under the terms of the Program, an arbitrator can award you anything you might seek through a court of law.
- **Preserve Work Relationships** — A quick and impartial resolution through arbitration may make it easier for you to stay on the job than years of costly, frustrating court battles.

Effective June 1, Brown & Root will adopt this four option program as the exclusive means of resolving workplace disputes for legally protected rights. That means, if you accept or continue your job at Brown & Root after that date, you will agree to resolve all legal claims against Brown & Root through this process instead of through the court system. Use of Options One and Two of the program for cases not involving legal rights is voluntary.

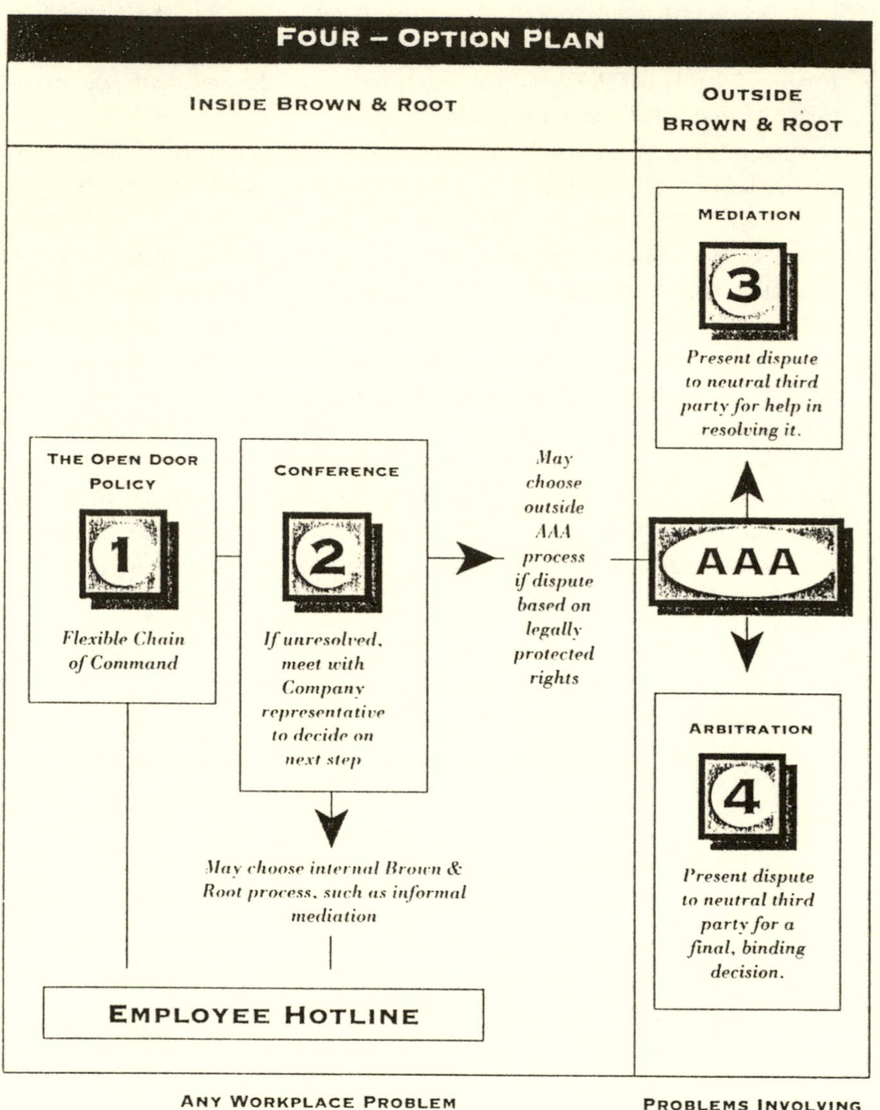

FOUR – OPTION PLAN
INSIDE BROWN & ROOT
OUTSIDE BROWN & ROOT
MEDIATION
3
Present dispute to neutral third party for help in resolving it.
THE OPEN DOOR POLICY
1
Flexible Chain of Command
CONFERENCE
2
If unresolved, meet with Company representative to decide on next step
May choose outside AAA process if dispute based on legally protected rights
AAA
ARBITRATION
4
Present dispute to neutral third party for a final, binding decision.
May choose internal Brown & Root process, such as informal mediation
EMPLOYEE HOTLINE
ANY WORKPLACE PROBLEM INCLUDING LEGALLY PROTECTED RIGHTS
PROBLEMS INVOLVING LEGALLY PROTECTED RIGHTS

QUESTIONS AND ANSWERS

1. How does the strengthened Open Door Policy differ from the old Open Door Policy?

For the first time in the history of the Company, the Open Door Policy has been put into writing. It has also become Option One of a four-option dispute resolution process. Both old and new Open Door Policies call for resolving workplace disputes through the Chain of Command. Improvements to Option One include an Employee Hotline, the potential for an Adviser and, if desired and approved, a legal consultation for those disputes involving legally protected rights. Brown & Root will be training all of its managers and supervisors how to use the new program. Helping employees resolve their problems at work will be part of every manager's and supervisor's job.

2. What's the difference between the Employee Assistance Plan (EAP) and the Open Door Program?

Although they are both assistance programs, they deal with different issues. The EAP offers short-term counseling for such things as family and marital conflicts, problems related to stress and anxiety, and those involving substance abuse. These problems can affect employees both at work and at home. The Open Door Policy offers you help in resolving conflicts at work specifically with your supervisors, managers and coworkers.

3. What do I do if the supervisor I approach ignores the Open Door Policy?

If the first person you approach under the Open Door Policy is unresponsive, proceed immediately to another level of supervision in the Chain of Command. You may also want to call the Employee Hotline at (800) 947-7658 and ask your Adviser for guidance or call your Business Unit Personnel manager or Employee Relations.

4. What happens if my supervisor starts to make things difficult for me after I complain?

Brown & Root encourages you to take full advantage of its programs and policies. The Company forbids retaliation against you for using the four-option program. If you feel that a supervisor is retaliating against you for using any or all of the options, you should take it to a higher level in the chain of command, or an Adviser through the Employee Hotline. The

Adviser will help you decide on a strategy for handling your problem or refer you to someone in the Chain of Command.

5. Can I use the Brown & Root Dispute Resolution Program to solve any problem that happens at work?

You may use Option One, **the Open Door Policy** to address any concerns, questions or problems you may have with your supervisors or coworkers. You may also request a Conference with someone from the Dispute Resolution Program and a Company representative for any workplace dispute if the Open Door Policy proves unsuccessful.

Options Three and Four, the outside resolution processes through AAA, can be used to resolve only those problems or disputes involving legally protected rights, such as: discrimination for age, sex or religion; on-the-job harassment, or being asked to commit unlawful acts. Whether or not a dispute truly involves a legally protected right may also be determined at this time.

6. How does arbitration differ from a court trial?

With arbitration, the decision is final; except under rare circumstances, it may not be reversed by subsequent proceedings. With a court trial decision, an appeal may be filed causing lenghtly [*sic*] delays. Also an arbitration proceeding is usually much more informal than a case in court. The arbitrator is usually a lawyer or a person with Employee Relations or legal background or who serves as a neutral on a part-time basis. The proceeding is held in private offices instead of in a public courthouse. The biggest difference, however, lies in the reasonable cost of arbitration. Because arbitration is faster and less formal, it ends up costing much less to prepare the case.

7. What's the difference between mediation and arbitration?

Mediation is a process in which those involved in a dispute try to resolve it with the aid of a neutral third party, the mediator. In this process, the mediator helps to open up lines of communication but does not hand down a final decision. With arbitration, a dispute is submitted to an outside, neutral party for a final decision which cannot be overturned by the courts, except in rare circumstances.

8. Do you have to go through mediation before proceeding to arbitration?

No, in some cases involving legally protected rights, you or the Company may wish to proceed directly from the Conference to arbitration for a final, binding decision.

9. Does the Program require me to go through each step completely before going through the next one?

The steps are arranged in the most logical pattern applicable to most disputes. However, a number of factors can effect [*sic*] the order of the steps you wish to utilize including: whether it involves a legally protected right, your own preference, the Company's preference and just plain common sense.

10. What happens if I file a lawsuit again the Company for a workplace dispute?

If you file a lawsuit, Brown & Root will ask the court to dismiss the case and refer it to our Dispute Resolution Program.

11. Is there any limit on the amount of award I can win through arbitration?

No. The arbitrator has the same authority as a judge in making awards to employees. That means in arbitration, it's possible for you to recover anything you might seek through the court system.

12. What can I do to seek relief if I believe my legally protected rights have been violated?

If you believe your legally protected rights have been violated, you may request a legal consultation through the Program Administrator. If you cannot resolve your dispute within the Company, you may pay $50 and request an outside process through AAA. The arbitrator will determine if a legally protected right has indeed been violated, and if so, the amount you recover.

13. What happens if I'm terminated or laid off from Brown & Root? Does the Dispute Resolution Program still apply to me?

If you are terminated or laid off from the Company, you must still resolve all legal claims against Brown & Root through the Dispute Resolution Program instead of through the court system. All four options of the program would be available to you.

14. What if the cause of my dispute is an on-the-job injury?

If you needed help with a problem regarding your claim for workers' compensation or unemployment insurance benefits, you could contact the Workplace Injury Administration Department at Brown & Root.

However, if you believe you have been fired, laid off or unjustly treated because you filed a claim for on-the-job injury, you would settle your dispute through the Dispute Resolution Program.

15. How can I be sure of confidentiality if I call the Employee Hotline?

The new Employee Hotline is designed to provide you with an independent and confidential source of advice and assistance. The Advisers are trained to make every effort to honor your requests for confidentiality. Also, whether or not, you disclose your name when you talk to your Adviser will always be your decision.

If you wish your Adviser to provide certain kinds of assistance, such as informal mediation, he or she may need your permission to contact other people about your problem. But again, none will be contacted without your permission.

Please note, however, that in certain rare instances, such as if criminal activity is reported, the Adviser may be requested to bring some information forward.

16. Are Brown & Root employees all over the world covered under the Dispute Resolution Program?

No. At this time, the new program applies only to domestic employees, i.e. those employees who work in the United States or are under the jurisdiction of its court system.

17. Will I still be able to go to the Equal Employment Opportunity Commission (EEOC) after the new program takes effect?

Yes. The Dispute Resolution Program applies to relief you might seek personally through the courts for a workplace dispute. You are still free to consult the appropriate state Human Rights Commission, the EEOC or any other government regulatory body regarding your workplace problem. The Dispute program may have some effect on the process for individual relief through such agencies. Of course, Brown & Root hopes the new program is so effective, you won't need to go anywhere else.

CONCLUSION

Our Dispute Resolution Program works for you and the Company in several ways. It strengthens Brown & Root's traditional Open Door Policy by formalizing a plan to keep communication open.

It promotes fair treatment of all employees by serving notice to supervisors that their decisions may be reviewed by higher management.

It saves all of us the financial and emotional expense of a long court battle which can weaken working relationships and careers.

It encourages teamwork by providing a system for working out differences within the Company. Working together as a team is the key to remaining a successful force in the industry — productive, efficient and responsive to our clients' needs.

The Brown & Root Dispute Resolution Plan and Rules

THE BROWN & ROOT DISPUTE RESOLUTION PLAN

1. Purpose and Construction

This Plan is designed to provide for the quick, fair, accessible and inexpensive resolution of legal disputes between the Company and its present and former employees. The Plan is intended to create an exclusive procedural mechanism for the final resolution of all disputes falling within its terms. It is not intended either to abridge or enlarge substantive rights available under existing law. The Plan contractually modifies the "at-will" employment relationship between the Company and its employees, but only to the extent as expressly stated in this Plan. The Plan should be interpreted in accordance with these purposes.

2. Definitions

A. "AAA" means the American Arbitration Association.

B. The "Act" means the Federal Arbitration Act, 9 U.S.C. § 1, *et seq.*

C. "Company" means Sponsor and every subsidiary of Brown & Root Holdings, Inc. (a Delaware Corporation), any Electing Entity, and all of their officers, directors, employees, and agents. "Company" also includes every plan of benefits, whether or not tax-exempt, established or maintained by any such corporate entity, and the fiduciaries, agents and employees of all such entities. “Company” also includes the successors and assigns of all such persons and entities. Provided, however, that in the case of an Electing Entity, “Company” shall include the Entity only to the extent provided in the Entity’s agreement to be bound by the Plan.

D. “Dispute” means a claim, demand or controversy to which this Plan applies, between persons bound by the Plan or by an agreement to resolve disputes under the Plan.

E. “Electing Entity” means any legal entity which has agreed to be bound to the Plan as provided herein.

F. “Employee” means any employee or former employee of the Company residing in the United States, or otherwise subject to the laws of the United States or any state, municipality, or other political subdivision.

G. “Party” means a person bound by this Plan.

H. “Plan” means this Brown & Root Dispute Resolution Plan, as amended from time to time.

I. “Referee” means a person selected under this Plan to decide or mediate a Dispute, such as an arbitrator or mediator. “Decision by Referee” means resolution of a Dispute by arbitration or any other method selected by the Parties under this Plan.

J. “Rules” means the Brown & Root Dispute Resolution Rules, as amended from time to time.

K. “Sponsor” means Brown & Root Corporate Services, Inc.

3. Application and Coverage

A. Until revoked by Sponsor pursuant to this Plan, this Plan applies to and binds the Company, each Employee who is in the employment of the Company on or after the effective date of this Plan, and the heirs, beneficiaries and assigns of any such person. All such persons shall be deemed Parties to this Plan. Provided, however, that this Plan shall not apply to any Employee in a unit of Employees represented by a labor organization, or to the Company with respect to such employees, except to the extent permitted in an applicable collective bargaining agreement.

B. Except as provided for herein, this Plan applies to any legal or equitable claim, demand or controversy, in tort, in contract, under statute, or alleging violation of any legal obligation, between persons bound by the Plan, which relates to, arises from, concerns or involves in any way:

1. this Plan;
2. the employment of an Employee, including the terms, conditions, or termination of such employment;

3. employee benefits or incidents of employment with the Company; or
4. any other matter related to the relationship between the Employee and the Company including, by way of example and without limitation, allegations of: discrimination based on race, sex, religion, national origin or disability; sexual harassment; workers' compensation retaliation; defamation; infliction of emotional distress; or status, claim, or membership with regard to any employment benefit plan.

C. Notwithstanding anything to the contrary in this Plan, the Plan does not apply to claims for workers compensation benefits or unemployment compensation benefits.

4. Resolution of Disputes

All Disputes not otherwise settled by the parties shall be finally and conclusively resolved under this Plan and the rules.

5. Confidentiality

The Company may employ confidential advisors to assist employees in management in resolving disputes. It is the intent of this Program that any matter brought to the attention of the confidential advisors in their capacities as advisors should be held in the strictest confidence in accordance with the terms and exceptions established in the Code of Ethics of the Corporate Ombudsman Association. The terms of that Code are incorporated into this Plan by reference. Any disputes [*sic*] resolution efforts or processes conducted by confidential advisors shall be confidential with the meaning of Section 154.053 and 154.073 of the Texas Civil Practice and Remedies Code and similar statutes.

The Dispute Resolution Program Administrator is authorized to conduct conferences for a purpose of assisting parties in selecting a dispute resolution process. The conferences conducted under this Program and all in-house dispute resolution processes including but not limited to mediation, fact finding, peer review, or any form of in-house arbitration shall be confidential within the meaning of Section 154.053 and 154.073 of the Texas Civil and Practice and Remedies Code. Any person conducting conferences or serving as an impartial third party under any in-house dispute resolution process under this Program shall be bound by the standards and duties established under Section 154.053 of the Texas Civil Practice and Remedies Code. The provisions of this section shall apply to the Program Administrator and any subordinate administrators.

6. Amendment

A. This Plan may be amended by sponsor at any time. However, no amendment shall apply to a Dispute of which Sponsor had actual notice on the date of amendment.

B. Sponsor shall adopt, and may amend the rules at any time. However no amendment will be effective:

1. until notice of the amendment is served on AAA, or
2. as to a Dispute of which Sponsor had actual notice (by notice of intent to arbitrate or otherwise) on the date of amendment.

7. Termination

This Plan may be terminated by Sponsor at any time. However, termination shall not be effective:

A. until 10 days after reasonable notice of termination is given to Employees or

B. as to Disputes which arose prior to the date of termination.

8. Applicable Law

A. The Act shall apply to this Plan, the Rules, and any proceedings under the Plan or the rules, including any actions to compel, enforce, vacate or confirm proceedings, awards, orders of a Referee, or settlements under the Plan or the rules.

B. Other than as expressly provided herein, or in the rules, the substantive legal rights, remedies and defenses of all Parties are preserved. In the case of arbitration, the arbitrator shall have the authority to determine and implement the applicable law and to order any and all relief, legal or equitable, including punitive damages, which a Party could obtain from a court of competent jurisdiction on the basis of the claims made in the Dispute.

C. Other than as expressly provided herein, or in the Rules, the Plan shall not be construed to grant additional substantive legal or contractual rights, remedies or defenses which would not be applied by a court of competent jurisdiction in the absence of the Plan.

D. Notwithstanding the provisions of the preceding subsection, in any proceeding before an arbitrator, the arbitrator, in his discretion, may allow a prevailing Employee a reasonable attorney's fee as a part of the award. The discretion to allow an award of fees under this subsection is in addition to any discretion, right or power which the arbitrator may have under applicable law. However, any award of fees shall be reduced by any amounts which have been or will be paid by the Brown & Root Employee Legal Assistance Plan.

9. Administrative Proceedings

A. This Plan shall apply to a Dispute pending before any local, state or federal administrative body unless prohibited by law.

B. Participation in any administrative proceeding by the Company shall not affect the applicability of the Plan to any such dispute upon termination of the administrative proceedings. A finding, recommendation or decision by an administrative body on the merits of a dispute subject to this Plan shall have the same legal weight or effect under the Plan as it would in a court of competent jurisdiction.

10. Exclusive Remedy

Proceedings under the Plan shall be the exclusive, final and binding method by which Disputes are resolved. Consequently, the institution of a proceeding under this Plan shall be a condition precedent to the initiation of any legal action (including action before an administrative tribunal with adjudicatory powers) against the Company arising out of the employment of an employee by the Company and any such legal action shall be limited to those under the Act.

11. Electing Corporations

A. Corporations or other legal entities not otherwise Parties may elect to be bound by this Plan by written agreement with Sponsor.

B. Election may be made only as to some types of Dispute, or only as to some persons, in the discretion of Sponsor.

12. Effective Date

The effective date of this Plan shall be June 15, 1993.

13. Severability

The terms of this Plan and the rules are severable. The invalidity or unenforceability of any provision therein shall not affect the application of any other provision. Where possible, consistent with the purposes of the Plan, any otherwise invalid provision of the Plan or the Rules may be reformed and, as reformed, enforced.

14. Administration

Sponsor shall appoint one or more persons to administer this Plan who shall be known as the "Dispute Resolution Program Administrator". The Administrator shall be responsible for the management and administration of the Plan. Any communication with the Company which is required or permitted by this Plan or the rules shall be made to the Administrator.

15. Assent

Employment or continued employment after the Effective Date of this Plan constitutes consent by both the Employee and the Company to be bound by this Plan, both during the employment and after termination of employment.

BROWN & ROOT DISPUTE RESOLUTION RULES

1. Definitions

All definitions included in the Brown & Root Dispute Resolution Plan apply to these Rules.

2. Application

A. If different rules, applicable to a specific class of disputes, have been adopted by Sponsor and served on AAA, these Rules shall not apply.

B. These Rules apply in the form existing at the time proceedings are initiated under them.

C. To the extent consistent with these rules, the Employment Dispute Resolution Rules of AAA also apply to all proceedings governed by these Rules.

3. Initiation of the Process

A. A party may initiate proceedings under these Rules at any time, subject to any defenses applicable to the timeliness of the claim, including limitations and laches.

B. A party may initiate proceedings by serving a written Request to initiate proceedings on AAA and tendering the appropriate administrative fee.

C. Copies of the Request shall be served on all other parties to the Dispute. The Request shall describe the nature of the dispute, the amount involved, if any, the remedy sought, and the hearing locale requested.

D. Proceedings may also be initiated by an Employee against the Company by serving the Company. In such a case, the Company shall promptly forward any properly served notice it has received to AAA.

E. Parties on whom notice is served shall file an answering statement within 21 days of receiving notice of intent to arbitrate or a specification of claims, which shall include any counter-claims and any request that the arbitrator (if any) prepare a statement of reasons for the award.

4. Administrative Conference

As soon as possible after receipt of the answering statement, if any, AAA shall convene an administrative conference. The conference may be held in person or by telephone. At the conference AAA will determine whether the Parties are in agreement on a method to resolve the dispute. If the Parties agree on a procedure, AAA will implement this agreement to the extent consistent with AAA's rules upon payment of any applicable fee. If the Parties cannot agree, or if the Parties have previously attempted and failed to resolve the Dispute by mediation or another non-binding mechanism, the Dispute shall be arbitrated under these Rules.

5. Appointment of Arbitrator

Immediately after payment of the arbitration fee, AAA shall send simultaneously to each party an identical list of names of persons chosen from a panel of qualified arbitrators which AAA shall select and maintain. Each party to the Dispute shall have fourteen (14) days from the transmittal date to strike any names objected to, number the remaining names in order of preference, and return the list to AAA. If a party does not return the list within the time specified, all persons therein shall be deemed acceptable. From among the persons who have been approved on both lists, and in accordance with the order of mutual preference, AAA shall invite the acceptance of the arbitrator to serve. Any party shall have the right to strike one list of arbitrators in its entirety. When a party exercises this right, AAA shall issue a new list of arbitrators consistent with the above procedures.

6. Qualifications of the Arbitrator

No person shall serve as an arbitrator in any matter in which that person has any financial or personal interest in the result of the proceeding. Prior to accepting appointment, the prospective arbitrator shall disclose any circumstance likely to prevent a prompt hearing or create a presumption of bias. Upon receipt of such information from the arbitrator or any other source, AAA will either replace that person or communicate the information to the parties for comment. Thereafter, AAA may disqualify that person and its decision shall be conclusive.

7. Vacancies

If a vacancy occurs for any reason or if an appointed arbitrator is unable to serve promptly, the appointment procedure in Section V shall apply to the selection of a substitute arbitrator.

8. Date, Time and Place of Hearings

A. The arbitrator shall set the date, time and place of the hearing.

B. Notice of any hearing shall be given at least ten days in advance, unless the arbitrator determines or the parties agree that a shorter time is necessary.

C. If one party is an Employee, the arbitrator shall make every effort, without unduly incurring expense, to accommodate the employee in the selection of a hearing location.

9. Conferences

At the request of AAA or of a party or on the initiative of the arbitrator, the arbitrator or AAA may notice and hold conferences for the discussion and determination of any matter which will expedite the hearing, including:

A. venue,

B. clarification of issues,

C. determination of preliminary issues, including summary determination of dispositive legal issues,

D. discovery,

E. the time and location of hearings or conferences,

F. interim legal or equitable relief authorized by applicable law,

G. pre- or post-hearing memoranda,
H. stipulations,
I. any other matter of substance or procedure.

10. Mode of Hearings and Conferences

In the discretion of the arbitrator or by agreement of the parties, conferences and hearings may be conducted by telephone or by written submission as well as in person.

11. Prehearing Discovery

A. On any schedule determined by the arbitrator, each party shall submit in advance, the names and addresses of the witnesses it intends to produce and any documents it intends to present.
B. The arbitrator shall have discretion to determine the form, amount and frequency of discovery by the parties.
C. Discovery may take any form permitted by the Federal Rules of Civil Procedure, subject to any restrictions imposed by the arbitrator.

12. Representation

Any party may be represented by counsel or by any other authorized representative.

13. Attendance at Hearings

The arbitrator shall maintain the privacy of the hearings to the extent permitted by law. Any person having a direct interest in the matter is entitled to attend the hearings. The arbitrator shall otherwise have the power to require the exclusion of any witness, other than a party or other essential person, during the testimony of any other witness. The arbitrator shall determine whether any other person may attend the hearing. Upon the request of any party, the arbitrator shall exclude any witness during the testimony of any other witness.

14. Postponement

A. The arbitrator, for good cause shown by a party, or on agreement of the parties, may postpone any hearing or conference.

B. The pendency of court proceedings related to the same matter is not good cause for postponement.

15. Oaths

Before proceeding with the first hearing, each arbitrator may take an oath of office and, if required by law, shall do so. The arbitrator may require witnesses to testify under oath administered by any duly qualified person and if required by law or requested by any party, shall do so.

16. Stenographic Record

There shall be no stenographic, tape recorded, or videotape record of the proceedings unless requested by one of the parties or the arbitrator rules otherwise. The party requesting the record shall bear the entire cost of producing the same. Copies of the record shall be furnished to all other parties on request and payment of the cost of reproduction.

17. Procedure

The hearings shall be conducted by the arbitrator in whatever order and manner will most expeditiously permit full presentation of the evidence and arguments of the parties.

18. Arbitration in the Absence of a Party

The arbitrator may proceed in the absence of parties or representatives who, after due notice, fail to be present or fail to obtain a postponement. An award shall not be made solely on the default of a party. The arbitrator shall require any party who is present to submit such evidence as the arbitrator may require for the making of an award.

19. Evidence

A. The arbitrator shall be the sole judge of the relevance, materiality and admissibility of evidence offered. Conformity to legal rules shall not be necessary.

B. The arbitrator may subpoena witnesses or documents at the request of a party or on the arbitrator's own initiative.

C. The arbitrator may consider the evidence of witnesses by affidavit or declaration, but shall give it only such weight as the arbitrator deems it entitled to after consideration of any objection made to its admission.

20. Post-Hearing Submissions

All documentary evidence to be considered by the arbitrator shall be filed at the hearing, unless the arbitrator finds good cause to permit a post-hearing submission. All parties shall be afforded an opportunity to examine and comment on any post-hearing evidence. The arbitrator shall permit the filing of post-hearing briefs at the request of a party and shall determine the procedure and timing of such filings.

21. Closing and Reopening of Hearing

A. When the arbitrator is satisfied that the record is complete, including the submission of any post-hearing briefs or documents permitted by the arbitrator, the arbitrator shall declare the hearing closed.
B. The hearing may be reopened on the arbitrator's initiative or upon application of a party, at any time before the award is made.

22. Waiver of Procedures

Any party who fails to object in writing after knowledge that any provision or requirement of these procedures has not been complied with, shall be deemed to have waived the right to object.

23. Service of Notices and Papers

Any papers, notices, or process necessary or proper for the initiation or continuation of any proceeding under these Rules (including the award of the arbitrator; for any court action in connection therewith; or for the entry of judgment on an award made under these procedures) may be served on a party by mail addressed to the party or his representative at the last known address or by personal service. Service may be made at any place, provided that the party served has had a reasonable opportunity to be heard with regard to service. The AAA, the parties, and the arbitrator may also use facsimile transmission, telex, telegram, or other written forms of electronic communication to give any notices required by these procedures.

24. Communications with the AAA and the Company

A. Any party may notice, serve or communicate with AAA by contacting:

Regional Administrator
American Arbitration Association
1001 Fannin St., Suite 1005
Houston, Texas 77002
(713) 739-1302
Fax: (713) 739-1702

B. Any party may notice, serve or communicate with the Company by contacting:

Dispute Resolution Program Administrator
Brown & Root, Inc.
4100 Clinton Drive
Houston, Texas 77020-6299
(713) 676-5383
Fax: (713) 676-4514

25. Communication with the Arbitrator

There shall be no communication between the parties and the arbitrator other than at any oral hearings or conferences. Any other oral or written communications from the parties to the arbitrator shall be directed to the AAA (and copied to the parties) for transmission to the arbitrator, unless the parties and the arbitrator agree otherwise.

26. Time of Award

The award shall be promptly made by the arbitrator and, unless otherwise agreed by the parties or specified by applicable law, no later than thirty days from the date of the of [*sic*] closing of the hearing or the closing of a reopened hearing, whichever is later.

27. Form of Award

The award shall be in writing and shall be signed by the arbitrator. If any party requests in its Notice or Answering Statement, the arbitrator shall write a summary of reasons for the decision. The award shall be executed in any manner required by applicable law.

28. Modification of Award

On order of a court of competent jurisdiction, or on agreement of the parties, the arbitrator shall modify any award. The arbitrator may modify an award on the motion of a party if the arbitrator finds that the award as rendered is ambiguous or defective in form, or if the award requires an illegal or impossible act. These are the only circumstances under which an arbitrator shall have jurisdiction to withdraw or modify an award.

29. Settlement

If the parties settle their dispute during the course of the arbitration, the arbitrator may set out the terms of the settlement in a consent award.

30. Scope of Arbitrator's Authority

The arbitrator's authority shall be limited to the resolution of legal disputes between the parties. As such, the arbitrator shall be bound by and shall apply applicable law including that related to the allocation of the burden of proof as well as substantive law. The arbitrator shall not have the authority either to abridge or enlarge substantive rights available under existing law. The arbitrator may also grant emergency or temporary relief which is or would be authorized by applicable law.

31. Judicial Proceedings and Exclusion of Liability

A. Neither the AAA nor any arbitrator is a necessary party in any judicial proceeding relating to proceedings under these Rules.

B. Neither the AAA nor any arbitrator shall be liable to any party for any act or commission in connection with any proceeding within the scope of these Rules.

C. Any court with jurisdiction over the parties may compel a party to proceed under these Rules at any place and may enforce any award made.

D. Parties to these Rules shall be deemed to have consented that judgment upon the award of the arbitrator may be entered and enforced in any federal or state court having jurisdiction of the parties.

E. Initiation of, participation in, or removal of a legal proceeding shall not constitute waiver of the right to proceed under these Rules.

F. Any court with jurisdiction over the parties may issue any injunctive orders (including preliminary injunctions) if the necessary legal and equitable requirements under applicable law are met pending the institution of proceedings under these Rules.

32. Fees and Expenses

A. The expenses of witnesses shall be borne by the party producing such witnesses, except as otherwise provided by law or in the award of the arbitrator.

B. All attorney's fees shall be borne by the party incurring them except as otherwise provided by law, by the Plan, or in the award of the arbitrator.

C. Employee Parties: Except as provided in this rule, Employee Parties shall not be responsible for payment of fees and expenses of proceedings under these Rules including required travel of an arbitrator, expenses of an arbitrator or of AAA representatives, and the cost of any proof produced at the direction of an arbitrator. If proceedings are initiated by an Employee, the Employee shall be responsible for the following fees.

i. $50 with service of a demand by an Employee;
ii. $50 if the Parties agree to mediation or other non-binding means to resolve the Dispute requiring one neutral; and
iii. $50 for arbitration initiated by an Employee.

D. If the demand for mediation or arbitration is initiated by the Company, all fees will be paid by the Company.

E. Other Parties: Except as otherwise provided by law or in the award of the arbitrator, all other expenses, fees and costs of proceedings under these Rules shall be borne equally by the Parties who are not Employees.

33. Interpretation and Application of These Rules

The arbitrator shall interpret and apply these Rules insofar as they relate to the arbitrator's powers and duties. All other rules shall be interpreted and applied by the AAA.

34. Applicable Law

A. These proceedings and any judicial review of awards under these rules shall be governed by the Federal Arbitration Act, 9 U.S.C. §1 *et seq.*

B. Except where otherwise expressly provided in these Rules, the substantive law applied shall be state or federal substantive law which would be applied by a United States District Court sitting at the place of the hearing.

35. Mediation

At any time before the hearing is closed, the parties may agree to mediate their dispute by notifying AAA. AAA shall determine what procedures apply to any such mediation.

Employment Legal Consultation Plan

BROWN & ROOT EMPLOYMENT LEGAL CONSULTATION PLAN

Brown & Root Holdings, Inc., a Delaware corporation, hereby establishes this Employment Legal Consultation Plan for its employees and the employees of its subsidiaries and affiliates, as set forth below.

The Plan hereby established has been approved by the appropriate officers of Brown & Root. The Plan is not intended to qualify under Section 120 of the Internal Revenue Code of 1986, as amended from time to time. Therefore any benefits received under this plan may be taxable to the employee or other recipient.

The terms and conditions of the Plan are as follows:

1. Purpose

The purpose of this Plan is to provide certain specified legal services for all Employees of Brown & Root who have a Dispute with the Company which is subject to the Brown & Root Dispute Resolution Plan, the provisions of which are incorporated herein by reference. This Plan is established and shall be maintained for the exclusive benefit of its Participants.

2. Definitions

Where the following words and phrases appear, they shall have the respective meanings set forth below, unless their context clearly indicates to the contrary.

A. Attorney: Any person who is licensed to practice law and to render any legal services subject to reimbursement of payment under this Plan.

B. Company: Sponsor and every subsidiary of Brown & Root Holdings, Inc. and every subsidiary of Sponsor adopting the DR Plan, any "electing entity" within the meaning of the DR Plan, and all of their officers, directors, employees, and agents. "Company" also includes every plan of benefits, whether or not tax-exempt, established or maintained by any such corporate entity, and the fiduciaries, agents, and employees of all such plans. "Company" also includes the successors and assigns of all such persons and entities.

C. Director: The person or persons appointed to administer this Plan in accordance with its applicable provisions.

D. Dispute: A claim, demand, or controversy to which the DR Plan applies between persons bound by such plan or by an agreement to resolve disputes under such plan.

E. DR Plan: The Brown & Root Dispute Resolution Plan, as amended from time to time.

F. Effective date: June 15, 1993.

G. Employee: Any employee or former employee of Brown & Root Holdings, Inc. and every subsidiary and electing corporation.

H. Panel: A list of one or more Attorneys maintained by the Director who are qualified to perform legal services reimbursable or payable under this Plan.

I. Participant: An Employee who has met the eligibility requirements set forth in Section 3 of this Plan.

J. Plan: This Brown & Root Employment Legal Consultation Plan, the terms of which are stated herein, as amended from time to time.

K. Referee: A person selected under the Rules to decide or mediate a Dispute, such as an arbitrator or mediator. "Decision by Referee" means resolution of a Dispute by arbitration or any other method selected by the parties under the DR Plan.

L. Rules: The Brown & Root Dispute Resolution Rules, as amended from time to time.

M. Sponsor: Brown & Root Holdings, Inc. or its designee.

3. Eligibility and Contributions

A. Participation: All Employees who are or are deemed Parties to the DR Plan are Participants in this Plan.

B. Termination of Participation: Participation in the Plan will terminate when and to the extent a Participant ceases to be a Party to the DR Plan.

C. Contributions: All costs associated with and benefits provided under the Plan will be paid by Sponsor. Sponsor may establish one or more trusts to fund this Plan in its sole discretion.

4. Benefits

A. General: The funds held pursuant to this Plan shall provide benefits with respect to services rendered by an Attorney representing one or more Participants in connection with a Dispute. The services must be performed by an Attorney or by a person who works under the direct supervision of an Attorney such as an associate attorney, paralegal, law clerk, or investigator. The services rendered must have a direct connection to the resolution of a Dispute by the means provided in the DR Plan. The Attorney and the Participant must have agreed to such representation in a written document satisfactory to the Director.

B. Benefits Provided: On and after the date an Employee becomes a Participant hereunder, benefits may be provided as detailed below for the provision of legal assistance to the participant by an Attorney:

i. Initial consultation regarding the Participant's Dispute with the Company
ii. Negotiation or mediation of the Dispute prior to Decision by Referee
iii. Representation of the Participant during any proceeding before a Referee, including any necessary discovery and preparation for the proceeding
iv. An amount equal to the participant's federal, state, and local income taxes and the Participant's portion of payroll taxes on the benefits provided to the Participant under the Plan (including the benefits provided pursuant to this paragraph), the amount of which shall be deemed to be equal to the tax withholding requirement with respect to such benefits

C. Benefits Not Provided: No benefits are payable for services rendered after Decision by Referee.

D. Limitation on Benefits: No benefits will be paid in excess of $2,500 with respect to the representation of any one Participant per calendar year.

E. After a $25 deductible for each dispute, the Plan shall pay 90% of the fees approved by the Director up to the pre-approved amount in relation to each dispute.

F. Qualification for Benefits: Participants may apply to the Director for benefits from this Plan under any procedures established by the Director. Unless such procedures provide otherwise, application may be made either before or after the Participant has consulted with an Attorney. The Director may approve payment of a reasonable fee as benefits if he determines in his sole and absolute discretion that the Participant has or may have a Dispute which requires legal assistance. In making this determination, the Director may consider the cost and value of the services rendered or to be rendered and any budgetary constraints applicable to the Plan.

G. Prohibition of Duplicate payments: No benefit shall be paid hereunder to the extent that attorneys' fees have been awarded by a Referee or a court for performance of the same legal services.

5. Selection of Panels

The Director may, in his discretion, establish Panels from which Participants may select Attorneys. However, no Participant shall be required to consult an Attorney from a Panel as a condition of receiving benefits under this Plan. Separate Panels may be maintained for different geographical areas, different classes of Dispute, or on such other basis as the Director may determine. The Director shall determine the number, types, and qualifications of Attorneys to be placed on any Panel in his or her sole and absolute discretion. The Director may provide a unique Panel for a particular case. Neither the Company nor the Director shall assume any liability beyond the payment of benefits provided for hereunder. However, any person placed on a panel must be:

A. Licensed to practice law in a state of the United States;

B. Regularly engaged in the practice of law; and

C. Qualified to represent Participants hereunder within the scope of his or her license.

6. Payment of Benefit Claims

Payments for services rendered hereunder shall be made directly to the Attorney involved by or on the order of the Director. Payment will be made only after the services have been rendered and in no event will such payments be made prospectively. Payment of the benefit described in Section 4.B.iv. shall be made directly to the applicable taxing authority in satisfaction of the tax withholding requirements with respect to the benefits provided hereunder. A claim for benefit payment shall be made on such forms and in accordance with such procedures as the Director shall prescribe for such purpose.

7. Administration

A. Appointment of Director: The Sponsor shall from time to time appoint one or more Directors who shall be responsible for the administration of the Plan. To facilitate the administration of the Plan, the Director may employ such persons as the Director from time to time shall designate.

B. Confidentiality: The Company shall have no right at any time to require the Director or his agents to reversal information which is privileged under applicable law. Subject thereto, the Sponsor may conduct audits of the Plan or of any claim at any time.

C. Powers of the Director: The Director shall have such powers as may be necessary to discharge his duties hereunder including, but not limited to, the sole discretionary authority and power to construe and interpret the Plan, prescribe operational rules for the Plan, and to employ such agents for the Plan as he or she deems advisable.

D. Authorization of Benefit Payments: The Director shall issue directions concerning all benefits which are to be paid pursuant to the provisions of the Plan.

8. Miscellaneous

A. Amendment: The Plan may be amended by the Sponsor at any time and from time to time. However, no amendment will affect the rights of a Participant to benefits under the Plan which accrued under the Plan prior to the date of such amendment.

B. Termination: The Plan may be terminated at any time by the Sponsor. However, termination will not affect the rights of a Participant to benefits under the Plan which accrued under the Plan prior to the date of such termination. Upon notice of termination, the Director shall secure all privileged or confidential documents of the Plan and shall cause them to be maintained at the Company's expense for a period of at least ten years from the date of termination.

C. Application of DR Plan: The DR Plan shall apply to all claims or controversies of any kind growing out of or related to this Plan, including any disagreement between or among the Director and the Company.

D. Governing Law: The Federal Arbitration Act (9 U.S.C. § 1 *et seq.*) and the Employee Retirement Income Security Act (29 U.S.C. § 1001 *et seq.*), as they may be amended from time to time, shall apply to this Plan.

BIBLIOGRAPHY

Abrams, Douglas E. "Arbitrability in Recent Federal Civil Rights Legislation: The Need for Amendment." *Connecticut Law Review* 26 (Winter 1994): 521–84.

Allison, Loren K. and Eric J. Stahlhut. "Arbitration and the ADA: A Budding Partnership." *Arbitration Journal* 48 (September 1993): 53–60.

Apruzzese, Vincent J. "Selected Recent Developments in EEO Law: The Civil Rights Act of 1991, Sexual Harassment, and the Emerging Role of ADR." *Labor Law Journal* 43 (June 1992): 334.

Bass, Stuart L. "Recent Court Decisions Expand Role of Arbitration in Harassment and Other Title VII Cases." *Labor Law Journal* 46 (January 1995): 38–47.

Baxter, Ralph H., and Evelyn M. Hunt. "Alternative Dispute Resolution: Arbitration of Employment Claims." *Employee Relations Law Journal* 15 (Autumn 1989): 187–207.

Berenbeim, Ronald. *Nonunion Complaint Systems: A Corporate Appraisal.* New York: The Conference Board, 1980.

Berkeley, Arthur Eliot, and E. Patrick McDermott. "The Second Golden Age of Employment Arbitration." *Labor Law Journal* 43 (December 1992): 774–779.

Blancero, D. "Nonunion Grievance Systems: Perceptions of Fairness." In *The Proceedings of the Forty-Fourth Annual Meeting (Industrial Relations Research Association) Held in New Orleans 3 – 5 January 1992*, edited by John F. Burton, 458–64. Madison: Industrial Relations Research Association, 1992.

Boroff, Deborah. "Loyalty — A Correlate of Exit, Voice, or Silence?" In *Proceedings of the Forty-Second Annual Meeting of Industrial Relations Research Association Held in Atlanta 28–30 December 1989*, edited by John F. Burton, Jr., 307–14. Madison: Industrial Relations Research Association, 1990.

Boroff, Karen E. "Measuring the Perceptions of the Effectiveness of a Workplace Complaint Procedure." In *Advances in Industrial and Labor Relations*, Vol. 5, edited by Donna Sockell, David Lewin, and David B. Lipsky, 207–33. Greenwich: JAI Press, 1991.

Committee on Labor and Employment Law of the Bar Association of the City of New York. *Final Report on Model Rules for the Arbitration of Employment Disputes* (50 The Record), pp. 629–59. New York City: The Bar Association of the City of New York, 1995.

Committee on Long Range Planning Judicial Conference of the United States. "Proposed Long Range Plan for the Federal Court, Draft for Public Comment." November 1994. Washington, D.C.: U.S. Government Printing Office, 1994.

Coulson, Robert. "Title Seven Arbitration in Action." *Labor Law Journal* 27 (March 1976): 141–51.

Delaney, John Thomas, David Lewin, and Casey Ichniowski. *Human Resource Policies and Practices in American Firms*. Washington D.C.: Bureau of Labor-Management Relations, 1989.

Dertouzos, James N., Elaine Holland, and Patricia Ebener. *The Legal and Economic Consequences of Wrongful Termination*. Santa Monica: The RAND Corporation, 1988.

Donohue, John J., III, and Peter Siegelman. "The Changing Nature of Employment Discrimination Litigation." *Stanford Law Review* 43 (1991): 983–1033.

Employment Discrimination: How Registered Representatives Fare in Discrimination Disputes (GAO/HEHS-94-179), p. 9. Washington, D.C.: General Accounting Office, 1994.

Employment Discrimination — Most Private-Sector Employers Use Alternative Dispute Resolution (July 1995, GAO/HEHS-95-150). Washington, D.C.: General Accounting Office, 1995.

Epstein, R. L. "The Grievance Procedure in the Non-Union Setting: Caveat Employer." *Employee Relations Law Journal* 1 (Summer 1975): 120–27.

Edwards, Harry T. "Arbitration of Employment Discrimination Cases — A Proposal for Employer and Union Representatives." *Labor Law Journal* 27 (May 1976): 265–77.

Edwards, Harry T. "Advantages of Arbitration over Litigation: Reflections of a Judge." In *Proceedings of the Thirty-Fifth Annual Meeting, National Academy of Arbitrators May 25–28 1982*, edited by James L. Stern and Barbara D. Dennis, 16–19. Washington D.C.: Bureau of National Affairs, 1983.

Edwards, Harry T. "The Rising Work Load and Perceived 'Bureaucracy' of the Federal Courts: A Causation Based Approach to the Search for Appropriate Remedies." *Iowa Law Review* 68 (May–July 1983): 871–936.

Estreicher, Samuel. "Arbitration of Employment Disputes Without Unions." *Chicago — Kent Law Review* 66 (1990): 753–97.

Ewing, David W. *Justice on the Job: Resolving Grievances in the Nonunion Workplace*. Boston: Harvard Business School Press, 1989.

Fleming, R. W. *The Labor Arbitration Process*. Illinois: University of Illinois Press, 1965.

Gettman, Julius G. "Labor Arbitration and Dispute Resolution." *The Yale Law Journal* 88 (April 1979): 916–49.

Gordon, Michael E. "Grievance Systems and Workplace Propositions about Procedural and Distributive Justice." In *Proceedings of the Fortieth Annual Meeting of the Industrial Relations Research Association Held in Chicago 28–30 December 1988*, edited by Barbara D. Dennis, 390–97. Madison: Industrial Relations Research Association, 1988.

House, Nancy C. "Grievance Mediation: AT&T's Experience." *Labor Law Journal* 43 (August 1992): 491–95.

Kaufmann, Steven M., and John A. Chanin. "Directing the Flood: The Arbitration of Employment Claims." *The Labor Lawyer* 10 (1994):217–38.

Kuhn, Peter. "Sex Discrimination in Labor Markets: The Role of Statistical Evidence." *American Economic Review* 77 (1987): 567, 579.

LaVaute, James R. "Alternative Dispute Resolution and Deferral to Arbitration." *The Labor Lawyer* 6 (Winter 1990): 87–96.

Levine, David I. *Reinventing the Workplace — How Business and Employees Can Both Win*. Washington, D.C.: The Brookings Institution, 1995.

Lewin, David. "Conflict Resolution in the Nonunion High Technology Firm." In *Human Resource Management in High Technology Firms*, edited by Archie Kleingartner and Carolyn S. Anderson, 137–55. Lexington, Massachussets: Lexington Books, 1987.

Lewin, David. "Dispute Resolution in the Nonunion Firm." *Journal of Conflict Resolution* 31 (September 1987): 465–502.

Lewin, David, and Richard B. Peterson. *The Modern Grievance Procedure*. New York: Quorum Books, 1988.

Lewin, David. "Grievance Procedures in Nonunion Workplaces: An Empirical Analysis of Usage, Dynamics, and Outcomes." *Chicago — Kent Law Review* 66 (1990): 823–44.

Lind, Allan, E., and Thomas R. Tyler. *The Social Psychology of Procedural Justice*. New York: Plenum, 1988.

Lynch, Edward P., and Courtney E. Redfern. "Committing employees to out-of-court resolution." *HR Magazine* 38 (May 1993): 97.

Mackenzie, Susan T. "Arbitration and the ADA: Is Avoidance of External Law in Grievance Arbitration Appropriate?" *Labor and Employment Law Section*

Newsletter New York State Bar Association 19 (March 1994): 12–17.

Malin, Martin H., and Robert F. Ladenson. "Privatizing Justice: A Jurisprudential Perspective from the Steelworkers Trilogy to Gilmer." *Hastings Law Journal* 44 (August 1993): 1187–1240.

McCabe, Douglas M. *Corporate Nonunion Complaint Procedures and Systems.* New York: Praeger, 1988.

McDermott, Edward P. "Time Involved in Litigation Makes ADR an Attractive Option." *The Daily Record*, August 1992.

McDermott, Edward P. "Fleet, Discrete and Complete — The Use of ADR in Employment Law." *Maryland Bar Journal* 26 (March/April 1993): 6–11.

McDermott, Edward P. "Survey: Using ADR to Settle Employment Disputes." *Dispute Resolution Journal* 50 (January 1995): 8–13.

Miller, Christopher S. "Arbitrating Employment Claims: The State of the Law." *Labor Law Journal* 46 (April 1995): 193–204.

Moberly, Michael D. "Truth and Consequences: The Impact of Arbitration in Employment Defamation Cases." *The Labor Lawyer* 9 (1993): 577–94.

Nye, David L. "Issues in Alternative Labor Dispute Resolution: Views of Members of the National Academy of Arbitrators." Ph.D. diss., Auburn University, 1994.

Peterson, Richard B., and David Lewin. "A Model for Research and Analysis of the Grievance Process." In *Proceedings of the Thirty-Third Annual Meeting of the Industrial Relations Research Association Held in Denver 5–7 September 1980*, edited by Barbara D. Dennis, 303–12. Madison: Industrial Relations Research Association, 1981.

Piskorski, Thomas J., and David B. Ross. "Private Arbitration as the Exclusive Means of Resolving Employment Related Disputes." *Employee Relations Law Journal* 9 (September 1993): 5–15.

Sheppard, Blair H., Roy J. Lewicki, and John W. Minton. *Organizational Justice — The Search for Fairness in the Workplace*. New York: Lexington Books, 1992.

Spelfogel, Evan J. "Alternative Dispute Resolution and Deferral to Arbitration." *The Labor Lawyer* 6 (Winter 1990): 87–96.

Subcommittee on Alternative Dispute Resolution. *Report of the Subcommittee on Alternative Dispute Resolution, Corporate Survey of Alternative Dispute Resolution in the Wake of Gilmer v. Interstate/Johnson Corp.* Chicago: American Bar Association, 1992.

Thomas, Todd J. "Using Arbitration to Avoid Litigation." *Labor Law Journal* 44 (January 1993): 3–17.

Tien Wendy S. "Compulsory Arbitration of ADA Claims: Disabling the Disabled." *Minnesota Law Review* 77 (June 1993): 1443–76.

Ury, William L., Jeanne M. Brett, and Stephen B. Goldberg. *Getting Disputes Resolved — Designing Systems to Cut the Costs of Conflict.* New York: Jossey-Bass Publishers, 1989.

Westin, Alan F., and Alfred G. Feliu. *Resolving Employment Disputes without Litigation*. Washington, D.C.: The Bureau of National Affairs, Inc., 1988.

Yenney, Sharon L. "In Defense of the Grievance Procedure in a Non-Union Setting." *Employee Relations Law Journal* 2 (Spring 1977): 434–43.

Index

ABOUT THE AUTHORS

E. PATRICK MCDERMOTT is a general attorney in the New York City office of Capital Cities/ABC Inc., a subsidiary of The Walt Disney Company and is continuing his graduate studies at the School of Business and Public Management, George Washington University.

ARTHUR ELIOT BERKELEY holds a J.D. from the New York University School of Law, and both an M.S. and D.B.A. from George Washington University. He has taught at the University of Baltimore, Memphis State University, Vanderbilt, and most recently, Johnson C. Smith University. The author and editor of six books, he has published over 100 articles on a wide variety of subjects. A member of the National Academy of Arbitrators, he has an active practice in resolving employment disputes.

Correspondence of JAMES K. POLK

Volume VIII

September – December 1844

WAYNE CUTLER

Editor

ROBERT G. HALL II

JAYNE C. DEFIORE

Associate Editors

1993

The University of Tennessee Press

Knoxville

Manufactured in the United States of America.

Cloth: 1st printing, 1993

The paper in this book meets the minimum requirements
of the American National Standard for Permanence
of Paper for Printed Library Materials.
∞
The binding materials have been chosen for
strength and durability.

LIBRARY OF CONGRESS CATALOGING IN PUBLICATION DATA (Revised)
Polk, James Knox, Pres. U.S., 1795–1849.
Correspondence of James K. Polk.
Vol. 8 edited by W. Cutler
CONTENTS: v. 1. 1817–1832.—v. 2. 1833–1834.—v. 3. 1835–1836.—
v. 4. 1837–1838.—v. 5. 1839–1841.—v. 6. 1842–1843.—v. 7. 1844.—v. 8. 1844.
1. Polk, James Knox, Pres. U.S., 1795–1849. 2. Tennessee—Politics and
government—To 1865—Sources. 3. United States—Politics and
government—1845–1849—Sources. 4. Presidents—United States—
Correspondence. 5. Tennessee—Governors—Correspondence. I. Weaver,
Herbert, ed. II. Cutler, Wayne, 1938–
III. Title
E417.A4 1969 973.6'1'0924 75–84005
ISBN 0–87049–777–4

Sponsored by

The University of Tennessee, Knoxville

The National Historical Publications and
Records Commission

The National Endowment for the Humanities

The Tennessee Historical Commission

To

Harriet Chappell Owsley

PREFACE

James K. Polk's correspondence during the last ten weeks of the 1844 presidential campaign contains a fairly extensive but unorganized stock of the aging Democracy's political, economic, and social ideas. Suffused as they are in almost every letter of instruction or advice, these bits and pieces of the Jacksonian perspective provide a somewhat innocent witness to one side of the partisan debate then in progress, the central focus of which was that the Old Democracies north and south must unite to regain control of the general government and block further consolidation of political and economic power at the national level.

Satisfied that the wealth of the nation already was widely distributed among the mass of its citizenry, Democrats assumed that a stronger general government would reverse that favorable distribution of wealth. The young Republic's chronic shortage of investment capital could not be overcome through wealth transfers extracted from the producing classes through centralized banking, protective tariffs, transportation monopolies, and emigration barriers. Democrats scorned what they assumed to be the covert Whig agenda—that the general government would take care of the rich and let the rich take care of the poor.

In negating Whig economic initiatives the Old Democracy thought it was sustaining the true interests of an economic democracy, the surplus wealth of which should accrue for the most part to those who labored. Numerically the largest portion of middling folk came from the ranks of yeoman farmers, factory workers, skilled craftsmen, and shopkeepers. Even had the producing classes willingly passed their surplus wealth to the general government for development purposes, they would not have been so naive as to assume that their elected representatives would distribute the largess equitably among the peoples of twenty-six states or that the political system itself would remain uncorrupted by special interests.

Many Democratic apologists assumed that the several sections of the Union moved in conflicting economic directions and that the basis for an organic, integrated national economic order did not exist. Many worried that a voluntary political Union composed of such incompatible interests could not survive Whig attempts to force unification beyond the limits of the fundamental compromises of the Constitution and its Bill of Rights. The Democrats of 1844 often spoke of the Whig consolidation agenda in apocalyptic terms, a rhetoric of angst almost universally disparaged by contemporary urbane financial savants eager to discard the archaic pleadings of agrarian republicanism. Silly or wise, those same draconian fears dividing the electorate in 1844 would tear the Union apart in 1861 and leave the course of American political economy to the fortunes of warfare between the northern and southern states.

According to the accepted dogma of the Old Democracy, Henry Clay's American system proffered an illusory vision of economic realities. Northern agricultural and manufacturing production required substantial development of an internal market economy protected by closed frontiers and high tariffs. The price of northern labor must be contained by keeping the work force as large and as far east as possible, for territorial expansion worked against sustaining eastern land values and lowering the price of labor. Without tariff protection northern manufacturers must turn to cheap immigrant labor, which for the most part would mean the unwanted introduction of large numbers of Irish Catholics into New England's body politic and the political and cultural alienation of that region from its Protestant owners. Nativist thinking held it to be axiomatic that Catholic rule brought superstition, sloth, poverty, and disorder. Thus the economic future of northern capital consolidation rested on such seemingly unrelated policies as would govern expansion, protection, immigration, and religion.

On the other hand, Southern cotton production found its best credit and export opportunities in Liverpool and Manchester, not in New York City or New England mill towns. Territorial expansion would throw more land into production, enhance the demand for slaves, and thus benefit the older agricultural areas of the South where soil exhausion had greatly reduced the values of both land and slaves. Although politically unconcerned about Irish immigration or papist domination in their region of the Union, southern farmers, yeoman and planter alike, understood fully what would happen to the price of their cotton exports and the length of their credit lines should British textiles lose their edge to protected American manufacturers. If it came to a choice between economic ruin or political separation, the South would choose secession. Among the Jacksonians of 1844 the fear of disunion stamped one side of their ideological coin and the lure of expansion, the other. Texas annexation would further diffuse political and economic power within the Union, thus retarding the growth of anti-democratic power centers and so preserving the objectives of the American revolution.

Partisans of the Old Democracy wanted to keep the political Union free and united; their Whig opponents wanted to make it rich and powerful. Most voters had inherited their political identity much in the same fashion as their religious faith: transmission of political dogma did not depend upon institutional affiliation; rather sons kept faith with fathers and grandfathers through a clan culture that helped to shape the individual's universe of choices, most particularly those that were of political, religious, social, and vocational significance. Probably the trauma of the revolutionary war tested that generation's basic ideological preferences more deeply than any other defining event in colonial history. For the most part those radicalized by the war feared despotism more than anarchy and subsequently supported the decentralizing policies of the anti-federalists, Jeffersonian republicans, and Jacksonian democrats. For the more moderate revolutionaries the threat of anarchy far outweighed any latent fears of their own misrule, and they accordingly attached themselves to the centralizing goals of the Hamiltonian federalists, national republicans, and Whigs. In the formative years of the Union the electorate's political and religious persuasions sprouted from the same soil and grew as two vines around the same stump.

Devout Protestants of an authoritarian bent generally kept company with the Whigs, whose quest for political and economic security matched the zealots' search for religious and moral absolutes. According to the Biblical covenant, Jehovah required of His people a strict obedience to His righteous laws, and in return He would shower them with material blessings, just the kind of rewards promised by the Whig elect. Conversely, the original contract provided that Jehovah would punish unrighteous individuals and nations; and from His wrath in this world none could or should escape. Poverty, disease, and degradations of all kinds clearly marked those who had broken faith with Jehovah and lapsed into moral anarchy. Nothing less than the ascendancy of the Protestant religion and the salvation of the republic stood at risk in adopting the laissez-faire politics of the Democrats, dominated as they were by their alliance between the unruly locofocos and the godless slavocracy.

Thus viewed from the dictates of an uncompromising, moral absolutism, the young republic must be purified or punished, for its societal ills, particularly the evils of chattel slavery, could not be tolerated, much less excused. Militant Protestant sectarians, highly vocal but few in number, demanded immediate, total abolition and in doing so pushed the slavery debate far beyond the limits of political action. Their support for the Liberty party provided a platform for their abolition crusade, but it also opened as it were unoccupied ground upon which less extreme, more secular Protestants could take a stand against slavery by opposing its expansion into the western territories. In the North the anti-slavery, anti-expansion movement helped Whig candidates hold their Protestant constituencies against the abolitionist challenge, but in the South the argument that slave holding was immoral touched the integrity of almost every voter's social, religious, economic, or political connection. In 1844 the anti-slavery movement hurt southern Whigs more than it helped their northern brethren.

At the close of one of the hardest fought political campaigns in American history, the Union stood almost evenly divided as to its choice of directions as well as its leaders. The ticket of James K. Polk and George M. Dallas defeated that of Henry Clay and Theodore Frelinghuysen in the Electoral College by a vote of 170 to 105, but the Democratic electors won only 49.5 percent of the popular vote and gained a plurality of only 39,490 votes. The Liberty party polled 62,103 or 2.3 percent of the popular vote for their candidate, James G. Birney. Although the Native American party did not run a presidential candidate, it did form alliances with the Whigs in both Pennsylvania and New York, thus bringing anti-immigrant, anti-Catholic influence to bear on the electoral voting in two very critical states.

In 1844 neither party could expect to carry the Electoral College without winning at least two of the four largest electoral states in the Union: New York, Pennsylvania, Ohio, and Virginia. In 1840 Democrats had lost Pennsylvania by 351 votes, New York by 13,268, and Ohio by 24,099; they had carried Virginia by a narrow majority of 1,120 votes. In the 1844 race they considered their chances better than even for taking Pennsylvania and Virginia; overcoming the 1840 deficit in New York would prove very difficult; and winning Ohio would require a very large number of Whigs going over to the Liberty party ticket. If Democrats could retain the seven states won in 1840, they would need 78 additional electoral votes to gain the necessary 138 majority. Their hopes ran high for picking up Maine, Michigan, Mississippi, and Tennessee; prospects for adding Georgia, Indiana, and Louisiana remained indeterminate until very late in the campaign. The most casual of calculations suggested that they must win in Pennsylvania, New York, and Virginia.

Electoral College Voting

STATE	1840 WHIG	1840 DEMO	1844 WHIG	1844 DEMO
Alabama	–	7	–	9
Arkansas	–	3	–	3
Connecticut	8	–	6	–
Delaware	3	–	3	–
Georgia	11	–	–	10
Illinois	–	5	–	9
Indiana	9	–	–	12
Kentucky	15	–	12	–
Louisiana	5	–	–	6
Maine	10	–	–	9
Maryland	10	–	8	–
Massachusetts	14	–	12	–
Michigan	3	–	–	5
Mississippi	4	–	–	6
Missouri	–	4	–	7
New Hampshire	–	7	–	6
New Jersey	8	–	7	–
New York	42	–	–	36
North Carolina	15	–	11	–
Ohio	21	–	23	–
Pennsylvania	30	–	–	26
Rhode Island	4	–	4	–
South Carolina	–	11	–	9
Tennessee	15	–	13	–
Vermont	7	–	6	–
Virginia	–	23	–	17
TOTALS	234	60	105	170

—from the Congressional Quarterly's *Guide to U.S. Elections* (1975).

Whig strategists saw with equal clarity that they must carry Ohio and New York. They could count on holding Connecticut, Delaware, Kentucky, Maryland, Massachusetts, New Jersey, North Carolina, Rhode Island, and Vermont, thus leaving another 69 votes to be won elsewhere. Conceding to the Democrats the seven states won in 1840, plus for local reasons Maine, Michigan, and Mississippi, the Whigs must then find the winning combination among the seven states of Georgia, Indiana, Louisiana, New York, Ohio, Pennsylvania, and Tennessee. Prospects for sweeping New York, Ohio, and Pennsylvania did not seem promising, but the prize in each case could not be ignored. The dynamics of the campaign itself gave both parties occasion to intensify their efforts in Pennsylvania and New York.

Having prepared for three years to campaign against Martin Van Buren, the Whig party had suffered a temporary loss of momentum as a result of Polk's unexpected nomination in May of 1844. By September, however, their vastly superior financial resources had put their newspapers and organizers into virtually every post village and city in the Union. Party faithful began to respond in greater numbers to the countless rounds of processions, barbacues, and courthouse speeches. For their part the Democrats adopted similar techniques designed to heighten party spirit; but as post-convention euphoria over their newfound unity subsided, party leaders became concerned that early indicators might have lulled local operatives into a false sense of optimism. Trial heats for both parties came in early October, when New Jersey, Ohio, Pennsylvania, and Georgia held state legislative and gubernatorial elections.

Although Democrats expected to lose in New Jersey and did, hopes for an upset victory in the Ohio governorship race remained high until returns from the northern part of the state revealed that the abolition party had drawn very few Whigs into their column and had attracted mostly Democrats to their abolitionist ticket. Having worked so hard and come so close—less than one-half of one percent of the total vote, Democrats nursed that grief along with an even more painful realization that if Whig abolitionists in other states, particularly in New York, chose not to support Liberty Party candidates as expected, the consequences might be devastating. Predictions for a great victory in Pennsylvania proved to be inflated, for angry memories of the recent riots and anarchy in Philadelphia had invigorated the Whig campaign and brought nativists out in large numbers. Catholic influence in state affairs had increased, as had their allegiance to the Democrats. Whig editors had paid considerable attention to the fact that the Democratic gubernatorial candidate, Francis R. Shunk, had moved so far into the orbit of Rome as to oppose Bible readings in the schools and to genuflect during the dedication of a Catholic church. Shunk won his race, but by less than half of his projected majority. Only in Georgia did the Democrats find relief from the torrent of disappointment. There the Whigs had failed to win on local issues and the respectability of their leading men. The loss of Georgia suggested that Whiggery might be in trouble in the deep South. Still the October elections did not bode well for Democrats in the large electoral states, and the critical question had now become whether or not the Whigs would get the Native and abolition votes in Pennsylvania and New York.

In Philadelphia Whig managers had made concert with the Native American party to trade their congressional and city election votes for the Natives' electoral votes. That the Whigs had failed to give up the city government and had delivered only two of the three congressional districts in Philadelphia County gave Democrats some reason to think that the alliance would break apart. John K. Kane calculated that two or three thousand of the Natives might have been angered enough to ignore the bargain in the presidential question; he also noted that many of those Natives were formerly Democrats, carried away at present with religious fanaticism. Holding the Whig-Native alliance together in Philadelphia was crucial elsewhere, for Pennsylvania's election results would be known to the New Yorkers before they began voting. Arrangements between Whigs and Natives in New York City mirrored the Philadelphia pact, although the New York Natives played a stronger hand in the deal making, for they already had won control of the City government. Democrats could do little to bargain for the Natives' support, but they did nominate for governor their party's most popular office holder, Silas Wright, Jr. No better boost could have been given the electoral ticket than having Wright's name heading the state ticket.

The abolitionist movement in Pennsylvania was less active than in Ohio and New York, and the failure there of Whig abolitionists to vote Whig would not be missed in the Empire State. Perhaps both Whigs and Democrats went to excessive lengths in convincing their former partisans not to throw their votes away on the third party candidate. Just prior to the election the Washington *National Intelligencer* published a letter purportedly from James G. Birney to the Democrats of Saginaw, Mich., accepting their nomination for the state legislature and acknowledging that he then was and always had been a Jeffersonian Democrat. The Saginaw forgery aimed a clear message to Whig abolitionists that a vote for Birney really was vote for a Democrat. In New York an Ithaca Democrat planted with the local Whig newspaper an extract purportedly taken from a popular travel journal, *Roorback's Tour through the Western and Southern States in 1836.* Once the Whigs had circulated the phony story alledging Polk's mistreatment of his slaves, Democrats gleefully exposed the Roorback forgery and urged their brethren with abolitionist views to reject a movement led by men of such questionable morals. Warnings of dirty tricks and pipelaying (election fraud) came from all quarters and most particularly from Tennessee, where the election would prove to be the closest in the Union.

Whigs in the home state of the Democratic nominee put together a well-organized and well-financed campaign and bet their hats and boots on their handing Polk a fourth straight defeat. Polk had campaigned vigorously for Martin Van Buren's reelection in 1840 and sustained a 12,243 vote rout, the worst of his career. Unwilling to diminish his attachment to Van Buren and the party's North-South alliance, Polk had lost his gubernatorial races of 1841 and 1843, although by fairly small majorities of about 3,000 votes. The excitement of the 1844 campaign in Tennessee attracted 11,812 or 11 percent more voters than that of 1840. Democrats gained 11,966 votes or 25 percent; and the Whigs polled 154 fewer votes for Henry Clay than for William H. Harrison. Tennessee Democrats had hoped that their favorite son's heading the ticket would reverse the Whig lockhold on Tennessee; they turned up 123 short. From 1836 through 1852 the Whigs held sway in five straight presidential races with an average majority of 6,018. Fortunately for the Democrats in 1844 they did not need Tennessee's electoral vote, although the vote count there would have been hotly contested had New York gone Whig.

The Democratic victory belonged more to the party than to the candidate, for James K. Polk attended no rallies, made no speeches, and wrote but one public letter throughout the entire course of the campaign. Party ideology rather than candidate personality dominated the Democratic campaign, and in most quarters the electorate knew little more about the Democratic nominee at the end of the campaign than at its beginning. On the other hand, no one of voting age needed to ask who Henry Clay was, for he had glowed in the nation's political spotlight for over thirty years. Yet with each new public letter on campaign issues the "Great Embodiment" appeared more and more soft of center. Clay's defeat probably belonged more to his pen and his past than to his party. Following the election Whigs blamed their defeat on the Catholic vote and for a brief period considered forming a more formal alliance with the American Native party. For an equally short time victorious Democrats celebrated their success and then fell to factional quarrels over the spoils of office.

Letters of recommendation and advice flooded Polk's desk in the next six weeks, but he kept close counsel about his choice of personnel. He did make one offer and that was to Silas Wright, Jr., who had just been elected governor of New York. Knowing that Wright probably would decline serving in the cabinet, Polk nevertheless promptly asked him to take any post he might wish. Wright replied that divisions in the New York Democracy had forced him to run for governor and that those same concerns required that he serve his full term, to which course he had committed himself during the campaign. Polk understood the factional divisions of his party and accepted Wright's declination with relief, for on the southern side of the party there was the difficult and equally divisive decision of including or excluding John C. Calhoun in the new administration. Although most of Calhoun's friends understood the difficulty of keeping him as secretary of state, they loyally urged his retention; some suggested that the South Carolinian might be willing to go as minister to Great Britain if Polk and the Senate would give him prior approval for his settlement of the Oregon dispute on whatever terms he might arrange! Most of the northern Democrats wanted all new faces in the cabinet.

Not limited to sectional splits, the post-election struggle saw state leaders and party newspapers divide along pre-election lines. In Pennsylvania the friends of George M. Dallas arrayed themselves against those of James Buchanan, and in New York the Barnburners sought supremacy over the Hunkers. Something would have to be done about changing the editorial direction of the Washington *Globe,* including the selection of a new editor or even a new publisher. The president-elect determined that most of the key decisions would be made in Washington City after personal consultations with party leaders from across the Union. Expecting to leave Columbia in early February, Polk made short visits to Nashville and to Murfreesboro, arranged as much liquidity as his financial situation would allow, and prepared to move his household to the National Hotel in Washington City by February 20th, thus allowing two weeks to form the new administration.

This Volume

Always concerned that the reader's primary focus fall on the text of the document, the editors have limited their annotations to textual criticism and identifications. Persons, subjects, and oblique references have been noted on the occasion of their first mention in this volume; for the full name of persons mentioned subsequently in the text only by surname, the reader will want to consult the index. The editors have transcribed the text faithfully with a strict regard for original spellings, punctuation, and text placement, except for the following rules of normalization:

1. initial words of sentences have been capitalized and ending punctuation marks have been supplied when the syntax is clear (uncertain constructions are noted and rendered without normalization);
2. conventional spellings have been followed except when misspellings have been clearly written;
3. conventional upper and lower case usage has been followed when

the writer employed multiple and/or irregular forms of the same character, thus indicating no discernible meaning behind the writer's use of capitals;

4. interlineations, cancellations, and unintentional word repetitions have been ignored unless something more than writing errors may have been indicated;

5. short dashes on the base of the line have been transcribed as commas or periods as the syntax may suggest;

6. redundant punctuation and random flourishes or ink marks have been ignored;

7. superscripts have been brought down to the line, and markings beneath or beside superscripts have been transcribed as single periods;

8. punctuation marks following the abbreviations *st, nd, rd,* and *th* have been deleted;

9. regardless of their position in the original manuscript, the salutation, place of composition, and date have been set on the line or lines immediately below the document's heading;

10. place of composition and full date, if omitted but known to the editors through content analysis, have been supplied in brackets and noted, and misstatements of place and date have been corrected and supplied in brackets with the misinformation noted;

11. the complimentary closing has been omitted, and the omission of same has been indicated by an ellipsis if the closing was written as part of the ending paragraph;

12. the author's signature has been rendered in capitals and small capitals at the end of the text (or supplied within brackets if unwritten or clipped);

13. the inside address has been omitted, but the information has been stated in the head note, along with the document's classification and repository location;

14. textual interventions (ie., words supplied within brackets) have been made only to complete probable meanings (garbled texts have been transcribed without intervention and so noted); and

15. bracketed ellipses have been added to indicate that a portion of the text has been obliterated by ink blots, sealing wax, or some other kind of damage, and the nature and extent of same has been noted.

The editors' identification and explanatory annotations often have been assembled from standard reference and monographic sources that are so well known and reliable as to obviate the need for citation. These considerations, coupled with a desire to ensure that the endnotes do not overwhelm the presentation of the textual material, have persuaded the editors to forego the naming of sources in their endnotes.

Acknowledgments

In dedicating this eighth volume of the *Correspondence of James K. Polk* the editor acknowledges his profound regard for the extensive and valuable contributions of Harriet Chappell Owsley to southern historical scholarship. In her varied roles as researcher, writer, archivist, and editor she has set the highest of standards for uncompromising fidelity to her witnesses and texts. Her love of scholarship has touched the career of this writer, and it is as a well meant but poor trade that he offers this dedication in grateful exchange.

One of the great pleasures in editing this volume has come from working with a very able and supportive staff. Associate Editors Robert G. Hall II and Jayne C. DeFiore shared fully in all phases of the book's editorial preparation, including document selection, transcription, and annotation; Connie L. Lester, Ralph W. Brown III, Brian E. Crowson, and James L. Rogers II each served one year as graduate research assistants and made important contributions in calendaring, indexing, typesetting, and proofing the documents. To all of the staff members the editor extends his sincere appreciation for their good services and kind regards.

Together we express our gratitude to those librarians and archivists who have assisted us in our labors at the University of Tennessee Library, the Tennessee State Library and Archives, the National Archives, and the Library of Congress. For grant support and wise counsel we are particularly indebted to the members of the National Historical Publications and Records Commission, the National Endowment for the Humanities, and the Tennessee Historical Commission and to the staff personnel of the above-mentioned agencies. We also wish to acknowledge the helping hand so kindly extended by Jennifer M. Siler and her staff at the University of Tennessee Press.

Knoxville, Tennessee
July 1992

WAYNE CUTLER

CONTENTS

SYMBOLS

Document Classification

AC	Autograph Circular
ACI	Autograph Circular Initialed
ACS	Autograph Circular Signed
AD	Autograph Document
ADI	Autograph Document Initialed
ADS	Autograph Document Signed
AE	Autograph Endorsement
AEI	Autograph Endorsement Initialed
AES	Autograph Endorsement Signed
AL	Autograph Letter
AL, draft	Autograph Letter, drafted by writer
AL, fragment	Autograph Letter, fragment
ALI	Autograph Letter Initialed
ALI, draft	Autograph Letter Initialed, drafted by writer
ALS	Autograph Letter Signed
ALS, copy	Autograph Letter Signed, copied by writer
ALS, draft	Autograph Letter Signed, drafted by writer
ALsS	Autograph Letters Signed
AN	Autograph Note
ANI	Autograph Note Initialed
ANS	Autograph Note Signed
C	Circular, authorship attributed
CI	Circular Initialed
CS	Circular Signed
D	Document, authorship attributed

DI	Document Initialed
DS	Document Signed
E	Endorsement, authorship attributed
EI	Endorsement Initialed
ES	Endorsement Signed
L	Letter, authorship attributed
LI	Letter Initialed
LS	Letter Signed
N	Note, authorship attributed
NI	Note Initialed
NS	Noted Signed
PC	Published Circular, authorship attributed
PD	Published Document, authorship attributed
PL	Published Letter, authorship attributed
PN	Published Note, authorship attributed

Repository Designations

CSmH	Henry E. Huntington Library, San Marino
CSt–V	Stanford University, Nathan Van Patten Library, Stanford
CoLHi	Litchfield Historical Society, Litchfield
DLC–AB	Library of Congress, Andrew Beaumont Papers, District of Columbia
DLC–AJ	Library of Congress, Andrew Jackson Papers
DLC–AJD	Library of Congress, Andrew Jackson Donelson Papers
DLC–FP	Library of Congress, Franklin Pierce Papers
DLC–GW	Library of Congress, Gideon Welles Papers
DLC–HC	Library of Congress, Henry Clay Papers
DLC–JKP	Library of Congress, James K. Polk Papers
DLC–Johnson	Library of Congress, Andrew Johnson Papers
DLC–LW	Library of Congress, Levi Woodbury Papers
DLC–Misc. Coll.	Library of Congress, Miscellaneous Collections
DLC–MVB	Library of Congress, Martin Van Buren Papers
DLC–WA	Library of Congress, William Allen Papers
DLC–WLM	Library of Congress, William L. Marcy Papers
DNA–RG 15	National Archives, Records of the Veterans Administration, District of Columbia
DNA–RG 28	National Archives, Records of the Post Office Department
DNA–RG 42	National Archives, Records of the Office of Public Buildings and Grounds

DNA–RG 45	National Archives, Naval Records Collection of the Office of Naval Records and Library
DNA–RG 46	National Archives, Records of the United States Senate
DNA–RG 49	National Archives, Records of the Bureau of Land Management
DNA–RG 56	National Archives, General Records of the Department of the Treasury
DNA–RG 59	National Archives, General Records of the Department of State
DNA–RG 60	National Archives, General Records of the Department of Justice
DNA–RG 75	National Archives, Records of the Bureau of Indian Affairs
DNA–RG 77	National Archives, Records of the Office of the Chief of Engineers
DNA–RG 92	National Archives, Records of the Office of the Quartermaster General
DNA–RG 94	National Archives, Records of the Adjutant General's Office, 1780–1917
DNA–RG 99	National Archives, Records of the Office of the Paymaster General
DNA–RG 107	National Archives, Records of the Office of the Secretary of War
DNA–RG 156	National Archives, Records of the Office of the Chief of Ordnance
DNA–RG 217	National Archives, Records of the United States General Accounting Office
GU	University of Georgia, Athens
ICHi	Chicago Historical Society, Chicago
IHi	Illinois State Historical Library, Springfield
Ia–HA	Iowa State Department of History and Archives, Des Moines
IaU	University of Iowa, Iowa City
InHi	Indiana Historical Society, Indianapolis
KyLoF	Filson Club, Louisville
MB	Boston Public Library, Boston
MH	Harvard University, Cambridge
MHi	Massachusetts Historical Society, Boston
NHi	New-York Historical Society, New York
NN–Kohns	New York Public Library, Kohns Collection, New York

NcD	Duke University, Durham
NcU	University of North Carolina, Chapel Hill
NjMoHP–LWS	Morristown National Historical Park, L. W. Smith Collection, Morristown
NjP	Princeton University, Princeton
NjP–BLL	Princeton University, Blair-Lee Letters, Princeton
PHi	Historical Society of Pennsylvania, Philadelphia
PPAmP	American Philosophical Society, Philadelphia
PT	Temple University, Philadelphia
ScCleU–JCC	Clemson University, John C. Calhoun Papers, Clemson
T–ARW	Tennessee State Library, A. R. Wynne Family Papers, Nashville
T–BG	Tennessee State Library, Boling Gordon Papers, Nashville
T–GP	Tennessee State Library, Governor's Papers
T–JPH	Tennessee State Library, John P. Heiss Papers
T–JKP	Tennessee State Library, James K. Polk Papers
T–Misc. File	Tennessee State Library, Tennessee Historical Society File
T–RG 5	Tennessee State Library, Internal Improvements Papers
T–RG 80	Tennessee State Library, Secretary of State's Papers
Tx	Texas State Library and Historical Commission, Austin
WHi	State Historical Society of Wisconsin, Madison

Published Sources

AHR	*American Historical Review*
ETHSP	*East Tennessee Historical Society's Publication*
NCHR	*North Carolina Historical Review*
PMHB	*Pennsylvania Magazine of History and Biography*
THM	*Tennessee Historical Magazine*
THQ	*Tennessee Historical Quarterly*

CHRONOLOGY

1795	Nov. 2	Born in Mecklenburg County, N.C.
1806	Fall	Moved to Maury County, Tenn.
1812	Fall	Underwent major surgery by Dr. Ephraim McDowell in Danville, Ky.
1813	July	Began study under Robert Henderson at Zion Church Academy
1816	Jan.	Entered University of North Carolina as sophomore
1818	June	Graduated from University of North Carolina
	Fall	Began reading law in office of Felix Grundy of Nashville
1819	Sept.	Elected clerk of the Tennessee Senate
1820	June	Admitted to the bar
1823	Aug.	Elected to the Tennessee House
1824	Jan. 1	Married Sarah Childress of Murfreesboro
1825	Aug.	Elected to the U.S. House
1827	Aug.	Reelected to the U.S. House
	Nov. 5	Death of his father, Samuel Polk
1829	Aug.	Reelected to the U.S. House
1831	Jan. 21	Death of his brother Franklin, aged 28
	April 12	Death of his brother Marshall, aged 26
	Aug.	Reelected to the U.S. House
	Sept. 28	Death of his brother John, aged 24
1833	Aug.	Reelected to the U.S. House
	Dec.	Chosen to chair the U.S. House Committee on Ways and Means

1834 June	Defeated by John Bell for Speaker of the U.S. House
1835 Aug.	Reelected to the U.S. House
Dec. 7	Elected Speaker of the U.S. House
1836 Aug. 6	Death of his sister Naomi, wife of Adlai O. Harris
1837 Aug.	Reelected to the U.S. House
Sept. 4	Reelected Speaker of the U.S. House
1839 Aug.	Elected Governor of Tennessee over Newton Cannon
1840 May	Withdrew candidacy for the Democratic vice-presidential nomination
1841 Aug.	Defeated in gubernatorial election by James C. Jones
1843 Aug.	Defeated in gubernatorial election by James C. Jones
Nov.	Recommended by the Tennessee Democratic State Convention to be the party's 1844 vice-presidential nominee
1844 May	Nominated for the presidency by the Democratic National Convention
Nov.	Elected President of the United States over Henry Clay
1845 Mar. 4	Inaugurated President of the United States
1849 Mar. 4	Yielded office to his successor, Zachary Taylor
June 15	Died in Nashville of cholera

Correspondence of James K. Polk

VOLUME VIII, SEPTEMBER – DECEMBER 1844

SEPTEMBER 1844

FROM ANDREW JACKSON

My dear Sir, Hermitage Septr 2nd 1844

The enclosed just received, and as requested by the author, I enclose it to you.[1] The withdrawal of P. Tyler I have no doubt will strengthen us in ohio & connecticutt—we wanted strength in ohio, where the course of Allen & Tapen against the Texean treaty had much weakened the democracy, & where Col Bentons speeches, as I am informed, has done us much harm, with his abuse of Tyler.[2] From all quarters accounts are gratifying. There are lively hopes of little Delaware & Rhode Island. If Col Thos. Marshall[3] strengthes holds out to canvass Ky, as he intends, Clay looses the state. In one county adjoining Tennessee that give owlsly[4] a majority I am creditably informed, a very wealthy man offers to pledge one of his plantations that the county will give Polk & Dallas upwards of 500 majority. N. Carolina I view amonghst the most doubtfull states. I think if the present enthuseasm can be kept up in the democracy to the election & all be brought to the polls, you will carry the state by ten thousand. Let the Texean question be kept up; and the vote of our senators againts the Treaty with the German league be fully exposed to the people.[5] The treaty which secured such important benefits to the growers of pork Tobaco, Rice, & cotton, & ensured, from the reduction of the revenue upon these articles one cent a pound to the raiser of Tobaco, perhaps more, and the aditional consumption of these articles by

27, millions of people. This conduct of our senators ought to be kept before the people (and this too, because great Britain complained of it, & would have had to reduce her Tariff on those articles or lost this trade[)]. *There never was such treachery to the laborer of the South & west, as the rejection of this treaty.* I have been greatly astonished, that the democratic papers have said so little about it. It must, when explained to our farmers, arrouse them against Whigery. Have it laid before the people. I am quite low, low & greatly debiletated, with shortness of breath that I cannot do more than walk twice across my passage without great oppression. My whole family join me in kind salutations to you & yours.

ANDREW JACKSON

ALS. DLC–JKP. Addressed to Columbia. Published in Lyon Gardiner Tyler, ed., *The Letters and Times of the Tylers* (3 vols.; Richmond and Williamsburg, Va., 1884–96), III, pp. 148–49.

1. Reference is to a letter dated August 20, 1844, from Joel B. Sutherland to Andrew Jackson. ALS. DLC–JKP.

2. John Tyler, William Allen, Benjamin Tappan, and Thomas Hart Benton. A lawyer, farmer, and stockman from Chillicothe, Ohio, Allen won election as a Democrat to one term in the U.S. House in 1833 and sat in the U.S. Senate from 1837 until 1849. A lawyer in Steubenville, Ohio, Tappan served as judge of the Fifth Ohio Circuit Court of Common Pleas in 1816 and as U.S. district judge of Ohio in 1833; he won election as a Democrat to one term in the U.S. Senate, 1839–45. He opposed slavery; but unlike his brothers, Arthur and Lewis Tappan, he rejected the abolition movement. A strong supporter of Jackson and hard money, Benton represented Missouri in the U.S. Senate for thirty years. In a letter addressed to members of the Texas Congress and published in the Washington *Globe* on April 29, 1844, he objected to the immediate annexation of Texas in the same spirit as Martin Van Buren's public letter to members of Congress of April 20, 1844. Benton's letter was followed by a "postscript" in the *Globe* on May 2, 1844. On June 13, 1844, Benton spoke for about two hours on the question of annexing Texas. He focused particularly on John Tyler's message of June 11, 1844, on that subject to the U.S. House and excoriated the administration for carrying the Texas treaty to the lower house. Benton's address of June 13, 1844, was not carried in the Washington *Globe* until June 20 and 24, at which time Francis P. Blair published the speech in full, but misdated it as June 12, 1844.

3. A Kentucky lawyer, Thomas F. Marshall served in the U.S. House from 1841 until 1843.

4. William Owsley was the Whig candidate for governor of Kentucky in 1844.

5. Reference is to a commercial treaty signed in April 1844 by the United States and the Zollverein, or German Customs Union, which had been formed in 1834. The Senate voted to table the treaty on June 15, 1844.

FROM JOHN K. KANE[1]

12 o'clock, M

My dear sir, Harrisburg, Pa. 2 Sept. 1844

We have just made the nomination of Francis R. Shunk[2] by a unanimous vote on the call of ayes and noes, 125 delegates present, absent 7. The nomination was presented by the Berks County delegation; and was received with such absolute cordiality by every one as to make the scene one of the deepest feeling. Our state is now *secure* by at least 15000: such is the concurring sentiment of all the delegates and of the many distinguished men whom the convention has brought to witness or to guide its proceedings.

An admirable letter of Mr. Dallas was presented and was ordered to a place among the proceedings.[3] It contributed not a little to the happy result.

J. K. KANE

ALS. DLC–JKP. Addressed to Columbia.

1. A Philadelphia lawyer and an ardent Jackson Democrat, John K. Kane served from 1832 until 1836 as one of the spoliation claims commissioners appointed under the authority of the 1831 convention with France. He opposed rechartering the second Bank of the United States, an unpopular position to take in Philadelphia. Appointed attorney general of Pennsylvania in 1845, Kane resigned the following year to become U.S. district judge for the eastern district of Pennsylvania, a post that he held for twelve years.

2. A lawyer from Pittsburgh, Shunk had served as clerk of the Pennsylvania House and as secretary of the commonwealth, 1839–42. Elected governor in 1844 and reelected in 1847, Shunk served from 1845 until 1848, when ill health forced him to resign.

3. A Philadelphia lawyer, George M. Dallas served as mayor of Philadelphia, 1829; U.S. Senator, 1831–33; minister to Russia, 1837–39; vice-president under Polk, 1845–49; and minister to Great Britain, 1856–61. Dallas' letter is not identified further.

FROM GEORGE M. DALLAS

No. 7

My Dear Sir, [Philadelphia, Penn.] 3rd Sept. 1844

Our organization in Pennsylvania was, yesterday, once more completed by the unanimous nomination of Mr. Shunk, at Harrisburg, amid acclamations, as our candidate for Governor.[1] I conceived this to be of the utmost importance, and directed all my efforts to attain it. He who now doubts a great democratic triumph on the 8th of October in this State, knows little or nothing of our politics. Altho' I was personally attached to Mr. Muhlenberg,[2] and very cordially sustained him, with a conviction that he would succeed handsomely, I always thought and am more perfectly satisfied that Mr. Shunk is a stronger candidate.

My recent information from Ohio is not promising. Judge Stroud, of this city,[3] before whom I am constantly practicing and whom I know to be a sincere and candid friend, though a resolute Whig, has been travelling very extensively through that State and is just returned. He tells me that his conclusion as to Penna. is that the Polk ticket will carry every thing before it; but that in Ohio appearances are in favor of the Whigs. He does not think that the democrats exhibit their usual activity there. I am the more apprehensive of the correctness of the Judge's impressions, from knowing that he is in the confidence of the Abolitionists as an anti-slavery man; while he is in fact, nothing of a political partizan.

Major Davezac who is here, just from an immense Convention held at Winchester, Virginia, brings the most confident assurance of the auspicious state of things in the ancient dominion.[4] He has been indefatigable as an eloquent missionary from Tammany Hall and has nearly worn himself out in the Empire State; nevertheless, he is on his way, in the course of the next week, to Trenton, Baltimore, Wheeling, and Pittsburg. He represents New-York as, in the estimation of Mr. Van Buren, Mr. Wright, Mr. Flagg, Gov. Marcy,[5] and all the other sagacious and reliable judges, beyond, far beyond the reach of any danger, be the gubernatorial candidate who he may. This view is corroborated by an intelligent and independent Whig gentleman, from the Genesee region, who candidly acknowledged that the republican strength had considerably increased since the last election of Governor Bouck,[6] and that Mr. Clay had really no chance whatever, no matter what might be the course of the abolitionists. In the whole of my political experience, I have always regarded the finale of a canvass in New-York as more uncertain, than in any other State. If we are to believe the best attainable intelligence, she is safe now; and certainly much may be ascribed to the recent and most effective exertions of Mr. Wright.

I have had apprehensions about the State election of Maine, which takes place on monday next, the 9th Sept., and any cold draught from that quarter would be mischievous. Mr. Green,[7] of Macon, Georgia, has just returned from thence; he was there several weeks, saw the leading republicans and the popular movements, and assures me that I may dismiss all forebodings, founded on a supposed want of organization.

The Polk-men of New-Jersey are hourly more and more sanguine. Capt. Stockton's confidence,[8] I was told to-day, had manifested itself by an offer to bet twenty-five thousand dollars on the event. He is fairly embarked. I have carefully compared the estimates as to every one of the counties, and tho' I think you will carry the State, I cannot make out a majority large enough to warrant any strong confidence. Your ticket may succeed by two or three hundred votes; it is barely possible that it may, by a thousand. We shall have little Delaware as sure as a gun.

Notwithstanding the Whig bluster and banter, there would seem to exist among them a sort of instinctive dread that, after all, you are to be elected. This has gone so far as even to anticipate your Cabinet; and one of them brought me, in pencil, yesterday, the list made out in a corner of our Exchange. It may amuse you—perhaps set you thinking usefully—if I copy it. Buchanan, Sec. of State; Dromgoole, War; Flagg, Treasury; Fairfield, Navy; Guthrie, Post Office; Walker, or Slidell, Atty. Genl.[9]

Our mass meetings are countless in number and immeasurable in size. We have them springing up as rapidly as mushrooms all around us. It is impossible to keep pace with them. Our public speakers are all complaining of their throats, and yet will not repose. They say they have got the enemy down, and intend to keep him under; they have outargued him on every point, and delight in their victory.

Have you yet determined on the course to be pursued respecting the questions propounded by our friends the naturalized gentlemen of New-York?[10]

G. M. DALLAS

ALS. DLC–JKP. Addressed to Columbia. Polk's AE on the cover states that he answered this letter on September 17, 1844; Polk's reply has not been found.

1. Following the death of Henry A. P. Muhlenberg in August 1844, Pennsylvania Democrats placed Francis R. Shunk at the head of their gubernatorial ticket; he won his race in 1844 and again in 1847. Shunk served from 1845 until 1848, when ill health forced him to resign.

2. Henry A. P. Muhlenberg was elected as a Jackson Democrat to five terms in the U.S. House, where he served from 1829 until 1838. He declined offers by Martin Van Buren to be named secretary of the navy and minister to Russia in 1837 but accepted the appointment as minister to Austria and served from 1838 to 1840. Muhlenberg, a friend to both Polk and Andrew Jackson, was nominated by the Democratic party for the governorship of Pennsylvania in 1844 but died on August 11, 1844, before the election.

3. A native of Pennsylvania and an 1817 graduate of Princeton College, George M. Stroud served in the Pennsylvania legislature in 1824. He edited three editions of *Purdon's Digest* and published *A Sketch of the Laws Relating to Slavery in the Several States of the United States of America in 1827*. He served as judge of the district court of Philadelphia.

4. Auguste D'Avezac, a Creole emigrant from Santo Domingo and brother-in-law of Edward Livingston, served as Andrew Jackson's aide-de-camp during the

War of 1812; interrupting a successful legal practice in New Orleans, D'Avezac served consular and ministerial appointments to the Netherlands and to the Kingdom of Two Sicilies during the 1830's; in 1839 he settled in New York City and in 1843 won election to the New York legislature. D'Avezac returned to the Netherlands as chargé d'affaires for five years, 1845–50. He spoke before an estimated crowd of 10,000 on August 29, 1844, at Winchester, Va.

5. Martin Van Buren, Silas Wright, Jr., Azariah C. Flagg, and William L. Marcy. Silas Wright, Jr., U.S. senator from New York from 1833 until 1844, backed Martin Van Buren for the 1844 presidential nomination, declined the second place on Polk's ticket, won election to the governorship of New York in 1844, and served in that post until 1846. A New York legislator and leader of the Albany Regency, Flagg was appointed Secretary of State by DeWitt Clinton in 1826, a position that he filled for seven years. He later served as state comptroller of New York for nine years during the 1830's and the 1840's. He was a strong opponent of the Bank of the United States. In 1846 he joined the Barnburners and eventually led that faction of the New York Democracy. A lawyer and New York politician, Marcy served as state comptroller, 1823–29; associate justice of the state supreme court, 1829–31; U.S. senator, 1831–32; Democratic governor of New York for three terms, 1833–39; secretary of war in the Polk administration, 1845–49; and secretary of state, 1853–57.

6. A farmer from Schoharie County, N.Y., William C. Bouck served as a canal commissioner for nineteen years. Defeated in his 1840 bid for the governorship, Bouck, a leader of the Hunker faction of the Democratic party, won election as governor in 1842 and served a single term.

7. Not identified further.

8. Robert F. Stockton, a naval captain from New Jersey, entered the U.S. Navy in 1811 and rose to the rank of commodore. In October 1846, while on a joint maneuver with land forces in California, he captured Los Angeles and proclaimed U.S. authority over the Mexican province and its capital. Resigning his naval commission in May 1850, he won election as a Democrat to the U.S. Senate and served from 1851 until his resignation in 1853.

9. James Buchanan, George C. Dromgoole, Azariah C. Flagg, John Fairfield, James Guthrie, Robert J. Walker, and John Slidell. Dromgoole, a Virginia lawyer, served five terms in the U.S. House, 1835–41 and 1843–47. A Maine lawyer, John Fairfield was elected as a Democrat to the U.S. House and served from 1835 until 1838, when he resigned to become governor of Maine, 1839–43. Fairfield resigned the governorship in 1843 and filled the seat of Reuel Williams in the U.S. Senate from 1843 until his death in 1847. A lawyer in Louisville, James Guthrie served in the Kentucky House, 1827–29, and Senate, 1831–40; from 1853 until 1857 he was secretary of the Treasury in the cabinet of Franklin Pierce; in 1865 he won election to the U.S. Senate and served until 1868. Pennsylvania born, Robert J. Walker moved to Natchez, Miss., in 1826 and practiced law. He served in the U.S. Senate from 1835 until 1845, when he became Polk's secretary of the Treasury. Subsequently, he served as governor of the Kansas Territory and as U.S. financial agent in Europe during the Civil War. A native of New York City, John Slidell removed to New Orleans and established a legal practice. Elected

as a States' Rights Democrat to the U.S. House, he served from 1843 to 1845. In 1845 Polk appointed him minister to Mexico, but the Mexican government refused to receive him. Later, he served in the U.S. Senate, 1853–61, before undertaking diplomatic service for the Confederate States of America.

10. Letter not found. See Polk to Dallas, August 29, 1844, and Dallas to Polk, August 7, 1844.

FROM NATHANIEL EWING[1]

Dear Sir Vincennes I[ndiana] Sept. 3d 1844

A scetch of your biography happening to fall into my hands, I find that I am better acquainted with the early history of your family than perhaps any of your immediate relatives now alive.

Your forefathers and mine emigrated together in the same ship from the North of Ireland in the year seventeen hundred an twenty seven, landed at Newcastle & settled together in the upper part of Cecil County adjoining the Pennsylvania line and Lancaster County.[2] There was a large colony composed principally of Ewings Porters Gillespies & Polks. Your great grandfather and two Grand Uncles were of the number. Of your great grandfather and one of his brothers I have no recollection. They with some of my relatives of the names of Gillespie & Porter had removed to Cumberland County near Carlisle before my time.[3] One of the brothers John Polk remained where he first settled until he died which was about the year seventeen hundred eighty three.[4] Him I well recollect as his Land & that of both my Grandfathers joined, and a constant friendly intercourse alway subsisted between the families, during their lives. On his land was the place selected by the emigrants on their first arival for a burying ground and in it is inter'd both my Grand fathers & grandmothers my Father & Mother with Uncles Aunts & cousins without number. John Polk & his family also lie there.

In the year seventeen hundred & eighty eight I found living on Cripple Creek one of the head branches of New River a numerous band of my relatives desendants of those who had removed from Cumberland County Pa. and from the old settlement in Cecil Co. Md. I understood the Polks had settled further south in Carolina. In this tour I found my relatives scattered from Prince Edward Co Va. through Bortitort Wythe Washington and down to Knoxville,[5] all the desendants of the emigrants of seventeen hundred & twenty seven. I have this date from record. One of my aunts was born on sea on their passage to America & this is the recorded year of hir birth. Here ends my knowledge of the family of the Polks except the grandsons of John Polk by his daughter Isabella who maried Thomas Grubb.[6] With those I was raised and schooled three of whome are still alive all living in Pennsylvania one in Franklin Co. & ten in Erie Co near the Town of that name. One of the latter Judge Grubb[7] is a man of six feet four & half inches high of good proportions. About ten years ago I visited the anciant site of the Emigants[8] after an absense of more than forty years. I was much surprised to find so little alteration in the superficial appearance of the country. The lands were unaltered the woodland but little deminished the only and great change was in the improvement of the soil. The fields which I had left in the most decay state of poverty I found covered with luxurient crops of clover & wheat. The tracts of land which were originally large I found divided into small ones not much exceeding one hundred acres on each of which were fine brick houses & barns and every conveniance necessary for a neat farm.

In the year seventeen hundred & seventy nine there was one of your family living at Natches, placed there by the State of Virginia as their agent to accept & pay the bills of Genl. Clark when carrying on his expedition against the british forts at Kaskaskia & Vincennes.[9] Thus I have given you my recollections & traditions of your family from their first landing in America. Your family like mine were originally from Scotlant & emigrated from that Country during the Protectorship of Cromwell.

As to our politicks in this State the parties are verry warm. I never saw the democrats so active & determined. The whigs obtained a majority in the house of representatives but that was measurably owing to the manner the districts are laid off. The democrats have the popular vote. There are also a great many who voted for whig representatives who will not vote the Clay ticket. The most of the Presbiterians are whigs but the moral charater of Clay is rather more than they can digest. The Texes question altho but little understood is a new thing and as the mass is always delighted with novelty it takes well with them, and I have no doubt of the democrats taking this State.

I have always thought and still think that the Globe & Thos. Benton[10] has done the democratic cause more injury than the partizens of Clay—their violence against Mr. Tyler disgusted many for say what place agains him.[11] The thinking & honest democrats will always feel greatfull for the servises he tendered the party by his firmness in placing his veto on the bill creating a U.S. Bank with such powers to render a representation of the people a perfect farse.[12] Instead of representing those who sent them they would become the panders of the moneyed power.

This judging harshly of my fellow citizens but in justifycation of my opinion we have only to recur to the conduct of congress at the time. The Bank obtained a recharter as far as they had power to give it and to the legislature of Pennsylvania when that same Bank obtained its charter as a bank of that State. As to this last I have some personal knowledge, I was in Pennsylvania during the canvass for Governor when Ritner was elected.[13] He lived in Washington Co. which had always before then been a democratic county untill the Bank of the U.S. under the cloak of subscribing to a turnpike Road between Washington & Pittsburgh (a road which will never yeald toll to keep itself in repair) gave them fifty thousand dollars which compleatly changed the political complextion of the county & gave it to the Whigs. I am sorry some of my relatives had a hand in this business. John Sergeant of Philadelphia[14] at the head he acted as agent for the Bank in negotiating the business. The papers from all quarters give cheering news as it regards the Presidental election. For my part I have never doubted our success. Twenty years ago I made a bet with a friend who is now dead that Henry Clay never would be President of the U.S. This Election will determine it.

NATH EWING

P.S. You will excuse my writing you on so immeterial a subject but it may perhaps tend to relieve your mind from too intense an application to politicks.

ALS. DLC–JKP. Addressed to Columbia. Polk's AE on the cover reads, "History of the Polk Family."

1. Born in Cumberland County, Penn., in 1772, Ewing moved to Vincennes in 1807 to take up his duties as receiver of the public land office. He was the president of the first bank established in Vincennes and served in the Indiana territorial legislature.

2. According to the most widely accepted genealogical study, the Polks first came to America from Northern Ireland in the 1680's and settled in Somerset County, Md.; one branch of the family then moved to Cumberland County, Penn., in the 1730's and subsequently to Mecklenberg County, N.C., in the 1750's. This study does not display, however, such documentation as might verify the movement of Polks from Somerset County, Md., to Cumberland County, Penn. See Mrs. Frank M. Angellotti, *The Polks of North Carolina and Tennessee* (Columbia, Tenn.: James K. Polk Memorial Association, 1984), pp. 2–5; reprinted from *The New England Historic Genealogical Register*, LXXVII (April, 1923), pp. 134–36.

3. Angellotti's sources indicate that Polk's paternal great grandfather, William Polk, was the father of eight children, all born in Cumberland County, Penn. According to Angellotti, William Polk's brothers remained in Maryland.

4. Ewing's meaning is that John Polk, one of the three brothers who settled in Cumberland County, Penn., remained there and did not move to North Carolina.

5. References are to the Virginia counties of Prince Edward, Botetourt, Wythe, and Washington.

6. Not identified further.

7. Reference probably is to John Grubb, a resident of Mill Creek township and an associate judge of the Erie County Court from 1820 until 1841.

8. Reference is to Ewing's former home, which was located near Carlisle in Cumberland County, Penn.

9. Reference is to George Rogers Clark's conquest of the Illinois country. He captured Fort Kaskaskia on July 4, 1778, and followed in August with the capture of the British fort at Vincennes, Ind. The fort at Vincennes was retaken by the British, but Clark recaptured it in February 1779.

10. The Washington *Globe* of April 29, 1844, published a letter from Thomas H. Benton addressed to members of the Texas Congress in which he objected to the immediate annexation of that republic. Benton's letter was followed by a "postscript" in the *Globe* on May 2, 1844.

11. Syntax garbled. After the publication of Martin Van Buren's April 27, 1844, letter on the annexation of Texas, the *Globe* defended the former president and attacked his rivals for the Democratic nomination, including John Tyler.

12. On August 16, 1841, John Tyler returned the bill entitled "An act to incorporate the subscribers to the Fiscal Bank of the United States," to the U.S. Senate with his veto.

13. Joseph Ritner. Elected to the Pennsylvania House from Washington County, Ritner served seven years in that body, including two years as its Speaker from 1826–28. He won election as governor on the Anti-masons' ticket of 1835; renominated for a second term in 1838, he lost the election to the Democratic candidate, David R. Porter.

14. An accomplished attorney, Sergeant served seven terms in the U.S. House, 1815–23, 1827–29, and 1837–41; his political affiliation changed from Federalist to National Republican to Whig, successively. He served as chief legal and political adviser to Nicholas Biddle, president of the second Bank of the United States and its successor corporation, the United States Bank of Pennsylvania, which was chartered by the Pennsylvania legislature in 1837. Biddle claimed that the Pennsylvania charter cost approximately one million dollars in loans to members of the legislature.

FROM J. G. M. RAMSEY[1]

My Dear Sir Mecklenburg Sep. 3, 1844

Your several letters of 28 & 29. ult. inclosing the copy of the sketch of 1841 came to hand an hour ago.[2] I have looked it over & at pages 8 have erased what is supposed now to be incorrect, as probably refering to Col. Wm. Polk[3] instead of E.P. & like erasures made at page 12, & above[4] you have what will probably be found to be sustained by the certificates, which have been published in the news papers. These you have doubtless preserved. I gave all that met my eye to Eastman[5] & I cannot now refer to them, but more than one of them & I think Danl. Alexander[6] if I recollect right states that he served to the end of the war & some other one I think amongst those procured by Edwin[7] in N.C. mentioned that he was after taking protection injured in a campaign against the tories. Look over the certificates & have this distinctly ascertained. I speak from memory, but can hardly be mistaken. If you find the attestations as I remember them, they can be refered to in the blanks left for that purpose. The last Jeffersonian contains another certificate from Mr. McLeary which I suppose you have seen & will have inserted in the appendix.[8] I wish my Dear Sir I was more able or that time sufficient would allow me to hope I would be able to review & improve these sheets, but as it is I could neither do you, the subject nor my self justice in my present feeble state, part of my time in bed & the other far from well. I can scarcely try to suggest how it should be done but I would somewhere say *that the certificate out of which the whole charge sprang* (that of Thos. A.) *nowhere asserts that E.P. was a tory, or bore arms against his country but that it only charged taking protection & that on learning his statements had been perverted to mean disaffection to his country he had corrected that distortion by his last certificate.*[9] I would further add the extracts from Johnsons life of Greene[10] copied here by Edwin P. & which he I hope still has showing some very strong & remarkable instances of Protection. Having not the strength to do more I therefore return the manuscript corrected at pages 8 & 12 as already indicated & hope some one of our friends will improve & amend it in a manner that will make it as perfect as possible. This will be easily done. You have Jacks certificate.[11] The manuscript gives the other quotations, correctly. You have all the certificates, & when embodied & properly connected will make the vindication complete. I have cut out the reference to *Draytons S.C.*[12] (for a reason that you would approve) at the bottom of page 7. When published the candid will be convinced but nothing can prevent the malicious from fabricating & circulating counter certificates. The comtee. ought at the conclusion to guard the public against such. Have you seen that I am accused in N.C. of forging the name of E.P. a few years back to the Meck. Dec. of In. I have had to state that 18. years ago I did have struck off a copy literal & exact of the names & words from the Raleigh Pamphlet of 1822.[13] I hope you will see my *whole* card & not portions of it only as copied in some Whig papers. My health is bad but not worse than when I last wrote. Things all look well, & accounts every where favorable & especially from all the large States, N.Y., Va. & Pa. In E.T. our friends are active. A company is organizing in Knox to go to Kingsport.[14] That will be a large meeting.

J. G. M. Ramsey

ALS. DLC–JKP. Addressed to Columbia.

1. A Knoxville physician, railroad promoter, and banker, Ramsey wrote one of the early landmarks in Tennessee historiography, *The Annals of Tennessee to the End of the Eighteenth Century* (1853). Ramsey played a key role in campaign ef-

forts mounted by Polk and his friends to refute Whig charges that Ezekiel Polk, James K. Polk's grandfather, had been a Tory during the Revolutionary War. Ramsey had supplied William H. Haywood, Jr., material with which to answer such allegations; Haywood's "Vindication" article appeared in the Washington *Globe* of September 2, 1844. A similar "Vindication," edited and vetted by Polk, appeared in the *Nashville Union* of September 11, 1844; subsequently at Polk's urging the Nashville Democratic Central Committee issued a sixteen-page *Vindication* pamphlet, which was little more than a reprint of the *Nashville Union* "Vindication" article.

2. Neither the enclosed "Vindication," written in 1841 by Ramsey, nor Polk's correspondence of August 28 and 29, 1844, has been found.

3. A son of Thomas Polk and a nephew of Ezekiel Polk, William Polk of Raleigh, N.C., served as a colonel in the Revolutionary War and later became a successful businessman and a member of the North Carolina House, 1785–87 and 1790. A "Colonel Polk" commanded patriot forces at the Battle of Eutaw Springs, S.C., on September 8, 1781.

4. Above the place and date line of his letter, Ramsey wrote the following notation suggesting an alteration in the text of his 1841 "Vindication" of Ezekiel Polk: "Instead of the erased lines the following might be inserted if the attestations are as I recollect them. A. on page 8) 'According to the statements of Daniel Alexander & pages of the appendix it will be seen that he continued the firm friend of the cause of his country & of freedom to the close of the war. It is believed that he was with Col. Wm. Polk at the victory of Eutaw Springs & it is attested at page of the apendex that he served against the tories at .'"

5. E. G. Eastman established the Knoxville *Argus,* a Democratic newspaper, in 1839; he edited the *Nashville Union* from 1847 until 1849.

6. A native of Mecklenburg County, N.C., Daniel Alexander had settled in Fayette County, Tenn., after the Revolutionary War. In his statement, dated July 1844, Alexander, then eighty-seven years old, defended Ezekiel Polk's war record. While admitting that Ezekiel Polk had taken protection from the British, Alexander described Ezekiel and the Polk family as "Good Whigs of Seventy Six" and pointed out that *"it was considered by a majority of the Whigs as necessary, and not improper in those living near the encampment, and owning large property to take the benefit of the protection and thereby save their property from destruction."* For the full text of his statement, see the *Nashville Union,* August 6, 1844.

7. A Hardeman County lawyer and farmer, Edwin F. Polk was the youngest child of Ezekiel Polk and was twenty-two years younger than his nephew, James K. Polk.

8. Reference is to the Charlotte *Mecklenburg Jeffersonian.* Michael McLeary, a resident of Mecklenburg County, N.C., and a veteran of the Revolutionary War, served several terms in the North Carolina Senate, 1819–24 and 1826. His statement in support of Ezekiel Polk appeared in William Haywood's "Vindication," the *Nashville Union* article, and the Nashville *Vindication* pamphlet.

9. Thomas Alexander's statement of June 19, 1841, was widely published in

Whig papers as evidence that Ezekiel Polk was a Tory. Alexander, who had served under Ezekiel Polk in the militia, asserted that after two early campaigns, Ezekiel "did nothing to favor the Whigs during the war." He also noted that Ezekiel Polk had taken protection from the British. Democrats countered with a statement dated August 5, 1844, in which Alexander testified that Ezekiel Polk "never took sides in any shape, manner or form against his country."

10. Reference is to William Johnson, *Sketches of the Life and Correspondence of Nathanael Greene, Major General of the Armies of the United States, in the War of the Revolution*(1822).

11. Captain James Jack carried the Mecklenburg Declaration of Independence to the Continental Congress. His testimony, given December 7, 1819, was printed in both the Haywood "Vindication" article and the Nashville *Vindication* pamphlet.

12. Reference is to John Drayton, *A View of South Carolina*(1803). Ramsey's deletion of the Drayton reference is not further identified.

13. On May 19–20, 1775, Mecklenburg County militia delegates gathered at Charlotte, N.C., and declared their constituents' independence in a set of resolves that came to be known as the Mecklenburg Declaration of Independence. In 1826 Ramsey printed a copy of the Mecklenburg Declaration entitled "Declaration of Independence by the Citizens of Mecklenburg County, North Carolina." In his "card" Ramsey stated that his intention in printing a copy of the Declaration had been to provide a copy of the text of the principal resolutions. He added that he had included a list of participants from an earlier pamphlet which named those who had actively supported the cause; but he insisted that he had never claimed that this list was either a list of delegates or a list of the Declaration's signers. The Raleigh Pamphlet of 1822 was a reprint of documents first published in the Raleigh *Register* of April 30, 1819.

14. Reference is to a Democratic mass meeting held in Kingsport, Tenn., on September 12, 1844.

FROM JOHN P. GORDON[1]

Kenton, Ohio, September 4, 1844

Gordon solicits Polk's aid in retaining his appointment as postmaster of Kenton. He expresses fear that the recent North–South split in the Methodist Episcopal Church portends a like division of the nation.[2]

ALS. DLC–JKP. Addressed to Columbia. Marked "P.M. Please Forward."

1. John P. Gordon served as postmaster of Kenton, Ohio, from April 22, 1843, until September 16, 1846.

2. Convened in New York City in May 1844, the General Conference of the Methodist Episcopal Church became embroiled in the issue of slavery. A plan of separation, adopted by the conference, led to the organization of the Methodist Episcopal Church, South, at a conference held in Louisiville, Ky., in May 1845. The northern and western conferences of the church continued as the Methodist Episcopal Church.

FROM CAVE JOHNSON[1]

Wednesday morning
Dear Sir, Clarksville Sept. 4 [1844][2]

I was with Coe & Caruthers,[3] yesterday & the day before at Springfield. Henry[4] is reported sick. He is advertised for E. Ten. Starts at Cross-plains on the 14th Sept. & at Jasper the 20th. If it is possible Barclay Martin should follow or Kible or some one who can ridicule & laugh him out of countenance.[5] Cheatham[6] & myself meets at Waverly on Friday on our way to the district. I cannot yet find out anything of my appointments. I am pressed to go to Sumner & Smith & into Kentucky. Boyd[7] says at the great mass meeting at Princeton 26th they are likely to be without speakers & begs for Nicholson,[8] Martin or myself, I have sent his letter to Genl. Armstrong.[9] I can scarcely find time for answers to the pressing invitations.

Coe beat Caruthers badly at Springfield as I did also at night. Coe stated in strong language your vote for the pension law of 1832. Cheatham had the Register of debates[10] and read your vote agt. the *House* Bill of 1832, contradicting Coe, which produced great shouts in the whig ranks & I was afraid would produce difficulties between Coe and Cheatham. I rather forced my way on the stand & shewed that the *House* Bill you had voted agt. & was defeated in the Senate and that you voted for the Senate Bill which became the law. This was a damper upon them. I kept cool & kept Coe quiet & all went off admirably. An exposition should be made of these two Bills & your course. Caruthers was astonished at my explanation & said other explanations had been given by others that he had met.

The same difficulty occurred in Indiana, of which I was informed by letter asking explanation. If any journals can be found I will make a proper exposition for the Union.[11] If not it must be attended to at Columbia.

C. JOHNSON

[P.S.] My jaws are still much swollen but without pain.

ALS. DLC–JKP. Addressed to Columbia.

1. One of Polk's closest friends and political allies, Cave Johnson practiced law in Clarksville and served in the U.S. House as a Democrat, 1829–37 and 1839–45. Polk appointed him postmaster general in 1845.

2. Date identified through content analysis.

3. Levin H. Coe and Robert L. Caruthers. A popular lawyer and Democrat from Somerville, Coe sat two terms in the Tennessee Senate, 1837–41, and

presided over that body as Speaker during the latter part of his second term. A Whig lawyer in Lebanon, Caruthers represented Wilson County for one term in the Tennessee House, 1835–37, and sat in the U.S. House for a single term, 1841–43.

4. Gustavus A. Henry, Kentucky lawyer, businessman, and Whig, served one term in the Kentucky legislature, 1831–33, before moving to Clarksville, Tenn.; he won election to the electoral colleges of 1840, 1844, 1852, but lost bids for a seat in the U.S. House in 1841 and for the governorship in 1853.

5. Barkly Martin and Edwin A. Keeble. A Columbia lawyer and Democrat, Martin served three terms in the Tennessee House, 1839–41, 1847–49, and 1851–53, and sat for one term in the Tennessee Senate, 1841–43. He won election to the U.S. House and served from 1845 until 1847. A lawyer and editor of the Murfreesboro *Monitor*, Keeble served as mayor of Murfreesboro in 1828 and 1855, campaigned successfully as a Democratic presidential elector in 1856, and represented Tennessee in the Confederate Congress in 1864 and 1865.

6. Leonard P. Cheatham, Nashville lawyer and popular stump speaker, presided over the Democratic State convention held in Nashville on November 23, 1843.

7. Linn Boyd, a Democrat from Kentucky, served several terms in the U.S. House, 1835–37 and 1839–55.

8. A. O. P. Nicholson, Democratic member of the Tennessee House from Maury County, 1833–37, and of the Tennessee Senate, 1843–45, served an interim appointment in the U.S. Senate from December 1840 until February 1842. He moved to Nashville in 1844 and edited the *Nashville Union* before being named president of the Bank of Tennessee in 1846.

9. Robert Armstrong served as Nashville's postmaster from 1829 until 1845. An unsuccessful candidate for governor in 1837, he remained politically active and coordinated Polk's three gubernatorial campaigns. An officer in the War of 1812, Armstrong commanded a brigade of Tennessee militia in the Second Seminole War.

10. Until superceded in 1837 by the *Congressional Globe,* the *Register of Debates in Congress,* published by Joseph Gales, Jr., and William W. Seaton, provided daily coverage of congressional proceedings.

11. The *Nashville Union* of September 10, 1844, carried a full explanation of Polk's votes on the pension bills of 1832. Polk voted against the House bill "Because it did not embrace *all* the old soldiers who deserved pensions." The *Union* further reported Polk's votes on all pension bills up to 1832. "We shall now see whether Gov. Polk 'voted against all the pension laws *up to* 1832,' as charged at Springfield."

FROM J. G. M. RAMSEY

My Dear Sir Mecklenburg Sep. 4, 1844

The mail of this morning which carried my letter to you brought me one from Senator Haywood—I hasten to have it copied.[1]

Raleigh 24 Aug 1844

Dr J. G. M. Ramsey
Dear Sir.

Your several favours have remained unanswered but not unheeded. I have this day finished a vindication of E. Polk and the Central Com: composed of about 20 of our leading men have approved it and sent it to be published. As our papers are weekly papers and it would not come forth under 10 days we have sent the MS. to the *Globe* and it will be published in Dollar Globe & otherwise as our friends there may approve. I have directed Mr. Blair to send one to you *forthwith.*[2] I have been very constantly (& too closely) engaged for my health in an effort to rally our party & also to prepare this vindication and find I am broken down in health & unfit even to render a suitable return at present for your acceptable favours.

I shall be gratified to learn that my effort to vindicate E.P.'s fame & to serve my excellent friend J.K.P. is approved by you. I should have forwarded the M.S. to you for criticism & correction but it is so late in the campaign I could not do it. The same cause has operated against its revisal & my shortening it. Tho: our friends here kindly say it is short enough already. I look for its appearance with some anxiety. It not only exhibits our proofs but reviews that of the enemy. The Mecklenburg Decn. was not "signed" by any one. I have exposed that mistake. Contrary to my judgment, Mr. Saunders used part of the evidence at Charlotte in his speech, but perhaps he was right. *His* name does not appear in this vindication.[3] It seemed better to notice it in the form of a request from Central Com: to *me* to compile the evidence & write the vindication of the State & her departed son and that I should report to *the committee.* That is the form adopted.

I shall be glad to hear from you and will endeavor to show myself a better correspondent. I have written our friend J.K.P. to day.[4]

very truly
Will. H. Haywood

P.S. It is submitted to your discretion to publish an appendix or not. I relied upon you for it & it has not reached me. If you should do so I beg you will look carefully over Otho H. Williams narrative published in the appendix to "Johnson's Life of Green" to show the destitute & miserable conditions of Mecklenburg when Cornwallis was at Charlotte so that Whigs were obliged to take protection. Also ascertain how long Cornwallis *was at Charlotte. It was but a very short time.*[5]

I have omitted it in the *vindication* in the hurry of its preparation. W.H.H.

Not knowing but W.H.'s letter to you may not yet have come to hand I have thought best to send you the above copy of his to me. The plan adopted I conceive to be the best possible as giving the vindication an extensive reading & securing to it also the highest confidence. I answered him by this days (the 5th Sep.) mail—informed him how much obliged Gov. Polks friends were by his effort to vindicate E.P.s fame & memory—

that his plan of bringing it before the public was the best possible—that from one of Genl. Saunders letters I had supposed his speech at Charlotte would be considered an ample vindication (& so Edwin Polk informed me also was the impression at Charlotte when he left there) that if he had accompanied his paper with all the proofs I had furnished him with those afterwards procured in N.C. & also those recently published in the Nashville Union[6] the vindication would be complete, but that to make it more perfect I now sent to him lengthy & copious extracts from the histories refered to giving the Vol. & pages—showing the great extremites to which the Whigs in the Southern States were driven after the fall of Charleston, many & remarkable instances of the best Whig Commanders with their entire Regiments taking protection & even Commissions from the British Commandants, & that at the close of the war when laws were passed confiscating the property of the *tories,* those who had been compelled involuntarily to take protection did not suffer confiscation, nor lose the confidence nor esteem, nor gratitude of their contrymen—suggesting such comments upon these extracts as more time & better health would have allowed me to make—& requesting him to make them & forward immediately to the Globe for the succeeding number. I also answered his enquiry by extracts about the circumstances detailed in Otho Williams appendix to the Life of Greene, which happily is in my library & such other matters as occured to me. I did not mention that a Tennessee vindication was being prepared, & I hasten this letter now so as that being informed of Haywood's paper being prepared & circulated as extensively as it will be by going into the Dollar Globe you may be the better able to decide whether another will be really necessary. If as Haywood writes me a copy is *forthwith* sent to me I must receive it in a day or two & will then after examining it with great care write you immediately, pointing out its defects or omissions if it has any & suggesting the improvement of additions that may occur to me. Let me here say that as H. may not have seen the certificates lately published in Tennessee it will be well to forward printed copies of them either to him of directly to the Globe. My copies were handed to Eastman or distributed elsewhere, so that I had none to send him to day, but I mentioned them to him as being much to the point.

I received to day from Gen. R.M.S. a letter informing me that W.H.'s vindication would soon be out—that they had found in the journals of State that E.P. was appointed *Col. by the Legislature of N.C. immediately after the war.* I hope they will make the necessary & natural inferences from & comments upon this important fact.

All accounts from every where are good—very good. The Whigs hereabouts are desperate & more abusive (I mean the leaders) than ever. This augurs well. Saunders writes that they the Whigs are much disappointed about the vote of N.C.[7] & that the Democrats are making a noble rally for Nov. I am still unwell, but will write you if any thing occurs to make it necessary in a few days again.

J. G. M. RAMSEY

ALS. DLC–JKP. Addressed to Columbia.

1. See J. G. M. Ramsey to Polk, September 3, 1844. William H. Haywood, Jr., served several terms in the North Carolina House of Commons; elected as a Democrat to the U.S. Senate in 1843, he served until 1846, when he resigned in protest to unacceptable instructions issued by the state legislature. The text of Haywood's letter to Ramsey, printed below is in an unidentified hand; Ramsey resumed writing below Haywood's postscript.

2. Commissioned by the North Carolina Democratic Central Committee, Haywood prepared a *"Vindication"* article that appeared in the Washington *Globe* of September 2, 1844. Founder and editor of the Washington *Globe* from 1830 until 1845, Francis Preston Blair was one of the leading spokesmen of Jacksonian Democrats; Blair's grudging support of the ticket in 1844 led to the founding of the pro-administration Washington *Union.*

3. Reference is to Romulus M. Saunders' speech at the Democratic barbacue held in Charlotte, N.C., on July 23, 1844. A lawyer active in North Carolina politics since 1815, Saunders lost his bid for the governorship in 1840; having previously served three terms in the U.S. House, 1821–27, he returned to that body and served two more terms, 1841–45. In his letter to Polk of July 29, 1844, Ramsey reported that Haywood and Saunders would jointly publish a vindication of Ezekiel Polk. ALS. DLC–JKP. The authorship of the North Carolina "Vindication," however, was solely attributed to Haywood.

4. Letter not found.

5. Reference is to Otho Holland Williams, "A Narrative of the Campaign of 1780," which appeared as an appendix to William Johnson, *Sketches of the Life and Correspondence of Nathanael Greene, Major General of the Armies of the United States, in the War of the Revolution* (1822). Following his arrival in America in 1776, Charles, second Earl and first Marquis Cornwallis, served in a series of military campaigns in the northern colonies. After the surrender of Charleston in May 1780, Sir Henry Clinton, the British commander-in-chief, returned north and left Cornwallis in charge of military operations in the southern colonies. In late 1780 Cornwallis' army occupied the Charlotte area for several weeks.

6. In early August the *Nashville Union* published a series of testimonials defending the Revolutionary War record of Ezekiel Polk; for statements by George Alexander, John Smith, Thomas Gribble, and Daniel Alexander, see the *Nashville Union,* August 3 and 6, 1844.

7. Saunders' reference probably is to North Carolina's state elections held on August 1, 1844.

FROM JOHN STAATS[1]

Dr. Sir, Geneva, Ontario Co. N.Y. Sept. 4th 1844

In your letter to the citizens of Cincinnati, under date of April 28th 1844, you say: "I have no hesitation in declaring, that I am in favor of the *immediate reannexation of Texas* to the territory and government of the United States."[2]

As different and opposite constructions are put upon this declaration by Democrats and Whigs, will you please to state under what circumstances and upon what conditions you are in favor of such reannexation?

An early answer is desired.

JOHN STAATS

[P.S.] I hope you will not consider the foregoing impertinant. My object is to take away all subterfuge and quibbling from the Whigs on the subject of your declaration. They contend that you are in favor of "immediate" annexation on *any* terms, and without regard to circumstances or consequences. The only seeming ground they have, (and it has great influence with a certain class, and with some even in our own ranks,) is the word *"immediate,"* "immediate reannexation." The Democrats say that you are in favor of the annexation of Texas upon the same conditions and manner as Mr. Clay has stated in his last letter on this subject, viz: "without dishonor, without war, with the common consent of the Union [and][3] upon just and fair terms."[4] We, at the north, cannot [ta]ke any other course. It is or has been, an embarrassing question with many of our Democrats. Mr. Clay's letter has given us larger scope in contending with our antagonists, whilst it has produced much confusion amongst them, and their last resort is quibbling. New York will, without a doubt, give you a large majority. The newspapers will, to some extent, give you an idea how much enthusiasm prevails in your favor here. If you deem proper to return an answer with a view to publication, let it be as soon as possible, so that it may be of avail before the election in Novr. I am a Physician by profession and you may address me as such. Wishing you a triumphant election, and prosperity in private life.... John Staats

ALS. DLC–JKP. Addressed to Columbia. Postscript marked "private" and written on a separate sheet.

1. John Staats was a physician and member of the Medical Society of Ontario County, N.Y.

2. See Polk to Salmon P. Chase et al., April 23, 1844. Polk's letter was printed in the *Nashville Union* of April 28, 1844.

3. Manuscript damaged.

4. Quotation is from Henry Clay's second Alabama letter, which was addressed to Thomas M. Peters and John M. Jackson and was dated July 27, 1844; the Tuscumbia *North Alabamian* published Clay's letter on August 16, 1844. His first Alabama letter was addressed to Stephen F. Miller, editor of the Tuscaloosa *Independent Monitor*, and was dated July 1, 1844. In his second Alabama letter, Clay came out in favor of the eventual annexation of Texas, without war and with the consent of the Union. He further argued that it was unwise to link the questions of slavery and annexation because slavery was a temporary institution, one which was destined to extinction. For the texts of Clay's two Alabama letters, see *Niles' National Register*, August 3 and 31, 1844.

FROM PATRICK COLLINS[1]

Honored & Respected Sir Cincinnati Septr. 5th 1844

Although personally a stranger to you, I Take the liberty to address you this line the object of which is to encourage your hopes in the triumphs which await you next November as the Champion & chief of the lion hearted Democracy of the land.

I am an eye witness of the movements of the Democracy of Ohio & Indiana since the Baltimore nominations of last May. It has been my lot to witness the first meeting that I believe was held in the Valley of the Mississippi responding to the nomination of "Polk & Dallas," which took place in the City of Columbus, Ohio, on the 3rd of last June, and have had the honour to make the opening speech on that occasion, and from that day, until this, I have traversed most of the Counties in Ohio [and] beheld with pleasure the mighty gatherings of her freemen & their thorough & fixed resolve to battle

"For young Hickory
Dallas, Tod[2] & Victory."

I have had the honor also to accompany Gen. Cass[3] to Indianapolis where he was met perhaps by Twenty thousand Hoosiers. I have been in different parts of that State & the popular enthusiasm & determination is admirable. Gov. Whitcomb,[4] told me, they would carry the State for "Polk & Dallas" by at least 5000 Majority, as the abolitionists of that State are resolved to vote for *"Birney."*[5] Here, in Ohio, they are in like manner determined to vote for Birney. They are Three thousand in Indiana & Six thousand in this State. From my own personal observation; as well as from all the opinions I could collect, Ohio, will give a Democratic Majority of at least *Ten thousand* although some think Twenty & some think Thirty thousand. There [are] at least Twenty or Thirty thousand more Naturalized Citizens in this State at present than in 1840. I should suppose the number of Naturalized Citizens in Ohio is Sixty or Seventy thousand and nineteen out of every twenty of them are Democrats. In Several of these Meetings, (all of which I had the honour to address) I have seen 60 or 70 "Straightouts" so called because they voted for Gen. Harrison in 1840 and now they go for "Polk & Dallas." I have met with several of the stump speakers of 1840, who were then flaming Whigs—now thorough going Democrats &c &c. Sir, these are a few of the many reasons Why I consider your triumph, which is the triumph of the Democracy as certain in Ohio & Indiana at least. I have in my desk letters of invitation from Michigan the Valley of the Wabash Virginia & from 40 Counties in Ohio. As I have "burned the candle, I will burn the inch"[6] until the Campaign is over. "Mass Meetings" are being held all over this part. I will be at the great Meeting at Wheeling Va. on the 12th Inst. from thence through Eastern Ohio, to Cleaveland, thence to Terrehaute Ind. & I expect to hear some shouts for "Polk & Dallas." I am an Irishman by birth. I do not believe there are a dozen Irish Whigs in Ohio. If at any time you should be pleased to hear from me again, I should be happy to know it. My address is Patrick Collins Cincinnati.

PATRICK COLLINS

ALS. DLC–JKP. Addressed to Near Nashville.

1. Patrick Collins was a school teacher in Cincinnati, Ohio; in 1845 he received an appointment from Polk to be surveyor of the port of Cincinnati.

2. A Democrat, David Tod ran unsuccessfully for the Ohio governorship in 1844 and 1846, served as U.S. minister to Brazil from 1847 to 1851, and in 1862 won the governorship of Ohio.

3. Lewis Cass, presidential nominee of the Democracy in 1848, served as governor of the Michigan Territory, 1813–31; U.S. secretary of war, 1831–36; U.S. minister to France, 1836–42; U.S. senator from Michigan,1845–48 and 1851–57; and U.S. secretary of state, 1857–60.

4. A lawyer from Terre Haute, Ind., James Whitcomb served as a member of the Indiana Senate, 1830–36, and as governor, 1843–49. From 1849 until his death in 1852, Whitcomb sat in the U.S. Senate as a Democrat.

5. A native of Kentucky and a graduate of Princeton University, James G. Birney practiced law in Alabama and Kentucky prior to his founding the *Philanthropist* in 1836; he moved his anti-slavery operation from Ohio to New York in 1837 and headed the Liberty Party's presidential tickets of 1840 and 1844.

6. Quotation not identified.

FROM ALBERT GALLUP[1]

Dr. Sir Albany Sep't 5, 1844

The State convention has nominated S. Wright for Gov. & Addison Gardner for Liu't.[2] The ticket is a strong one. Probably the strongest that could have been made. The State of N.Y. is safe beyond the reach of a contingency. Gov. Bouck has been shabbily treated in certain quarters but feels as none but a democrat can feel; that the success of Republican principles is paramount to that of any individual.[3] He is satisfied—so are his friends. Whig stock is below par this morning. The Whigs are aghast at the nomination. They were not at all pleased with the "god-like"[4] when here. He spoke over 2 hours & did not utter the name of Henry Clay.

He could not have been much flattered with his own reception here. He peregrinated through the most of our principal streets, but no one smiled upon him—no one cried God save him. His speech was a stale one, & the meeting flat & unprofitable. You can put us down for 20,000. We will have a mass meeting here in all the current month. It will take all the wind out of the whig sails, & show such a mass of democrats as was never looked upon before in this section of the State.

ALBERT GALLUP

ALS. DLC–JKP. Addressed to Columbia.

1. A lawyer, Gallup served one term in Congress, 1837–39; Polk appointed him collector of customs for Albany, N.Y.

2. Silas Wright, Jr., and Addison Gardiner. Gardiner, a lawyer from New York, served as lieutenant governor, 1844–47; resigned to become judge of the N.Y. Court of Appeals, 1847–55; and presided over that court, 1854–55.

3. See Gallup to Polk, August 14, 1844.

4. Reference is to Daniel Webster, who delivered an address at a Whig mass meeting held in Albany, N.Y., on August 27, 1844.

FROM ROBERT P. FLENNIKEN[1]

Uniontown, Penn. September 6, 1844

Flenniken reports that he has just returned from the Democratic convention at Harrisburg, where delegates met on September 2 to select a candidate in place of Muhlenberg.[2] He emphasizes that harmony prevailed at the convention and assures Polk that Francis Shunk, the convention's nominee for governor, will carry the state by a majority of 20,000. "The moral influence of such a majority," he adds, "cannot fail of its effect throughout the Union." Polk's prospects in New Jersey are excellent, and if Maryland Democrats succeed in electing their candidate for governor, the electors are safe in November. Although Clay "represents a powerfull interest in this country consisting of the money power," Flenniken believes that efforts of "the hardy yeomanry" will ensure Polk's election.

ALS. DLC–JKP. Addressed to Columbia.

1. Robert P. Flenniken represented Fayette County in the Pennsylvania House in 1838 and 1840–41. Polk appointed him chargé d'affaires for Denmark in January 1847.

2. Reference is to the recent death of Henry A. P. Muhlenberg, the Democratic candidate for governor.

FROM ALLEN McLANE[1]

Respected Sir. Wilmington D. Sept. 6th 1844

Please accept my sincere thanks for your answer to my letter in June last.[2] We are doing all we can in little Delaware, but having the Patronage of the State and General Governments opposed to us, it is very much of an up hill business.

If Mr. Tyler is really anxious to defeat Mr. Clay, it is most extraordinary that he does not aid us. If we could get the Patronage of the Custom House in this District much could be done. Fifty votes might give us the State. In 1842 we lost it by only nine.

I have learned accidentally that a letter has been addressed to you by three Whigs of this city viz. Wm. H. Griffin, Wm. McCleeze, and George Richardson.[3] I am ignorant of its import, but take the liberty of stating to you the Politics of the signers, that you may be upon your guard if any fraud is contemplated.

ALLEN MCLANE

[P.S.] I would be pleased to have favourable accounts from Tennessee.

ALS. DLC–JKP. Addressed to Columbia.

1. A physician in Wilmington, Del., Allen McLane served as one of the first mayors of that city; he was the brother of Louis McLane.

2. McLane wrote Polk on May 31, 1844. Polk's AE on the cover states that he answered this letter on June 21, 1844; Polk's reply has not been found.

3. Reference is to the letter of George Richardson, W. H. Griffin, and William K. McClees to Polk, September 5, 1844.

FROM WILLIAM C. BOUCK

Dr. Sir Albany Sept. 7h 1844

Our state convention met on the 4h Inst. and nominated Silas Wright for Gov. and Addison Gardner[1] for Leiut. Gov.

A small fraction of the democratic party were hostile to my nomination in 1840, and also in 1842. In 1840 the Maj. against Mr. Van Buren was in this state 13,000 and against me 5,000. In 1842 I was unanimously nominated and Elected by 22,000 majority. During the Session of 1843 I made more than 1500 appointments out of more than 10,000 applications; the rush for office was unprecedented; nothing like it was ever seen before in this state.

The Small section of the party who were opposed to me in 1840 & 42, rallied the disappointed men, made a noise throughout the state, created a panic in the public mind in regard to myself, and with the apparently unauthorised use of Mr. Wright's name, succeeded in getting a majority of delegates in the state convention against me. Under such circumstances, and with the view of uniting the party I requested my friends not to present my name; this they did with the exception of 30 who were instructed to vote for me in any event. The nomination of Mr. Wright was finally unanimously concurred in, he will be supported by all my friends, and no doubt elected. His views in regard to the Texas question, are supposed not to accord with yours, and may embarrass us some.

In view of the importance of the Election, and knowing there were 10,000 men in the state who were disappointed applicants, I requested my friends last April to permit me to withdraw; and one of them said to Mr. Wright that if he desired the nomination I would unite in his support. He positively declined to be a Candidate on several occasions, and I was consequently kept in the field. After his refusal to accept the Baltimore nomination,[2] no body dreamed that he would accept that for Governor.

I send you the Argus which contains his last letter and the authorised remarks of the Editor[3]; which will show you his and my position before the public. Although he said that he would not be a competitor before the people, nor the convention; yet not a newspaper reached him which did not show him that he was my competitor before the people. He sent no letter to the convention, and was my competitor there. These are matters that cannot fail to affect the fame of Mr. Wright, but they will not be canvassed until after the election. I have the gratification to know that not a word of complaint is uttered against my administration, except from the applicants for office.

There is a section of the party in this state, that were to say the least of it, cold towards your nomination, & at one period gravely discussed the question whether it would not be best for them in regard to the future, to have you defeated. Hence the confidential circular which you have doubtless seen.[4] This scheme was discovered in its bud, and exploded. These men were the peculiar friends of Mr. Wright, and his nomination, removes all difficulty. We cannot I think fail to carry the state by a large majority.

I have during forty years of active life been the warm supporter of Van Buren; but many of my friends prefer your nomination to his, and I have no doubt we can give you a larger vote than we could him.

You will pardon me for trobling you with this long letter, my only object is to apprise you of the position of things in this state, supposing that you had heard of dissentions in the party, and might feel some apprehensions about the result.

My Brother[5] who was in Congress with you desires to be remembered to you; you have not a warmer friend in this state.

WM. C. BOUCK

ALS. DLC–JKP. Addressed to Columbia and marked *"private."*

1. Addison Gardiner.

2. In a letter to the Democratic National Convention dated May 29, 1844, Silas Wright, Jr., declined the vice presidential nomination.

3. Edwin Croswell edited the *Albany Argus* from 1823 to 1854.

4. George P. Barker, William Cullen Bryant, Isaac Townsend, J. W. Edmonds, Theodore Sedgwick, Thomas W. Tucker, and David D. Field were signers of a confidential circular letter that surfaced in New York in late July 1844. The circular supported Polk and Dallas but rejected the immediate annexation of Texas.

5. Joseph Bouck of Middleburg, N.Y., served one term in the U.S. House, 1831–33.

FROM WILLIAM TYACK[1]

My Dear Sir New York Sept. 7, 1844

I arrived home on the Monday after I left Nashville with the same Mail in 7 days, in good Health & spirits. The enthusiasm is intense on the whole Road. Hickory Trees were up and others being Raised at almost every place where there was a Store or Blacksmith shop, and where there was a Coon Pole there was Sure to be a Hickory Pole much Higher. Polk stalks on the Fences, and over the doors, in their Travelling Wagons, & Democracy. I stated to you that N. York was safe for 20,000. We shall give I think nearer 50. We are now all united. We have Nominated Silas Wright for Govr. and Addison Gardner[2] for Lt. Governor. A very strong Ticket, that sweeps all before it. Although I must say we have not treated Governor Bouck with Justice, yet he and his Friends must submit for the General Good. The Tyler Custom House Clique have now hauled down their Colours and wish to Compromise, and are to have what they can.[3] A Union Meeting of themselves with the Democrats, to enable them to hold their situations in the Customs House. I say let them come if they Choose, although we do not want them. We are strong enough without them, but we must watch them. They are of the Native American Party & Tyler Men. But the Native American Party here is entirely dead. We are all alive to Mass Meetings here. We had a Glorious Time at Trenton—New Jersey is as I informed you safe and will give a Handsome Majority for Col. Polk. Old Connecticut is doing well.

We also had a Glorious Time of Rhode Island Mass Meeting. The Poor Rhotes had their Prison Guarded with a Heavy Park of Artillery and a Strong Body of Infantry. All passed off without the least Disturbance although they were very anxious to provoke one. I advise our Friends to say nothing about Dor[4] untill after Col. Polk is Elected President. Then we will take up the Matter in earnest, and Dor will yet be the Govr. of Rhode Island. We are all alive to Mass Meetings here. Perfect Harmony I believe reigns throu out the whole Democratick Ranks. The Poor Coon Whigs look very Blue at our Proceedings. They cannot withstand the Mighty Torrent of Democracy that is Sweeping them out of Power so Rapidly. But after this Campaign I will give them a quarter of a Century at least to Rest. Nothing can look better here. We have a Mass Meeting in our Congressional District this Week. We intend to keep Moving. We are to have a Mass Meeting, sometimes this month which we intend shall be a Great Gathering. While I am writing I have this Moment Recvd an Invitation to attend the Mass Meeting at Tarrytown W. Chester County 30 Miles from this City—on the spot where Major Andre was taken in the Revolution.[5] I hope you arrived home safely, and that your Amiable Lady Mrs. Polk[6] is in Good Health, for I do assure her that all is Safe an Sure as She and you live.

I cannot expect you to write me. You have so much to do where you are obliged to answer. But Sir I will Keep you advised of Matters and things Generally.

Will you please to accept of my sincere Regard for the future Welfare, Prosperity and Hapiness of yourself, your Amiable Lady, Family, and all Friends.

WILLIAM TYACK

[P.S.] The Texas Fever is raging here to a great extent with strong symtoms of an Oregan Charracter.

ALS. DLC–JKP. Addressed to Columbia.

1. William Tyack, associated with the "Hunker" faction of the New York Democracy, resigned his post as master warden for the Port of New York to campaign for Polk in 1844; he served as president of the Polk and Dallas Association of New York City and spoke at the Democratic mass meeting in Nashville of August 15, 1844.

2. Addison Gardiner.

3. At the urging of Robert Tyler, Joel B. Sutherland, and John Lorimer Graham, John Tyler appointed Cornelius P. Van Ness in place of Edward Curtis as head of the Customs House in New York City. Van Ness, a strong Tyler Supporter, dismissed some sixty Whigs employed in the Customs House. Afterward, on August 21, 1844, Tyler announced his withdrawal from the presidential contest in a notice published in the Washington *Madisonian*.

4. Popular dissatisfaction with suffrage restrictions led to Rhode Island's "Dorr Rebellion" of 1841–42. In late 1841 a popular but extralegal convention framed and ratified a "People's Constitution," which provided for white manhood suffrage and new state elections; Thomas W. Dorr won the new constitution's gubernatorial election. The legislature declared the new constitution illegal and sponsored a regularly scheduled spring election under authority of the colonial charter of 1663. Incumbent governor, Samuel W. King, gained reelection under the old charter. Both Dorr and King applied to John Tyler for military aid. In a letter dated April 11, 1842, Tyler assured King that if an actual insurrection were raised against the charter government, the general government would furnish that protection guaranteed to each state under Article 4, Section 4 of the U.S. Constitution. In a private letter of May 9, 1842, Tyler urged King to exercise conciliation and restraint, including a general amnesty and a new constitutional convention. On May 18 the Dorrites attempted and failed to seize the state's militia arsenal; the "rebellion" rapidly lost support thereafter. Dorr received a sentence of life imprisonment but won release in 1845. A Democratic mass meeting was held on September 4, 1844, in Providence one mile from the prison in which Dorr was incarcerated.

5. Reference is to John André adjutant general of the British army and intermediary in an exchange of correspondence between Benedict Arnold and Sir Henry Clinton. On the evening of September 22, 1780, André met with Arnold to finalize plans for the delivery of West Point to the British. The following morning, André, disguised as a merchant and traveling under the alias "John Anderson," was stopped by three militiamen on the Tarrytown Road. Upon finding papers of a suspicious nature in André's boot, the three militiamen turned him over to the revolutionary army. André was tried and convicted as a British spy and executed on October 2, 1780, in Tappan, N.Y. Arnold escaped to safety behind British lines.

6. Sarah Childress Polk.

FROM JAMES HAMILTON, JR.[1]

Oswichee Bend
Russel County (Ala) Sept. 8, 1844

My Dear Sir.

As I have taken a somewhat active part in the canvass for your election, and have recently returned from New York, I desire to make a suggestion on which I think it would be well for you to act without a moment's delay. Which is, that you cause some of your friends in Tennessee to write pressingly to the Leaders of the Democracy in New York to be up & doing for I remarked with much regret the extreme indifference many of the friends of Mr. Van Buren expressed as to the result of the Contest. I think if we can carry New York, your election is certain, or if we lose New York if we are able to carry Ohio & Tennessee, it is equally beyond doubt. On my way home I saw enough to satisfy me that Pennsyl. &

Virginia were quite safe. But, the Democracy of New York require to be warned. I have written most pressingly to Silas Wright who I believe is sincerely devoted to the cause.

As I reside on the Banks of the Chattahoochee within sight of the Georgia Shore my social relations with that State are much more active than with Alabama. I therefore have thrown my whole force whatever it may be on the parties in Georgia, where we have a majority of some 5 or 6000 in favor of the Whigs *to reverse.* The utmost activity prevails among your friends and the Democrats are *efficiently* organized. I attended two immense mass meetings, the last fortnight at Macon & Columbus and until the election I shall successively address the people of Georgia at all the points at which I can be present. The vote of Georgia may be the casting vote & therefore it is of infinite importance we should carry that State. I have a strong hope of success but the weight of the combination against us is not to be conceded. I shall go to Savannah to address the people there the first Saturday in Oct. Judge Berrien's[2] stronghold where I hope to make a dash into his ranks.

With the exception of 500 Whig votes in So. Carolina you carry that State almost by a perfect unanimity. Those of us who feel most strongly on the subject of the Tariff (and certainly no one entertains a stronger opposition to that measure than myself) regret Mr. Calhoun with the rest of us Mr. Rhett's premature & intemperate view on this matter & have I am happy to say successfully conteracted the evil consequences which might result from it in the other States.[3] I send you a paper containing my view of the course it behoves the South, to take [in][4] the present crisis.[5]

I regret that my engagements prevented my attending the Nashville Convention which I hope is a faithful exponent of the public feeling of your own State.[6]

But let me revert to the principal object of this Letter, that your friends in Tennessee write instantly to the Leaders of the Democracy in New York that every thing depends on their zealous & untiring exertions.

I desire to express my gratification of renewing our long suspended correspondence[7] & intercourse & to assure you of the esteem with which I am....

J. HAMILTON

[P.S.] My address is usually Fort Mitchell (Ala) but a Letter directed [to][8] Savannah will find me there the last of the month.[9] Let me know what Reports your friends make from Ohio, Indiana, Missouri & Louisianna—and what your own candid opinion is as to the vote of Tennessee.

ALS. DLC–JKP. Addressed to Columbia.

1. Hamilton, a lawyer and planter, served as a member of the U.S. House, 1822–29, and as governor of South Carolina, 1830–32. Initially an ardent supporter of Andrew Jackson, he became an outspoken advocate of free trade and a leader of the states' rights party in South Carolina. After the nullification crisis of 1833, he invested in land in Russell County, Alabama. Enthusiastic in his support for Texas, he served as one of its European commercial agents and later advocated its annexation to the the United States.

2. A Savannah lawyer and judge of the eastern judicial circuit of Georgia, 1810–21, John M. Berrien served in the U.S. Senate as a Democrat, 1825–29, and then as a Whig, 1841–52. He also held the post of attorney general in Andrew Jackson's cabinet, 1829–31.

3. An extreme advocate of states' rights and a South Carolinian loyal to John C. Calhoun, Robert Barnwell Rhett served in the U.S. House from 1837 until 1849. During the summer of 1844, he defied Calhoun's wishes and launched the "Bluffton" movement for separate state action on the tariff. Rhett succeeded Calhoun in the U.S. Senate in 1850, but resigned his seat two years later. Through his newspaper, the *Charleston Mercury,* he espoused the right of secession and inveighed against the South's reliance upon the Democratic party; he led South Carolina out of the Union in late 1860.

4. Manuscript damaged.

5. Enclosure not found. Hamilton later referred to it as "a published Letter to my former Constituents of Beaufort District." See James Hamilton, Jr., to James K. Polk, November 29, 1844.

6. Reference is to the Democratic mass meeting in Nashville on August 15, 1844. Hamilton had received an invitation from the Nashville Central Committee, but had been unable to attend. See "Gen. James Hamilton's Letter" in the *Nashville Union,* October 10, 1844.

7. Letters not found.

8. Manuscript damaged.

9. The first sentence of the postscript was written in the left margin of the third page; the remainder, at the top of the cover sheet.

FROM LEVIN H. COE

Dear Sir Camden Sept. 9th [1844][1]

I met Carruthers at Springfield, There we got into a snarl about Revolutionary voters which you will in a few days see the finale of in the Union[2] & I think we have them bugged & Clayism defending on the votes of Clay.

I addressed a letter to Foster[3] from Nashville inviting him to my appts. & if this did not suit him asking if I could take an equal partnership in his. He has declined to *answer. Mum* again & it is reported will leave for home & probably for E. Ten: in a few days.[4]

I attended to Caruthers appts. to Waverly. Few Whigs out to hear him.

Cheatham is here. D. Craighead[5] expected at Paris. I have written by this mail to H.L. Turney to mail to N. Watkins at Somerville Ben Hardin's letter to C. Johnson & such other documents as will aid me in meeting Bell if he can't come down.[6] I see Bell & N.S. Brown[7] commence at Savannah on the 16th & if Turney don't come down I will meet him at Bolivar & have *equal time* or divide the crowd & publish my speech.

I was on Saturday at a Dem. Mass meeting at the mouth of White oak in Stewart 2500 present. Judge Harris[8] & myself addressed them.

To Day to a good crowd Cheatham & myself spoke. After Court adjourned this evening Mjr. Dougherty[9] of Perry made a speech on our side. A fellow by the name of Saunders[10] answered him & I replied to him.

I am confident Clay can't get 1000 maj. in the District perhaps not 500. Pavatt,Caldwell, Douglas of Perry, Chase, Genl. Dunlap[11] & others are here. All report a fine state of things.

L. H. Coe

ALS. DLC–JKP. Addressed to Columbia.

1. Date identified through content analysis.

2. A Whig lawyer in Lebanon, Robert L. Caruthers represented Wilson County for one term in the Tennessee House, 1835–37, and sat in the U.S. House for a single term, 1841–43. Reference is to Polk's position on Revolutionary soldiers' pensions reported in the *Nashville Union* of September 10, 1844.

3. Ephraim H. Foster, a Nashville lawyer and one of the founders of the Whig party in Tennessee, served three terms in the Tennessee House, 1827–31 and 1835–37. Appointed to the U.S. Senate following the resignation of Felix Grundy in 1838, Foster won election to a full six-year term beginning March 4, 1839. Having pledged to resign should a Democratic majority be elected to the next legislature, he redeemed his promise in November of 1839; the Tennessee General Assembly elected Grundy to the vacancy; and Grundy served from November 19, 1839, until his death on December 19, 1840. Polk appointed A. O. P. Nicholson to the vacant seat; and he served until February 7, 1842, when the Assembly adjourned without electing a successor and thus terminated the interim appointment. The seat remained vacant until the Assembly elected Foster to the place in October of 1843; Foster finally completed the term on March 3, 1845.

4. Reference is to a letter Coe sent to Foster requesting joint appointments at mass meetings. Coe's letter and Foster's reply were published in the Nashville *Republican Banner* of September 20, 1844.

5. David Craighead, a wealthy Nashville lawyer, served one term as a Democrat in the Tennessee Senate, 1835–37.

6. Hopkins L. Turney, N. Watkins, Benjamin Hardin, Cave Johnson, and John Bell. Turney, a lawyer from Winchester, served four terms in the Tennessee House, 1825–31 and 1835–37; three terms in the U.S. House, 1837–43; and one term in the U.S. Senate, 1845–51. N. Watkins and Coe founded the Somerville *Spy* in October 17, 1843. A Bardstown lawyer, Hardin served several terms in

the Kentucky House and Senate and was secretary of state of Kentucky from 1844 until 1847; he served five terms in the U.S. House between 1815 and 1837. John Bell served a partial term as Speaker of the U.S. House, 1834–35, but was defeated by Polk in his bid for reelection to that post in 1835; he headed Hugh Lawson White's Tennessee presidential campaign in 1836 and subsequently became one of Tennessee's most powerful Whigs.

7. A Pulaski lawyer, Neill S. Brown represented Giles County in the Tennessee House, 1837–39; ran an unsuccessful race for Congress against Aaron V. Brown in 1843; won election as a presidential elector on the Whig ticket in 1844; served one term as governor of Tennessee, 1847–49; and went to Russia as U.S. minister from 1850 to 1853. Joining the Know-Nothing party, he served one term as Speaker of the Tennessee House, 1855–57.

8. William R. Harris. A lawyer from Henry County and an older brother of Isham G. Harris, William R. Harris was judge of the Ninth Judicial Circuit from 1836 until 1845. Six years later Harris removed to Memphis.

9. James W. Dougherty, a lawyer, represented Perry County in the Tennessee House for one term, 1837–39.

10. Not identified further.

11. Stephen C. Pavatt, probably Samuel Polk Caldwell, probably Joseph S. Douglas, Lucien B. Chase, and William C. Dunlap. A lawyer from Huntington, Pavatt served as a Democrat in the Tennessee House, 1833–37, and in the state Senate, 1851–53; ran unsuccessfully for Congress in 1839, 1841, 1843, and 1853; and moved from Huntington to Camden in 1846. Caldwell was the eldest son of Silas M. Caldwell and Lydia Eliza Polk Caldwell, Polk's sister. Douglas, a colonel in the Tennessee militia, occasionally served as Polk's agent in managing properties in Perry County. Chase practiced law in Charlotte, Tenn., until 1843, when he moved to Clarksville and formed a partnership with Willie B. Johnson; Chase won election as a Democrat to two terms in the U.S. House, 1845–49; at the end of his second term he moved to New York City. A lawyer from Bolivar, Tenn., Dunlap served as a Democratic congressman, 1833–37, prior to his election as a state judge in 1840.

FROM JOHN M. DAVIS[1]

My dear Sir, Wilkins P.O. ally, co. Pa. Septr. 9th 1844

Should the purity of my motives fail to plead an apology for the liberty I am taking in addressing you at this time, I can scarcely expect that my acquaintance with you *Will,* as it was so limited, that I presume you will not recollect me, which happened at the time Genl. Jackson was retiring from the Presidency, that I fell in with the company passing through Washington county in this state. But, under the present Political crisis of affairs I have thought that perhaps it might not be unacceptable for you to hear how our elections in Pennsylvania are progressing; and at the same time give you my candid opinion relative to the final result.

Both the great leading parties are highly excited. The Whigs are immensely so, and appear determined to carry their point at all hazards. They are in the field as in 1840 with all their usual foolery, of the most unmeaning character, such as live Racoons, old Racoon skins, gourds, hard cider in Logcabins, together with the most ridiculous songs, and singers hired for the campaign to sing them. Also they have a number of stump speakers hired who attends their public meetings, and promulgates such falshoods as their committees chooses to dictate to them, and seldom are they instructed to utter a word of truth.

Permit me here to inform you, that all their parade and falshoods will be unavailing. They are doomed to be defeated in Pennsylvania. They hoodwinked the unsuspecting class of this community by their display of racoons, racoonskins, Banners, vulgar songs & false promises of Two dollars a day and roast beef. But I am thoroughly convinced, they cannot do it the second time. There never has been a period since the second election of Genl. Jackson that the Democratic party in Pennsylvania were so completely united as they are at the present juncture: and when united they cannot be defeated.

The Whigs are making large calculations on the success that attended them in 1840, when Genl. Harrison gained from three to four hundred votes over Mr. Van Buren, but they never appear to take into consideration how their novel mode of electioneering, promising a change of times for the better, (which has not been realized,) played upon the feelings of the unweary[2] & unsuspecting class of the community. Moreover they don't seem to know that many of Mr. Van Buren's former friends had lost confidence in him, and actually did not attend the election, which was clearly demonstrated at a more recent election in 1843 for canal-commissioners, wherein a complete strength of parties was manifested, and the democratic candidates were elected by 14,000 of a majority.

I have been a close observer of the political movements of both parties for a considerable time, and my opportunity for obtaining information in the Western district of Penna. has been good having contracted an extensive and intimate acquaintance throughout the same, during the time I was marshal under the Administration of Genl. Jackson; and I do candidly say to you, without exagerating in the slightest degree, that my opinion is from every thing I can learn, that the Democratic majority for President & vice President will fall but little if any short of from 15 to 20,000 in this state.

At our last election for Govr. in 1840 the democratic candidate as he was called had 23,000 of a majority but that was not a fair test, as there were as many Whigs as democrats voted for him believing him more favorable to the Banking system than their own candidate.[3]

I am one of those who firmly believes that the fortuitous events which has occured within a few years past amongst some of our great men, was intended by the Supreme ruler of the Universe to favor our beloved nation. The death of Genl. Harrison I shall always consider relieved our country from the scourge of a National Bank, as I am firmly of opinion had he lived he would have been so importuned by his party, that he would have signed the Bill which Mr. Tyler had nerve and courage enough to Veto.[4] And again in Penn. the recent death of Mr. Muhlenburg will undoubtedly make a very great and favorable change in our approaching elections. Mr. M. was the democratic candidate for Gov. and he having been in 1835 improperly smuggled upon the party in opposition to the regularly nominated candidate, George Wolf, (both democrats) which created a division in the ranks[5]; and the consequence was Joseph Ritner the Whig & anti Masonic candidate was elected; and in the first session of the Legislature under his Administration was passed that odious Bill granting the charter to establish that *Hydra headed monster* the U.S. Bank in Penna.[6]; and the recollection of Mr. Muhlenburg having coincided in this mismanaged step, and suffering himself to be run by a minority of the party in 1835 *could* not have failed if he had lived, but to create another division in the ranks of the democratic party as respects the election of Governor, at our October election; and there is no knowing what effect it would have produced on the Presidential election in Novr. But, we are now relieved from that catastrophe. Mr. Muhlenburg is no more; and Francis R. Shrunk has been nominated by acclamation at a recent convention held on the 2d. Inst:[7] who is certainly the most Popular man at this time in Penna. for that office; and who will completely unite the whole strength of the democratic party at the October election, which will have a benificial influence on the Presidential election in November. For if we were to loose the governors election on the 8th of October it would arrouse and greatly encourage the Whigs with fresh vigour, and discourage the Democrats; and no doubt induce many to Join the whigs believing them the strong party, and others would become careless and not attend the election. But as that difficulty is now obviated, We can stand like faithfull Sentinels on the Watch Tower and *Cry all's Well.*

I have spun this communication out, more lengthy than I intended when I commenced, but I hope you will excuse me when I assure you that I am actuated by pure phlantropy; and if I convey any information you are not in possession of I flatter myself it will be found correct. Should you not recollect me I beg leave to refer you to my venerable, worthy and much esteemed friend General Jackson, from whom I have recd.

more disinterested friendship than I ever did from any other man, and to whom I owe a greater debt of gratitude than I will ever be able to pay.

JNO. M. DAVIS

P.S. The Revd. Doctor Campbell[8] desires me to present his best wishes to you; and say to you that he is sincerely your friend, and prays that you may be successfull in your election. J.M.D.

ALS. DLC–JKP. Enclosed without seal or cover in Andrew Jackson to Polk, September 17, 1844.

1. John M. Davis held commissions in the U.S. army, 1807–15 and 1816–21, and fought at the Battle of New Orleans. An ardent Jacksonian, he later served as U.S. marshal for the western district of Pennsylvania during the 1830's.

2. Misspelling of the word "unwary."

3. David R. Porter, as iron manufacturer and Democrat, defeated Joseph Ritner in Pennsylvania's gubernatorial race of 1839. Serving in the governor's chair from 1839 to 1845, Porter took a conciliatory approach toward the banking industry and favored protective tariffs. During his second term, opponents in the legislature tried unsuccessfully to impeach him.

4. John Tyler vetoed two Whig-sponsored bank bills in 1841.

5. George Wolf served two full terms and one session of a third term in the U.S. House, 1824–29. Governor of Pennsylvania from 1829 until 1835, Wolf was nominally a Jacksonian Democrat; but many Pennsylvanians believed that he was too friendly toward the Second Bank of the United States. The anti-Wolf wing of the Pennsylvania Democracy nominated Henry A. P. Muhlenberg for governor in 1835, thus occasioning a public split between the "Wolves" and the "Mules."

6. Upon expiration of the federal charter of the Second Bank of the United States in 1836, Nicholas Biddle secured from the Pennsylvania legislature a state charter creating the Bank of the United States of Pennsylvania.

7. References are to the death of Henry A. P. Muhlenberg, Democratic candidate for governor, and to the substitute nomination of Francis R. Shunk by a specially-called meeting of the Pennsylvania State Democratic Convention at Harrisburg on September 2, 1844.

8. Allan D. Campbell of Pennsylvania served as pastor of Nashville's First Presbyterian Church from 1820 to 1827.

FROM HOPKINS L. TURNEY

Dear Sir Winchester Sept. the 10th 1844.

I have just received your Second Letter.[1] Since my answer to your first,[2] I Should have answered your before this[3] but for the fact, that I had writen to John Bell to know if a democratick Speaker would be admitted at his appointments. Seeing that Coe had a long list of appointments which conflicted with Bells, I had determined on meeting

Bell at his appointments and had made every arrangement to do so, but as Coe has made his arrangements to do so, I will not, and now I find myself without any appointment or arrangement whatever. Henry only has three appointments 1 in Robinson[4] & 2 in Sumner, & then the next at Pikeville, &c. It is too far to ride for these appointments especially as we know he will be met in Sumner. As you know all the arrangements and also the Sections of the State that has been canvassed, as well as those that has not, and as my only object is to promote the cause, I have determined to troope about here and the adjoining counties until you designate my work between this and the election, and in laying off for me I desire you to Send me where I can do the most good, regardless of where I have been. Do this as Soon as may be conveneant. Publish the appointments and write me I am now willing to go it fron this to the election.

I would gladly give you a history of My Tour in East Tennessee but can not in the Limits of a Letter. I will say however I tracked Bell privately and publicly on this state.

I do not know what was done in the middle division while I was in the east. Has the counties of Decalb, White, Putnam, Jackson, Smith, &c on the North Side of the State been canvassed?

H. L. TURNEY

ALS. DLC–JKP. Addressed to Columbia. Polk's AE on the cover states that he answered this letter on September 16, 1844; Polk's reply has not been found.

1. Letter not found.

2. Neither Polk's letter of August 31, 1844, nor Turney's reply has been found.

3. Syntax garbled. Turney probably intended to say that he would have answered Polk's "first letter sooner"; apparently Turney had responded to Polk's letter of August 31 just prior to receiving Polk's second letter.

4. Turney probably intended to write "Robertson."

FROM JOHN ANDERSON[1]

Portland, Me. September 11, 1844

Anderson states that Maine's electoral vote will go to Polk and Dallas; explains that both houses of the legislature are strongly Democratic and will cast their state's votes for the party's ticket.

ALS. DLC–JKP. Addressed to Columbia.

1. A Portland lawyer, Anderson won election to four terms in the U.S. House, 1825–33; became mayor of Portland in 1833; served as U.S. attorney for Maine, 1833–36; and twice held the post of customs collector for Portland, 1837–41 and 1843–48.

FROM JONATHAN I. CODDINGTON[1]

My dear Sir New York Sept. 11, 1844

Permit me to congratulate you on the glorious result of the Election in Maine. Anderson the Democratic candidate for Govr. is elected by about 7000 majority over his whig competitor & by about 4000 over abolition & all others.[2] This is a very different result to what we had in Sept 1840.[3] This result in Maine together with the nomination of Silas Wright in this State which secures it to you & settles the Presidential question in the judgement of our most intelligent Democrats. I have witnessed every election in this city since 1798 and I can say without any exaggeration that I have never seen as much zeal & enthusiasm from that time to this as exhibitted at our mass meetings of last evening & the night before at Tammany Hall & Castle garden.[4] Your old friend Mr. C. C. Cambreleng[5] made a very excellent speech last night to a very numerous audience & which was most enthusiastically received by them. The Elections that are to take place in Octr. in the States of Maine N. Jersey & Pena. will no doubt follow suit with Maine & elect the Democrat governors and there is not the shadow of a doubt but of your election to the Presidency in November. At all events this is now the firm and decided opinion of your democratic friends in this city and I know it is the opinion of our mutual friend Mr. Van Buren and no one knows better he having information from most every state in the Union. (In great haste.)

J. I. CODDINGTON

ALS. DLC–JKP. Addressed to Columbia.

1. Jonathan I. Coddington, a merchant and postmaster of New York City since 1836, ran as the Democratic candidate for mayor in 1844; he lost that contest to James Harper, the Native American candidate. In 1845 Silas Wright, Jr., and Martin Van Buren supported Coddington's application for customs collector of New York City.

2. A friend and supporter of Martin Van Buren, Hugh J. Anderson won two terms in the U.S. House, 1837–41, and served as governor of Maine from 1844 until 1847. In the 1844 gubernatorial election he received a majority of the votes cast in the election, thus defeating both the Whig candidate, Edward Robinson, and the Liberty party candidate, James Appleton.

3. In mid-September 1840 the Whigs won Maine's gubernatorial election and a majority of both the congressional and state legislative races. In the presidential election of that year, Maine went for the Whig candidate, William Henry Harrison.

4. On the evenings of September 9 and 10, 1844, the Democrats of New York City held mass meetings and endorsed the party's nomination of Silas Wright, Jr., for governor and Addison Gardiner for lieutenant governor.

5. A party stalwart and member of Martin Van Buren's inner circle, Churchill C. Cambreleng was engaged in mercantile business in New York and served nine terms as a Democrat in the U.S. House, 1821–39. Van Buren appointed him minister to Russia, 1840–41. In his speech at Castle Garden, Cambreleng praised the nominations of Polk and Wright.

FROM WILLIAM H. HAYWOOD, JR.

My Dear Sir Raleigh 11. Sept. 1844

Before this time you have seen the vindication[1] &c and all I have to regret about it is that our distance apart and my distance from Mecklenburg prevented its being made *more conclusive.* I wanted and tried very hard to procure a copy of *Record* showing his appointment as Sheriff so as to state it as a *fact* instead of "it is believed." But I wrote for it until I got tired of receiving no reply. So of his Commn. as a *Militia Col:* The State kept no record or list of such appointments. Being called & known as Col. is to be sure strong proof but not so strong as *Record evidence.* If that Commn. is still in the family I want a *Certified Copy without delay.* I apprehend there is to be a reply as it is thought *here* that Mr. Badger[2] is preparing one, tho: he will keep his name off of it. They are a reckless pack & will no doubt bring out *Col. Wm. Polks* declarations heretofore alluded to by me. How will the old man's *sons like that?*[3] I have my own opinions but will not write them even to you. A confidential letter of Bishop Polks to Dr. R.[4] is in my hands but of course nothing shall or ought to alude of its publication without his leave. If any thing occurs to you or is in your possession that I might counteract such a statement with, lose no time in sending it. I want nothing sent to my address *jointly with any one else.* Please do not forget that. I have sent to Mecklenburg for the Genl. Davie Copy of Declaration[5] and hope it will be forwarded to me. I lost a great deal of time & spent some labor before publishing vindication to possess myself of *record* proof Sheriff appoint., and Col. of Militia and to get an *inspection of the Document left by Genl. Davie.*

I think it is probable that the address or vindication will be met by abuse of E.P.[6] and your *humble servant.* Indeed it is so much the habit of Federalists to abuse *me* when they get frightened that I almost take hope from their *fears* this week that North Carolina may vote for you in Nov. But I cannot count upon it.

I rejoice to perceive that in other sections and especially in Tennessee our friends are so full of reasonable expections. But really it is too bad for men to be abused as political candidates are in our Country: "N'Importe."[7] The Raleigh paper of today has in it an address to No. Caro. which will do for N.C. *if any thing will do.* I shall send you a

Copy. It is mine of course.[8] For I find my reputation amongst friends as a writer the *people can understand* quite onerous to me. They oblige me to labour all the time & my health is indifferent enough any way. Another will follow this address in a different shape, not to say a *reply* to such answer as it may provoke.

You are no doubt too much engaged however to read such things. Our friends in Tennessee I presume will attend to the circulation of the Vindication. If it is approved. The Committee *here* were not able to do much that way. F. P. Blair is pleased with it and published it in Daily, semi-weekly, and Dollar Globe.[9] He wrote me that he thought it "admirable" & conclusive.

R.M.S.[10] you observe is not associated with me in the defense for many reasons. The chief of which (not personal) is that he had been one of the *Blunderers* about *"signers"*[11] and it was due to the subject & to the integrity of history to correct that matter and our friends here thought it better not to have his name to the exposure of an error that he had fallen into as deeply as any one before him.

The *honest!!!* defamers of your Grandfather who published the Copy of Declaration *"as one taken from the executive office" when there was none other to copy from* were not exposed because I designed to give effect to *truth* by avoiding censure of any one, to put the cause of your Grandfather in no degree upon the malignity of your enemies.

I shall be gratified to know that my efforts are not without approbation on success but more so that I have had it in my power to show you that the affection of early youth has matured into a friendship of maturer life which I hope will continue always.

My warmest regards to you and to Mrs. Polk.

WILL H. HAYWOOD, JR.

P.S. If by a quiet systematic organization of our party we can bring to the Polks the *Whole of Hoke's vote* it will elect you in No. Caro.[12] The Federalists have not yet discovered the fact that Hoke's vote falls very little below *Harrisons* in 1840. Not more than 600 or 700 behind it. They are under the false impression that the Federal vote *fell off* in 1844. Not so. Both sides increased their vote. We *the most* & hence our approach within 3000 of Grahams vote in 1844.[13] We are endeavoring to possess our party of this fact & not to apprize the Feds of their mistake. If the People of N.C. Get an alarm about *altering the Constitution* they will *not* vote for *Clay*.[14]

ALS. DLC–JKP. Addressed to Columbia. Published in Elizabeth Gregory McPherson, ed., "Unpublished Letters from North Carolinians to Polk," *NCHR*, XVI (July 1939), pp. 344–45.

1. Haywood published his *"Vindication"* article, which defended Ezekiel Polk's loyalty to the revolutionary cause, in the Washington *Globe* of September 2, 1844.

2. George E. Badger, a North Carolina lawyer, legislator, and superior court judge, served as secretary of the navy under William H. Harrison and John Tyler in 1841; subsequently he served as a Whig in the U.S. Senate, 1846–55.

3. In 1844 Lucius J., Leonidas, George Washington, and Andrew Jackson Polk survived their father, William Polk of Raleigh, N.C.

4. Leonidas Polk and J. G. M. Ramsey. An 1827 graduate of the U.S. Military academy at West Point, Leonidas Polk resigned his army commission after one year to prepare for a ministry in the Protestant Episcopal Church; he was ordained priest in 1831. In 1838 he was elected missionary bishop of the Southwest; three years later he was chosen bishop of Louisiana. During the Civil War he served as a lieutenant general in the Confederate army; he was killed in action at Pine Mountain near Marietta, Ga., in 1864.

5. Reference is to William R. Davie's copy of John McKnitt Alexander's narrative account of a meeting of Mecklenburg County militia delegates held on May 19–20, 1775, and of subsequent proceedings of a court of inquiry held, according to Alexander's narrative, by authority of the resolves adopted on May 20 and of additional resolves issued on May 31, 1775. ADS, copy. Davie's copy is dated September 3, 1800. NcU–SHC. Alexander's narrative includes the putative text of the May 20th resolves, which collectively formed the Mecklenburg Declaration of Independence as it was known to and denominated by Haywood and his contemporaries. Davie was reared near Charlotte, N.C., in the Waxhaw settlement; was graduated from Princeton College in 1776; fought in the Revolutionary War and attained the rank of colonel in the North Carolina line; served in the North Carolina legislature, 1786–98; represented his state in the Constitutional Convention; played an important role in founding the University of North Carolina; became governor of the state in 1798; and retired in 1805 from public life to his plantation in Lancaster County, S.C. Following Davie's death in 1820, his copy of the Alexander narrative was sent to Alexander's heir and son, Joseph McKnitt Alexander; the "Davie copy" subsequently passed into the hands of David L. Swain, governor of North Carolina, 1832–35, and president of the University of North Carolina, 1835–68; upon the resignation of Swain from the University's presidency, the "Davie copy" was misfiled in the collections of the North Carolina Historical Society and thus lost to scholarship until found in 1917 by J. G. de Roulhac Hamilton. For a thorough review of the historiographical controversies relating to the historicity of the Mecklenburg Declaration of Independence, see Richard N. Current, "That Other Declaration: May 20, 1775–May 20, 1975," *The North Carolina Historical Review*, LIV (April 1977), pp. 169–91. For the provenance and significance of the "Davie copy" of Alexander's narrative, see V.V. McNitt, *Chain of error and the Mecklenburg Declarations of Independence: A New Study of Manuscripts: Their Use, Abuse, and Neglect* (Hampden Hills Press: Palmer, Mass., & New York, 1960), pp. 93–98.

6. Edwin F. Polk.

7. French phrase meaning "it's no matter."

8. Haywood's anonymous article, probably published in the Raleigh *North Carolina Standard,* is not identified further.

9. Reference is to the several editions of the Washington *Globe.*

10. Romulus M. Saunders.

11. Speaking at a Democratic mass meeting in Charlotte, N.C., on July 23, 1844, Saunders claimed that Ezekiel Polk had signed the Mecklenburg Declaration of Independence; Haywood did not accept the notion that the resolutions had been written as a separate document and signed by those attending the militia delegation meeting of May 20, 1775.

12. Michael Hoke lost his bid for the North Carolina governorship in state elections held on August 1, 1844. A lawyer and Democratic member of the North Carolina House from 1835 to 1842, Hoke died on September 9, 1844.

13. In the 1844 gubernatorial election in North Carolina, Michael Hoke received 39,433 votes and William A. Graham, 42,486.

14. Haywood's point of reference is not identified.

FROM WILLIAM C. HAZEN[1]

Dear Colo. Covington Tenn. Sept. 11th 1844

I recd. yours of the 2nd inst. on yesterday[2] & rejoice at the prospect of the success of the Democracy in Tennessee. We have been gaining I believe all over the State but the great question is can we *gain enough* to carry the State. I know that our friends are sanguine, and so is the press, but I fear they do not look at the matter right. They do not properly estimate the determination of the Whigs, their perfect organization, and their *desperation,* for it is now "neck or nothing."[3] They will make a desperate effort to have *every* voter to the polls, and I really believe in some places, more *votes* than *voters.* What I most fear is, that *minute, thorough,* and *complete* organization will not be had by the Democrats. If they do, I believe we will carry Tennessee.

I have just seen Wm. Gillespie,[4] formerly of Maury, who has been in Hardeman & Fayette. He says they are making large preparations to be at our mass meeting near Wesley. (You will see by the Spy,[5] that the committee of arrangements thought it best to postpone the meeting until the 3rd of October). He also says at the Democratic meeting at bluff Creek all was in the right spirit, that the company of *squatters* numbering 200 marched into Somerville, and the best of the proceedings was that *eleven* Whigs marched in with them, and renounced their allegiance to the Coon.

We are rather increasing in this county.[6] Since I last wrote you, We have secured *four* whom we considered doubtful and I think there is a good chance for several more. If it could possibly be arranged so that some of the distinguished speakers from other states could be procured to speak at Wesley, I really believe we should have 8 or 10,000 persons in council. Can this be done in time and published in the Union? It is of vast importance. It would bring such a crowd as would infuse enthusiasm into our ranks heretofore unknown in this end of the State. There is as much opening in the District as any other portion of the State. I believe as much or more capital can be made here than either division. Our people are ripe for it, particularly in Tipton, Hardeman Haywood Lauderdale & Fayette. If we had Mellville or Marshall[7] I would insure 100 votes from the direct & subsequent effects.

I had almost forgotten the *money* in troubling you about my notions for political movements. Mr. Adams paid me the balance of the note I held on him of yours three or four days since, amounting to $49. 49/100 with intst., if I have made no mistake.[8] I enclose to you forty nine dollars, and will hand you over the balance some time or other, *probably the 4th of March next!* as I design going to Philadelphia about that time.

Our cotton crop is pretty good though injured by the drought. Other crops fair.

WM. C. HAZEN

ALS. DLC–JKP. Addressed to Columbia. Polk's AE on the cover states that he answered this letter on September 24, 1844; Polk's reply has not been found.

1. William C. Hazen, a Democrat and Covington merchant, presided over the Tipton County Court for two years, 1832–33.

2. Letter not found.

3. Quotation by David Crockett, printed in *Narrative of the Life of David Crockett of the State of Tennessee Written by Himself* (7th ed.; Baltimore: Carrey, Hart & Co., 1834), p. 198.

4. Not identified further.

5. Somerville *Spy*.

6. Tipton County.

7. Gansevoort Melville and probably Thomas F. Marshall. A New York Democrat, Melville was appointed secretary of legation to Great Britain in 1845.

8. Hazen served as Polk's agent in collecting two promissory notes held on Benjamin Adams, a Tipton County planter.

FROM WILLIAM L. MARCY

My dear Sir: Albany 11th Sept. 1844

I intimated in my former letter[1] that I would probably write you again after we had past some of the difficult places in our way in this state.

We have now got over the worst and well over it. Gov. Bouck was in his first term and had been faithful to the party & its principles, & he & his friends claimed what had been usual at least a second term; it seemed to imply a censure not to give it to him. Mr. Wright was properly, of course highly esteemed by all and those who appreciated him most highly wished to have him remain as he is, a national man; he himself was much opposed to the position which has been assigned him. The current in the rank & file ran so strong for him for Gov. that it could not be resisted. He is very popular and adds great strength to the tickets both national & state. The feeling is confident and my best judgment fully endorses it. There is but one thing & that is not likely to happen which can at all shake this confidence. We have had the national issues both as to measures & candidates long enough before us to be convinced that they *take well* and good policy therefore requires that they should be kept up as the main issues, and all State questions should be regarded as subordinate. There is some danger that the placing Mr. Wright on the ticket will give too much prominence to state affairs. In regard to these there is not quite so much harmony as we could wish. Though the whigs broke down the credit of the state during the short time they were at the head of our affairs since the restoration of the democratic party it has been completely invigorated. To do this it was necessary to suspend the public works, & they were left in an unfinished though some of them far advanced state. Many sections of the state are directly interested in the resumption of them. The Whigs advocate that measure generally and democrats in the interested localities really wish it success; and as money can now be borrowed by the state at less than 5 per cent, they see not sufficient reason for delaying resumption very long. Mr. Wright is supposed to be strongly opposed to the policy and so indeed are the mass of the Democratic party. If this should be, as the whigs intend it shall, a prominent question in the election, it may disturb its harmonious action. Local interests act, as you are aware, more intensely than general policy. It is not certain we should lose by such an issue yet as the present condition of things is well I would if possible avoid new issues, particularly as we are in our best judgment in the majority. Minorities may safely experiment.

We are fully aware that the force of the enemy will mass upon our line. They think or at least greatly fear that without New York Mr. Clay cannot be elected with it they hope he may. We mean to be prepared for them and act as if the destiny of the country depended upon us.

We dread the profuse use of money but it is not a new element. Our adversaries have for a long time used it lavishly [. . .][2] we have generally prevailed.

I am now satisfied that they cannot get the whole or even a large portion of the abolition vote for Mr. Clay, but some part of it they will get; but I do not think they can do without the whole of it & even with the whole their success would be quite doubtful. I know that I am not up to the confident tone of our party but I am not a sanguine man & hitherto have not been deceived on the wrong side. Yet I unhesitatingly say that the indications which have in past times foreshadowed events are decidedly favorable. They promise success to our cause.

W. L. MARCY

ALS. DLC–JKP. Addressed to Columbia.

1. See William L. Marcy to Polk, June 28, 1844.

2. Manuscript damaged.

FROM JAMES M. WILLIAMSON[1]

Somerville, Tenn. September 11, 1844

Acknowledges receipt of Polk's September 8th favor[2] and agrees to go to Memphis and urge Stanton[3] to participate in the campaign. Relates that Stanton and his family are unwell. Notes that since August 1 there has been unparalleled sickness with many deaths in that part of Tennessee. States that the mass meeting at Wesley, scheduled for September 12, has been postponed until October 3. Expects that the Texas Blues, a Fayette County militia company, will attract a large gathering in Somerville tomorrow.

ALS. DLC–JKP. Addressed to Columbia via Nashville.

1. Williamson, formerly a resident of North Carolina and a member of that state's House of Commons, 1834–36, moved in 1838 to Somerville in Tennessee's Fayette County and took up the practice of law. He served in the Tennessee Senate from 1845 until 1847.

2. Letter not found.

3. A Memphis lawyer, Frederick P. Stanton, served as a Democrat in the U.S. House, 1845–55, and as governor of the Kansas Territory, 1858–61.

FROM EDWIN F. POLK

Dear Sir. Bolivar Sept. 12th 1844

Yours dated Sept. 4th reached me on yesterday,[1] and I take the first opportunity to answer it. Enclosed according to request I send you the *"extracts"* which I copied while at Dr. Ramseys.[2] Dr. Ramsey was then pursuing his historical investigations as to *protection,*[3] and doubtless will furnish other interesting facts, the fruits of his research expecting that he would propose the vindication to be published in pamphlet form.[4] I wrote him a long letter detailing all that I had heard concerning the case of E.P.'s story, and also advised him to speak something as to his claims to the authorship of the *"Mecklenburg Declaration."* From what I learned in *Mecklenburg* and from the manner in which it came out I have not the *slightest doubt* that he either wrote the instrument, or assisted materially in doing so. As for examining into Shocco Jones history of N.C.[5] since my return, I find there that in detailing the evidence as to the authenicity of the *"Declaration"* much reliance is placed on the letter of Gen. Graham[6] as to the details of getting up the Declaration. He says that the duty of preparing the Declaration was left to a committee of *three,* Brevard a Mr. Kennon and a *third person not recollected.*[7] I would like to know who prepares the pamphlet before it is prepared so that I may write him on these subjects or get Dr. Ramsey to forward what I wrote to him. My last "Mecklenburg" Jeffersonian[8] contains the statement of old Query one of the old revolutionary soldiers, of whom I told you & whose statement I did not procure.[9] I saw the *heresay* testimony of two or three old persons published from the Charlotte Whig paper. I consider it very lame & foolish. I did not hear of such persons whilst I was in Mecklenburg. I will procure the statement of Paris Alexander[10] and send it by next tuesday Wednesdays mail. I cannot go before that. I could procure it to be done before but not so well *perhaps* as I could do it. I left the Statements which I procured in N.C. with Col. Laughlin, and he told me that they should appear *that week.*[11] I was surprised at their non appearance, but expected that you had so [...][12] it.

Several Whigs whose fathers were from N.C. in this part of the Country have openly denied the charge though in remote parts of the country they are or have been using it. Wardlo Howard & H. G. Smith[13] came near fighting about it in Clay club room some time ago & Howard openly left the party on account of it & is a warm Democrat. I have just heard this a day or two since. I think it highly necessary that a full statement should appear *immediately.* A letter from Gen. Sanders[14] says that the Democrats will turn it their advantage in N.C. Cave Johnson spoke near Whiteville yesterday, as the Wesley meeting was postponed and there was some misunderstanding as [...][15] the time of his speaking *here* on account different [...] being struck. I thought it best to leave out the place & have a grand rally at Whiteville a barbecue & there were over 2,000 persons present & a fine impression made. Our military companies are concentrating wherever he goes. We will *increase* our majority *here* over 400 votes. If McNairy is well canvassed we will carry it. A. V. Brown[16] can do more there than any one else. Stanton wants to go to *M. Tennessee* but our friends have thought that he could do more in Perry Henderson & Carroll. I will tell him the wishes of the Democracy there & urge him to so. He is doing nobly here. Our Democratick forces ought to be canvassing every nook & corner of the District for the canvass will be fixed by first of Oct. Every meeting of the Democracy is a mass meeting in this part of the District. A mass meeting in McNairy on the 20th.

E. POLK

[P.S.] The mail about to close. Let me know who prepares the pamphlet. EP

ALS. DLC–JKP. Addressed to Columbia. Polk's AE on the cover states that he answered this letter on September 17, 1844; Polk's reply has not been found.

1. Letter not found.
2. Enclosures not found.
3. Reference is to patriots who during the Revolutionary War protected their property from sequestration by swearing loyalty to the British crown.
4. The *Nashville Union* of September 11, 1844, carried a revision of J. G. M. Ramsey's 1841 "Vindication" of Ezekiel Polk's conduct during the Revolution.
5. Reference is to Joseph Seawell "Schocco" Jones, *Memorials of North Carolina* (1838).
6. On October 4, 1830, Joseph Graham wrote to Joseph McKnitt Alexander and recalled the events of the meeting of May 20, 1775; Graham's letter was printed first in David L. Swain, ed., *The Declaration of Independence by the Citizens of Mecklenburg County on the Twentieth of May, 1775, with Accompanying Documents and the Proceedings of the Cumberland Association Published by the Governor, Under the Authority and Direction of the General Assembly of the State of North Carolina* (1831). Graham, a native of Pennsylvania, moved as a youth with his family to Mecklenburg County, N.C., in 1768. He fought the Revolutionary War, sat in the North Carolina Senate, served as a trustee of the University of North Carolina, and acquired a substantial fortune from the profits of his iron mine, furnace, and forge in Lincoln County, N.C.
7. Ephraim Brevard and William Kennon. Brevard, a 1768 graduate of the College of New Jersey, and Kennon, a lawyer from Salisbury, N.C., are not identified further.
8. Charlotte *Mecklenburg Jeffersonian*.
9. William Queary's certificate, dated August 10, 1844, was included in the Nashville "Vindication" article of September 11, 1844.
10. A resident of Madison County in 1840, Alexander is not further identified.
11. Reference is to the publication of additional certificates in the Nashville *Star Spangled Banner.* A McMinnville lawyer and founding editor of the *Nashville Union,* Samuel H. Laughlin agreed to return to the *Union* in 1844 and edit its campaign newspaper, *The Star Spangled Banner;* he served three terms as a Democrat in the Tennessee Senate, 1839–45.
12. Word illegible.
13. Wardlow Howard and H. G. Smith. Howard married Mary Wilson Polk, daughter of William Wilson and Elizabeth Dodd Polk, in Hardeman County, Tenn., on December 27, 1834. H. G. Smith is not identified further.
14. Romulus M. Saunders.

15. Manuscript damaged here and one line below.

16. Aaron V. Brown, Polk's former law partner and longtime friend from Pulaski, served in the Tennessee Senate and House, 1821–33, in the U.S. House, 1839–45, and in the governorship, 1845–47. From 1857 until his death in 1859, Brown was postmaster general in the administration of James Buchanan.

FROM J. G. M. RAMSEY

My Dear Sir Mecklenburg Sep. 12, 1844

Yours of the 8th from Nashville came by this days Mail.[1] I wrote you four days ago[2] & I hope my letter may reach you in Nashville. It contained a copy of one received from Mr. Haywood & informing me that he had forwarded to the Globe[3] a full *vindication,* &c., & that it would be forthwith forwarded by Mr. Blair to me. It has not yet appeared in the Globe, but certainly will in the next. I sent on to H. *extracts* to be forwarded by him to the Globe to be inserted as an apendix with the proofs already in his possession. I hope tho you got my last, & therefore will repeat no more of it, only that I think it well to furnish the Globe with the Union[4] that contains the Tennessee proofs as H. may not have seen them before he finished the vindication.

We have all written to A. Johnson,[5] urging him to meet Henry. I wrote also to Lowry[6] & other friends above to join us in the application, & last Monday morning as all our friends were leaving my house on their way to the Kingsport Barbacue[7] the last thing I mentioned was for them to bring Johnson back with them so as to meet Henry either at Pikeville of the appointment the day after. I look for him confidently here on the 15th. We sent a very respectable delegation to Kingsport: Reynolds, Eastman, Crozier, Lyon,[8] indeed all our most active friends, are up there to day, so that Barton & Jones[9] will have a thin house tomorrow in town. I have rode out into the neighborhood & requested our country friends that are at home to go to Knoxville tomorrow. I will be there myself as I wish to see Jones & Barton with a view to change some of their appointments. They ought to propose to Barrow[10] to draw in his appointments & adopt theirs. If this is not done tho, we will have some one to meet Barrow every where. The moment Crozier returns from Kingsport he will either meet him or some one else will. Crozier was all last week in the Clinch counties[11] attending to the Sub-elector Wm. Williams[12] in the 2nd Dist. On Friday last W.W. abandoned the field. C. reports favorably from all that country, & my accounts are all very favorable—even Jefferson[13] is doing well, & I am glad to hear from abroad that every where the most perfect Union & active zeal characterise the Democrats. The withdrawal of Mr. Tyler[14] has dispirited our

Whig neighbours, & must I think be followed in these States with decisive results.

But on all these subjects I need not say a word more to you. This letter will be mailed at this office but after I go to town if I learn anything further I will write you from there. My health is rather better & I hope after a few frosts that "Richard will be himself again" [15] but I have been extremely debilitated, & am still weak but ride about some every day.

I am anxious to see both the Globe & the Union. The slanders against E.P.[16] have hurt the Whigs I believe, & they are evidently getting tired of it, & the better ones ashamed of it & even censuring it.

J. G. M. RAMSEY

[P.S.] Conner[17] has not yet written me from New-York as I believe I wrote to you he had promised to do. He is every way reliable & I will be impatient till I hear from him. So soon as I do you shall hear from me.

ALS. DLC–JKP. Addressed to Columbia.

1. Letter not found.

2. See J. G. M. Ramsey to Polk, September 4, 1844.

3. Washington *Globe.*

4. *Nashville Union.*

5. Andrew Johnson's early political career included service in the Tennessee House, 1835–37 and 1839–41, and in the Tennessee Senate, 1841–43; he won five terms as a Democrat in the U.S. House, 1843–53, and two terms as governor of Tennessee, 1853–57; and in 1857 the Tennessee legislature elected him to a seat in the U.S. Senate.

6. A business, personal, and political friend of Andrew Johnson, William M. Lowry served as postmaster of Greeneville, 1843–50, and as U.S. marshal for the Eastern District of Tennessee during the years before the Civil War.

7. Reference is to a meeting held at Kingsport on September 12–13, 1844.

8. Robert B. Reynolds, E. G. Eastman, Arthur R. Crozier, and either William or Thomas C. Lyon. Reynolds, a lawyer and key member of the Knoxville Democratic Central Committee, served as attorney general for Tennessee's Second Judicial District from 1839 until 1845. Crozier was the son of John Crozier, Knoxville's postmaster from 1804 until 1838. William Lyon, a Knoxville Democrat, is not identified further. Thomas C. Lyon, a son of William Lyon, was appointed U.S. attorney for the Eastern District of Tennessee in 1844.

9. Roger Barton and George W. Jones. A lawyer, planter, and jurist, Barton was born in Knoxville and moved in 1827 to Bolivar, where he practiced law, won election to a single term in the Tennessee House, 1829–31, and held the post of attorney general for the Eleventh Judicial District from 1831 until 1836; he subsequently moved to Holly Springs, Miss., and won election to two terms in the Mississippi legislature. A native of Virginia, Jones followed a saddler's trade in Fayetteville, Tenn. He served two terms in the Tennessee House, 1835–39, and sat one term in the Tennessee Senate, 1839–41. An unsuccessful candidate

for presidential elector on the Van Buren ticket in 1840, Jones first won election to the U.S. House in 1843 and served as congressman until 1859.

10. A lawyer from Tennessee and briefly a resident of Mississippi, Washington Barrow served as U.S. chargé d'affaires to Portugal, 1841–44; edited the Nashville *Republican Banner,* 1845–47; and won election to one term in the U.S. House as a Whig, 1847–49. In the summer and fall of 1844, Barrow toured Middle and East Tennessee and campaigned on behalf of Henry Clay for president. Barrow had scheduled his first appearance at Gallatin on Saturday, July 13.

11. Reference to the Clinch River district probably included Anderson, Campbell, Claiborne, Grainger, and Morgan counties.

12. William Williams, a Whig from Grainger County, served one term in the Tennessee House, 1839–41, and one term in the Tennessee Senate, 1841–43. He headed the arrangements committee for a Whig mass meeting held at Cumberland Gap on September 18–19, 1844.

13. Jefferson County.

14. John Tyler announced his withdrawal from the presidential contest in a notice published in the Washington *Madisonian* on August 21, 1844.

15. Paraphrase of the quotation, "Richard's *himself again,*" from Colley Cibber's adaptation of *Richard III* (rev. ed., 1718) act 5, scene 3.

16. Ezekiel Polk.

17. Reference is to James Conner, grand sachem of the Tammany Society of New York City.

FROM ROBERT ARMSTRONG

Govr. [Nashville, Tenn. September 13, 1844][1]

Wright has the unanimous nomination in New York. Shunk in Pennsyl. and Thompson[2] in New Jersey. You see every thing yields to the advance of our party. Not an obsticle is suffered to remain or interfair with the interest of the party.

Not a word from Turney. Stanton will *not* come up. Send Barkly Martin after Jarnigan.[3] I can hear nothing of Keeble. Bell returned this evening from Clarksville. It is said he is going on to Savanah tho "in bad health & spirits." Whig stock declined 50 percent this evening on receipt of Wrights nomination.

I will attend to your commands as directed. The enclosure will appear in the Union of Monday.[4] Craighead was to day in Nolensville. Ewing[5] tomorrow at poplar Creek. The News is good from all quarters. McLemore[6] & Keeble will soon be off. The letters for the counties are nearly complete.[7]

R. Armstrong

ALS. DLC–JKP. Addressed to Columbia. Polk's AE states that he answered this letter on September 16, 1844.

1. Place and date identified through content analysis.

2. John R. Thomson left the College of New Jersey his junior year and entered the China trade; from 1823 to 1825 he served as U.S. consul at Canton; returning to New Jersey and settling in Princeton, he engaged in business pursuits. In 1844 he failed to win his race for the governorship but subsequently won election as a Democrat to the U.S. Senate, where he served from 1853 until his death in 1862.

3. Spencer Jarnagin studied law under Hugh L. White and practiced in Knoxville from 1817 to 1837, when he moved to Athens, McMinn County. A Whig presidential elector in 1840, he failed to win election to the U.S. Senate in 1841 but two years later achieved his goal and served in that body from 1843 until defeated for reelection in 1847.

4. Polk's instructions and enclosure have not been identified.

5. Andrew Ewing, a Nashville Democrat, shared his legal practice with his Whig brother, Edwin H. Ewing. Andrew Ewing won election to a term in the U.S. House, 1849–51, but did not stand for reelection.

6. John C. McLemore, an early settler of Nashville, married Elizabeth Donelson, daughter of John Donelson, Jr., and niece of Rachel Donelson Jackson. McLemore, a wealthy land developer, assisted in the financing of Democratic party newspapers and campaign promotions in the Western District of Tennessee. In 1840 Memphis Whigs, anxious to protect their control of the river trade and in turn their political hold on the Western District, blocked McLemore's scheme to develop Fort Pickering, which he had laid off on his Chickasaw Bluffs tract south of Memphis. Had his Fort Pickering development proven successful, the LaGrange and Memphis Railroad company was prepared to run a spur from its main line to the new river port.

7. Armstrong, a member of the Nashville Democratic Central Committee, coordinated the speaking schedules of the state party's most able and available orators; he sent "county letters" to the local party leaders telling who would speak where and when.

FROM GEORGE BANCROFT[1]

My Dear Sir, Boston. Sept. 13, 1844

There was a good detail of work to do, this year, to bring the Democracy harmoniousy into line in all their strength. But *the work is done.* Our opponents here as in Tennessee, were more zealous, more ready to spend time & money, more determined than in 1840. But they have found no access to the hearts of the people; their orators and active partizans have been hurrying to and fro, flooding the country with false newspapers and documents, calling mass meetings; but all is passing away without enthusiasm, and with a hopeless despondency as a consequence. Tomorrow I will go to New York to spend a fortnight in that state & New Jersey. But the battle is already won. In New England the

Democratic ticket will receive more votes than the whig ticket; summing up the popular vote of all the N. England States in November, you will lead Clay here in New England by several thousands; but owing to our laws in the Presidential elections, the localities of our Majorities, & to other causes, I still think, that the Democratic Electors will be chosen only in *Maine* & in *New Hampshire.* In this state I consented, reluctantly enough, to be the candidate for governor with a certainty of defeat; but it aided, what all as the North depends upon, *Union.* To Maine & N. Hampshire you may add as *certain,* New York, New Jersey & Pennsylvania.

Three great causes have operated everywhere in our favor; your own good judgment and sound discretion in all your letters and movements; the honorable & open adhesion of Mr. Van Buren and his friends and the absurdly contradictory letters of Henry Clay.... *Wright's* nomination,[2] and Clay's *Pro-texas letter,*[3] have annihilated the last gasp of whiggish hope in New York. In attending their mass meetings, I shall rather enjoy the general exultation, than argue as though any thing were in doubt. Be assured, that the support in the North is as hearty as could possibly be given. The alacrity is universal. Ohio & Indiana & even your own Tennessee, & Georgia & North Carolina may go as they will; your success is certain, most probably by a vote in the electoral College of more than three to one. This I write soberly, being well informed of the state of feeling in New England & the nearer states. Here in Massachusetts the whigs have grown downcast and vituperative but their abominable calumnies, like the Abyssinian belles among their slave gallants, smell sweetly only in the nostrils of their own self-complacent respectabilities. The sober judgment of the people refuses to be deceived.

GEORGE BANCROFT

P.S. Our New England customs do not permit candidates to take the field before their own people; yet our friends signify a readiness to have the respective candidates meet the masses, and jointly address them. I should like for once to try the game you played with Carroll[4]; but our opponents will never consent to it. Their strength lies in making up false issues.[5]

ALS. DLC–JKP. Addressed to Columbia.

1. Historian and diplomat, Bancroft was influential in securing Polk's nomination to the presidency and subsequently served as his secretary of the navy.

2. See William Tyack to Polk, September 7, 1844; and William C. Bouck to Polk, September 7, 1844.

3. Reference is to Henry Clay's second Alabama letter; see John Staats to Polk, September 4, 1844.

4. Bancroft probably meant to write "Cannon" instead of "Carroll." His reference is to Polk's 1839 campaign for governor against incumbent governor, Newton Cannon. Although the two men began the campaign with joint speaking engagements, Polk's oratory drove Cannon from the stump and back to Nashville. This anecdote was reported in Polk's presidential campaign biography, which Bancroft had previously read in its drafting stage and which subsequently was published in part in the *Nashville Union* of September 4, 1844.

5. Bancroft wrote his postscript at the top of his first page.

TO JOHN P. HEISS[1]

My Dear Sir: Columbia Sept. 13th 1844

I send you to day, under cover to *Genl. Armstrong,* a *Nashville Union* of the 11th Instant, containing with the additional matter attached by wafers, the material for the Pamphlet which I wish published.[2] The *"Vindication,"* as published in the Union of that date, with the additional matter attached, by wafers, will constitute the Pamphet. Let there be a title page, if there is room, upon which the title, must be printed. I wish you to print $10.000 copies, in neat style.[3] I wish you to advise me on what day they will be out and ready for distribution. I hope they can be ready by monday or tuesday. The title or heading of the Pamphlet, must be the same as that printed in the Union.[4] I wish it properly done & must therefore ask your personal attention to its publication. Not being a printer I do not know that you will understand where I wish the additional matter to come in, from the manner in which I have attached it by wafers. Lest you may not I state that I wish the *statement or letter of John Wallace* to be inserted immediately after the statement of *Jacob Lowrence.*[5] I wish the *Extracts* from *Mr Senator Haywood*'s Report, to come in at the close of the whole, and immediately after the address of the North Carolina committee. There are two *extracts* from *Mr Haywood*'s Report. I wish the more lengthy *Extract* pasted as wafered on the left hand side of the page, to come in first; and the other *Extract,* to come in after the x x x, and to conclude the Pamphlet.[6] I hope I have made my[self] understood. I have noted several typographical errors, in the paper as published in the Union of the 11th, which you will please have corrected in the Pamphlet impression. If you get this letter in time to answer by saturday's mail, let me know when the Pamphlet-copies will be ready.

JAMES K. POLK

ALS. T–JPH. Addressed to Nashville and marked *"Private."* Published in St. George L. Sioussat, ed., "Papers of Major John P. Heiss of Nashville," *THM,* II (June, 1916), p. 144.

1. Heiss, a native of Pennsylvania, and his partner, Thomas W. Hogan, had published the *Nashville Union* since late April 1842. Heiss managed the newspaper's financial affairs until May 1845, when he became business manager of the *Washington Union*.

2. Polk's enclosures have not been found. Reference is to the publication of testimonials defending the Revolutionary War record of Polk's grandfather, Ezekiel Polk.

3. Polk's instructions to print "$10.000 copies" refers to the number of copies, not printing costs. Previously Heiss had estimated that ten thousand copies of the Nashville *Vindication* pamphlet would cost $160. John P. Heiss to Polk, September 11, 1844. ALS. DLC–JKP.

4. The lengthy article, entitled "Vindication of the Revolutionary Character and Services of the late Col. Ezekiel Polk of Mecklenburg, N.C.," appeared in the *Nashville Union* on September 11, 1844.

5. John Wallace and Jacob Lowrance were veterans of the Revolutionary War. A native of Mecklenburg County, N.C., and a friend of the Polk family, Wallace defended Ezekiel Polk's war record and asserted that he and his brothers were "all true Whigs of the right stamp." His statement appeared in the Nashville *Vindication* pamphlet; for the text of this pamphlet, see Mary Winder Garrett, "Pedigree of the Pollok or Polk Family, from Fulbert, the Saxon, (A.D., 1075) to the Present Time," *American Historical Magazine,* III (April 1898), pp. 157–90. Lowrance, who had served in several campaigns in the Carolinas, declared that Ezekiel Polk was "always a true friend of the American cause in that struggle." His statement appeared both in the *Nashville Union* article of September 11, 1844, and in the Nashville *Vindication* pamphlet.

6. The Nashville *Vindication* pamphlet drew upon material that had appeared in the *Nashville Union* article and in William Haywood's "Vindication" article, which was printed in the Washington *Globe* of September 2, 1844. The Nashville *Vindication* pamphlet concluded with two lengthy extracts from Haywood's "Vindication" article.

FROM WILLIAM E. VENABLE[1]

Sir Winchester 13 Sept. 1844

Turney, who is filling appointments in Coffee and this county,[2] requested me to say to you, that he cannot possibly meet Henry in Sumner, but that he will be with [him] at Pikeville, and will accompany him until Johnson[3] or some other Democrat, "good and true," shall take him in hand.

We have had, at Winchester and at other places in this county, and, if I may judge from the past, we will have, many large, enthusiastic and joyous meetings of Democratic men, women and children. We raised, last Wednesday, in Winchester, a stately and graceful hickory Pole; at its head, flies a beautiful national flag, 18 ft. by 13, the work of fortyfour of our democratic ladies. At night we had a delightful democratic reunion, an uncommonly large number of Ladies honoring and blessing the occasion with their presence and their smiles. The assemblage was addressed by Turney, Fletcher[4] and myself. The exercises of the day were closed by the exhibition of twentyseven brilliant transparencies, so strikingly emblematical of our attachment to the existing confederacy, and of our wish as to what it should be. Order and innocent hilarity triumphantly presided over the whole affair.

Our party in Franklin is thoroughly organized. The men are active—the women, enthusiastic—and the children perfectly musical.

I remember the closing scenes of the War.[5] I have been an insignificant actor in many of the political contests since, particularly in the furious conflict in So. Carolina,[6] but never have I seen a party, so enthusiastic, so united, and so energetic, and at the same time, so perfectly under legal and constitutional restraint, as is ours now. We remember the struggle of '40—the battle—the rout and the orgy. They, in turn, are dispirited and dumb. We hear the shouts of our hosts encompassed by the prestige of victory. We must and will succeed, not to avenge insult and defeat, but to vindicate the constitution, to destroy federalism, and to purify the government from its contaminating touch.

Turney, Bright,[7] and Fletcher and myself will visit Salem tomorrow. We will do what we can for the invincible democracy of that section.

Good judges think, and I believe, that the democratic majority of our county will be increased by from one to two hundred votes.

Dr. William Estill has just shown me a letter from Mr. Guess,[8] a wealthy and influential citizen of Marietta, Georgia. At the request of Dr. Estill, Mr. G. has been making numerous inquiries in Georgia, and he gives it as his opinion founded upon the result of his inquiring that the democratic majority in Georgia will range from 6000 to 8000. He says that there is almost a perfect Union between the old Nullifying and Union parties in favor of Democracy leaving but few except the original federalists for Whiggery.

WILL EDW. VENABLE

ALS. DLC–JKP. Addressed to Columbia.

1. A Winchester lawyer and educator, Venable represented Franklin and Lincoln counties as a Democrat in the Tennessee Senate from 1847 until 1849.

2. Franklin County.

3. Cave Johnson.

4. A farmer and Democrat, John D. Fletcher sat for Rutherford County in the Tennessee House, 1839–43, and for Franklin and Lincoln counties, 1845–47, in the Senate.

5. Reference probably is to the end of the War of 1812; Venable was eleven years old in 1815.

6. Reference is to the nullification controversy in South Carolina.

7. A Fayetteville lawyer, John M. Bright ran as a Democratic presidential elector in 1844 and 1848; he served both in the Tennessee House, 1847–49, and in the U.S. House, 1871–81.

8. A physician from Winchester, William Estill was the brother of Wallace W. Estill. William A. Guess represented Cobb County in the Georgia Senate from 1836 to 1840.

FROM JOHN GALBRAITH[1]

Dear Sir, Erie. Sept. 14. 1844

Since I wrote you last,[2] I have been round on the circuit attending the courts in Crawford Venango & Warren counties & have seen many gentlemen from other parts of the state, & am fully confirmed in the opinion that I then expressed that the Democratic party in this state was never better united, & I feel convinced beyond all question, as far as there is any certainty in politics that we shall carry the Keystone by a large majority. I have addressed meetings all round & find a spirit & life & energy in the party that I have never seen exceeded before. I send you the papers printed here that you may see some of the doings on the 10th here & at Meadville in Crawford county.[3] The account in the Gazette[4] is terribly exaggerated, as I am well informed by candid men of both sides. You will see by that also that C. M. Clay[5] has been here & addressing our people on the subject of having to induce abolitionists to vote for *Henry Clay!* H. Clays letter however of the 2d has come here[6] & plays the duces with C.M.'s beautiful argument here, as well as that of the Whig orators generally, the burden of whose song has been for the last three months against annexation & slavery which they argue would be perpetuated by it. I thought perhaps the speech of C. M. Clay as reported here in a Whig paper[7] might be of some service in your quarter, as showing the course pursued by the Whigs here in the North, very different I presume from those South of Mason & Dicksons line.

I have frequent opportunities at this place of seeing gentlemen from New York & Ohio. Since the nomination of Mr. Wright for Governor & Gardner[8] for Lieut. Govr. I think there is little or no doubt of the Empire. Indeed before that I considered there was not much doubt about it unless our party should be thrown into confusion in the nominiation of the State officers. Now I think there can scarcely be a doubt as to the result—not only a very popular nomination, but that made with great unanimity & general satisfaction. Wright stands high all over the state

(& indeed everywhere) & Gardner has the general confidence of the people in the Western part of the state of all parties.

Ohio, I regard as exceedingly nearly equally balanced between the two great parties, & if the issue stood between them alone, I think it would be a very doubtful one, & the result there will depend much upon the course of the abolitionists. It may seem strange that there should be any doubt of their course in relation to Mr. Clay, but I know it is so with many avowed abolitionists. It goes to show how far they are governed by motives of honesty. I think however a large portion of them cannot swallow his last letter, however they might do with those which preceded it. The third party[9] will take 3 whigs to 1 democrat, & should it obtain anything like a considerable vote, we shall certainly succeed in that state.

We met with a great loss in the death of our lamented friend Muhlenburg. Its sudden occurrence struck a damp upon us for a short time, but I am satisfied with so unanimous a nomination of Mr. Shunk it will make little if any difference on the result of the State election.

Please present my kindest respects to Mrs. P.

JOHN GALBRAITH

[P.S.] I should have been delighted to have attended your mass meeting at Nashville to which I was politely invited by our friend Hon. C. Johnston, but business prevented me. I should have been highly gratified to have had another opportunity of taking by the hand Old Hickory, the patriot of the Hermitage.[10]

ALS. DLC–JKP. Addressed to Columbia.

1. A Pennsylvania lawyer and judge, Galbraith won election as a Democrat to the U.S. House, where he served three terms, 1833–37 and 1839–41; subsequently he was elected presiding judge of Pennsylvania's Sixth Judicial District in 1851 and served until his death in 1860.

2. See John Galbraith to Polk, June 17, 1844.

3. Enclosures not identified.

4. Reference probably is to the *Erie Gazette,* which began publication in 1820.

5. An 1832 graduate of Yale College, Cassius M. Clay supported internal improvements and promoted the abolitionist cause through publication of his Lexington *True American,* which was founded in 1845. Clay served two terms in the Kentucky House, 1835–37 and 1840–42. Although opposed to Texas annexation, he volunteered for military service in 1846 and fought in the Mexican War. Running for governor on an emancipation platform in 1849, he gained sufficient support to defeat the Whig candidate. In 1856 Clay joined the Republican party, and from 1863 to 1869 he served as U.S. minister to Russia.

6. Galbraith's reference is to Henry Clay's Lexington letter of September 2. In a widely reprinted letter of July 10 to J. J. Speed, Cassius Clay expressed his belief that Henry Clay and his friends sympathized with the cause of abolition. On September 2nd Henry Clay published a letter in a Lexington newspaper in

which he denied any such sympathies. He claimed that Cassius Clay had written without his consent or knowledge and had misrepresented his views. Henry Clay went on to declare that Congress lacked the authority to interfere with the institution of slavery either in the states or in the District of Columbia. For copies of those letters, see the Washington *Globe,* September 6 and 10, 1844.

7. Cassius M. Clay's speech is not identified further.

8. Addison Gardiner.

9. Reference is to the Liberty party ticket of James G. Birney and Thomas Morris.

10. Galbraith's note refers to Cave Johnson and Andrew Jackson.

FROM J. GEORGE HARRIS[1]

My Dear Sir, Nashville Sept. 14. 1844

It was impossible to get Mr. Walker's article into the Union of to-day, but it will be promptly inserted on Monday as you will see.[2]

I will attend to the additional evidence for the pamphlet[3]; and in the course of the next week I shall make an article[4] embracing all the points contained in Mr. Haywood's defence[5] for the Union. On the whole I think that a most important paper for the canvass. Its reacting force is great.

Wright for Gov. of New York, Thompson for N.J. & Shunk for Pa., have great *reinforcing* power, and nothing can now prevent entire success. The letters to Counties are off. McLemore and Keeble start on Monday with *minute* instructions. I will *closely* calculate the cost of that pamphlet.

J. GEO. HARRIS

ALS. DLC–JKP. Addressed to Columbia. Polk's AE on the cover states that he answered this letter on September 16, 1844; Polk's reply has not been found.

1. A staunch New England Democrat, J. George Harris had been associated with the New London *Political Observer* (Conn.), the *New Bedford Daily Gazette* (Mass.), the Boston *Bay State Democrat,* and the Boston *Morning Post* before assuming the editorship of the *Nashville Union* on February 1, 1839. In March 1843, Harris received a commission from Secretary of State Daniel Webster to be a commercial agent of the United States, with special regard for American tobacco sales in Europe.

2. The lead article in the *Nashville Union* of Monday, September 16, 1844, argued that the gubernatorial nominations of Silas Wright, Jr., in New York, of Francis R. Shunk in Pennsylvania, and of John R. Thomson in New Jersey rendered Polk's election a near certainty; authorship of the article was unattributed. Throughout the 1844 presidential campaign Robert J. Walker wrote articles and distributed pamphlets in behalf of the Democratic party's national ticket.

3. Nashville *Vindication* pamphlet.

4. Harris' article appeared in the *Nashville Union* of September 30, 1844.

5. Reference is to the "Vindication" article by William H. Haywood. Jr., in the Washington *Globe* of September 2, 1844.

FROM JOHN P. HEISS

Dear Sir, Union Office Nashville Sep. 14 1844

On account of not receiving your letter[1] until this morning I was unable to answer it by return mail.

As our edition of the Star Spangled Banner is very large—rising six thousand copies, it will not be from press before Tuesday: when we will commence the "Pamphlet"[2] and have between one and two thousand copies ready for distribution by Wednesday night.

With the additional matter you have sent us, we will have but little room for a title-page—not more than a quarter of a page.

I shall hurry it through the press as fast as possible, but, as we work hand presses altogether, we cannot print the whole number during the coming week. You will please inform me, what disposal I shall make with those which will be ready for circulation on Wednesday night.

Democracy seems to have recieved new energy in this city since the nomination of Silas Wright for Governor of New York.

Several large bets were made to-day by our friends on the general result; and, some Whigs from the surrounding counties sent us word in the morning, that they would put up an amount on a certain number of States they named, but found the Democrats so eager to close the bets with them, that they made sundry excuses to get off; and as our friends followed them up so closely, they were *run out of town by 12 Oclock A.M.*

David Craighead Esq. returned to-day from the Nolensville meeting, and gave a glowing description of it. He says there were between two and three thousand persons present, and, that after he had concluded his address to them, several came and gave him the *"hand of fellowship"*[3] and said: "they were with us hereafter." Everything at present—politically, looks very encouraging.

JOHN P. HEISS

ALS. DLC–JKP. Addressed to Columbia. AE by Polk states that he answered this letter on September 16, 1844.

1. See Polk to John P. Heiss, September 13, 1844.

2. Reference is to the Nashville *Vindication* pamphlet.

3. Probably a corruption of the scriptural phrase, "The right hands of fellowship." Galatians 2:9.

FROM ANDREW T. JUDSON[1]

My Dear Sir Canterbury Ct. Sept. 14th 1844

Your position before the public, renders it proper that you should know, from time to time, with what spirit the canvas, progresses, and what are or may be the prospects of success or defeat, both results being now of very general interest. It is with that view I now address you a few lines. Yesterday I returned from the City of N.Y. where I had been spending a few days, and was there at the great ratification meeting, held in Castle Garden, after the nomination of Silas Wright as a Candidate for Govr. of the Empire State. The meeting was immense and the enthusiasm all-pervading. The whole day previous was spent by the Empire Club in erecting a tall Hickory, and suspending from it a broad Banner *"Polk & Dallas Wright & Gardiner."* Cambrelling[2] was there and made one of his eloquent declamations. Nothing could have been more fortunate to the general result, than the nomination of Silas Wright. *It settles the question as to N. York.* This is a great point to gain. Give us N. York & Pennsylvania and there can be no doubt, as to the residue of the matter. My own opinion is, that *these two* states are *now secure.* I may misjudge, but this is my opinion, after careful and dispashionate examination of the matters. While in N. York, the news of the Main election was recived and its effects were visibly to be seen on every Coon's face as he walked up broadway. I think the ultimate majority of Anderson over the Whig Candidate[3] may be 10.000. In 1840, as you will remember the vote was far diffent. Whig 45574—Demo. 45507. This favorable change is an indicative of the feeling there, and elsewhere.

I do indeed anticipate a change somewhat like this in N. York & Pennsylvania. The democratic vote in Massachusetts will be highly gratifying though not enough to silence whig authority.

You will be glad to hear what is doing in our old Connecticut, and I will tell you that the democracy are buckling on their armor for such a fight as they have never seen. It will be man to man, breast to breast. In 1840 the Coons beat us 6000, and now, if they beat us at all, they may be thankfull. The Democratic mass meetings began last week, in each old congressional District. In this County, Windham, it was held on Wednesday, and a real barbacue it was, more than 4000. This was indeed a large number considering the place of meeting was remote from any large town, and away from any rail road or boat communication, with a farming population. The democracy of the district never saw such a meeting before. The true spirit is up and awake. Our State is very nearly divided, and if every voter was called out no man could say which side could count on ten the most. I cannot assure you, under such circumstances that Con. will be given you, though many of our well informed friends believe it. One thing I do know, that we can give you more votes than we could poll for any other, except the good old Patriot Jackson.

ANDREW T. JUDSON

ALS. DLC–JKP. Addressed to Columbia and marked "Confidential."

1. A native of Windham County, Conn., and a practicing attorney, Judson served in the Connecticut House, 1822–25, before his election as a Democrat to the U.S. House in 1835; he resigned his seat the following year to accept an appointment as U.S. district judge for Connecticut, in which position he served until his death in 1853.

2. Churchill C. Cambreleng.

3. Edward Robinson, a Thomaston merchant, represented Knox County in the Maine Senate for one term, 1836–37, and served in the U.S. House, 1838–39, in place of Jonathan Cilley, deceased; failing in his gubernatorial race in 1844, Robinson resumed his commercial pursuits in Thomaston, where he died in 1857.

FROM BROMFIELD L. RIDLEY[1]

Govr. Polk McMinnville 14th Septr. [18]44

Until yesterday I had expected to hold the September Term of your Chancery Court at Columbia by arrangement with Judge Cahal[2] to interchange but since my arrival at this place I have received a letter from him changing the settled arangement between us. I therefore take the liberty to communicate now by letter what I had promised myself the pleasure to have told you in a personal interview. Whilst I have been holding Court through the Summer I have endeavoured in a still quiet way by enquiries of leading Whigs & Democrats to form an opinion satisfactory to myself; of the probable result of the November election in the several Counties in which I have been. And as I do not doubt that the information will be acceptable to you I forward to you a coppy of my memorandum.

The Democratic Vote will be increased in the following Counties as follows. Franklin 85. Coffee 75. Bedford 75 Rutherford 60. Cannon 55 Wilson 90 Smith 50. Jackson 150. Dekalb 65. Overton 50. Fentress 81. White 75 Van Buren 25. Bledsoe 50. Warren 50 making a gain in these Counties of 1076 votes if my addition is right.[3] I have taken much pains not to deceive myself and in every instance have put down the amount at less that the testimony makes it. The Whigs in most cases say there are no gains either way or if any that the increased vote which will fall with them will neutralize it. In this they are *greatly deceived*. I saw Mr.

Lyon[4] & others from E. Tennessee at Pikeville the past week. They are sanguine that E. Tennessee will give to Clay a mere nominal majority *if any.* In a word the Democrats are all enthusiasm & confident of victory in Tennessee at least. I have seen nothing to equal the Democracy in Warren. They have had speaking in this village every night this week (Court Week) have erected a hickory pole 100 feet & since the Whigs have erected one 10. feet higher, they the Democrats are prepared to raise another on Monday next 200. feet.

From the signs of the times in & out of Tennessee who can doubt that a victory awaits the Democracy equal in its importance & consequences to that of Jefferson over Burr.[5]

BROMFIELD RIDLEY

ALS. DLC–JKP. Addressed to Columbia.

1. A Tennessee lawyer, Ridley represented Warren County for one term in the Tennessee House, 1835–37. He moved to Rutherford County in 1840 and served as judge of the Chancery Court from 1840 until 1861.

2. Terry H. Cahal, a prominent Columbia Whig and lawyer, served twice in the Tennessee Senate, 1835–36 and 1837–39; he became mayor of Columbia in 1840.

3. Ridley's figures total 1,036.

4. Reference probably is to Thomas C. Lyon or his father, William.

5. In the presidential election of 1800 Thomas Jefferson and Aaron Burr each received 73 Electoral College votes and the tie forced the election into the U.S. House of Representatives, where the representation of each state had one vote and where the Federalist party controlled eight of the sixteen state delegation. On the thirty-sixth ballot the House elected Jefferson president; many Democrats believed that Burr, the Democratic party's candidate for vice-president, had conspired with the Federalist opposition to elect himself president in Jefferson's place. The Twelfth Amendment, which was ratified in 1804, provided that the Electoral College would cast separate ballots for president and vice-president, thus preventing a repetition of the Jefferson-Burr election dispute.

FROM JAMES M. WILLIAMSON

My dear Sir — Sommerville Sept. 14th 1844

On the morning of the 12th when I had expected to start to Memphis, I was myself taken with a slight chill and could not ride with safety that distance. I am home to day pretty well, and trust that by prudence I will not be sick; I dispatched an express horse to Mr. Stanton, not waiting for the mail as that would be leaving to day. I enclosed yours[1] to him which he writes me came safely to hand. I sent it by one of my boys with whom I knew it would be safe.

He writes me for reply to mine urging upon him not to disappoint our friends in Middle Ten: and to go by all means. "I have been confined to the house by sickness ever since I saw you here, and have not yet been in town. I was determind however to go out to day, and would have done so but for the bad weather.

I regret exceedingly, the circumstances which render it necessary for me to disappoint my friends in Middle Tenn. No personal inconvenience expense or difficulties, would prevent me from granting their wishes if it were at all possible for me to go.

I might probably make arrangements to Start on Monday, but I presume that would be too late for the Opportunity."

If he gets up to our County Sunday evening, as he writes me He expects to do, I will urge him by all means to go on if he feels strong enough to ride. I can put him in my sulky and I know the road and stands and he can reach Spring Hill on the 20th. This however will depend entirely upon his health and strength.

Yesterday we had Cave Johnson with us, and we are *perfectly delighted with him.* He was at Whiteville on the 11 and met near 2000 people. There were two uniform companies present, Our Somerville boys & the Bolivar Company marching 200 and a company of Squaters 70 or 80 strong with horns and trumpets made of polk stalks (what an idea!) The whigs were indeed astounded. Cave Johnson made one of his happyest efforts. Some theretofore Whigs openly proclaimed they were changed men. Yesterday also was a proud day for democracy. Early in the morning Col. Johnson was waited on to know if he would divide the time with whig speaker (Col. Searcy).[2] This he readily assented to upon condition the same courtesy should be extended to our friends when Bell came around. As a Whig Speaker had the reply the last time Col. Johnson met an opponent, we insisted Searcy should lead. After the presentation of the flags, a star spangled banner and a Texas flag to the Texas Blues, a beautiful and moving ceremony, Searcy took the Stand and made the most of his speech from a little Whig primer yclept Defense of the Whigs by a senator of the 27 Congress. The worst of his harrangue was standard perororation and the other part of it was taken up with the stale slang about the defalcations; he did not touch any of the main issues, and what was still more unfortunate for his frinds, or rather for us his voice gave out by the time his first hour was over. Cave Johnson then took the stand and like a kind preceptor and in the most benevolent humor in the world applied the rod to him soundly and then proceeded to enlighten him as to some of the truths of history and the actings and doings of the Whig Congress & Administration. The effect was most triumphant and elicited a continued round of applause, and Whiggery was smitten to the dust in one of its [...][3] a Bank and Court house village. Cave Johnson is a powerful man and I will heartily wish we could get him to some of our large mass meetings that are to come off in a week or two. We would like to get Bartly Martin[4] at our Mass meeting at Westly[5] on the 3 of October.

J. M. WILLIAMSON

ALS. DLC–JKP. Addressed to Columbia and marked "private."

1. Reference is to Polk's letter to James M. Williamson of September 8, 1844. Letter not found.

2. A lawyer, Granville D. Searcy served two terms in the Tennessee House and represented first Tipton County, 1835–37, and then Shelby County, 1849–51.

3. Word or words illegible.

4. Barkly Martin.

5. Reference is to a Democratic mass meeting in Wesley, Tenn.; originally scheduled for September 12, 1844, the Wesley appointment was postponed until October 3.

FROM JAMES McKISICK[1]

My Dear Sir Fayetteville Arkansas 15th Sept. 1844

We are extremely anxious to hear from you & to know what your calculation is in regard to the result of the great approaching political contest. It is not expected however that you would undertake to write answers to your friends & correspondants on this all absorbing question. I have no doubt but you are literaly inundated with communications; my apology for intruding this upon you at this time is, that when I wrote you from Little Rock shortly after your nomination I among other things had reference to a political calculation that your friend Genl. Maclin & myself made at the time on the subject of the Electoral votes.[2] It may be, that I made a clerical error in writing the name of Genl. Caruthers, instead of Genl. Maclin. If I did, you would be at a loss to know to whom I had reference. I do not know that I made the mistake alluded to, but think it probable I might from the fact, of my having commited an error of the same kind in a letter to Governor Yell[3] about the same time.

We are all on tiptoe in regard to the way Tennessee will cast her vote in this Election: we have great hopes she will repent for her Sins & again espouse the true faith, but she has departed so far from her original creed that altho I fondly cherish a hope of return, it is not without fear. The accounts however of changes & recruits in the democratic ranks in Tennessee are quite flattering if true, which I hope & am induced to believe will be realized at least to a considerable extent. If Tennessee perseveres & holds out against republican men & measures through this contest, I shall consider her irretrievably gone.

It seems to me from the general tenor of accounts from all parts on the Union, that whiggery is on the wane, & that democracy is gaining strength. Mr. Vanburen & Col. Benton I think took a strange course in relation to the Texas question.[4] I am strongly inclined to the opinion, that each of those Gentlemen, knew the position the other would assume in regard to that question: & were totally mistaken in their calculations, as to the affect the ground they took would have upon the democratic party. Tho I think Mr. Vanburen evinced a commendable liberality in placeing his letter in the hands of Genl. Butler to meet contengencies[5]; I would be sorry for the party to loose the talents of Col. Benton, tho I think he ought to be punnished some for the peak he thot proper to take, & he has received a pretty castigation, & is perhaps rather whipped back into the traces, & seems now to be doing pretty good service.

I confidently believe that if you get the vote of New York or Ohio you must be elected with the addition of the States which I consider certain. I do not think Mr. Clay can get Ohio, & I see one of the Gentlemen from N. York who addressed the mass meeting at Nashville gave it as his opinion, that N.Y. would go for the democracy by a majority of 15 or 20.000.[6] This is first rate news if there is no mistake about it. But you know Mr. Vanburen himself lost that State. I however make strong calculations on the influence of Silas Wright. I think it quite probable he can now command more strength in that State, than Mr. Vanburen, tho I apprehend the Walstreet money influence in the City, is a powerful opposition to contend against.

We calculate on Electing Governor Yell to congress by a majority of 2000 or 2500 over his opponant Mr. Walker who I believe is the most popular man of the Whig party in the State.[7] We have no fears but you will get the electoral vote of this State, tho it is but a drop in a Bucket. The whigs however are making a most tremendous struggle: & we have made so many balks & bad starts in relation to our candidate for Governor, that I would not be surprised if the Whigs were to Elect the Governor.[8]

I would like verry much to get a letter about this time from Mr. Frierson, Col. Moore,[9] or some of my old Tennessee friends about matters or things in general, & Tennessee in particular. There will be several asperants to fill the Senatorial vacancy, occasioned by the death of Governor Fulton.[10] At this time I consider it quite uncertain who the legislature will fix upon. Genl. Maclin I think bids fair to be popular in this State. But on account of his short residence among us it perhaps would not do to take him up yet. Col. Ashley one of our Electors, is a man of verry respectable talents, & could sustain himself as Senator, at least equal to any man in the State, tho I do not know that his name will be presented. Heretofore he has not been verry popular with the party.[11] He has however traveled & spoke all over the State as a candidate for Elector, & is decidedly an overmatch for any of the whig candidates.

JAS. MCKISICK

P.S. I was gratefyed that you put your veto upon a reelection to the presidency in the event of your succeeding, which God grant. I have uniformly thot where there are so many distinguished men as the U.S. affords, one time only ought to be allowed. In the infant State of the Republic when Genl. Washington was called to the presidency it was necessary to have the influence of his name, & the weight of his character a second time to inspire confidence in our institutions, & when Mr. Jefferson came into power, perhaps it was necessary also for him to serve two terms, to give effect & perminancy to his policy, but I consider the reasons in the above cases, do not apply to the present state of things, & I hope the example proposed by you will have its Just influence on the determination of all succeeding presidents.

ALS. DLC–JKP. Addressed to Columbia.

1. A political ally of both Archibald Yell and Polk, McKisick served as court clerk of Bedford County, Tenn., before moving to Arkansas about 1836.

2. Reference is to McKisick to Polk, June 18, 1844. A Democrat, Sackfield Maclin represented Fayette, Hardeman, and Shelby counties in the Tennessee Senate, 1841–43. After his legislative service, he moved to Texas.

3. A close personal and political friend of Polk, Archibald Yell practiced law in Fayetteville, Tenn., until his appointment as U.S. judge of the Arkansas Territory in 1832. He won election to several terms in the U.S. House, 1836–39 and 1845–46, and served as governor of Arkansas from 1840 until 1844. Yell died at the Battle of Buena Vista in 1847 during the Mexican War.

4. Martin Van Buren's Texas letter was published in the Washington *Globe* on April 27, 1844. Van Buren stated that he would support Texas' annexation provided that the state of war between Texas and Mexico were resolved first. He did not think, as did some, that a European power would annex Texas if the United States failed to do so; however, as president he would resist any such encroachment by a European power. Van Buren argued that immediate annexation would render an injustice to Mexico. Yet if Mexico attempted to reconquer Texas and if Texas then requested annexation, he would submit the question to Congress. In a letter addressed to members of the Texas Congress and published in the Washington *Globe* on April 29, 1844, Thomas H. Benton also objected to the immediate annexation of Texas.

5. A former law partner and close confidant of Van Buren, Benjamin F. Butler served as U.S. attorney general, 1833–38, and twice as U.S. attorney for the southern district of New York, 1838–41 and 1845–48. Prior to the meeting of the Democratic convention at Baltimore in May 1844, Butler, the chairman of

the New York delegation, had received from Van Buren a letter authorizing him to take such action as might be necessary to bring the nominating process to a harmonious decision.

6. Reference probably is to a speech by William Tyack at the Democratic mass meeting in Nashville on August 15–16, 1844. Tyack's remarks were reported in the Nashville *Star Spangled Banner* of August 31, 1844.

7. A native of Kentucky and a successful lawyer, David Walker settled in Fayetteville, Ark., around 1830. He was a member of the Constitutional Convention of 1836 and served in the Arkansas Senate, 1840–44, as a Whig. In 1844 he ran for Congress but lost the election to Archibald Yell.

8. In December 1843 delegates from only sixteen of Arkansas' forty-six counties nominated Elias N. Conway for governor and Daniel J. Chapman for Congress. Dissension within the ranks of the Arkansas Democracy led to the calling of another convention to be held in May 1844; delegates to the second convention nominated Chapman for governor and Archibald Yell for Congress. Chapman subsequently withdrew from the race, and party leaders placed in nomination Thomas S. Drew, who went on to defeat the Whig candidate, Lawrence Gibson.

9. Reference probably is to Erwin J. Frierson and William Moore. Frierson studied law in Polk's office at Columbia and later practiced law in Shelbyville. He served as attorney general for the Eighth Judicial Circuit, 1827–36, and represented Bedford County in the Tennessee House, 1845–47.

10. William S. Fulton, a Tennessee lawyer and military aide to Andrew Jackson in the 1818 Florida campaign, moved to Alabama in 1820 and then to Arkansas in 1829. He became governor of Arkansas Territory, won election to the U.S. Senate as a Democrat in 1836, and gained reelection to the Senate in 1840. Fulton died in Little Rock on August 15, 1844.

11. Chester Ashley, a lawyer, settled in Little Rock, Ark., around 1820. He was elected as a Democrat to the U.S. Senate in 1844 to fill the vacancy caused by Fulton's death. Ashley was reelected in 1846.

FROM JOHN T. ANDREWS[1]

Sir North Reading Steuben Co. N.Y. Sept. 16. 1844

Since I wrote you last,[2] I have visited various parts of this state and Pennsylvania. Our political prospects are good. I have never known a better feeling among the Democracy than prevails at present. Our state convention could not have made a better nomination.[3] Every dissension is healed, and all feel the fullest confidence that we shall carry the state by a large majority. The whigs are doing all in their power but evidently with less effects than in 1840. Large numbers who supported Harrison will not vote for Clay, while scarcely an individual can be found who has heretofore voted with us who will not now warmly sustain the Democratic Candidates. Let me repeat it, there is scarcely a doubt that the state of New York will be Democratic by a large majority, and very few intelligent whigs can now be found who will not admit it—within the last few days bets have been freely offered on 10,000 majority and declined by the whigs.

JOHN T. ANDREWS

ALS. DLC–JKP. Addressed to Columbia.

1. A school teacher and merchant, Andrews served as sheriff of Steuben County prior to his election as a Democrat to a single term in the U.S. House, 1837–39; he subsequently served as postmaster of North Reading, N.Y.

2. See Andrews to Polk, June 13, 1844.

3. New York Democrats nominated Silas Wright, Jr., for governor.

FROM ROBERT ARMSTRONG

Dr Sir Nashville Septmr 16th [1844][1]

Craighead leaves in the morning. What we will do at the great meeting at Paytons Creek[2] on wednesday I cannot tell. That meeting will [be] greatly disapointed in Craighead's leaving.

Tomorrow Foster & Henry go near Hendersonville. The "terms" of the meeting to devide time. We have no one. *Boddie*[3] in very bad health and Guild[4] filling appointments in Smith. I will send *"Sykes."*[5] He is able for *both* Foster & Henry.

I have not heard a word from Keeble or Turney. Foster goes to *East Tenns* so it is said. If he does some one ought to be assigned him (Turney.)

Bell has gone on to his appointments with an ulcer in his throat and a cancer in his heart. It is said he was *"tight"* at Clarksville,[6] in argument I *suppose*. He looked badly as he passed on as tho he was sick. He will not stay *out* Long. Crittenden returns to Kentucky.[7] Let me say to you that Tennessee is the field. We must gain it. I am preparing all our *forces* for Spring Hill.[8] Let it be a large meeting. I will attend to your letters received to Night.

Try and make *McClung*[9] go to East Tennessee. You will see the *bet* proposed Dr. [...][10] in the Banner this morning.[11] It was promptly taken.

On your precinct	250
On your County	250
On Tenssee &c	250
The Result	750
	$1500

Tell our friends to arrange for *Having it* to commence *in* time. It was made at *you and for effect abroad.*

Several bets on the *result*. Money put up to day *even*.

It is all effort *for Tennessee*.

Send in Barkly Martin, or send him *Out* to work. He can do as much as any man. I wish we had him for Foster tomorrow. In haste....

R. Armstrong

ALS. DLC–JKP. Addressed to Columbia. Polk's AE on the cover states that he answered this letter on September 18, 1844; Polk's reply has not been found.

1. Date identified through content analysis.
2. The Democrats scheduled a mass meeting for September 19, 1844, following the Whig mass meeting at the same location on September 13, 1844.
3. A lawyer in Gallatin, Elijah Boddie served four terms in the Tennessee House, 1827–29, 1831–33, 1835–37, and 1843–45.
4. A Gallatin lawyer and Democratic elector in 1844, Josephus C. Guild served three terms in the Tennessee House, 1833–36, 1845–47, and 1851–53, and sat for one term in the Tennessee Senate, 1837–39.
5. A Democrat from Huntsville, Ala., William J. Sykes represented Madison County in the Alabama state legislature for one term, 1843–44.
6. Reference is to the Whig mass meeting held in Clarksville, Tenn., on September 12, 1844.
7. A Kentucky lawyer and prominent Whig politician, John J. Crittenden's public career spanned five decades. He served in the U.S. Senate, 1817–19, 1835–41, 1842–48, and 1855–61; the U.S. House, 1861–63; the U.S. attorney generalship, 1841 and 1850–53; and the Kentucky governorship, 1848–50.
8. Reference is to the Democratic meeting planned for September 20, 1844.
9. Nephew of Hugh L. White and native of Knoxville, James W. McClung practiced law in Huntsville, Ala.; served in the Alabama House as its Speaker in 1835, 1837, and 1838; failed to win the governorship in 1841 as an independent; but won election in 1845 to the Alabama Senate and served until his death in 1848.
10. Word illegible.
11. Nashville *Republican Banner* printed a notice with the caption "Attention Locos," but the author of the proposed bet was not named.

TO ROBERT ARMSTRONG

My Dear Sir — Columbia Sept. 16th 1844

A letter received to day from *Williamson* of Somerville,[1] renders it probable that *Staunton*[2] may still come up in a few days. If he does, *Nicholson* will immediately take his place.

I promised to send you the names of the Democratic Speakers, to whom the letter is to be sent by the committee. I can only give you a part of them to night. In Counties where there are two or more speakers, one letter addressed to them jointly will answer. The list is herewith enclosed.[3]

Majr. Heiss writes me that the Pamphlet Edition of the "Vindication of E. Polk &c." will be out this week, a part of them on wednesday evening.[4] I wish you to send 100. of the first that are struck to *Edwin Polk Esqr* Bolivar, through the mail. Send them in such way that he will only have newspaper postage to pay.

Send one copy, of the first that are out to each Democratic member of Congress. When all are out send 25. copies to each Democratic member of Congress.

Send 10 copies to each Democratic Elector in the Union, as far as their names can be ascertained from the newspapers.

Send one copy, to each Democratic newspaper in the Union.

Request *Mr. Southall*[5] to send one copy to each one of the list of persons in this State which he has.

Send one copy to each Democratic Speaker in this State.

Send to any others in any part of the Union whom you may think of.

Reserve 1.000 copies for me and 1.000 copies for Edwin Polk Esqr of Bolivar. Send them to Edwin & myself, by the first safe opportunity, so as to avoid Postage if it can be done.

I wish 100. of the first that are struck sent to me. Send them out to *Mr. Langtry*[6] on thursday, if you can get them.

JAMES K. POLK

ALS. T-JPH. Addressed to Nashville and marked *"Private."* Published in *THM*, II, pp. 144–45.

1. Reference is to James M. Williamson to Polk, September 11, 1844.
2. Frederick P. Stanton.
3. Armstrong's circular letter arranging campaign appointments in each county is not identified further; Polk's enclosed list has not been found.
4. Reference is to John P. Heiss to Polk, September 14, 1844.
5. Joseph B. Southall was appointed to the Democratic Central Committee by the state convention in November 1843. Other Nashville operatives included Felix Robertson, Andrew J. Donelson, Willoughby Williams, and Timothy Kezer. The Central Committee also conducted operations from Knoxville and Jackson.
6. A Columbia merchant and bank director, Hillary Langtry became the postmaster of Columbia in January 1844 and served in that post until June 1845.

FROM LEONARD P. CHEATHAM

Dr. Sir: Dresden Sept 16th 1844

In my last[1] I refered to the Pension question at Springfield. Johnson's journals proved the assertions, that it was the Senates bill that passed &c &c.[2] Caruthers surrendered the point. I found before I left home Crockets speech, which shows the reasons why *he you & others* voted as you did,[3] it has done good here. I filled most of *Coes* appointments while he was with Caruthers. Crockett[4] followed a while & has now backed out. Saturday Coe & myself had *Dresden* to ourselves. To day *Coe & Brown*[5] will meet at Trenton, I am staying *here* to meet Caruthers to-morrow & then to remain with him until I hand him over to Coe at Troy.[6] On *Thursday* last I left *Coe* & went to a barbecue at Robertsons on the Jackson road. I met *Houston*[7] there who says Cave is going on with Staunton[8] South &c. If Nicholson does not or some other person accompany Bell, Houston will endeavour to meet him tomorrow & remain with him until *Coe* can come up.

Crittenden & Foster have been through here. Foster has left, his friends say to put out the *fire* in the mountains. Carroll & Gibson have been neglected by our Speakers. Still gain is going on; in this County a decided gain, from what I see & learn, we will come over Tennessee locked or *nearly* so. On Saturday several changed & among them *Davis* who had put up the Whig pole came out openly, on the ground he said of the Tariff question. He came to our room & remained until nearly bed time, as decided a democrat now as any.[9]

The excitement here is not equal to Middle Tennessee but the harvest is more *abundant*. In haste.

L. P. CHEATHAM

ALS. DLC–JKP. Addressed to Columbia and franked by Robert Armstrong.

1. Cheatham wrote to Polk on September 4, 1844.

2. See Cave Johnson to Polk, September 4, 1844.

3. David Crockett, a political and military leader in Tennessee's Western District, served two terms as a Democrat in the U.S. House, 1827–31; during his third and final term in Congress, 1833–35, he sided with those who opposed Jackson's administration. In a speech delivered before the House of Representatives on March 19, 1830, Crockett objected to the Revolutionary soldiers' pension bill on two counts. The House bill allowed too high a ceiling ($1,000) on veterans' cash assets and thus provided some with unneeded assistance; the bill also excluded militia veterans and individual volunteers.

4. John Wesley Crockett, son of David Crockett, practiced law in Paris, Tennessee. He was elected as a Whig to Congress for two terms, 1837–41.

5. Born in Ohio, Milton Brown moved to Tennessee and lived in Nashville and Paris before settling permanently in Jackson. A member of the Madison County bar, he served as chancellor of West Tennessee, 1837–39, and sat in the U.S. House for three terms, 1841–47.

6. Reference is to the Democratic mass meeting scheduled for Troy on September 28, 1844.

7. George S. Houston of Athens, Ala., served in the U.S. House, 1841–49 and 1851–61; he later served as governor of Alabama, 1874–78, and as U.S. senator in 1879, the year of his death.

8. Frederick P. Stanton.

9. In a letter to the editor of the *Nashville Union* of September 23, 1844, W. L. Davis confirmed his affiliation with the Democratic party.

TO JOHN P. HEISS

My Dear Sir: Columbia Sept. 16th 1844

Yours of the 14th came to hand to day. You say you will have one or two thousand of the Pamphlet[1] out by wednesday night, and the balance during the week, and desire to know how you are to dispose of the first copies, which you get out. Send one copy to every Democratic newspaper in the Union. I suppose you have the name and title of a large number of them on your exchange list. Send 100. copies addressed through the Post office to *Edwin Polk Esqr.* Bolivar Tennessee. You can put them up in bundles of 25 or 50, and mark on the envelope the number of printed sheets which each bundle contains. Put up 200. copies for me and give them to Genl. Armstrong to be sent out. Furnish to Mr. *Southall* two or three hundred of a sufficient number put up in single copies, to send one to each of the list of names which he has in this state. Have a single copy sent also to each Democratic member of Congress. Genl. Armstrong has a *directory* containing their names and Post office. Put up all the balance in bundles of 25. each and deliver them to Genl. Armstrong and I will inform him how I wish them distributed.

Send me one of the first copies which you strike off.

I suggest that you put into the next *Star Spangled Banner,* the additional matter: viz *Wallace*'s statement & the extracts, from the North Carolina vindication, which will appear in the Pamphlet, and which did not appear in the last Star-Spangled Banner.

My news from New York and New Jersey is very fine.

James K. Polk

ALS. T–JPH. Addressed to Nashville and marked *"Private."* Published in *THM,* II, p. 145.

1. Reference is to the Nashville *Vindication* pamphlet.

FROM HERSCHEL V. JOHNSON[1]

Dear Sir: Milledgeville Geo. Sep. 16th 1844

I have the pleasure to acknowledge the rect. of your kind letter of the 29th ult.[2] I regret exceedingly that you may not honor our State with a visit. But while I regret I must own, I approve your course. Perhaps the tenor of my letter on this point was indiscreet & in bad taste. If so, you will find my apology in my zeal for the success for the Democratic cause. However much I would be pleased & feel honored, by such a visit to my own State & to my house, yet I gladly forego that, rather than you should compromit the dignity of your position before the American people, or subject yourself to censure.

Knowing the flood of letters with which, you are doubtless deluged daily, I should not trouble you with this, did I not think its contents would be of sufficient interest to repay you for the time consumed in its perusal. By this I do not mean to claim any thing on account of its authorship or its merits as an epistolary production. Its interest (if it should possess any) will consist in the statement which I will give you of the prospect of "Young Hickory" in Georgia. In my first letter, I said, we expected to carry the state for you, by a handsome majority. That opinion was based upon data, much less satisfactory, than that which I now have in possession. At that time, public opinion was still in its forming state; now I think it is made up. I have travelled extensively in the prosecution of the labours of the campaign; and upon anxious and honest inquiry, from every part of the State, I have no reason to doubt the correctness of the opinion which I then gave you. Indeed, at every step of my inquiry, my opinion has been confirmed. Our party are thoroughly united and zealous. And when *united,* all prior elections in Georgia, have shown that we have the numerical strength, even without accessions from the Whig ranks. Now we are not only united and aroused, but there are tangible and visible changes in our favour, in almost every county in the State ranging from Ten to Fifty, and in some few counties from Fifty to one hundred. How then can we fail of success? We cannot, unless extensive frauds and corruption are perpetrated at the ballot box by our opponents. This they will do, if they can. But we hope by vigilance to prevent it. We are sure of Four Members of Congress out of Eight, and we expect, not without good reason, to elect Six. The following is my calculation on the best information, I can obtain, as to the result in October.

The 1st Cong. Dist. *may* be Whig by 250 maj.
The 3rd Cong. Dist. *may* be Whig by 150 maj.
The 7th Cong. Dist. *will* be Whig by 700 maj.
The 8th Cong. Dist. *will* be Whig by 1500 maj.
aggregrate Whig Maj 2600
The 2d Cong. Dist. *will* be Dem. by 1000 maj.
The 4th Cong. Dist. *will* be Dem. by 300 maj.
The 5th Cong. Dist. *will* be Dem. by 2000 maj.
The 6th Cong. Dist. *will* be Dem. by 1500 maj.
aggregate Dem Maj 4800
Nett Democratic majority of the popular vote 2200

In this estimate, I give the 1st & 3rd Dist. to the Whigs. But we hope to carry them. The 1st is Tom. Butler King's[3] (Whig) who is personally very unpopular; the 3d is Chappel's,[4] who occupies a very proud & commanding position before the Democracy. If we carry the State by 2000 majority in October, we shall carry it by 4000 in November. There are a great number of voters who will vote with the Whigs in the congressional election, who will not vote directly for Mr. Clay. And besides, if we succeed in October, it will inspire the Democracy & discourage the Whigs. But Georgia is a fickle State & all calculation on her must be recd. with caution. Still, unless our friends are wofully decieved, the above is a safe calculation.

But let Georgia do as she may, I can but think victory will be ours in the final result. I have no fears of Pennsylvania, and I like the recent movements in New York exceedingly. For a time, I greatly feared that the anti-Texas, Tariff and ultra Van Buren Democrats would give us only a cold shoulder. But the nomination of Wright for Gov. & Butler for Elector has quieted my apprehensions & I now feel strong confidence, in the vote of N. York. With the vote of these two states and Virginia and Tennessee & the other states, which we know to be certain for Democracy I can but think your success is sure.

I send you an old paper containing the official returns of 1842.[5] That was a pretty fair test of the relative strength of parties in Georgia. It is true that Crawford has beaten Cooper for Govr.[6] since then, by near 4000 votes. But the Democratic party were not all satisfied with Cooper's nomination. They did not *unite* on him. But that Election table may be of some little interest & use to you, in comparing the returns of an approaching election. It so happens that the same paper also contains an address of mine delivered before the Alumni of our State University. Its perusal may serve to while away an evening hour. If you should deem it worth reading, you will find that I am a pretty good Democrat. Although the occasion required a purely literary production, still my Democracy would ooze out occasionally. It abounds in typographical errors but your eye will correct them as it glances along.

I dislike to draw a moment in your time; but really I am strongly tempted to ask a line from you about Tennessee & the prospect as to the final result. For of course you are in possession of the best information from all points. But being personally interested yourself, you might deem such a request indelicate & impertinent. But of one thing, you may rest assured, that if you should deem such an anxiety on my part worthy of gratification, any thing which you might think proper to communicate in a spirit of confidence & candor, touching the prospects of the cause of Democracy, will be as sacred as the grave.

When that *"vindication"*[7] of your grand father, to which you refer, shall appear, please furnish me with it. But I can assure you, *that* slander is dead in Georgia: it will not influence ten votes in the State. If any thing, it has rebounded upon the Whigs themselves.

Mrs. J.[8] joins me in expressions of high regard & sincere esteem.

H. V. JOHNSON

ALS. DLC–JKP. Addressed to Columbia.

1. A Milledgeville lawyer and 1844 Democratic presidential elector, Johnson served as U.S. senator, 1848–49; as judge of the Superior Court of Georgia, 1849–53; as governor of Georgia for two terms, 1853–57; and as senator in the Confederate Congress, 1863–65. In 1860 he ran unsuccessfully for vice-president on the Democratic ticket with Stephen A. Douglas.

2. See Polk to Herschel V. Johnson, August 29, 1844.

3. A lawyer from St. Simons Island, Ga., Thomas B. King served several terms in the Georgia Senate, 1832–37, and two terms in the U.S. House as a Whig, 1839–43. An unsuccessful candidate for reelection in 1842, he was returned to the U.S. House in 1845 and served until his resignation in 1850.

4. A lawyer from Macon, Absalom H. Chappell served in both houses of the Georgia legislature prior to his election as a states' rights Whig to one term in the U.S. House, 1843–45.

5. Enclosure not found.

6. George W. Crawford and Mark A. Cooper. A Georgia Whig, Crawford served in the state legislature, 1837–1842; the U.S. House, 1843; the governorship of Georgia, 1843–47; and the cabinet of Zachary Taylor. Cooper, a states' rights Whig, won a seat in the U.S. House in 1839; lost his bid for reelection; filled the congressional seat the late William C. Dawson, 1842–43; and ran unsuccessfully for the Georgia governorship in 1844.

7. Reference is to the Nashville *Vindication* pamphlet and its defense of Ezekiel Polk's loyalty to the American revolutionary cause.

8. Ann Polk Johnson, born in 1809 in Somerset County, Md., married Johnson in 1833; she was the daughter of William Polk, who served as a judge on the Maryland Court of Appeals from 1806 until 1812.

FROM JOHN K. KANE

My dear sir, Phila. 16 Sept. 1844

I take the liberty of sending you our two most recent pamphlets. The one addressed to the Native Americans is by Mr. Richard Rush. The other is mine[1]

This last will show you the course which we are taking on the Tariff question. It is one that all Mr. Clay's letters cannot affect, and which so far at least has made the topic a harmless one. On the whole, I am glad that the Whigs have said so much about it. They have forced our people to reflect more full than they have heretofore done on the effects of the protective policy, and have prepared them to listen favourably to a discussion of its character. Before your four years are out Pennsylvania will be disembarassed on the subject.

Our Majority for Shunk promises now to be 20,000; and it is doubtful whether the majority for Electors will be the larger or the smaller of the two. Of New Jersey, we have ceased to doubt: it is our's by at least 2000. Delaware is debateable ground: 100 will turn the chances there. Maryland too is full of promise. Taking in the whole horizon, it really looks as if you were to have 20 States of the 26.

J. K. KANE

ALS. DLC–JKP. Probably addressed to Columbia. Polk's AE on the cover states that he answered this letter on October 4, 1844.

1. A lawyer, diplomat, and writer, Richard Rush served as U.S. attorney general, 1814–17; as acting secretary of state, 1817; as minister to Great Britain, 1817–25; as secretary of the Treasury, 1825–29; and as minister to France, 1847–49. An unsuccessful vice-presidential candidate on John Q. Adams' ticket in 1828, he moved into the Democratic ranks during the fight over rechartering the Second Bank of the United States. In 1844 Rush wrote the pamphlet, *To the Democratic Citizens of Pennsylvania. Remarks on the Rise of the Native American Party.* Kane's pamphlet has not been identified.

FROM J. G. M. RAMSEY

Mecklenburg, Tenn. September 16, 1844

Ramsey notifies Polk that Haywood's "Vindication" of Ezekiel Polk has been printed in the Washington *Globe;* however, the extracts from the histories of the Revolutionary War in the South were not included.[1] Ramsey notes that the barbecue in Kingsport "was the largest meeting ever held in East Tennessee."[2] Concerned about the possibilities of election frauds in Tennessee, he suggests that the penalties for illegal voting should be published in the Nashville newspapers and perhaps in the Columbia newspapers as well.

ALS. DLC–JKP. Addressed to Columbia.

1. See J. G. M. Ramsey to Polk, September 3, 1844.
2. A Democratic mass meeting was held in Kingsport, September 12–13, 1844.

FROM ROBERT ARMSTRONG

D Sir 17 Septemr [18]44

I am *not* satisfied of the propriety of answering all the mass of trash and nonsense put out by the Whig paper here. Still I urged Harris on to a defence of what you see in the Whig of to day.[1] I could find but *little* data. Your course in Congress on the Land bill is not at hand tho it is publish some place fully.[2] Where is it? I told Harris he must Charge upon Clay every thing and let them answer and defend as Clay is doing in letter writing, mixing himself up.

Foster is back to *night* from Hendersonville. I will ascertain his route. It is said to be back to the District.

We are geting the letters off for the different Counties. The Letters to the speakers will be attended to. McLemore is dangerously *Ill* at the Inn. *Keeble* will leave in a few days. If Maine is only True it will be a Damper. Have the meeting as Large at Spring Hill[3] as posible. In haste.

R. ARMSTRONG

ALS. DLC–JKP. Addressed to Columbia. Polk's AE on the cover states that he answered this letter on September 19, 1844; Polk's reply has not been found.

1. A lengthy editorial criticizing the *Nashville Union*'s campaign biography of Polk appeared in the *Nashville Whig* on September 17, 1844. It attacked in particular the campaign biography's account of Polk's stand on the public lands and occupancy questions. The next day the *Nashville Union* defended Polk's position on those questions as having been held uniformly and consistently. On September 23, 1844, the *Union* published a longer, more detailed answer to Whig charges about Polk's record on the public lands and occupancy issues.

2. Armstrong's reference to a published account of Polk's position on the land bill is not identified further.

3. Reference is to the Democratic mass meeting at Spring Hill, Tenn., on September 20, 1844.

FROM JOHN BLAIR[1]

Dr freind: Jonesborough Sepr. 17 1844

I have cautiously omitted writing you, ever since your nomination to the Presidency because of the disposition which was apparent amongst your freinds both at Baltimore & elsewhere to tax you with their correspondence. I now feel that I must break silence & add to the *stock* of *taxation a moment.* East Tennessee as you know has been the region of darkness and an extraordinary effort has been made on the part of our Democratic freinds to effect a change. We have called our freinds to all the public meetings Barbacues &c & furnished cloathing to the naked & subsistence to the destitute & so far all things have gone well. The Whigs are holding on, or trying so to do to their party with a *death-like grip* & everything that money can affect is done & still they are lavishing their means to regain their losses, (for losses they have sustained) and deluging the country with documents & pamphlets & papers: in this they have the advantage of us for our Editors are both poor our itenerant speakers mostly so, & those of us who could or would open the purse have contributed to pay an Editor for the Sentinel,[2] to defray the expenses of travelling speakers to cloathe feed & carry out the poor & penniless amongst us, until money cannot be raised for further prosecuting the war. What is to be done? As a last expedient we have concluded to address our wealthy friends at Nashville & Gifford[3] is the bearer of a communication to the committee of correspondence at Nashville in order to see if any thing can be done. I have more faith in you, than all others to put this thing into operation, & take the liberty of thus freely communicating with you. It will not do to *loose hold* at this stage of the game. The skies are bright & if overclouded between this & November it must be, from the use of means not within our controul, in possession of our opponents. I have just returned from the convention at Kingsport[4] where were more persons assembled than has ever assembled in E Tenn & the spirit of Democracy aroused for any emerge[ncy].[5] That feeling must be kept up & if permitted to wane must ensue in our loss of what we have gain[ed]. I did, & do believe, that Tennessee could be carried without a single postate[6] if the fire could be kept up so as to insure a full turn out at the polls of the lazy Democrats. But we are not left to rest on the plans. We have changes every where, in our favour if we can hold on to them, & rest assured we can do [so] if invested with means to carry on the combat. You will see that the Argus[7] is advertised *for sale,* & an attempt is made to *silence* that portion of our *artillery.* Gifford can prise[8] you with his difficulties whilst the whigs are deficient in no means but even Nashville is contributing to their freinds here on the Whig side, some sixty to eighty documents a week to each little Country Post office, and that too of matter most *false* & *foul.* I will forbear further to write as it is now near 12 oclock in the night & Gifford is waiting for me to close. I refer you to him for further particulars. I hope & pray, yes, I believe the next letter which I address you will be after you shall have been elevated to the summit of earthly promotion for which I mean to earnestly contend until the last vote shall be cast.

JOHN BLAIR

ALS. DLC–JKP. Addressed to Columbia.

1. A merchant, manufacturer, and lawyer in Washington County, John Blair served as a Democrat in the U.S. House from 1823 until 1835; he lost his bid for reelection in 1834 to William B. Carter.

2. Reference is to the Jonesboro *Tennessee Sentinel,* which was founded in 1835 to serve the Democracy of Washington, Sullivan, Greene, and Hawkins counties.

3. Lawson Gifford helped establish the Jonesboro *Tennessee Sentinel* in 1835.

He also assisted in founding the Knoxville *Argus*, a Democratic newspaper edited by E. G. Eastman and first published on June 27, 1839.

4. Reference is to a Democratic mass meeting held at Kingsport, September 12–13, 1844.

5. Word ending obliterated here and on lines below, probably by mending tape.

6. Misspelling of "apostate."

7. Knoxville *Argus*.

8. Misspelling of "apprise."

FROM WILLIAM E. CRAMER[1]

Albany Argus office

Gov Polk [Albany, N.Y.] Septem 17th [1844][2]

I have delayed writing you, until after the Whigs had made their nominations.[3] We can now better ascertain "the lay of the land." The campaign will not only be animated but contested beyond all example. Both Parties look upon this State as the battle ground—the debateable country of the Presidential canvass.

The Nomination on both sides are the strongest names that could have been presented and both Parties are now perfectly united.[4] The exertion will therefore be intensive and corresponding to the might of the Stake.

Our friends feel sanguine. I think too sanguine. There is much yet remains to be done. I an happy to say *that work is now* doing. We are organizing effectively in every District in the State. This will be the lever to lift us in.

The Whigs are also well organized, but I think not so effectively as in 1840. Their late *decreased* vote in Maine shows that some of their system is out of gear. Mr. Clay's *two last* letters have injured him seriously in all the Northern States and particularly in Western New York. In the one, he is a quasi Texas man and in the other he repudiates Cassius M Clays celebrated invitation to the Abolitionists.[5] This puts an impassable gulf between him and them. If they vote their own ticket the State is ours beyond a question. They will poll from 15 to 20,000 votes and therefore hold the balance of power. Before Mr C's false letter they were hesitating whether they should not vote for him. For a few weeks we were on a volcano. But just in time have come these missives from Ashland. You in the Southwest cannot appreciate the commotion they have created. You see that he has placed himself at war with the positions taken by Webster, Choate, Seward Granger Fillmore and Corwin.[6] But while in their own hearts they feel *deeply indignant,* they are now busy in trying to explain away some of the unfortunate paragraphs. *But it is too late.* I think Mr C has doomed himself. The judgment you have exhibited in abstaining from writing letters for the Public, is in singular and proud contrast with the course of your great competitor. I have heard more than one or our able men allude to it. The Whig papers are busy half their time in explaining Clays letters. This puts them on the defensive While our friends are constantly assuming the offensive.

In New York city our friends claim at least 4000 majority. In St. Lawrence County, we shall have 1000. In 1840 that county gave Harrison 52 majority. New York gave Van Buren only 994. This will certainly be a handsome gain in two counties. The rest of the State will not do as well but after a careful look over the whole ground my impression is that we will carry this State. Mr Wrights nomination knits us together with cords of steel and Texas and Anti-Texas Democrats are all in the same boat.

On the strength of the representation from leading democrats Tennessee, our friends here are betting heavily on that State. I pray they may not deceive us.

We have a mass convention here on the 2nd of October. We then expect Gansevoort Melville.

WM. E. CRAMER

ALS. DLC–JKP. Addressed to Columbia.

1. William E. Cramer, son of Polk's former colleague in the U.S. House, John Cramer, had been associated with the *Albany Argus* since March 1843.

2. Date identified through content analysis.

3. On September 11, 1844, the Whig state convention at Syracuse nominated Millard Fillmore for governor and Samuel J. Wilkin for lieutenant governor.

4. Reference is to Silas Wright, Jr., and to Millard Fillmore.

5. Reference probably is to Henry Clay's second Alabama letter and to his Lexington letter of September 2.

6. Daniel Webster, Rufus Choate, William H. Seward, Francis Granger, Millard Fillmore, and Thomas Corwin. Having won elections to single terms in the Massachusetts House and Senate, Choate served as a Whig in the U.S. House, 1831–34, and in the U.S. Senate, 1841–45. Governor of New York from 1838 to 1842, Seward served two terms in the U.S. Senate, 1848–60; he served as secretary of state under Abraham Lincoln and Andrew Johnson. A New York lawyer and Whig, Granger served two terms in the U.S. House, 1835–37 and 1838–41, before resigning to accept an appointment as postmaster general in William H. Harrison's cabinet; he held that post from March until September 1841, when he returned to the U.S. House to fill a seat vacated by John Greig. An Ohio lawyer, Corwin served as a Whig member of the U.S. House, 1831–40, and as governor of Ohio, 1840–42; elected to the U.S. Senate in 1845, he resigned to become secretary of the Treasury under Millard Fillmore and held that post from 1850 to 1853.

FROM J. GEORGE HARRIS

Tues. morn

My Dear Sir Nashville Sept. 17. 1844

Late on Saturday night before starting on my homeward ride I dropped you a line, advising you of sundry matters referred to in your letter of the day before.[1] Your letter to Gen. Armstrong received last night[2] enclosing a paragraph, induced me to rise this morning at the ringing of the market-bell to prepare as far as I could the defence of your course on the public lands, occupants, &c, and ere I had written a page along came the Whig of this morning[3] groaning under *nine* columns of a poor attempt to review my biographical sketches—a batch of old slanders revised, nothing more. It is evidently from Meig's[4] pen upon *items* furnished by Bell, who is nettled at the position which he is given in the sketch. Accordingly I shaped an article to the point on the subject of Pub. lands &c., which you will see in to-morrow's paper,[5] and made sundry other paragraphs for the same number calculated to repel the slanders contained in the Whig, which are evidently intended for *foreign* use.

The article describing your course on the public lands goes as far as *my data* run, and I have not desired to make it *long,* lest it should not be as readily copied by contemporaries in refutation of these charges.

Their object is *clearly* to put us on the *defence,* which I tell Laughlin must be avoided as much as possible.

If you have additional *data* which will further illustrate your course in favor of "the settlers" after you have seen the article in tomorrow's Union please send it to me under cover to Genl. Armstrong, and I will use it according to your direction.

Kendall's "Clay & the Squatters" has been published in the Star Spangled Banner,[6] is now standing in type, and Mr. Heiss tells me he is about to print a quantity more extra copies. I have advised him to insert in the Union and he will do so.

You will have seen by the morning's paper that *bets* are being made very freely by our friends here.[7]

I met the Whig handbill of last night by an *exposé* under P.S. in this morning's Union as "a weak exertion of the enemy."[8]

If Maine, in spite of the "money and men of Boston" proves right; we shall be overjoyed. If not we must make the best of it as not affecting the general result.

J. GEO. HARRIS

[P.S.] The presses are at work on the "Vindication." It will take several nights and days to run off 10,000 copies.[9]

ALS. DLC–JKP. Addressed to Columbia. Polk's AE on the cover states that he answered this letter on September 19, 1844; Polk's reply has not been found.

1. See J. George Harris to Polk, September 14, 1844.
2. See Polk to Robert Armstrong, September 16, 1844.
3. Reference is to the *Nashville Whig.*
4. Return J. Meigs, a Davidson County lawyer, served briefly as general and court reporter for the state from early 1839 until November of that year. He became U.S. attorney for Middle Tennessee in 1841 and represented Davidson County as a Whig in the Tennessee Senate from 1847 until 1849.
5. In his article in the *Nashville Union* of September 18, 1844, Harris argued that Polk had pursued a "uniform course" in favor of the occupants.
6. A newspaperman and member of Andrew Jackson's "Kitchen Cabinet," Amos Kendall served as postmaster general from 1835 until 1840. In 1842 he edited a Washington biweekly, *Kendall's Expositor.* The following year, Kendall issued a prospectus for a biography of Jackson, but never finished it. The text of his pamphlet, *Mr. Clay Against the Frontier Settlers* (1844), appeared in the Nashville *Star Spangled Banner* of September 21, 1844. The *Nashville Union* had published the same text under the caption, "Henry Clay Against the Frontier Settlers," on July 9, 1844, and repeated it on October 14th.
7. Reference is to an article in the *Nashville Union,* which correctly states that Nashville partisans had bet $3,000 on Polk's presidential campaign. See Robert Armstrong to Polk, September 16, 1844.
8. Reference is to the Postscript section of the *Nashville Union* in which Harris accused the *Carlisle Statesman* of duplicity. According to Harris, the *Statesman* raised the Polk standard in order to pull it down.
9. Harris wrote his postscript in the left margin of the last page of his letter.

FROM WILLIAM HENDRICKS[1]

Dear Sir — Madison Indiana Sept. 17. 1844

I had the pleasure of receiving a line from you during the past summer[2] and events since the commencement of this campaign are as far as I am capable of judging more and more cheering. In this quarter the party are certainly gaining strength continually and although a strange series of incidents in some 5 or 6 counties have given the Whigs a small majority on joint ballot yet the popular vote was certainly with us on the first Monday of August last by about 1700 over and above the vote of last year which selected a democratic Gov.[3] by about 2000. We are too, unquestionably stronger now than we were then. Moreover before the Presidential election we shall have time to hear from the annual elections of Pennsylvania and Ohio and should their results cheer us as we doubt not they will we shall carry this state by a very respectable majority and feel Kentucky our neighbor quivering like an aspen leaf.

Business took me last month into Ohio, through Columbus Mount Vernon and to Mansfield not very far from the Lake.[4] Ohio is engaged with all her powers on both sides in a mighty struggle. The Whigs pretend to be sanguine and confident of success, and the Democrats certainly are so. And unless our political friends are much deceived, they will certainly carry the state. Never were parties better organized or more generally active. It was said and believed that the Whigs in summing up their reports from the entire state in its various counties and townships were discouraged; that their returns shewed 4 columns No. 1. Whigs. No. 2 Democrats. 3. Abolitionists and the 4th doubtful, and that they had come to the conclusion that unless new impulses could be given and new ground gained, that they must be beaten, and that renewed & desperate efforts were making.

At Mansfield I saw Mordecai Bartley whom you know; an excellent man and the Whig candidate for Governor.[5] He talked freely and candidly about the conflict: has not travelled much through the state: thinks it will be a hard battle, and expects to be elected; but bases his calculation on the results of 1840. He was you will probably remember 2 or 3 congresses in the Ho Reps with you.

I have just been receiving and answering some cheering intelligence from N.W. Penna. and Western N. York. My information does not at all doubt the results of those states and we think here that New Jersey is more certain than either. Last nights mail brought us accounts of victory in Maine which you will know as much about as we do ere this reaches.

You must be overloaded with correspondence and I shall not expect you to trouble yourself with a reply to this letter but hope and expect to know that you have been successful in the final result before the close of November.

William Hendricks

ALS. DLC–JKP. Addressed to Columbia.

1. Born and educated in Pennsylvania, Hendricks migrated first to Ohio, where he taught school and read law, and then to Indiana, where he enjoyed a lengthy political career. He served as a member of the U.S. House, 1816–22; as governor of Indiana, 1822–25; and as U.S. Senator, 1825–37.

2. Reference is to Polk's letter to Hendricks of July 4, 1844.

3. Reference is to James Whitcomb.

4. Lake Erie.

5. A farmer originally from Pennsylvania, Mordecai Bartley removed to Richland County, Ohio, in 1814. He served two years in the Ohio Senate, 1817–18; held the post of land office register for the Virginia military district of Ohio from

1818–23; and sat four terms in the U.S. House, 1823–31. He removed to Mansfield, Ohio, in 1834 and subsequently served three years as governor of Ohio, 1844–46.

FROM ANDREW JACKSON

My dear Col, [Hermitage September 17, 1844][1]

The within letter is from one of my compatriots in arms, now Genl. Davis & for many years Marshal of Western District of Pennsylvania, and on whose information I greatly rely. The Revd. Mr. Campbell within named,[2] is our old friend and preacher in Nashville. He like all good christians who knows Clays immoral character will not vote for him. How different this is to the majority of our Protestant clergy in these parts. New York & Pennsylvania, are now both certain for the Democracy & let Ohio go as she will, your election is sure if you live. We all kindly salute you & Lady.

ANDREW JACKSON

ALS. DLC–JKP. Addressed to Columbia under the frank of Andrew Jackson.

1. Date identified through content analysis. Jackson appended his letter to one received from John M. Davis and dated September 9, 1844. Jackson also forwarded a letter from Davis to Polk of September 9, 1844.

2. Davis wrote Jackson that Allan D. Campbell had paid him a visit the previous week, had asked to be remembered to Jackson, and had mentioned that he intended to vote for Polk.

FROM ROBERT ARMSTRONG

Nashville, Tenn. September 18, 1844

Armstrong urges Polk to secure McClung's campaign services in East Tennessee and Sykes' assistance in Wilson and Smith Counties. He notes that McLemore is very ill. While news is good from every quarter, Armstrong remains a little anxious about state elections in Maine.

ALS. DLC–JKP. Addressed to Columbia.

FROM JOHN P. HEISS

Union Office
Dear Sir, Nashville Sep. 18 1844

It happens to be an unfortunate moment for us to print as neat a pamphlet[1] as we could wish on account of paper. The Cumberland River has been so long *low* that we are compelled to use an inferior article.

I have procured a ream of superior paper which will print near five hundred copies for your own especial use. You write for only two hundred copies, and, if you desire the balance forwarded to you, please inform Gen. Armstrong or myself. I send but twenty five copies by this evenings mail on account of the quality of the paper as stated above but will print on the fine paper to-morrow and send you the balance you desire.

While sending a copy to each Democratic Member of Congress, would it not be as well at the same time, to send one to each Democratic Elector in the different States?

JOHN P. HEISS

ALS. DLC–JKP. Addressed to Columbia. Polk's AE on the cover states that he answered this letter on September 20, 1844.

1. Nashville *Vindication* pamphlet.

FROM DANIEL KENNEY[1]

Dear Sir, Jonesborough Sep. 18. 1844

Among the thousand letters which I know you must receive, I deem it not out of place to also address a line at this very momentous crisis in our affairs, to yourself. I scarcely know whether or not it is proper, that I should do so. But such is the importance of the present canvass, I have ventured to make you this approach. Judging from the past I know you have the fullest confidence in in the uprightness of my course and the integrity of my purpose. I have been for some time past devoting all my time to the canvass, and intend up to the election to do nothing else. My opinion is, that as much depends upon the success of our *party* and our *principles,* as depended upon the success of the struggle of our Revolutionary Fathers in 1776. In view of this who can be still by day or by night? All! All! ought and must work to Land the Ship of State safely to its Republican moorings. The great Mass meeting at Kingsport is just over. We had from Twenty five to Thirty Thousand present. It lasted Two days. We had upwards of six hundred waggons and carriages on the ground; and old Va God bless her poured out her thousands. We shall carry her by more than the old Jackson Majority, no mistake. Many of her distinguished sons were present, and addressed the meeting. Many of the Virginians informed me, that in 1844 they were fighting over again the Battle "98"[2] and as they then Triumphed by the powers of the Constitution, and the right arm of Republican freemen, so they would do again in 1844.

In this part of the state East of the mountains, we shall make a great and glorious gain upon our opponents and they know it. The great Mass meeting at Athens comes off on the 25th. Two of our talented, and best speakers will be there—the Hon R. W. Powell, and Col. Landon C. Haynes.[3] East Tennessee will be her self again like she was in 1832. The old Jackson men are coming into their old Republican course. It is highly important that every county in the state should be thoroughly organized by classing all the voters but especially the doubtful, or those who can be opperated upon. Every one of this class should be noted down in a Book by the central committee in each county and then we should know on Whom to opperate and by what kind of Documents, as well as by the man or men, who could exercise over them the most influence until the election is over. This to my mind is a great matter!

I know that you ought not, nor will not do any thing in a public way, but through your friends at Columbia or at Nashville much good may be done by wholsome private advice. The Whig Banner[4] published at Nashville, is pouring in upon us by thousands to every post office in this section of the state, free of charge. The excitement here never was as great as at present, and the Democracy feel confident of success, and are fighting the Battle like men fighting for Liberty as did their Father's in the days of the Revolution. The fact is we must succeed and the the Democracy must open if needed their *purses* as well as their mouthes, and that too over the whole American Union. The Whigs having the money will spend almost the last cent they have rather than be defeated. The central committee at Nashville must be stired up to double their diligence. They have been doing much but I think they can do more. I hope therefore from this onward that all, yes, every Democrat will renew the contest, with double vigour. The time will soon be over, and all should attend to the election instead of his private affairs, and no one will regret it after the election is over.

DANL. KENNEY

ALS. DLC–JKP. Addressed to Columbia.

1. A Jonesboro physician and merchant, Kenney served a single term in the Tennessee House, 1843–45, for Greene, Hawkins, and Washington counties.

2. Kenney probably refers to the Virginia Resolutions of December 24, 1798, which were written by James Madison in response to the passage of the Alien and Sedition Acts earlier that year.

3. A native of Maryland, Robert W. Powell practiced law in Elizabethton and for two terms, 1841–45, represented the counties of Carter, Johnson, Sullivan, and Washington in the Tennessee Senate. Born in Elizabethton, Landon C. Haynes sat for Washington County in the Tennessee House for one term, 1845–47; represented Carter, Johnson, Sullivan, and Washington counties in the Tennessee Senate for one term, 1847–49; and in 1849 returned for one additional

term in the Tennessee House, where he served as Speaker. Haynes was a presidential elector both in 1844 and 1860.

4. Reference probably is to the Nashville *Republican Banner.*

FROM ROBERT WEAKLEY[1]

Dear Sir, Lockeland September 18th 1844

Permit me to introduce to you acquaintance Mr. Lyman C. Draper[2] my freind as a gentleman whos traveling over our state to obtain information from all the first settleler he may be able to see that are now living—any aid you can be able to give, will be thankfully acknowledged, by your old friend. Mr. Draper's Object is to Publish a History of the old pioners of Tennessee & Kentucky. He likewise as a wish to become acquainted with you as he is your political friend. He is Just on from the East. My health is not good I can Scarcely get about, wishing good health, and success in the approaching Election.

R. WEAKLEY

[P.S.] Please excuse this scrall as I can scarcely see to write. R.W.

ALS. DLC–JKP. Addressed to Columbia.

1. Surveyor, planter, and bank director, Weakley served two terms in the Tennessee House, 1796–99, and six terms in the Tennessee Senate, 1799–1805, 1807–09, 1819–21, and 1823–25. He won election to one term in the U.S. House, 1809–11; but lost his bid for the Tennessee governorship in 1815.

2. Historian, collector, and librarian, Draper gathered oral histories from pioneers residing in the western part of New York, his native state; he pursued that line of research southward to Alabama and Mississippi. Often Draper supplemented his oral accounts with articles from contemporary newspapers, court records, letters, diaries, and other manuscript sources. In 1854 he moved from northern Mississippi to Wisconsin, where he served as secretary of the Wisconsin State Historical Society, 1854–86. He published *King's Mountain and Its Heroes* in 1881 and edited ten volumes of *Wisconsin Historical Collections.* Upon his death he bequeathed his collection to the Wisconsin State Historical Society.

FROM ALFRED BALCH[1]

My Dear Sir, Nashville 19th Sept [18]44

Strangers from every point of the compass are dropping into our hotel every day and such is the public anxiety about the Presidential elections that all feel themselves authorized unceremoniously to inquire of each man the state of the public sentiment in the part of the country whence he comes. Since you left I have made it by business to gather up what these strangers report and as Grundy used to say "to put this and that together."[2] In all the news coming to us in this way there is one grand feature to wit "that you have gained, that you are now gaining and that you must continue to gain."[3] The Whigs themselves admit this important fact. It is of great consequence to all of us whether successful or beaten that we should carry Tennessee. I have a bushel of news from very many of our counties. I have noted it down as well as the sources where they were entirely *reliable*—have turned it over in my mind cooly and I assure you that I entertain a perfect conviction that we shall carry our state and possibly by a majority which will astonish our adversaries as well as ourselves. The tendency of *every* thing we hear points to such a glorious heart cheering result. Your friends are coming up boldly and cheerfully to their work. The leaders of the Whigs are down hearted and their tone is evidently subdued. The general *tone* of a party is in ninety cases out of a hundred the best possible evidence of its strength in a hotly contested election. I was not in Pen. or Va. more than three days before I decided that both states were irrecoverably lost to Clay. I formed my judgt on this general tone & confident feeling of all our friends.

In the District our forces are increased. Likewise in Middle Ten. and east of the mounties. Even in Dn[4] we shall reduce the Whig majority *somewhat* and in Cave Johnsons whole District add largely. As I have belived for sixty days that you will be elected our President I should be profoundly mortified at our defeat in cheated defrauded, deluded democratic Tennessee for in truth her people are decidedly democratic if they could get to understand themselves! If you are President they will soon come to this point. Mr. Senator Foster reached here Monday night last and left Wednesday morning for the conventions of East Tennessee soon to be held.[5] Ephraim cannot see further into a mill-stone than his neighbours but I am very certain from what a whig told me who saw him in the West, that he sees a probable defeat ahead.

It seems to me that a victory in Ten. will kill John Bell outright and downright. His bosom is hotter than the centre of Aetna[6] when it is pouring forth its burning lava.

Had these men possessed real hard sense they would have foreseen in 1835 the terrible fate which now awaits them. Old Bob[7] requested me in 35 to talk to Ephraim which I did and told him what he would come to. His friends however say that if he is whipped he will laugh it off, will resign and become once more the agent of the Planters Bank by which he can "put money in his purse."[8]

I expect to receive a frank and comprehensive letter from Butler[9] which I will enclose to you.

When I was travelling with Houston and his wife[10] I told her to say to Mrs. Polk that I expected to stand very near her on the 4th of March next whilst you were delivering your inaugural in the portico of the Capitol. She replied that she hoped so but she was afraid my phrophecy would not be verified. If Mrs. H has forgotten to deliver my message I now repeat it.

ALFRED BALCH

[P.S.] Saturday Ev. 21st. The news from Maine altho expected cheered our friends throughout the City; and was unpalatable to our opponents. It is not difficult to tell how they will feel should we succeed in Jersey & Maryland as well as in Pena. N. Hampshire Ohio &c &c &c. Your course from this till the 4th of November is a plain one—to be still—keep at home say little and *do* nothing but eat up your rations and take excellent care of your health. We are all in the best possible spirits! AB.

ALS. DLC–JKP. Addressed to Columbia.

1. A Nashville lawyer and an influential political strategist, Balch was named to a four-year term as judge of the U.S. Middle District of Florida in 1840; He resigned his judgeship before the end of his term and declined all subsequent overtures to run for public office.

2. Mentor for Polk's legal training and early political career, Felix Grundy served as chief justice of Kentucky's Supreme Court prior to moving to Nashville in 1807. He won election as a War Democrat to two terms in the U.S. House, 1811–14; sat in the Tennessee House for two terms, 1815–19; and served in the U.S. Senate from 1829 until 1838, when he resigned to become U.S. attorney general. Grundy returned in 1839 to the U.S. Senate and served until his death in December of 1840. Balch's Grundy quotation is not identified further.

3. Paraphrase of the motion proposed by John Dunning, Baron Ashburton, and passed by the British House of Commons in 1780: "The influence of the Crown has increased, is increasing, and ought to be diminished."

4. Davidson County.

5. While en route to a Whig mass meeting in Athens, Tenn., Ephraim H. Foster was notified that his father, Robert C. Foster, was gravely ill. He returned to Nashville.

6. Reference is to Mount Etna, an active volcano in eastern Sicily.

7. Reference is to Ephraim H. Foster's father, Robert C. Foster.

8. Paraphrase of a line from William Shakespeare's *Othello,* act 1, scene 3.

9. Probably Benjamin F. Butler.

10. George S. and Mary Beatty Houston.

FROM JOHN I. DEGRAFF[1]

My Dear Sir Schenectady N.Y. Sepr 19, 1844

I need not congratulate you on your unexpected Position as a candidate for the Highest Honor in the world. You must long ere this be surfeited with salutations of that sort but I will simply congratulate you on the cheering prospects before us. We are daily gaining ground in this state as well as elsewhere. I have never at any time witnessed a better feeling a better spirit and a more animated desire for success. The rank & file or rather a portion of them which left us in 1840 have returned to our ranks. Your nomination has afforded them *an apology* when they would not so generally have come out under Mr. Van Buren. You know Van has no better friend in the U states than your Humble servant, yet I have well known for two years past that we should have been beaten with him in 1844. While I feel confident we shall carry everthing with young Hickory at our head, Mr. Van Buren has been so long before the public the common people wanted *a new man*. They wanted a common ground upon which they can travel with their old associates and comrades & with whom they travelled prior to 1840. The avalanches that fell upon his administration although not arising from any fault of his, had its effect and made impressions upon common minds that are not easily removed. Many of them would not return to the Demo Ranks under Van Buren. They are now with us here and elsewhere. Mr. Clay has injured himself greatly by answering too many Letters. His late Letters do him much injury.[2] I now think most of the Abolitionists will vote their own ticket. If they do there can be no doubt at least scarcely any doubt in regard to N. York state [...][3] The Whigs will not hazard any *bets* on this state, so I am credibly informed. All will however depend upon the feeling that may exist with moderate men of the Demo Party on the Texas question. Some few are alarmed at any acquisition of Territories of states, beyond the Limits of the Present states & Territories. The alarm on that subject is daily lessening and will in all human probability not be thought of on the day of Election. I have from the first been in favour of the annexation. The Whigs here calculate some upon Tennessee. It seems to me they calculate without their Host, although you will have a severe Battle in Tennessee. Indeed Tennessee & NY will be the Main Battle Grounds. With best regards for Mrs. Polk I remain....

JOHN I. DEGRAFF

ALS. DLC–JKP. Addressed to Columbia. Polk's AE on the cover states that he answered this letter on October 3, 1844; Polk's reply has not been found.

1. DeGraff was a merchant and banker who served two terms in the U.S. House, 1827–29 and 1837–39. He declined an offer to become secretary of the Treasury in Martin Van Buren's cabinet.

2. In addition to Henry Clay's two Alabama letters, reference probably is to his Lexington letter of September 2, 1844.

3. Word illegible.

FROM ARNOLD S. HARRIS[1]

Dr Sir Nashville Sep 19 [1844][2]

The "Star in the East" has risen and shines brightly—Maine glorious Maine comes in beyond our most sanguine hopes.[3] The Coons in town took to their hollow stumps soon after the mail came in. The democrats are in a perfect delerium of joy. Tomorrow night the "big gun" will be brought out and the death knell of whiggery will be sounded. This great and decisive victory will strike a panic among the Whigs and throw every fence man over on our side. Its effect will be irresistable. The ball started at Maine with such a momentum cannot be stopped short of the Gulf of Mexico.

Enclosed is the slip, made up from others recd. here to night.[4]

A. HARRIS

ALS. DLC–JKP. Addressed to Columbia.

1. Arnold S. Harris, a resident of Arkansas, was Robert Armstrong's son-in-law.

2. Date identified through content analysis.

3. News bulletins in the *Nashville Union* often appeared under the caption, "Star of the East"; below the display type would be printed a drawing of a "Democrat rooster" crowing over a "Whig coon." For particularly good news, the late news column would be headed by the caption, "Bring out the Big Gun!"; below the display type would be printed a drawing of a smoking cannon. On September 20, 1844, the *Nashville Union* carried a "Big Gun" column detailing the Democratic party's recent victory in Maine's state elections.

4. Enclosure not found.

FROM SAMUEL H. LAUGHLIN

My dear Sir, Nashville, T. Sept. 19, 1844

Under cover of this you will receive the Vindication of Col. E. Polk in the final form which it has assumed,[1] after having gone through the Daily, Tri-weekly, and Weekly editions of the Union, and a more than full edition of the Star Spangled Banner.[2] I have thought, that after these are all passed through the press, and started out in all directions, that the Report at length of Mr. Haywood,[3] *without the proofs,* ought to be published through the Union and Star S. Banner. I have reviewed it in a careful reading, and find that *in and of itself,* it is an able, persuasive, patriotic democratic document, calculated to do good. I have only kept it back in that form, because it is too long to be crowded into the same papers and pamphlets containing the present publication. I wish you would take the trouble to look over it, leaving out the testimony, and see whether you do not think it deserves such an insertion. We owe Haywood and North Carolina the compliment of a publication, and a respectful and thankful notice of the services of Haywood and the Committee. Do please favor me with your suggestions on the matter.

For a week and more the papers here have teemed with charges against you,[4] most of them contemptable and frivalous, but deserving notice and reprehension. Harris and myself upon daily consultation, have tried to keep up with them, he taking some of the topics and I others. In the meantime, I have attended to preparing such articles as the review of the Prospect before us, answer to Clayton on the tariff,[5] the old documents quoted from Morford and Falkner, as White and Harrison Electors[6] etc. The calls and appeals, to keep the fire burning, I urge Col. Harris to keep up. Tomorrow I shall have a good paper, a letter from Buffalo &c. showing how glorious and certain our prospects are east, and a *new view* of the Bargain question from a writer in Arkansas.[7]

Mr. Kezer[8] will, though very inconvenient, make the travel we talked of. He goes with our cavalry to Spring Hill,[9] and will see you. He has put his matters in train[10] to go out as a missionary. I hope in God he may be able to do something. We are too poor here. Distressed as I have been, I have not asked our friends to raise me a cent since the $100 they furnished me to go to Baltimore, and that fell $50 short of my expenses. Seeing the necessity of forbearance, I have had Dr. Smartt[11] commissioned for a month to sell a negro for me to keep constables off of me, rather than annoy our friends here who are, I hope, contributing to other purposes as liberally as they can. My case shall be no additional annoyance to them, if I am never paid. I went into the contest determined that no sacrifice I could make of time and labor—money I had none—should be spared. For the paper I could write more, especially could have written more before it became daily, but I made up the time in letters and documents, for I have sent more pamphets, news papers, letters &c. than any man in the state, having continually hunted up our friends at the taverns from all the remote counties and sent packets by them.

We are now, my dear sir, ten years earlier than I expected it, engaged in the very battle which I foresaw, and prayed for, from the first hour after I headed the first movement to bring your name before the nation as a candidate for the Vice Presidency. And however I may be deemed of, and however short of my own wishes or the wishes of my friends my exertions may fall, I have in every movement of my life politically, had an eye single, in all my exertions, to promote and hasten the advancement of the time when the present contest, with you in your present position, should come. It has come, come sooner than I expected, but not sooner than desired, because success must be the result. This being truly the case, and because I have not been able fully to please all here, my position has been sometimes painful, distressingly so; because I have kept up and toiled day and night, have sat up, read and compared trash, stuck to my post in privacy, doing always what I deemed best, when my health for a great portion of the spring and summer has been such that I have been sometimes for weeks unable to stand on my feet and walk even as far as Kezer's. Yet I have complained not. I have not held back from any work or responsibility and will not. I will not, and do not write this in the tone of complaint. I only wish *you* to know the truth, for it is long since I have ever had a thought to conceal from you.

Please confer with Kezer. You may with perfect safety advise him what to do, though your name must not appear in any thing he may do in raising means. I am sorry that McLemore is sick and likely to die without speedy change. Kezer will report his case at a later date than the hour of this writing.

S. H. LAUGHLIN

ALS. DLC–JKP. Addressed to Columbia and marked "Private."

1. Reference is to Ezekiel Polk and the Nashville *Vindication* pamphlet. Enclosure not found.

2. *Nashville Union* and Nashville *Star Spangled Banner.*

3. William H. Haywood, Jr. Extracts from Haywood's report to the Democratic State Committee of North Carolina were printed in the *Nashville Union* of September 30, 1844.

4. The *Nashville Whig* of September 17, 1844, attacked the credibility of a Polk campaign biography that had appeared serially in the *Nashville Union.* The Nashville *Republican Banner* also printed numerous articles denouncing Polk's position on the sub-treasury plan, his views on the tariff, and his record as governor of Tennessee.

5. The *Nashville Union* of September 18, 1844, printed an article charging that John M. Clayton of Delaware had misrepresented Polk's tariff views in a speech delivered on September 5, 1844, at Lancaster, Penn. Clayton, a lawyer, won election to a seat in the Delaware House in 1824; served as Delaware's secretary of state, 1826–28; sat in the U.S. Senate as a National Republican, 1829–36, and as a Whig, 1845–49 and 1853–56; presided as chief justice of the Delaware Supreme Court, 1837–39; and negotiated the Clayton-Bulwer Treaty with Great Britain during his tenure as U.S. secretary of state, 1849–50.

6. Reference is to an article in the *Nashville Union* of September 19, 1844, that included extracts from circular letters written in 1835 by Josiah F. Morford and Asa Falkner. Morford, a lawyer in McMinnville, served as a Whig in the Tennessee Senate, 1835–36; he also held the post of clerk and master of chancery court for thirty-five years, beginning in 1836; and he served as a presidential elector in 1840 on the presidential ticket of William Henry Harrison. Born in

South Carolina, Falkner established cotton and woolen mills near McMinnville; he won election as a presidential elector on Hugh Lawson White's ticket in 1836.

7. In a letter to the editor printed in the *Nashville Union* of September 20, 1844, the writer suggested that John Q. Adams had purchased Henry Clay's support in 1824 with the office of secretary of state.

8. A Nashville merchant and hatmaker, Timothy Kezer married Ellen, eldest daughter of Samuel H. Laughlin.

9. The Democrats held a mass meeting at Spring Hill on September 20, 1844.

10. Meaning "to put matters in order."

11. Thomas C. Smartt, a McMinnville physician, married Laughlin's daughter, Sarah Louise. Smartt's father was William C. Smartt, also of Warren County.

FROM ROBERT ARMSTRONG

at night

Dr. Sir [Nashville Tenn.] 20 Septemr [1844][1]

The birds have been fluttering a little to day under the lash of the Union. They must stand it and have more of it. The news from Maine is almost too good. Since its receipt the Whigs are really desperate to mend the matter. Their *rotton pole* broke the other night and came down with the flag while the Hickory stood.

They made some little noise about it charging on the Democrats &c. &c. It is all over. Yesterday McNairy (Doctor)[2] offered his land at $50 an acre pay'l when Clay was Elected. It was taken and when the news from Maine came out this morning he backed out.

I will attend to the hand bills for Turney &c. I wish Currin & Claiborne[3] to go into Wilson Smith Jackson White & DeKalb. I think great good would result from their visits.

Keep East Tenss. in motion. Old Mr. Foster[4] is at the Point of Death and I think Ephraim will be sent for to come back. Spur on *Rowles* Maxwell Andrew Johnson[5] &c. and if possible get James McClung to go over. His trip just after Barton would be very sensable.

Virginia every one says is safe. *It is close,* and there is much talent and influence that seems to be doing nothing. The Whigs *will* make an exertion such as has never been made, to carry that state and may find our men *sleeping on their post.* They do not seem to be up and doing there as in other states. There is *now* a fine spirit in Ohio and the Texan Question since Genl Jacksons Letter to Dawson[6] is just sprung.

The Maine Election will have most glorious influence. It has here. Those scamps are all quiet. In haste.

R. ARMSTRONG

ALS. DLC–JKP. Addressed to Columbia.

1. Date identified through content analysis.

2. Educated at the University of Pennsylvania, Boyd McNairy returned to his native Nashville after completing his medical studies and practiced medicine there until his death in 1859; McNairy was an ardent Whig and great admirer of Henry Clay.

3. David M. Currin and probably Thomas Claiborne. A Murfreesboro lawyer, Currin ran as the Democratic candidate for elector in the Seventh Congressional District in 1844; he later moved to Memphis and served one term in the Tennessee House, 1851–53. A major on Andrew Jackson's staff during the Creek War and a Nashville lawyer, Claiborne served three terms in the Tennessee House, 1811–15 and 1831–33, and one term in the U.S. House, 1817–19.

4. Reference is Robert C. Foster, Sr., the father of Robert C. Foster, Jr., and Ephraim H. Foster.

5. George W. Rowles, probably William Henry Maxwell, and Andrew Johnson. A Bradley County lawyer and Democrat, Rowles won election to two terms in the Tennessee House, 1841–43 and 1857–59; in the presidential campaign of 1844, he ran on the Democratic slate for elector from the Third Congressional District. A farmer and lawyer in Washington County, Maxwell switched from the Whig to the Democratic Party in 1844.

6. On August 28, 1844, Andrew Jackson responded to a letter from Moses Dawson, an Ohio Democrat and newspaper editor. Dawson had asked Jackson for his views "in relation to the advantages likely to flow from the annexation of Texas to this country, and the injury that would result to us if Great Britain succeeded in her designs upon that territory." For a copy of Jackson's reply, see the *Nashville Union,* September 3, 1844.

FROM GEORGE M. DALLAS

No. 8

My Dear Sir, [Philadelphia, Penn. ca. September 20, 1844][1]

Very general indignation has been excited here by the libellous forgery called Roorback's Tour.[2] It's absurdity was, indeed, too obvious to an intelligent mind to permit even a momentary deception. We have taken measures to pourtray in it's true colors the grossness and baseness of the falsehood, and I think what was intended to injure you will yet be made the means of extensive benefit. A party that can descend to penitentiary crimes, in order to undermine a fair political adversary, loses all confidence when once caught and exposed. The forgery is ascribed to the pen of Thurlow Weed.

You may have noticed that the Democratic Executive Committee here has claimed the reward of $1000 offered by the Whig Clay Club if their extracts from your speeches and letters on the Tariff were proved to be unfairly made. Their unfairness is palpable to the commonest apprehension, and the Whig pamphleteers know it; so they have attempted to wriggle out of the scrape and to save the reward; but they will be coolly held to this original proposal; and their shameful conduct exposed. Our friend Kane pursued this matter with firmness and discretion, and the adversary cannot foil him.

These two subjects will constitute *brochures* for circulation at a propitious moment. Our friends are all alive with hope and conscious strength. The Whigs are overawed and dispirited. Mr. Webster canvasses, not so much for Mr. Clay in '44 as for himself in '48. He is summoning the Whigs to the crusade against Slavery; and while it is clear that he does not expect to bring the abolitionists to vote the Kentuckian, it is equally clear that he says to both Whigs and Abolitionists that they can hereafter rally in union upon Daniel Webster. He is making, too, his own pedestal.

We are to have a Whig Mass Convention, drained from all our eastern counties, and from New York, New Jersey, and Delaware, in this city on the 1 of October. The movement is one of sheer despair, and will be marked by extravagance in all it's features. No expenditure will be spared; nothing that can subdue our spirits will be left undone; Mr. Webster will harangue, from the marble colonnade of our Exchange, thirty thousand people; Mr. Berrien and Genl. Coombs are enlisted.[3] Yet, do as and all they will, the Whigs can make no capital by mass meetings now, in this quarter; our democrats will only be excited to renew the overwhelming manifestations of popular feeling which they have been making recently by scores in Trenton, West Chester, Norristown, Bristol, Harrisburg, &c. &c. &c.

We are agreed, nem. con., that New-York, Pennsylvania, New-Jersey, Delaware, Virginia, and, not unlikely, Maryland, will be democratic in their electors. Mr. Bancroft writes, in doubt whether he may not be elected, and Massachusetts vote for Polk. Should so strange an incident happen—it can hardly be considered a fortunate one—the equivocal course and probably private arrangements of Mr. Webster may explain it. There are several States which you may possibly get, and which I should prefer your not getting; but I fervently hope that our friends in Tennessee will triumphantly silence the Whig boast that their candidate will have your State.

Have you noticed certain givings out by letter-writers at Washington that some critical movement as to Texas is contemplated by the Cabinet? May it not be the detention of the Mexican Steamers at N. York, so necessary to an aggressive step to Galveston?[4] May it not be *the loss* of a few regiments to President Houston, as a sort of intimation to the Mexicans that the U. States and Texas are too *nearly* united not to have their colors blended? It is rumoured, too, that the Secretary of State[5] has accomplished some diplomatic conclusion about Oregon. I did not like Mr. Calhoun's speech in the Senate on this subject—nor Mr. McDuffie's—and, therefore, I hope this rumor is unfounded.[6]

We shall have *three* tickets, in the city and county of Philadelphia, at the election on the 8 of October. In the City, the Whigs and Natives will probably strike a bargain, and unite on the *Native Mayor* and the *Whig Member* of *Congress;* if they do not, the democrats may edge in both their candidates. In the 1 Cong. district—known to you perhaps as Sutherland's old district—the three sided conflict rages fiercely, but, I am inclined to believe that our friend, Lehman, will succeed by a plurality of about 250. In the 3d Cong. District, the odds seem to be in favor of *the Native.* In the 4 Cong. District, Mr. C. J. Ingersoll's,[7] I hope, but yet painfully doubt. This particular region of Pennsylvania is doomed to be always infested by factions, or unrelentingly ruled by federalism.

I receive and am obliged to answer so many letters that I am sure you, who are probably much worse afflicted in that way, will excuse the haste and carelessness with which I write.

G. M. Dallas

ALS. DLC–JKP. Addressed to Columbia. Polk's AE on the cover states that he answered this letter on October 7, 1844; Polk's reply has not been found.

1. Approximate date identified through content analysis.

2. On August 21, 1844, the Ithaca *Chronicle* published an article purporting to have been extracted from *Roorback's Tour through the Western and Southern States in 1836.* The *Chronicle's* article, signed "An Abolitionist," recounted Roorback's story of having met a slave trader who had in his custody forty of James K. Polk's slaves, all of whom bore Polk's initials branded on their shoulders. The *Chronicle* subsequently retracted the article and claimed that William Linn, a Democrat office holder in Ithaca, had invented the Roorback book and had lifted the slave trader story from a travel memoir by G. W. Featherstonhaugh. The *Chronicle* noted that Featherstonhaugh had never connected Polk's name with that incident. The *Chronicle* also printed an affidavit by Daniel McKinney of Ithaca stating he had been misled by Linn as to the truth of the Roorback story and had been misused by Linn in placing the article in the *Chronicle.* The Albany *Evening Journal,* edited by Thurlow Weed, reprinted the Roorback story before the *Chronicle's* retraction; Weed thus gave additional circulation to the forgery. *Niles' National Register,* October 5, 1844.

3. John M. Berrien and Leslie Combs. A veteran of the War of 1812 and a lawyer by profession, Combs served in the Kentucky legislature several terms during the period from 1827 to 1859; an ardent Whig and friend of Henry Clay, he served as an elector in the presidential contest of 1844.

4. On September 14, 1844, *Niles' National Register* reprinted under the caption, "Outrageous," the following notice: "It appears by a card from the Mexican consul general in New York, (Mr. Granja) that the officers of the two Mexican frigates have been harassed by lawsuits, and subjected to much vexation

in prosecuting their duties, from the prejudices excited among the people with whom they have to deal, by the Texas question. The sailors have been tempted to desert, and then to institute suits against officers on frivolous pretences, and shameless misrepresentations have been made of the order and condition of the crews. The courtesy of the U.S. officers, however, is gratefully acknowledged."

5. John C. Calhoun.

6. Participating in the U.S. Senate's debate on Lewis F. Linn's bill for the occupation and settlement of Oregon, George McDuffie spoke on January 25, 1843, and John C. Calhoun, on January 31, 1843. McDuffie, a lawyer, won election to seven terms in the U.S. House, 1821–34; served as governor of South Carolina, 1834–36; and went to the U.S. Senate for parts of two terms, 1842–46. McDuffie and Calhoun argued that treaty agreements with Great Britain concerning Oregon must be legally ended before Congress undertook regulation of the occupation and governance of the Oregon country.

7. In Pennsylvania's first congressional district, previously represented by Joel B. Sutherland from 1827 to 1837, the Whig party supported Lewis C. Levin, the successful candidate of the Native American party over the Democrat candidate, George Lehman. In the third congressional district of Pennsylvania the Native American party elected John H. Campbell. The incumbent Democrat candidate in the fourth district, Charles J. Ingersoll, won reelection.

FROM DAVID T. DISNEY[1]

Dr Sir Cincinnati 20 Sep. 1844

I have the pleasure of acknowledging the receipt of your favour in reply.[2]

I am perfectly sensible that your position must cause you to be overborne with correspondence and as I have been absent from home nearly all the summer I have not thought since upon the points suggested by me in my former communication especially as matters seemed to take a course which rendered it unnecessary.[3]

I have just closed a tour with immense fatigue, and have now pretty thoroughly traversed our state in every direction. Both parties are armed for the fight and indeed are making herculean exertions. We shall poll an enormous vote and I have the satisfaction of saying to you that my impressions which I communicated to you in my former note remain unchanged with regard to the result in this state.[4]

The majority for our gubernatorial candidate[5] will not be large but I am satisfied that it will be decisive.

I learn accidentally from a whig friend who visited Mr. Clay a day or two since that he is very uneasy and apprehensive of the result in Ohio. A number of the leading whig stumpers from Kentucky are now traversing our state and the whole whig party seem to be aroused not only to the importance of our October election but to the danger they are in of having its results adverse to them. But our people appreciate these things just as well as they do and every nerve is strained upon our part to secure the victory. For myself I am nearly jaded down with this incessant travelling and speaking.

But two weeks more will close this campaign as our election for state officers will take place on the 2d Tuesday of October and many of us here believe that Tods election on that day will crush alike the hopes and the spirits of Mr. Clay and his friends. A decisive vote in Ohio must have an immense effect upon other states and remove all doubts if any yet exists with regard to Indiana.

Congratulating you upon the glorious victory achieved by the democracy of Maine and the cheering prospects in Ohio I remain....

D. T. DISNEY

ALS. DLC–JKP. Addressed to Columbia.

1. A Cincinnati lawyer, David T. Disney served three terms in the Ohio House, 1829 and 1831–32, and two terms in the Ohio Senate, 1833–34 and 1843–44. A delegate to the Democratic National Convention of 1848, he represented Ohio in the U.S. House from 1849 to 1855.

2. Polk wrote to Disney on August 3, 1844. His letter has not been found.

3. See David T. Disney to Polk, June 11, 1844.

4. Reference is to the above letter.

5. David Tod.

FROM JOHN FAIRFIELD

My Dear Sir, Saco Sept. 20, 1844

The election is over, and the result verifies my prediction in a letter to you written on Saturday before our election on monday,[1] except that I did not estimate our majority high enough. Returns are now all in, and our majority is from 4500 to 4700 over Whigs and abolitionists. The difference between our papers I presume to be a difference of addition merely. Maine may now be set down by others what we have always known here to be, as sure for Polk & Dallas in November. This state is essentially democratic, and whenever pains are taken to inform the people so as to prevent their being *cheated* by the whigs they will always go right. This year uncommon efforts have been made upon both sides. Evans, Gov. Kent, Fessenden[2] & many of the strong men of the whigs have been over the State and done all that mortal men could do to seduce the people. But wherever they have been, and it must be very mortifying to them, the Whigs have sustained a loss. While on the other hand every place visited and addressed by myself and others on our side, have given large democratic gains. For this however we claim no merit. We give all the glory to the *power of truth,* to the *goodness of our cause.* What course the Whigs intend pursuing in reference to the November election we are not yet apprised of. I think however they can do but little more than show their teeth. Their bark will be harmless and bite they cant. We shall look sharp after them nevertheless, and take the stump again, if need be.

I regret that differences about men have prevented an election in two, if not three of our Congressional Districts. Another trial will settle these I think. At all events the vote for Electors will not be affected by them.

I have received a letter from Mr. Van Buren since the election in this State, and he seems to be as much rejoiced at the result as if he occupied your position himself. His course has been magnanimous, and such in all respects as his best friends could wish. The Texas question has not excited much feeling in our contest. The whigs have used it, but not with much effect. Upon several occasions I have answered the Whigs and advocated the annexation as strongly and ardently as I could, although as you are aware I voted against the treaty, and with the abolitionists, it is said, my views have had considerable effect.

The tariff and Bank however have been the principal topics on both sides, and on these the Whigs have been sadly beaten. But not to exhaust your patience I close by subscribing myself....

J. FAIRFIELD

ALS. DLC–JKP. Addressed to Columbia.

1. Reference is to Fairfield's letter to Polk of September 7, 1844.

2. George Evans, Edward Kent, and William Pitt Fessenden. Evans, a Whig, served six terms in the U.S. House, 1829–41, and one term in the U.S. Senate, 1841–47. Kent won election as a Whig to two terms as governor of Maine, 1838–39 and 1841–42. A lawyer and a strong anti-slavery man, Fessenden was a member of the Maine House from 1832 until 1840; won election as a Whig to one term in the U.S. House, 1841–43; and later served in the U.S. Senate from 1854 to 1864, when he resigned to become secretary of the Treasury in Abraham Lincoln's cabinet.

FROM J. GEORGE HARRIS

My Dear Gov, Nashville Sep 20 [18]44

We are really overjoyed to night. Maine has done nobly. I rec'd a letter from Boston two or three days ago in which our friends said they expected to elect Anderson by only 2000. It is now almost certain that he is elected by 5000 at least over all. This will be a *glorious* beginning in the East.

You will have seen by this morning's Union that I held up Jones[1] in his *true colors.* It was *sucre*—it *deserved* to be so.[2] It was the only way, to give him *a rough-hewing.* His hide is so *thick,* he *feels* nothing else. Nothing *short of that* would silence his foreign letters,[3] and I do *honestly* think it was *true* and simply *put.* He *feels* it to the quick, so do his friends. You will see some *squirming* in the whig papers.

I have just finished preparing the defence of you on the Occupant Question, according to your notes. It will be in type to-morrow and appear in the Union on Monday. It is *conclusive.*

Kendall's "Clay agt the settlers" appears for a second time in the Star Spang Banner to day, making 12,000 impressions of it in the two nos. It has appeared in the Union already, and Heiss says it may appear again if thot best.

We have them on the *hip* here now, decidedly. What with Jones, & his friends "under [. . .],"[4] the breaking of the Whig pole and the Maine news, they are *already* defeated.

J. GEO. HARRIS

[P.S.] I have *burned* your manuscript notes.[5]

ALS. DLC–JKP. Addressed to Columbia.

1. James C. Jones, a Wilson County farmer and one-term member of the Tennessee House, 1839–41, defeated Polk in the Tennessee gubernatorial elections of 1841 and 1843. In 1850 he moved to Shelby County and became president of the Memphis and Charleston Railroad. Jones was elected as a Whig to one term in the U.S. Senate, 1851–57; after the demise of the Whig Party, he joined the Democrats in supporting James Buchanan for the presidency in 1856.

2. Harris' use of the French noun "sucre" in this context suggests the idiomatic phrase, "casser du sucre le dos de quelqu'un," which translates "to make a scurrilous attack on someone."

3. Reference probably is to Jones' public letter of August 5, 1844, printed in the *Pittsburgh American* and reprinted in *Niles' National Register* of September 14, 1844.

4. Word illegible.

5. Harris wrote his postscript in the left margin of the last page of his letter.

TO JOHN P. HEISS

My Dear Sir: Columbia Sept. 20th 1844

Your letter the 18th is at hand.[1] I wish you to reserve for my own use 1.000 copies of the "Vindication."[2] I have written to Genl. Armstrong,[3] particularly how I wish the balance distributed. I directed him to send 1.000 copies to Edwin Polk of Bolivar, and pointed out to whom the balance were to be sent. He has my letter. I wish of course one or more copies sent to each Democratic Elector throughout the Union as far as their names can be had.

Will you put up 600 of the 1.000 which I wish to reserve for myself, in *single copies,* as your printers do your newspapers, so that I may direct them to individuals. Deliver all reserved for me to *Armstrong* as soon as they are ready, and he will send them out. In haste....

JAMES K. POLK

ALS. T-JPH. Probably addressed to Nashville; marked *"Private."* Published in *THM,* II, pp. 145–46.

1. See John P. Heiss to Polk, September 18, 1844.
2. Nashville *Vindication* pamphlet.
3. See Polk to Robert Armstrong, September 16, 1844.

FROM BARNABAS BATES[1]

Dear Sir. New York Septr 21. 1844

The interest I feel for the diffusion and perpetuity of democratic principles must be my apology for addressing you, but having witnessed the zeal & enthusiasm of our friends in this City, I deemed it not impertinent in giving you a candid statement of the meetings which have been held here the present week.

On Monday last, we held a Union meeting of all the democrats in this County, which brought together as large a political assemblage as I have seen in this city for the last 20 years.[2] There were 10 different stands for speakers in the Park & vicinity, besides the meeting in Tammany Hall which contained from 4 to 5,000 persons. At these several stands there were from one to three thousand people, addressed by different speakers. One consisted of Germans, who were very eloquently addressed in the German language by one of their countrymen. I have never seen on any occasion more enthusiasm and unanimity. Old democrats who had not been at a public meeting for many years came out on this occasion, and the friends of the different candidates merged all their personal preferences in a cordial & united determination to support the nominees of the Baltimore Democratic Convention. It is difficult to say what number was present, but 30,000. would be a moderate estimate.

Last evening a meeting of the young men was held in the Park, and although it was not quite so numerous as that on Monday, yet it was none the less enthusiastic and effective. I visited eight different stands, exclusive of the large stage erected in front of the City Hall. Two of these groups were addressed in French & German. All the speakers addressed these several assemblages with great animation; which was interrupted only by cheers of the people, the thunder of the cannon & the bands playing some national air. The questions of Bank, Tariff, Distribution, Assumption, Texas & Oregon were handled in a masterly manner; and the false promises and humbuggery of Whigism were exposed in a masterly manner. Our friends felt that they were "right & would go ahead."[3]

The present contest is very different from that of 1840. Then the Whigs made no avowal of their principles or measures. The cry of *change, change,* down with the Sub-treasury & Martin Van Buren! was to be heard in every direction: the low price of produce & labor was owing to democratic measures, and a change would set all right: the laborer would get $2.00 a day, & roast beef, & the bankrupt would be released from his debts by the passage of the bankrupt law to which Mr. V.B. was opposed. They also had a new candidate in the field,[4] against whom little or nothing could be said; he had done nothing, avowed nothing, very obnoxious, but was bank or anti bank, just as his friends were pleased to interpret his sayings & had made few or no enemies by his public course. But our candidate was in many points obnoxious, & notwithstanding he was one of the best of Presidents and purest democrat, he was unmercifully assailed and unjustly treated not only by his enemies, but by many who had once been his friends.[5] His actions & measures were grossly misrepresented & thousands of democrats were deceived by the false & wicked representations of the Whigs. Besides, he had been long before the public, & disappointed & ambitious men had become his enemies because he could or would not gratify their wishes, and our opponents resorting to the most unscrupulous measures to defraud & cheat the people at the polls, our candidate was defeated, when 14.000 more votes would have elected him.

But the position of parties is now reversed. They have a beaten & obnoxious candidate,[6] who has many of his own party arrayed against him as personal enemies: we have a candidate fresh from the people, who has no political sins or offences against individuals to atone for, & whose moral character is without a stain: he has no clique to gratify, no resentments to indulge in, because the friends of all the other aspirants to the Presidency have united in his nomination. Hence all feel that he is their peculiar candidate, & will emulate each other in their exertions to secure his election. We have these advantages over our opponents which we had not in the last presidential campaign.

The *native* party in this city may do us some injury in our election for Congress & the Assembly this autumn; but for Presidential electors we shall no doubt give from 4 to 5,000 majority. Our friends were never in better spirits, & the Whigs are depressed. We feel that every man must do his duty, & not one vote must be left which can be brought to the polls.

You will probably recollect that I saw you at the Astor House on your visit to this city,[7] as well as frequently in Washington when I was connected with the P.O. Department, at which time I could not venture to hope that you would have been unanimously called so soon to be the Presidential candidate of the democratic party.

With my sincere & earnest wishes for your election, & a firm determination to employ my pen, purse and tongue to effect it, I subscribe myself....

B. BATES

ALS. DLC–JKP. Addressed to Tennessee.

1. A minister from Rhode Island, Bates moved in 1824 to New York City where he started a weekly journal, *The Christian Inquirer;* in 1828 he retired from the ministry. Serving as assistant postmaster of New York during Andrew Jackson's administration, he became an advocate of postal reform and in 1840 published an article, "Post-Office Reform–Cheap Postage," in *Hunt's Merchants' Magazine.* In 1843 he arranged a public meeting in New York, reportedly the first of its kind, to promote postal reform. On March 3, 1845, John Tyler signed a bill reducing postal rates to five cents an ounce. Bates served as corresponding secretary of the New York Cheap Postage Association, which was organized in 1846. The first authorized issue of postage stamps came in 1847, six years prior to Bates' death.

2. Reference is to a Democratic mass meeting held in New York City on September 16, 1844.

3. Paraphrase of David Crockett's maxim, "Be sure you are right, then go ahead." James A. Shackford and Stanley J. Folmsbee, eds., *A Narrative of the Life of David Crockett of the State of Tennessee by David Crockett* (Knoxville: The University of Tennessee Press, 1973), page 13, note 1.

4. Reference is to William Henry Harrison.

5. Reference is to Martin Van Buren.

6. Henry Clay.

7. In June and July of 1842 Polk traveled to Washington City, Philadelphia, and New York City for purposes both political and financial.

FROM JOHN W. GOODE ET AL.[1]

Sir — Pulaski Sept. 21st 1844

At a meeting of a portion of the Citizens of this County, at the Court House in this Town on yesterday evening, the undersigned were appointed a Committee to address you, transmitting a copy of the preamble and resolutions adopted at said meeting, and to solicit an early reply, without reference to your addresses and speeches, to the interrogatories therein propounded. In discharge of the duty imposed, we now enclose you a Copy of said preamble and resolutions, and respectfully request a response to said interrogatories, in the manner mentioned in the resolutions.

Doctor J. N. Brown[2] will deliver this with its enclosures, and awaits your reply, which we hope your Convenience will permit you to make at an early day.

JNO. W. GOODE

[Giles County Whig Interrogatories]

Whereas pending the election for Governor in this state in 1843, between the Honorable James K. Polk and his Excellency James C. Jones, Messrs Wyatt Christian, J. T. Leath and others of Memphis, propounded to said Candidates several interrogatories,[3] and among them the 7th which was in the following words to-wit: "Are you in favor of the election of U.S. Senators by joint ballot of both Houses of the Legislature? If not, by what mode should they be elected?" And whereas Gov Polk under date of May 15th, 1843, replied to said 7th interrogatory in the following words to-wit: "I answer, that by the Constitution of the United States it is provided that "The times, places, and manner of holding elections for Senators and Representatives shall *be prescribed in each state by the Legislature thereof,* but that Congress may at any time by law, make or alter such regulations, except as to the places of choosing Senators." The Legislature of this State have never *by law prescribed the times, places or manner* of electing Senators. Our practice has been to elect by joint ballot. In other states a different mode has been adopted, and in some of them the practice has been to choose by the concurrent vote of the two Houses, each House acting in its separate and distinct Legislative character, as it does in passing laws or performing any other Legislative act. Senators elected in each of these modes have been permitted to take their seats and serve as such, no Constitutional question as to the *"manner"* of their election, so far as I know, having been raised. I think then, in the absence of any Legislative provision prescribing the *"manner,"* that it rests in the sound discretion of each House of the Legislature, to select the mode or manner, which in its judgment will best subserve the public interest, the mode by *concurrent vote* of each House is Concededly Constitutional, and if by insisting upon it as the preferable mode, that be the only means of effecting a great public good, or preventing a great public injury, such as preventing the election of persons to the Senate of the United States who conceal their opinions upon public subjects interesting to the people, and who refuse to make them known, or to say whether they admit or deny the right of instruction, when respectfully interrogated upon these points by any portion of the Constituent body. In such cases, or similar, I hold that either branch of the Legislature, would not only be justified in adhering, but it would be due to the rights of their Constituents whose interests were to be deeply affected that they should adhere, to the *manner,* by which these rights would be protected and preserved. The chief, if not the only value of the right of suffrage consists in the fact, that it may be exercised *understandingly* by the constituent body. It is so, whether the immediate constituency consists of the Legislature, as in the case of the election of United States Senators, or of the people in their primary capacity, in the elections of their Executive Legislative agents. In either case the Constituent has a right to know the opinions of the candidate before he casts his vote." And whereas Gov Polk is now a candidate for the Presidency of the United States, many questions, and "public subjects interesting to the people," are involved in the canvass, and it is much desired that before the election, his present opinions in regard to the measures and policy, which in the event of his election, would be adopted in the administration of the General Government, should be made known to, and understood by, the people; and whereas a variety of opinions are expressed and published, as we are credibly informed, in different parts of the Union, and even here among his neighbors and former constituents there is a want of agreement, as to his present sentiments and views upon two highly important subjects, to-wit: the Tariff, and annexation of Texas to the United States. And whereas we a portion of the Citizens of Giles County, in the same Congressional District with Gov Polk, his neighbors, and many of us his old supporters and constituents, consider that, as above quoted, he recognises the obligation upon those who may be designated for office to answer "when respectfully interrogated upon these points *by any portion of the constituent body,"* that "it is so, whether the immediate constituency consists of the Legislature, as in the case of the election of United States Senators, *or of the people in their primary capacity, in the elections of their Executive or Legislative agents,"* that *"in either case the Constituent has a right to know the opinions of the candidate before he casts his vote."* We have a guaranty, that if interrogated he will promptly respond, and remove all doubts as to his present opinions on the above two subjects. Therefore

Resolved. That the chairman appoint a Committee of seven persons, respectfully to address a letter to Gov Polk, enclose him a copy of this preamble and resolutions, and solicit an early reply, without reference to his former addresses and speeches, to the following interrogatories to-wit:

1st Are you in favor of the Tariff Act of 1842?

2nd If not, are you in favor of its repeal, and the reestablishment of the Act of 1833, commonly called the Compromise Act?

3d If not in favor of said act of 1842, nor of its repeal and the reestablishment of said act of 1833, are you in favor of modifications of said act of 1842? If so, what modifications, in your opinion, should be made of the present duties, upon the following articles to-wit: brown sugar, hemp, Iron, in bar and bolts rolled & not rolled, and in pigs, Muskets and rifles, coal, wool, fur and wool hats, shoes and boots, ready made cloathing, coarse domestics, blankets, and salt?

4th Are you in favor of Tea and Coffee remaining free articles, or should a duty, and what duty, be imposed upon them?

5th In your letter to J. K. Kane Esqr. of Philadelphia, do you intend to be understood, as being in favor of discriminations for revenue, or for protection?

6th You have said that you were in favor of the immediate annexation of Texas to the United States: are you in favor of the terms and conditions of the treaty made at Washington for that purpose, and rejected by the Senate?

7th If not, are you in favor of the bill introduced by Mr. Benton, into the Senate for the same purpose?

8th If not in favor of either, are you in favor of providing, at the time of the annexation of Texas, in whatever mode may be selected, for the admission of the states, thereafter to be formed out of the territory of Texas, into the Union with slaves, if they desire to be so admitted? or would you be in favor of leaving that an open question to be settled by Congress when such states might petition for admission?

Resolved. that said committee select some suitable person or persons to deliver said letter to Gov. Polk.

LS. DLC–JKP. Signed by Goode and six other citizens of Giles County, Tenn.; addressed to Columbia. Polk sent a copy of this letter and its enclosure to Robert Armstrong on September 24, 1844. Copy. DLC–JKP. Polk's AE on the cover reads, "Giles Whig Interrogatories. Delivered to me by Dr. *J. N. Brown,* in presence of T. H. Cahal & S. D. Frierson, witnesses called to see it delivered, Sept. 23rd, 1844. Delivered in Genl. Pillows office and in Genl. P.s presence."

1. A Pulaski lawyer, Goode served as an officer in the Columbia, Pulaski, Elkton, and Alabama Turnpike Company; he won a seat for one term in the Tennessee House, 1843–45.
2. Not identified further.
3. See Polk to Wyatt Christian et al., May 15, 1843.

FROM GEORGE S. HOUSTON

My Dear Sir Athens. 21st Septr 1844

I have just got home from the W. Dest.[1] I found & left our friends in the *very best State of feeling*. They are up & doing every where in that part of the State, while the Whigs look somewhat dispirited. I heard none of the demos give more that 1000 in the Dest against you & many claim it as a stand off. Of course my opinion cannot be worth much on that point. I am thoroughly well satisfied of this that we are gaining considerably in every county I have been in except Wayne. In that our gain will be little or nothing. I saw Col. Harry Brown & Dougherty[2] of Perry. They say that there will be a change of 100 votes in Perry—Henderson, Madison, Gibson, Carroll, Hardin, McNairy all count great gains. Col Johnson came to us at Pleast Exchange,[3] where Col Gordon[4] left for home. Johnson & I were at Jackson together he then went south & west to fill the appointments. I was kept in Jackson[5] to fill or attend meetings there & in Carroll. On Sunday I left Jackson for home & to meet Bell at Savannah.[6] I met him, Shields & N. S. Brown[7] & made a fight with them all day. It of course is not or me to say how I *"held my hand"*[8] with them. The democrats were well satisfied & *crowing loud* after we got through—the Whigs were silent. I am satisfied with the days work *"inter Nos."*[9] I was much disappointed on Bells speech. I had never heard him before. He is greatly behind what I had anticipated altho I had heard he was not an interesting speaker.

Upon the whole, if the balance of the State begins to equal the Dest in gains to us we must carry the state triumphantly. I am aware you are probably more than busy. Yet I should like very much to hear yr news if you have any very interesting. Craighead[10] will be in the Dest tomorrow. McClanahan of Jackson[11] is doing good service. He was a little reluctant to go out but we succeeded in induceing him to take the field. He was with me at all of my meetings after I got to Jackson & is a good speaker.

The nomination & acceptance of Mr Wright has wonderfully *cut down* the Whigs. They fear that will use them up. I think we can beat them without N.Y. Yet I must believe the position of Mr Wright removes all doubt of our carrying it. What think you of it?

GEO. S. HOUSTON

ALS. DLC–JKP. Addressed to Columbia.

1. Western District of Tennessee.

2. Henry Hill Brown and James W. Dougherty. A resident of Perry County and a veteran of the War of 1812, Henry Hill Brown served four terms in the Tennessee Senate, 1823–25 and 1835–41.

3. Cave Johnson. Reference is to a Whig mass meeting held at Pleasant Exchange on September 7, 1844.

4. A Hickman County planter, Boling Gordon served three terms in the Tennessee House, 1829–35, and two terms in the Senate, 1835–37 and 1843–45.

5. Reference is to a Whig mass meeting in Jackson on September 12, 1844.

6. Reference is to a Whig mass meeting held in Savannah on September 16, 1844.

7. Ebenezer J. Shields and Neill S. Brown. Shields, a Pulaski lawyer and a political ally of John Bell, served two terms in the U.S. House 1835–39, but lost his bid for reelection in 1839.

8. Quotation not identified further.

9. Latin expression meaning "between ourselves."

10. David Craighead.

11. Samuel McClanahan, a Madison County lawyer, is not identified further.

FROM EDWARD J. MALLETT[1]

Providence, R.I. September 21, 1844

After congratulating Polk on receiving the nomination, Mallett recalls their college days together at the University of North Carolina, where they had shared the same boarding table and had "imbibed learning & science from the same fountain." He describes at length the adverse effects of the Dorr War on the Rhode Island Democracy. Although he had supported the initial movement for suffrage extension, he had opposed the use of military force against "the existing government" by Dorr's followers and had felt bound to take up his musket in defense of women and property. He warns Polk about certain Democrats who are seeking to identify the party with "Dorr-ism" and names in particular Dutee J. Pearce, Burrington Anthony, John B. Barton, Walter R. Danforth, John S. Harris, and Benjamin Cowell.[2] In his postscript Mallett mentions that at a meeting the previous evening "the suffrage party" proposed to raise $500 "in sums not exceeding one dime each" to pay the fine of Martin Luther.[3]

ALS. DLC–JKP. Addressed to Columbia.

1. Edward J. Mallett, like Polk, received his A.B. degree from the University of North Carolina in 1818; he served as postmaster of Providence, R.I., from 1831 to 1845.

2. Dutee J. Pearce, a Democrat and lawyer from Newport, R.I., won election to six terms in the U.S. House, 1825–37. Burrington Anthony, formerly U.S. marshal for Rhode Island, won election as sheriff of Providence County in 1842 on the People's ticket. A lawyer and newspaper editor, Walter R. Danforth was collector of customs for Providence from 1829 to 1841; he served ten years on the town council and won election as mayor of Providence in 1853. Benjamin Cowell was appointed collector of customs for Providence in 1848. Dorrites John B. Barton and John S. Harris have not been identified further.

3. A Dorr supporter, Martin Luther was indicted for the crime of acting as moderator of a town meeting in Warren, R.I., under the People's Constitution. He was sentenced to pay a fine of $500 and to serve six months in jail. In a related matter, Martin Luther and his mother, Rachel, filed suits in federal court against Luther Borden and several militiamen who had broken into their home during the "Dorr Rebellion" of 1842. The case of *Luther* v. *Borden* subsequently went to the U.S. Supreme Court on appeal; in 1849 the U.S. Supreme Court denied the Luthers' appeal on grounds that the Court lacked jurisdiction in such political questions as that of Rhode Island's disputed sovereignty.

FROM JAMES BUCHANAN

My dear Sir, Lancaster 23 September 1844

I have delayed to write to you on purpose, until I could express decided opinion in regard to the vote of Pennsylvania. I was so much mistaken in the result of our State election in 1840, that this has made one cautious. We have had much to contend against; especially the strong general feeling in favor of the Tariff of 1842; but notwithstanding all, I am now firmly convinced that you will carry the Keystone by a fair majority. Your discreet & well advised letter to Mr. Kane, on the subject of the Tariff, has been used by us, with great effect.[1]

There may, I fear, be some falling off in the City & County of Philadelphia, both on account of the native American feeling[2] & for other causes. We have been much at a loss for an able & influential Democratic paper there possessing the confidence of the party throughout the interior & devoted to the cause rather than to men. The Pennsylvanian[3] is owned by a clique of the exclusive friends & office holders of Mr. Van Buren, most of whom are obnoxious to the mass of the Democracy. It *now* does pretty well; but it harped too long upon the two thirds rule &c. &c.[4] I have had several times to assure influential individuals in that City, without pretending, however, to know your sentiments, that as you were a new man yourself & would be anxious to illustrate your administration by popular favor as well as sound principles, you would not select old party hacks for office, merely because they had already held office under Mr. Van Buren. By the by, this gentleman's conduct, since your nomination, deserves all commendation.

In my late political tour through the Northern Counties of Pennsylvania, I met many New Yorkers at Towanda. Among the rest were some of the members of the late Syracuse Convention.[5] They assured me, that after canvassing the information brought by the Delegates from all parts of the State, they had arrived at the confident conclusion, it would vote for Polk & Dallas. I have this moment received a letter from the Hon. Mr. Hubbell of Bath,[6] in that State, a member of the present Congress, which assures me that we shall carry it by a majority of from 15 to 20 thousand; and so mote[7] it be! Indeed, all my information from New York, since the Syracuse convention, has been of a similar character.

Please to remember me, in the very kindest & most respectful terms, to Mrs. Polk. Tell her, that although I have nothing to ask from the President, I shall expect much from the President's lady. During her administration, I intend to make one more attempt to change my wretched condition, & should I fail under her auspices I shall then surrender in despair.

JAMES BUCHANAN

P.S. I intend to go to Jersey next week where our friends are high in hopes. The Texas question is decidedly popular in Pennsylvania.

ALS. DLC–JKP. Addressed to Columbia. Polk's AE on the cover states that he answered this letter on October 3, 1844. See also AL, draft. PHi. Published in John Bassett Moore, ed., *The Works of James Buchanan* (reprint edition; 12 vols., New York: Antiquarian Press, 1960), VI, pp. 70–71.

1. See Polk to John K. Kane, June 19, 1844.

2. In early May 1844 armed conflict in Philadelphia between Protestant nativists and Irish Catholic immigrants produced several deaths and substantial property damage.

3. Philadelphia *Pennsylvanian*.

4. Buchanan's reference probably is a floor fight over rules governing the 1844 Democratic National Convention, which adopted the practice of earlier conventions requiring a two-thirds vote for presidential and vice-presidential nominations. Although a majority of the delegates voted for Martin Van Buren on the first ballot, the same majority could not be obtained in efforts to block adoption of the two-thirds rule.

5. On September 3, 1844, New York Democrats met at Syracuse, N.Y., for their state convention. See Albert Gallup to James K. Polk, September 5, 1844.

6. William S. Hubbell served as postmaster and then town clerk of Bath, N.Y., and later turned to banking. He won election as a Democrat to one term in the U.S. House, 1843–45.

7. Archaic variant of "might" or "must."

FROM DAVID M. CURRIN

D Sir: Murfreesboro Sept. [23, 1844][1]

I arrived here on yesterday (Sunday) afternoon, leaving Turney (who met me at Cornersville)[2] with Jarnagin. I have seen Yoakum.[3] He consents to accompany McClung in the route Eastward, which you suggested when I was in Columbia—prefers that the list of appointments should begin at Bradyville, Cannon County on the 5th of October; thence Eastward. About this, however, he will not be tenacious.

I consented, at Cornersville, to accompany Turney in his appointments. The publication of them as *joint* appointments may prevent Whig speakers from presenting themselves. I do not know that I shall accompany him, during the whole route. I shall be ready to go where our friends may think that I would be more efficient.

I wrote you from Pulaski; but, on learning that the stage did not leave that place until Monday (this) evening, did not mail the letter. Topp and myself spoke there, during the whole afternoon, on Friday last.[4] The crowd was almost exclusively Whig, the Democrats not knowing that they would have a speaker present. On that night, as I was informed, some resolutions were adopted by the Whigs, to call on you for *another* declaration of your Tariff opinions.[5] Our friends there laughed at the whole matter as perfectly ridiculous, a mere proceeding on the part of some half a dozen village wiseacres, striving to assume the imposing form of "a large and respectable public meeting."

I suppose, however, that Pulaski friends have advised you of the character of the proceedings; and, if they have not, you will best know how to treat it.

I find on reaching home, that a meeting of committee-men from each civil District of the County was held at my office on Thursday last. Their

Report is as follows:

Dem.	1585
Whig.	1481
Doubtful	160
(1843)	
Dem.	1367
Whig	1586

This seems to me to be too flattering; but judicious friends who were present (amongst the number, Yoakum who knows every body) assure me that it is correct and that the committee-men from each District could mention them, *nomination*.

DAVID M. CURRIN

[Addendum]

I would prefer a list like this:

1. Bradyville Cannon 5 Oct. where I have an appt. already
2. Some point on hickory creek
3. Some point about 10 miles below Pikeville
4. Pikeville
5. About 10 miles above P.
6. Washington
7. Prigmore's
8. Holt's McMinn Cty
9. Madisonville
10. Athens
11. County seat of Polk
12. Cleaveland &c backwest

I cannot go further east. H. Yoakum[6]

ALS. DLC–JKP. Addressed to Columbia. Polk's AE on the cover states that he answered Henderson K. Yoakum's letter on September 30, 1844; Polk's reply has not been found.

1. Currin mistakenly dated his letter September 24; corrected date has been identified through content analysis.

2. Marshall County.

3. A graduate of the U.S. Military Academy, Henderson K. Yoakum served as mayor of Murfreesboro, 1837–43; won election to one term in the Tennessee Senate, 1839–40; moved to Texas in 1845; and authored a two-volume *History of Texas,* which was published in 1855.

4. A Whig mass meeting was held at Pulaski on September 20, 1844. A lawyer, landowner, and railroad promoter, Robertson Topp represented Shelby County

in the Tennessee House from 1835 through 1839; in the 1844 election he was the Whig presidential elector for the Tenth Congressional District of Tennessee.

5. Reference is to the Giles County Whig Interrogatories of September 20, 1844. See John W. Goode et al. to Polk, September 21, 1844.

6. Yoakum's addendum was written on the reverse of Currin's cover sheet.

FROM RANSOM H. GILLET[1]

My Dear Sir. Ogdensburgh Sept 23 1844

Since the nomination of Mr. Wright for Gov. I have been so busy that I have hardly written a word to any body. Courts speechmaking & something for our paper have kept me constantly engaged. I can say, without a doubt on my mind, that New York is as certain for us as any state in the union. The only hope of our opponents rests in their appeals to the abolitionists. Mr. Clay's letter to Wickliff[2] has nearly blasted this hope. Gov. Seward is the emissary sent about to court Birneys friends & to persuade the Irish that they should vote for "Patrick O'Clay." It is too late for him to accomplish much.

Mr. Wright has ceased to make speeches. His correspondence is heavy. He "goes like a book"[3] on all subjects & his administration will be easy & free from all trouble on questions of public policy.

Every day there is a public meeting some where in this part of the state. Tomorrow morning, I leave to attend five, before I return. Next week I go to Lewis Co. (Dayan's residence)[4] to attend one. In fact our talking men are put upon *circuits* with as much regularity as if they were "regular clergy."

Letters from all parts of the state speak as cheeringly, as I feel authorized to speak of this region. I cannot doubt that every man I vote for at this election will be triumphantly elected. Unless we are deceived in Ohio & Tennessee this is certainly so.

R. H. Gillet

ALS. DLC–JKP. Addressed to Columbia.

1. A Democrat, Gillet won election to two terms in the U.S. House, 1833–37; during Polk's administration he served as register of the Treasury, 1845–47, and as solicitor of the Treasury, 1847–49.

2. Reference is to Henry Clay's Lexington letter of September 2, 1844. See John Galbraith to Polk, September 14, 1844. Daniel C. Wickliffe became editor and proprietor of the *Lexington Observer and Reporter* in 1838 and served in that capacity for twenty-seven years.

3. Quotation not identified further.

4. Probably Charles Dayan of Lowville, N.Y. Dayan served in the New York Senate, 1827–28, and as acting lieutenant governor from October to December

1828; won election to the U.S. House, 1831–33; sat in the New York House, 1835–36; and served as district attorney for Lewis County, N.Y., 1840–45.

FROM WILSON LUMPKIN[1]

My dear Sir, Athens Ga. Sep. 23d. 1844

In my retirement from public life, I still feel an abiding interest in all that concerns the common & vital interests of our beloved Country, and since your nomination for the Presidency, my faith & hope for the ultimate success of the good cause of Democracy, has revived & strengthened every day. The Democracy of Georgia are perfectly & fully united in your support, and I believe you will recive the vote of the State. No man living has so large an acquaintance personally with the people of Georgia as myself, & I have taken some trouble to inform myself correctly on the subject, & think we can scarcely fail to carry the State by a handsome majority. The whigs of Georgia have been forced to assume their proper position. They are now boldly advocating all the old Federal principles of Hamilton[2] &c. as well as the new federal measures dictated by Clay. They are *Anti*-Texas to the core. Indeed the Federalist of the present day, are identical with the old federal Party—with the addition of becoming Demagogues, playing off their fantastic tricks & mummeries, upon what they deem the ignorant masses of the people. They stoop to conquer. I was always more successful at *still-hunting*[3] than driving, and have taken much pains in a quiet still way to effect something in the approaching Election, and know that I am not mistaken, in assuring you, that I know of a vast number of changes from whigery to Democracy in the course of the last few months. The following states I think will vote for you. Maine, New Hampshire, Pennsylvania, Virginia, So. Carolina, Georgia, Alabama, Mississippie, Louisiana, Missourie, Arkansas Illinois, & Michigan—Tennessee, Indianna, Ohio, New York & New Jersey—I consider somewhat doubtful, but have strong hope for Tennessee, New York & New Jersey. I have less faith in Indianna, & but weak hope for Ohio. Indianna & Ohio, have a great deal, of the abolition & anti-Texas spirit. Clay will get the vote of Massachusetts, Vermont, Rhode Island, North Carolina, Kentucky, Delaware & perhaps Maryland & Connecticut, but in most of these states, our friends will make a creditable fight. Indeed the great Democracy of the Country, are fairly in the field & united.

Now my old friend, let me say, Texas must come into our Union. Texas & the Slave holding States of the Union, must be one & indivisable. If J. Q. Adams[4] & Co. leave us, let them go. They are Englishmen in heart & principle, and if it was not for my love & veneration, for the Democrats of the north, I should before God desire to get rid of the Hartford Clan.[5] I have no questions to propound to you as a candidate for the Presidency. Upon a critical examination, I find we have always thought & voted alike upon every important National question involving principle, and our views coincide upon the all important subject of Texas. In your success, none of your numerous friends will be more gratifyed than myself. My poor prayers & best wishes await you.

WILSON LUMPKIN

ALS. DLC–JKP. Addressed to Columbia. Polk's AE on the cover states that he answered this letter on October 3, 1844; Polk's reply has not been found.

1. A lawyer from Athens, Lumpkin served two terms in the Georgia House 1808–12; sat for three terms in the U.S. House, 1815–17 and 1827–31; won election to two terms as governor of Georgia, 1831–35; and filled the unexpired U.S. Senate term of John P. King serving from November 1837 to March 1841.
2. Reference is to Alexander Hamilton.
3. Expression meaning "a quiet or secret pursuit of any object."
4. John Quincy Adams.
5. Reference is to the Federalists and the 1814 Hartford Convention.

FROM WILLIAM MOORE[1]

My D. Sir. Mulberry 23d. Septr 1844

As the time approaches when the great Battle of Battles, is to be faught, so increases my anxiety, and with strengthened zeal we will meet the Enemy, the Enemy of our Countries Glory.

And unless the late tamperings (such as C. M. Clay)[2] gives strength to the North, Victory is ours.

I am pleased that you have not suffered yourself to be drawn out by cunning devises. Your position is fair and understood. I know that your enemies are anxious to get something new, on which they may comment & misrepresent. I need not say be on your guard, for you never sleep on your post.

The South is safe even Georgia is in our ranks. My old friends of all parts of the South, & particularly my old Soldiers are saying to me, for Gods sake save Tennessee. Well I think she is safe, but the better to insure it, my plan is fight the Enemy in the last ditch. One Man may save the State, this State may save the Election & save our *Country.* It was my wish to be at Spring hill[3] but I am a cripple & riding injures me verry much. I am getting much beter. I wish you could be placed on an eminance to see old Fayetteville next thursday. It will far surpass every thing that has been witnessed in "old Lincoln."[4] We are still gaining, & with our strength zeal is renewed or increased.

I have just wrote a letter to Prest. *Sam* Houston,[5] in which I say to him, that "the U.S. are now reeling like the drunken Man, & the Battle now to be faught is of as much importance to us, as was Jacinto,[6] to Texas, and that the Salvation of Texas is identified with the Democracy of the U.S. Give us *Houston, & Polk,* we have nothing to fear, but let the sceptre pass into the hands of Clay & Co. and darkness will prevade our happy Land." "But God forbid."

I could write more but my scrawl may be in the way of more important communications. If you write to Mr. Dallas, say to him, he shall have a triumphant Vote in old Lincoln which is one of the Counties composing your old District. And that shall tell in time to come. Yes and I will look at it with pride.

I have a few enimies round me & have been disposed to shew no quarters, was near having a fight, made my charge & caught two Men to a certainty, but have no fight yet. I think I can get 2 more to compromise if as I will make it up.[7] I feel admonished to stop all those little matters although they are true.

I would be glad to see you, or hear from you.

WILLIAM MOORE

ALS. DLC–JKP. Addressed to Columbia.

1. An early Lincoln County settler with large landholdings, Moore served two terms as a Democrat in the Tennessee House, 1825–29, and sat two terms in the Senate, 1833–37. He became state adjutant general in January 1840.

2. Cassius M. Clay urged abolitionists to vote the Whig ticket in the presidential contest. See John Galbraith to Polk, September 14, 1844.

3. Reference is to the Democratic mass meeting held at Spring Hill on September 20, 1844.

4. Reference is to the Democratic mass meeting scheduled at Fayetteville, September 26, 1844.

5. Sam Houston, a former Tennessean, won election to two terms as president of the Republic of Texas, 1836–38 and 1841–44. After Texas' annexation to the United States, he served as U.S. Senator from Texas, 1846–59, and as governor, 1859–61.

6. Reference is to the Battle of San Jacinto, which was fought on April 21, 1836.

7. Syntax garbled.

FROM FRANKLIN PIERCE

My dear Sir, Concord N.H. Sept. 23. 1844

I have been intending to write to you ever since our Delegates returned from Baltimore, but have been prevented by constant and pressing professional engagements, which have called me much of the time from home. That I was highly gratified personally with the selection of that Convention you will not doubt, but I was still more gratified on other and higher grounds than those based upon any strong predilection or personal friendship.

Mr. Van Buren altho' a sagacious and very able Statesman, commanding almost universal respect, had not that hold upon the hearts of the people that is essential to success in a violent political contest. He would have been decidedly my first choice under all the circumstances, if my vote alone were to settle the election, but it could not be disguised, that his name while it inspired respect, awoke enthusiasm no where. Prior to the publication of his Texas letter,[1] little doubt was entertained here of his nomination, but that expectation was accompanied by *hope* rather than *confidence* in success. The moment the auspicious result at which that body finally arrived was announced, the Democracy seemed to awake as from a slumber; and from that time to the present our prospects have been constantly brightening. The brilliant result in Maine has carried dismay to the whigs throughout the Country not on account of the number of electoral votes made certain there, but because it shows in connexion with the other elections conclusively the *setting* of the resistless current. The nomination & acceptance of Silas Wright is still more disheartening to them.

Johnson of course gave you a full account of the *unpublished* proceedings of the Convention on his return home. We think much credit is due to Mr Bancroft of Mass. & Mr Carroll[2] of this State for the noble stand they took in bringing your name before the Convention; indeed I believe all our delegates entered into the matter heartily when presented to them and a large portion of the Mass. delegation with Mr Bancroft & Gov Morton[3] at their head. Bancrofts name is a tower of strength in New England and indeed of vast service to us in the nation. It is a remarkable fact, but nevertheless a fact, that his prominence as a schollar & historian is fully equalled by his energy and power as a public speaker and political leader. Next after the noble conduct of Van Buren, Wright, Butler and the entire New York Democracy, I notice nothing in this canvass calculated to awaken higher admiration than the patriotic fortitude and favor with which our friends are contesting every inch of ground in Massachusetts and Kentucky. Altho in my judgment we stand no chance of success in either, still it is quite obvious that in both those states the whigs will find full occupation at home, with neither *men* nor *means* to spare to their neighbours in other states as in 1840. In Kentucky my conviction is that state pride will save the "Embodiment"[4] and that nothing else could. How sudden and afflictive the death of our friend Mr Muhlenburg! After he was put in nomination in Pensylvania and you for the Presidency, the two events recalled pleasantly to my mind the night when he presented the resolution of thanks to the *Speaker* and our agreeable meeting in your room soon after.[5] He was a true and worthy man. Our majority in this State will be from 6,000 to 10,000. The party is thoroughly organized and we are to have mass meetings in every County before the election. I have engaged to address the people of Grafton Co. next week. Have you an organization in Tenn. minute & thorough? In 1840 the whigs had the advantage of us in this as in everything else, except our principles & our candidates. What are the prospects in Tenn. and what is there thought of Georgia? Is it not very queer that Berrien should be in Massachusetts making tariff speeches at this time?[6] Does he think Georgia more safe than Massachusetts or is he in despair with regard to his own state? When you see Cave Johnson please to present to him my kindest regards & tell him that we give him credit for doing "Yeoman Service" in this great battle. Mrs Pierce[7] is now absent or she would unite with me in kindest regards to Mrs Polk & yourself.

FRANK PIERCE

ALS. DLC–JKP. Addressed to Columbia.

1. See Nathaniel Ewing to Polk, September 3, 1844.

2. George Bancroft and Henry H. Carroll. Formerly a law student under Franklin Pierce, Carroll edited the Concord *New Hampshire Patriot and State Gazette;* he served as one of the secretaries of the 1844 Democratic National Convention.

3. Marcus Morton, a lawyer and Democrat, won election to two terms in the U.S. House, 1817–21, and served as governor of Massachusetts from 1840 through 1844. Polk appointed him collector of customs for Boston.

4. The sobriquet, "Great Embodiment," referred to Henry Clay.

5. On March 3, 1837, the last day of the 24th Congress, the House of Representatives, on a motion by Henry A. P. Muhlenberg, passed a resolution of thanks to the Speaker, James K. Polk. Pierce's reference to the meeting in Polk's room has not been identified further.

6. On September 19, 1844, John M. Berrien, a Whig senator from Georgia, spoke in Boston and defended at length his party's support for a protective tariff.

7. Franklin Pierce married Jane Means Appleton, daughter of Jesse Appleton, a former president of Bowdoin College.

FROM J. GEORGE HARRIS

Nashville Sept 24 (eve) 1844

My Dear Sir,

The first question to be decided is "Will you answer the Giles whigs at all?"[1] Your *friends* throughout the Union would be glad to see you *absolutely silent* until the day of election. That is *their* feeling. Clay is killing himself by writing on all subjects and even to the editors of the newspapers without being called on. His friends *feel* that he has thus injured himself and they are trying to get our candidate into the same difficulty. Still, as you truly say, a *refusal* to answer would give them something to harp on. Now, Gen Armstrong concurs in the opinion that if you do answer, it should be a mere reference to your past acts upon the questions referred to, brief and pointed—careful to give them nothing out of which they can make capital.

Gen Armstrong is of the opinion that it would be best to answer them in some shape or other and the least said is the best. I will write you again and more in detail to-morrow.[2] Every thing is done according to directions in late letters.

J. GEO. HARRIS

[Addendum] Currin accompanies *Turney*. Nicholson & Keebles appointments will be out tomorrow. *Say* or *write* Nicholson that he must be at [...][3] in Wilson on the 3rd and at Hendersonville on 4th October. I stand pledged that he will. He can then rest untill the *7th* & take up his appointments at Cainsville. RA[4]

I send to Langtry a small sack containing *single* pamphlets enveloped as you directed.[5] No Eastern mail to *night*. Of course no news. In haste. RA

ALS. DLC–JKP. Addressed to Columbia. Polk's AE on the cover states that he answered this letter on September 26, 1844; Polk's reply has not been found.

1. See Giles County Whig Interrogatories in John W. Goode et al. to Polk, September 21, 1844.
2. Harris' letter has not been found.
3. Word illegible.
4. Robert Armstrong wrote his addendum on the verso of Harris' cover sheet.
5. Armstrong's references are to Hillary Langtry, the Columbia postmaster, and to copies of the Nashville *Vindication* pamphlet.

FROM BENJAMIN RAWLS[1]

Columbia, S.C. September 24, 1844

Rawls tells Polk that Whig newspapers are circulating untrue charges of Toryism against Ezekiel Polk. Rawls remembers that as a young boy he lived near Ezekiel Polk's farm and attended school with his eldest son and a daughter.[2] He requests that Polk write him and refresh his memory on the line of descent of the Polk and Knox families then residing on Sugar Creek and Steel Creek in Mecklenburg County, N.C.

ALS. DLC–JKP. Addressed to Columbia.

1. A Democrat from Columbia, S.C., Rawls was appointed postmaster during Andrew Jackson's administration, but lost his post following the Whig presidential victory of 1840.

2. Thomas Polk and probably Matilda Golden Polk Campbell.

FROM ROBERT ARMSTRONG

Nashville, Tenn. September 25, 1844

Armstrong advises Polk that a messenger from the State Department arrived tonight with an appointment for Andrew J. Donelson[1] to be chargé d'affaires to the Republic of Texas. Armstrong concludes that Tyler has chosen Donelson for this important and delicate assignment because he wants the "Old Chief's"[2] advice and influence with both Van Buren and Houston. Armstrong states that he has received Polk's two letters and will reply tomorrow.[3]

ALS. DLC–JKP. Addressed to Columbia.

1. A nephew of Rachel Jackson's, Andrew Jackson Donelson served as private secretary to Andrew Jackson, 1829–37. Donelson later guided negotiations for the annexation of Texas and served as U.S. minister to Prussia during Polk's administration.

2. Andrew Jackson.

3. Reference probably is to Polk's two drafts of a letter in reply to the Giles County Whig Interrogatories; see Polk to John W. Goode et al., September 25, 1844.

TO JOHN W. GOODE ET AL.[1]

Gentlemen: Columbia Sept 25th 1844

Mr *J. N. Brown* handed to me on the 23rd Instant, your letter of the 21st covering a Preamble and Resolutions which you state were adopted by a portion of the Citizens of Giles County on the preceding evening. I avail myself of the first leizure moment I have had since your letter reached me to respond to it.

Having long known you as leading and active members of the Whig party in your County, who have for years been politically opposed to me, and being apprized that your association has undergone no abatement in the present canvass, I should underate your intelligence if I were for a moment to suppose that anyone of you, had exerted his influence against me in *ignorance* of any sentiments on the subjects on which you now seek information. I can scarcely hope to be able to say any thing, in response to the call which you have made upon me, consistently with my known opinions and political principles, which could by possibility be satisfactory to *you*. Indeed you seem yourselves to have been aware of this. You are careful to notify me that you do not desire me to furnish the desired information by reference to my "former speeches and addresses." I had been in the habit of believing that a public man's public declarations & acts furnished the best means of learning his opinions. But I am now led to infer from your care in directing that you desire me to make no references to that source of information, that in my speeches addresses, and other public acts, you have found full answers to your interrogatives, and yet you desire me to spread before you, in some other shape, my opinions thus easily ascertained by the references which you inhibit me from making, and which you yourselves doubtless had made. If by your strange refusal to learn my opinions, from consulting them as laid down in my public declarations and acts, you hope to induce me to write out my opinions in different language, from that already employed in conveying them, and thereby to furnish carping political opponents, who really do not seek to know what thy are, with an opportunity by ingenious misrepresentation, to involve me in alledged inconsistences, I have no hesitation saying that such hope will be disappointed. If this be not the legitimate inference, I am at a loss, to conceive why you have been pleased to impose such a restriction. Allow me to assure you Gentlemen: that I by no means, recognize your right, to dictate the terms or the manner in which I am to respond to the call, which you have thought proper to make.

Satisfied as I am, from your standing for intelligence, from your prominent positions in your neighbourhoods, from the determined opposition which you are known to have exerted, against the Democratic party and its principles, from your familiarity with my opinions, and from the formal manner in which your call has been made, that your object has been not to procure information to aid you, in deciding how you will cast your votes, but most probably with the hope that you might derive, some benefit from it, to the political party of which you are members, I might with entire propriety decline any response to your interrogations. But as it is more than probable that you would be as much gratified at my refusal to answer, as by any answer I could give, I will refer you to the sources from which you may derive the information which you ask.[2]

When I accepted the nomination, by which I was placed in my present position before the country, I fully approved and ratified the political creed, which was laid down by the nominating convention in the Resolutions which were unanimously passed by that body. That creed embraces and covers, the subject matter of your Resolutions. The Doctrines therein, set forth, were such as I had entertained long before they were re-declared by that body.[3] I send you herewith a copy of the Resolutions embracing this creed. I send you also a copy a letter addressed by me on the 23rd of April last, to certain citizens of Cincinnati,[4] upon the subject of the annexation of Texas to the United States: a copy of my letter to which you refer addressed to Mr. Kane of Philadelphia, on the subject of the tariff.[5]

I could not in clearer and more unequivocal language, convey my opinions, upon the subjects to which you call my attention, than has been done, in the Resolutions of the Convention, and in the letters, copies of which I transmit to you: and I am happy to believe that my fellow-citizens generally fully comprehend and understand them.

[JAMES K. POLK]

AL, draft 1. DLC–JKP. Marked in unidentified hand, "1st Letter"; letter not sent. Copy, draft 1. DLC–JKP. Polk sent this copy of his "1st Letter" to Robert Armstrong on September 25, 1844.

1. Polk retained in his possession six different drafts of a possible response to the Giles County Whig Interrogatories of September 20, 1844, which had been communicated under cover of John W. Goode et al. to Polk, September 21, 1844. Polk sent copies of two of the drafts, hereafter identified as draft 1 and draft 2, to advisers in Nashville for their review and counsel; see Robert Armstrong to Polk, September 25, 1844.

2. On the copy of draft 1, which Polk sent to his Nashville advisers, the last three sentences of paragraph 2 and the whole of paragraph 3 have been marked for deletion; see John Catron to Polk, September 26, 1844.

3. On May 30, 1844, the Democratic National Convention adopted a set of ten resolutions treating the public issues of the day; for the published text of the platform statement, see *Niles' National Register,* June 8, 1844.

4. See Polk to Salmon P. Chase et al., April 23, 1844.

5. See Polk to John K. Kane, June 19, 1844.

TO JOHN W. GOODE ET AL.[1]

Gentlemen: Columbia Sept 25th 1844

Mr *J. N. Brown* handed to me on the 23rd Instant, your letter of the 21st covering a Preamble and Resolutions, which you state were adopted by a portion of the citizens of Giles County on the preceding evening. I avail myself of the first leizure moment I have had since your letter reached me to respond to it.

In your letter and in the Resolutions which you enclose to me, I am requested to reply to your interrogations, "without reference to my former addresses and speeches." I cannot Gentlemen: recognize your right to impose such a restriction. I had been in the habit of believing that the public declarations and acts of a public man, furnished the best means of learning his opinions. But I am now led to infer from the care you have taken in notifying me, that you desire me in my answers to make no reference, to that source of information, that in my speeches, addresses and other public acts, you have found full answers to your interrogations, and yet you desire me to spread before you, in some other shape, my opinions thus easily ascertained by the reference which you inhibit me from making. If by your strange refusal to learn my opinions, by consulting them as laid down in my public declarations and acts, you hope to induce me to write out my opinions in different language, from that already employed in conveying them, & thereby to furnish carping political opponents who really do not seek to know what they are, with an opportunity by ingenious misrepresentation, to induce me in alledged inconsistencies, I have no hesitation in saying that such hope will be disappointed.

When I accepted the nomination by which I was placed in my present position before the country, I fully approved and ratified the political creed, which was laid down by the nominating convention, in the Resolutions which were unanimously passed by that body. That creed embraces & covers, the subject matter of your resolutions. The political doctrines therein, set forth were such as I had intertained long before they were re-declared by that body. I send you herewith a copy of the Resolutions embracing this end.

I send you also a copy of a letter addressed by me on the 23rd of April last to certain citizens of Cincinnati upon the subject of the reannexation of Texas to the United States,[2] and a copy of my letter to which you refer, addressed to Mr Kane of Philadelphia on the subject of the tariff,[3] both of which avow sentiments in strict accordance with those laid down in the Resolutions of the Democratic convention at Baltimore. I could not on clearer or more unequivocal terms convey my opinions, upon the subjects to which you call my attention, than has been done in the Resolutions of the Convention, and in the letters copies of which are herewith transmitted to you, and I am happy to believe that my fellow citizens generally fully comprehend and understand them.

In regard to that portion of your proceedings, which relate to the minute details as connected with the subjects upon which you address me, it is enough to say, that having declared the general principles which I entertain, and to which I would conform in the event of my election to the Presidency, it cannot be expected that I should do more. No President of the United States, it is believed, has ever recommended to Congress, the minute details of any measure, brought to the notice of that body. General principles have been recommended and if in the adjustment of details, the action of Congress, has conformed to these principles, the sanction of the Executive has been given. Nor has any President in advance, proclaimed to the world, the minutes terms, and conditions upon which he would insist in any pending foreign negotiation. To do so would be to give foreign nations, an advantage over our own. Trusting, Gentlemen: that any legitimate purpose of your inquiries has been answered....

JAMES K. POLK

ALS, draft 2. DLC–JKP. Marked in unidentified hand, "2d Letter"; letter not sent. Copy, draft 2. DLC–JKP. Polk sent this copy of his "2d Letter" to Robert Armstrong on September 25, 1844.

1. Polk retained in his possession six different drafts of a possible response to the Giles County Whig Interrogatories of September 20, 1844, which had been communicated under cover of John W. Goode et al. to Polk, September 21, 1844. Following a policy set early in the presidential campaign, Polk chose not to answer the Giles County Whig Interrogatories, although the number and tenor of the drafts suggest that he gave serious consideration to making an exception to his general rule.

2. See Polk to Salmon P. Chase et al., April 23, 1844.

3. See Polk to John K. Kane, June 19, 1844.

FROM ROBERT ARMSTRONG

Dr Sir [Nashville, Tenn.] 26 Septemr. [18]44

Something like the enclosed[1] in reply to the Giles Committee I think would be well received by *your* friends and the *Whigs* could make nothing out of it. It is my view of the case as expressed to Harris. You must reply and the *least said* the *best;* it is a trick of Jarnagans,[2] and by the time any thing they can say on the subject will reach Pennsyl, Shunk will have received 15 or 20,000 Majority. I send a line from Catron.[3] In haste.

R. ARMSTRONG

[P.S.] I will write you tomorrow night and return the papers—and also of Giffords Matters &c.[4]

ALS. DLC–JKP. Addressed to Columbia.

1. Armstrong enclosed his and Harris' proposed version of a reply to the Giles County Whig Interrogatories of September 20, 1844; see John W. Goode et al to Polk, September 21, 1844, and J. George Harris to Polk, September 26, 1844.

2. Spencer Jarnagin.

3. One of Polk's staunch political friends, John Catron was appointed to the U.S. Supreme Court in the last days of the Jackson administration. A Tennessean, Catron helped the *Nashville Union* financially and occasionally wrote articles for it. See Catron to Polk, September 26, 1844.

4. For Lawson Gifford's planned visit to Nashville to raise money for campaign expenses, see John Blair to Polk, September 17, 1844.

FROM JOHN CATRON

Dr. Sir. Nashville, Septr 26 [18]44

This evening Genl. Armstrong put into my hands a letter from certain persons in Giles, propounding to you various interrogatories,[1] concerning an answer to which Genl. A. informed me you had some difficulty.

No further asperity can be added to the now existing bitterness operating on the minds of those gentlemen. The letter, and preamble accompanying the resolutions, prove this, aside from other evidence. They, and the resolution, show the petty tricks of a county election; and will decieve no one. No candidate for the Presidency has ever had presented to him, so far as my observation, and recollection extend so contemptable a paper; nor will any sober-minded man, feel for them the slightest respect, at home or abroad. They ask you to write a pamphlet on the Tariff bills of 1833 & 1842—and on the treaty for the acquisition of Texas: and it would require a heavy one, to cover the whole ground, including Mr. Benton's Bill.[2] And this you are asked to write and return by a messenger sent from a neighbouring village, and by men who declare your grand-father a tory, & call you all the hard names they dare, without a risk of injury to the cause they advocate. They ask of you *categorically* to answer forthwith papers that are an insult to you as a man; and comtemptious and arrogant in a high degree to a gentleman in your position.

Were it otherwise—still they ought not to be answered by you. Your opinions on the two subjects referred to are plainly stated, to Mr Kane, and to the Cinnti meeting.[3] These letters the Country understands fully. They have in them the general opinions you entertain on each subject. They are satisfactory to the party whose principles you profess, and whose support you recieve; and now to thrust on the party, any new issues, growing out of details, numerous and complicated, at this late day, would be in all probability as unfortunate for the Democratic party, as have been Mr. Clay's numerous and conflicting letters, to the Whig party.

Perfect silence on the subject ought to be observed as I *conclusively* think: and of this I have no doubt. No one has been consulted by me, because the matter is deemed too plain for doubt.

On this subject of letter writing, by those run for the Presidency, my opinions are known to you. If you answer these resolutions, you must almost of necessity answer all others. This would be impossible. Mr. Madison's course is the one I first remember: It was almost entire silence. Genl. Harrison's was *Silence;* it was the true and dignified course, after the first expression of opinion on the great landmarks of National policy professed, and correctly treated by Mr. Madison.

J. CATRON

P.S. When this letter was written I had not seen yours to Genl A. nor the proposed answers Nos. 1. [and] 2.[4] I think any answer improper, & neither 1 or 2, equal to the position you hold. Still your opinions formerly expressd. as to the duty of one before the people, when you & Gov. Jones were called on,[5] may require you to answer in some form, in the opinion of Gentlemen better qualified to judge of such matters than I am. I am a very poor Judge, and resentful in cases like the one presented. I deem it a barefaced *trick,* with condemnation on its face, and of no force. J.C.

P.S. By striking out all between the red marks in no. 1—it will then be better in my judgmt than no. 2. —and as good as such a thing could be.[6] That between the marks is rather *Carping.* I tried *Joking* in its stead. This wont. do. You must tell them they are *Whigs*—rank party scrubs, & in a decent way—& an earnest way is all that is allowed you. No. 1 does it well, down to the first mark, and your references after the 2d. mark are in true taste, and genuine ridicule of *assumed* ignorance.

I had doubts whether the last paragraph in no. 2, ought not to be added to no 1, curtailed—on reflection, I think *not.* You wd. be charged with seeking Sea-room,[7] be taking a new ground. Avoid this altogether. J.C.

ALS. DLC–JKP. Addressed to Columbia and enclosed in Robert Armstrong to Polk, September 26, 1844.

1. See John W. Goode et al. to Polk, September 21, 1844.

2. Reference is to Thomas H. Benton's Texas Annexation bill of June 1844, which authorized and advised the president to open negotiations with Mexico and Texas for fixing by treaty a new international boundary west of the Nueces River and for annexing Texas to the United States. Benton's plan also outlined terms under which a portion of Texas, not to exceed the size of the largest existing state, would be admitted to the Union and the remainder would be accorded territorial status, provided that the new territory's northern half would be forever free of slaveholding.

3. References are to Polk's letter to John K. Kane, June 19, 1844, and Polk's letter to Salmon P. Chase et al., April 23, 1844.

4. See Polk to John W. Goode et al., September 25, 1844, draft 1 and draft 2.

5. See Polk to Wyatt Christian et al., May 15, 1843, and Polk to George W. Smith et al., May 15, 1843.

6. See Polk to John W. Goode et al., September 25, 1844, draft 1, note 2.

7. Expression meaning "unobstructed space at sea in which a vessel can be easily maneuvered or navigated."

FROM J. GEORGE HARRIS

My Dear Governor, Nashville Sept. 26. 1844

This is the best that my poor judgment could conclude upon.[1] I have revised it and re-revised it in the presence of Gen. Armstrong. We have thought it over and over, and weighed every sentence. It can do no harm. It evinces a becoming sense of your devoted position. It will make them *sorry* they addressed you. I think it will please your friends, and show them that you are fighting your part of the battle as it should be fought. It charges the issue, and will *adjoin* the matter at least. A *Knotty* matter at best.

You are undoubtedly apprised of Donelson's apt as *Chargé* to Texas. He will make an efficient officer. The news from the North is glorious. New York was in a blase on the 16th. Bancroft in his glory at Tammany &c. &c. Tomorrow's Union will tell it.[2] All is now safe and certain, there is no doubt of it. But everything depends on your *prudent* letters when compelled to write.

J. GEO. HARRIS

[Addendum]

Gentlemen:

Yours of the 21st inst is at hand. For twenty years I was a chosen public servant of the People of Tennessee either in the State or General Government. During that period I took an active part in the great questions that agitated the public mind, and official records bear witness that I never occupied a doubtful position on any one of them or in a solitary instance avoided the responsibility of giving my vote at the calling of the roll.

In years past I have repeatedly addressed the citizens of this State in each and every county, clearly and unreservedly avowing and re-avowing my sentiments on all the leading public questions at length and in detail. And having no wish to disguise or conceal from friend or foe any sentiment that I ever uttered or any opinion that I ever entertained respecting the public welfare, it affords me pleasure, as a candidate for office, to answer all the questions that the people in their sovereign capacity have an indisputable right to ask. But, gentlemen, there is a *condition precedent* accompanying your interrogatories, to wit: *that they shall be answered by me "without reference to your (my) former addresses and speeches,"* which tells me that your object is not so much to obtain information as to *intimate* that there is a difference between my sentiments at the present time and my "former addresses and speeches" which difference you would seem to ask me (very respectfully) to aid you in establishing before the country.

This rather a misconception of yours than a fault of mine. It has been my constant aim as a public servant to be uniformly governed by a sense of strict propriety and exact justice; and my *past acts,* now serve me as *land marks* by which to preserve my republican position and direct my course. You will excuse me, therefore, from abondoning these ever faithful guides.

It is to my addresses, speeches, letters, votes, on the several questions to which you have referred—and others of a similar character too highly appreciated by the democracy of my country—that I feel indebted for the Presidential nomination. By them I am about to be tried before the great tribunal of The People—and it is to them—neither few or obscure—that I would refer you, gentlemen, for any further information you or your friends may desire. Your fellow-citizen, J.K.P.[3]

ALS. DLC–JKP. Addressed to Columbia and enclosed in Robert Armstrong to Polk, September 26, 1844.

1. Reference is to the addendum here printed below Harris' signature.

2. Reference is to an article in the *Nashville Union* of September 27, 1844, reprinted from an undated issue of the *New York Herald;* the account detailed events at a Democratic mass meeting attended by a crowd of 50,000 people at Tammany Hall on September 17.

3. At length Polk decided not to reply to the Giles County Whig Interrogatories of September 20, 1844, which had been communicated under cover of John W. Goode et al. to Polk, September 21, 1844.

FROM WILLIAM H. HAYWOOD, JR.

My Dear Sir | Raleigh 26 Sep 1844

I snatch a moments time to send you the enclosed,[1] written I have no doubt by *Geo E Badger,* the same who wrote the address of 1828 charging Clay with a corrupt bargain & coalition with J.Q.A.[2] Your kinsman by one marriage, mine by another.[3] It makes it prudent to circulate the vindication[4] more extensively. We have had the vindication inscribed in Standard & hope our friends elsewhere have circulated it.

I have rec'd to day the most positive assurances that N. York & Penna. are both *safe.* The letters are confidential & therefore more to be relied on than newspaper correspondents. If it were allowable to part with confidential letters I would send them to you. But suffice it to say that they come from the best qualified judges in N. York. Our good old mother (N.C.) cannot be *counted* on but we are struggling to effect a quiet organization & though we do not *count* on her *I hope.* If the October elections in Penna. & N. Jersey should be favourable it must operate in Tennee. &

here greatly in your favor. After you admn. commences I have no doubt N.C. will come to its support.

Judge Chevis' letter[5] is *ill-timed* & therefore *selfish* because it is likely to give countenance to the idea that Demos will go for Disunion: I am against it *out & out,* now and always, in the details & the aggregate, I am opposed to a self constituted Southern convention, opposed to resistence *any where* but the Ballot Box. How ridiculous to talk of dissolving our Union because we are afraid the abolitionists *may* do it. To cut our throats to keep from dying. May heaven bless you & yours.

W. H. HAYWOOD JR.

ALS. DLC–JKP. Probably addressed to Columbia. Published in *NCHR,* XVI, p. 347.

1. Enclosure not found.
2. John Quincy Adams.
3. Point of reference is not identified further.
4. Reference is to Haywood's "Vindication" article, which appeared in the Washington *Globe* of September 2, 1844.
5. Reference is to Langdon Cheves' letter to the editor of the *Charleston Mercury,* reprinted in *Niles' National Register,* September 28, 1844. A Charleston lawyer, Cheves served in the South Carolina House, 1802–10; won election as a Democrat to the U.S. House, 1810–15; succeeded Henry Clay as Speaker in 1814; sat as a justice on the South Carolina Court of Appeals, 1816–19; resigned to become a director and president of the second Bank of the United States, 1819–22; and held the post of chief commissioner of claims under the Treaty of Ghent, 1822–29.

FROM ANDREW JACKSON

My dear Sir, Hermitage Septbr 26th, 1844

This day I am greatly afflicted, but I cannot forbear trying to inclose, the within & others accompanying it.[1] As you will see *alls well* in N. York & Pennsylvania & Michigan & I have no doubt of Ohio.

I have recd, a letter also from Mr V. Buren who says Wrights accepting the nomination for govr. has secured beyond all doubt New York. Mr. Wright, he says accepted with much reluctance, but he yielded the moment he was told, it was the only way to insure the N.Y. vote to the Democracy.

Private. I have just recd a letter from Mr. Tyler—Howard our minister to Texas is dead.[2] Major A. J. Donelson is appointed and the means forwarded for his speedy outfit & journey, & urging me to use my influence with him to accept—tell Donelson of this & hurry him on, the crisis is important. P. Tyler has sent a despatch to our minister at Mexico[3] to remonstrate against the invasion of Texas, to say, cum multo in parvo,[4] that he will view it as war on the United States & present it as such to congress. This is the true energetic course. Yours in haste.

ANDREW JACKSON

P.S. Congress will not be called. A.J.[5]

ALS. DLC–JKP. Published in John Spencer Bassett, ed. *Correspondence of Andrew Jackson* (7 vols.; Washington, D.C.: Carnegie Institution, 1926–35), VI, pp. 322–23.

1. Jackson probably is referring letters from A. P. Stinson, September 11, 1844; John O. Bradford, September 16, 1844; and Joel B. Sutherland, September 17, 1844.

2. Born in South Carolina, Tilghman A. Howard practiced law in Tennessee and won a single term in the Tennessee Senate, 1827–29. In 1830 he moved to Indiana and served as U.S. district attorney from 1833 to 1837. He went to the U.S. House in 1839, but lost his gubernatorial race in 1840. Howard served briefly as the chargé d'affaires to the Republic of Texas.

3. Governor of Ohio, 1838–40 and 1842–44, Wilson Shannon served as minister to Mexico, 1844–45. He won election as a Democrat to a single term in the U.S. House, 1853–55, and moved to Kansas Territory, where he served two years as governor, 1855–56.

4. Variant of the Latin phrase, "multum in parvo," which translates, "much in little."

5. Jackson wrote his postscript in the left margin of the page.

FROM JOHN LAW[1]

My Dear Sir   Vincennes Septr 26 [18]44

The course is onward in Indiana, and the democratic majority for Polk and Dallas may be set down safely at from *three* to *five* thousand *majority* next November, and so our democratic friends in Tennessee may be assured. If "coming events" ever "cast their shadow before them"[2] Indiana is as safe as New Hampshire. Hannegan[3] and myself on yesterday united in a letter to our mutual friend Cave Johnson pledging Indiana for the majority above. I believe the highest number is less than what the majority will be, and we at the same time gave him full permission to use the letter as he pleased. I received last week a letter from Mr Dallas, of which the following is an extract "Genl Howard of Maryland[4] who has been actively canvassing that State writes me as his confident opinion that the Republicans would carry their Governor Carroll,[5] and if so, he does not doubt the success of their Electoral Ticket. As to Pennsylvania we are sailing before a spanking breeze without a rock, a shoal or eddy ahead, and as sure of success as we ever were in the course of our political history. The Tariff question is completely lulled by the manly letter of Gov Polk. The death of poor Muhlenburg, though a subject for sincere regret, in the political contest, opens a place for Francis R Shunk, who I doubt not will be elected." The letters received by me from all quarters are equally cheering, and I cannot and do not doubt of our complete and triumphant success.

I am well aware your correspondence is very extensive, and your time much occupied in attending to it. I should however be glad from some of our friends to learn the prospects in Tennessee. For my own part I have never doubted for a moment our success there.

JOHN LAW

ALS. DLC–JKP. Addressed to Columbia.

1. An Indiana lawyer and legislator, Law served as a delegate to the 1844 Democratic National Convention, as a judge for Seventh Circuit Court of Indiana, and as a two-term member of the U.S. House, 1861–65.

2. Quotation is a paraphrase of "coming events cast their shadows" from Thomas Campbell's poem, *Lochiel's Warning*.

3. An Indiana lawyer, Edward A. Hannegan served in the state legislature; in the U.S. House, 1833–37; and in the U.S. Senate, 1843–49. From March 1849 until January 1850, he was U.S. minister to Prussia.

4. Having won four terms as a Democrat to the U.S. House, 1829–33 and 1835–39, Benjamin C. Howard of Maryland served as reporter for the U.S. Supreme Court from 1843 until 1862; he succeeded Richard Peters, who had compiled the reports from 1828 to 1842.

5. A Baltimore judge and businessman, James Carroll won election as a Democrat to one term in the U.S. House, 1839–41; he was unsuccessful as a candidate for governor of Maryland in 1844.

FROM ROBERT ARMSTRONG

Nashville, Tenn. September 27, 1844

Armstrong informs Polk that Harris has prepared an article for the *Nashville Union* in answer to the Giles County Whig Interrogatories.[1] John P. Heiss has forwarded the Ezekiel Polk defense[2] to Democratic electors and members of Congress; handbills announcing A. O. P. Nicholson's appointments have been distributed. Armstrong notes that Nashville's city elections are tomorrow.

ALS. DLC–JKP. Addressed to Columbia.

1. J. George Harris' article, entitled "The Attempt to Misrepresent Gov. Polk, and Place Him in a Wrong Position–Gross Indecency of Modern Whiggery," appeared in the *Nashville Union* of September 30, 1844. See John W. Goode et al. to Polk, September 21, 1844.

2. Reference is to the Nashville *Vindication* pamphlet.

FROM JOHN W. GOODE ET AL.

Sir Pulaski Sept. 27th 1844

Under date of the 21st Instant we had the honor to address you a letter, enclosing certain preamble and resolutions adopted at a public meeting of a portion of the Citizens of this County at the Court House on the evening of the 20th[1] and which, at our request, were handed you by Doct. J. N. Brown on Monday last, the 25th instant. Not having been favored with an answer, we respectfully desire you to inform us whether a reply is to be expected, and if so at what time.

We trust that your engagements will permit an early notice of this communication.

JNO. W. GOODE

ALS. DLC–JKP. Addressed to Columbia.

1. Reference is to the Giles County Whig Interrogatories; see John W. Goode et al. to Polk, September 21, 1844.

FROM JOHN W. P. McGIMSEY[1]

Dear Sir, Baton Rouge 27th Sept 1844

In a previous communication to you,[2] soliciting the appointment of surgeon to the Troops stationed at this Garrison, in the event of your election, I stated that the present Incumbent was a Whig. I take pleasure in correcting this statement. I am informed that Dr Harny[3] is now, & always has been, a sound Republican & Democrat. Nevertheless, he has had the appointment upwards of 20 years, & it seems to me that rotation in office is more in harmony with true Republicanism; & I therefore hope that my humble claims may be remembered for the appointment, either here or near St Louis after you are installed as our Chief Magistrate. But if I were assured by you, that I would not receive any appointment, it would not change my course towards you. Altho I am no public speaker, you shall have my humble, but zealous support. I hope that I shall never be influenced by selfish motives, when I am required to act in reference to those great Republican principles, of which you are the able advocate; & which I deem to be of such vital importance to the strength & dignity, the prosperity & happiness of our whole Union.

We contemplate raising on tomorrow our democratic Hickory pole (in an open space near our Court house) intended to be 150 feet in highth, from which will be suspended a large & splendid flag, & upon the top will be perched a large & beautifully carved American Gold Eagle. Our

Democratic mass meeting will come off on monday next, at which we expect a crowded assembly.[4] I only wish that you could, consistently with your Views, be one of the number. The Zeal of our community increases with the approach of the comming contest, the great day of conflict. Not an individual seems to occupy a neutral stand. All have arrayed themselves under the standard of Polk & Dallas, or Clay & Frelinghuysen. This is perhaps as it should be. I hope the two great parties are influenced alone by a love of country. There has not been a time since the organization of our Government, when a greater necessity existed for giving an impulse to those great Republican measures under which our country has uniformly prospered. Hence I concieve the election of a Democratic President, of the first importance to its best interests.

Tell Mrs. Polk that Mrs. McGimsey is a thorough going Democrat, & full of activity & zeal, for the election of her Husband. I took her with me, day before yesterday on the high lands, the most beautiful part of our Parish, where I had some patients. We made several calls & at every place, she made a favourable impression & I hope several converts to the Republican faith. She stated that she was intimately acquainted with you both. She spoke of you, as an enlightened statesman a distinguished Jurist, an honest man & no gambler. And of Mrs. Polk, she said that no Lady could be found better quallified to grace the Capitol as Mistress of the Country. I verily believe that no Lady could electioneer better, or with more effect. She says she will continue in the good cause until the conflict is over. I shall be egregiously disappointed if you do not get Louisiana by a Very large majority.

J. W. P. McGimsey

ALS. DLC–JKP. Addressed to Columbia.

1. McGimsey had been a physician in Columbia, Tenn., before moving to Mississippi in 1834; he settled in Baton Rouge in December 1840.

2. See John W. P. McGimsey to James K. Polk, July 31, 1844.

3. Probably Benjamin F. Harney, a U.S. Army surgeon.

4. McGimsey's reference is to the Democratic mass meeting at Baton Rouge, La., September 30, 1844.

FROM JULIUS W. BLACKWELL[1]

Dear Sir, Athens Ten. Sept. 28th 1844

I cannot resist the impulse of feeling which now prompts me to write you. I attended three barbecues last week; the first at Decatur, 18th inst. Meags Co.[2] which was a Democratit concern, and about 5000 persons were present, nearly all democrats. All went off gloriously. The second at pikeville on the 20th inst. About 2500 persons were there.

Maj Henry spoke nearly three hours. Then dinner was announced; after dinner Maj. Rowles was allowed to answer Henry, but Henry put off to the village, and did not heare Rowles. The leading whigs moved off soon after Rowles got to speaking, and the rank and file followed. By the time Rowles finished, there very few left to heare him, and most of them democrats. The 3rd tooke place at Washington[3] on the 21st inst. and as it was very evident that there was a larger number of democratic voters than was of Whigs; and as it was threatened that the crowd would be divided if Rowles did not get a division of time, the whigs were quite condescending, and let Rowles speak first, and two hours was allowed for each (Rowles & Henry) before dinner. After dinner the crowd dispersed. Henry was eloquent, but Rowles is his superior in argument.

Our friends, *every where,* assure me that we are gaining votes. In 1840 the Democrats commenced arrangements for a barbecue, and invites the whigs to joine them and make a union barbecue; but they refused, and then pitched upon the same day, and made one for themselves. When the day came on, we out numbered them more than 2 to one. This year, the whigs pitched their barbecue on the day Henry had appointed to address the people in this place, and the democrats without determined to pay off old scores, and have a barbecue on the same day.[4] However much the whigs may grumble about it, and however much some of our moderate democrats may have condemned it, I do assure you it has had a most triumpant and glorious effect. We out numbered the coons at least three to one. Never did I see such enthusiasm in our ranks. The coons tried to sing, they tried to groane, but all could see that they felt whiped. The news from Maine,[5] which reached us on the evening before the barbecue, put a damper upon the whigs which they could not conceale. Altho great excitement pervaded both parties, yet nothing of a serious nature occured, altho there was but little needed to have brot. on a battle. On one occasion, where the two parties had to pass during the parade, a two-legged coon, bearing a four-legged coone on a pole, he impudently poked his coon towards the face of a democrat. The democrat seized the pole, shook off the coone, jumped down and stamed it to death in the street. The whig got down to defend the coone, and the democrat gave him a genteels flogging in less than a minute. The interfeareance of some of both parties put a stop to the matter just at this point.

The democrats evidently ruled the day, and had the coones under *cow.* The poor coons look whiped, they feel whiped, and they know they are badly whiped, but they dred the whipping which they must know they are to get in November next. Nothing gives them more pain than to see us out Herod Herod.[6] We fight the Devil with fire and have whipped him in evry engagement so far. Nothing plagues the coons more than to turn their songs against them.

They sing a corus to one of their songs, thus. "O! dear what a fine Joke, to have such a leader as little Jim Polk." Our little boys sing it thus. " O! dear, what a fine joke, To beat an old gambler with little Jim Polk."

The excitement is so high, I know not where it will end, but I hope no violence will take place. It is impossible to say how much we will gain in this end of the state. I have not the least doubt but that we will greatly reduce the coon majority in this Congressional district, if we do not over-run it. But the coons fight with desparation, and we are determined to meet them at evry point of attack.

J. W. BLACKWELL

P.S. L. C. Haines,[7] Geo. W. Jones, and Col. Robt. Powell, all Tennesseans, were our principle speakers. None from any other State. J.W.B.

ALS. DLC–JKP. Addressed to Columbia.

1. A Democrat from Athens, Blackwell won election to the U.S. House from the Fourth District in 1839 and from the Third District in 1843.

2. Misspelling of Meigs County.

3. Reference is to the town of Washington in Rhea County.

4. Both the Democrats and the Whigs held mass meetings at Athens on September 25, 1844.

5. Reference is to the state elections.

6. Paraphrase of "it out-herods Herod." William Shakespeare, *Hamlet,* act 3, scene 2.

7. Landon C. Haynes.

FROM ROBERT ARMSTRONG

Nashville, Tenn. September 29, 1844

After criticizing the Giles County Club's "Indecent *haste*" in sending out its letter,[1] Armstrong argues that the real intention of the Giles County Whigs was "to play out the *trick.*" He advises Polk that the latest letter removes any obligation on Polk's part to write a reply. Armstrong reports that the Democrats have been defeated in Nashville's city elections by 50 votes more than expected.[2]

ALS. DLC–JKP. Addressed to Columbia.

1. See John W. Goode et al. to James K. Polk, September 27, 1844.

2. On September 28, 1844, the Whigs won a decisive victory in Nashville's municipal elections; they elected the mayor, the town constable, and ten aldermen.

FROM LEONARD P. CHEATHAM

Dr. Sir: Memphis, Sept. 29th 1844

I have nothing particularly interesting to you, but presume you would be glad to know how your friends are geting on. Since Caruthers crossed the Tennessee, I have been with him at every point, but one up to *Covington.* [1]

Johnson, Coe & myself all met at Brownsville. [2] Cave gave us an excellent speech, his health is improving, for fear he might fail, Judge Wm. T. Brown & Th. Craighead [3] went on with him; I think he will have a good attendance hereafter, for at four places they promised me to have barbecues for him, so as to draw out all. *Coe* went home from Brownsville, to rest & be ready to join *Bell* at Portersville. [4] I met Bell the day before this (Yesterday) near Portersville, seemingly cowed. It is said here that Staunton [5] has only been able to meet him 3 times, & at each place gained a decided advantage; Bell gets vexed &c. The North part of the District has not been well canvassed & in no portion do I think the gain equal to Middle Tennessee, yet I have been in no County where our friends do not claim a gain of 50 votes & more, unless it be *Tipton.* There they say *30* & a few who will act vote at all.

I shall fill Coe's appointment here to-morrow, then go to *Westly,* [6] where we will have a meeting of some *15,*000 as they say: Monday after I shall be at Jackson with D. Craighead [7]: then on to several barbecues made to suit my return in Middle Tennessee. I shall reach home the 17th. Say to the *Madam* to *cheer* up a little; *Tennessee* is *certainly* safe & so must be *New York;* this County they say will give an increase of *150* votes.

I saw a man today just from Ohio, he says Clays response to C. M. Clay's letter will & *is now* injuring him there. [8] I have stood it well so far, feel dull to day from having road in the rain the day before yesterday. I wrote to you something about a *vest,* [9] if you have not heard of it, I am inclined to think it was left at that Doc's house we spoke at in Springhill. [10]

L. P. CHEATHAM

ALS. DLC–JKP. Addressed to Columbia.

1. Caruthers was scheduled to appear in Covington on September 25, 1844.

2. Democrats held a mass meeting in Brownsville on September 23, 1844.

3. William T. Brown, formerly a law partner of James P. Grundy in Nashville, served as judge of Tennessee's Sixth Circuit Court, 1836–38, before establishing a legal practice in Memphis. The son of Thomas B. Craighead and brother of David Craighead, Thomas Craighead studied law under William Williams of Davidson County.

4. The Portersville Whigs held a mass meeting on September 28, 1844.
5. Frederick P. Stanton.
6. A Democratic mass meeting was scheduled on October 3, 1844, at Wesley.
7. A Democratic mass meeting was scheduled on October 7, 1844, at Jackson.
8. On September 18, 1844, Henry Clay wrote Cassius M. Clay that he was neither an "ultra supporter of the institution of slavery" as northerners saw him nor "an abolitionist" as southerners saw him. Reprinted from the *Albany Evening Journal* in *Niles' National Register,* October 12, 1844.
9. On August 23, 1844, Cheatham wrote to Polk from Lynnville, "I left a black vest either at your house or at Mr. Alexanders at Mt. Pleasant, if it can be sent to Chappelhill or Shelbyville, I would be glad as I have only one with me & that is dirty & etc." ALS. DLC–JKP.
10. Democrats held a mass meeting at Spring Hill on September 20, 1844; reference to the "Doc's house" is not identified further.

TO JOHN P. HEISS

My Dear Sir: Columbia Sept. 30th 1844

I have received a letter from a leading Democratic friend in Louisiana,[1] requesting me to ask you to send the Nashville Union, in exchange to the *"Bayou Sara Ledger"* published at Bayou Sara Louisiana. I will thank you to do so.

Have you sent the 1.000 copies of the "Vindication"[2] to Edwin Polk Esqr. at Bolivar as requested? If you have not send them through the mail. Put them up in packages of convenient size or request Genl. Armstrong to do so, in such manner that they will be charged with newspaper or Pamphlet Postage only. Have all the balance been distributed? Send me the balance of my 1.000.

My news from Georgia is very good, as good as that from the north. In haste.

James K. Polk

ALS. T–JPH. Addressed to Nashville and marked *"Private."* Published in *THM,* II, p. 146.

1. Polk's reference is to a letter from William G. Austin, September 16, 1844.
2. Nashville *Vindication* pamphlet.

FROM J. G. M. RAMSEY

My Dear Sir Mecklenburg Sep. 30, 1844

Yours of the 23rd is just received.[1] I will immediately make the appointments for Col. McClung. The two last days will I think do the cause most good by being spent at Kingston & Campbells Station, as Monroe

& Blount have had a full share of effort already tho I will confer with our friends about that before the appointments are announced.

Clay (of A.)[2] should go to Grainger Jefferson & Sevier. When I hear from him or you I will have the list extensively circulated in the papers & will *write* to our friends at all the points in his & McClungs list to have barbacues &c. &c. Recently we have had such frequently. Our delegates have just returned from the mass meeting at Athens. We doubled the Whig Meeting held simultaneously.[3] Haynes & Jones were there & made a decided impression. Many of the Whigs were in our crowd. Haynes goes over to Olivers in Anderson on the 3rd. Speaks in Knoxville to day. Barton heard of the sickness of his family & was compelled to leave his & Jones list unfilled, but Bradley[4] & Maxwell will supply their places as low down as Guthries in Greene County. There West Humphreys[5] & A. R. Crozier will take them up on Wednesday & continue them through. Rowles is attending to Genl. Henry. We keep every point guarded, & I never knew our friends, speakers & hearers in such excellent spirits. As the time approaches the people pause & are giving a patient hearing to our friends. We are certainly making converts every where. Barton assured me that there were Whigs enough who will not vote to change the election even if we did not make a single convert in the State.

I have cases of sickness in Blount Sevier & the upper end of Knox which keep me constantly on horse back since I have got well & I make it subserve our cause as well as I can by circulating papers wherever I go, & by talking to the people. I was in all these counties twice last week & know of changes in every district. The Whigs are desperate, & I think are relaxing their efforts visibly. Their failure at Athens was obvious, & is admitted by the candid amongst them. I write this hasty note while my young men are replenishing my saddle bags with medicine & newspapers for a long list of visits to day. Will write soon when I have a little more leisure. I forgot to say that I have written to Philadelphia Charleston Cincinnati & Nashville for documents printed in the German language to be circulated in E.T. for the use of our Dutch citizens. They will do us essential service.

J. G. M. Ramsey

ALS. DLC–JKP. Addressed to Columbia. Polk's AE on the cover states that he answered this letter on October 9, 1844; Polk's reply has not been found.

1. Polk's letter of September 23, 1844, has not been found.

2. A lawyer and Alabama state legislator, Clement C. Clay won three terms as a Democrat in the U.S. House, 1829–35; he also served as governor of Alabama, 1835–37, and as U.S. Senator, 1837–41.

3. On September 25, 1844, the Democrats and Whigs held mass meetings at Athens, Tenn. Some ten thousand men, women, and "attentive youths" at-

tended the Democratic rally and heard speeches by George W. Jones, Landon C. Haynes, and Robert W. Powell.

4. Orville T. Bradley studied law under Hugh L. White and supported his mentor for the presidency in 1836. He served as a Democrat in the Tennessee House, 1833–35, and in the Tennessee Senate, 1835–37. A member of the Whig party after 1836, he backed William H. Harrison for the presidency in 1840 but supported Polk in 1844.

5. A lawyer from Somerville, West H. Humphreys won election to a single term in the Tennessee House, 1835–37, and served as state attorney general and reporter, 1839–51. He presided over the U.S. District Court for West Tennessee from 1853 until 1861.

OCTOBER

FROM JOHN H. LUMPKIN[1]

Dear Sir
Rome. 1st October 1844

I have just returned from a democratic mass meeting held at Marrietta, a central parish in my district. The assemblage was large, numbering from 6 to 8 thousand persons, all animated with the same burning zeal for democratic principles and measures. In this vast assemblage I do not think there was one solitary individual who even doubted that a glorious triumph awaits the Democracy on the first monday in this month, and also on the first monday in November.[2] All was hope, confidence & enthusiasm. One of the distinguishing features in this contest in Georgia is, the degree of personal and individual interest manifested in behalf of the democratic candidates is unparralled in the history of party contests. Our ablest and most talented statesmen and speakers it is true, are daily canvassing the whole state, but the humblest democrat in this state is fully alive to the importance of the contest, and all are doing whatever in them lies to promote and make certain a glorious triumph. And I now feel confident that we shall carry Georgia in November by not much less than five thousand majority. The majority will not be so large in the election for members of Congress, which takes place on Monday next. In this Congressional district my majority over my opponent[3] will not be less than 2500—and he is the open advocate of annexation *now* and professes to advocate a Tariff for revenue with incidental protection only. Col. Cobb informs me that his majority over his opponent will be at least 1500 and may reach 2000.[4] Col. Seaborn Jones[5] thinks he will carry his district by 1000 majority. It is believed that Genl. Harralson and Col. Chappell will both succeed by small majorities, but the contest will be very close in both districts.[6] Col. Thomas B. King (whig) will probably be elected over Col. Spalding (dem) in the first by a small majority but not more than 300 votes.[7] Col. Toombs (whig) will succeed in his district over the Hon. E. J. Black by 1200 votes.[8] And the Hon. A. H. Stephens will be reelected by probably 800 votes.[9] I have been thus particular in giving you the estimates in each district that you may see what is our present calculations. And by it you may see that we may even be defeated in the Congressional election, and only elect 3 out of the 8 members, and still carry the state from 2 to 3 thousand if our estimates are correct. You will I doubt not recognize the acquaintance I had the honor to make with you at Chattanooga in Hamilton County, Tennessee, something more than twelve months ago. My most ardent desire is that I may have the pleasure of meeting you at Washington City the fourth of March next, as the Chief magistrate of the people of the United States. That such will be the result of this contest I feel now an assurance that does not doubt.

JOHN H. LUMPKIN

ALS. DLC–JKP. Addressed to Columbia. Polk's AE on the cover states that he answered this letter on October 14, 1844.

1. A lawyer from Rome, Ga., John H. Lumpkin served one term in the state legislature; won election to three terms in the U.S. House, 1843–49; served as judge of the Georgia Superior Court, 1850–53; returned to the U.S. House, 1855–57; and lost his bid for the governorship in 1857.

2. Reference is to the state congressional elections of October 7, 1844, and the presidential election of November 4, 1844.

3. An Augusta lawyer, Andrew Jackson Miller served one term in the Georgia House, 1836–37, prior to his election to the Georgia Senate, where he served from 1838 until his death in 1856.

4. Howell Cobb and John W. H. Underwood. Cobb, an Athens lawyer, was appointed solicitor general of the western district of Georgia, 1837–41; was elected as a Democrat to the U.S. House, 1843–51; and was chosen Speaker during his final term. He won election to one term as governor of Georgia, 1851–53; returned for one term to the U.S. House, 1855–57; and served as secretary of the Treasury during James Buchanan's administration. Underwood, a lawyer from Rome, Ga., was appointed solicitor general of the western judicial district of Georgia, 1843–47; was elected to one term in the Georgia House, 1857–59, and to one term in the U.S. House, 1859–61; and was appointed twice to the Georgia Superior Court, 1867–69 and 1873–82.

5. Jones, a Columbus lawyer, served as solicitor general of Georgia in 1823;

he won election as a Democrat to two terms in the U.S. House, 1833–35 and 1845–47.

6. Hugh A. Haralson and Absalom H. Chappell. A lawyer, Haralson served several terms in the Georgia legislature before winning election as a Democrat to the U.S. House, where he served from 1843 until 1851.

7. Admitted to the bar in 1790, Thomas Spalding never practiced law but pursued his extensive interests in agriculture, which included cotton, sugar cane, silk, and grape cultivation. He served in both the Georgia House and Senate and won election in 1805 to one term in the U.S. House.

8. Robert Toombs and Edward J. Black. A lawyer from Washington, Ga., Toombs served in the Georgia House, 1837–40 and 1841–44; won election as a Whig to the U.S. House, 1845–53; and represented his state as a Democrat in Senate from 1853 until his withdrawal in 1861. Black served as a States' Rights Whig in the U.S. House, 1839–41; he subsequently won election as a Democrat to that body and served from 1842 until 1845.

9. Alexander H. Stephens, an attorney from Crawfordville, Ga., served both in the Georgia House, 1836–41, and in the Georgia Senate, 1842; from 1843 until 1859 he held a seat in the U.S. House, initially as a Whig and later as a Democrat. During the Civil War, he served as vice-president of the Confederate States of America. He was elected to the U.S. House in 1866, but was denied his seat. In 1872 he returned to the U.S. House and served in that body until 1882, when he was elected governor. Stephens served in that post but a few months prior to his death in 1883.

TO JAMES BUCHANAN

My Dear Sir: Columbia, Tenn. Oct. 3rd 1844

I thank you for the information which you give me, in your esteemed favour of the 23d ultimo.[1] The account which you give of the political prospects in Pennsylvania, accords with all the information which I have received from other sources. The great "Key-Stone State," will I have no doubt, continue to be, as she has ever been, Democratic to the core. I was glad to learn your opinion of the probable result in New York, as well as in Pennsylvania, because I have great con[fi]dence in your sober judgment, and know the caution with which you would express an opinion. I received a letter from *Gov. Lumpkin* of Georgia on yesterday,[2] giving me strong assurances that, that State is safe. We may not carry a majority of the members of Congress, at the election which takes place next week, because of the peculiar arrangements of the Districts, which were laid off by a Whig Legislature, but that we will have a decided majority of the popular vote he has no doubt. In this State our whole Democracy were never more confident of success. It is true we have a most exciting and violent contest, but I think there is no reason to doubt, that the State will be Democratic in November. A few weeks however will put an end to all speculation in the State, and in the Union.

The State elections in Pennsylvania and New Jersey, will be over before this letter can reach you. Will you do me the favour to give me your opinion, whether the vote in these elections may be regarded as fair and full test of the strength of parties in November?

Thanking you for your very acceptable letter....

JAMES K. POLK

ALS. PHi. Addressed to Lancaster, Penn., and marked *"Private."* Published in Moore, ed., *The Works of James Buchanan,* VI, p. 72.

1. See James Buchanan to Polk, September 23, 1844.
2. See Wilson Lumpkin to Polk, September 23, 1844.

FROM J. GEORGE HARRIS

My Dear Governor, Nashville Oct. 3. 1844

I have just finished directing to every quarter of the State the plan of organization suggested. It cannot help doing much good.

I perceive that the "Roorback" Hoax is recoiling on its inventors at the North, as a panic prevails in the Whig party there which is a premonitory symptom of its fate.

We have been trying to get up that pamphlet exhibiting a contrast between your course and the course of Mr. Clay on Pre-emption.[1] I trust we shall succeed, but we have some financial difficulties to encounter at this moment which it is difficult to overcome. I trust, however, it will be forthcoming.

You will receive Handbills for Gordon & Voorhies[2] with 100 blanks to be sent wherever a good soldier may need them. For the *handbill business* the General[3] & myself here chartered the Agriculturist Press,[4] all those of the Union Office running constantly on the St. Sp. Ban., Union[5] &c. Indeed the General and myself are *de facto* the State Committee, it having merely honorary (not *active*) members *de jure.*

I write before the in-coming of the Columbia Mail, and I believe every thing is attended to according to your suggestions up to this moment.

I fear Kezer did not take the best steps to secure aid.[6] He brought nothing to the treasury. The promises, on subscription lists, still in the hands of subscribers are not *par funds* with which to pay printing bills &c., and I am afraid he has given the State Committee to understand that *no reliance* can be placed on these promises for he told Maj. Heiss to day (himself & Dr. Robertson[7]) that the State Committee would not be *personally* responsible for printing bills. This was *un-*

wise. If this is the *fruit* of his mission, he had better have remained at home.

But this is a small matter of no consequence. We will *push on the column* so far as our strength goes.

The more I think of your course towards the Pulaski Whigs the more I approve it. They can make nothing out of it.

J. GEO. HARRIS

ALS. DLC–JKP. Addressed to Columbia and marked *"Private."* Polk's AE on the cover states that he answered this letter on October 4, 1844; Polk's reply has not been found.

1. Because of a shortage of funds, Harris set aside plans to publish a pamphlet and instead ran in the *Nashville Union* a lengthy article contrasting the positions of Clay and Polk on the pre-emption question. See the *Nashville Union,* October 14, 1844.

2. William Van Voorhies formed a law partnership with William H. Polk in 1844, went to California early in 1849 as a special U.S. postal agent, and in 1850 won election as California's first secretary of state.

3. Robert Armstrong.

4. Reference is to the printing office for the Tennessee periodical, *Agriculturist, and Journal of the State and County Societies.*

5. Nashville *Star Spangled Banner* and *Nashville Union.*

6. See Timothy Kezer to James K. Polk, October 6, 1844.

7. Felix Robertson, a physician, was the son of Nashville's founder, James Robertson. Elected Mayor of Nashville in 1818, 1827, and 1828, Felix Robertson headed the Nashville Democratic Central Committee in 1844.

FROM GANSEVOORT MELVILLE

Thursday 10 P.M.

My dear Sir Cleveland, Ohio. Oct. 3d 1844

In passing through Columbus I dropped to your address a hasty line in which I spoke of the great uncertainty of the result in Ohio.[1] Since then having attended and addressed a mass meeting every day, and conversed with hundreds of voters I feel myself constrained to say that I can not avoid continuing in the beleif that no reliable calculations have been arrived at as to the probable result of the approaching gubernatorial election.

In compliance with your request I mentioned to Mr. Medary[2] that which you desired. He said that he would write soon.[3] I presume that he has done so, but as in the multiplicity of his avocations he may not have found time to fulfill his intention I beg leave to submit a few remarks on the present state of affairs here.

And first as to individuals. At the mass meeting at Elyria on the Reserve I met Col. Tod our candidate for Governor and had with him a full and free conversation in which he stated without any proviso whatever that he is confident of being elected Governor of Ohio on Tuesday next by not less than 5,000 majority. Our mutual friend Mr. Hamer[4] (who is here now and in whose company I have had the pleasure of travelling for some days) assures me strenuously that the state is safe for Tod by a similar vote. He entertains no doubt of the result. Gen. Cass is still more sanguine than the gentlemen first named. Caleb J. McNulty late Clk H of Representatives and whom I met at Columbus anticipates a still heavier majority.[5] At Cincinnati I conversed with Jho B. Weller, David T. Disney, C. C. Brough and others, and all alike rely with implicit confidence on a favorable result.[6] Medary in our first interview frankly told me that things were not working to suit him and that he was apprehensive that our friends would be disappointed. Twenty four hours afterwards he was more confident and Twenty four hours having again elapsed, i.e. at the Zanesville meeting he assured me that fresh information of a favorable character had come in and that he no longer doubted the result and considered Tod's election certain. These gentlemen one & all unite in the opinion that the vote for Governor will be indicatory of the Electoral vote of Ohio.

Two or three things induce me to hesitate in according full credence to the views above expressed. First, the Texas question has not been argued before the people on the stump as it should have been fully, boldly and directly. In the 10 or 12 mass meetings which I have talked to in this state from the Ohio river to Lake Erie I found it to be universally the case that the people listened to a manly discussion of that issue with interest and even astonishment pictured in their faces and fairly with their mouths open—Again. The rank and file of the party are not so alive to the importance of this contest as they are in other states. In my humble judgment this is obvious—Kindly. The organization of the party is defective, at least to the eyes of a New York politician. There is no plan in operation by which the political pulse of the state can be felt from week to week. In the fourth place, in Fairfield, Wayne and other counties the Currency question is distracting our friends.[7] And yet again—there are slumbering jealousies among some half dozen of our leading men who now occupy in the public eye about the same position—each man being determined to assert his supremacy at the first convenient opportunity. The Whigs are evidently full of hope even while acknowledging the undeniable weakness of Mordecai Bartley as a candidate. If Spangler had accepted the nomination which they tendered to him or Corwin had run again,[8] little doubt could have been entertained of their success. King, the abolition candidate for Governor[9] is very active in canvassing the state. He attacks Clay with great ferocity, calls you a slave-holder and *that is all,* and advises his friends to vote for Birney and himself. Three quarters of the Abolitionists are Whigs. In the adherence of the third party men to their ticket lies, as I am persuaded, our only reasonable hope of carrying the state. In the present state of things, no man can tell whether they generally will adhere to their nominees or not, but the better opinion is that they will. Had it not been for Mr. Clay's letter disavowing Cassius M. Clay it would probably have been otherwise.[10]

Our meeting here to-day has produced an excellent effect. Even Cass, Mr. Hamer, and myself spoke each two hours to a most attentive and numerous auditory. Harrison's majority in '40 on the Western Reserve was over 9000. This year the democrats say that Clay's will be under 5000. As Ritchie[11] says Nous verrons.[12]

At this point I have recd. several letters from N.Yk., Albany, Buffalo, Lockport & other places the tenor of which is uniform as to the contest in the state of N. Yk. being already settled in favor of the Democratic nominees. In the firm hope and trust that this will prove to be the case & with my respectful regards to Mrs. Polk I am....

GANSEVOORT MELVILLE

ALS. DLC–JKP. Addressed to Columbia and marked "Private & *Confidential.*"

1. In his letter of September 24, 1844, Melville informed Polk that he planned to accompany Lewis Cass and Thomas L. Hamer on their speaking engagements in Ohio. He promised to write Polk providing information on the Democrats' chances for election in Ohio. ALS. DLC–JKP.

2. A native of Pennsylvania and printer by trade, Samuel Medary edited the Columbus *Ohio Statesman* and in that position exercised great influence in the Ohio Democracy; he subsequently served first as governor of Minnesota Territory, 1857–58, and then of Kansas in 1859–60.

3. Medary wrote to Polk on October 28, 1844, thanking Polk for his letter. ALS. DLC–JKP.

4. A lawyer and Democrat, Thomas L. Hamer of Ohio served three terms in the U.S. House, 1833–39; commissioned a brigadier general in the Mexican War, he died in the service in 1846.

5. A resident of Ohio, Caleb J. McNulty defeated Matthew St. Claire Clarke for the office of House clerk on December 6, 1843, and served until January 18, 1845, when he was dismissed from office. For the clerk's election, see Cave Johnson to Polk, December 11, 1843.

6. John B. Weller and probably Charles H. Brough. An Ohio lawyer, Weller served three terms in the U.S. House, 1839–45, and represented California in the U.S. Senate from 1852 until 1857. He fought with the rank of colonel in the Mexican War, won election to one term as governor of California, 1858–60, and went

as U.S. minister to Mexico in 1860. A resident of Fairfield County, Ohio, Brough served one term in the Ohio House before moving in 1841 to Cincinnati, where he and his brother, John, purchased Moses Dawson's *Cincinnati Advertiser* and renamed it the *Cincinnati Enquirer.* Brough served as a colonel in the Mexican War and afterward sat on the bench of the Ohio Court of Common Pleas; he died of cholera in 1849.

7. Reference is to a division in the Ohio Democratic party over rechartering the Bank of Wooster in 1844; "hard money" Democrats opposed the recharter legislation.

8. David Spangler and Thomas Corwin. A lawyer from Zanesville, Ohio, Spangler removed to Coshocton in 1832; he won election as a Whig to two terms in the U.S. House, 1833–37; he declined his party's nomination for the Ohio governorship in 1844.

9. Leicester King represented Trumbull County in the Ohio Senate, 1834–37, before running for the governorship on the Liberty party ticket in 1844.

10. See Leonard P. Cheatham to Polk, September 29, 1844.

11. Probably Thomas Ritchie, editor of the *Richmond Enquirer* from 1804 until 1845 and unofficial leader of the Virginia Democracy.

12. French expression meaning "we shall see."

FROM LEWIS CASS

My dear Sir, Cleaveland, Ohio, Oct. 4, 1844

I am just about to embark in the steamboat for Detroit, and I sit down to write you a hasty line.

I have been thru' the central and northern parts of this state, and have addressed the people at sixteen different places, and I have sought to ascertain the true condition of publick opinion. It is a large state and so divided, that no one ought to speak too confidently of the result. The Whigs are more active, and I may add more powerful, than I thought they were upon my former trip. However I have endeavoured to look at the matter dispassionately, and I am satisfied, that Tod will be elected next tuesday and that our vote in November will be still stronger than not. It is well ascertained, that the abolitionists will stick to their ticket, and they will number perhaps 10,000 votes. Our friends are every where sanguine and active. Hamer leaves here this morning for home, after having produced the most powerful effect, at the many places, where he has spoken, by his argumentative and eloquent speeches. I have rarely heard his superior. So Melville too has acquitted himself well, and parts from us today, to visit various places in the state of New york, before he reaches the City, Mr. Rantoul[1] of Massachusetts joined us at Elyria, and has spoken with great effect. He is a powerful man, the most powerful I have heard on the subject of the Tariff. He goes to

Cincinnati, and I think will lose no opportunity of addressing the people.

As to New york, and Pennsylvania, I feel certain they are right. We entertain no doubt of it. I read a letter from Gov. Dickerson[2] a short time since, who tells me we shall carry New Jersey. I think I can look upon the whole matter dispassionately, and I feel as confident, that the general result will be favourable, as I am of any event, which has not happened.

I will write you once more before the election. And that will be the day I leave Indiana. I trust I shall reach home tomorrow, Saturday, for I must set out for Indiana on Monday, where the Central Committee of that state have assigned to me nine different places to address the people. Hannegan will be with me and Wright[3] of the House. This will keep me till the last of the month. At its termination, I will communicate the result of my impressions, and then go home and vote. With my best respects to Mrs. Polk....

LEW CASS

ALS. DLC–JKP. Addressed to Columbia.

1. A Massachusetts lawyer and Democratic state legislator, Robert Rantoul, Jr., served as U.S. district attorney for that state from 1845 until 1849. Elected to the U.S. Senate to fill the vacancy caused by the resignation of Daniel Webster, he served there for one month and then won election to the U.S. House, where he remained from March 1851 until his death in August 1852.

2. Philemon Dickerson, a New Jersey lawyer, won election as a Democrat to the U.S. House in 1833 and served until 1836, when he resigned to become governor of New Jersey. He was re-elected to a single term in the U.S. House in 1839 but lost his bid for re-election. Dickerson was appointed judge of the U.S. District Court for New Jersey in 1841 and filled that post until his death in 1862.

3. Joseph A. Wright served as a Democrat in the U.S. House, 1843–45; in the governorship of Indiana, 1849–57; and in the U.S. Senate, 1862–63.

FROM WILLIAM E. CRAMER

Gov. Polk Albany Friday Oct. 4th 1844

Our Southern friends are throwing rather too much responsibility upon New York. The load may stagger perhaps capsize us. I understand that Senator Walker through the Central Committee at Washington has just issued a most inflammatory pamphlet titled "The South in danger."[1] If I read it aright it presses Annexation solely on the ground of *extending* and *perpetuating Slavery*. This will not do at the North. On this false and most *Anti-democratic* issue, the majority against us would not be thousands but tens of thousands.

It is hardly right that the North should bear the whole burden of the fight. We have already done more than our share, yet South politicians seem to think that we can do *all their fighting* in the Northern States. *The Whigs are reprinting this* pamphlet and in the language of Willis Green "are now circulating it throughout this wide Republic."[2]

All confess that the vote of New York *must be decisive* and yet these moves of Walker &c may embarrass us most seriously in Ohio. I still more fear its effect. Melville writes me that Tods chance *was fair*[3] "The South in danger" will do us no good there. It may turn that State against us. To devote their energies for the extension of Slavery must be odious to a free People and this is the issue, from the first of the campaign which the Whigs have tried to fasten on us, but which we have most *properly repudiated.* I write freely because it is important fully to appreciate the difficulties under which we are thrown, should the result be not so favorable as was anticipated.

During the last month we *have been* gaining ground in this State. The Texas question as it became better understood, as a *national* but *not as a Slave* question has become more popular. Mr. Clays shuffling on Texas angered some of the most distinguished and devoted Whigs. And Mr. Wrights nomination withal, gave us the vantage ground. The Whigs seemed to be aware of this. The leaders have at last chalked out their final plan and they are now carrying it out with the energy of desperation.

The South is to be left to take care of itself. *The whole onset* is to be made *on Pennsylvania New York and Ohio.* The Tariff is to be the hobby in Penn. Webster has gone there to remain until after the election. His appeals are sectional but powerful.[4]

Slavery is to be the question in this State and Ohio. Cassius M. Clay is their emissary. His denunciations of Slavery are terrible. His picture of Slave-breeding for the Texas Market is ingeniously calculated to arouse every passion that freemen can feel. *He will use* the manifesto, "The South in danger."

To crown all, Mr. Clay has been got (I say got because I believe there is a combination) to write his *final letter*[5] going with Seward and Webster *against* the Annexation of Texas. This is his last card. He thus hazards even Kentucky but it will unquestionably strengthen him at the North. Now Sir, this is our position. You must admit that the *whole battle is to be fought in this State.* We have a fair prospect of carrying it and triumphing over the most desperate political army that ever was marshalled, *if we are not still farther embarrassed by Southern firebrands.* But if we are, the consequences are inevitable. Most fortunately, the exposure of the Roorback Forgery has strengthened you materially. If the Abolitionists maintain their separate organization (as I believe they will) we carry this State. They poll at least 20.000 votes, and therefore, manifestly hold the balance of Power. They are well educated and as resolute as they are enthusiastic.

I will write again in a few days.

WM. E. C.

[Insert sheet follows.]

The Pamphlet alluded to came as I understand *from the Spectator Office.* Mr. Calhoun should be more careful about the action of his friends.[6]

[Cover sheet follows.]

P.S. The meeting here on the 2nd was truly an imposing Demonstration. We think it the largest collection of voters ever gathered in this State.

You perceive that Clay has come out dead against Assumption. So did Webster at Philadelphia. They are trying to get rid of every issue but Slavery and the Tariff. Ingenious are they not.[7]

ALS. DLC–JKP. Addressed to Columbia.

1. Reference is to Robert J. Walker's pamphlet entitled, *The South In Danger! Read Before You Vote: Address of the Democratic Association of Washington, District of Columbia.* A copy of Walker's pamphlet was printed in *Niles' National Register* on November 2, 1844.

2. In the Washington *Globe* of October 1, 1844, James Towles, chairman of the Democratic Association of Washington, denounced *The South In Danger!* as a Whig forgery. Willis Green, a Kentucky Whig, responded to Towles' denouncement in the Washington *National Intelligencer* of October 2, 1844. Green claimed that the pamphlet was printed in the office of the Washington *Spectator,* a Calhoun paper. He accused Walker of surreptitiously preparing the pamphlet for distribution only in the South. Green tried unsuccessfully to purchase 1,000 copies from the *Spectator* office for distribution in the North. He then turned to the office of the *Intelligencer* to reprint the pamphlet. Walker responded to Green in the *Globe* of October 3, 1844.

3. Reference is to David Tod's gubernatorial race in Ohio.

4. The text of Daniel Webster's speech, delivered in Philadelphia on October 1, 1844, was reprinted in *Nile's National Register* on October 12, 1844.

5. Reference is to Henry Clay's campaign letter of September 23, 1844, which was printed in the Washington *National Intelligencer* of October 1, 1844; in that pronouncement he stated that he was "decidedly opposed to the immediate annexation of Texas to the United States."

6. Here were cancelled the words, "He has never been North." This addendum was written on a separate sheet; on its verso was penned the address, "Gov. Polk Columbia Tennessee." Oil stains from the cover sheet's sealing wax indicate that this sheet was inserted next to the addressed cover sheet.

7. Cramer wrote his postscript on the inside folds of his cover sheet.

TO CHARLES J. INGERSOLL

My Dear Sir: Columbia Ten. Oct. 4th 1844

I have examined the Journals of the Legislature of 1823 & 1824, of which I was a member, and find that I was right in my recollection, that the *yeas* and *nays* were not taken on the passage of the Bills for "the encouragement of iron works." I gave the titles of these Bills, and an abstract of their provisions, in my letter two days ago.[1] In regard to the law of 1823, to which I referred you, the Journal contains, the following to wit,

"A Bill supplemental to an act entitled 'an act to encourage the building of iron-works, passed Nov. 2nd 1809,' was read the third and last time, passed & ordered to be engrossed." On the same day (Nov. 28th 1823) it was signed by the Speakers, of the two Houses and became a law.

In regard to the law of 1824, to which I referred you, the Journal contains the following, to wit,

"A Bill for the encouragement of iron-works, was read the third and last time, passed, and ordered to be engrossed." On the same day (Oct. 5th 1824) it was signed by the Speakers of the two Houses, and became a law. So that, if you make any use of the facts, you can truly state, that both laws passed without objection, and had my assent & support. Such was my recollection of what had been my course, but as I had not thought of it for twenty years, and as you intimated in your letter,[2] that you might wish to use the facts, I thought it safest to turn to the Journals, and see what record had been made. Such was the settled policy of the State, and so unanimous were the Legislature that passed these laws, that no division or *yeas* & *nays* were called on their passage.

You may rely upon the facts which I gave you in my last, and in this letter as correct, though as I desire to avoid appearing before the public, you will not of course, in any thing you may do, have any reference to my letters or to me as the source of your information.

The *"Roorback" forgery & falsehood,* is the grossest & basest I have ever known. It is in all its facts an infamous falsehood. I am glad the Democratic press, at the East, have been able so promptly to meet and expose it.

JAMES K. POLK

ALS. PHi. Addressed to Philadelphia and marked *"Confidential."*

1. Letter not found.

2. In his letter to Polk of September 4, 1844, Ingersoll asked Polk if by an act of the Tennessee legislature bounty land had been allowed those establishing or improving iron factories or forges. ALS. DLC–JKP.

TO JOHN K. KANE

My Dear Sir: Columbia Ten. Oct. 4th 1844

Before this letter reaches you, the State elections in Pennsylvania & New Jersey, will be over. I hope the estimate which you made in your letter of the 16th ult. of the probable majorities, may be realized by the result.[1] As soon as you receive full returns I would be pleased to have your opinion, whether the vote in these elections, may be fairly regarded, as a test of the strength of parties in November.

I received a letter from *Gov. Lumpkin* of Georgia two days ago, giving the strongest assurances that, that state is safe.[2] We may not carry a majority of the members of Congress, at the election of which takes place next week, because of the peculiar arrangement of the Districts, which were laid off by a Whig Legislature, but Gov. L. has no doubt we will have a decided popular majority. The confidence of the Democracy of this state is daily strengthening. They have now no doubt, but that they will carry the state. If Pennsylvania & *New Jersey* come in handsomely next week, as you think they will, the contest will I think be settled. My information from Indiana derived from reliable sources, satisfies me that, that state is safe.[3] I have doubts of Ohio. The contest there will be close. I have had great fears for two months, past, that enormous frauds would be attempted at the ballot box in November, & I so wrote to Mr. Dallas. In *that* I think lies our only danger. The cry which has been set-up by the Federal presses, about Brittish Gold, to aid the Democracy, is I fear intended to draw off public attention, and to enable the Federalists to do what they falsely charge upon the Democracy.[4] Rely, upon it there is danger that immense frauds, will be attempted, and they can only be prevented by the closest & most minute organization. This danger is greatest in the large cities, and in their neighbourhood. New *Jersey* and *Delaware* in your neighbourhood are close states, and may be lost by means of imported and fraudulent votes, unless, they are closely watched. Too much care cannot be taken, to put the Democracy in those states on their guard, in time to prevent it.

You will see in the Whig paper of this village that an attempt has been made, by a clique of Whig–partisans, to force me to make another Declaration of my views upon the tariff and Texas.[5] From the Nashville Union of yesterday, a copy of which I send you, you will see how I have treated them.[6] My opinions have been fully declared and are well understood, and it cannot be necessary, or proper that I should write any more. I shall treat their communication, with the silent contempt which it deserves.

The two Pamphlets which you forwarded to me came safely to hand.[7]

James K. Polk

P.S. You can if you choose show this to *Mr. Dallas.*

ALS. PPAmP. Addressed to Philadelphia and marked *"Confidential."*

1. See John K. Kane to Polk, September 16, 1844.
2. See Wilson Lumpkin to Polk, September 23, 1844.
3. Reference probably is to John Law to Polk, September 26, 1844.
4. The *Nashville Whig* of October 1, 1844, and October 3, 1844, reported that manufacturers in Great Britain were raising substantial funds to bring and distribute tracts in the United States supporting free trade in order to influence the outcome of the American presidential election.
5. See John W. Goode et al. to Polk, September 21, 1844.
6. The *Nashville Union* of October 3, 1844, declared "that no more should be required of a candidate for the Presidency than to state the general principles upon which, if elected, he would act."
7. Enclosures not found.

FROM JOHN O. BRADFORD[1]

Dear Sir Philad. Oct. 5th 1844

With this you will receive a paper containing an account of our great torch light procession last night.[2] It was the most splendid political demonstration ever witnessed in this city. The Whigs had their great convention a few days since for *eastern Pensylvania.* Quite a number of counties were represented and they counted all told not exceeding five thousand seven hundred persons. Ours last night was to embrace only the voters of *Philad city and county* and we numbered over twelve thousand. Our opponents were at work for weeks drumming up for their procession. They procured a reduction of fares on all the principal routes and used all the other devices for which they are famous to attract a large gathering, but after all had it not been for the whig merchants shutting up their stores and the manufacturers their factories the whole affair would have been a perfect failure. As it is they feel that they have been badly beaten. They realize the painful fact that the general sentiment of the county is against them and that they are doomed to defeat.

You will I am apprehensive not receive as good a report from this county as we could wish on the Governor election. Advantage has been taken of a perfectly proper movement of Mr. Shunk to slander and traduce him in the vilest manner and I fear that in the present excited state of the community upon the subject of native Americanism we will lose thereby some two thousand votes in this city and county. This question will have no influence upon the presidential vote and I only mention that our folks in Tennessee may not be disappointed should our majority not be as large as previously expected on our Governor. Do not for a moment imagine that we are not right. We are all in glorious spirits, cheered and encouraged by any breeze that blows. Delaware the Banner State of the Whigs the home of John M. Clayton has come in Democratic and under such circumstances too as render assurance doubly sure that she is indeed regenerated disenthralled. The old Maryland line too has been broken and if our friends in the county had known their strength they would have elected their Governor by more than two thousand votes. As it is we have triumphed most gloriously and unexpectedly. If the Whigs cannot succeed in Maryland and Delaware where can they hang a hope?

The most exciting topic now before the public is the Rhode Island question and the imprisonment of Gov Dorr. The eastern Democracy and I may add the yeomanry every where feel that they are outraged in the imperious persecution of this excellent man. And it has been much wondered why in the account of the recent celebration with the letters of Mr. Van Buren Genl. Jackson Mr. Wright Woodbury[3] &c none appeared from yourself. If Connecticut and Massachusetts are gained to us it will be upon this question. I am apprehensive that the fact of no letter appearing from you upon this subject may at the eleventh hour be used against us. I know you well enough to know that you desire no concealments and knowing moreover your sentiments upon the great question of political rights, I would suggest whether it would not be well, whether in fact Justice to yourself and friends does not require that your opinion upon this deeply exciting question should not be made known. If they are not you may rest assured that you will be most villainously misrepresented, and at a time when it will be too late to make amends. I would be much gratified to see your sentiments upon this subject made public, and if you think proper you may consider this letter as a call and write me accordingly. I will take care that the proper use is made of it.

J. O. BRADFORD

P.S. You may have seen my name mentioned as a candidate for congress in the 3rd dist by the native party. I was brought forward without my knowledge or consent. I had no affinities with them and gave them to understand that if run by them it must be with the distinct understanding that I was a democrat out and out. I fear they will carry the district.

I would further say that although Mr. Tyler took a course upon the Rhode I. subject which the democrats condemn I am perfectly sure that he never contemplated the inhuman punishment of Gov. Dorr. On the contrary I heard Judge Sutherland who is considered here as the special friend of the President a few evenings since at a large Democratic meeting denounce the punishment inflicted upon Dorr as monstrous and inhuman. I mention this because I should dislike to see anything occur that would seem to indicate conflicting opinion among democrats, as we are now, all united; The Tyler men are working nobly and I honor them for it; they are well drilled and are doing good service. Judge Sutherland[4] is a host himself. O'Connell is free in England.[5] Dorr is in chains in free America.

I would strongly advise your attention to the Rhode Island business. I am fearful a mine may be sprung. The Roorback forgery shows what the Whigs will do.

ALS. DLC–JKP. Addressed to Columbia.

1. Bradford served briefly in 1837 as editor of the *Nashville Union;* the following year he went to Puerto Rico as U.S. consul at St. Johns; and in March 1845 Polk appointed him to the post of purser in the navy.

2. Enclosure not found.

3. Levi Woodbury headed the U.S. Treasury Department from 1834 until 1841. Earlier he had served as governor of New Hampshire, Democratic senator from that state, and secretary of the navy. In 1841 Woodbury returned to the U.S. Senate and served until his appointment to the U.S. Supreme Court in 1845.

4. Joel B. Sutherland won election as a Jackson Democrat to five terms in the U.S. House, 1827–1837, and served as associate judge of the Court of Common Pleas of Philadelphia, 1833–1834. He broke with the Democratic party over the tariff and the rechartering of the national bank and lost his congressional seat in the 1836 election. Appointed Naval Officer of Philadelphia by John Tyler in 1843, he advised Tyler on the distribution of patronage in Philadelphia and worked closely in 1844 with the president's son, Robert, to facilitate the return of Tyler's friends to the Democratic party.

5. Known as the "Liberator," Daniel O'Connell championed the cause of Irish nationalism. Elected to Parliament, he served for many years before he was arrested and sentenced to prison in 1844 on a charge of creating discontent and disaffection. Upon appeal his judgment was reversed, and he was released from prison.

FROM J. GEORGE HARRIS

Nashville, Tenn. October 6, 1844

Confirms Polk's assumption that he did not write the tariff article in the *Nashville Union* and gives assurances that great care has been taken to avoid all discussion of the tariff in the *Union.*[1] Yesterday Laughlin furnished two columns on a similar topic that could not be published. Caution is required in dealing with "different *cliques*" of the Boston Democracy. Rantoul's visit to Tennessee probably is "a *fishing excursion*" undertaken with a view of obtaining Polk's future patronage. McKeon[2] reports that New York, New Jersey, and Pennsylvania are safe, and Gardner[3] sends encouraging news about Polk's prospects in the Western District.

ALS. DLC–JKP. Addressed to Columbia.

1. Harris probably refers to one of the tariff articles in the *Nashville Union* of October 4 or October 5, 1844.

2. John McKeon, a New York City lawyer, served as a Democrat in the New York Assembly, 1832–34, and in the U.S. House, 1835–37 and 1841–43.

3. A Weakley County lawyer, John A. Gardner served three terms as a Democrat in the Tennessee Senate, 1843–47, and a single term in the Tennessee House, 1879–81.

FROM TIMOTHY KEZER

Dear Sir Nashville, Oct. 6, 1844

You were pleased to ask me to give you some account of my trip [and] of business arrangements after my return home. I have been at home just one week, but have delayed writing sooner, from runing about to public gatherings of the Democracy.

After I left Columbia, I visited Pulaski where I collected $165, to be appropriated for one hundred numbers of the "Star Spangled Banner" to be circulated in each civil district in Giles County.

Our friends there seem sanguine of carrying the county by a small majority. I found an old anti-Tarriff document there, giving an account of a Meeting held in Pulaski in 1831, in which E. J. Shields and some others now whigs, were prominent actors. You will find it in yesterdays "Union."[1]

At Lewisburg, I collected but little, but was promised one hundred Dollars to be remitted by mail. There all was confidence, zeal and activity. Mr. Thomas,[2] made a good speech to a very large audience in the evening, at least 1000 persons present. Gen. Record[3] and others assured me that "Marshall" would give a majority of 800.

At Fayetteville, all were so busy, on account of the mass meeting, that nothing was effected farther than good promises, which they said might be relied on. The Mass Meeting was a very large lively and spirited one. The particulars of which I have no doubt reached you.[4]

I saw there Dr. Estle, Mr. Finch, Mr. Frances,[5] who also assured me they would take the matter into serious consideration on reaching home, and remit whatever could be raised.

The prominent men of "Lincoln" think that 2000 majority is not an extravagant calculation for that county. Some person seemed confident of a higher number.

Our friends in Rutherford are doing extremely well for that county. It is well, and thouroughly organized, and every vote closely canvassed. The result is about 100 majority for Democracy, giving all doubtful, near 160 votes, to the whigs.

They are spending for that county, all that they can well stand, I trust however, we will get a little more out of them.

The plan of organization recommended by friends here, was favorable received at all places.

I was at "Shallow Ford" in Sumner County on Friday, with the "Hickory Cavalry" Capt. Campbell[6] being unable to go. The number present was variously estimated from 4 to 500 voters. There was 13 military companies, numbering little over 500 voters. A large proportion of Ladies were present. Mr. Currin, Mr. Nicholson and Powel[7] of East Ten. were the speakers.

A good barbecue, lively democratic songs with the able speeches, pleased all tasters, and made the day pass off with good effect.

T. KEZER

ALS. DLC–JKP. Addressed to Columbia and enclosed in Samuel H. Laughlin to Polk, October 6, 1844.

1. On October 4, 1844, the *Nashville Union* ran an article on an anti-tariff meeting at Pulaski held on August 15, 1831; the article focused on those Whigs who had reversed their tariff views.

2. Reference probably is to either James H. Thomas or Jonas E. Thomas. A Columbia lawyer and district attorney, 1836–42, James H. Thomas became a law partner of James K. Polk in 1843 and later won election as a Democrat to three terms in Congress, 1847–51 and 1859–61. A successful lawyer and farmer, Jonas E. Thomas represented Maury County in the Tennessee House, 1835–41, and sat for Maury and Giles counties in the Tennessee Senate, 1845–47.

3. Kezer's reference probably is to James C. Record of Marshall County, Tenn.

4. On September 26, 1844, Democrats held a mass meeting at Fayetteville, Tenn. For details, see the Columbia *Tennessee Democrat,* October 12, 1844.

5. References probably are to Wallace W. or William Estill, Thomas H. Finch and Hugh Francis. Wallace W. and William Estill were both prominent physi-

cians in Franklin County. Wallace W. served two terms as a Democrat in the Tennessee House, 1835–37 and 1841–43. Finch, a Franklin County farmer, won election as a Democrat to a single term in the Tennessee House, 1839–41. Francis served as clerk of the Franklin County Chancery Court from 1838 until 1858.

6. On October 4, 1844, Democrats held a mass meeting in the northwestern division of Sumner County at Shallow Ford. Volunteer militia companies from Davidson and other counties attended and made "a brilliant display" with flags, banners, and bands of music. John Campbell was a company commander of the Hickory Cavalry, a unit of the Nashville Texas Volunteers. Kezer also served as one of the officers of that unit. See the *Nashville Union,* October 7, 1844.

7. David M. Currin, A. O. P. Nicholson, and Robert W. Powell.

FROM SAMUEL H. LAUGHLIN

My dear Sir, Nashville, Sunday night, Oct. 6, 1844

The news this evening in letters to Gen. Armstrong from Gardner & others from the West, is exceedingly cheering. *A thousand squatters,* caparisoned in their own uniform escorted Old Cave[1] into Dresden the other day. Craighead is achieving great good. One leading man, followed by about thirty others, *flung up Whiggery* and changed under his ministry at one of his late meetings.

The N.Y. Herald to-night,[2] contains a full account of the Organization and result of the Utica consultation of the Abolitionists, and copious extracts from their report or Address as it may be called, or perhaps still more properly their Manifesto. They have nominated Birney of Michigan for President, and Morris[3] of Ohio for Vice President, and as appears, will run their own separate, independant ticket. If this be so, I can see no ground to doubt that it will finally be their course everywhere, it finally destroys Clay's *last hope,* and our *only remaining fear.* Laus Deo![4] The grand final result is now certain.

I enclose you with this, (under cover of a blank invelope of Blackwell's, which I received in blank covering a copy of one of Owen's speeches)[5] I send you late letters from Bowlin, Croswell and Flennken.[6] Bowlins letter will give a fuller *inside* look into the real state of men and parties in Missouri than I expect you have yet had. Croswell's letter will give you a real view and calculation of what our friends in New York were relying on at its date than you have perhaps seen. Flinnikens letter gives a fair view of the real state of things in Western Pennsylvania. After reading these letters, *please return them to me under cover immediately.* I take the liberty of sending them, knowing how anxious you must be to know the *real* state of things everywhere. I have many other letters lately of less important character, from Mississippi, Georgia, Kentucky &c. all speaking with confidence of the result.

I am trying to make most I can of old documents, such as the meeting at Giles in 1831, and of the tobacco treaty, factory system &c. &c.[7] I think I have successfully answered the charge about British Gold.[8]

From Maryland no news from which to make any reasonable conjecture. I understand the Hon. Mr. McKeon from N. York has arrived, and says N.Y. and Pennsylvania are perfectly safe, but that we will most likely loose Maryland. I have always doubted that state.

I send also under cover, a letter Mr. Kezer[9] handed me to-night when I was at his house to supper.

S. H. LAUGHLIN

P.S. Gifford informed me when he came from Columbia that it was his Hon. Judge Dillahunty,[10] and not his Honor T. H. Cahal, who figured in the grand diplomatic mission to you from Giles.[11] I have just recd. the Pulaski Whig, with the *after* proceedings,[12] and shall handle the affair as it deserves. You forgot to favor me with any instructions or information as to distribution of the Col. E.P. pamphlets[13] to members of Congress. I hope one has been sent to each. Croswell's call for pamphets, which has been complied with, reminds me of it.

ALS. DLC–JKP. Marked "Private" and addressed to Columbia. Polk's AE on the cover states that he answered this letter on October 7, 1844; Polk's reply has not been found.

1. Cave Johnson. The Democrats held a mass meeting at Dresden, Tenn., on September 30, 1844.

2. On September 28, 1844, the *New York Herald* reported that the abolitionists had held a convention at Utica, N.Y., about a week earlier. The convention platform rejected both Clay and Polk on grounds that neither candidate supported abolition of slavery; however, the convention did not oppose in principle the annexation of Texas.

3. James G. Birney and Thomas Morris. Elected as a Democrat to the U.S. Senate in 1833, Morris broke with Ohio Democrats by publicly defending, the abolitionist cause in an 1839 Senate debate with Henry Clay. Morris' political sacrifice earned him second place on the Liberty Party ticket in 1844.

4. Latin phrase meaning "praise God."

5. Reference probably is to Robert Dale Owen. Son of Robert Owen, British industrialist and social reformer, Robert Dale Owen assisted in the founding of the New Harmony community in Indiana in 1826; he served three terms as a Democrat in the state legislature, 1836–38, and two terms in the U.S. House, 1843–47. On May 21, 1844, he delivered a House speech on Texas annexation, the text of which later appeared, under various titles, in pamphlet form.

6. James B. Bowlin, Edwin Croswell, and Robert P. Flenniken. A lawyer and

resident of St. Louis, Missouri, Bowlin served as a Democrat in the U.S. House from 1843 to 1851.

7. Articles on these subjects appeared in the *Nashville Union* on October 1, 4, and 5, 1844. On October 1, 1844, the *Union* attacked those Whig Senators who had voted against the treaty with the Zollverein, a German customs union; the article also claimed that the treaty's defeat severely hurt the agricultural interests of Tennessee and the West. To illustrate that point, the paper ran a copy of the address, "To the Tobacco Planters,"which had been prepared by the Democratic Association of Washington City.

8. Reference is to Whig charges that the Democrats were receiving large sums of money from British industries opposed to protective U.S. tariffs.

9. See Timothy Kezer to Polk, October 6, 1844.

10. A prominent Columbia lawyer, Edmund Dillahunty was Maury County solicitor, 1831–36, and judge of the Tennessee Eighth Judicial Circuit, 1836–51.

11. See John W. Goode et al. to Polk, September 21, 1844.

12. Laughlin's reference probably is to the second attempt by the Giles County Whigs to elicit a response from Polk. See John W. Goode et al. to Polk, September 27, 1844.

13. References are to Ezekiel Polk and to the Nashville *Vindication* pamphlet.

TO ROBERT ARMSTRONG

My Dear Sir: Columbia Oct. 7th 1844

I received the enclosed letter to day.[1] The whole statement is a base falsehood. I know nothing of the writer *Aaron Wagar.* I never had such a transaction or agency as that of which he speaks, with him or any one else. I never was at *Helena* or Little Rock in my life. I am at a loss to know what is meant by it. It may be an attempt to extract money, by an unprincipled man; or it may be that, it is intended to put the base falsehood into circulation, on the eve of the election & when it will be too late, to expose it. I suspect the latter. To guard against any use which may be intended to be made of so base a falsication, you can if you think it necessary, enclose the letter of *Aaron Wagar* to some friend at New Orleans, furnishing him with the facts here stated, to be used only in the event that the story shall be put in circulation there. I would do so myself but I do not at this moment know that I have any intimate acquaintance who is now in the City.

JAMES K. POLK

ALS, draft. DLC–JKP. Addressed to Nashville and marked *"Copy."*

1. In his letter of September 12, 1844, Aaron Wagar claims that in 1835 he sent Polk $2.25 and a deed intended for delivery to William E. Woodruff. According to Wagar, Polk handed over the deed but not the money; now Wagar requests that Polk return the money to him in New Orleans. L. DLC–JKP.

FROM JOHN A. GARDNER

Gardnersville, Tenn. October 7, 1844

Gardner reports on campaign activities in the Western District. He notes that on September 30th some twelve to fifteen hundred friends "marched out on horse back" to escort Cave Johnson into Dresden, that the mass meeting of Democrats in Obion County on October 5th drew a crowd estimated at fifteen hundred or more, and that tomorrow he will address the regimental muster at Troy. Gardner adds that on October 15th he and Fitzgerald[1] will speak at a mass meeting in Dresden.

ALS. DLC–JKP. Addressed to Columbia and marked *"Private."* Polk's AE on the cover states that he answered this letter on October 11, 1844; Polk's reply has not been found.

1. William Fitzgerald served as circuit court clerk in Stewart County, 1822–25; sat one term in the Tennessee House, 1825–27; and held the position of attorney general of Tennessee's Sixteenth Judicial Circuit before winning election in 1831 to a single term in the U.S. House. He moved to Henry County in the late 1830's and in 1841 became judge of Tennessee's Ninth Judicial Circuit.

FROM LAWSON GIFFORD

Dear Sir, Nashville, Oct. 7, [1844][1]

After waiting in this place 2 weeks in daily expectation of getting some assistance, I find I have to leave without one dollar. It may be all right in the end. I hope it will be, but with the aid of a little money I know it would have been better. Powell, (R.W.) is here & receivd some letters from Elizbethton & Jonesboro to-day that makes things look some what doubtful. Dr. Chester & Haynes write from Jonesboro' & Wm. Rhea from Eliz'ton.[2] They urge Powell to return & assist in keeping the Carter voters in the traces. Stories recently invented & put afloat by Brownlow[3] & others have made our friends some what alarmed. The result in the Union is settled. Polk & Dallas will be elected. But Tennessee is rather doubtful unless our folks can be kept together. They[4] least giving way will endanger every thing. Write to Blair just on the eve of the election. He is prudent & careful & will do evry thing in his power. With the best wishes for your success & the success of our party in this state....

L. GIFFORD

ALS. DLC–JKP. Addressed to Columbia.

1. Date identified through content analysis.

2. John P. Chester, Landon C. Haynes and William R. Rhea. A Jonesboro physician and an ardent Democrat, Chester served twelve years as postmaster,

1829–37 and 1842–44. William R. Rhea was an elder in the Elizabethton Presbyterian Church.

3. A minister, editor, and politician, William G. Brownlow became editor of the Elizabethton *Tennessee Whig* in 1839. The following year he moved the paper to Jonesboro, where it was known as the *Jonesborough Whig and Independent Journal.* Ten years later Brownlow again changed his residence and moved to Knoxville, where he published his *Brownlow's Knoxville Whig.* A Whig congressional candidate in 1843, he was defeated by Andrew Johnson; but later he twice won election as governor and served from 1865 to 1869. He also served in the U.S. Senate from 1869 to 1875.

4. Gifford probably intended to write the definite article, "the."

TO BOLING GORDON

My Dear Sir: Columbia Oct. 7th 1844

Your letter was handed to me this morning by *Mr. Jones,*[1] and I am greatly gratified that you have consented to go with *Mr. Voorheis.*[2] Since the change of the route which you thought it best to make, I do not know the *times* and *places* of the *appointments.* Will you send me up a list of your appointments, and I will if possible, to prevail on some of our Speakers, to relieve you at *Douglass's Springs in Perry.* I wish you to send me the whole list, as well before reaching Douglass's Springs as afterwards. If I find no Speaker can be had in this part of the State, I will write to *Jackson* to have one sent from there. I think you may count certainly on being relieved at Douglass's. If you are not I hope you can keep on a day or two longer when you will certainly be relieved.

A. V. Brown starts to East Tennessee on thursday.

JAMES K. POLK

ALS. T–BG. Addressed to Hickman County, Tenn., and marked *"Private."*

1. In his letter to Polk of October 6, 1844, Gordon agreed to speak in the Western District at some of the places recommended, but in reverse order.

2. William Van Voorhies.

FROM ADAM HUNTSMAN[1]

Dear Sir Jackson 7th October 1844

Yours of the 23d & 27th[2] was duly received upon my return from Shelby, on the 5th Inst, and the appointments for Mr Thomas[3] has been made. Also for James L. Totten[4] of Mississippi whose aid we have envoked. Craighead is doing sterling business where ever he can get good meetings, but the Whigs are making every exertion to prevent any of their party from hearing him. The battle will be kept up incessantly here untill the day of the election. My own opinion is somewhat settled, as to the result in the District & is as follows:

Democratic Majority		Whig Majority	
Benton	100	Perry	175
Henry	450	Henderson	600
Weakly	400	Madison	500
Obion	250	Gibson	600
Hardeman	400	Carroll	700
Fayette	75	Dyer	75
Hardin	100	Lauderdale	50
Haywood	50	McNairy	50
Tipton	150	Shelby	175
	1975		2925
			1975
		Whig Majority	950

This is 1000 votes better than when you beat Cannon.[5] There will be a *gain* of upwards of twelve Hundred upon the last election and two members of the Legislature next August. These counties may vary a little from what I have set them down but in the aggregate the vote will be even larger than my allowance. Betts are running even upon the general result. We consider our success certain but as to Tennessee the letters that I receve from E. Tennessee vary so much that I am induced in splitting the difference and allowing one fourth for calculations too sanguine to put it down at 1500 against us. So that to make it certain we must get 3000 in Middle Tennessee. In the Counties of White Overton Jackson & Fentress my old district my information is that we will gain 4 or 500 and [....][6] The ballance must come from the other Counties. We must have 3000 from Middle Tennessee. In making calculations you know I generally underate the mark for safty but this is not far from it. State Pride makes it desirable to get Tennessee but I do not consider it absolutely necessary. I claim Michagan Maine N Jersey New York Pensylvania Virginia South Carolina Alabama Missisippi Arkansaw Massouri & Illinois as certain which is enough & I consider our chances best for Georgia Tennessee, Ohio & Indiana & Lousiana. Clay will get R Island Massachusetts Vermont Connecticut Maryland, Delaware N Carolina & Kentucky & some chance for Georgia Tennessee Ohio Indiana & Lousiana. What say you to this calculation?

If the abolitionists in Ohio & Indiana vote a seperate Ticket we have these States. If not we are *licked.* If Georgia goes for Clay she ought to be put in the mad House.

Our cause is still improving here and if you will act out in proportion in Middle and E Tennessee we will send Harry of the west[7] to Davy Jones locker. Put up the 3000 and all is set. Harry will be in a worse fix than he was in Washington City when he teazed a little Milliner for six months before he could get her to meet him & then he could not *come it.*

There is a pretty strong objection to you which is well founded, as Washington Madison & Jackson had no children. If you succeed the world will believe that the qualifications of an American President lies *all* in his head, and *none* in his Breeches.

ADAM HUNTSMAN

ALS. DLC–JKP. Addressed to Columbia. Published in Emma Inman Williams, ed., "Letters of Adam Huntsman to James K. Polk," *THQ,* VI (December, 1947), pp. 362–63.

1. Born in Virginia, Adam Huntsman had moved by 1809 to Overton County, where he practiced law and engaged in extensive land speculations until 1821. He sat three terms for Overton County in the Tennessee Senate, 1815–21, and later represented Madison County in the Senate for two terms, 1827–31. A loyal Jacksonian Democrat, he defeated David Crockett for a seat in Congress and served one term in the U.S. House, 1835–37.

2. Letters not found.

3. Probably Jonas E. Thomas.

4. A lawyer, Totten represented Marshall County in the Mississippi legislature from 1844 until 1846; he served as Speaker of that body during both legislative sessions.

5. Newton Cannon, a Williamson County planter and supporter of Henry Clay, lost races for the Tennessee governorship in 1827 and 1839, but won bids for that office in 1835 and 1837.

6. Word or words illegible.

7. Henry Clay.

FROM GEORGE M. DALLAS

No. 9

My Dear Sir [Philadelphia, Penn.] 8 Oct. [18]44

The State Election is under way, and proceeds in this City with great briskness but, as yet, perfect order. A placard was posted on Sunday night of a highly inflammatory character, calling upon all Protestants, Presbyterians, Methodists, Baptists etc. to unite in putting down the Catholics by voting the Whig ticket. This dreadful element of religious fanaticism, thus introduced into the political contest at a moment of excitement, will, I fear, create scenes of disorder and violence in the districts adjoining the City. The Nativists are said to have joined our opponents, under a bargain which gives them the three County Congressional districts and the City Corporation, and exacts from them votes against Shunk. If this be true, the Whig candidate for Governor, Markle,[1] will leave this City and County with a large majority; and if the same Coalition has been effected throughout the State, Mr. Shunk cannot be expected to reach a majority exceeding ten thousand.

On the Electoral struggle, your vote will every where gain upon that of Mr. Shunk, and our majority may probably double his. The adversary has so managed as to assail Mr. Shunk for tendencies to Catholicism, and thus to provoke the prejudices of the Nativists, and of many others too, against him.[2] These feelings cannot bear on the Presidential question.

The accounts from New-Jersey and New-York continue to be of a promising character. The State Election of the former began today and goes on through tomorrow. A letter from the democratic Candidate for Governor, Mr. John R. Thompson,[3] written last evening, is full of confidence. In reality, however, I am not as well assured about N. Jersey as I felt some weeks ago. Gov. Wall,[4] whom I casually met, seems disatisfied with the nomination of Mr. Thomson, and others complain bitterly of a speech made by Capt. Stockton at the Trenton Convention.[5] Still, appearances remain decidedly favorable. Of New-York, Webb, the Editor of the Courier,[6] who had been on here for several days, spoke with certainty of its giving Mr. Clay a majority of 20,000; but information from every other source is precise and emphatic in the opposite direction. Very generally, in the City of N. York, the Whig merchants and conversational politicians acknowledge that the nomination of Mr. Wright had destroyed all their prospects. Such, too, is the calm and deliberate opinion, of Chief Justice Jones,[7] of that State, who was good enough to visit me this morning, and who expressed him[self] decidedly. I have, this instant, also parted with an intelligent farmer of our Berks County, who tells me that he has just returned from a tour of business through New-York, and that he found throughout that State that the outcry of 1840 was reversed, and that where Tip and Ti[8] were then sounded P. & D. were now universal. He spoke of 15000 at the least as our majority.

I have nothing from Ohio, but general declarations. Our friends in Maryland are dejected by their overthrow, and efforts will have to be made to re-animate them to another trial. In Delaware, we feel confident of success.

Your suggestion as to warning the democrats every where against pipe layers[9] has been vigorously and effectually attended to. The Empire Club of New-York has signalized its sagacity and perseverance on this subject: it has a committee in attendance in this city to aid in detecting imported voters; and one of its members is said to be detailed to each of the endangered townships of N. Jersey. The main body of the rogues are supposed to diverge from N. York.

Mr. Webster's speeches, though not generally supposed to have done the cause of Mr. Clay much service, have perhaps artfully and successfully aimed at effecting a single important object, that is the drawing to his standard, the abolitionists of New-York and Ohio. I am not quite sure that after all their professions, they will not yield to the plausible persuasions of Mr. Webster. We hear, to be sure, rumors of their inflexibility; but I have seen nothing that does not leave them a locus penitentiae.[10] If we depended on their remaining true to their principles, we should have a sorry chance. They are considered a gradually increasing party, but I much doubt their having augmented to the extent represented. Should the democracy fail in November, by the course taken in Louisiana, Georgia, Tennessee, North Carolina, Virginia, and Maryland (these states are still claimed by the Whigs) the avalanche of abolition will become irresistible, as I should think it impossible any longer to keep the northern democrats battling on that point. If, on the contrary, the South stands manfully and unitedly by the cause, the abolitionists will rapidly retrograde and disappear. In very truth, the great question of union or disunion is at issue, though not in the shape in which it is put by some hot partizans in S. Carolina.

Nothing can be learnt as to our election before tomorrow, the voters and tickets being very numerous and consuming much time in counting: I would otherwise keep this letter open.

G. M. Dallas

ALS. DLC–JKP. Addressed to Columbia. Polk's AE on the cover states that he answered this letter on October 19, 1844; Polk's reply has not been found.

1. Joseph Markle, a Westmoreland County farmer, was the unsuccessful gubernatorial candidate of the Whig party in 1844; in previous political contests, he had failed to win election to the Pennsylvania House and the U.S. Senate.

2. See Jesse Miller to Polk, October 12, 1844.

3. John R. Thomson.

4. A lawyer, Garret D. Wall sat in the New Jersey General Assembly in 1827, served as U.S. district attorney for that state in 1829, won election as governor but declined to serve in 1829, sat in the U.S. Senate as a Democrat, 1835–41, and served as judge of the Court of Errors and Appeals of New Jersey from 1848 until his death in 1850.

5. The second edition of the *New York Herald* of September 6, 1844, carried the text of Robert Stockton's speech.

6. James W. Webb, publisher of the *Morning Courier and New York Enquirer*, supported Andrew Jackson and the Democratic party until 1831; Webb's critics

claimed that he changed his political views following receipt of a $50,000 loan from the Second Bank of the United States.

7. Samuel Jones served as a justice of the Superior Court of New York from April 1828 until May 1847; he served two more years as a justice of the Supreme Court of the First District of New York City.

8. Reference is to the 1840 Whig campaign slogan, "Tippecanoe and Tyler too," in behalf of the ticket of William H. Harrison and John Tyler.

9. A few weeks before the presidential election of 1840, a Whig operative named "Glentworth" was arrested and charged with voting frauds alledged to have been committed in the 1838 New York gubernatorial election. According to Thurlow Weed in his *Autobiography,* Glentworth had received the office of tobacco inspector as compensation for having recruited gangs of Pennsylvania laborers to lay water pipes between Lake Croton and New York City; Glentworth's out-of-state pipe layers only worked on election days and in such places as their illegal votes could be counted with safety. Legislation designed to prevent election fraud came to be known as "anti-pipelaying" bills.

10. Variant of the Latin phrase, *locus poenitentiae,* which translates "place for repentance." Used as a legal term, the phrase means "an opportunity for changing one's mind" or "an opportunity to undo what one has done" or "a right to withdraw from an incompleted transaction."

FROM EDWIN F. POLK

Dear Sir Boliver Oct 8. 1844

Yours of Oct 1st came duly to hand and I handed your letter to Coe who happened to be here on yesterday and just left.[1] He & Maj. Harvey[2] of Miss addressed the people here on yesterday. Harvey is doing good service and goes back to Fayette to morrow to fill some appointments there. By the last mail I received 900 copies of the *"Vindication,"* 100 having been previously sent. I wrote to W. Howard at Memphis & requested him to write to brother William[3] (as I was fearful a direct letter might not reach him) and asking him to contribute to the payment of the cost of the publication, telling him also the amount of the cost. Howard writes me that he sent my letter to him and that he doubts not that he will contribute. I have been waiting to hear from him, is the reason that I have not written before. The amount is more than I at first anticipated else I should not have written to him. I have no doubt that he will pay half, and Perry[4] & myself will pay the other half. If I had the money I would advance it immediately without hesitation, but a few days can make no difference with the *Printer.* I think that brother William would pay the whole of it if he were asked, but this I do not want him to do. He has seven thousand dollars deposited in Memphis to bet on the election. I expect to hear from him by the last of this week—if he does not contribute, I will immediately have a bill drawn on Bank and send you a check for the amount.

I saw old Paris Alexander. He is too young to remember any thing that occurred in the revolution and gave me a statement of something similar to that of his brother Augustus.[5] He has a son named after my father.[6] I did not think it very material or should have sent it.

EDWIN POLK

P.S. The Eagle has published the old Gentleman's Epitaph, but I hear nothing said about it. His paper[7] is in almost as low a standing as Brownlow's. E.P.

ALS. DLC–JKP. Addressed to Columbia.

1. Letter not found.

2. Not further identified.

3. Wardlow Howard and William Wilson Polk. Fourth son of Ezekiel Polk, William Wilson "Stingy Bill" Polk received a captain's commission in the Maury County militia in 1808; he subsequently moved to Middleburg in Hardeman County. By 1840 he had removed to Phillips County, Ark., where he owned one of the South's largest and most profitable plantations.

4. Charles Perry Polk, fifth son of Ezekiel and Sophia Neely Polk, was born in Maury County in 1813; his family moved to Hardeman County in 1820.

5. Augustus Alexander contributed a certificate attesting to Ezekiel Polk's loyalty to the patriot cause; his statement was published in the Nashville *Vindication* pamphlet.

6. Paris Alexander's son, Ezekiel, is not further identified.

7. Francis S. Latham established the Memphis *American Eagle,* a Whig sheet, in January 1842.

FROM GEORGE M. DALLAS

No. 10

My Dear Sir [Philadelphia, Penn.] Oct. 9, 1844

Your letter of the 30, Sept.[1] has just reached me. On the question you submit for reflection, I entertain no doubt whatever. The discourtesy manifested in the manner of questioning you, as well as the avowed and notorious hostility, both in general action and in special purpose, of those who interrogate, deprive them of all claim to any reply whatever.[2] Public opinion will, I feel assured, promptly reach this conclusion. But were they ever so well entitled, by civility and fairness, to an answer, I think the democratic party generally would regret to see you induced, by any consideration whatever, at this stage of the canvass, to open anew a speculation as to your sentiments on a topic already sufficiently developed and in which your legislative speeches and vote leave nothing for candor to desire. No statement, however explicit, will satisfy your adversaries, and your friends are content with what they have and know.

The result of the election yesterday in this City and County was a Waterloo defeat to the democrats. It was brought about by a very reckless and profligate bargain between the whigs and the natives, under the terms of which they divided the spoil and coalesced to obtain them. Thus the Natives were to be secured by Whig votes in carrying their Candidates for Congress in the *first, third,* and *fourth* districts,[3] together with their members of Assembly and some local officers, and the Whigs were to be secured in carrying their congressional candidate in the second district,[4] their members of Assembly, Select and Commons Councils and Mayor in the City[5] by native votes, and both whigs and natives, in City and County, were to rally on the Whig candidate for Governor.[6] This bargain, which was not ascertained with certainty by our friends until about noon produced a panic which in some measure aided in it's consummation. Every thing was carried out by the allies according to contract, except in the *fourth* Congressional district, where our friend Charles J. Ingersoll gallantly weathered the storm and has been re–elected by a majority of 167.

On the leading point at issue, the Governor, the Majority of the Whigs is larger in the City and County than I yesterday anticipated. It will probably be very little above or below 6000. This is a heavy item to start with against the democrats in counting up the results; but I believe that we shall find our candidate has succeeded, notwithstanding, by seven or ten thousand. The news comes in pretty rapidly this morning, but not with the exactness as to amounts which is desirable. Enough is known to make it apparent that the democratic Counties have asserted their customary overpowering strength; and if in Lancaster & Pittsburg, and Huntingdon, the Whigs have not transcended all their past exploits and present expectations, we have the State secure. As matters now are, we are almost a tie.

Whig			*Democratic*	
City & County of Phila	say	5737	Berks	4451
Chester		665	Montgomery	1168
Delaware		575	Schuylkill	1100
			Bucks	265
		6977		6984

I don't want to close this letter before obtaining the returns which are looked for by the western car at about 2 o'clock. I must, however, have it ready for the Southern mail by 3 o'clock. I will add on the opposite page what may arrive. The belief is that we have carried N. Jersey; but I don't like to say so, until the vote is safely posted.

Lancaster is just in, and instead of Whig 6000, it is only 3967! This relieves my mind wonderfully.

G. M. DALLAS

[P.S.]

Dauphin	900	Whig.
Adams	700	Whig.
York	1000	*Dem.*

ALS. DLC–JKP. Addressed to Columbia. Polk's AE on the cover states that he answered this letter on October 19, 1844; Polk's reply has not been found.

1. Letter not found.
2. See John W. Goode et al. to Polk, September 21, 1844.
3. Lewis C. Levin, John H. Campbell, and Jacob Shearer. Shearer served multiple terms in both the Pennsylvania House, 1805–11, and in the Pennsylvania Senate, 1813–17.
4. Joseph R. Ingersoll, a Philadelphia lawyer and brother of Charles J. Ingersoll, served as a Whig in the U.S. House, 1835–37 and in 1841–49; in 1852 Millard Fillmore appointed him minister to Great Britain, where he served until 1853.
5. A descendant of one of Pennsylvania's oldest families, Peter McCall graduated from Princeton in 1826; read law in the office of a Philadelphia attorney; and served several terms on the Philadelphia City Council before running for mayor in 1844.
6. Joseph Markle.

FROM ALBERT GALLUP

Albany, N.Y. October 9, 1844

Gallup acknowledges receipt of a copy of the Nashville *Vindication* pamphlet. He fears that the "whigs in Philadelphia & in the city of New York are about to coalesce with the natives." Yet in his twenty–eight years as a New York politician, he has never seen the Democrats "better united than they now are." The "old fashioned democrats," in whose number he counts himself, are satisfied with their state nominees; certainly the "Barnburners," [1] as they call themselves, are well pleased and united. He calculates that New York is safe for the Democrats in the presidential election. Many participants at the mass meeting at Kinderhook, N.Y., on October 5th expected to meet Martin Van Buren, but the former president declined to attend in deference to the honor of the presidential office. Such "mock dignity" cannot be sustained by republican principles. Democrats will win in Pennsylvania by a small majority, but Ohio remains in doubt.

ALS. DLC–JKP. Addressed to Columbia.

1. In 1843 the radical wing of the New York Democracy took the nickname "Barnburners," which recalled the Dutch story of a farmer who burned his barn to get rid of the rats.

TO CAVE JOHNSON

[Dear Sir,] [Columbia, Tenn.] October 9, 1844

I was glad to learn from your letter of the 4th that you had reached home in improved health, and that you bring good news from the District.[1] I am glad to learn that you will return and spend 10 days before the election in that part of the State. I think it very important that it should be canvassed closely up to the election. *Fitzgerald* wrote pressingly for help in the Northern part of the District, some two or three weeks ago.[2] I immediately saw *Nicholson* who was here, who authorized me to write to him as I did so to make a list of appointments for him commencing at *Paris* on the 21st and at such other points as he might select. I have received no answer from *Fitzgerald* and fear he may have been absent from home. Will you write immediately to *Fitzgerald* or some other friends at *Paris* to make the appointments for *Nicholson* if they have not done so, commencing at *Paris* on Monday the 21st and continuing up, to the 1st Nov. He must be back at Nashville at the election. *Nicholson* will be at *Clarksville* on the 21st and his calculation is to go from there to *Paris*.[3] He desires also that one appointment shall be made for him in *Stewart* on Saturday the 19th which he can attend on his way from *Clarksville* to *Paris*. Will you write to *Cherry*[4] or some one else in *Stewart* to have it made. Let them get up a *Barbacue* and have an exclusive Democratic mass-meeting if possible. *Boling Gordon* and *Wm. V. Voorhees*[5] start on a tour through *Wayne, Hardin, McNairy* and *Perry* today. *A. V. Brown* and *Gov. Clay* of Al. will start to East Tennessee on tomorrow.

The State is now *safe,* if we can keep her so. To do this will require all our energy and vigilence. There is great danger of illegal voting and frauds upon the ballot box, and especially in the Counties bordering the Kentucky line. The election comes on different days in Kentucky and Tennessee, and unless you have the boxes in your District in every precinct bordering on the *Kentucky* line guarded by men chosen for that purpose, there will be hundreds of *Kentuckians* imported, who will vote in Tennessee. I beg you to attend to this in your counties. Do not leave it to accident or general promises of our friends to guard these *boxes.* Let the men be appointed by your Committee before hand, let them be sure and take their pledges that they will stand by the box in their respective precincts and watch. A general rule which I think should be adopted all over the State, is, to swear every man who offers to vote out of his own precinct, that he has not voted at any other place and will not attempt to do so in that election. Urge this upon our friends wherever you go.

All my news from abroad is of the most cheering character.

[JAMES K. POLK]

P.S. Do not fail to write the letter about *Nicholson's* appointments as soon as you get this letter. He will go to *Clarksville* calculating to make the trip, and will be greatly disappointed if the appointments are not made for him. Have it attended to without fail.

PL. Published in St. George L. Sioussat, ed., "Letters of James K. Polk to Cave Johnson, 1833–1848," *THM,* I (September, 1915), pp. 250–51. Addressed to Clarksville and marked *"Private."*

1. In his letter of October 4, 1844, Johnson observed that their meetings were "generally good," and he predicted that the Democrats would carry the Western District. ALS. DLC–JKP.

2. On September 22, 1844, William Fitzgerald solicited Polk's assistance in obtaining prominent speakers from outside the Western District. ALS. DLC–JKP.

3. The Democratic mass meeting in Clarksville was held on October 17, 1844, and the meeting in Paris on October 21, 1844.

4. A farmer, William B. Cherry represented Stewart County in the Tennessee House as a Democrat for three terms, 1839–45, and served as sheriff of that county from 1837 until 1840.

5. William Van Voorhies.

FROM J. G. M. RAMSEY

Mecklenburg, Tenn. October 9, 1844

Ramsey reports that he has received from a friend in Charleston[1] several newspapers and a manuscript address in the German language and has begun to circulate the papers among the Germans of East Tennessee. He notes that in *"Little Germany"*[2] many of the people have only their "Dutch Bible & Almanac" to read; consequently, these newspapers have been received with great avidity. Ramsey expects the newspapers to do good service during the campaign and plans to send additional papers to other counties. His Charleston friend also writes that Calhoun considers Polk's election "as near certain as any thing political can be." Calhoun has commented that for the first time since Jackson's election, the Democratic party is united upon principles and is aroused to vigorous action.

ALS. DLC–JKP. Addressed to Columbia. Polk's AE on the cover states that he answered this letter on October 15, 1844; Polk's reply has not been found.

1. Not identified further.

2. The Mosheim Community of Greene County constituted the largest concentration of German-speaking East Tennesseans prior to the settlement of Wartburg in Morgan County in 1845; Ramsey's "Little Germany" also may have referred to Washington and Sevier Counties.

FROM GEORGE M. DALLAS

No. 11

My Dear Sir, [Philadelphia, Penn.] 10. Oct. 1844

I am busy in court, but cannot allow a mail to be lost at present.

The returns from our interior continue to cheer us. We have gained largely, and the whigs have lost largely, in every county, on the returns of 1840. *The majorities* that came in last evening exceed our hopes. Cumberland, dem. 35. Northampton, dem. 1100. Lebanon, Whig, 735 (instead of 967). Franklin, Wh. 375 (instead of 694). Adams, Wh. 500 (instead of 825), Columbia, Dem. 1689 (will be more), Northumberland 1226. Dem. Monroe, dem. 1238. Perry, dem. 1126. We are now elated at the prospect of a majority exceeding 10.000, if our northern counties do as they usually do.

As I feared, we have lost N. Jersey—probably by about 2000—a large majority for that State. This is certainly owing to the causes to which I have heretofore alluded, causes which may not operate at all at the electoral election.[1]

G. M. DALLAS

ALS. DLC–JKP. Addressed to Columbia. Polk's AE on the cover states that he answered this letter on October 21, 1844.

1. See Dallas to Polk, October 8, 1844; and John K. Kane to Polk, October 13, 1844.

FROM FRANCIS W. PICKENS[1]

My dear Sir Edgewood near Edgefield 11 Oct: 1844

I take great pleasure in stating that my letters to-day leave no doubt but that Georgia will go for you in November. We have gained in every part of the State & although the Whigs laid off the State into congressional districts so as to secure them, yet the probability now is that we have carried 4 out of the 8, with evidence certain that the popular majority is with us.

I think there can be no reasonable doubt but that you will be elected President, & probably by a large majority. If so, God grant that you may be enabled to administer the government so as to acquire fame & honor to yourself & confer a lasting blessing upon your country. Your difficulties may be great; but firmness, fidelity, & truth will carry you through gloriously & triumphantly. If it be true that Mexico is moving upon Texas it can only be done through British councils & British funds

& we will be bound to meet the issues tendered with temperance & dignity, but in a lofty spirit. Mr. Monroe's message at the period when the Holy Alliance meditated a re-conquest of the Spanish colonies who had declared & maintained their independence furnishes a precedent & a noble model.[2] You have seen that since my return home things have taken a great turn in this State.[3] Although there is a united and determined intention in this State to bear the present odious and oppressive Tariff, yet I think there is a settled disposition amongst all reflecting & just men to wait events & look with confidence to the triumph of the Rep. party, which seems now to be inevitable. I trust every thing will work right.

If Clay is now defeated it will be forever, & the organization of the Whig party will be broken up as far as the South is concerned. The young & aspiring men will fall back into their true and natural position. If your administration takes the course that I believe it will, there will be no division in the South in its support—there *can be none.* Webster will lead the opposition & this will but consolidate our friends & drive off the Southern Whigs. You & he represent the extreme wings of the two great parties that have always existed, & the middle men & *tacticians* will necessarily fall into the stronger wing. This will give us the ascendency for years to come, exactly as we had it under Jefferson. The difficulty with us since Jefferson's time has been, that there has been no great battle fought upon radical *principles throughout.*

Present [...][4] most respectful [...] to Mrs. Polk & to your bro[ther] also, and accept for yourself....

F. W. PICKENS

ALS. DLC–JKP. Addressed to Columbia.

1. Francis W. Pickens, a South Carolina lawyer and planter, first won election to Congress as a nullifier and sat from 1834 until 1843; a member of the Nashville Convention of 1850, he served as governor of South Carolina from 1860 until 1863.

2. Reference is to the Monroe Doctrine, first set forth in James Monroe's Annual Message to Congress of December 2, 1823.

3. Pickens probably refers to the Bluffton movement in South Carolina.

4. Word or words here and below obliterated by sealing wax oil.

FROM ALFRED BALCH

My Dear Sir, Nashville 12th Octr 44

The Whigs have carried Maryland, having run in Pratt[1] only 500 or 1000—this result was anticipated by every sound headed Democrat in the Union.

It is impossible for me to describe the anxiety which I feel to hear the news from Ohio Pen & Jersey. We have letters from Cincinnati up to the night of Tuesday the 7th in which our friends assure us that the skies were bright and that they were full of auspicious hopes. My faith in Ohio, as I wrote you when in that State,[2] is by no means *strong* altho we have tens of thousands of faithful friends within her length and breadth. I saw too many full blooded *federal* Yankees in that quarter. Still we may have succeeded by "the skin of our teeth."[3] It is to the great states of Pen New York and Va that we are to look for the decision of the pending contest—the most important that has been waged since November 1800. On Thursday we had partial returns from Maryland and some believed that we had succeeded there, altho I was not one of them. I have known too much of Maryland from my youth upwards to repose the least confidence in her *Democracy.* But, whilst our friends were that elevated in the hope and our adversaries a little depressed, I sallied out with a view to pick up the notions of A B and C. I soon perceived that the Whigs who are not leading manifested a docile spirit and that no small number of them were quite reconciled to the prospect of your election. If we have carried Penn. *and* Ohio by the election of Shunk & Tod I am thoroughly satisfied that we shall lead the Whigs in Ten on the 5th Nov by at least 5000 votes. The moment we ascertain this fact, if it has occurred we shall begin to gain every where throughout our state to a greater or lesser extent. You may rely on this. I have never known the population of Nashville to be in such a condition as at this moment. Every one looks & feel grave and anxious.

I saw Foster yesterday for the first time for nine months as I never go near him or Bell. As for the latter gentleman I have not spoken to him since April 35 except once on business. I have the honor of enjoying his eternal hatred a matter of small moment to me. Ephraim had at one time a notion to follow Bells example but soon found that it was useless. So yesterday he approached me with great cordiality and addressed me in a subdued and most polite tone and manner. Spoke of politics like a *gentlemen* and seemed anxious to press the subject quite in a cozy way. I told him laughingly that I was too earnestly engaged in endeavouring to blow him and his party up to talk with him any longer then but that we would meet again.

ALFRED BALCH

P.S. We have cheering accounts from Indiana and we may carry her. But, there are rather too many *full blooded* Yankees there. Ever since the 1st of August my faith has been perfect as to Maine N. Hamp. Michigan, New York, Pennsylvania Va S. Carolina Ala Mississippi Arkansas Missouri & Illinois, being 142. As to our success beyond there I shall look on each one that we gain (and we have at least an equal chance for several) as a *windfall*. Our numerous accts from this state continue to be favorable and all point to a successful result. AB.

ALS. DLC–JKP. Addressed to Columbia.

1. Thomas G. Pratt, a lawyer, held seats in both the Maryland House, 1832–35, and Senate, 1838–43, prior to his election to the governorship of Maryland in 1844; he subsequently served in the U.S. Senate from 1850 until 1857.

2. See Alfred Balch to Polk, August 12, 1844.

3. Paraphrase of the Biblical quotation, "with the skin of my teeth." Job 19:20.

FROM DAVID T. DISNEY

Dr Sir Cincinnati Saturday 12 Oct. 1844

Contrary to my expectation, we are beaten in this State. Our governor[1] is beaten probably by a vote less that *1000,* out of a poll of nearly or quite 300,000. Congressman 13 D. 8 Whig. State Legislature Senate 20 W. 16 D. H of R. 40 W. 32 D. The abolition party deceived us. All the whigs of that party voted with the whigs and left the democratic abolitionists to vote the abolition ticket. The struggle has been tremendous. I fear that we cannot rally our folks for the november fight, *but we will try.*

Four counties from Pennsylvania have come in; they indicate that we have swept that state by an overwhelming vote.

D. T. Disney

ALS. DLC–JKP. Addressed to Columbia.

1. David Tod.

FROM SAMUEL H. LAUGHLIN

10 o'clock Saturday night
Nashville, Oct 12, 1844

My dear sir,

The within coming open to Gen. Armstrong,[1] we have used it privately, in confirming a printed slip from the Enquirer office, in the preparation of a little Extra slip which we will issue to night. The contents of this letter, without names given and the slip from Enquirer[2] have been read and proclamed to an immence mass of the Democracy collected around the Post office, and Union office. While I write, the drums are beating a call for parade, and guns are being fired in every direction all over the city. The news has run over town with the rapidity of a cry of fire. In addition to this letter, we learn that we have carried Delaware, by a majority it is reported in papers, of less than 200. I presume the mail will take you the same news we have recd. here.

On the whole, from all news, notwithstanding state of things in Maryland, we have most abundant cause to rejoice. I can say thank God, from the bottom of my heart. Whig final majority for Gov. in Maryland is only about 300.

While I still write, our boys have already got their full band of music out, and are in full march through the streets. Such a sudden outburst of enthusiasm, as now pervades Nashville, all raised in half an hour, no man has ever seen.

S. H. LAUGHLIN

ALS. DLC–JKP. Probably addressed to Columbia; marked "Private."

1. On October 9, 1844, Moses Dawson wrote Polk that the Ohio state election returns for Cincinnati indicated "a Waterloo defeat of the federal ticket" for governor, Congress, legislature, and county offices; Dawson estimated that the Democratic majority was twenty-one hundred votes, a reversal of the sixteen hundred margin garnered by the Whigs in the 1840 elections. ALS. DLC–JKP.

2. Enclosed offprint from the *Cincinnati Enquirer* not found.

FROM JESSE MILLER[1]

Dear Sir [Harrisburg, Penn. October 12, 1844][2]

The above is a copy of a letter I sent this day to our old friend John Adams of Catskill, New York,[3] and as I wish to keep you correctly inform'd of things here I have thought it most convenient to send you a copy. We entertain the hope that the union between the natives and Whigs cannot be continued or carried out to the same extent in the Presidential Election. The only hopes of the Whigs now both in this State and N.Y. is in getting the Natives & abolition vote. One of our Western Counties in this state (Mercer) poll'd 1000 abolition votes from which I entertain the hope that they will adhere to their own candidates in New York & Ohio. It is the present intention of a large portion of them to do so and they will do it unless the Whigs can cajole them by some bargain. We feel confident however of carrying Penna. under any and all circumstances but we have to work constantly.

J. MILLER

[Addendum]

My dear Sir Harrisburg Oct 12th 1844

The Combination of the *native* Americans in the City and County of Philada. a few days before the election deranged all our Calculations. We have however notwithstanding this Coalition elected our Candidate for Govr (Mr. Shunk) by about 5.000 majy.

We lost in the City and County alone 7,000 votes by this union. That is, we ought to have had a majority in the two of about 1000 instead of which there was near 6000 against us. We also lost in other Counties of the state at the very lowest estimate 3000 votes in consequence of the slanders circulated against Shunk about him being a Roman Catholic and opposed to the use of the Bible in the Common Schools. Thus you will perceive when I told you that we would not have less than ten and probably 15.000 majority I had good *datum* for my opinion, as the two causes which opperated against us had not then developed themselves so as to indicate their effect. Now let me tell you, the origin of these slanders against Shunk. Some time in the spring of 1842 the Catholics were building a Church in Pittsburg and had the usual Ceremony of laying the Corner stone. On the day of the procession a Catholic friend of Mr. Shunk (a Mr. Berlin)[4] accidentally met Mr. Shunk and took him by the arm, and invited him to walk with him in procession. Mr. Shunk at first declined but being pressed, he went along, and was present as any other Citizen at the Ceremonies. In Consequence of this act of Courtesy to a friend, the Whig got evidence to prove that Shunk had been seen in a Catholic procession. That he had bowed to the Cross, and laid down the american flag for the Priests to tread on and desecrate. It was in vain that we contradicted the story, and proved that his bowing to the Cross and desecrating the flag were all as false as *Hell.* They persisted in asserting it. But the story of the Bible was still worse in its effects, and now let me explain this. About four or 5 weeks ago a *whig* friend of Mr. Shunks (by the name of McClure)[5] invited him to dine with him. During the sitting, the subject of using the Bible as a Common School Book became the topic of conversation in the Course of which Mr. Shunk observed that "When there was much division among the parents of the Children about the use of it, it would perhaps be better to dispense with the Book than to be quarelling about a good thing." This Conversation leaked out from the family and an unprincipled editor by the name of Biddle[6] put it in his paper. It at once produced some excitement and Mr. Shunk wrote a letter to a friend for publication in which he stated that he himself was in favor of the use of the Bible in the schools and as an evidence of that fact he referred them to a resolution which he had introduced when a school director in Harrisburg requiring the Bible to be read regularly in the schools of which he was a director, but in the honesty of his nature admitted that he used the language attributed to him. This was a most unfortunate admission. They at once issued handbills and papers to show that by his own admission, all the Catholics had to do would be to get a Catholic family in each school district to object to the use of the Bible in the schools and then its use would have to be discontinued.

It is difficult to estimate the number of votes we lost on this question but I know they were numerous.

Great efforts will now be made to perpetuate the union between the *natives* and the whigs with what success we cannot tell. I have understood that the whigs had a meeting last night in this Borough, at which they determined to call themselves "Democratic *native* whigs," but do not know it certainly.

We feel confident however, that we can carry the state for Polk and Dallas by an increased majority over Shunk.

We think they have done the most they can do under any Circumstances and that by the exertions which we intend to make, we believe, we can increase our vote. Indeed it was not until a very few days before the election that we had any apprehension of Shunks defeat.

ALS. DLC–JKP. Addressed to Columbia.

1. Jesse Miller sat in both the Pennsylvania House and Senate prior to his election as a Democrat to the U.S. House, where he served from 1833 to 1836. Appointed first auditor of the Treasury Department in 1836, he served in that post until 1842.

2. Date identified through content analysis.

3. Reference is to Miller's letter to John Adams of October 12, 1844, the text of which is printed below as an addendum. A lawyer from Catskill, N.Y., Adams served both in the New York General Assembly, 1812–13, and in the U.S. House, 1833–35.

4. Not identified further.

5. Not identified further.

6. Not identified further.

FROM JAMES HAMILTON, JR.

My Dear Sir, Savannah Geo Oct 13h 1844

I feel peculiarly gratified in being able to assure you that the vote of Georgia *is now secure for you beyond all contingencies.* We have reversed the Whig Majority of 5000 which they had at the last election and are now ahead in the aggregate returns some hundred votes. On the choice of presidential Electors we shall largely augment our majority, as Mr. Clay is less popular in this State than the Whig candidates for Congress.

The Contest has been a very severe one and so close that nothing but the utmost vigilance and zeal can enable us to hold our ground. The Leaders of the Clay party have become perfectly desperate for they feel, that their over throw *now involves their total subversion.* I shall remain here until the election is over before I return to Alabama, where everything is safe by an overwhelming Majority. Here I am able to confer with the most active & intelligent of the Leaders of the Democracy and by Mail to communicate with all parts of the State.

I am exceedingly happy *to know* that all Mr. Calhouns friends in Georgia have done their duty towards the Democracy and sustained your nomination in the most manful & cordial manner; indeed they have been the effective Leaders every where in this State. Nor have I ever seen a party who came up to the mark with a more enthusiastic zeal. It is due to Mr. Calhoun that I should say to you, that he wrote me immediately after your nomination requesting me to quit my retirement & to come out and exert my influence with all his friends and my own in Georgia to sustain the Baltimore nomination. I hope My Dear Sir this will again lead to a cordial Reunion between Tennessee & S.C. so unnaturally separated by some of the unfortunate events which occurred in Genl. Jacksons administration, and redound to the Peace Security & honor of our Country.

Judge Berrien instead of staying at home to take care of his own State such was his false security has been playing sattelite to Webster in the midst of the abolitionists.[1] If he returns before the electoral election the 1st Tuesday in Nov. the Democratic Central Committee have determined to challenge him to meet me before the whole people of Savannah & Chatham County without distinction of party on the Tariff, Annexation Question and respective claims of the Candidates for the Presidency. If he does come up to the scratch, I shall try my best to floor him before *his own people* of which his recent servile walk in Websters wake will afford me rich materials.

In order to keep the Georgians up to concert pitch, I am endeavoring the produce without depressing them the impression that *on them* may devolve the casting vote.

As soon as the election is over in this State I shall hasten to Alabama as private business will take me to Texas the last of the next month where I hope to meet Major Donelson & to do him all the service in my power in the deeply interesting objects [of][2] his mission.

I think My Dear Sir that I may congratulate you on the auspices looking bright & that we shall attain "a famous Victory." In any event be assured of the esteem with which I am....

J. HAMILTON

P.S. We have carried exactly 1/2 of the Delegation in Congress by an increased vote of 5000, being now 1700 a head of the Whigs. My address here to the 10th Nov. After that Oswichee P.O. Alabama. I must apoligize to you for paying the Postage on this Letter but you have doubtless so many Correspondents that as you have not the franking priviledge yet, it is mercy to do so.

ALS. DLC–JKP. Addressed to Columbia and marked "via Washington City."

1. John M. Berrien had addressed the citizens of Boston, Mass., on September 19, 1844; his speech defending a protective tariff included appreciative remarks about Daniel Webster, who presided over the meeting. For the text of Berrien's address, see *Niles' National Register,* October 12, 1844.

2. Manuscript torn.

FROM JOHN K. KANE

My dear Sir, Philada. 13 Oct. 1844

I have this moment received your letter.[1] You will have seen before this that Mr. Shunk is elected by a majority between 4500 and 5000. The estimate which I sent you[2] is falsified by this result; but those who take the pains of comparing the returns with it, will see that in the Democratic counties we were not mistaken. The errors occur in the counties which were against us, and are in a very great, an enormous degree, referrable to frauds either on the polls or the voters. Not however to occupy time with the past, let me speak of the future. What remains to us is absolutely our's: our party has been so thoroughly *winnowed* that nothing is left but grain of standard weight. For the electoral ticket we begin our calculation then with some 5000 majority. To this we add some two or three thousand, perhaps more, from *natives* in Philadelphia city and county, principally the latter. Many of these are indignant at the knavery as they term it of their recent allies, in not yielding up the city government and in not electing the native candidate in C. J. Ingersoll's district, both of which had been stipulated for. Again, many of them are at heart Democrats, led away by Religious fanaticism. Our success with Shunk moreover brings others back, who are unwilling to stay on the losing side. These & other causes counted, we look to a reduction of some 3000 on the majority in Philadelphia. I have no doubt myself, indeed I have letters from twenty counties to show it, that Mr. Shunk lost a thousand or more of our party vote in consequence of the Slanders against him, the flag & corner stone stories, &c.[3] These come back to us in November. In several counties besides Philada., the influence of the Native bargain has lost us some hundreds more. Now, reckon as we may upon the more direct operation of the tariff dispute in some parts of the State, an operation apt to be greatly overrated. I hold it to be *absolutely impossible* to lose us the State. I do not hesitate to say so *to you.*

We have a letter this morning from Nashville, informing us of the last device of Gov. Jones & his associates to operate on Pennsylvania by certificates distorting your opinions about the Tariff. Our newspapers tomorrow[4] will prepare our people to receive the poison without harm.

From N. Jersey our letters explain our defeat by reference to the dissatisfaction of Gov. Vroom, General Wall, & others with Thompson's nomination.[5] They certainly gave it a very niggard support; but the East & West Jersey question no doubt helped Stratton[6] to our disadvantage and Capt. Stockton & his railroads did us more harm than good, by the jealousies they excited among our friends, who have always had the instinct of opposition to the mammoth corporations of that State. On the whole, our chances in New Jersey for the electoral vote are, as near as may be, *even*.

I write in the midst of a din of voices at the Pennsa. office,[7] & have no time to revise. The most guarded calculation, just made in my hearing, brings down Shunk to some 4200. We have *certain*, 52 members of one Legislature, probably 53, in Senate 21, in Congress 12 certain, 3 doubtful, of whom 2 probable, besides 2 natives.

J. K. KANE

ALS. DLC–JKP. Addressed to Columbia.

1. See Polk to John K. Kane, October 4, 1844.

2. See Kane to Polk, October 1, 1844.

3. See Jesse Miller to Polk, October 12, 1844.

4. On October 14, 1844, the Philadelphia *Pennsylvanian* published an address on "a gross and outrageous fraud" alledged to have been committed by the opposition Whigs. The centerpiece of that address, issued by the Democratic Executive Committee of Philadelphia, was a letter from an unnamed correspondent in Nashville, Tenn., under date of October 3, 1844. The Nashville letter, probably written by J. George Harris, charged that James C. Jones, at the urging of some Pennsylvania Whigs, had drawn up false statements about Polk's tariff views; those statements had been signed by a number of well-known Tennessee Whigs.

5. Peter D. Vroom, Garret D. Wall, and John R. Thomson. Vroom, a lawyer, served as governor of New Jersey, 1829–31 and 1833–36, and won election as a Democrat to one term in the U.S. House, 1839–41. Appointed minister to Prussia, he held that post from 1853 to 1857. The nomination of Thomson, a Tyler Democrat, rendered New Jersey Democrats vulnerable to charges that they were the party of monopoly and privilege; Thomson was the brother-in-law of Robert F. Stockton, president and major stockholder of the Camden and Amboy Railroad Company. New Jersey Whigs thus claimed that through Thomson the railroad interests were attempting to extend their control over the state's executive and judicial branches and thereby further protect the railroad's east-west monopoly, which linked Philadelphia and New York City. The Camden and Amboy Railroad Company and the Delaware and Raritan Canal Company had merged their stock in 1831, thus giving the "Joint Companies" one of the most complete transportation monopolies ever granted by state charter.

6. Charles C. Stratton served as a Whig in the U.S. House, 1837–39 and 1841–43, and as governor of New Jersey, 1845–48. Kane's reference to the "East & West Jersey question" is not identified further.

7. Philadelphia *Pennsylvanian*.

TO CAVE JOHNSON

[Dear Sir,] [Columbia, Tenn.] October 14, 1844

The returns from the elections as far as they have reached me are most favourable. Whilst we are doing so well in other states, we must look closely to our operations at home. Our opponents in this State are at this moment making a noiseless but desperate struggle. All their small as well as large debaters are out. In this and the Counties between this, they are holding small meetings in remote places daily. Many of their appointments are never published in the newspapers, and some of them pass off before it is known out of the neighborhood that there is to be a meeting. You know this is a very closely contested State. I think she is now safe, but we must not relax our exertions or be too confident. When our debating friends meet at Clarksville I hope they will hold a consultation, and act in concert, so as to cover every part of the ground that is possible. I wrote to you[1] that *Nicholson* had authorized *Fitzgerald* to make appointments for him commencing at Paris on the 21st. I was surprised to receive a letter from *Fitzgerald*[2] on Saturday informing me that *Nicholson* had written to him subsequently and requested to be excused from attending any but the one at *Paris* on the 21st. When you see him at Clarksville, inquire how this is. Where will he be after the 21st? Has he any other appointments made? I see your appointments with Heiskell[3] as published in the Jackson paper commence in Henry on the 21st. I hope you will not fail to attend them. As I said to you in my last, the contest in the State is in my calm judgment to be decided by the vote—of the Western District and of East Tennessee. But little is now to be done in the Middle Division. Our opponents know this, and hence *Jernigan*[4] has gone to the District, and their main forces have gone either to the East or West. I do not know where *Jernigan*'s appointments in the District are. They are not published and probably will not be, because he will desire to go alone. If *Nicholson* has no appointments beyond *Paris,* urge him to ascertain where *Jernigan* is, and go with him.

Do not fail to guard the Northern border of your District against imported and fraudulent votes from Kentucky. This you can do during your great meeting at Clarksville. Let me hear from you.

[JAMES K. POLK]

P.S. *Boling Gordon* and *W. V. Voorhees* are now making a tour through *Wayne, Hardin,* and *Perry* and will probably extend it to *Benton* and *Humphreys*. I hope whilst you are gone to the District, that *Garland, Voorhees* of Dickson[5] and every other debating man we have will throw out appointments and hold small meetings in remote places, in your District, every day until the election. This is important, for I tell you all our energies are necessary to keep the State safe, as I believe she now is. The least relaxation at the close of the canvass might loose her.

PL. Published in *THM,* I, p. 252. Addressed to Clarksville, Tenn., and marked *"Private."*

1. See Polk to Cave Johnson, October 9, 1844.
2. Polk's reference is to William Fitzgerald's letter of October 10, 1844.
3. William T. Haskell, a leading Madison County Whig, fought in the Seminole War under Robert Armstrong's command and served one term in the Tennessee House, 1841–43. A presidential elector for Henry Clay in 1844, he later sat for one term in the U.S. House, 1847–49, and ran unsuccessfully for governor in 1859.
4. Spencer Jarnagin.
5. Hudson S. Garland and Jacob Voorhies. A native of Virginia, Garland studied law at the University of Virginia prior to establishing a law practice in Clarksville, Tenn., where he took an active part in local politics; he was a son of James Garland. A Dickson County merchant and farmer, Voorhies represented Dickson, Benton, Humphreys, and Stewart counties as a Democrat in the Tennessee Senate from 1843 until 1847.

TO CAVE JOHNSON

[Dear Sir,] [Columbia, Tenn.] October 14, 1844

Yours of the 10th came to hand today. It will I fear be disastrous to our prospects in that part of the State if you fail to attend your appointments in the Western District. It will certainly be so, unless you can prevail upon Mr. *Nicholson* to take your place. He has no engagements to prevent him from doing it. It will never do to rely on *Ewell* to meet *Heiskell.*[1] The notices having gone out in your name, large crowds will no doubt be out, and they will be greatly disappointed unless you or *Nicholson* attend them. If you find you cannot possibly go, request Mr. *Nicholson* from me to do so. Show him this letter and urge him without fail to attend your appointments.

The Whig party in Tennessee seem to regard this State is the turning point in the Presidential election. I scarcely think it is so, but still it may be. I am satisfied that the State is now ours, but it will require great energy and constant effort up to the day of the election to keep her so. I think your appointments are arranged through a country where more good can be done than in any other part of the State, provided that an able and [____][2] speaker can attend them. Say to *Nicholson* that I think he can do vastly more good by attending your appointments with Heiskell (if you cannot) than in any other part of the State, and that it is my urgent request that he will do so. One of you *must* attend them. Nothing must prevent it. We all know that Tennessee is a closely contested State. She is as we all think now safe, but the smallest accident might lose her.

You will have received all the returns of the elections—that I have, unless it may be from Georgia. I have two letters today by the Southern mail giving cheering accounts from that State. *Hon. David Hubbard*[3] (Formerly of Congress) writes me on the 11th from the Eastern part of Alabama, where he was travelling in the stage—as follows—to wit,

"We have beat them in Georgia, carrying 5 certain and 6 probable of the Congressmen, and an estimated popular majority from 5,000 to 8,000, so says an intelligent traveller in the stage who joined me today in Eastern Ala. near the Georgia line." In a postscript he adds "I have no doubt of the truth of what has been reported, three other travellers all agree." This is confirmed by a letter from the Post Master at *Tuscumbia,* Alabama,[4] of the 13th Inst., who says he got it directly from an intelligent traveller, who left Washington Wilkes Cty, Georgia, on the morning after the election and had come directly on. If you use this information at your mass-meeting on the 17th[5] of course you will not say that you derived the information from me.

The last word I have to say is, to beg that you or *Nicholson*—will one of you fill your appointments with *Heiskell.* Say so to *Nicholson.*

[JAMES K. POLK]

PL. Published in *THM,* I, pp. 251–52. Addressed to Clarksville, Tenn., and marked *"Private."*

1. Thomas Ewell and William T. Haskell. A Jackson lawyer, Ewell ran unsuccessfully for a seat in the Tennessee House in 1843; in 1844 he was the presidential elector on the Polk ticket for the Eleventh Congressional District.

2. Bracketed blank previously supplied to indicate illegible word or words.

3. A lawyer, merchant, and dealer in Chickasaw lands in Alabama, David Hubbard served several terms in the state legislature and won election to two terms in the U.S. House, 1839–41 and 1849–51; he was a cousin to Sam Houston.

4. In 1844 the postmaster of Tuscumbia, Ala., was Jonas J. Bell, who had been employed some thirty years before as clerk to Joel Childress, the father of Sarah Childress Polk.

5. Polk's reference is to the Clarksville meeting of October 17, 1844.

FROM JOHN K. KANE

My dear Sir Phila. 14 Oct. 1844

I wrote to you yesterday a hasty and, I fear confused letter from the printing office of our paper.[1]

The returns as they now stand show a majority for Mr. Shunk of over 4000, and this will be increased perhaps 300 from the counties not yet in. No one here has a doubt but that we shall give a larger majority for our electoral ticket. The only trick by which it can be prevented must be an extension, or rather a renewal of the coalition, for it is now nearly broken up by mutual reproaches. We are industriously at work to prevent this reunion, and have reason to hope that before many days a public demonstration on the part of the Democratic natives will be made of a conclusive character. We are striving in this as much for the sake of our New York friends as ourselves. In the City of N.Y., nativism has been entirely reanimated by the election here, and the Whigs are tempting it to a similar compact with that which disgraced Philadelphia. In fact, I apprehend that after the present canvas we shall hear no more of Whiggery. It will merge in nativism, taking in abolitionism as the other member of the firm. I learn today that the Whigs at Harrisburg formally resolved to bear hereafter the new name; Mr. Thaddeus Stevens having acted as godfather.[2] This is only the advanced-guard movement.

But change and coalesce as they may, though the increase of our majority may be prevented by it, our electoral ticket must receive at least as sound a victory, as we have had at the past election.

I send you the Pennsylvanian of this morning, that you may see how we have anticipated the Tennessee project.[3] The "Union" which you sent me did not arrive, and I was obliged therefore to advert to the call on you in merely general terms.[4]

The news from Georgia shows that we have nothing to fear in that quarter. If we can hold Delaware, we have now a majority; no matter what comes of N. York, N. Jersey, Maryland, North Carolina, or even your own state; though I should be sorry to give up either of them, and am not without hopes from Connecticut.

Mr. Dallas, who comes in while I am writing, asks me to say to you that a vexatiously protracted trial in which he is engaged has made him for a few days delinquent in writing to you.

J. K. KANE

[P.S.] 15 Oct. My letter was too late for the mail of yesterday. The "Union" came to me this morning.

The natives to the extent of 150 were to have met in convention last night in one of the adjoining Districts, for the purpose of making arrangements to come out for the Democratic Electoral ticket: I have not heard the result.

The Pennsylvanian of this morning has the address to the Iron interests. J.K.K.

ALS. DLC–JKP. Addressed to Columbia.

1. Philadelphia *Pennsylvanian.*

2. A native of Vermont and graduate of Dartmouth College, Thaddeus Stevens moved to Pennsylvania in 1816 and began the practice of law in Gettysburg; he won election to the Pennsylvania House on the Anti-Masonic ticket in 1833 and served in the legislature for eight years before moving to Lancaster in 1842; he won election to the U.S. House twice as a Whig, 1849–53, and five times as a Republican, 1859–68. Throughout his public career Stevens uncompromisingly supported tariff protection, public education, and immediate abolition; following the Civil War he pushed through Congress his program of radical reconstruction.

3. Enclosure not found. Reference is to certificates signed by Nashville Whigs, who asserted that in Tennessee Polk had campaigned as a staunch opponent of tariff protection of all kinds, direct and incidental. See Kane to Polk, October 13, 1844.

4. Reference is to the Giles County Whig Interrogatories. See Polk to Kane, October 4, 1844.

FROM J. G. M. RAMSEY

Mecklenburg, Tenn. October 14, 1844

Ramsey acknowledges receipt of Polk's letter of October 7th.[1] After discussing speakers' appointments and upcoming meetings and barbecues, he assures Polk that prospects look favorable in East Tennessee and adds that the Democrats hope to attract good crowds to the meetings. The season, however, is advanced; and voters are "busy with their corn." Ramsey reports that he has received from Kane some German newspapers and the confidential circular of the Democratic Committee of Philadelphia and that he has begun to circulate the papers among "our Dutch citizens"; those papers have caused the Lutherans to see "new light." He hopes that the papers will have a similar effect in Washington and Green counties; Ramsey also plans to send some papers to "the Dutch Settlement in Sevier."

ALS. DLC–JKP. Addressed to Columbia.

1. Letter not found.

FROM FRANCIS R. SHUNK

Dr. Sir. Pittsburg Octo. 14 1844

A hard fought political battle has just been fought in our state and the Victory is ours. The democratic majority in the state is upwards of four thousand. It would have been much larger but for a Compromise between the Native Americans and Whigs in Philadelphia. The particulars of which you will learn from our newspapers. I sincerely hope and have good reason to believe that this influence will not be brought to bear against you and that you will rally the entire democratic vote of Penna. Our friends have had a hard contest in this state. The tariff question has been forced upon them. Their opponents on the stump will discuss nothing but the tariff & distribution.

I leave this evening for the Eastern section of the state of which I am native and will probably be absent until the election; my visit will be a political one. I shall unite my efforts with those of our friends to secure the desired result. It is thought by many that Clay will not receive Markle's vote and that your majority will be greater than mine. We will have a majority in both branches of our Legislature, and Consequently a democratic U.S. Senator.

FRS. R. SHUNK

ALS. DLC–JKP. Addressed to Columbia.

FROM SAMUEL P. WALKER[1]

Memphis, Tenn. October 14, 1844

Reporting on the state of the campaign in the Western District, Walker states that the two parties are in a "perfect fever." Last Saturday, when the Democrats and Whigs both held meetings, the Democrats' procession, which included the Irish and Germans, outnumbered that of the Whigs two to one. Although the Democrats have made important gains, he notes that Memphis has "the most fluctuating population" in Tennessee. Since last winter hundreds of newcomers have arrived, and the outcome of the election in this county[2] depends in part on the votes of those who have settled here since the last election. Walker believes that the party can reduce the Whig majority in town and county to one hundred; he adds that favorable results in the Ohio and Pennsylvania elections will improve the prospects of the Democrats.

ALS. DLC–JKP. Addressed to Columbia. Polk's AE on the cover states that he answered this letter on October 22, 1844; Polk's reply has not been found.

1. A Memphis lawyer, Samuel P. Walker was the eldest son of James and Jane Maria Polk Walker; Polk was his uncle.

2. Shelby County.

FROM ROBERT ARMSTRONG

Nashville, Tenn. October 15, 1844

Armstrong relates that by tomorrow night he will have distributed all copies of the squatters document[1] and that he has sent copies to Chester and to the river counties. He notes that appointments have been made for Nicholson and Johnson and that a list of the same has been sent to Clarksville. Armstrong assures Polk that all possible efforts are being made to win Tennessee and adds that the "deep mortification" of losing it would be "too much." The Whigs claim to have won back all those in Giles County who had deserted their party.

ALS. DLC–JKP. Addressed to Columbia and marked *"Private."*

1. Reference is to the article "Henry Clay Against the Frontier Settlers," as printed in the *Nashville Union Extra* of October 14, 1844.

TO CLEMENT C. CLAY

My Dear Sir: Columbia Ten. Oct. 15th 1844

Your letter of the 12th was received to day.[1] *Brown* has gone to East Tennessee alone. I have written to *Dr. Ramsey* that you will not be there, and that, some one of their local debaters must join *Brown* and accompany him.

Relying upon you to be at Lawrenceburg *certainly* & *without fail,* at the great mass-meeting at that place on the 25th, our friends, will have several mass-meetings for you for the following week, commencing on Monday the 28th. Can you bring *Genl. Geo. S. Houston* over with you? All our debaters have gone either to the Western District, or to East Tennessee, and our friends will rely solely upon you to be at Lawrenceburg, and at the other Barbacues which they will make for you. It will be almost too hard on you to speak on successive days, alone, and I hope you will bring *Genl. Houston* or Mr. *Clements*[2] over with you. We feel confident that Tennessee is now *safe,* but it will require all our energy and a constant effort to keep her so. Our opponents are making a desperate struggle to carry the State.

The contest in Ohio has been a very close one. The abolitionists, almost in a body, voted the Whig ticket. 12 Counties remain to be heard from. The majority either way will not reach 1000 & will probably fall under 500 votes. We will know the precise vote tomorrow. The chances are in favour of the Whigs.

Georgia from what we hear I have no doubt has done well.

Write me on receipt of this, whether you can spend a week in the State, commencing at Lawrenceburg on the 25th. If you can we will have large meetings for you. I hope you can do so & that *Houston* or *Clements* can be with you. In anticipation that you can do so, some of the appointments will be made, before your answer can be received, & others afterwards, if you write you can spend so long a time here.

JAMES K. POLK

P.S. As you say, my letters to you which may arrive in your absence from home will be regarded as *confidential* by your son.[3] I address this directly to you. J.K.P.

ALS. NcD. Addressed to Huntsville, Ala., and marked *"Confidential."*

1. Letter not found.

2. Jesse B. Clements, a Lincoln County planter, was elected Brigadier general in the Tennessee militia in 1836. He was probably a son of Benjamin Clements, who in 1838 served as one of the state-appointed directors of the Fayetteville and Shelbyville Turnpike Company.

3. A lawyer from Huntsville, Ala., Clement Claiborne Clay, Jr., served as a member of the Alabama House, 1842–44 and 1845, and as judge of the Madison County Court, 1846–48. He won election to the U.S. Senate and served from 1853 until 1861.

TO J. GEORGE HARRIS

My Dear Sir: Columbia Oct 15th 1844

I see the pre-emption document is out in yesterday's Union,[1] & I have only time before the mail closes to say, that I hope the *Extras* will be distributed to the proper points *forthwith*. Send several hundred of them to me, & I will send them to the River Counties.

Unless they are dispatched immediately, it will be too late to do good.

We have carried *Georgia* (see my letter to Genl. Armstrong).[2]

JAMES K. POLK

ALS. ICHi. Addressed to Nashville and marked *"Private."*

1. On October 14, 1844, the *Nashville Union* carried an article, without attribution, under the caption, "Pre-emption Rights and Reduction of the Price of the Public Lands. James K. Polk's Course." The same issue of the *Union* also ran an article entitled, "Henry Clay Against the Frontier Settlers."

2. Letter not found.

TO A. O. P. NICHOLSON

My Dear Sir: Columbia Oct 15th 1844

I have reced. a letter from *Fitzgerald* of the 10th saying that you had written to him desiring to be relieved from attending the Western District appointments, under the belief that you could do more good elsewhere. He says he had yielded to your request, except for the meeting at *Paris* for the 21st where there would be a Barbacue which he thinks will collect a large crowd. On yesterday I received a letter from *Cave Johnson*[1] expressing doubts whether he could attend his appointments with *Heiskell*[2] commencing in *Henry* on the 21st. Now I write for the purpose of making an earnest request of you, to attend *Cave Johnson's* appointments with *Heiskell,* if he fails to do so. Either *Johnson* or yourself *must* attend them. If he cannot I hope you can. These appointments run through a most important part of country, and I am fully satisfied you can do more good by attending them, than you can possibly do in any other part of the State. Will you see *Johnson* before you leave Clarksville and have it settled definitely which of you attend them. One of you I insist earnestly *must* do so.

Hon. David Hubbard writes me from Eastern Ala. near the Georgia line, under date of the 11th, that we have carried *Georgia,* having elected 5. and probably 6. out of the 8, members of Congress, & having a large popular majority. You will of course have more news from the Northern elections than I can give you.

JAMES K. POLK

P.S. *Brown* has gone to East Tennessee. *Gov. Clay* could not go with him, but writes me that he had accepted the invitation to the mass-meeting at Lawrenceburg on the 25th and would certainly attend it,[3] so that you need give yourself no uneasiness about that meeting. It will be well attended without you. J.K.P.

ALS. NHi. Addressed to Clarksville, Tenn., in "care of Hon. C. Johnson" and marked *"Private."* Published in Joseph H. Parks, ed., "Letters from James K. Polk to Alfred O. P. Nicholson, 1835–49," *THQ* III (March, 1944), pp. 74–75.

1. Polk's reference is to Cave Johnson's letter of October 10, 1844.
2. William T. Haskell.
3. Reference probably is to Clement C. Clay's letter of October 12, 1844. See Polk to Clement C. Clay, October 15, 1844.

FROM JOB PIERSON[1]

My Dear Sir, Troy Oct. 15. 1844

Ever since our Baltimore Convention, I have been extremely desirous of writing to you and of taxing you with an answer. I have feared however that you were so overburthened with letters, you would regret that my name should be added to the list of your correspondents, and I have forborne until the time has arrived when, as I hope you will have leisure to peruse a few lines from an old friend.

I was at the Baltimore Convention. I went there not only instructed to vote for Mr. Van Buren but without such instruction should have voted for him as I preferred his nomination to that of any other person. He has been my old an intimate friend through life. I am sure he can never be otherwise. And I shall ever cherish his friendship with more than earthly fondness. There are those we can love, or affect to love to day, and cast off to morrow. Mr. Van Buren is not that man. He is a democrat without being a demagogue a statesman who has a single eye to the best interests of the people, the whole people and nothing but the people.[2] I say this of him because he merits it. I have neither had or sought any personal or political favor of him. I speak disinterestedly & I am sure that you entertain the same sentiments respecting him. You were with me four years in Congress at a most exciting period and during all that time our views of men and measures, and our votes, were alike in every particular, unless perhaps a slight variance on the subject of the Tariff. I will not stop to inquire who was the more correct on that subject. Both of us no doubt represented the views of our respective constituents. Suffice it to say that your opinion where it differed from mine corresponded with that of the two best friends I have on earth Viz Mr. Van Buren & Mr. Wright, neither of whom censured me for my views and I am sure you did not.

Mr. Van Buren as I have lately had occasion jacosely to remark on the Texas question committed as Talleyrand said, "more than a crime. It was a *Blunder.*"[3] Yet his letter was that of a Statesman.[4] I regretted it, but I respected him for the frankness of his avowal. His friends supposed he lost his nomination in consequence of writing that letter. Such however was never my opinion. During Mr. Van Burens administration he had as every President will have, numerous applicants for every office. Many must necessarily have been disappointed, and they did not desire, his reelection. They wanted a new deal & a new shuffle. The result I apprehend does not quite satisfy that particular class of politicians. They desired a more pliant man than the Hon James K Polk.

I have said that the N.Y. delegates were instructed to vote for Mr. Van Buren. They were not however instructed in relation to Vice President. It is right to say that Mr. Butler with my humble self & a majority of our delegates would have cast their votes for you as Vice President. It is also right to say that before the termination of our proceedings at Baltimore all the New York delegates were not only reconciled to your nomination, but were entirely satisfied with the result. There was no other name presented for the Office of Chief Magistrate that would have reconciled them. They believed (whether right or wrong I will not say) that the other nominees had intrigued to defeat Mr. Van Buren. No one believed you had any art or part in the transaction. And I was gratified on my return home to find that my constituents & the democrats throughout our State received the nomination with enthusiasm.

And now a word or two respecting your prospects. I cannot entertain a doubt of your receiving the electoral vote of this State. The nomination of Mr. Wright will insure it. We cannot get a bet that he will not be elected, and I see no reasons why our electoral ticket will not run even with that of the Governor. Every thing looks favorable. All democrats are certain of success.

The late Elections in other States seem to me more flattering for you than I anticipated. In Philadelphia City & County we were defeated by an unexpected combination.[5] In the City of N.Y. they are attempting the same game. It was successfully played there at the Charter election last Spring. It is said that lightning never strikes twice in the same place. It is rare if ever that such an unhallowed combination is twice successful. I am sure that the effort there making will help us greatly in all other parts of this State, and I repeat, that you must & shall have the vote of the Empire State. Have you any fears of Tennessee? I want you to have it because it is your State, but we can elect you without it.

When you have nothing else to do drop me a line for old acquaintance sake and believe me now as ever....

JOB PIERSON

ALS. DLC–JKP. Addressed to Columbia.

1. A native of Suffolk County, N.Y., and a graduate of Williams College, Pierson practiced law in Rensselaer County; served as district attorney from 1824 to 1833; won election to two terms in the U.S. House, 1831–35; lost his bid for reelection; and attended the four Democratic national conventions from 1844 through 1856.

2. Paraphrase of the witness oath "to tell the truth, the whole truth, and nothing but the truth."

3. Quotation from Antoine Boulay de la Meurthe, *On the Execution of the Duc d'Enghien* (1804).

4. Reference is to Martin Van Buren's public letter of April 20, 1844, on the annexation of Texas.

5. Reference is to a temporary combination of the Whigs and American Natives in Pennsylvania's 1844 state elections.

TO RICHARD H. STANTON[1]

My Dear Sir: Columbia Ten. Oct. 15th 1844

I thank you for your two letters of the 7th & 10th Inst, the latter giving returns from several Counties in Ohio. In your list of votes in Ohio, in your letter of the 10th you gave me the returns from seven Counties, which reached me through no other channel. The contest in Ohio is very close, and as far as I am enabled to judge from the returns received, the results in the State may be regarded as very doubtful.

The *Hon. David Hubbard* (formerly a member of Congress) writes to me from Eastern Alabama near the Georgia line, under date of the 11th Inst, that the Democracy have carried that State, having elected 5. and probably 6. out of the 8. members of Congress, and carried a decided majority of the popular vote. In your letter of the 7th you inquire what our prospects are in Tennessee. We have a most exciting and violent contest. Our whole Democracy are perfectly united, and roused to the most energetic action, and have the greatest confidence that they will carry the State. Judging from all the information which I have, I think there is no reason to doubt that the State will be Democratic in November.

Thanking you for your letters....

JAMES K. POLK

P.S. I mark this letter *Private*, as it is intended for yourself alone. J.K.P.

ALS. PHi. Addressed to Maysville, Ky., and marked *"Private."*

1. Editor of the Maysville *Monitor* from 1835 to 1842, Stanton served as the postmaster of Maysville in the late 1840's and as a Democrat in the House of Representatives, 1849–55; he was a brother of Frederick P. Stanton, a Memphis lawyer and Democrat.

FROM GEORGE M. DALLAS

No. 14

My Dear Sir, [Philadelphia] 16 Oct. [18]44

Nothing can well be more flagitious and base than the system of electioneering which is now being pursued by the Whigs in this particular district, and in New-York. They are literally bargaining right and left, courting the Roman Catholics and promising every thing to the Natives, and even avowing that Abolition is a fundamental article of the Whig creed. Our friends have a hard task to ferret them out in all their windings and doublings; but they persevere stoutly and with success. You will hardly credit what I have most solemnly been assured of, that there are, at this moment in this city, two letters from Mr. Clay, to be used in opposite channels, one all bland and courteous [to] Catholicism, the other all decided nativism. The former of these two letters is circulating in a pamphlet, and I have seen it; the latter I am promised a copy of, but it is kept *in petto*, to be suddenly handed round on the day preceding the election, in order to rally once more the coalition of the 8. instant! In New-York, I am told they have another letter from Ashland, in which a distinct pledge is given that if the Abolitionists will vote for Mr. Clay, and he should succeed, he will emancipate all his slaves the day after his inauguration! In times of extreme excitement like the present, poor human nature seems capable of any absurdity; otherwise, I should not conceive it possible that such wretched tricks and strategems could work beneficially—otherwise indeed than injuriously—for the party who resorts to them. If they are measures necessary to election, God grant that you and I may never be elected!

The movements here are unceasing, though comparatively noiseless, to effect, if possible, a return by the democratic natives from their recent whig association. I think these movements will succeed to a considerable extent—not, however, to the extent which some of our sanguine friends anticipate. Many say that you will leave the City and County of Philadelphia with a handsome majority—more say, that you will tie your competitor; I shall be perfectly content if we reduce the late 6000 majority by two thirds. If this be effected, my conviction is strong that we shall more than treble the majority of Shunk in the State, for all my correspondents assure me that every democratic county will augment its majority, and that in every whig county (except perhaps Lancaster) we shall cut them down. These results are to be anticipated as *natural*. The State patronage for the next three years is now secured to the democratic party. The Legislative body, towards which many local interests look anxiously, is decidedly democratic. The Congressional representation is of the same character. All who wish to attract attention, and to lay the foundation for future claims upon the party which is dominant in the State, must seize the opportunity to do so on or before the 1. of November. We are, therefore, stimulated to redoubled energy by what has been accomplished. On the other hand, at least two thirds of the zealous and efficient partizans of Whiggery have had all the glittering inducements with which they decorated their future suddenly and irreparably swept away; they limited their pretensions within the boundaries of *General Markles* way, and feel that all the avenues to Mr. Clay's possible patronage are choaked up by friends and associates of higher aspirations and claims. They have lost their cue to action; and will do very little more for their party than keep up appearances. Besides all these operating causes, another is working perceptibly. The elections in New-Jersey, Georgia, and Ohio—especially that in Georgia—have so dreadfully belied the Whig prophets, that the prospect of your election seems rapidly and irresistibly realizing itself, to the sober reflection of every man. Our adversaries are shaken, and wear dismally long faces—faces with which they alarm each other quite as much as we alarm them. They seem now sure of nothing! They look at a string of reduced majorities in their boasted strongholds—Maryland, N. Carolina, Delaware, N. Jersey, and Ohio—and they cannot tell what one of all these will certainly survive another conflict. Now, to be beyond the pale of both State and National Administration and parties is by no means, agreeable to the mere politicians of this region. The Whigs don't like the idea; the Natives cannot bear it; the former would be pleased to subside into moderate courses, to avoid, if possible, retributive proscription; the latter see no earthly reasons why they should, at this juncture, abandon their past professions of indifference, as a party, to the Presidential contest, and cannot consent unnecessarily to sacrifice themselves with a cause already defeated. These are not mere speculative views; within my own reach, and under my own eye, are many cases attesting their practical truth.

There is an active intercourse going on between the leading political men of this City and New York. The Natives in N. York have been suddenly made to swarm by the noise from here; and I conjecture that *our* managers having established a high reputation for skilful and unscrupulous contrivances, are engaged in teaching the *modus operandi:* in other words, they are adjusting the bargains by which a Coalition is to be effected. Should they succeed, our friends must look out not merely for a squall, but for a tempest. And if, as I believe, this union of all honest men is designed to embrace within its circle the rampant abolitionists, we shall require all the buoyancy and strength of Mr. Wright's best popularity to enable us to ride out the tornado.

Altho' I sincerely and firmly believe that you are on the eve of as honorable an election to the chief magistracy of our country as any man has enjoyed, and altho' I rely with the utmost confidence on the wise and virtuous policy you will pursue, yet I feel, my Dear Sir, a melancholy and disheartening foreboding of what awaits the union from the progress of combined Abolitionism and Nativism. Rest assured that before the 4. of March next, the Whig party will have merged, throughout the East and North, into another party constituted of itself, the abolitionists, and the natives, under the common designation of the *Liberty Party.* It is their inevitable tendency and termination. I foretold it in 1840, in a letter to the Virginia Convention when the abolitionists were scarcely an ominous force; their increase has out stripped my apprehensions, and there has arisen, in the fanatic hostility to papal power, another organized and excited band ready to form a junction with them, and to force the Whigs to their purpose. You will have this imposing confederacy of factions to encounter first on the Texas question, then on the Naturalization laws, and finally on a Convention to alter the Constitution in order to destroy the slave representation in Congress. There are calamities enough involved in this prospective view. But I see others to arise out of the uncompromising nature of the southern aversion to the very terms of tariff and protection. If southern politicians could be brought to unite all their strength with the northern democracy—to postpone the everlasting tariff question—until the Country was effectually secured against the alarming strides of abolition and her kindred bigotry—you might achieve an exploit worthy of immortal fame and universal gratitude; but if they distract your councils and enfeeble your measures by preferring to triumph over custom-houses, I cannot see whence you are to draw force enough to beat back the amalgamated and fierce onset that is threatened. I know and feel that, come what may, you will hold the helm undauntedly; and, while there is a fragment of the constitution left, you may be assured that I will stand by your side to defend and restore it.

G. M. DALLAS

ALS. DLC–JKP. Addressed to Columbia. Polk's AE on the cover states that he answered this letter on October 28, 1844; Polk's reply has not been found.

FROM WILLIAM C. BOUCK

Dr Sir. Albany Oct. 17. 1844

A few days since I returned from a visit to the Northern counties in this state. From my information from the different parts of the state, I feel persuaded we shall carry the state, but not by so large a majority as I contemplated four weeks ago.[1]

I do not know of any cause very prominent, why we should be loosing ground, and it may be mere conjecture.

WM. C. BOUCK

ALS. DLC–JKP. Addressed to Columbia.

1. See Bouck to Polk, September 7, 1844.

FROM J. GEORGE HARRIS

My Dear Sir, Nashville Oct 17. 1844

Supposing Gen. Armstrong kept you advised of all important information from this point & having nothing special to communicate, I have not written for several days.

What an alarming speciman of *corruption* was that open and downright bargain between the Whigs & *the Natives* of Philadelphia? It came upon us like an avalanche, but thanks to the yeomanry of the interior counties they served as an *efficient barrier.* We believe Shunk will be elected about 7000 majority, that the bargain with the Natives expires with the State election and will not hold good in November, and that our Presidential majority will be from 10 to 15 thousand. On this we rally, and meet the Whigs at every point.

I perceive that the Ohio Whig State Central Com. in their congratulatory bulletin *boast* of having secured "the naturalized citizens" of Ohio. Will not the Whig bargain with the Philadelphia Natives *open* their eyes? I think so. Then is Ohio safe. Medery writes, truly no doubt, that Walker's most *injudicious* "South in Danger"[1] was put into every abolitionists house on the day before election. I say "injudicious" as to *time & place.* His short sightedness in that particular instance is astonishing. Medary says "but for that we would have carried Ohio."

I think, on the whole, that this corrupt bargain between the Philad. Whigs and church–burners will redound to our advantage both in Pa. & Ohio. It stands to reason.

The editor of the Baltimore Argus[2] writes me that the tide continues to set in our favor in Maryland, and he says our friends are rallying with more earnestness than before.

Humphreys has just returned from the East with glad tidings. His opinion is we cannot be beaten more than a thousand votes East of the mountains. Gardner & others in W. Ten. write that "it will be a throat-latch race from the district across the Tennessee River." Foster was heard to say the other day in Murfreesboro that "Polk will maintain his majority of '39 in the Middle Division." If so, with constant energy all is well in Tennessee. If with a revolution going on in Ky Geo and other border States, the spirit does not cross our State line it will be strange indeed.

The Whig news from Arkansas is nonsense—not a word of it reliable.

I sent a thousand of the "Squatter Extras" into the West. Dist. by Dr. Lea whose letter was on the back of them.[3] He promised to ride through different counties & distribute them with his own hand. He is active, resolved, proud of the reception given to his letter, and will circulate them faithfully.

I shall endeavor to induce our State Committee to publish a rallying card, calling on the voters to be vigilant, active and firm; and to be well supplied with true tickets on the day of election.

I have written this at a moment of leisure. I will not close it until to–night's mail arrives.

Eve. The night's mail brings not a line of intelligence concerning the eastern elections. We stand therefore, on the calculations in the morning's Union.

Another letter to Gen A. from Mr. Hubbard of Ala. states that our maj. in Geo. will probably be about 3000—he also expresses his belief that [it] is not only *safe* now but will be safer in November.

We made *the best* of last night's news and sent it off to Clarksville, to cheer our friends there to–day. The Whigs made a terrible noise over Philad Co. & city, and sent an express to Clarksville to throw a *wet blanket* on the meeting. The Express stopt 10 miles from town on account of darkness & the storm, concluded to wait for the stage, fell asleep, overslept himself until the stage had passed and so their news did not get on.[4]

J. GEO HARRIS

ALS. DLC–JKP. Addressed to Columbia.

1. See William E. Cramer to Polk, October 4, 1844.

2. Not identified further.

3. Reference is to the article, "Henry Clay Against the Frontier Settlers," published in the *Nashville Union Extra* of October 14, 1844. William W. Lea, a Gibson County physician, served as a presidential elector for Hugh L. White in 1836; and in 1844 he bought the Whig *Trenton Journal* with partners John A. Taliaferro and Thomas B. Claiborne and conducted it as a Democratic newspaper under a new name, the Trenton *True American.* Lea confirmed his change in party allegiance in a public letter addressed "To the People of Tennessee," which was published in the *Nashville Union* of October 9, 1844, and in the *Nashville Union Extra* of October 14, 1844.

4. Harris concluded his letter in the right margin of his last page.

TO JOHN K. KANE

My Dear Sir: Columbia Tenn. Oct 17th 1844

We have returns from 31. Counties in Pennsylvania including the City and County of Philadelphia. The result in the City and County is astounding. Still I think Mr. *Shunk* will be elected by a small majority. I shall be anxious to learn your opinion, whether the alliance which was found between the *Natives* and *Whigs,* in your City and County, will be carried into the Presidential election, and if so, whether it will operate to the same extent. Will the Gubernatorial vote be a fair test of the strength of parties in November? I have some fears, that a similar *alliance* may be formed in the City of New York, in the election of members of Congress, and State officers, and that it may weaken the whole ticket. Have you any information from New York, on this point? I hope our friends there will take timely precautions to prevent it. We have received no information from the New Jersey election, but I am prepared to learn that she has gone against us. The immense Whig majority in your City & County, must have operated most unfavourably on the second day's voting in that state.

The vote in Ohio has been very close. The abolitionists in that State as in Pennsylvania seem to have voted almost in a body with the Whigs. Will they maintain their distinctive organization, and vote for their own candidate in the Presidential election, or will they unite with the Whigs? The opinion of my friends in Ohio is, that in that State they will generally adhere to their own candidate, and will not vote with the Whigs.

In that event we will carry Ohio without doubt, and indeed some of my friends think that our chances are best against the combined vote of Whigs and abolitionists, it being ascertained that many of the Society of Friends cannot be induced to vote the Whig ticket for President. Every day adds increased confidence that the Democracy will carry this state in November. My information justifies the opinion that Louisiana and Georgia, may be set down as certainly Democratic in November. With either Pennsylvania or New York I think our success is placed beyond reasonable doubt. A few weeks however will put an end to all speculation. I hope you will give me your opinion of the present prospects in Pennsylvania on the receipt of this letter.

JAMES K. POLK

ALS. PPAmP. Addressed to Philadelphia, Penn., and marked *"Confidential."*

FROM GANSEVOORT MELVILLE

Thursday
Utica October 17th 1844

My dear Sir,

Mine from Cleveland expressing an unfavorable opinion as to the probabilities of Tod's election was I presume received in due course of mail.[1] It is a source of regret that the returns corroborate that view. But then, how much more the Whigs had pending upon the result of that election than we. The slender majority by which they have carried Bartley deprives them of all moral power in New York, Pennsylvania & New England arising from their success in Ohio, and if Bartley had been beaten, they could not have brought up the rank & file of their force to have voted for Clay in the face of a certain adverse result and the general election would have gone as it were by default.

Of the contest in Pennsylvania I will not speak as you are doubtless particularly well informed of the causes which rendered Shunk's majority smaller than it should have been to be absolutely decisive. Our friends in this state are not at all cast down by the defeat of Thompson[2] in New Jersey. It was owing to a decided anti-Stockton, anti-accumulation of wealth, & anti-combined-monopoly feeling which for several weeks previous to the election gathered strength every day, and which it was impossible to resist. The news from Georgia has inspirited our voting masses to a great degree. Chancing to speak of it last eve'g in a speech here the response was most overwhelming, and of a character denoting a confidence in the result of the general election throughout the Union which is a powerful element in a contest like the present.

The excitement in this state is very great and rising day by day. Since my return I have been constantly moving from point to point, speaking every day, not infrequently twice a day, and sometimes as at Syracuse & Ithaca speaking 2 1/2 hours in the afternoon & the same time again in the eve'g at the same place. I mention this to evince the great desire of the people to hear the principles at issue discussed, a thing that is not usual with us on the very verge of the day of election as we now are. Everywhere in meetings & in private conversation I am constantly questioned as to our prospects in Tennessee, and even our friends seem surprised at the confident manner in which I claim it by a handsome & decisive majority. This is peculiarly obnoxious to the Whigs who abuse me heartily for it, because it interferes somewhat with their loud & brawling assertions that "Polk can not carry his own state." In every speech since my return I have pledged myself for a Democratic victory in Tennessee and my trust is unswerving that Tennessee will redeem the pledge. *Here,* there is not a cloud on our political horizon. *Every thing is right.* We feel a calm confidence that we will carry the state decisively. I am interrupted and must close. In two or three days I will write very fully as to matters and things with us. With my most respectful regards to Mrs. Polk and your mother[3] & remembrances to other friends....

GANSEVOORT MELVILLE

ALS. DLC–JKP. Addressed to Columbia and marked *"Private & Confidential."*

1. See Gansevoort Melville to Polk, October 3, 1844.
2. John R. Thomson.
3. Reference is to Sarah Childress Polk and Jane Knox Polk.

FROM WILLIAM TAYLOR[1]

Dear Sir Manlius N.Y. October 17, 1844

I hope you are not so badly off as Mr. Clay, who according to his own account is nearly killed by his extensive correspondence. He has at last determind he will write no more letters,[2] the wisest step he has taken since his nomination; for his friends have been grievously perplexed to keep track of him. I will however at once relieve you from any anxiety on my account by saying, that it is neither my wish nor expectation to trouble you with a reply, for I well know that your time and attention must be too much occupied to engage in any unnecessary correspondence.

I thank you for the token of remembrance in the pamphlets relative to Ezekiel Polk, which as they were mailed at your place, I suppose were by your direction. But I am happy to say they were not needed in this quarter, for I believe the Whigs have become as heartily ashamed of their assaults upon the character of the old patriot as they are of the paternity of the "Roorback" forgery. These things only serve to show the desperation to which they are driven, and that they can find in their ranks tools base enough for the vilest of purposes.

The excitement in this State is beyond anything I have ever before witnessed. The whigs opened the campaign early, as in 1840, and much in the same way, evidently anticipating similar results. But they have been met very differently by the democracy. Then we did not believe they could hold out; and it seemed impossible to arouse any thing like a suitable energy or enthusiasm on our part; but now they have been met with a spirit they hardly anticipated, and with a firmness and determined energy which they have not been able to resist. The enthusiasm of the democracy is unparalleled, and I feel confident that nothing but a lavish expenditure of money, pipe laying, bargain, and fraud, can save the whigs from defeat. But my reliance upon the integrity, firmness, and patriotism of the masses is too strong to permit me to doubt the result. My greatest fear in this state is from a bargain in the city of New York like that we have recently witnessed in Philadelphia. It is even said such a bargain is already consummated, or at least in negociation. This being understood so long beforehand I hope may be conteracted. Nativism has no foothold out of the city, and its alliance with whiggery being generally understood may in the aggregate operate as much in our favour as against us. The mission of C. M. Clay to bring over the abolitionist to the support of H. Clay will not succeed to any considerable extent. Smith[3] and Birney are in the field to keep their party together and preserve its seperate organization, and will, I think, succeed. It was believed by the leading whigs that to ensure any hope in this state the abolitionists must be brought over. The Texas question was the pivot on which they were to be turned. Hence Ex Gov. Seward and others took the stump professing great regard for their cause. C. M. Clay was sent for and H Clay was ready to exclaim "help Cassius or I sink."[4] But Cassius cant help him. At least such are present appearances.

I am gratified to learn that Tennessee is likely to wheel into the democratic column. Mr. Melville informs me he has no doubt she will be democratic. I hope so most sincerely, not only for the cause sake, but also for the gratification it will afford both yourself and the old patriot at the Hermitage.[5] I believe we can succeed without Tenn. but in this contest we want her to share by her vote in the glory of the triumph. It will be wormwood to Bell, but will richly pay him for the trick he played off with old Judge White, whom he so adroitly used to enable himself to step off the more gracefully into the ranks of whiggery.

Although my long letter will hardly pay the trouble of its perusal, yet it will assure you of the hearty zeal and efforts of your old friend in the cause, and in the fulfilment of a prediction made 3 years since, when at a public dinner in this village I gave your name as a future President of the U.S. an event I did not then anticipate as early as I now confidently expect. Please make my respectful regards to Mrs. Polk.

WILLIAM TAYLOR

ALS. DLC–JKP. Addressed to Columbia.

1. William Taylor, a physician in Onondaga County, N.Y., won three terms in the U.S. House, 1833–39, and sat in the New York Assembly in 1841 and 1842.

2. Taylor's reference probably is to Clay's letter of September 23, 1844, to the editors of the Washington *National Intelligencer;* for that letter, see the Washington *National Intelligencer,* October 1, 1844.

3. A wealthy New York philanthropist and reformer, Gerritt Smith was one of the founders of the Liberty party. In 1848 the "true Liberty party" men, those who refused to support the Free Soil party, nominated him for the presidency; but he declined the nomination. Smith served a partial term in the U.S. House, 1853–54.

4. Paraphrase of a quotation from William Shakespeare, *Julius Caesar,* Act 1, scene 2, line 92.

5. Andrew Jackson.

TO WILLIAM ALLEN

My Dear Sir Columbia Ten. Oct. 18th 1844

The democracy of Ohio fought nobly, in your late election. The contest has been very close, and it is manifest was finally decided, by a union of the body of abolitionists with the Whigs. Will this union be kept up at the Presidential election, or will any considerable portion of the abolitionists maintain their distinctive organization, and vote for their own candidate? I will thank you My Dear Sir: to give me your opinion of our prospects in Ohio, and Indiana, at the November election.

Every day increases the confidence of the Democracy in this State, that they will succeed in November. We have a most exciting and violent contest. Our whole democracy are roused to the most energetic action, and are perfectly united, and I think there is no reason to doubt but that the State will be Democratic in November. My information derived from intelligent correspondents satisfies me that Louisiana and Georgia are safe. We have received returns from only 31. Counties in Pennsylvania, including the County and City of Philadelphia. The large loss, which the Democracy sustained in the City & County, it is clear was produced by an alliance between the *Natives & Whigs.* It is not probable that this *alliance* to the same extent at least, can be made to operate in the Presidential election.

I have observed the immense labour which you have performed in canvassing your State during the summer. From your extensive intercourse with the people, you will be enabled to give me an opinion approximating correctness, of the probable result in the State in November, and I will thank you to do so. If we carry either Pennsylvania or New York (and I think our prospect is good to carry both) the result in the Union, would be in favour of the Democracy without Ohio. With Ohio, we would probably succeed by a large majority.

Hoping to hear from you soon.

JAMES K. POLK

ALS. DLC–WA. Addressed to Chillicothe, Ohio, and marked *"Confidential."*

FROM EDWIN A. KEEBLE

Murfreesboro, Tenn. October 19, 1844

Keeble reviews campaign efforts in Rutherford County and calculates that they are on "the verge of a tremendous political revolution." He cites the example of a prominent family in the Versailles district, "the Patriarch" of which has reversed his political affiliation and brought with him his eight sons and numerous relations—a total of some thirteen changes in Polk's favor.

ALS. DLC–JKP. Addressed to Columbia.

FROM ISAAC TOUCEY[1]

My dear Sir. Hartford Ct. Oct 20, 1844

Having just returned from a tour through this State, & addressed the people in large meetings in every part of it, I am able to speak with some confidence of the result, even here. I have never known so perfect unanimity & such ardent zeal, as now exist in the Democratic ranks. We have fought, & are fighting, the battle on the great question of a "Republic without a Bank, or a Bank without a Republic"[2]; & we carry the war into the enemies camp on the Texas & Tariff questions, & other kindred topics. The masses are moving, spontaneously, with a degree of feeling unexampled with us. I defy all the bank-men, the high-tariff men, the sticklers for partial interests & special privileges in the whole Union, to resist the spirit now roused in the people to assert the equal & just rights of all, & to re-establish a Democratic Administration at Washington. Permit me to congratulate you, as I do with heartfelt satisfaction, upon the enviable position assigned you at the head of this great & patriotic movement, which is destined to restore the Government to its "Republican task."

In this State we do not intend to be left behind. In the last election, when more than 60,000 votes were cast, we lacked but 12 or 1300. We had the Conservatives & the Govt at Washington against us. We needed but to change 700 votes to carry the State. It is my opinion, we have already accomplished *that,* & no effort will be spared to maintain it.

With most respectful regards to Mrs Polk I remain, dear Sir....

I. TOUCEY

ALS. DLC–JKP. Addressed to Columbia.

1. A lawyer from Hartford County, Conn., Toucey served as a prosecuting attorney, 1822–35 and 1842–44; as a member of the U.S. House, 1835–39; as governor of the state, 1846; as U.S. attorney general in Polk's cabinet, 1848–49; and as a U.S. senator for one term, 1851–57.

2. Paraphrase of a line in Polk's speech delivered in the U.S. House, January 2, 1834, printed in the *Register of Debates in Congress,* 23rd Congress, 1st Session, Appendix, Vol. X, pt. 2, p. 2289.

FROM ARCHIBALD YELL

Dear Polk Waxhaws Ark 20th Octr 1844

We in Ark. have "fought the good fight and have kept the faith."[1] Our little gallant state is determined to be the Banner state in the approaching Presidential election. Your old and steadfast friends, such as, Col. McKisick Genls. Whinery & Mitchell, Maclin, Dr. Borland the Editor of the Ark. Banner,[2] and hundreds of others have done their duty. The state election is just over, which sittles the contest in this state; and will ensure your Majority to be 5000 if we have a fare turnout. One fourth of the population was sick at our state election, and still we have exceeded our most sanguine expectations. My Majority will be about 4000 over a popular & talented competitor and Genl Druis[3] the true blue Democrat for Gov will not fall short of my[4] Majority more than 1000 or 1500 which will elect him by 2000 majority tho there was an Indpt. Disorganizer in the field, who had canvassed the state thorerly.[5] I had also an *Indpt,* Judge Tully,[6] a Democrat, to embaris my prospects but my majority will be but little short of 4000 over the *Whigs* & *Indpt.* There will be about 15 or 20 Whigs in bothe Houses out of 100 members.

I have been constantly engaged, not even the *Sabath* excepted since the 27th day of April last, and tho I was forced into the contest, I do not now regret it.[7] The state is saved and our party once more *united.* A few words now on your prospects. I may perhaps be too sanguine but I look upon your election as cirtain. I put down as almost cirtain, Maine N Hampshire N York N Jersey Pensyla Michgan Illinoise Mo Arkansas

Louisiana Missi Tennessee Alabama Georgia S Carolina & old Virginia (God help her), and a good chance for Ohio & Indiana.

You have no friend in this Union that will be more gratified at such a result than myself. I shall if alive be in the Ho of Repts. to give my feble aid to the support of your administration.

If you are elected I shall try and see the enaugeration, I have besides a few removal cases to lay before you. Mr. Clay has stuck full a set of the most vile and unscrupilous set of scamps in all or nearly all the Public offices in the state; they have not only warred openly upon our candidates for state offices but have used unsaparingly & unblushingly the slang about your *Ancesters.*[8] Your friends here have met that charge as became them, and have succeeded in makeing those who try to use it ashamed of their damnable slanders. You know me well enough to be sattisfied that I would not attempt to impose upon you, or deceive you. But there are cases here that will require and demand of you the *corrective.*

We have a U.S. Senator to elect in the place of our old friend Gov Fulton. Who it will be I am not now prepared to say. He will be cirtain sound in politics. Many of my friends desire me to be a candidate. I should not object, but for the position I now occupy. To leave the Ho. if cirtain of success would weakin our party in the State; believing so I can not consent to change my situation to gratify my ambition or pride. I shall therefore not be an applicant for the station. I feel under too many obligations to my friends the *people* to leave them so soon and men seldom loose by *modesty you know.* I shall content myself therefore with the fresh Laurils just won.

Our mutual friend Genl Maclin is poor. Can he not be provided for with some situation which he is capable of filling. Think of it and old *Jimmy* McKisick too is one of the best men living and could die for you. You must not forget Jimmy. The same may & ought to be said of Genl Whinery. But sir its rather too soon to trouble you about appts. for *several* reasons. More when I see you.

I leave in a few days for Little Rock where I shall remain a few months & where a letter will reach me up to the 1st Decr. if you can spare time to drop me a line.

Present me most kindly to the Madam & tell her I am still a *Young Widdower* and that without the influence of some friend I am likely to remain so.[9]

Give my respects to your Bro. W. Henry.[10]

A. YELL

ALS. DLC–JKP. Addressed to Columbia.

1. Paraphrase of the verse, "I have fought a good fight, I have finished my course, I have kept the faith." 2 Timothy 4:7.

2. James McKisick, Abraham Whinnery, Samuel Mitchell, Sackfield Maclin, and Solon Borland. A resident in Polk's congressional district and a colonel of the Tennessee militia during the late 1820's, Whinnery moved to Arkansas and served in the territorial legislature. A southern planter, Mitchell owned sixty-five slaves and vast landholdings in Arkansas County. Solon Borland, a physician, had published the *Western World and Memphis Banner of the Constitution* prior to becoming editor of the Little Rock *Arkansas Democratic Banner* in 1843. During the Mexican War he served as a major in Yell's Arkansas Volunteer Cavalry. In 1848 the Arkansas legislature sent Borland to the U.S. Senate; in 1853 he resigned to become U.S. minister to Nicaragua. During the Civil War he rose to the rank of brigadier general in the Confederate service.

3. Thomas S. Drew.

4. Here Yell cancelled the word "vote."

5. Reference is to Richard C. Byrd, who subsequently served in 1849 as acting governor of Arkansas in place of Thomas S. Drew, resigned.

6. Not identified further.

7. See James McKisick to Polk, September 15, 1844.

8. Reference is to the accusation that Ezekiel Polk was a Tory during the Revolutionary War.

9. Yell's correspondence to Polk, 1842–44, often contained humorous entreaties to Sarah Polk to procure for him a suitable marriage partner. See, for example, Yell to Polk, June 25, 1842; October 31, 1843; and January 10, 1844.

10. Reference probably is to Polk's only surviving brother, William Hawkins Polk. William practiced law in Columbia and served three terms in the Tennessee House, 1841–45 and 1857–59, and one term in the U.S. House, 1851–53. He went to Naples for two years as U.S. minister, 1845–47, and attained the rank of major during his service in the Mexican War.

FROM ALFRED BALCH

My Dear Sir, Nashville Octr 21 [18]44

I have very recent accts from Benton who is now speaking at many points in Missouri to large crowds. He believes firmly that you will be elected and I am sure that he will give to your administration an able cordial zealous support. As he evidently fell into great error under the influence of his love for Van Buren and his hatred to Tyler we must give him a fair chance to fall back slowly upon his former position. I have been greatly gratified that Benton has become so moderate and that he has taken in perfect good temper my earnest entreaties made to him from time to time. Rest assured that with him every thing will be straight. You will need strong and faithful friends in the Senate for there you will be weak for your first two years. We will loose Tappan and Maryland will elect a Whig, as well as Indiana. But, of all these things here after. You have the news from Pena & Georgia as well as from N. Jersey. The unprincipled plan devised and consummated by the native Americans is disgraceful. I have no doubt but that your majority will be greater in old Penn than Shunks and that the fact of Shunks election will add to our strength. All those who have lately voted with us will I should think stand any fire. They have certainly been sifted to the bran. Clays letter in which he declared that he was *utterly opposed to a repeal of the present tariff* was intended to secure Pen which is lost to him and it killed him stone dead in Geo in 48 hours with Websters speech on Boston Common.[1] We may now count with perfect confidence on Georgia. Now every thing depends on La. Indiana Tennessee and the Empire State as has always been the fact since you were nominated. I trust that we shall not have to fight against nativism in the great city.

News has reached me yesterday and to day from many points east of this, particularly from Wilson Smith and Jackson. It is decidedly favorable and what is better it is authentic. We have gained and are still gaining in those counties in which such large numbers have so long offered an idolatrous worship to the "Great embodiment."[2]

You must have patience and be tranquil as possible. Your friends are doing their work like brave fellows. We have a blaze of light from Pen & Georgia which will fill our path and shew us our way to a glorious victory. The skies are bright.

I almost forgot to mention that our information from Indiana is more and more favorable by every mail. Genl Walter Overton[3] of Red River La. writes, *set down this state for Polk & Dallas.* Our majority will certainly be 1500, or 2000, or 2500 votes.

Alfred Balch

ALS. DLC–JKP. Addressed to Columbia.

1. Henry Clay's letter of September 9, 1844, was printed in *Niles' National Register* on October 4, 1844. Reference is to Daniel Webster's speech delivered in Boston on September 19, 1844, and printed in *Niles' National Register* on September 28, 1844.

2. Henry Clay.

3. Walter H. Overton entered the army from Tennessee in 1808 with the rank of lieutenant. He was advanced in grade to major and during the War of 1812 was brevetted lieutenant colonel for gallantry during the Battle of New Orleans. From 1815 until his death in 1845 he lived on his plantation near Alexandria, La. He won election as a Democrat to one term in the U.S. House, 1829–31, but did not stand for reelection.

FROM DAVID CRAIGHEAD

Dr Sir Raleigh 21 October 1844

I do not now write to report my progress nor to give in my trials or my experience. I will only say that Bell Carruthers Heiskell Neil S. Brown[1] and all the makers of the pack have left you and all others and make me their copious text and conclusion. I write this to suggest to you as I do by this mail to the central committee the propriety of ending their speeches and deliberations and coming to action. The enthusiasm is all on our side. I advise that we avail ourselves of it to the utmost. It is a powerful agent & if you agree with me let a jubliee and general show and parade and assembling together commence and be promoted and encouraged from the earliest practicable moment until the evening of the election. I think this will be the most efficient to retain our own and to draw in the floating. I will as at present advised return home through Columbia and I hope to find you all in motion rejoicing and assembling and feasting as on the eve of our approaching and certain Conquest. The influence and the ingenuity of our ladies can now be of service if they are properly called into action. I am to speak here to morrow and next day at Memphis.

If I make any more speeches they shall be short and exceeding Cheering and annimating.

D. CRAIGHEAD

ALS. DLC–JKP. Addressed to Columbia.

1. John Bell, Robert L. Caruthers, William T. Haskell, and Neill S. Brown.

TO GEORGE M. DALLAS

My Dear Sir: Columbia Ten. Oct. 21st 1844

I have just received your two letters of the 10th and 11th.[1] The Democratic majority in Pennsylvania is I think a safe one, even if you should not be able to recover the heavy loss, which we sustained in the City and County of Philadelphia, in consequence of the alliance which was formed between the *Natives* & *Whigs* in your late elections. I hope however that you may be able to regain that loss, partially at least. Your reduced majority may and probably will encourage the Whigs to make great efforts to overcome it, on the 1st of November. Our friends will of course see the great importance of vigilance in guarding against pipe-laying.

What I now fear most is, that an alliance may be effected between the

Natives and *Whigs,* in the City of New York, similar to that which we have just witnessed in your City and County. I hope our Democratic friends in New York, being "forewarned will be forearmed,"[2] and take timely precautionary measures to prevent it. I have called Mr. Kane's attention to the subject, and hope he has written to our friends in New York.[3] I have ventured to write Mr. *Croswell* and Mr. *Wright,* but neither of them reside in the City, where the danger is.[4]

Genl. Armstrong of Nashville enclosed to me to day, the letter of Mr Henry Johnson, which I thought it important you should see, and therefore I transmit it to you.[5] When you have noted its contents, will you be pleased to enclose it back to me, that I may return it to Genl. Armstrong.[6] I think the writer may be mistaken in some of his impressions, but I thought it proper, perhaps important, that you should be placed in possession of the facts which he states, that you might thereby be enabled, to guard against the dangers, which he apprehends. I do not know *Mr. Johnson,* but he seems to be a man of some intelligence.

We may all be mistaken about Tennessee. The contest is a very bitter one and will no doubt be close. Every day however increases the confidnece of our democracy that they will carry the State. I think they will do so. *Georgia, Indiana & Louisiana,* I think may be put down as certain Democratic States. To enable our opponents to succeed in the Union, they must carry, in addition to their certain strength the *five* closely contested States of *Connecticut, New Jersey, Maryland, N. Carolina* and *Ohio,* and also both *New York* & *Tennessee.* If *Pennsylvania* remains firm & we can carry any one of these *seven* States, we must carry the election. In this view of probable results in the several States, we are fully impressed with the vast importance of carrying Tennessee. No effort within our power will be spared to effect it. My last letters from New York continue to give strong assurances, that, that great State is safe. I hope our friends are not mistaken. If New York shall be Democratic, the contest will beyond all doubt be settled in our favour. Our opponents see and know this, and all the power of money, and of fraud and corruption will be brought to bear on New York, and it will require all the energy, and vigilance of our friends to counteract the effect of such means. I have still some hope of *New Jersey,* but more of *Ohio.* It would not surprise me too, if that good old great State of *N. Carolina,* should vote for us. It will not do however to rely on any of these States. If *New York* and *Pennsylvania* vote with us all is safe. Should we loose either, then we must carry *Tennessee* to save the election. Every Democrat here is roused, to the importance of carrying the State, and will work every hour until the election is won. A few days more will put an end to all speculation as to the result in the State, and in the Union.

Hoping that we may have safe deliverance from the most unprecedented contest.

JAMES K. POLK

P.S. I will [send] to you Mr. *Johnson's* letter to *Genl. Armstrong,* under cover of a separate envelope. J.K.P.

ALS. Private Collection of Deanna McQueen. Probably addressed to Philadelphia; marked *"Confidential."*

1. In his letter to Polk of October 11, 1844, Dallas described gains made in all other counties in Pennsylvania outside the city and county of Philadelphia and informed Polk that Charles J. Ingersoll had been reelected by a majority of 175 votes. ALS. DLC–JKP.

2. Paraphrase of a quotation from Miguel de Cervantes, *Don Quixote de la Mancha,* Part II, Book III, Chapter 10.

3. See Polk to John K. Kane, October 17, 1844.

4. Polk's letters to Edwin Croswell and Silas Wright, Jr., have not been found.

5. Polk's reference probably is to a letter from Henry Johnson to Robert Armstrong of October 16, 1844, in which he accuses David Porter of having secretly supported Joseph Markle, the Whig candidate for governor of Pennsylvania. ALS. DLC–JKP. Armstrong probably forwarded Johnson's letter under a separate cover; Armstrong wrote Polk on October 21st but did not mail his letter until the following day. Henry Johnson, brother of Richard M. Johnson and a resident of Lexington, Ky., was a delegate to the Democratic National Convention of 1844.

6. Dallas returned the Johnson letter on November 1st.

FROM DAVID T. DISNEY

Dr Sir Cincinnati 21 Oct 1844

I merely write to advise you that the first shock of our defeat in this State being over our friends are rallying with unexampled vigour for the final struggle on the 1st prox. Exasperation has succeeded to mortification and we shall contest every inch of ground in Ohio.

The whig leaders are alarmed—secret circulars are flying in every direction and as Clay said of the friends of Adams[1] they are calling upon the *abolitionists* "with tears in their eyes"[2] to vote for Mr. Clay "this once." We are doing all that men can do, all that inflexible determination and untiring industry can accomplish. If the abolitionists stand firm or even vote as they voted at our recent election, we shall carry the state, but *every thing now depends upon them.* The fact has been developed that they hold the balance of power and their own councils are diversely agitated. What their final course will be none can tell. Both parties are quivering in the scale, with about equal hopes and prospects. Ohio is more doubtful than ever. I start in the morning for Columbus our seat of government. I shall keep you advised of matters.

D. T. DISNEY

ALS. DLC–JKP. Addressed to Columbia.

1. John Quincy Adams.

2. Quotation taken from a letter written by Henry Clay to Francis P. Blair on January 8, 1825; on October 26, 1844, the *Nashville Union* reprinted the text of Clay's letter as it appeared in Whig newspapers current in 1844.

FROM WILLIAM E. CRAMER

Gov. Polk Albany Oct. 22nd [18]44

The excitement in this State widens and deepens. The Whigs are now making their final onset. They have worked themselves up to the belief that they can carry New York. Their present confidence arises from the coalition they are now *trying to make* with Nativism in New York. Abolitionism in the Western part of this State, with the Anti-Renters (about 4000 voters) in this Senate district,[1] and the immense supplies of money they have already, or rather recently raised from the Merchants of New-York and the Manufacturers of Boston. The report is that the Bostonians promised $100.000 provided they could receive ample assurances that it would secure New York for Mr. Clay!

The history of every day shows that we shall have the most terrible fight in this State that ever before occurred in all our past history: 1840 was remarkable but 1844 will be far more so. New York is emphatically the Battle ground of the Union. Every means that can be obtained and every engineering that can be devised by desperation will be let loose upon us.

We are preparing to meet that shock with all our power. We are now stronger than we were a week ago. Our friends at first were a little scared at their responsibility, but they are now coming square up and are willing to meet the issue in New York *for the Union*.

It begins to be the impression that the efforts for a coalition of the Whigs and Natives on the *Presidential* ticket cannot go through. I should not be at all surprised if on the local ticket, the coalition was carried out.

It is also more than probable that in spite of every seduction, half of the Abolitionists will not go for Clay. The exertions now making to secure this strength to Mr C. are tremendous.

Our most sagacious friends still have full confidence that against all combinations, we shall carry this State both on Governor, and President, but our majority must be small. It has been rated altogether too high in the South West, and thus, I fear our friends may be disappointed.

Mr. Melville has returned in fine spirits. His valuable and efficient labors in Tennessee, Kentucky, Ohio and the Western part of this State have already given him a very marked position among our Public men. His sagacity and forecast seem no less creditable than his oratorical powers. His estimate of the result in Ohio prepared us for the defeat of Tod. On Saturday evening Mr. Melville gave us a short talk at Waterford my Fathers residence.[2] He, very appropriately alluded to his visit at Columbia. See Argus of the 21st instant.

He spoke in Troy, the preceding evening where the Irish are very strong. His popularity with this large and true-hearted class of democrats is inferior to that of no one in the State. His course on the Repeal question is known to every Irishman in the Northern States.[3] I might almost add in the Union.

It is not improbable that Mr. M will speak at Philadelphia and Baltimore before the canvass is over and also in this city. He was here yesterday. He feels sanguine of the general result. He says Ohio trembles in the balance. He left this morning for New York as he is very anxious to understand the full aspects of this new Coalition with Nativism.

My Father feels a confidence in the general result and of course of our triumph in this State.

WM E. CRAMER

ALS. DLC–JKP. Addressed to Columbia.

1. Attempts to force back rent payments on tenant farmers working lands under the Dutch and English system of perpetual leases precipitated agrarian unrest in the Albany region of New York State; the farmers' resistance, sometimes violent, led to the adoption of a more liberal constitution in 1846. The Antirent War of 1839–46 also brought about legislative action designed to restrict the length of farm leases and to abolish distress for rent action on new leases.

2. A lawyer and Democratic politician from Waterford, N.Y., John Cramer sat in both houses of the state legislature and served two terms in the U.S. House, 1833–37.

3. Reference probably is to repeal of the Act of Union of January 1, 1801, which provided for a single parliament and union of the churches of Ireland and Great Britain into one Protestant Episcopal Church.

FROM J. G. M. RAMSEY

My Dear Sir — Mecklenburg Oct. 22. 1844

Yours of Oct. 15th[1] I have just received & read. Before this you will have seen from my two last[2] (one of which covered the appointments of McClung as published in the Argus) letters that your requests have all been promptly complied with. I wrote twice to McC.,[3] sent him the first Argus (from my own office here) that contained his list of appointments. Wrote specially to Blackwell to meet & attend him & to be sure to have his list put in the Athens Courier, such other publicly given to them as our friends down there could furnish. Got Mr. Reynolds to write to Rowles at the same time urging him to see whether Blackwell could meet McC. & if he could not that then he Rowles must. We all gave as early notice of the appointments for Clay & Brown as they came to hand. At Kingston they had a barbacue & of course a good crowd—between 2 & 3,000. At Clinton it rained all day & I hear the crowd was very inconsiderable, just such as Barrow had a few weeks back when he suspended operations. At Blains X Roads the day was also stormy & I am without advices how the people turned out. The weather has been rainy all the time till this afternoon—hope he will have a good day to morrow at Dandridge—& I have just got off my horse from a long ride up French Broad trying to get the Whigs notified of the appointments at Sevierville & Trundles on the 24 & 25th. The Democrats there as you know are scarce but I find them elastic & determined. They all will attend but the Whigs have appointed meetings the same day in the same neighborhoods & I count upon but few of them attending, especially as every farmer is using what few fair days we have in getting in their corn. I shall meet Brown myself tomorrow. Clay had written to Eastman explaining why he could not come to E.T. I advised him to publish his letter. If McC. should not come, of which I have no intimation from himself, we will all urge Brown to fill his list. Supply his place at home if he remains with us, as it is essential that he fill the appointments of McClung if he fail on account of his brothers death[4] to canvass before the people. Reynolds wrote to him just last Friday by no means to disappoint us. I think he will not or he would so have informed us before now. We have taken all possible pains to guard the Ky & N.C. frontier, & illegal & fraudulent voting elsewhere as far as we can. I went to town yesterday, had the tickets[5] struck off *correctly* (see that is done in the West) & got the Marshall Woods[6] to tell us who were reliable men of the jury & witnesses & parties, so as to have the tickets thoroughly distributed in each District in each county we have to supply. That will be done to morrow or the day the court adjourns. Woods says they are providing tickets above, & Lowry writes me to day. Promises to circulate the German papers which had come to him from Pa. Says that Johnson had used up Barrow on the 15th & that they are constantly gaining ground & will give a Dem. majority of 1000 in the 1st District. If we fail any where to realise our expectations in E.T. it will be in the 2nd District. In Ocoee & Hiwassee we are certainly gaining every day or every ones judgment misleads us.

I may be deceived but still think you will get your vote of 1839 & will carry the State. I still receive Dutch papers & have circulated them extensively. Will write the moment this is finished to such friends in other counties as I suppose can use them advantageously. The Pa. news have dampened the ardor of the Whig voters but excited the leaders. We will make the most of it & also of the result in Georgia.

J. G. M. RAMSEY

ALS. DLC–JKP. Addressed to Columbia and marked *"Private."*

1. Polk's letter has not been found.
2. Ramsey's reference probably is to his letters of October 15 and 17, 1844.
3. James W. McClung.
4. Matthew McClung.
5. On October 17, 1844, Ramsey wrote Polk a letter about the state of the campaign in East Tennessee and mentioned that "the news-papers at Sommerville & in the Lincoln District have the names wrong on the electoral ticket." He urged that the problem "be at once corrected as many voters cut the names from a news-paper & use it for a ticket & what is worse give copies from it to others for the day of election." ALS. DLC–JKP.
6. Appointed U.S. marshal for East Tennessee in 1838, Richard M. Woods held that post at least until 1843; he had also served as sheriff of Greene County, 1826–40.

TO AARON VANDERPOEL[1]

My Dear Sir: Columbia Ten. Oct. 22nd 1844

The returns of the Pennsylvania election, shew that the "Keystone," is still Democratic by a safe majority, notwithstanding the heavy loss, which we sustained, in consequence of the alliance which was formed between the *Natives* & *Whigs* in the City and County of Philadelphia. I have apprehensions that a similar alliance, between the *Natives* and *Whigs* may be attempted in the City of New York, at the November election. Should it occur and be as successful as that in Philadelphia, our whole ticket would be weakened several thousand votes, and the State possibly endangered. I know you will excuse the liberty I take in suggesting that our Democratic friends in New York, should, adopt energetic and timely precautionary measures to prevent it. I cannot too strongly impress, upon you, the great importance, of giving immediate attention to this matter. In the present aspect of probable results, in the several States, the result of the contest in the Union, *may* depend on the vote of New York. Should she vote against us we may still carry the election. If she votes, for us, our success, is placed beyond all doubt. How vastly important then that we should carry her: I think you may put down

Georgia, Indiana & *Louisiana* as certain Democratic States. If I am right in this, then to enable the *Whigs* to succeed, they must in addition to their certain strength, carry all the clearly contested States of *Connecticut, New Jersey Maryland, N. Carolina,* & *Ohio,* and also both *New York* and *Tennessee.* Should they loose any one of these seven States I think they must still be defeated. Every day increases the confidence of our Democracy here that we will carry this State. The vast importance of doing so, is fully appreciated, and I think the State will be Democratic but by a small majority. If *New York* shall be democratic, we can loose all the doubtful & closely contested States, and still succeed in the election. I hope you will not fail to see *Mr. Butler* and other friends, and impress upon them, the great importance, of guarding against the danger which I have suggested in your City. The *Whigs* see their danger & know that, without New York they will certainly be defeated, and with a view to carry the State, will not only resort to pipe-laying, but will leave no means untried to effect an alliance between the *Natives* & *Whigs.* You may if you choose shew this letter to *Mr. Butler,* but *confidentially* of course.

Hoping that we may have a safe deliverance from this most unprecedented contest....

JAMES K. POLK

ALS. CoLHI. Addressed to the City of New York and marked *"Confidential."*

1. A lawyer, Aaron Vanderpoel served in the New York Assembly, 1826–30; in the U.S. House, 1833–37 and 1839–41; and on the Superior Court in New York City, 1842–50.

FROM ANDREW BEAUMONT[1]

My Dear Sir Wilkes Barre. Pa. Oct. 23d 1844

I have not tormented you with my correspondence because I presumed that you must be almost overwhelmed with other of vastly more interest and importance. You will have perceived that we have fought thro' the preliminary battle and although staggered by the astounding defection of the City and County of Philad yet the *northern* and *western* bulwarks have withstood the violent shock of Whiggery and corruption. We still have our armor girded on awaiting the final and all important struggle. It may be the last day of liberty to the people of this Republic. It may be the day of our redemption. God grant us success. We have just been apprised of the last diabolical plot of the enemies of liberty. We have been advised this morning by our mutual friend Jesse Miller that more than $100.000 has been raised by the great Bank and

Tariff aristocracy of Boston N York and Philada to crush the sturdy Democracy of Penna. Salvation alone depends upon the yet pure and unbought democracy of the country districts. The Cities are a dead mass of corruption and hirelingism. All that can be done to save the Country from this threatened scourge, by the true hearts and Strong hands, will be done. Contrary to my usual habits, (for I have always doubted my powers for public speaking) I have taken the stump on many occasions this Season, and endeavored, to the extent of my humble abilities, to vindicate your cause and that of the country before the patriotic population of this portion of Penna. The sacredness of the cause has given me courage and strength and I feel encouraged that my exertions have not been wholly useless. These are truly "the days that try mens souls."[2] Mr. Bidlack[3] is doing all he can and I trust Luzerne will acquit herself with her usual energy and gallentry. Our Democratic paper the Farmer, edited by my Son-in-law,[4] is conducting the campaign with much energy & skill. We have been recently informed that a sum of near $200.000 has or is to be raised by the Federalists of Boston N. York & Philada to be applied to crush the democracy of Penna. You see we have a most formidable and insidous enemy to grapple with but bitter issue as it may we will meet them with all firmness and determination that democrats are capable of and if we succeed then most cheering and rich will be our reward and if we are conquered by the power of fraud and corruption we shall have the abiding consolation of having done our duty.

A. BEAUMONT

P.S. As I had commenced this letter and my attention been called off by another matter I have twice alluded to the scheme of raising money to crush us. I have learned the fact more circumstantially. Boston was to raise $100.000 City of N. York $50.000 & Philad $35.000. Fearful indeed is the crisis of our Republic when the State of our affairs and the tone of public opinion should have room even to suspect such nefarious appliances. Every patriot has cause, great cause to shudder for the fate of his country and for liberty when he looks upon this hideous picture. If the people however shall safely pass thro' this ordeal and come out unscathed & victorious then indeed will they show themselves worthy of the character and dignity of freemen, then indeed will they have demonstrated that they are capable of self government. God grant it may be so. A.B.

ALS. DLC–JKP. Addressed to Columbia.

1. Andrew Beaumont served several terms in the Pennsylvania House, 1821, 1822, 1826, and 1849, and in the U.S. House, 1833–37. Polk nominated him to

be commissioner of public buildings for the District of Columbia in December 1846, but the Senate rejected the nomination in March of the following year.

2. Paraphrase of a quotation taken from the introduction to Thomas Paine's *The Crisis.*

3. Benjamin A. Bidlack, a successful farmer in Luzerne County, Penn., is not further identified.

4. Reference is to Samuel P. Collings, proprietor of the Wilkes-Barre *Republican Farmer and Democratic Journal.* In 1852, Franklin Pierce appointed Collings consul to Tangier.

FROM JOHN CARR[1]

Clark County, Ind. October 23, 1844

Writing soon after his return home from a short tour through Indiana, Carr assures Polk that he will receive the vote of the Hoosier state. The Central Committee in Indianapolis estimates Polk's majority at six thousand, but Carr believes that this estimate is probably too high. The Democrats are well organized and will battle the Whigs in their own way, "by show and parade, and all sorts of fandangoes." They raise hickory poles, carry polk stalks, build ships, fit out crews, and unfurl appropriate flags and mottoes. Today the ship "Charlestown," fifty feet long, spreads her sails and steers northward with her crew to attend a barbecue. Although Carr prefers other modes of electioneering, he sees no alternative.

ALS. DLC–JKP. Addressed to Columbia.

1. A veteran of the Battle of Tippecanoe, Carr rose to the rank of major general in the Indiana militia and served in the U.S. House, 1831–37 and 1839–41.

FROM JOHN McKEON

My Dear Sir, New York Oct. 23. 1844

I arrived last night in this City & found as I anticipated the most intense excitement prevailing amongst politicians. I have spent the day endeavouring to learn the probable result in this City & State. I have seen democrats of standing in the Interior of the State amongst the rest. Mr. Flagg our Comptroller who handed me this circular. I send it to you for the purpose of shewing how active & zealous the party is.[1] Mr. Flagg informs me 1250 of these circulars have been issued. He is you are aware a man of great judgment—very sagacious, & cool. His opinion is that the *State is safe for Polk & Dallas under all circumstances.* As to the abolitionists & Native Americans, they will certainly affect us but not sufficient to vary the result. Much depends on this City. I have had conversations with some of the leading Natives amongst the rest one of their candidates for Congress. They all assure me they will not make any arrangement on the Presidential ticket. Their party will divide on that subject. Our friends here give up the Congressional & legislative tickets if the Whigs & Natives unite as they probably will in those tickets but our friends also are confident on a majority of 1500 to 2000 for the Presidential electors. Our county friends say if we keep the Whigs from obtaining any majority we shall succeed in the State beyond question.

Pennsylvania is safe. Of Ohio I have some hopes. Maryland I now give up to Clay.

I am aware of the anxiety you naturally feel in relation to this state and for that reason I send you the opinions I have collected immediately on my arrival. I assure you the greatest zeal & enthusiasm prevail & nothing will be wanting to achieve a victory.

I will write again soon. I leave next Monday to attend a meeting up the North River. I had a committee to request my attendance & this Committee give me every assurance of the great spirit of our friends in the section they come from.

JOHN MCKEON

P.S. I broke the seal of this circular, as it was sealed when handed to me by Flagg.

ALS. DLC–JKP. Addressed to Columbia and marked *"Private."*

1. Enclosed was a circular, dated October 14, 1844, written from Albany, and attributed to Azariah C. Flagg and four others; the circular requested that the names of all voters and their political preferences in each recipient's town, county, or school district be returned to Albany for compilation and analysis. C. DLC–JKP.

FROM JOHN K. KANE

My dear Sir, Philada. 24 Oct. 1844

We have felt a good deal of anxiety for some ten days past in consequence of the more sanguine tone of the Whigs around us and the well ascertained fact that they had made up a Secret Service purse of at least $20,000. Happily we received intelligence yesterday, which shows the manner in which the fund is applied; and I am much mistaken now if we do not make it a most effective party engine against those of whose money it was made up. Mr. William B. Reed, Mr. John Sergeant's nephew,[1] the same who reported the bill rechartering the Bank U.S. in 1836–7, and who received some $12000 at least of the unexplained disbursements of Mr. Biddle,[2] made a blunder in the address of one of his friends. The result you will see in the Penna. of this morning.[3] Now, the letter itself is a small matter; but connected with the past history of Mr. Reed and his relationship to Mr. Sergeant, at whose instance and in whose office the $20000 was subscribed, it becomes one of the most interesting facts in the canvas. It enables us to make palpable the attachment of the native leaders and of their presses to the Whig cause, and thus to detach the masses from them. It gives us a fine topic, on which to rally the pride of the Country people, whom the arrangement was to buy. And more important than all, it throws our people into action again, excites them, and gives a new topic for public speaking, on which Democrats and Natives can meet. I have no doubt now that the majority against us in Philadelphia city and county will be reduced 2000 at least: this reduction would have been 1000 more, but for the folly of our party men in the Board of Commissioners of the Northern Liberties in refusing to elect a *Native* mayor, there being no choice by the people, but the native being highest on the return.

From the interior our accounts are somewhat diversified, but on the whole cheering: I look for a majority on the 1st about the double of that of the 8th. We are arranging expresses to bring in the returns from all the principal counties, and shall transmit them by express to New York.

I still expect that we shall carry New Jersey. There were causes at work against us, quite as potent as the railroad monopoly, which are now on our side: Mr. Wall and the Senior *Coterie* of our party are now fairly at work, which they were not before the late election. Besides this, I am assured that we are to have some hundreds of Natives for us who voted against Thompson.[4]

Our letters from New York too have resumed much of the confidence which they expressed before our Pennsylvania Election. For some days their spirit was *muffled*.

On the whole, things look well here. Our Governor[5] is doing us much good wherever he goes, less by his argument in favour of the Presidential ticket, though he is an excellent stumper on that subject, than by the quiet refutation which he makes every where of the slanders against himself, thus demonstrating the dishonesty of the Whig partisans. I have seldom heard a better speech than he gave us three days ago at Downingstown.

J. K. KANE

ALS. DLC–JKP. Addressed to Columbia and franked by John T. Smith.

1. The nephew of John Sergeant and a close associate of Nicholas Biddle, William B. Reed first supported the anti-Mason movement and then became a Whig. He served in the Pennsylvania House, 1834–35, and Senate, 1841–42. In 1838 Governor Joseph Ritner appointed him attorney-general of the state.

2. A native of Philadelphia, Nicholas Biddle served as the president of the Bank of the United States from 1822 until 1836. At the expiration of the Bank's

charter, Biddle secured a charter from Pennsylvania and continued as president of the Bank of the United States of Pennsylvania until his resignation in March 1839.

3. Kane's reference is to the letter of William B. Reed to W. Selfridge, October 19, 1844; a copy of Reed's letter appeared in the Philadelphia *Pennsylvanian.* In this letter Reed authorized Selfridge to draw one hundred dollars and entrusted him with "its judcious and effective expenditure" in Lehigh County during the final days of the campaign. For a copy of this letter, see the Washington *Globe,* October 25, 1844.

4. John R. Thomson.

5. Francis R. Shunk.

FROM JOHN T. HUDSON[1]

Buffalo Erie County New York
October 26h 1844

Sir

The undersigned was the Delegate from this, the 32d Congressional District in this State in the Democratic National Convention held at Baltimore in May last & had the pleasure to give his vote for you Sir as the Democratic Candidate for the Presidency. As the course which this state may take & the vote it may give at the approaching Election, which takes place a week from next tuesday is to have great weight in the final result, it has occurred to me that information in relation to this fact, added to what you doubtless receive from the other parts would not be unacceptable, in order to enable you to form from the aggregate some opinion of what the probable result will be in the state. This part of the state is the extreme Western part. I have been long a resident here & have an extensive acquaintance, constant correspondence & frequent intercourse with people in all parts of this section of the state. It is *the* Whig stronghold of the state. The Seven Western Counties compose collectively the 8h Senatorial District of the state & from its having been the District in which Anti-masonry originated, it is commonly termed the "infected district." The District was, before the advent of Anti-masonry, Democratic, strongly so; but the spirit of anti-masonry which arose from the outrage committed in the abduction of Morgan[2] took so decided a hold of it that the mass of the people were carried away with it & as soon as anti-masonry was made *the* politics of the District that faction carried it by large majorities. This faction was subsequently, in the year 1832, transferred to the Whig party & from that period until 1840 the majorities for the Whigs in the Counties composing the District have been steadily increasing.

In 1840 however they reached their maximum. Harrisons majority in the District exceeded the most sanguine expectations of his party. In these seven Counties he obtained within a hundred of 10000. The majority, however on Governor & Senator in that year did not exceed 10000 & if my recollection serves, the majority on the latter against myself who was that year the Democratic Candidate for Senator did not quite reach 10000. The difference between the majority for Harrision & the remainder of the Whig ticket can be accounted for by the pecuniary embarassment of the Country[3] which was most sensibly felt in this District & the hope that in change, men might produce a change of times. The actual Whig majority of the District in the year 1840 may be set down at 10,000 in round numbers. This is the highest majority that party has ever attained & I may add the highest that it ever will attain in this District. In that year the abolition vote in these Seven Counties was 441, which if added to the Whig majority would have made it about 10500. Since 1840 the Whig majority has been diminishing. It is true that no Election since that period has called out as many votes as were cast in 1840, & that test is wanting to prove this assertion. The highest vote cast throughout the state since that year was at the election for Govr in 1842, but then the Democratic vote cast was not so large by 4400 nor the Whig vote by 3900 as in 1840. The vote in this District in 1842 does not however shew so great a falling off as in other parts of the state, the Democratic vote being a little over that of 1840 & the Whig vote being less by 6500 while the abolition vote increased from 441 the number in 1840 to 1387 in 1842. This last added to the Whig vote (where it properly belongs) cast in 1842 & the Whig & abolition vote cast in the District in 1842 will be only 5500 less than the vote of the same parties in 1840. But the Whig majority has been as steadily diminishing since 1840 as it steadily increased up to that time.

One cause of its diminution is the increase of the abolition vote. I have stated above the increase from 1840 to 1842 a space of only two years. This increase is taken from the Whig vote. It is possible that a few of the abolitionists may have been Democrats—such are however few. As evidence that the increase of abolition votes in this section does not come from the Democratic side I will mention the vote of this (Erie) County in which the Democratic vote has increased from 3100 in 1840 to 4100, while the Whig vote has not increased, but the abolition vote has increased from 36 votes in 1840 to 360 votes in 1843. This abolition vote will I think be increased at this election. At all events if not increased it will not be diminished. C. M. Clay has been here & endeavoured to induce them to support Mr Clay but without effect. They are more strongly confirmed in their determination to support their own ticket. If there is any increase of their vote as it is probable there will be in this District, it will be from the Whig ranks, or if the vote remains the same as in 1843, the Whig majority will be diminished by that much in the district over 1840. But aside from this the Democratic party has made a large gain in this District since 1840 as the result will prove.

So far as this County is concerned we have an accurate canvass of it taken by personal application to each elector & I can assure our friends that the Whig majorities which in 1840 was 3099 cannot this year exceed 2200. In the adjoining County of Chautauqua the Whigs cannot claim over 2200 when they had 2800 in 1840. Our friends in this County advise that the Whig majority cannot go up to 2000. In the adjoining County of Niagara the Whig majority in 1840 was 745. This year it will not exceed 600. Genesee & Wyoming which together gave 3248 Whig majy in 1840, will not I am assured by discreet men who reside there give over 2200 together. Orleans County which in 1840 gave 579 Whig majy is now claimed by our friends there by a small majy. Of this I have however no confidence, but believe it will give the Whigs about 200 majy. Monroe County gave a Whig majy of 1634 in 1840. It is the residence of Judge Gardiner our Candidate for Lieut Gov. He assures us that it will not give to exceed 1000 Whig majy this year. His judgement in regard to it may be depended on. The above named Counties Comprise the 8th or "infected" District. The majority our friends may rely will be reduced at least 3500 below what it was in '40 whether the abolits stand fast or not, & still more if they increase. There are other western Counties which in '40 gave large Whig majs which will be diminished very much. But I will trespass on your patience no longer. We here consider this state beyond a doubt safe for the Democratic candidate. For myself I considered it certain when I returned from the Baltimore Convention since the nomination & acceptance of Mr Wright I consider it safe for us beyond all peradventure. Our people are active energetic & enthusiastic & every thing fair that can be done will be done to ensure a victory. In the hope that you will pardon this liberty....

JOHN T. HUDSON

ALS. DLC–JKP. Addressed to Columbia. Paragraphing supplied.

1. John T. Hudson served as alderman of the third ward in Buffalo, N.Y., and as canal commissioner, 1846–47.

2. In September 1826, William Morgan was abducted outside the jail at Canandaigua, N.Y., ostensibly to halt the publication of his book, *Illustrations of Masonry, By One of the Fraternity Who Had Devoted Thirty Years to the Subject,* and thus to prevent disclosure of the secret works of Freemasonry. In January of 1827, four men were tried, convicted, and sentenced for the Morgan kidnapping. Judicial process failed, however, to defeat the Masons' conspiracy of silence regarding Morgan's fate; and the Anti-Masons took as their organizing principle the rule of civic duty over fraternal loyalities.

3. Reference is to the Panic of 1837.

FROM GANSEVOORT MELVILLE

My dear Sir New York October 26th 1844

Political excitement in this state has reached a high and almost fearful point. It rages to a greater degree than at any time in the bacchanal canvass of 1840. It spreads wider, is more deeply seated and burns more fiercely. It is unexampled in the history of New York politics. Coming from one theatre of action into another and still stormier one, and desirous of obtaining that full and accurate information and preserving that equilibrium without which the best man's opinion is valueless, I have kept both eyes and ears open, have conversed with prominent men of the respective parties, have striven to keep my mind free from prejudice and passion so as to look at things as they are through an undistorted medium—and now not as a politician, but if I may presume so far as an humble personal friend, I avail myself of the permission so kindly granted to write to you freely and frankly—with a sincere desire to spread before you the actual condition of things as they now exist with us without color or concealment so far as they lie within the scope of my apprehension.

At the Democratic State Convention of 1840 our first and best calculation beat Van Buren 3000 votes. This of course would not do and was altered without sufficient reason so as to give him about 10.000 majority. At the Convention of the present year various canvasses of the state ranging from 9.500 to 25.000 Democratic majority were submitted, compared revised and re-revised by competent persons and a result arrived at giving us the state by 12.000 majority. This was considered to be done on the basis of giving our opponents the benefit of all doubts. In this calculation the City and Co of New York were put down as good for 2.500, which at that time was perhaps a low figure. The estimate throughout was made on the basis of the electoral ticket. For several weeks afterward there was manifest a steady increase in the intensity of the Democratic feeling and numerous reputed changes in our favor until about the 1st of October at which time there was an evident depression in the Councils of the Whig party and a general want of spirit among their voters. This was their lowest point. From it they have gradually recovered. By degrees a change has taken place in the Whig camp. They have become more determined in their action much more lavish in the use of money, more hopeful, exhibiting greater activity than heretofore, and at this moment *to my knowledge* count confidently upon carrying the state by from 8 to 10.000 on a poll of 490.000 votes.

On the contrary our best informed and most judicious friends are at this time not only confident but sanguine of carrying the state by a majority somewhat less than that settled upon at the Convention but still sure, handsome and decided. The rank and file of the Democracy throughout the state are perfectly uproarious in their confidence of an overwhelming victory not only in the state but in the nation. Our gatherings are more largely attended than those of our opponents, and in the more than a dozen meetings which I have addressed since my return home the attendance has been in every case far greater than had been anticipated and the enthusiasm more obvious than I have elsewhere witnessed. Still to my mind matters are not working as they should *to ensure and place beyond doubt* a Democratic victory.

Our organization altho' fair is not what it has been in one or two preceding conflicts. We have relied too much on popular impulse and enthusiasm. Our people in the expense, excitement, and hurry-scurry of repeated mass-meetings have in some portions of the state been less attentive to organization than is desirable. The organization of the Whigs is I am inclined to think rather better on the whole than ours but not nearly so perfect as it was in 1838 when they beat us by the force of an organization unequalled in either party before or since.

Every possible effort has been made by the Whigs to operate upon the Abolitionists and induce them to vote for Clay. Cassius M Clay has been in all the strong abolition counties but has proved himself unequal to his mission and failed in equalling public expectation. He has exercised little influence in any way and certainly none against us. Each successive attempt made by the Whigs to produce a favorable impression upon the Abolitionists has recoiled upon themselves. But a new element has lately been introduced by Mr Birneys course in relation to and his acceptance of the Saganaw nomination [1] which has produced a great sensation in the Abolition ranks, has alarmed a portion of that large section of the Abolitionists who were originally Whigs, and caused an uncertainty as to their position in this contest which until lately did not exist and in my humble opinion *if* properly taken advantage of by the Whigs (which is doubtful) paved the way for an unexpected accession to Clay's strength from that quarter. That the entire abolition strength can be polled for Mr Clay I do not for a moment suppose but that a considerable portion of it can (if judiciously managed) I do not doubt. The feelings of the Abolitionists are much more embittered towards Mr Clay than towards yourself, but their surprise at Mr Birney's recent avowal of Free Trade and Anti-Land Distribution doctrines followed up by his acceptance of the Saganaw Nomination and his clumsy attempt to explain it, [2] all heightened by the great unanimity with which the slave-holding states are coming up to your support, have super-added to their first surprise a distrust of the propriety and policy of voting for their own candidates and thus not making themselves so powerful an element as otherwise, in the decision of the great question so far as the state of New York is concerned. Time alone will develope their course, but the position of that portion of their rank and file who were originally Whigs is one calculated to excite some apprehension.

The "Native Americans" have no seperate existence or distinct party organization in our state except in this County and Kings & Queens with one or two trifling exceptions. They had apparently collapsed owing to internal feuds, jealousies, and an alleged mal-administration of our municipal affairs, but have recently been aroused, united and re-organized in direct consequence of the result in the City and County of Philadelphia, and are now in the field with a complete ticket for the State Legislature and Congress which they count confidently upon carrying. They present no candidate for Governor and no electoral ticket. Last April the Native American and Whig vote for Mayor—Franklin & Harper[3] combined—showed a majority of 9000 over the Democratic candidate. It is the object of certain intriguing leaders of these respective parties to effect a combination now on the basis of procuring the support of the Native Americans for the Whig electoral and gubernatorial ticket giving in return the Whig support to the Native American ticket for Congress and the State Legislature. This it will be next to impossible to carry into effect fully. Natural obstacles exist which will be increased by our friends who are alive to the importance of frustrating this movement. Every nerve will be strained on either side. Tammany Hall is confident of success in preventing this formidable coalition. Mr Harper the Native American Mayor as we have ascertained from private and reliable information is active aided by other leading men in his party in the attempt to transfer the "Natives" to Clay and expects to succeed in so doing on the strength of the fact that the mutual trading capital exists to do it with. Each interest is strong on the expectation of its own triumph in the great struggle now in progress on this point. After looking over the whole ground I cannot avoid differing from both, and it is my deliberate opinion, that the proposed coalition will be carried into effect—not fully by any means—but partially—and to an extent which will probably overturn our undoubted majority of say at least 2.600 on the general issues before the people, and give to the Clay electoral ticket in this city a majority, uncertain, and to which a reasonable approximation can not be made for the reason that these elements are so corrupt their mutual interests so varying and their mutual distrust so great that the extent to which such a plan would be operative admits of no well grounded opinion. These last considerations apply measurably to any settled, distinct, general opinion upon the whole subject because these causes unite in producing a constantly shifting aspect which it is most difficult to fix, and in their operation admit of phases varying from day to day. The opinion above expressed is in my humble judgment the better opinion now, but it may not be so, three or four days hence.

I regret to be compelled to say that so far as the city is concerned the Democratic nominations for Congress and the State Legislature are not of a character to strengthen the electoral ticket. The same may be said though in a lesser degree of the nominations of the Whigs. Both parties have erred here—particularly ours—our best and strongest men should have been brought forward and forced to stand.

A Democratic association started here within a few months known as "the Empire Club" (one of those fighting and bullying political clubs which disgrace our city politics) some of the leading officers and members of which including its President[4] are men of reputed and believed suspicious and *criminal* character, and which owing to its reckless boldness and activity in the contest has been over-much petted by the Democratic press has of late committed some unprovoked outrages upon Whig processions and meetings injuring and insulting many quiet persons, (and among others Jno. C. Hamilton (son of Alexander Hamilton) who on the 23d inst was knocked down and damaged by a party of the Empires).[5] This course of conduct has re-acted and hurt us a great deal among sober and thinking men of our own party, who in a city populated like ours have a perfect horror of any approach to banded and collected ruffianism.

On the other hand great activity and a most confident spirit exist among the Democrats in the city and in all parts of the state. The naturalized citizens are all devotion and will poll an almost unanimous and greatly increased vote. The accession to our strength from that quarter will be larger than is generally supposed. Our city courts are now naturalizing over 60 every day—yesterday between 90 & 100—every man of them Democrats. The Native American paper[6] and one Whig paper, the Express,[7] are publishing the lists daily, a thing unusual and now done with an object apparent on its face.

Many Counties will do nobly. All *promise* to do better than in 1842 when we elected Gov Bouck by 22.000. The Whigs are destined to be greatly disappointed in their strong-hold, the 8th Senate district. Their lowest mark there is 10.500. It will be difficult for them to obtain over 6.250. Let us instance three counties in that district. Erie gave Harrison 3.300. It can not give Clay over 2.250. Chatauqua gave Harrison 2.660. That figure will be reduced to 1.800. Genesee gave Harrison 3.000. Since '40 Wyoming has been taken from it. Now Genesee & Wyoming together (i.e. the old County of Genesee) will be pushed hard if they roll up combined 1.900 or 2000. In the powerful County of Onondaga, our central county we have sound reasons to anticipate great gains. Tompkins will be revolutionized. In St Lawrence alone we shall gain 1550 on the vote of 1840. Then the Democrats in that County stayed at home on account of Mr Van Buren's course in regard to the affair of the Caroline.[8] Now they will all be out. In Jefferson, Oswego, Orleans, Niagara—in all those frontier counties where the Anti-British feeling is strong we shall gain largely. We shall increase our majorities in Suffolk, Putnam, Rockland and other staunch Democratic strong-holds. In some *strong Tariff* counties as Rensselaer, Saratoga and others where we are running Congressmen who acknowledge *the principle* of protection the local Democratic tickets will lead the electoral. Considerations connected with the Direct Tax and state-debt-paying policy[9] will induce many Whig capitalists to vote for Wright on that ground only. Other considerations connected with the Canal & Improvement system of the state will induce many good democrats to vote for Fillmore. It is my devout hope that the gubernatorial and electoral tickets will in the aggregate run side and side. A score more considerations might be offered but having already occupied much more space than I had intended and fearing that I may trespass too far on your time, I will conclude by the expression of my unassuming though deliberate and candid judgment as to the probable result, which is that the full vote of the state will be more nearly polled than ever before, that the contest will be *much closer* than either party anticipate, that the majority will not exceed from 7/8 to 1 3/4 % on the aggregate vote, and that unless the "Native Americans" and Abolitionists support the Whig electoral ticket with unexpected and considerable unanimity, we shall give you the six and thirty votes of the Empire State. The aspect on the whole is therefore a good deal in our favor. Elements exist which skilfully and thoroughly combined can beat us. That they will combine to a degree sufficient to compass that end is improbable. Still it is possible.

Governor Marcy returned from Pennsylvania two or three days since. He expresses a firm conviction that 5000 will be added to Shunk's majority. Our friends all unite in the utmost confidence as to the result there. For myself I would be glad to compromise for the Governor's vote. The result in Pennsylvania known as it will be in the cities of New York, Brooklyn, Albany and Troy on the morning of the election will exercise a great influence on our large floating vote and may in case the Whigs (*against all our advices*) should succeed give them this state. If our friends in Pennsylvania only do half so well as the letters from men who ought to know in Harrisburgh and Philadelphia indicate, we are not authorized to indulge a single apprehension as to the Key Stone.

The leading Whigs of this city Graham (David) Greeley, Reynolds[10] and others are evidently looking of late with some hope to Virginia. A letter from Ritchie Sr. under date of the 14th inst bids us be of good cheer and says that the Democratic majority in that ancient commonwealth can not be less than 5000. From Maryland the letters of our friends promise much. So too from Ohio, and Indiana. The result in Georgia affords I trust some evidence of a progressive Democratic sentiment in North Carolina, and distinctly foreshadows our triumph in "the Home of the Hickories."[11] As things now stand the vote of Tennesee is most important. The Whigs here count upon it with entire confidence and laugh at me with apparent real sincerity for the distinct expression of a contrary opinion. It is my fervent hope and trust that three things will be evolved in this momentous canvass. First a decided majority on both the electoral and popular votes for our nominees. Second that Tennesee will cast her 13 votes for Polk and Dallas. And thirdly that New York will do likewise with her six and thirty. Then things would be placed at once in that condition most favorable to sustaining triumphantly the four years of embittered warfare which will be attempted by our opponents against your administration.

For the views here-in expressed I am alone responsible. They conflict in some particulars of importance with the views of older more experienced and more sagacious men. Mr Croswell, Mr Cramer, Gov Bouck, Mr Van Buren, and all our other friends feel a greater and some of them a *much* greater degree of confidence than I do, and I would not now venture to write with such entire frankness as I have done, were it not that the more than kindness, the friendship with which I was treated by yourself and Mrs. Polk while in Tennesee have left with me a gratitude so warm and an impression so indelible, that whenever it shall be my lot to write or speak to you, I shall make bold to do again what I have done to day, which is without regard *to any interest* that may be thereby affected, to utter my candid and conscientious convictions.

On my way down I stopped at Lindenwald whence I scribbled a hasty line to your brother William. Mr Van Buren is in excellent health and evidently growing fat. It is his opinion that we will carry the state and succeed largely in the general National canvass. His confidence is much more lively than when I saw him previously a few months since.

In case you may think fit to honor me with any communication to which the words Private or Confidential or both may be prefixed I need not say (after the conversation we held on that point) that anything so marked shall be sacredly inviolate, not to be seen or the contents in whole or in part divulged to any person, *without any exception whatever*, unless expressly directed to the contrary under your own hand.

Be pleased to present my most particular and respectful regards to Mrs Polk, as also to your mother.[12] Remember me with kindness to Mrs. Hayes and the ladies of Mr Walker's family, not forgetting the gallant Major, that puissant general who wields the sword of Gideon and his excellent lady, the Messrs Walker, Mr. Thomas & Barkley Martin, and believe me....[13]

GANSEVOORT MELVILLE

ALS. DLC–JKP. Addressed to Columbia and marked "*Private & Confidential.*"

1. In September of 1844, a Democratic convention meeting in Saginaw, Michigan, nominated James G. Birney as a candidate for the state legislature. On November 2, 1844, the Washington *National Intelligencer* carried a letter purportedly written by James G. Birney to J. B. Garland in which Birney authorized Garland to say to the nomination convention, "I am now and ever have been a Democrat of the 'Jeffersonian school.'" It was not until after the election that the letter was proved a forgery.

2. Letters from James G. Birney remarking on his nomination were published in the *New York Tribune* of October 9 and 15, 1844.

3. Morris Franklin and James Harper. Franklin served in the New York House, 1837, and in the New York Senate, 1842–44. Harper, co-founder of Harper Brothers publishing house, won election to the mayoralty of New York City in 1844; during his one term he created the first organized metropolitan police force in the United States.

4. Reference is to Isaiah Rynders. In 1849 Rynders was involved in an anti-British riot in New York City that left more than a dozen men dead. He was arrested, tried, and acquitted. In 1857 he was appointed U.S. marshal of the Southern District of New York by James Buchanan. On August 28, 1844, Rynders wrote a letter informing Polk of his election to honorary membership in the Democratic Empire Club of New York City. ALS. DLC–JKP.

5. The *New York Herald* of October 24, 1844, reported that members of the Empire Club threw lumps of clay at Whig party supporters taking part in a procession in New York City on October 23, 1844.

6. Reference probably is to the *New York Citizen and American Republican*.

7. Reference is to the *New York Express*.

8. In the fall of 1837 William Lyon MacKenzie, an immigrant journalist from Scotland and assemblyman for Upper Canada, led an uprising against Canadian authorities. Defeated by British regular and Canadian militia units, he fled to safety on the American side of the Niagara River. In January of 1838 hostilities broke out along the Niagara River when British soldiers seized a small rebel vessel, the *Caroline*, which was anchored on the American side of the river. Shots were exchanged, several Americans were killed, and MacKenzie's ranks were swelled by New York militiamen. Martin Van Buren dispatched Winfield

Scott to restore order; both Rensselaer Van Rensselaer, the American leader, and MacKenzie were arrested.

9. In 1842 Michael Hoffman, chairman of the New York House Ways and Means Committee, proposed a bill to stop further canal construction in the state and to levy a property tax to pay off the state's substantial debt. The bill, popularly known as the "stop and tax act," was passed by the legislature.

10. David Graham, Horace Greeley, and J. N. Reynolds. A New York criminal defense lawyer, Graham wrote a number of treatises on judicial processes relating to the New York Supreme Court, trial practices in both civil and criminal cases, and the organization and jurisdiction of courts of law and equity in New York. He served as an alderman of New York City in 1834 and as chairman of the General Committee of Democratic Whig Young Men in 1844. Former editor of the Whig weekly, *Log Cabin*, Greeley founded the *New York Tribune* in April of 1844. Elected as a Whig to the U.S. House to fill a vacancy, he served from December 1848 until March 1849. Subsequently, Greeley ran for the U.S. Senate in 1861 and for the U.S. House in 1870 but lost both elections. He was also defeated in his bid for the presidency in 1872 by Ulysses S. Grant. Reynolds served as president of the Central Clay Committee of New York City during the presidential campaign of 1844.

11. Reference is to Tennessee's "Old" and "Young" Hickories, Andrew Jackson and James K. Polk.

12. Sarah Childress Polk and Jane Knox Polk.

13. References are to Ophelia Clarissa Polk Hays, the James Walker family, William H. Polk, Gideon J. Pillow, Mary Martin Pillow, James and J. Knox Walker, James H. Thomas, and Barkly Martin. A Columbia lawyer and general in the Tennessee militia, Pillow played a key role at the 1844 Democratic National Convention. He later served as a general officer in the Mexican War and commanded a Confederate brigade during the Civil War. Joseph Knox Walker, third son of James and Jane Maria Polk Walker, served as a private secretary to Polk during his presidency. Walker subsequently practiced law in Memphis and represented Shelby and Fayette counties as a Democrat in the Tennessee Senate from 1857 until 1859.

FROM COLLIN S. TARPLEY[1]

My Dear Sir　　　　Clinton 26th Oct 1844

Knowing as I do that you are greatly troubled with correspondents about this time, it is with much reluctance that I can consent to add to your troubles. But the political campaign just about to close in this state presents a prospect to gratifying to every Democrat that I cannot forbear to congratulate the country upon the anticipated result. We have fought the battle bravely nobly and at every point we have met and overcome the enemy. Every inch of ground has been contested, every energy of a sinking cause has been displayed, but every where we have triumphed and the whigs are forced at last to concede that Missi is a democratic state. I have attended mass meetings and addressed the people at various places particularly in the whig counties of Warren Yazoo & Hinds and from a whig majority in those three counties of about 1200 the aggregate majority will not now exceed 300. Every other whig county except Adams has been revolutionised and there the majority has been greatly diminished. We confidently expect a majority of from 6 to 8000. Missi being entirely safe I shall spend the coming week amongst the squatters of La. where a series of public meetings will take place. Such enthusiasm has never been seen as these squatters exhibit, and if by proper management we can carry the Parishes of Carroll & Madison, settled almost entirely by squatters, we shall carry Louisiana by a hansome majority. These men have always voted with the whig party. Even in the last summers election[2] they went with that party. But when Clay is presented to them with his string of denunciations against them, they cant "go it" and they have come out for the democracy; I mean the largest portion of them. I think from the arrangments for next week that we shall manufacture democrats out of nearly all the rest of them. As cotton has gone *down* and cotton goods have *gone up* people begin to inquire the cause and trace it to the Tariff of 1842. This has produced very many changes. The Texas question also operates finely for our party more particularly since it is opposed at the North by the Abolitionists. I consider the whole south united upon these questions and if Tennessee can prove an exception and support Mr Clay in defiance of principle I shall not only lose my respect for the state but consider that John Bell spoke truly when he pledged her to stand side by side with the Federal State of Massachusetts. The news from Ohio is rather discouraging, but I do not yet despair of that state particularly if the Abolitionists will stick to Birney; but we can do without her, and if New York goes right (Wright) as I doubt not she will the sage of Ashland[3] is again doomed to defeat.

But I will not trespass longer on your valuable time. I merely set out to say that the battle in Missi was fought and gallantly won, and before I know it I am going out into conjectures about the result of the Election. Well pardon me for it has been my study by day and my dreams by night ever since the 1st of June.

My kindest respects to Mrs P. and believe me as ever . . . .

C. S. TARPLEY

ALS. DLC–JKP. Addressed to Columbia.

1. After reading law in Pulaski under Aaron V. Brown, Tarpley moved to Florence in 1831; five years later he moved from Tennessee to Hinds County, Miss.

2. Tarpley's reference is to state elections held in Louisiana on July 1, 1844 to elect congressmen, state legislators, and delegates to a state constitutional convention.

3. Henry Clay.

TO FERNANDO WOOD[1]

My Dear Sir: Columbia Ten. Oct. 26th 1844

Your letter of the 16th Inst reached me on yesterday. I hope you may not be mistaken in the opinion you give of the f[l]attering prospects of the Democracy in New York. The moment I saw the effect of the alliance between the Native Americans and Whigs in the City and County of Philadelphia, I had apprehensions that a similar Union might be attempted in your City. I hope however that our friends in New York being apprized of the danger have taken timely and energetic precautionary measures to prevent it.

Our whole democracy here are mistaken, or we will carry this state. Never were our party more confident of success.

I will thank you to forward to me the earliest information of your Election returns.

JAMES K. POLK

ALS. DLC–JKP. Addressed to the City of New York and marked "*Private*."

1. A shipping merchant in New York City, Fernando Wood won election as a Tammany Democrat to one term in the U.S. House, 1841–43. He held the post of dispatch agent for the State Department at the port of New York from 1844 until 1847. After serving as mayor of New York City, 1855–58, 1861, and 1862, he won nine terms in the U.S. House, 1863–65 and 1867–81.

FROM J. GEORGE HARRIS

(Sunday morn)

My Dear Sir Nashville Oct 27. 1844

Immediately on the receipt of yours of Oct 26,[1] communicating an extract of a letter from Mr. Dallas,[2] Gen Armstrong and myself had an interview "upstairs" and concluded to call in your bro: Wm. We thought it over and over, read it again and again, discussed it in all its bearings, saw the enormity of Clay's course, and came to the conclusion that an authentic and *authoritative* exposure of his double-dealing and especially of his offer to *sell the South* for the abolition votes of New York &c would have an *all-powerfull effect* at this moment in Kentucky, North Carolina, Georgia and Tennessee. Especially *because* (as Mr.Clay acknowledged in his letter to Cassius)[3] that any show on his part to favor abolitionism would *endanger* the whig character of those four States, and especially because he has, the better [to] carry out this deceptive rascality (it is nothing better) written a long letter to the National Intelligencer pledging and promising that he would write *no more* letters on public matters.[4]

To make an editorial exposure of this, would, in our judgement, scarcely accomplish the object. We therefore concluded that if the State Central Committee would but make use of it as the State Central Committee of Penn made use of the letter of Gen. Armstrong & myself exposing the letter of Jones & his cronies,[5] there could be no doubt that *it would tell with* great power in the four States referred to.

Dr. Robertson being below we called him in as Chairman of the State Com. & communicated the whole matter to him. He inclined to the opinion that *an editorial* would be all sufficient—that all was "well enough" &c. Your brother will give you all the particulars. We concluded to sleep upon it.

This morning Gen. A., Wm. & myself met at the Post office. The *importance* of an authoritative exposure of this shameful and abominable course which Clay has pursued, seems to impress us more deeply than ever. Wm. has concluded that it is advisable for him to visit you to-day and obta[in][6] your opinion. We are anxious to load the mails of tomorrow night with an authorative exposure signed by the State Committee.

J. GEO. HARRIS

ALS. DLC–JKP. Delivered by hand of William H. Polk and marked "*Confidential.*" Harris' inside address, "Col. Polk," has been overwritten to read, "Wm. Polk."

1. Polk's letter has not been found.
2. See George M. Dallas to Polk, October 16, 1844.
3. Harris' reference is to Henry Clay's letter to Cassius M. Clay of September 18, 1844. See Leonard P. Cheatham to Polk, September 29, 1844.
4. Harris' reference is to Henry Clay's letter to the editors of the Washington *National Intelligencer* of September 23, 1844. See William Taylor to Polk, October 17, 1844.
5. See John K. Kane to Polk, October 13, 1844.
6. Portion of one word obliterated by sealing wax oil.

FROM SAMUEL P. CALDWELL

Dear Sir

Memphis Oct. 28th 1844

Believing that the vote of Shelby Cty: is of the highest importance in the approaching election, I have concluded that a fair account of her political feeling would be interesting. The County exclusive of Memphis will do better for the democrats than it ever has. This fact I *know*. As to the City of Memphis, we will battle for it with a resolution and confidence never approximated in this place. We will increase our strength greatly here. This I also *know*. The numerous and spirited displays of the democrats here, have thrown the Whigs here into the greatest consternation, accustomed as they have been to carry the city with little or no oppostion. The only advantage the whigs have of us, is, that the new citizens are considerably in their favor. Of the old vote we will gain largely.

Mr. Topp nor any other person can rein over the democrats here as formerly. The democrats of this place have been very much brow beaten heretofore. But *now*, we are respected as a party.

The vote of Tennessee will evidently have great influence in the coming election whic fact we have not overlooked and I trust that the democrats in the other portions of the State will not. The Hon: Robert J. Walker, passed here yesterday on his way home. He gives the most pleasing account of the North. He says New York is safe by many thousands. No combinations, can prevent our success there. We are *ready* and eager for the fight. *Shelby* will do her duty.

David Craighead has been here and done much good. He is the most effective Stumper, who has been amongst us. The democrats are taking all the bets they can get, on the *general* result *even*. Fear not for the Western District. All is well here.

SAMUEL P. CALDWELL

ALS. DLC–JKP. Addressed to Columbia.

FROM DAVID T. DISNEY

Dr Sir Cincinnati 28 Oct 1844

I have the pleasure of acknowledging the receipt of your favour.[1]

On last evening I returned from Columbus our seat of state of Government where I had an opportunity of seeing many of our friends from different parts of the state. We have fairly and fully compared notes and I believe are ready now for the shock of battle. At last however as I wrote you before all depends upon the vote of the abolitionists. And how they will go no man can tell, for the simple reason that they do not know themselves. They are agitated by diverse counsels and antagonist influences. The whigs are using every means to secure them and you may well believe that we are not idle. Indeed *Ohio never witnessed such a contest as the one we are now engaged in*. The two great parties are so nicely balanced that a straw may decide the fight.

The result in our northern counties at our October election developed an antagonist influence which I fear from the connexion and intimacy which exists between that part of our state and western New York, is also at work in New York. I allude to the movements of the Whig abolitionists. It was them who beat us in Ohio and I dread their movements in New York. I have however written to some of our friends in that state warning them of what they may expect, in the hopes that they may not be deceived as we were.

Our advices from Indiana confirms the belief that it will be carried by the democracy.

There is one matter connected with our own state which I have not breathed to any person but which *may become important.* In the event of its going for Clay and that being decisive of the contest. I am satisfied that her vote *can be contested* on fair broad and substantial grounds. How far it would be expedient to do so is another question and will be judged of hereafter. I merely hint the matter to you at this time in order that you may not be surprised if the course of events should decide us to make the effort to throw out her vote.

D. T. DISNEY

P.S. I shall write you by every mail giving the vote so far as our state is concerned.

ALS. DLC–JKP. Addressed to Columbia.

1. Polk's letter has not been found.

FROM J. GEORGE HARRIS

My Dear Sir, Nashville October 28. 1844

We have just given notice in the Union of tomorrow that Mr. A. G. Jewett[1] of Maine who came to our town a day or two ago as a volunteer will speak at Franklin, Spring Hill, and attend your great rally at Mt. Pleasant on Saturday. We have caused handbills of his appointments to be sent on, some of which accompany this letter.

Mr. Jewett made a very good speech at the Court House last night, and has gone to Lebanon to-day with Dr. Duncan[2] to attend the mass meeting there to-morrow. Our Military Companies have gone with them, so we shall make *quite an invasion of Wilson.* Dr. Duncan goes from Lebanon to Hartsville 31st, Gallatin 31st where he will probably be met by Gov. Pope[3] who did not arrive here last night as expected.

General Armstrong has just written to Messrs Potter and McKissek[4] at Spring Hill, forwarding handbills to them containing Jewett's appointments—also a letter to Park and Bradley[5] at Franklin giving notice of his apts. at Franklin.

Our canvass for this county goes on finely. We thoroughly, *efficiently* organised and we confidently expect to reduce the whig majority one to two hundred.

From the signs in New York I cannot believe the enemy will succeed in their late attempts to trade with the factions. If they do, it is my belief that the South will save us.

J. Geo. Harris

[Addendum]

I have received the *hand Bills* & printed Notices and cannot find Heiss. *I send the bills*, Those for *Spring* Hill & *Franklin*. I send *them* & for Mt Pleasant to *you*. [Robert Armstrong][6]

ALS. DLC–JKP. Addressed to Columbia.

1. Albert G. Jewett, lawyer with an extensive practice in Bangor, Maine, was appointed chargé d'affaires to Peru in 1845.

2. Alexander Duncan, a Cincinnati physician, sat for several terms in both the Ohio House and Senate, 1828–34; he served three terms in the U. S. House, 1837–41 and 1843–45.

3. John Pope, a lawyer, served several terms in the Kentucky House before his election to one term in the U. S. Senate in 1807. He later won election to two terms in the Kentucky Senate, 1825–29; went to Arkansas as territorial governor, 1829–35; and served three terms in the U. S. House, 1837–43.

4. Harris' references probably are to James O. Potter and Spivey McKissack. Prior to succeeding Pleasant Nelson as circuit court clerk in Maury County in 1844, Potter served as postmaster at Spring Hill. An early settler in Spring Hill and a leading merchant, McKissack had served as the town's first mayor.

5. Harris' references probably are to James Park and Thomas H. Bradley; they have not been identified further.

6. Robert Armstrong wrote the last two sentences of the addendum on the inside fold of Harris' cover sheet.

FROM SAMUEL H. LAUGHLIN

My dear Sir, Nashville, Oct. 28, 1844

I think with only two or three rather short Editorials, two being prefaces merely to articles from the Yeoman and Globe, in reference to Clay and Adams,[1] and the other a brief call for the last Rally meeting here next Monday,[2] that I have made the best paper for immediate effect, with just time to circulate before the election, that we have made for several weeks. The enclosed came to-night from Indiana.[3] To-day, to appear in the morning, Col. Harris wrote the article you will see in the Union on the same subject, which goes out in time to do good here and south, but *not* in time, as we calculate it, to do harm north.[4] The evidences of this damnable combination I think are sufficient. Dr. Duncan, still here, thinks the abolition matter in no event can be as injurious as we have been led to fear. The event is with God and the people. The same exposure that goes out in the Daily Union of tomorrow morning, went out *south* to-day in the Weekly.

I have a letter from Gen. Haralson of Georgia, pledging a large increase of the late vote in that state.

I have a letter from Twyman,[5] an able Virginia politician, dated from Albemarle, giving most sensible calculations of results all over that state, proving as I think clearly, that our majority in the Old Dominion must be at least 4500 at lowest, and possibly between 6 and 7 thousand. He writes after consultations with some of the first men of the state.

A letter from Judge Bowlin of 22nd instant, written at the close of Col. Bentons speech in St. Louis, and after he had seen its effects, gives an account of that speech, so as to make it appear even stronger for you than the Missourian's Report, which you will have seen.[6] I know by the letter, that Benton feels the awkwardness of his position most keenly, and that in coming back, in the event of your election, he will set up instantly as one of the main stays of your administration. Bowlin says Len Sims, when he goes into the next Congress, will be a pure radical democrat—a fully reclaimed man.[7]

Gov. Yell writes me from Waxhaws, Arkansas, (where is Waxhaws?) since his election, that he will keep the field till the close of the war, and that Arrington, a popular lawyer, whom we have gained from the Whig Electoral ticket to which he was regularly nominated, is also in the field for us, being a popular speaker.[8] These are things, however, where all is safe.

Mr. A. G. Jewett, who is here from Maine, whom Gen. Pillow will remember as a leading member of the Convention at Baltimore, brings good news from the East. He spoke several times as he came out in the interior of N. York, and at Louisville. Croswell, in his letter of introduction, calls him "excellent friend," and says he is an able man, ready to speak and fight *for* and *with* us here, up to the election. He will go to work. He has great desire to make your, and Gen. Jackson's acquaintance.

Croswell in writing, and Cramer who also writes for the Argus in a letter of two days earlier date and who wrote for documents which I have sent to him, speak confidently and confidentially of certain success in New York.

Danforth, Gen. Jackson's and Mr. Van Buren's Collector at Providence, who was beheaded by Gen. Harrison, and who is President of a Democratic Association, in sending me Dorr's Trial, and thanking me for the Vindication,[9] Humphrey's Corruption Proofs,[10] and a bundle of the most important Nos. of our Banner which I sent him, says they are hopelessly under Algerine Dominion in Rhode Island, and that they *know* there, that if Clay is elected, that Gov. Dorr will be put instantly to *hard convict labor*. He says they have issued an *Expose* of the matter in a pamphlet, and in their democratic papers, which his Association are sending all over New England.[11] He says he is the principal writer for the Republican Herald, and has published a large part of my letter to him, being answers to enquiries as to what sort of man you are morally, religiously, and as a "lawful and justifiable owner of slaves."[12] These words were in the enquiries. He says our chance is excellent in Connecticut, and that we will run the Whigs to the eyes in Massachusetts. Of New York, though I suppose his means of information are not better than ours, he entertains no no doubt.

H. C. Williams, under Gen. Dawson's frank,[13] has sent to use here, to Gen. Armstrong, and myself, copies of some of the villain Willis Green's last *Roorbacks*.[14] As I use a frank, taken off one of Owens speeches, thereby saving you postage, and they may not have been sent to you, I send you a specimen of each. I know you preserve such things, for future reference, and as part of the History of the times. Williams in writing, under date of the 20th, says Joe Gales[15] had been heard privately to say to a friend, since the Pennsylvania Election, that Clay's case was *gone*, but that they must and would fight it out. Jewett says, all intelligent democrats in the North, think the contest settled for us—in our favor. I know you are worried to death with letters, and the intense pain and affliction I have suffered, more than I have ever suffered on any account of my own or any man's before, on account of your dissatisfaction and displeasure about the publication of the Col. Polk papers, and when I thought I was doing what was for the best as much as if my soul's salvation had depended on it, has been a reason why I have not, when I had occasional leisure from writing to others, written you oftener, or several times asked your advice in relation to several matters in which I have ventured to pursue my own judgment, always being cautious of saying too much, for fear of Comprietting[16] some one, or giving a handle to enemies, when perhaps I ought to have said more. I have permitted base, vile, absolute lies in regard to myself to pass unheeded, unwilling to make any new issue, or to connect in the smallest degree your interests, or the interests of the party to be trammelled in any manner in my humble and unimportant affairs. I state these matters now, because the war is nearly ended, and I have nothing to ask or wish, but to be correctly understood. I have had to do, and to bear, and forbear, with a very disagreeable, and very selfish man as a publisher,[17] who was always opposed to publishing many things which I desired, and nothing more than the whole of the extended and continued Col. Polk papers—because, after most of them had once appeared, he thought the case so clearly and strongly settled, that no harm could be done to us in the case. In the end, I did not get in near so much of Mr. Haywoods admirable report as I desired, not because the *full defence* needed it, but is due to Haywood and North Carolina. I manifested my own wishes and earnestness, by going to Warren and Van Buren, taking part of the proofs with my own hand, and coming back to my post here in three days and nights. After stating these matters in self justification, and which altogether have cost me sleepless nights and much sorrow, I will never trouble you by the slightest reference to them hereafter. My whole hopes and prospects in life having been crushed and destroyed by providential afflictions in the last few years,[18] leaves me but little to desire except the good opinion of good men as I shall deserve it by my acts and motives. To have this, and deserve it, would be all the riches I would covet—with it I would esteem myself rich in the midst of poverty. Excuse all this—it is the last word I shall ever say to you on the subject....

S.H.L.

P.S. If you shall answer this letter, unless by return mail, please direct to McMinnville, as I shall be there after leaving here on Saturday morning, until Wednesday of next week, when I shall return here to aid in posting up the books til all the returns come in. S.H.L.[19]

ALI. DLC–JKP. Addressed to Columbia. Polk's AE on the cover states that he answered this letter on October 29, 1844; Polk's reply has not been found.

1. The article from the Frankfort *Kentucky Yeoman* dealt with Henry Clay's refusal to pay the gambling and tavern debts of his son Thomas. The Washington *Globe* article reviewed the long-standing disagreement between John Q. Adams and Andrew Jackson over the Adams-Onís treaty of 1819.

2. On Monday, November 4, 1844, the Democrats met to make preparations for the "security and purity of the ballot box" in Nashville and Davidson County.

3. Enclosure not found.

4. On October 29, 1844, the *Nashville Union* ran an article with the caption, "Alarming Facts. The Last Bargains of the Great Bargainer." Drawing on information from "unquestionable authorities at New York and Philadelphia," the *Nashville Union* charged that Henry Clay had attempted to strike bargains with the abolitionists of New York and with both the immigrants and Native Americans of Philadelphia.

5. Reference probably is to Travis J. Twyman, who served one term in the Virginia General Assembly for Madison County, 1847–48.

6. Laughlin's reference is to Thomas H. Benton's speech at St. Louis on October 19, 1844. In that speech Benton condemned Tyler's annexation treaty but gave his support to the annexation of Texas and Oregon.

7. Leonard H. Sims, a Missouri Democrat, served one term in the U. S. House, 1845–47.

8. A lawyer and poet, Alfred W. Arrington served briefly in the Arkansas legislature; in 1844 he was nominated an elector on the Whig ticket, but he withdrew his name and declared himself a Democrat. Soon after the election, he moved to Texas.

9. Nashville *Vindication* pamphlet.

10. Laughlin's reference probably is to materials relating to Henry Clay's alledged "corrupt bargain" in 1825. On March 12, 1844, West H. Humphreys wrote Polk that the Democrats intended to publish a pamphlet on the "corrupt bargain." ALS. DLC–JKP. Humphreys' pamphlet is not identified further.

11. The Dorr *Exposé* is not identified further.

12. Laughlin's letter to Walter R. Danforth, published in the Providence *Republican Herald*, is not identified further.

13. Hampton C. Williams and probably John B. Dawson. A native of Georgia, Williams was a clerk in the Bureau of Construction, an office in the Navy Department, and a party operative. A native of Tennessee, Dawson won election in 1826 as major general of the Louisiana militia; he subsequently served two terms in the U.S. House, 1841–45.

14. A Kentucky Whig, Willis Green served three terms in the U.S. House, 1839–45. Since the adjournment of Congress, he had supervised Whig committee activities in Washington City. On October 18, 1844, the Washington *Globe* charged that Green and the committee had sent out bundles of pamphlets and handbills "consisting of all sorts of libels" against Polk. In the next issue, James Towles and C. P. Sengstack of the Democratic Association attacked, in particular, a pamphlet reviving allegations about the use of British gold to buy votes for Polk and Dallas.

15. Joseph Gales, Jr., and William W. Seaton published the Washington *Daily National Intelligencer*, the *Register of Debates in Congress*, the *Annals of Congress*, and *American State Papers*. Gales served three terms as mayor of Washington City, 1827–1830.

16. Misspelling of the archaic word "compromiting."

17. John P. Heiss

18. Laughlin probably refers to the death of his wife, Mary C. Bass Laughlin, in 1840 and that of his daughters, Cora Kezer and Isabella Laughlin, in 1842.

19. Laughlin wrote his postscript in the upper left-hand corner of the first page of his letter.

FROM J. G. M. RAMSEY

My Dear Sir — Mecklenburg Oct. 28. 1844

I attended the speaking at Trundles[1] on the 25th & handed your letter to A. V. Brown[2] & he directed me to be very sure to tell some friend the condition of things in Jefferson County that it may be distinctly known & understood at Nashville when the votes are counted out there.

Major Newman[3] was at the county election last spring re-elected Sheriff of that county gave bond & security which were approved & he duly sworn into office, & has continued to perform its duties till the first Monday in this month at the county court *ten* magistrates being present out of *thirty* they pretended to remove him & elected over him a new sheriff to whom they directed Newman to hand over his official papers, Jail-key &c. He refused to do so, holds on to his office & has taken the necessary measures for holding the election 5th Nov. The new sheriff intends also to open a poll at each precinct. Our friends have been advised & have determined to vote at *each poll*. The Whigs generally say Newman is not sheriff & as he is said to have turned out on account of his change to Democracy it is believed that party efforts will be made to get them all to vote at the poll of Parrott[4] the new Sheriff. Newman has taken counsel from a Whig Attorney who has advised him to continue to act. He has since his reelection avowed himself a Democrat & it is believed that is the reason why he has been superseded. This circumstance has disaffected a great many Whigs who had voted for him & some that had not, & Brown believes we will not be beaten more than five hundred votes there. But some one (the Secretary of State?) has to compare the returns. Whose poll will be counted? Our friends have taken the best advice & are making every exertion, & using every caution to have their votes counted. If the poll of Newman is the correct & lawful one & I cant see how it can be otherwise the Whig vote will be vastly diminished. I promised him to give the case as it stands so that if any thing is to be done at Nashville, they may be prepared to act in time.

Brown is the best speaker decidedly I have heard during the canvass, & made a decided impression wherever he has been. A. R. Crozier, who has accompanied him the whole round & has assisted him occasionally says so. They were met Friday by a delegation from Louisville, were to breakfast Saturday at Maryville & be joined there by a large body of voters & go on immediately after to Louisville to the speaking. They will have had quite a crowd. Brown told me after he had read your letter that he would certainly be at the Meeting (was it at Shelbyville?) in time on the 2nd, to take part in the discussion there.

I have no advices from McClung—presume he has certainly determined to come. Our friends are much encouraged every where I hear from & are relaxing nothing from their exertions. A barbacue 30 & 31 at Panther Springs will close the campaign in that quarter. Haynes & Johnson[5] both to be there.

J. G. M. Ramsey

P.S. Since writing the above yours of the 22 have been received.[6] The notice for public speaking for Turney & Brown I will forward by mail to day to Kingston but he will be at Shelbyville even if it should not reach him, & the other suggestions have all been attended to. I add this post-script principally to say that I have just received a note from A. R. Crozier requesting me to write that the paper published in Lincoln, the Fayetteville Democrat or Spartan[7] has still got the *electoral ticket wrong*. We have all written & cant get it corrected. It may loose us at least a thousand votes. Crozier also wishes me to have some one at Nashville apprised of the state of things in Jefferson county. I have detailed it above, but I will write to you more fully giving the latest aspect of the case so soon as he returns from Panther Springs. He starts in the morning & will see & confer with every friend we have at that barbacue. He is prepared to give wise & safe counsel. If Newman is not *enjoined* as is threatened we will get 5 or 600 votes & if he is the vote may be even larger. J.G.M.R.

ALS. DLC–JKP. Addressed to Columbia and marked "Private."

1. Reference is to Trundell's Cross Roads.

2. Reference probably is to a letter from Polk to Aaron V. Brown of October 21, 1844. Letter not found.

3. Benjamin F. Newman served three terms as Jefferson County sheriff, 1840–46.

4. M. J. Parrott served one term as sheriff of Jefferson County, 1846–48.

5. Andrew Johnson.

6. Letters not found.

7. Not identified further.

FROM JULIUS W. BLACKWELL

Athens, Tenn. October 29, 1844

Blackwell writes that Rowles and P. B. Anderson[1] will probably meet McClung in Chattanooga. He assures Polk that the "Democrats are wide awake and full of hope, and are active." Acknowledging the lack of his own appointments, Blackwell tells Polk that he has met the Whigs at county militia musters. He believes that his most effectual service has been to frank and distribute "documents sent me by thousands from Washington City and from Nashville." He reports optimistically on Polk's chances in East Tennessee.

ALS. DLC–JKP. Addressed to Columbia.

1. An Athens lawyer, Pierce B. Anderson represented McMinn County as a Democrat in the Tennessee House from 1843 to 1847.

TO CLEMENT C. CLAY

My Dear Sir Columbia Oct. 29th 1844

I learn from *Majr Lewis*[1] who returned to day that you will be at Chappel Hill on thursday. I learn further that two Whig orators[2] of this town were in that part of the country on saturday last, and misrepresented my votes on the *Pension Bill.*[3] *Mr. Hancock*[4] will deliver this note to you, as also the *Journal of Congress*, containing my votes, and I must ask you to correct the misrepresentation. On page 793–4, you will find my vote recorded in favour of the Bill, which passed and which is now the law, under which the old-soldiers have ever since, and now draw their pensions. I voted for the Bill but the Journal shows that *John Bell*, and *Daniel L. Barringer*,[5] both now Whig candidates for Elector, in this State, (the latter for this District) voted against it. These men and their party now falsely charge me with doing what they themselves did. You can turn the tables upon them and put them to defending.

You will see on page 792 that a motion was made to extend the pension to all who served *three* instead of *six* months. The Previous question was moved, the effect of which (if carried) was to cut off the amendment. I voted against ordering the main question, that is to preserve the amendment. The Previous question was carried & I voted for the Bill. At page 820 the Bill was finally passed, without the yeas and nays being taken.

The fraud and deception which these Whig orators practice on the people is this. At that Session, there were two Pension Bills before Congress, the one originating in the House & the other in the Senate. The House Bill was taken up first. Pending its consideration a motion was made to include the defenders of the frontier in the Indian wars: I voted for this amendment but it was rejected. You voted with me. (See Journal page 679.) A motion was made to include the soldiers who fought at King's Mountain & Guilford Court House. I voted for this amendment but it was rejected. You voted with me (See Journal page 679, 680). A motion was made to include the Widows of those who fell in battle. I voted for this amendment, but it was rejected. You voted with me (See Journal page 689). All these amendments being rejected, I voted against the Bill, & so did you, and so did *John Bell* & every member of the Tennessee delegation except *Arnold*[6] (See Journal page 691). This was on the 1st of May 1832. On the 24th of May 1832, the Senate's Bill, was taken up. I voted for it. It passed, and is now the law of the land. Now these Whig orators quote the vote on the 1st of May 1832, on the House Bill and take special care to suppr[ess][7] my vote for the Senate Bill that passed on t[he] 24th May 1832, about three weeks afterwards. I wish you would take pains to make this plain & to expose them. You can truly state that both *Clay & Frelinghuysen*,[8] voted against extending the Pension system to the Indian fighters &c., whereas I voted in favour of such extension. If you speak at Cedar Springs on thursday evening as Majr Lewis informs me you will, I will be obliged to you to make the same exposition and then deliver the Journal back to Mr Hancock to bring to me.

JAMES K. POLK

ALS. NcD. Addressed to Chapel Hill, Tenn., and marked "*Private*."

1. Micajah G. Lewis operated a tavern in Columbia; previously he had held a part-interest in the *Columbia Observer*, 1834–35.

2. Not identified further.

3. See Cave Johnson to Polk, September 4, 1844.

4. Probably Stephen M. Hancock, a Democrat and Polk supporter from Maury County.

5. A lawyer from Raleigh, N.C., Barringer served as a Democrat in the North Carolina House, 1813–14 and 1819–22, and in the U.S. House, 1826–35; he moved to Bedford County, Tennessee, in 1836. Having changed to the Whig Party, Barringer lost his 1839 Congressional race to Harvey M. Watterson. Elected to one term in the Tennessee House, 1843–45, Barringer served in that session as House Speaker.

6. Formerly a resident of Knoxville, Thomas D. Arnold moved to Greene County, where he practiced law; he won election to two terms in the U.S. House, 1831–33 and 1841–43.

7. One word here and one below obliterated by sealing wax oil.

8. Selected by the Whigs as Henry Clay's running mate in 1844, Theodore Frelinghuysen of New Jersey served in numerous positions of public trust: state attorney general, 1817–29; U.S. senator, 1829–35; mayor of Newark, 1837–38; chancellor of New York University, 1839–50; and president of Rutgers College, 1850–62. Active in many private organizations, he served as vice-president of the American Colonization Society and as vice-president of the American Sunday School Union.

FROM JOHN McKEON

My Dear Sir, New York Oct 29. 1844

This week opens brightly for the Democratic cause in this City. Last night at Tammany Hall we had an immense meeting & I addressed the immense multitude and gave them a statement of my journey to the West, my interview with Genl Jackson & told them of Jackson's intense anxiety for your success. I asked them if they were willing to allow Clay to triumph over the Old Hero. Were they ready to disappoint Andrew Jackson in the last wish expressed by him to me that New York should not desert Polk & Dallas. You should have heard the shouts the cries of "we will not." I told them the truth of the Roorback fiction & also stated that I had held in my own hands the commission of your ancestor.[1] The greatest spirit prevailed and every thing augured well. Although the rain fell in torrents there was not only a large meeting but a great procession. Another movement is a meeting of the Native Americans. I send you the Herald from which you will learn that upwards of 1500 Natives proclaim their determination to go for Polk & Dallas.[2] At a meeting of the Executive Committee of the Natives a few evenings since a resolution was passed that in the procession which is to take place the 5th Nov.[3] no banner making any allusion to either of the Presidential candidates shall be borne. This shows they will not coalesce. We have every hope & belief that the Democratic Natives will sustain our Presidential candidates. Our people are ready to make any sacrifices to save our Presidential electors and I am prepared to see every thing lost except them and the Governor. I congratulate myself on the advice I gave you some months since. The opposite course to that so wisely pursued by you might have kept the natives against us. As it is they will go with us on President and desert us on almost every thing else.

I have no doubt but Pennsylvania will go right. I am aware that the Whigs are working hard to produce a change but it will be in vain. The Whigs here have raised a large sum I hear but our friends have also been making subscriptions and I understand have succeeded thus far very well. The Whigs will have a grand procession on tomorrow evening.[4] They have called a meeting of the Whig lawyers with Dudley Selden[5] & others in the head to join the procession. I have in connexion with others called a meeting of the Democratic lawyers for the purpose of countering with our procession.[6]

Let not our friends be disheartened. I feel confident of the "great hereafter."

JOHN MCKEON

ALS. DLC–JKP. Addressed to Columbia and marked "Private."

1. McKeon probably refers to Ezekiel Polk's commission as a captain in the South Carolina militia during the Revolutionary War.

2. Reference is to an article in the *New York Herald* of October 29, 1844.

3. The Native American party cancelled its November 4th procession because of rain.

4. Details of the Whig procession held in New York City on October 30, 1844, were reported the following day in the *New York Herald*.

5. A New York lawyer, Dudley Selden served one term in the New York House, 1831, and one term in the U.S. House, 1833–34.

6. New York City Democrats held a torchlight procession on the evening of

November 1, 1844; details of their parade were reported the following day in the *New York Herald*.

FROM SYLVESTER S. SOUTHWORTH[1]

New York City. October 29, 1844

Southworth writes that Polk can count on receiving New York's electoral vote and notes that there are three thousand names on the Native American party's recent manifesto vowing support for Polk and Dallas.[2] Throughout the campaign he has kept up a constant correspondence with the *Nashville Union* but now plans to change his signature.[3] Southworth believes that the Native American movement has "united the whole adopted population together."

ALS. DLC–JKP. Addressed to Columbia.

1. Employed as an inspector in the New York customs house, Southworth wrote for the *New York Aurora* in 1844; formerly he had served as a Washington City correspondent for newspapers in Baltimore, Philadelphia, and Boston.

2. See John McKeon to Polk, October 29, 1844.

3. Southworth corresponded regularly with the *Nashville Union* beginning on June 18, 1844; he wrote under the pseudonym, "John St. Tammany." In the *Union* of November 9, 1844, "St. Tammany" announced the conclusion of his correspondence and introduced his successor, "R.R.R."

TO CAVE JOHNSON

[Dear Sir:] [Columbia, Tenn.] October 30, 1844

In the present aspect of probable results in the several States, it has become vastly important that we should carry Tennessee. If possibly we should lose New York, the vote of Tennessee may and probably will decide the contest in the Union. My friends in New York write to me up to the 16th Inst. expressing great confidence that they will carry that State, but they may be mistaken. A powerful effort is now making to induce the *Natives* and *Abolitionists* to unite with the Whig party proper. If this movement is successful and a complete union of these factions with the Whigs shall be effected, the contest in New York will be close and the result doubtful. I think the following states may be put down as reasonably sure for the Democracy—to wit—Maine, N. Hampshire, Pennsylvania, Virginia, S. Carolina, Georgia, Alabama, Mississippi, Louisiana, Arkansas, Missouri, Illinois, Michigan, and Indiana. These States give 134 electoral votes, and if we carry Little Delaware (for which our chances are best) we will have 137 electoral votes, or within one vote of enough to make our election, it requiring 138 electoral votes to make choice by the Colleges.

Our opponents must carry all of the five closely contested States of Connecticut, New Jersey, Maryland, N. Carolina, and Ohio, and also both New York and Tennessee, to enable them to succeed. If they lose any one of them, they will be defeated. They think they will carry the five first States named. Of New York and Tennessee they have more doubt.

How vastly important therefore is it, that we shall carry Tennessee. We *can* and we *must* save her, but to do it will require our whole energy, and the unceasing labour of every man whether he be a debater or not, every hour until the election is over. My information satisfies me the State is now safe, but by a close vote, and if we lose her it will be by the superior vigilence of our opponents, or by fraudulent and illegal voting. There is great danger of double voting and of imported Whig votes from Kentucky. Two or more active men should be appointed to watch every poll and challenge suspected persons who offer to vote. Let every man who offers to vote out of the Civil District in which he resides—be sworn that he has not voted at any other place and that he will not offer to vote at any other place in that election. This is very important and especially in the border and strong Whig Counties. For the few remaining days before the election, I hope that our leading friends at Clarksville will mount their horses and ride through Robertson and Montgomery and have these suggestions carried out. Let our friends ride on Saturday and Monday through every [...][1] District, see every Democratic voter, and urge him to attend the polls. Let not Democrat, not one remain at home on the day of the election. I make these suggestions to you because I am deeply impressed with their importance, and because if they are observed throughout the State, we must I think carry the State by a handsome majority.

James K. Polk

P.S. After writing this letter, it occurred to me that you might be absent at the Gallatin meeting on Friday, and therefore I address it jointly to yourself and Mr. Garland.

PL. Published in *THM*, I, p. 253. Probably addressed jointly to Cave Johnson and Hudson S. Garland in Gallatin, Tenn., and marked "*Confidential*."

1. Bracketed ellipsis previously supplied.

FROM KENEDY LONERGAN[1]

Cincinnati, Ohio. October 30, 1844

Lonergan reports that John Y. Mason[2] thinks Virginia is safe. Lonergan explains that Ohio Democrats lost their recent state elections by about a thousand votes because the "Democratic liberty men" did not vote and the "liberty Whigs" did. He assures Polk that no Liberty party men will vote for a slaveholder for president; thus he predicts a Democratic victory in the state. Lonergan claims that of the 480 people in Cincinnati who have become naturalized citizens since the last election "19 out of 20 of them are Democrats."

ALS. DLC–JKP. Addressed to Columbia.

1. Kenedy Lonergan was an Irish construction contractor on the Hiwassee Railroad, 1837–39.

2. John Y. Mason served as a member of the U.S. House, 1831–1837; as U.S. district judge for the eastern district of Virginia, 1837–1844; as secretary of the navy, 1844–45 and 1846–49; and as U.S. attorney general, 1845–46.

TO JAMES HAMILTON, JR.

My Dear Sir: Columbia Tenn. Oct 31st 1844

I had the pleasure some days ago, to receive your very acceptable and friendly letter of the 13th Inst[1] giving returns of the Georgia election, for which I thank you. I had learned from numerous other sources, the fact which you state, that Mr Calhoun and his friends had given a very cordial support to our ticket, throughout the canvass, and need not say to you that I am much gratified that is so. A few days more will decide the great contest in which we are engaged, and it would be useless to indulge in speculations as regards the probable result. I will say however, that our prospects for success, as I have them from my numerous correspondents, are of a cheering character. My friends in New York write to me most confidently that they will carry that state. Great efforts are however now being made by the Federal leaders to unite the *Natives & Abolitionists* with the *Whig party proper*. If these efforts shall be successful, and a complete union shall be effected between these factions and the Whigs, the contest in New York will be close and the result doubtful. If we carry New York the contest will be settled. If we loose her, and carry any one of the six closely contested states of Connecticut, New Jersey, Maryland, N. Carolina, Ohio or Tennessee, I think we will still succeed. All our information in this state justifies the confident belief that we will carry her, though by a close vote.

I shall be pleased My Dear Sir: to hear from you again, whenever your leisure may permit.

James K. Polk

ALS. ScCleU–JCC. Addressed to Savannah, Ga. and marked "Private."

1. See James Hamilton, Jr., to Polk, October 13, 1844.

FROM SILAS WRIGHT, JR.

My Dear Sir, Canton 31 October 1844

Your very acceptable favor of the 19th[1] reached me this morning. I hasten to give you a very brief answer, so that the results of which I speak may not go before my letter.

My position is truly one which I desired most extremely to avoid, but the command of my friends ended my resistance. I will not pretend to believe that I am not fairly popular with the democracy of this State, and with the true and faithful portion I have no doubt I shall receive the most faithful, and a very cordial support, but with the untrue portion, those whose politics hang upon Banks, canals, rail roads, and other like local, and personal, and corporate interests, I never was, and never expect to be a favorite. I shall not, therefore, add the strength to the combined tickets which some of my too partial friends hoped and believed, and yet I am satisfied I shall be as well supported as any candidate could be in this contest. I shall be disappointed if you do not get more votes in the State than I do, and for the simple reason that these local interests do not touch you. Yet I *believe* we shall both get a majority over our whig competitors, though not large. Our contest is such an one as I have never seen before, and many degrees are added to its desperation every day now, as the time for the trial so nearly approaches.

If you have noticed our cause on the Tariff, you will understand me, when I tell you I think we have gained rather than lost by that question. We have treated the matter fairly and frankly and honestly, and addressed the intelligence and judgements and personal knowledge, observation, and experience of all classes of our citizens upon it. Our greatest obstacle, at the start, was to explain away, and remove from their minds, certain arbitrary and ill chosen terms, such as "anti-tariff," "free trade,"and the like, and to define what is in fact "protection," in a legitimate sense, and what "prohibition" in a practical sense. Where we could get these *terms* understood, we could take up the present law, and show its defects, inequalities and partialities, and our farmers would listen to us; and I assure you: so far as I was allowed personally to observe, they listened, not merely with a deep interest, but with a will.

Upon the other questions our course was what it has always been, and what is the course of our friends every where. And I am not mistaken when I tell you we were driving the whigs out of the field of argument and into despair, when the Pa. election came off. The moment the news from the city and county of Philadelphia spread over our State, the whole scene changed with the rapidity of lightning.

The whigs had been courting and tampering with our abolitionists before, and Cassius M. Clay was moving about the State, with very indifferent success, or rather with very questionable utility to his friend and Kinsman.[2] The success of the coalition with the natives in Philadelphia awakened new hope and new life in the whole party, and from that moment coalitions form their only hope, and they are openly and shamelessly attempted with every faction, every interest, every prejudice, and even every fanaticism to be found within our wide limits. A coalition with a small band of "Millerites"[3] in one town in this county came to my knowledge yesterday.

To guard against the influences of these movements I assure you every thing has been done, and is doing, which honest men can do. There is no negligence in any quarter so far as I can gain information, and as I verily believe, and if we are overpowered, it will be because we cannot guard ourselves against the corrupt and corrupting efforts of an unprincipled party.

I rejoice to say that my latest information from the city is more favorable than I had any right to hope a week ago. We shall loose our legislative and congress tickets there, because the Natives have made their nominations and will adhere to them, and the whigs will abandon their own tickets and vote for the Native Candidates to beat us; but our best men say that the Democratic Natives declare they will make no coalitions and that they will support the Democratic Electoral and State tickets. A single correspondent[4] yet expresses apprehension, and upon grounds which I fear have too much foundation. He says there is the most constant intercourse between the Natives of New York and Philadelphia, and that committees pass almost daily from city to city. He fears they may act in concert upon these points, and that if the Philadelphians go for Clay the New Yorkers will follow, while he says, if the Philadelphia democratic Natives shall, tomorrow, go for you, we are safe, but he feared that point was not determined when he wrote me, on the 25th. Tomorrow must decide that.

My opinion of this state is that we are safe without the city, but that, if the city comes in with from 5000 to 8000 against us, like Philadelphia at the State election, we shall be in the most imminent danger. I may say in desperate circumstances. I think the city will not do worse than to be neutralized, and yet while I write a different direction may be giving thus, which will astound us like the news from Philadelphia, after their 'state election.'

The conduct of the whigs, for the last few days, induce the hope that they have ceased to expect the aid from the city they so confidently counted on two weeks ago, for *money* seems now to be their sole dependance, and it flows like water. A purse of $180.000 is said to have been brought from Boston, within ten days, and letters received today tell me that the distributing agents are on the wing to every quarter of this State. We fear the effect of this, but not so much as the threatened coalition in the city. Whether this purse comes from the manufacturers, or the British Bondholders, we do not yet learn.

I have serious fears for Pennsylvania, if the Natives in the city and county of Philadelphia stick to Clay. Our friends in that State have poised themselves upon the present tariff law, and dispute with the whigs which party is most friendly to it. If all had done this we should have been beaten out of sight, and I cannot but fear the effect then when the electoral election is alone involved. Indeed I have a very alarming letter from *Henry Horn*,[5] and when I find him alarmed I conclude there is danger of the Key Stone. Tomorrow will settle it, but at this moment I feel about as confident of Ohio as Pa. In the former State our friends are fighting upon their own principles, while, in the latter we fight upon the enemy's ground. I never could make our Democracy fight well in such a position. Yet we feel quite confident of the vote of Pa. after all, and hope strongly for that of Ohio; and yet all say to ourselves, and feel and act, that the Battle is not and cannot be safe without our vote and that we intend to give. One thing I can truly say to you, and that is that I never have seen a time when I am compelled to feel, let the result be as it may, so perfectly satisfied that our democracy has done, and is doing, its whole duty.

SILAS WRIGHT

ALS. DLC–JKP. Addressed to Columbia.

1. Letter not found.

2. Reference is to Henry Clay.

3. A self-educated preacher from New York, William Miller attracted a band of followers who accepted his predictions that the Christian Messiah would return to Earth sometime between March 1843 and March 1844; subsequently Miller recalculated his prediction and fixed the "Second Coming" at a date no later than October 22, 1844. The following year the Millerites formed the Adventist Church.

4. Not identified further.

5. A Philadelphia hardware merchant, Henry Horn served as a Democrat in the U.S. House for one term 1831–33.

NOVEMBER

FROM GEORGE M. DALLAS

No. 15

My Dear Sir, [Philadelphia] 1 Nov. 1844

Our time for decisive action has arrived. I believe all that could be done by a noble party has been done. We have nothing to fear but fraud, and against that every precaution which ingenuity and zeal could devise, has been taken. If you do not obtain the vote of Pennsylvania, it will be owing to treachery in a certain quarter, of which we have had vague and forewarning hints, only within the Past 24 hours. I regard the story as unfounded, and as involving an accusation too base to be repeated without proof. You will have seen that the Kentucky rumor about Gov. Porter was untrue.[1] He has emphatically disputed it by a short letter published at Pittsburg in which he avows his belief that your election is "*absolutely certain*."[2] I return to you by this mail the letter of *Col. Johnson's brother* to Col. Armstrong.

Our city is crowded with New-Yorkers and Baltimoreans, anxious to report to their respective homes the signs of the day. Our native Americans *profess* to maintain their allegiance to the democracy. We have pursued a course, since the 8th of October, calculated to win them right again. In the city proper, the whig government may seduce many of them by promises of employment and petty office. New-York and Ohio, I believe, irreversibly secure to you. Indeed, I see no cause any where for changing the opinion expressed in my last,[3] that your election is achieved. I can send you nothing by this mail, but the next will convey the first great development of the electoral struggle.

G. M. DALLAS

ALS. DLC–JKP. Addressed to Columbia.

1. See Polk to George M. Dallas, October 21, 1844.
2. David Porter's "letter published at Pittsburg" is not identified further.
3. See George M. Dallas to Polk, October 16, 1844.

FROM JOHN W. P. McGIMSEY

Baton Rouge, La. November 1, 1844

McGimsey describes a lively Democratic mass meeting held at Baton Rouge. Enthusiasm runs high even among the Democratic ladies. When a Whig lady says "that if She had a 100 thousand dollars She would be willing to bet it that Mr. Clay would be elected" McGimsey's wife[1] answers, "we all know that you have not 100,000 dollars to bet; but you have an excellent house Servant–will you madam bet your house Servant against another as good, & equal Value." McGimsey predicts that Louisiana will go for Polk.

ALS. DLC–JKP. Addressed to Columbia.

1. Rowena Jossey married John W. P. McGimsey on November 9, 1821.

FROM GANSEVOORT MELVILLE

Friday
New York November 1st 1844

My dear Sir

Your welcome favor of the 21st[1] reached me in due course of mail and would have been replied to at once were it not that under date of the 26th ult I had mailed to your address a long and very full letter covering in the main the ground suggested in yours of the 21st.

Your suggestion as to the danger to be apprehended in case an alliance should be consummated between the Whigs and Native Americans meets precisely the view which I have earnestly entertained since my return. A full conviction of the great importance of frustrating this movement has induced me to give a nearly undivided attention for the last ten days to the prevention of this threatened and threatening coalition. Others have labored assiduously for the same end. Our efforts have been thwarted to some extent by one or two ill-advised movements which those who had them in hand absolutely refused to give up, spurred on by a desire for temporary prominence and local notoriety, and unwilling or unable to see that no good end can possibly be accomplished and much harm may be done by a certain course of action in the present state of affairs. For instance a political meeting *exclusively* of "French citizens" being the first ever called in this city was held night before last; at which after a speech in the French language from Major Davezac[2] it was gravely resolved to support Polk and Dallas. All well informed men knew this before. Of this accession of not less than 750 or 800 votes we were all well aware. Under any circumstances in *this election* they would be polled to a man on our side. Not one individual vote was to be gained by such a demonstration. It was therefore impolitic. Besides in point of principle it will scarcely bear examination. These gentlemen are either French citizens or American citizens. If the latter their right to meet in reference to American politics as Frenchmen is to say the least questionable, and by so doing the popular mind which in the Atlantic cities is already inflamed to an extraordinary degree on the subject of an alleged and increasing so called "foreign influence" is needlessly irritated still further. The same remarks will in the main apply to a very numerous and well appointed "German Democratic" procession which in defiance of a heavy storm of rain came off five or six nights since. Such movements can only tend to perpetuate and exasperate feelings which if suffered to continue and increase may yet prove a fruitful source of turbulence and evil, and which every good citizen must desire to see allayed. Allow me to say in conclusion that everything honorable and possible will be done to prevent so formidable a coalition from taking place. The aspect on this point is certainly no worse than it was on the 26th inst and probably somewhat better. By to-day's mail private letters from various points in the state indicate great sanguineness as to the result. As far as I can observe this feeling for a week past has been steadily progressive.

The suggestions made by you in regard to danger to be apprehended from fraudulent voting on the part of our opponents have been borne constantly in mind, and have been acted upon in a manner which will prove a great bar to anything of this sort except upon a most limited scale.

Saturday m[ornin]g Nov 2nd

The news from Philadelphia City and County which is just in & by which it appears that Clay leaves the City & County with but 4000 majority, instead of the 6000 which Markle had in October, and the 7 or 8000 which leading Whigs confidently claimed until a very late hour last evening, has cast a damper on the Whigs and elated our rank and file to a most unusual degree. The Democratic procession of last evening was a surprising turn-out. It was a magnificent demonstration of the *man-power*—full of life, energy and enthusiasm. Our voters are eager for the contest. The Whig procession of Wednesday last was far less numerous but more costly and imposing in its splendor. It was an exhibition of the strength of the Money-power. Ours, of that which after all controls the wealth, the masses.

The last rally of the Democracy of the powerful Whig county of Essex in New Jersey takes place at Newark this eveng. I leave town in a few moments to attend it. Our friends in New Jersey seem to be making a silent but most determined effort to retrieve the defeat of October. On the evening preceding the election here I may write again. Meantime with my most respectful regards to Mrs Polk and remembrances to other friends....

GANSEVOORT MELVILLE

P.S. By this mail I send to yr address to-day's Tribune and also one of the Native American prints.[3]

ALS. DLC–JKP. Addressed to Columbia and marked "Private & *Confidential.*"

1. Polk's letter has not been found.
2. Auguste D'Avezac.
3. Enclosures not found.

FROM ALEXANDER BEST[1]

Dear Sir

Danville Pa Nov 2d 1844

I have the pleasure to send you the results of the Election in Columbia and Northumberland County.[2] The unconquerable Democracy of those two noble counties have done their duty notwithstanding every mean that could be resorted to was caried out by threats bribes & persuasion.

You will observe that I have marked Bloom, Franklin & Mahoning Townships. In these Townships all our large Iron Works are located. The propriators led up all there men for which they had prepared red Tickets so that There men could not deceeve them. The Whigs said Columbia County should be redeemed and no longer disgraced by being a Democratic County. How successful they have been the returns will shew.

Hon David Petriken[3] who has been confined to his room for 18 months was yesterday carried to the court house by his neighbours on a bed and voted. He said it was one of the last desirse he had to gratify to be able to assist to defeat Clay.

ALEXR. BEST

P.S. Dr Petriken sends his best respects to you.

ALS. DLC–JKP. Addressed to Columbia.

1. Best served as register and recorder of Columbia County, Penn., from 1836 to 1839 and as postmaster of Danville from 1842 to 1849.

2. Enclosure not found.

3. A physician in Dannville, Penn., Petrikin won election as a Democrat to two terms in the U.S. House, 1837–41.

FROM CAVE JOHNSON

Dear Sir, Clarksville 2nd Nov. 1844

We have all arrangements made as far as practicable to prevent frauds in our election, particularly at the precincts near the line. We shall do better every where than in Montgomery.

I recd yesterday a letter from Lund Washington,[1] with the enclosure which I send,[2] desiring it to be presented with his respects to Mrs. Polk. He says, they have *certain* information, that no combination can be made between the Natives & Whigs in NY further than for Congress & the legislature. Several other letters from NY confirm it. Wright, Marcy & many of our leaders believe that we can defeat all possible combinations but express the opinion that none can be made with the abolitionists. I enclose you a hand-bill circulated all over Ky.[3] It shews their alarm as well as rascality. It was enclosed me by Hardwicke,[4] who *thinks* he will return by the election. I do not understand, why Doct. Duncan & Jewett are not at home.

I have had for the last week a painful attack of rheumatism, tho I have not been confined & it yet troubles me much.

We were blessed this morning with the birth of another son & my wife[5] is doing well.

C. Johnson

ALS. DLC–JKP. Addressed to Columbia.

1. Polk appointed Lund Washington justice of the peace for Washington County, D.C., in 1847.

2. Enclosure not found.

3. Enclosure not found.

4. Johnson's reference probably is to Jonathan P. Hardwicke. A tavern keeper in Dickson County, Hardwicke served as a Democrat in the Tennessee Senate from 1837 until 1843.

5. Cave and Elizabeth Dortch Brunson Johnson had three children who survived infancy. James Hickman and Thomas Dickson Johnson were born in 1840 and 1842, respectively. Polk Grundy Johnson was born on November 2, 1844.

FROM ALEXANDER JONES[1]

241 8th Avenue
Dear Sir New York Nov. 2d 1844

I sent you a copy of the Journal of Commerce of the 31 Ult.[2] which gave what appeared to be a fair exposition of the course the Native Americans will pursue in the election next week. I send you another to day, with some extraordinary things in it![3]

There is no question but *Clay* since, he has said he would write no more letters, has written two to the Natives of this City, intended for private circulation among them; in which, he states was the time sufficiently long he would come out openly in favour of their cause, and, that, he is opposed to the present naturalization laws! But, as the publication of these letters would be highly offensive to Naturalized Citizens, the Whig portion of the Natives only make a private use of them among such as can be worked upon. This intrigue may defeat us in the city, but we shall struggle hard for victory, and fight manfully to the last, combatting as far as possible fraud and corruption at every point.

The Democrats had one of the most numerous and splendid processions last evening, ever seen in this, or probably in any other city. It far exceeded the boasted Whig affair, both in numbers, & brilliancy.[4] The streets, houses and windows of the 6 or 8 miles of streets, through which it passed, were thronged by 1 or 200.000 spectators! A great many houses were brilliantly illuminated, and the air made bright by the continual display of fire works amidst which splendid rockets were darting in every direction!

Such a scene has never been witnessed in New York before.

Next Tuesday, we go into Action, and God grant us Victory. In much haste....

ALEXR. JONES

ALS. DLC–JKP. Addressed to Columbia.

1. Author, physician, and journalist, Jones was born the son of a North Carolina planter. He practiced medicine in Mississippi before removing permanently in 1840 to New York City, where he wrote regularly for the *New York Journal of Commerce*. Quick to grasp the potential use of the telegraph in news distribution, Jones organized a cooperative press among several American cities and served as the first general agent of the New York Associated Press.
2. Letter not found.
3. Enclosure not found.
4. See John McKeon to Polk, October 29, 1844.

FROM JOHN McKEON

2. P.M.
My Dear Sir, New York Novr. 2. 1844

I read your letter of the 21st[1] two days since and have delayed writing until this moment with the view of giving you the result of our Torchlight demonstration[2] and the effect of the Philadelphia news. Our display last night was magnificent beyond any description. It struck terror into the Whigs who all admit that as to numbers it far exceeded any thing ever seen in this City. I saw Mr Butler and all our leading men out. These men are not in the habit of joining in processions. I never until last night took part in any such affair but as it was understood that it was to be a sort of display of strength I with the rest went into the movement. The affair has given great hopes to our friends. If the demonstration shows any thing it must be the premonition of a large democratic majority in this City but for certainty sake I still keep to my estimate of 1500 to 2000 majority.

But if the Whigs were astonished last night at our review they have been astounded this morning with the news from Philadelphia. There they expected not only to hold the majority Markle received in the City & County but also to increase their majority. The returns show a falling off and the effect of the Pennsylvania returns now coming in will be very great in our favor not only on this City but in the state. Our friends dispatched a locomotive printing office in one of the steam boats up the North River this morning to scatter the good news through the river counties & through the state. The Boat went off with the first news and will carry good tidings to our people who will vote on Tuesday next. We have been active in spreading throughout the state the impression that we have carried Pennsylvania. To show you that the Whigs believe we have been successful I will state that I saw a bet offered of $100 to a prominent man of their party on Pennsylvania being Democratic and he refused to take it. The consequence of the Philadelphia decrease certainly increases our prospects in this City. I have reason to believe that the Whigs expected the whole Native force in Philadelphia to stand by their candidate Clay. In this they have been disappointed & I should not be surprised if they now refuse a cordial coalition with the Natives here. I have heard some of them this morning complain bitterly of the Philadelphia Natives and shows sympathies against our New York Natives. There is no doubt however the result does not help the union they wish to perfect. Let them do their utmost I sincerely believe we are safe on our electoral ticket. The feeling of the party have been thoroughly aroused & from all quarters of the state I see individuals of different political opinions. There is but one opinion I can come to and that is of our triumph. The Western part of this state will not do any thing as well for the Whigs as it did in 1840.

Our friends are active in watching the movements of the Whigs in their efforts to defraud us—Double Tickets so ingeniously put together as to drop apart (& make two votes instead of one) when deposited in the ballot box have been discovered & notice given of them in our papers.

I will write you on Monday (the day preceding our election) the impressions and expectations of our people.

John McKeon

ALS. DLC–JKP. Addressed to Columbia and marked "Private."

1. Letter not found.

2. On the evening of November 1st a Dorrite delegation from Rhode Island led by Martin Luther, members of New York's Empire Club and German Democratic Association, and numerous local fire engine companies, ward associations, and craft unions marched through the streets of New York City with banners and bands of music; about 12,500 persons participated in the torchlight procession.

FROM SYLVESTER S. SOUTHWORTH

My Dear Sir, New York Nov. 2d 1844

I have the honor to inform you that the Democracy of the City and County of New York, turned out *en-massee* last night, and numberd in its ranks as nearly as could be estimated, sixty thousand souls. The procession was upwards of three miles long; and, before the gala had done, it was encreased to seven miles in length.

The events of the last twenty four hours, have, I believe satisfied the Whigs that Mr Clay has been *already* defeated. The intellgence we received to day for the City and County of Philadelphia, gives us full assurance that we have carried Pennsylvania.

That New York, will follow next, I have not a doubt, nor have I a single doubt of your Election. As early as June last, I sat the thing down as decided in your favor. If I am disappointed in this instance, and, if by any possbility the Whigs should succeed I will forever abandon political speculation. But they are defeated, and there can be no doubt of it.

S. S. Southworth

ALS. DLC–JKP. Addressed to Columbia.

FROM DAVID T. DISNEY

Dr Sir Cincinnati 3 Nov. 1844

I regret to be compelled this morning to confirm the apprehensions which I expressed to you yesterday in relation to this state. Ohio has gone for Clay by probably about 5000. I am determined however if our friends here will back me to contest the vote upon the ground that the statutes of our state have disfranchised tens of thousands of legal voters under our constitution. Of course I shall need strong support but I am willing to make the effort and I am honestly convinced that I am right in the legal opinion and that the vote ought to be rejected as having been cast in opposition to the fundamental law regulating it.

I learn that C. M. Clay has just arrived in the City and has advised the Whigs to bet freely on Pennsylvania. They are acting upon his advise.

D. T. DISNEY

ALS. DLC–JKP. Addressed to Columbia.

FROM JOHN P. HEISS

My Dear Sir Nashville Nov 3rd 1844

The great contest ere this has been fought in Pennsylvania and Ohio and I anticipate a most glorious result.

The news from those states for the last few days has been indeed gratifying; and, I have no doubt but everything will result in a manner satisfactory to our most sanguine friends.

The last letter of Gov. Jones,[1] written to have effect in Pennsylvania has fallen *still-born* by the publication of another letter written from this place on the 3rd of Oct to counteract a plot we believed at that time to be brewing by our opponents. *Harris* penned a letter for the Globe,[2] of which, I took a copy and forwarded them to my friends in different parts of Pennsylvania. The corresponding committee of Philadelphia embodied this letter in an address, and have had it published in *english* and *german* and circulated by thousands and tens of thousands.

Jones' letter was published a few days afterwards, and I am informed by Jno. M. Read Esq[3] that the publication of our letter by the Democratic Corresponding Committee not only counteracted it, but was having a beneficial effect wherever it had been circulated.

I feel confident that we have succeeded in carrying Pennsylvania. My old County—Bucks has done nobly. She is generally Whig by a small majority; but have given Shunk a majority of upwards of 300, and has assisted materially in electing Erdman (Dem)[4] to Congress over the present member M. H. Jenks (Whig).[5] My old friend Hon. Jno. Davis[6] fought the battle most nobly.

Our advice from Ohio Saturday night was most cheering, and lead us to believe we have carried the state by a handsome majority. If we have, Sam Medary deserves a crown of laurels, for he has contested every inch of ground most manfully. Medeary is one of the greatest editors of the age, and I would consider my fortune made if I could procure the services of a man who had one half of his talent and capacity to edit the "Union." So I am going to improve the Union by making it larger etc. etc. I must ask your assistance in procuring some gentleman to take it in charge.

One more sentence in regard to Penna. *I should not be surprised if we get a majority in the county of Philadelphia of One Thousand.*

Your advices in regard to these suppositions, I have no doubt are equally as cheering as my own. In New York, you know it has been very strongly intimated that a coalition was about being entered into by the "Whigs" and "Native Americans." I have received letters daily, for several days, informing me differently. Such an attempt was made, but it failed. On the other hand I am informed that a large majority of the Natives will vote our ticket, and, that the Democrats will drop their ticket for Congress and the assembly in the different districts composing the city of New York and vote for the Natives. As two thirds of the "Native American Party" were originally Democrats I am inclined to believe there is some truth in this information. If such a combination is made by our friends in New York, I shall not blame them much, for the party which professes to be composed of all the honesty and decency, has shown them the example. As Gov. Jones has made himself conspicuous of late by writing letters, our friends in the East have taken up his "Brownlow case" and are making him appear in a beautiful character before his "Silver Pitcher" friends of Philadelphia and New York.[7]

John St. Tamany of the "Union" has given "Slim Jimmy" considerable uneasiness.[8]

JOHN P. HEISS

ALS. DLC–JKP. Addressed to Columbia.

1. James C. Jones' letter to Charles Gibbons of Pennsylvania, dated October 3, 1844, was printed in *Niles' National Register* on October 26, 1844. The purport of Jones' letter was that Polk always had opposed tariff protection and that voters in Pennsylvania should not be led to think otherwise by northern Democrats.

2. J. George Harris' letter, dated October 3, 1844, and printed without attribution, appeared in the *Washington Globe* of October 15, 1844. Harris warned that Pennsylvania Whigs had "plotted" with James C. Jones to gather an impres-

sive collection of signatures from Tennessee Whigs certifying that Tennesseans understood Polk to be an ardent opponent of tariff protection.

3. A lawyer from Philadelphia, John M. Read served in the Pennsylvania House for one term, 1823–24; he was appointed U.S. district attorney for eastern Pennsylvania and served from 1837 until 1841. John Tyler nominated Read to be associate justice of the Supreme Court but the U.S. Senate refused confirmation. Read pursued a private law practice until 1858, when he was elected to the Pennsylvania Supreme Court.

4. A farmer residing in Lehigh County, Jacob Erdman was elected to one term in the Pennsylvania House, 1834–36, and sat in the U.S. House for a single term, 1845–47.

5. A farmer from Bucks County, Penn., Michael H. Jenks served as associate judge of the Court of Common Pleas, 1838–43, before winning election as a Whig to the U.S. House for one term, 1843–45.

6. A merchant and farmer, John Davis rose to the rank of major general in the Pennsylvania militia; he won election as a Democrat to one term in the U.S. House, 1839–41. Polk appointed him surveyor of the port of Philadelphia where he served from 1845 until 1849.

7. On June 6, 1844, Andrew Jackson wrote James C. Jones asking him to verify newspaper accounts of an alledged conversation with William G. Brownlow in which the governor reportedly claimed that Jackson had insisted for personal spite upon the expulsion of a female member of the Hermitage Presbyterian Church. On June 10, 1844, Jones denied all knowledge of the supposed conversation with Brownlow and the supposed incident relative to any female member of the Hermitage congregation. Both letters were published in the *Nashville Union* of October 21, 1844.

8. Writing under the pseudonym, "John St. Tammany," Sylvester S. Southworth commented on James C. Jones' letter to Charles Gibbons of Pennsylvania of October 3, 1844. See the *Nashville Union* of October 30, 1844.

FROM JAMES BUCHANAN

My dear Sir, Lancaster 4 November 1844

I think I may now congratulate both yourself & the Country on your election to the highest & most responsible office in the world. After our glorious victory on Friday last, I can entertain no doubt of the final result. I feel confident that New York will follow in our footsteps, notwithstanding their majority may be greatly reduced, as ours has been, by an unholy union of Native Americans with the Whigs.

Never have there been such exertions made by any party in any state, as the Whigs have made since our Governor's election, to carry the Keystone. They have poured out their money like water; but our Democracy has every where stood firm, except the comparatively few who have been seduced on the Tariff question & those whom the Native American humbug has led away. Immediately after the first election we requested our honest & excellent Governor elect[1] to come East of the mountains & stump it in your favor: & this was no sooner said than done. He produced a powerful impression wherever he went. I attended two mass meetings with him & he made speeches at several other places. In "Old Berks," he gave it to them both in Dutch & English much to their satisfaction.

Whoever has observed with a reflecting eye the progress of parties in this Country must have arrived at the conclusion that there is but one mode of re-uniting & invigorating the Democratic party of the Union & securing its future triumph; and that is, whilst adhering strictly to the ancient land marks of principle, to rely chiefly upon the young, ardent & efficient Democrats who have fought the present battle. These ought not to be forgotten in the distribution of offices. The old office holders generally have had their day & ought to be content. Had Mr. Van Buren been our candidate, worthy as he is, this feeling which every where pervades the Democratic ranks, would have made his defeat as signal as it was in 1840. Clay would most certainly have carried this State against him by thousands; and I firmly believe the result would have been similar even in New York. The Native American party in Philadelphia never could have become so strong, had it not been for the impression which to some extent prevailed, that your patronage would be distributed in that City amongst those called "the old hunkers" by the Democratic masses.

Yours is a grand mission; and I most devoutly trust & believe, that you will fulfil it with glory to yourself & permanent advantage to the Country. Democrats, from year to year, have been dropping off from the party on questions not essentially of a party character. It will be your destiny to call home the wanderers & marshal them again under the ample folds of the Democratic flag. It is thus that the dangerous Whig party will be forever prostrated, & we will commence a new career of glory & usefulness under the guidance of our ancient principles.

From the violence of the Southern papers & some of the Southern Statesmen,[2] I apprehend that your chief difficulty will be on the question of the Tariff. They seem to cling with great tenacity to the horizontal ad valorem duty of the Compromise Act,[3] which independently of the injury inflicted on the Country, would in practice prostrate the Democracy of the middle & northern states in a single year; because it would destroy all our mechanicks who work up foreign materials. If the duty on cloth & ready made clothing were but twenty per cent ad valorem, we should soon have no use for tailors in our large cities & towns. So of shoemakers, hatters etc etc. Foreigners would perform the mechanical labor.

The Tariff ought to have been permanently settled in 1842. That was the propitious moment. With much difficulty, I then prevented myself from being instructed, that I might be free to act according to my own discretion. I proposed to our Southern friends at that time to adopt the Compromise Act as it stood in 1839. The Treasury required fully that amount of duties; whilst such a measure would have saved their consistency. For some time, I thought they would have gladly embraced this proposition which was presented by Mr. C. J. Ingersoll in the House; but at a great caucus of the party, several of the ultras[4] opposed the measure; & the consequence has been the extravagant Tariff of 1842. Had my proposition been adopted, the country would have been just as prosperous as it is at present, and this would have been attributed in the North to that measure as it is now to the existing Tariff. You would then have received a majority of 20,000 in Pennsylvania.

JAMES BUCHANAN

P.S. I find I have omitted to say than when your letter[5] arrived I was absent from home on a political excursion & when I returned it was so near the election that I concluded I would not write till the result was known.

ALS. DLC–JKP. Addressed to Columbia. Published in Moore, ed., *The Works of James Buchanan*, VI, pp. 72–74.

1. Francis R. Shunk.
2. Buchanan probably refers to the Bluffton movement in South Carolina and to Langdon Cheves' letter to the editor of the *Charleston Mercury*.
3. Buchanan's reference is to the Tariff Act of 1833.
4. In a draft of this letter, Buchanan here cancelled words "Mr. Calhoun & his immediate friends" and interlined "several of the ultras." ALS, draft. PHi.
5. See James K. Polk to James Buchanan, October 3, 1844.

FROM ALEXANDER JONES

New York, N.Y. November 4, 1844

Jones reports to Polk that out of desperation the New York Whig newspapers of November 4, 1844, told of a flag in the Democratic procession of November 1, 1844, inscribed with the words, "Americans, They *shall not rule over us*." According to Jones, all of the Whig newspapers plan to carry a letter from Henry Clay on the morning of November 5, 1844, "declaring openly his opposition to the Naturalization laws."[1] Jones believes that since the Whig newspapers of November 4, 1844, "have all come out for Native Americans," there is the possibility of a Native and Whig combination that "will carry a majority of the Assembly and Members of Congress in this City." He predicts that the Democrats will carry the state for Silas Wright, Polk, and Dallas.

ALS. DLC–JKP. Addressed to Columbia.

1. See Alexander Jones to Polk, November 2, 1844.

FROM JOHN K. KANE

My dear Sir, Philada. 4 Nov. 1844

I sent you yesterday[1] by the conductor of the southern train the news which reached us by express some ten minutes before. I was lucky enough to get off the same returns to our friends of the Richmond Enquirer and Globe.[2]

The game, so far as regards Pennsylvania, has now been played out. We have had fraud and falsehood and bribery and forgery to deal with, in all their most dangerous varieties, first as interest and fanaticism and pride and venality could combine them; and I believe that we have won our victory without masking principle or soliciting a faction.

As I think I foretold in my first letter after the nomination,[3] our only real embarassment has proceeded from the Tariff question. Our political guides in this State were to blame for this. They had never met the subject fairly before the people; and when the Convention adjourned, there was no time left for abstract discussion. Your letter[4] happily marked out for us the general ground; and for the rest, each section took counsel of its own discretion. There has not therefore been as much concert of action on this topic as there has been on others. But almost every where, we were forced by the manufacturing Interest to argue the policy of *protection*; and I am convinced, that so far as there was danger in that subject, we have encountered it all. Hereafter, with a little more nerve on the part of our leading men, Pennsylvania may be secured against all risk of being divorced by the Tariff from the Democracy of the Union.

We are assured by all our New York friends that they will do better than we have done. If they do only as well, we may save ourselves the trouble of reading further election returns. Our majority here will not fall much below 7000.

J. K. KANE

ALS. DLC–JKP. Addressed to Columbia.

1. On November 3, 1844, Kane sent Polk the latest Pennsylvania returns. ALS. DLC–JKP.

2. Reference is to the *Richmond Enquirer* and to the Washington *Globe*.

3. In his letter of May 30, 1844, Kane urged Polk to use "dignified reserve" in approaching the tariff question, the only issue on which Pennsylvania Democrats were vulnerable. ALS. DLC–JKP.

4. See Polk to Kane, June 19, 1844.

FROM JOHN McKEON

2 PM

My Dear Sir, New York Novr. 4, 1844

The glorious news from Pennsylvania which comes rolling in by every mail has added to our strength very materially. The Whig papers admit that Clay has lost the state by at least 4000 majority. Our friends are in the highest excitement and they begin the contest with the greatest confidence in the result. The Whigs are desperate. They have lost so much money on Pennsylvania & have risked so much on the result that they will not stop at any thing to effect Clays election. This morning their papers are loud in praise of the Natives. They say they stood by Clay in Philadelphia and it is evident they expect that the Native strength will be given to Clay. Archer (Senator)[1] has been in to this City and I have heard he & Gales of the Intelligencer have had interviews with Harper the Native Mayor. The object of that interview was to have some understanding between two parties and they believe they have had a transfer made of the Natives to Clay. Unless we are deceived no such union has been effected so far as a large portion of the democratic natives is concerned. We still hold to the opinion we shall carry the City for President & Governor. Our committees are active in naturalizing. Our organization is perfect as to finding out fraudulent voters, and we all feel in the best spirits.

Fortunately this day has been ushered in with a most disagreeable rain. The Native procession was to have come off to day but it has been postponed until after the election. We were fearful that a riot might occur. We had heard the Whigs were about attacking the procession & then charging it on the democrats. Any disturbance will lose us votes and we are extremely anxious to keep the peace. Most opportune has been this postponing rain.

JOHN McKEON

P.S. There is a rumor that one County in Ohio has given an increased democratic vote. It is doubtful whether any report can have reached us from Ohio yet.

ALS. DLC–JKP. Addressed to Columbia and marked "*Private.*"

1. William S. Archer, a Virginia lawyer and Whig, served in both the U.S. House, 1820–35, and in the U.S. Senate, 1841–47. During 1844 he supported the Native Americans' demand for a change in the naturalization laws and introduced a number of their petitions and memorials; in the closing weeks of the 1844 campaign, he visited Philadelphia and New York City.

FROM J. G. M. RAMSEY

My Dear Sir Mecklenburg Nov. 4, 1844

A. R. Crozier returned last night from a tour to Panther Springs where there was an excellent meeting on the 30th. ult. Next evening they were at Russellville where an unexpected number attended. On Saturday a discussion was held between Newman & Center[1] in Bradshaws District[2]—the attendance good. An injunction has been got out against Newman.[3] If it is served upon him to day of course he cannot open a poll. Mr. Newman was to write to Mr. Crozier stating the real position of things. The moment it arrives if anything important occurs we will write to our friends at Nashville.

I fear we will not realise as much from the apathy of the Whigs as at first was expected but we are doing & I will do up to 4 Oclock to morrow everything we can for our cause & our principles.

J. G. M. Ramsey

[P.S.] McClung wrote me that he would fill all our appointments but Maryville & Knoxville.[4] We had no one to supply them with & they are recalled.

ALS. DLC–JKP. Addressed to Columbia.

1. Reference probably is to William T. Senter. A Methodist minister and farmer in Grainger County, Senter won election as a Whig presidential elector in 1840 and represented Tennessee's Second Congressional District in the U.S. House for one term, 1843–1845.

2. Probably Richard Bradshaw, who represented Jefferson County in Tennessee's Constitutional Convention of 1834.

3. See Ramsey to Polk, October 28, 1844.

4. McClung was scheduled to speak in Maryville on November 2, 1844, and in Knoxville on November 4, 1844.

FROM JOHN M. READ

Dear Sir Philadelphia November 4: 1844

The triumph in this state is a complete one, and the returns received leave no doubt that under all circumstances our majority will not fall below 6000.

The reduction of 1400 in this city and county, was perhaps the most important element in our late canvass, as it has enabled our friends in New York and New Jersey, to think, feel and speak confidently, *at once* of the result in Pennsylvania, and has prevented the whigs from offering any encouragement to their friends in these states. Pennsylvania has in fact been the battle ground in the middle states, for I cannot but believe that if we had lost the Governor's election, with the disaster in Ohio, and the Native Americans in The City of New York, and the abolitionists in the interiors, that the whole three states of Ohio Pennsylvania and New York might have gone by the board. And as our Party has only a plurality in New York I should have feared that an unfavourable result in the presidential contest *here* would have produced a similar result in the former state.

The Pennsylvania News has spread through the whole of New York, and I believe will secure the state, and will induce the abolitionists to adhere to their own ticket and will prevent a complete coalition in the City between the Whigs and Natives.

Pennsylvania has under all circumstances held up surprisingly. The death of Mr. Muhlenberg, the nomination of Mr. Shunk, but a month before the election, and the coalition in this district were all new elements, which did not enter into the earlier part of the canvass, and gave our opponents the means to engage in a contest which they had previously thought almost hopeless.

We had other difficulties, which could not be explained to our friends abroad, arising out of the peculiar situation of our State Administration.[1] So great a drawback was this, that I feel entirely confident, if such a man as Mr. Muhlenberg had been governor and Mr Shunk the candidate in October, that we should have had a majority of at least 15,000 which would have placed the presidential election beyond all doubt or cavil.

It can therefore be easily understood, that the Democracy of Pennsylvania has gone through a fiery trial unscathed, and that their success ensures a victory in the Empire State.

I wrote to a friend in Alabama,[2] that New Jersey was safe, and I believe he communicated that opinion to you. At the time I expressed it, I had every reason to do so, with entire confidence, and I believe if there had been the same cordiality evinced, that there was in Pennsylvania towards Mr. Shunk, by the friends of Mr. Muhlenberg, that the results could have been the election of Mr. Thomson. I know well that if there had been the slightest hesitation here, on the part of the leading friends of Mr. Muhlenberg, Mr. Shunk never could have been elected. Expressed dissatisfaction in a state so close as New Jersey, must produce defeat, because it leads the rank and file, to believe the falsehoods of the opposition, and allow our enemies to use the names of the dissatisfied to influence the votes of our own people.[3]

New Jersey was in a peculiar position. A number of prominent democrats were friends of Mr Tyler, a large number of Gen Cass and other candidates. Nothing but an union of the whole and more particularly of the Tyler section which included some Whigs who were desirous of acting with the Democratic Party could possible give us the State.

Mr. Thomson, the brother in law of Captain Stockton [and] a man of fine talents and excellent sense, had been an unwavering democrat, and always in favour of a reform of the state constitution. After our defeat in 1842, when the Whigs carried the Legislature against the popular majority in the State, it became evident, that a new issue must be presented at the next election to give the Democratic party any Chance whatever. This new issue was the reform of the constitution, and in a conversation I had with Mr. Thomson in October 1842, a few days after the election, I urged it upon him, as he was thoroughly acquainted with the subject, at once to make it the question of the next campaign, and to treat it not as a mere party question, so as to secure the votes of the liberal portion of the whigs who disliked the provisions of the old defective charter of 1776. Mr Thomson did so—he lectured, wrote, traversed the State, enlisted in the cause many prominent men, and the consequence was the entire success of the State in 1843. Mr. Thomson pressed it before the Legislature, procured the passage of an act to call a convention, became a member of that body, and a participates in its most important deliberations and acts, and at the close of its session he was called the father of the new constitution. While the convention was in session the nominations were made at Baltimore, and the whole Tyler section without hesitation raised the Polk and Dallas flag and the party became actively united.

The general sentiment of the Democratic Party pointed to Mr Thomson (who had around him all the going and active politicians of the State) as the proper individual to be made the first governor under a constitution, to which he had contributed so largely, and by the most respectable convention ever assembled in New Jersey he was nominated almost unanimously on the first ballot.

It was known that the accession of Capt. Stockton and his friends[4] brought a peculiar kind of aid essential in New Jersey and without which we should never have seen the very large democratic vote given in October last.

When I wrote therefore to Major Hubbard, I had a well grounded confidence of success, for I knew we would act cordially together in Pennsylvania, and I supposed the same could be the case in New Jersey, but just previous to the election I saw matters which made me doubt the results. Immediately upon his defeat Mr Thomson issued an address,[5] honourable both to his head and his heart, and as far as I can learn, all have gone in cordially, and unitedly to support the electoral ticket. I have urged the leading men of all sections to make a bold push tomorrow and next day. They promise to do so, and some promise success. Our news will have a powerful effect in New Jersey. It had [...][6] us in October. The loss of the Governor and Legislature is difficult to encounter but I still hope that the certainty of your election as President & the downheartedness of the Whigs here, may give us the electoral vote of the state.

JOHN M. READ

[P.S.] A friend who knows says our maj in Penn. will be about 7000.

ALS. DLC–JKP. Addressed to Columbia.

1. Read's reference is to the rift between David R. Porter and the Pennsylvania Democracy. Estranged from the Democratic party by his views on protective tariffs and by his support for John Tyler's candidacy in 1844, Porter withdrew from Democratic politics upon completion of his second term as governor.

2. Read's reference probably is to David Hubbard; Hubbard's letter to Polk on the situation in New Jersey has not been found.

3. For the divisions within the New Jersey Democracy, see John K. Kane to Polk, October 13, 1844, and Gansevoort Melville to Polk, October 17, 1844.

4. A supporter of William Henry Harrison in 1840, Robert F. Stockton eventually returned to the Democratic party and came out in favor of Polk and Dallas in 1844. Closely identified with railroad and canal interests in New Jersey, he had invested heavily in the Delaware and Raritan Canal and in the Camden & Amboy Railroad.

5. In his address "To the Democratic Electors of the State of New Jersey," John R. Thomson thanked New Jersey Democrats for their support and attacked the Whigs' use of "false issues" in the campaign. While portraying their party as "*anti-monopoly*," the Whigs had emphasized Thomson's "supposed connection with the canal and railroad company." After pointing out that Henry Clay supported the greatest of all monopolies, a national bank, Thomson urged his fellow citizens to support Polk and Dallas and thus preserve "the existence of republican government." See the Washington *Globe*, October 16, 1844.

6. Word or words illegible.

FROM JOEL B. SUTHERLAND

My dear Sir. Philada Novr. 4th 1844

The election is *now* over in Penna & I think you will find, that all that has been promised for Penna has been fully realized.

During the last week of the campaign I went among my old constituents in Southwark & I think did some service. I also went into Kensington. Both of these Districts are deeply embued with Native Americanism. They have large bodies of ship carpenters among them, who voted many of them for the *Native Congress* & *Legislative* ticket. I thought, however, that I could do something with them particularly as they about *a year ago*, sent me a cane of *live oak*, with a fine *gold* head with the Inscription, that it was presented to me by the Mechanics of the Port of Philadelphia. When I met them, I was met, most enthusiastically. I went into a full argument of the importance of the contest. The necessity of adhering to Democratic principles, & contending that as they had nobly sustained Old Hickory in former times, that I expected they would come up in the same enthusiastic manner for Young Hickory. This suggestion was recd with hearty cheers and it is my opinion that every Democratic Ship Carpenter in Southwark & Kensington in the Native ranks votes for Messrs Polk & Dallas.

They reduced the majority given at the Shunk election between 6 & 7 hundred. A large[1] of the *Methodist* Democratic natives on the *Bible* question,[2] went over to the Clay ticket *in Southwark*. I trust however, by proper attention we will get them all *back* again. Some of our *orators* at the Gubernatorial election assailed the *Natives*, without mercy in *Southwark & Kensington*. This we in a great measure arrested at the Presidential election & hence our success. I was *specially* invited to *speak* & no *other named in the Handbill*, *but myself*, so as to keep off, the *vituperation* of *short sighted speakers*. I also shew'd by electing Mr Dallas we gained 2 votes in the Senate. For if the Whigs Vice Presidential candidate should be chosen, we would not only lose Mr Dallas; but have a Whig elected in his place. The ship carpenters & other working people here are very anxious about a *Dry Dock* at this Port. This I said Mr Dallas could carry & I have no doubt of it. I also added, that if he were there, to Preside over the Senate, he might be authorized, to appoint the Naval & Commercial committees, & aid largely in confirming Democratic appointments. I prepared a handbill about the Dry Dock & had 500 of them put up in Kensington & Southwark.

But enough of this. Our victory is so perfect & thorough in Penna. that we shall not hereafter be seriously troubled & our triumphs, will not require again any minuteness of detail. Hereafter we shall sweep them *here* by the *Board*. If we act prudently, every thing *is within our grasp*. Present my respects to Mrs Polk.

J. B. SUTHERLAND

ALS. DLC–JKP. Address to Columbia and franked by Andrew Jackson.

1. Sutherland probably intended to write "large number."

2. See Jesse Miller to Polk, October 12, 1844.

FROM DAVID T. DISNEY

Dr Sir Cincinnati 5 Nov. 1844

Thank God the torrent of Whig triumphs is *checked* at last. Five counties from Pennsylvania show a majority for us *increased over Shunks* of about 700 votes and the indications give us that State by 11 or 12,000. *Pennsylvania is safe.*

Ohio has gone for Clay by 6 or 7000. The rumors from the adjoining counties in *Indiana* are favourable.

The news from Pennsylvania has caused a perfect revulsion in the feelings and speculations here. It has taken me from the cellar and placed me on the house top. The rumours from Pennsylvania for the last 48 hours all indicated that it had gone for Clay. And I gave up all for lost. I would not that my worst enemy had the hopes and the agonies which I have undergone the last 48 hours, but light is breaking. My hopes of New York are much raised by an inspection of the returns of our northern counties. They show that the abolitionists there have adhered to their ticket much better than any other part of the state—from this I reason that the same influence has extended into western New York. If so a great danger will have been escaped in that state. For it was that and *that alone* which beat us in Ohio.

D. T. DISNEY

Pennsylvania		
Alleghany	2369	Clay
Fayette	600	Polk
Green	940	do
Washington	140	do
Westmoreland	2380	do

ALS. DLC–JKP. Addressed to Columbia.

FROM ANDREW JACKSON

Dear Col., Hermitage, [November] 5, 1844[1]

I inclose at th[e re]quest[2] of Judge Hayward,[3] the within paper.[4] I have just recd. from Mr. Blair a letter. He thinks Pennsylvania is safe notwithstanding all the attempts of bribery and fraud. He also says VanBuren writes him that Newyork is safe. This day clo[sed] the resu[lt]. I Tru[st] in a kind providence, that it is in favour of democracy.

Have you any thing from N. Carolina, I fear it is Federal.

In haste adieu with our kind regards to Mrs. Polk.

ANDREW JACKSON

ALS. DLC–JKP. Addressed to Columbia. Published in Bassett, ed., *Correspondence of Andrew Jackson*, VI, p. 324.

1. Date identified by postmark and through content analysis. Bassett dated this letter "October 5."

2. Bracketed word-completion supplied.

3. A strong Jackson supporter and editor of the Cincinnati *National Republican*, Elijah Hayward served in the Ohio House from 1825 to 1828; he won election to the Ohio Supreme Court in January 1830, but resigned later in the year to become commissioner of the General Land Office, a post that he held until August of 1835.

4. Enclosure not found.

FROM FERNANDO WOOD

Tuesday night

My dear Sir [New York, N.Y.] Nov. 5, 1844

Our election has closed and we have had the severest struggle ever witnessed in this city. Every means of the most dispicable and corrupt character have been resorted to by our opponents. Money has been lavished upon the disolute and indigent without stint, and where intrigues, gold and calumny could not effect the object, threats have been resorted to, but without avail. The alliance you dreaded took place. The whig candidates were withdrawn and a formal agreement made with the natives, thus securing their votes for the electoral ticket. Against these adverse circumstances have our lion hearted democracy contended with success. Our majority is 2088. Again I congratulate you upon your tryumphant election. We look upon it here as the most decided and brilliant victory ever achieved by the democracy. Never have they had such an array of power and combination to contend against and never have they more completely covered themselves with glory.

FERNANDO WOOD

[P.S.] Nov. 6, 4 AM. The returns from Westchester County are in—540 Democratic majority. Richmond 178 Demo Maj. Kings 314 Whig. All is safe. Hurrah! FW

ALS. DLC–JKP. Addressed to Columbia.

FROM GEORGE M. DALLAS

My Dear Sir, [Philadelphia] 2 p.m. 6. Nov. [18]44

We are full of glee and exultation. You must have got the Virginia news, which confirms all Mr. Ritchie's promises. The result in the City of New York meets the expectations of our friends—2154 majority for Polk—and is an index which points unerringly to a great triumph throughout the State. Pennsylvania! Virginia!! New York!!! Are we still to invoke our philosophy to be prepared for defeat? Not a jot of it! The thing is rounded off. I repeat my sincere congratulations, and send them, from the bottom of my heart, to the noble old Sage of the Hermitage.[1]

New Jersey cannot but be affected on this her second day with the clap of thunder from N. York. But she is at liberty to stand by her broad seal if she likes, and will not be missed.

G. M. DALLAS

ALS. DLC–JKP. Addressed to Columbia.

1. Andrew Jackson.

TO GEORGE M. DALLAS

My Dear Sir: Columbia Ten. Nov 6th 1844

Our election took place on yesterday. The Democratic majority in Maury County (this County) is 707 votes. In the Gubernatorial election of 1843 my majority was 379, making a gain of 328 votes. We have the returns from Marshall County except one precinct. The Democratic majority is about 750. In 1843 it was 640. We have the returns also from Giles County: The Democratic majority is 70 votes. In 1843 the Whig majority was 81 votes.

	1843		1844		
	W	D	W	D	D. Gain
Maury	do	379	do	707	328
Marshall	do	640	do	750	110
Giles	81		do	70	151
		Dem. Gain in 3 Counties			589

The Whig majority in the state in 1843 was 3833. There are 82 counties in the state, and unless the strong Whig Counties have increased their majorities beyond all reasonable calculation, we have carried the state, by a majority ranging probably between 1000 & 3000 votes. I think the state is safe, but by a close vote. I will keep this letter open that I may add any further returns which may be received before the mail closes. In haste....

JAMES K. POLK

[P.S.] The returns are just in from Lawrence County.

1843		1844		
W	D	W	D	D. Gain
5	do	do	63	68

ALS. MH. Addressed to Philadelphia.

FROM ANDREW J. DONELSON

Dr Sir New Orleans Nov 6 1844

You will be desirous of knowing the result of the elections here. That of this city can only be assumed as the basis of calculation for the parishes of the state where the polls will not close until 4 oclock to day. The vote of this city gives Clay a majority of about 400, Seven hundred less than his friends bet on the day previous to the election. Our party have now no doubt that the vote of the whole state will give you a majority ranging between 900 and 1200.

If the lst days returns from Penna should show that the natives of Philadelphia are separated from the Whigs, or even so far as to make you 2000 stronger in that city and county, I shall set it down as evidence of your success throughout the union. But unfortunately I shall not have this information for some weeks after it will be known to you as the vessel on which I am to sail will be off in the morning and the communication between this place and Galveston is yet irregular.[1]

It is wonderful what ignorance prevails with many of the citizens in this section of the Union respecting the bearing which the Presidential election has on the Texas question. Many honest men have been led to believe that Clay's influence will be exerted to acquire the Territory and even some citizens of Texas are so much duped as to countenance the idea.

The Texas congress will assemble about the time ours will. When Houstons term expires I wish to be there before the message of his success is delivered, so as to turn to the best account the result of our elections whatever it may be. If you arê elected I shall use the fact as decisive of the wish of the people of the U States to incorporate Texas immediately into our Union, and shall calculate that the response to this wish on the part of the Government of Texas will be such as to shut out effectually all machinations of Great Britain and other powers to defeat it. Mexico's war will then terminate in a protest, and Great Britain will tell her that it is better to stop at that point than enlarge the national debt.

But if Clay should be elected what then? How undefined become all the speculations respecting the existence of slavery. What a dark clould will at once hang over the prospect of all our southern states. Great Britain will forthwith resume her projects for the abolition of slavery, and with the aid of Webster and Adams will consider that her game is insured.

But it is useless to look at this side of the picture. Enough for the day will be the evil thereof.[2]

I will give you a particular account of the state of our affairs in Texas, as soon as I am informed of them.

In the mean time believe me....

A. J. DONELSON

ALS. DLC–JKP. Addressed to Columbia.

1. Reference is to Donelson's appointment as chargé d'affaires to Texas. See Robert Armstrong to Polk, September 25, 1844.

2. Paraphrase of the scriptural verse, "Sufficient unto the day is the evil thereof." Matthew 6:34.

FROM ALEXANDER JONES

241 8th Avenue
New York Nov. 6th 1844

Dear Sir

As regards this city, "*we have met the enemy and they are ours!*"[1] We have carried the city in favour of Polk & Dallas by 2127 majority, beating *Whigs, Native Americans*, and *Abolitionist*, all combined. The day proved fine and clear. The Whig Candidates for Congress & for Members of the State Legislature all withrew; the entire Whig party voting for the Native American nominations in their stead, under the expectation, that, the natives in return would vote the Whig Electoral Ticket and for the Whig Candidate for Governor.[2] In this expectation the Whigs only partially succeeded. Had it not been for this base coalition intrigue, our Electoral Ticket would have left the city with a clear majority of from 4 to 5000. As it is, are[3] friends have fought nobly, and gained a great Victory. Over 50,000 votes were cast. Our opponents fought with desperation. They "left no stone unturned."[4] They left no lie, or fraud untried. To the last hour, to sunset they exerted their strength and influence to the utmost. They tried all kinds of bribery and corruption, offering poor people employment for the winter, if they would only vote *for Clay*! It would not all do. To day the Polk & Dallas flags are waving in triumph over this great city.

All the native and whig combination could accomplish was to elect several members to the Legislature, and two, or three members to Congress on the Native American Ticket. We have elected two members to Congress and how far else we have succeeded is not yet fully ascertained.

The county returns from the interior are now arriving, all of which look favourable. Our friends are sanguine, that, we have carried the entire State; if so, you may make your arrangements to leave for Washington, for your election will thereby be placed beyond all doubt.

I write this letter in the Office of the Journal of Commerce, which has received the latest and most correct information (as far as ascertained) with regard to the election in this state. The Editors have heard from *nine* counties including our New York, which give a Democratic Electoral Majority of 4,781, being a gain over 1840 of 1,549, when Harrison beat Van Buren in the whole state about 13,000 votes. In 1842 the Democratic Majority for Governor was about 21,000. On that large majority we have thus far sustained a loss of about 2,367. The final result in this state, will depend very much, probably, upon the disposition of the Abolition vote in the interior of the state. If they vote *en mass* for the Whigs, it is barely possible we may fail in carrying the state, or carry it by a moderate majority otherwise we must carry it by a large majority. *Wright*, it is said, run about 1000 ahead of his ticket in this city.

22 Minutes of *2 Oclock P.M.* We have reported returns from 16 counties in Virginia; they show no material difference over the election of 1840. Only 14 being set down as Whig gain.

As soon we have sufficient returns in to determine the result in this state, I will write to you again.

My sincere Respects to your amiable Lady....

ALEXR. JONES

ALS. DLC–JKP. Addressed to Columbia.

1. Variant of a quotation from Oliver H. Perry's dispatch to William H. Harrison, September 10, 1813. Perry wrote, "We have met the enemy, and they are ours."

2. Millard Fillmore.

3. Here Jones probably meant to write "our" instead of "are."

4. Variant of the quotation "To leave no stone unturned," a phrase commonly attributed to Euripides, *Heraclidae*, 1002.

FROM JOHN McKEON

My Dear Sir, New York Novr. 6. 1844

My prophecy is fulfilled. The City of New York has given a Polk & Dallas Majority of 1941. This is indeed a triumph over the coalition of Whigs & Natives. Mr. Van Buren received in 1840 the majority of 900. in this City. We have now more than doubled his majority. The increase is almost the number we have naturalized since last spring. Never have men acted more faithfully than the entire democracy of this City. Every man worked as if the safety of the party rested on him alone. Great efforts were made by Whig & Native inspectors to exclude our votes but three of us legal gentlemen rode to the different polls & gave advice to our voters how to act. We soon found the enemy giving way under our movements.

There are flying rumours from the river counties. Some of the Whigs still claim the state but I believe we have carried it but by a very small majority. I heard one of the editors of the Tribune (Clay) admit that in his opinion the state had gone for us.[1] I hear that Weed the editor of the Evening Journal (the state paper of the Whigs) admits we have carried the state.[2]

You should have witnessed the wild enthusiasm of the democracy last night. The City rang with their shouts & with the roar of cannon. I have never witnessed such exultation. We have probably elected two congressmen. This is doing better than we expected.

So far as heard from we have gained largely on our vote of 1840. Unless Flagg & all our friends have been greatly deceived we must be safe in the state.

Give us Tennessee and we are triumphant.

J. McKeon

P.S. Connecticut is against us.

ALS. DLC–JKP. Addressed to Columbia and marked "Private."

1. Founded by Horace Greeley in 1841, the *New York Tribune* endorsed Henry Clay in the presidential contest of 1844.

2. Thurlow Weed, editor of the *Albany Evening Journal* and opponent of the New York Democracy, supported John Q. Adams' presidential bid in 1824; joined the Anti-Mason party in 1830; organized New York Whigs in the state elections of 1834, 1836, and 1838; led his party to gubernatorial victories with William H. Seward in 1838 and 1840; and carried New York for William H. Harrison over Martin Van Buren in 1840. Although an ardent anti-slavery man, he approached politics from a pragmatic perspective and often scorned radical proposals, such as those put forward by the abolitionists. He followed Seward into the Republican

party in 1854, but failed to win for his friend the party's presidential nominations in 1856 and 1860.

FROM J. G. M. RAMSEY

My Dear Sir Mecklenburg Nov. 6 1844

I drop you a line before the stage arrives. I have sent to town by my son Crozier[1] for the results of the election yesterday in Knox County. If it arrives before the mail closes it will be appended. I have returns from but three districts. This one the 17th gave last year 100 Whigs & 33 Democrats. It voted yesterday 96 W. & 32 D. & we sent off to neighbouring Districts 4 active Democrats to watch the polls etc. & colonised 6 timid or doubtful voters each of whom voted right making our Dem. vote 42 & one old man unable to be brought to the polls. The other two districts have not done quite so well but both have given a Dem. gain & a Whig loss. Putting the three together & supposing the State at large to have voted in the same ratio we have carried the State. Knox County, where the White & Williams parties[2] have each been vying for the last 6 years which of them is the most active in & can do the most for the Whig cause, is I believe the hardest county in the State to operate in for our cause, & in these three Districts the Whigs have laboured more to retain their strength than any others in the county. So that I have some reason I think to hope you have carried the State. The remaining 14 Districts I hope have done better. If the returns reach me in time they will be inclosed.

I hear nothing further from Jefferson. I hope our friends have availed themselves of every lawful advantage the peculiar condition of things there offered.[3]

We had recalled McClungs appointment for Knoxville on the 4th. But a large number of citizens attended & A. R. Crozier spoke two hours Monday afternoon with great spirit & effect & closed the campaign by an earnest appeal to his Democratic hearers to repair to their respective polls to morrow & rescue Tennessee from Federalism.

The battle is now over & I still hope the victory is won. If the amalgamation of all the pernicious *isms* in the north[4] has not been effected you are the President of the United States. God grant that it may be so!

J. G. M. RAMSEY

[P.S.] I unfold my letter to give you as I have this moment received the vote of Knox Count "Polk 502 Clay 2013—last year P. 454 J. 1911. thus gaining some upon the Whig vote of 1843. Anderson County *reported Whig* majority 305. Precinct at Louisville Blount Cty Dem. Gain 17."

That will do if it is so all over the State. I still keep this letter unsealed to get accounts from Sevier & Jefferson if the driver or passengers bring me any reliable intelligence.

	P.	C.	
Jefferson	252	1600	
Cocke	111	506	three Dist. to hear from

ALS. DLC–JKP. Addressed to Columbia.

1. John Crozier Ramsey was the eldest son of J. G. M. and Peggy Barton Crozier Ramsey.

2. Hugh L. White and John Williams, both connected by kinship or marriage to Knoxville's founder, James White, dominated East Tennessee politics for over two decades. Williams, whose wife, Melinda, was a sister of Hugh L. White and a daughter of James White, fought in the War of 1812 as a regimental commander under Andrew Jackson and served in the U.S. Senate from 1815 until 1823, when he lost his bid for reelection to Jackson. Williams' two sons, Joseph L. and John, both pursued political careers: Joseph won three terms as a Whig in the U.S. House, 1837–43; and John represented Knox County two terms in the Tennessee House, 1845–59. White broke party ranks in 1836 when he allowed his name to be put forward as the South's presidential candidate; his supporters subsequently provided much of the leadership for the Whig party's formation and management in the southern states.

3. See J. G. M. Ramsey to Polk, October 28, 1844, and November 4, 1844.

4. Reference is to nativism and abolitionism, some proponents of which had formed alliances with like-minded Whigs in Ohio, Pennsylvania, and New York.

FROM JOEL B. SUTHERLAND

My Dear Sir Philad. Nov. 6th 1844

I sent you a line this morning[1] in which I said we would I thought carry New York, & that we would also run a very good chance for *New Jersey* & *Delaware*. I am still more confirmed in this opinion. This morning I recd a letter, requesting me to see that the Revenue Cutter be allowed to come up the Bay of Delaware, to give the men & officers belonging to Delaware a chance to vote. I have attended to this request. Every freeman, entitled to vote, ought to have the opportunity afforded to him. A committee waited upon R. Tyler Esq.[2] to day to go down to Delaware to address the Irishmen at the factories. We hope his visit will prove advantageous. He is a very eloquent speaker. He promised me to day to go down at the time fixed for the meeting. The News from New York you will read with immense pleasure. I feel very anxious for Tennessee for your sake & for the sake of the Old General.[3]

I take it for granted that you recd as good a share of the votes of the Democratic *natives* in N.Y. as you did in Philada. Some of our speakers, & Editors, north & South have not handled the native question with sufficient caution. For myself, I think it best (at least for the present) not to disturb the question. By a proper course of procedure, we may possibly keep the *native Democrats* from acting with the Whig Natives *for the future.* In the city & county of Philada. many of our Democrats were distressed with the Maryland Ohio & Conn. news yesterday, & last night I met them at a Public meeting & cheered them in a speech in which I promised them glorious *news to day.* I am glad, that all I promised has been so fully realized.

I think enough of the abolitionists will *stand by* Birney, to make our success certain in New York. Birney's letter exposing their forgery on him, was dated at Batavia the hotbed of abolition.[4] It is right therefore to expect that *he* will get the abolitionists *there*. Remember me to Mrs. Polk and tell her that I say that you are elected President & that I shall be greatly delighted to see her in the White House next March.

J. B. SUTHERLAND

[P.S.] 3 p.m. A friend just from New York says we will have a majority of 5 thousand. If the *abolitionists* stand up to Birney, all is safe. I herewith send you all the papers from New York.[5]

ALS. DLC–JKP. Addressed to Columbia; franked by Andrew Jackson.

1. Letter not found.

2. Robert Tyler, eldest son of John Tyler, served in the Land Office at Washington during his father's tenure as president. Later he practiced law in Philadelphia, served as register of the Confederate Treasury, and edited the Montgomery *Daily Advertiser*.

3. Andrew Jackson.

4. See Gansevoort Melville to Polk, October 26, 1844. James G. Birney's letter, dated October 26, 1844, was published in the *New York Herald* of November 5, 1844.

5. Enclosures not found.

FROM JAMES D. WASSON[1]

10 O.C. P.M. Post Office
Albany Nov. 6. 1844

Dear Sir

It gratifies me much to assure you that I have this evening recd returns from different portions of this State to assure you that you have the Electoral vote of this State from 5 to 7,000 & Gov. will be higher probably 2 or 3,000. All is safe in this State after a dreadful struggle and all kinds of lies & deception with a great quantity of money 5 to 10 Dolls was freely paid in this City for votes but the Democracy were on the alert and thank God are successful.

I have not the pleasure of a personal acquaintance with you, and I had determined not to write you unless we were successful. This morning Gov. Marcy, A. C. Flagg, Genl. Dix, John Van Buren & myself were cooped up together,[2] almost in despair from the returns then recd, & the Whigs in high spirits offering any amount of Bets, which were not taken, by the way they have suffered much in that way. On the arrival of the Rail Road Cars & Steam Boats all doubts were dispelled *and no mistake* ....

JAMES D. WASSON

ALS. DLC–JKP. Addressed to Columbia.

1. Wasson served as postmaster of Albany, N.Y., through Polk's term as president.

2. William L. Marcy, Azariah C. Flagg, John A. Dix, and John Van Buren. Soldier, lawyer, and railroad president, John A. Dix served two years as adjutant general of New York, 1831–33, and one term as a member of the New York House in 1842. Elected as a Democrat to the U.S. Senate seat vacated by Silas Wright in 1845, Dix ran unsuccessfully in 1848 as the gubernatorial candidate of the Free Soil party, served in the Union army as a general officer during the Civil War, and won election to the governorship on the Republican ticket in 1873. A lawyer and member of the radical wing of the New York Democracy, John Van Buren won a single term in 1845 to the office of attorney general; he married Elizabeth Vanderpoel, the daughter of James Vanderpoel, who was a prominent Albany lawyer and wealthy landholder in Kinderhook.

FROM HENDERSON K. YOAKUM

My Dear Sir — Murfreesboro Tenn Nov 6, 1844

The election is over, and your destiny is in some way determined. I hope for the best, but almost despond. Whatever may be the result however I feel that your wisdom & philosophy will enable you to bear it with dignity. And I know the world will not find any thing in the manner in which you have conducted the canvass wherewith to reproach you. In this county we have fought against the wealth & power of the Bell & Foster Kith, and have gained 44 votes on the election of 1843, counting the Williamson fraction.

For my own part I have long since determined to leave the State. I have spent ten years here in almost fruitless controversy. The necessities of a growing young family require that I should go away from strife & make wherewithal to buy them food & raiment. Should I see a fair prospect of annexing Texas, I shall go there; if not, elsewhere.

Maj Hickerson[1] met with a serious accident at Woodbury on Saturday last. The story is that while he was speaking in the court house he said "E. Polk is a tory, JKP is a tory, & those who support him are tories." Just as he finished the last words a rock hit him in the mouth, breaking his jaw and knocking out some of his teeth. It is not known who threw the rock. You have a large increase upon the vote of 43 in that county–say 135.

The election here was attended with some of the richest scenes you ever witnessed. There was kidnapping enough on both sides to put half the county in the penitentiary. I hope never again to witness the like. Indeed I am fully persuaded this country cannot stand another such campaign, and I am sure no one can judge of the policy decided upon, when the balance of power is determined by bargain and sale.

H. YOAKUM

P.S. just as I signed my name I heard a gun fire. It was Bailey (whig) shot at Sanders (dem).[2] No harm done. The news from Ohio is distressing.

ALS. DLC–JKP. Addressed to Columbia.

1. Yoakum's reference probably is to one of the Hickerson family of neighboring Coffee County; the Hickersons were staunch Whigs.

2. Bailey and Sanders have not been identified further.

FROM ROBERT ARMSTRONG

12 Oclk

Dr Sir [Nashville, Tenn.] 7 Novmr [18]44

The Democrats of Nashville are Indeed in their Glory. I have never seen anything like it. The news from Pennsyl. is almost too good to stand. Great God what a Triumph. I send you the slips of the Union and the letters to me giving the Information.

This state is close but our majority will not fall below my estimates of 1400 unless Huntsman, Rowles, Crozier, Geo. Powell &c are *greatly* deceived.[1]

We have only the Whig Report from Lincoln of 175 majority. I hope it is more. We have no other returns but what you have. None in to day but Warren. Laughlin says our gain there will be 54 to 70. Several Districts not heard from. Tomorrow night's (12 Oclk) mails will show us how the state has gone. I will start the mail or an Express *after* 12 Oclk of the news &c &c. I am in haste.

R. ARMSTRONG

ALS. DLC–JKP. Addressed to Columbia.

1. Adam Huntsman, George W. Rowles, Arthur R. Crozier, and George R. Powel. Powel represented Hawkins and Sullivan counties in the Tennessee

House for one term, 1835–37, and served as circuit court clerk of Hawkins County from 1840 until 1852.

FROM JOHN P. CHESTER

My Dear Sir [Jacksboro, Tenn. Nov. 7, 1844][1]

I have just time to enclose you a slip containing the votes of this county[2] with the majorities in Sullivan 1212 in Green about 700 a small gain in Carter of 20 or thirty and a few in Johnson.

In the evening after the Coons heard the vote of this County, they formed a procession with transparencyes, marched up until they came opposite my house where they commenced swearing & abusing the company on the porch and boastering them to come down. They went down and faced them, when one of the Coons threw a rock at some of the democrats and hit a Coon boy of 18 years of age who died this morning of the wound. His scull was fractured from one ear to the other across the head.

J. P. CHESTER

ALS. DLC–JKP. Addressed to Columbia.

1. Place and date identified by postmark cancellation and through content analysis.
2. Enclosure with vote of Campbell County not found.

FROM JONATHAN I. CODDINGTON

Thursday Evening
My dear Sir New. York Nov. 7. 1844

The Boat is just in from Albany & we have carried the State by at least 5000 & it may reach 7000. On the Electoral ticket, this is rather less than your Democratic friends here expected to give you, but considering what base lies & forgeries our political opponents resorted to to deafeat us, it is the most glorius victory that we ever achieved in this City or State, not excepting that of 1800. Altho. this secures your Election, yet we hope to hear that Indiana & Tennessee has done likewise.

Some of the newspapers are attempting to create a jealousy against the friends of Mr. V Buren but there is not the least foundation for it. Mr Wrights vote over the electoral ticket is owing to the Whigs voting for him in prefference to giving their votes to Fillmore beleiving that Mr. Wright would manage the State finances much better than his Whig opponent. A great many Whigs told me on the day of the Election that they should vote for Mr W. on this account.

The Whigs were much elated here last evg. after the arrival of the Boat bringing a few returns from the abolition counties which induced them to beleive that they had dropd. Birney & gone over to Clay. But they have given up the State this afternoon. Maine votes on Monday next & will follow in the foot steps of the Empire State, which will only increase your majority as you are elected without.

J. I. CODDINGTON

ALS. DLC–JKP. Addressed to Columbia.

FROM ALEXANDER JONES

1/2 past 8 P.M. 241 8h Avenue
New York Nov. 7h 1844

Dear Sir

I congratulate you on the result in this state! We have heard from all the counties but 14 or 15. Our friends feel assured that you have carried the state.

In no event can your majority over Clay be less than 2000, even allowing Clay to get the same vote in the counties to hear from that Harrison obtained in 1840. Your majority may be increased to 4 or 5000. The *Albany Argus* claims the state for you and Dallas by 5000!

Virginia is safe! Tamany Hall is illuminated! And our cannon is firing in the Park. This all being true, the election in your favour is settled!

God be be praised therefore. I have requested the Editors of the Journal of Commerce to send you their paper, till all the election returns are pretty well recieved. They have taken much pains and expense to collect the latest and most correct official returns.

I have sent you two copies by this mail.[1]

I write in great haste amidst great excitement among our friends. Indeed the whole city seems thrown into commotion by the news this evening by the gratifying news from the west of the state. The streets are full of people.

News paper offices Hotels, & public political houses, all crowded. The Whigs, are all thunder struck and in utter astonishment, give up the contest!

I again congratulate you! My highest respect and Esteem to your amiable & kind Lady.

ALEXR. JONES

ALS. DLC–JKP. Addressed to Columbia.

1. Newspapers not found.

FROM JOEL B. SUTHERLAND

My dear Sir 3 P.M. Philada Novr 7th 1844

Thus far, we have gained 8000 on the Whigs. We have seventeen counties east of the bridge[1] yet to be heard from & I think we will have enough to beat the Whigs, who think they can bring 10 thousand from the West. They I do not believe can do as much as they anticipate. The Harrison majority was very large on the Western & Lake borders on account of our Canadian difficulties.[2] I by no means dispair. I think we will carry the state of New York from the fact, that the abolitionists have not gone in for the Whigs. In Ontario County, we have a decrease of the Whig strength about 300 votes & in that county, there are 300 abolitionists. It will be remembered that in Oneida our majority is 769 & in that county the abolitionists [...][3] votes in 1840, & Harrisons majority 613. Our majority being about 140 more than Harrison—so the abolitionist have not *here* gone for the Whigs. Monroe (Rochester)[4] abolition, gave Harrison about 2000. Not[5] it gives Clay 1200. So here the abolitionists have not helped the Whigs. It is fair to presume, that we will carry the state. Oswego gave for Harrison 285 majority. It now give our candidate 600. St. Lawrence, the adjoining County (Wrights),[6] will give 1500 majority. It gave [...][7] for Harrison before. This was one of the Lake counties in which the Canadian excitement operated so severely—Jefferson a strong Democratic *Lake* county gave 600 for Harrison & now gives 787 for Polk. I think on the whole we may fairly therefore count upon success in New York. New Jersey it is said is lost to us by a small vote. In haste.

J. B. Sutherland

ALS. DLC–JKP. Addressed to Columbia.

1. Reference is to the bridge over the Seneca River at Cayuga, N.Y.; constructed of wood and extending over a mile in length, the Cayuga bridge served as the principal passage way for early nineteenth-century immigration into western New York.

2. See Gansevoort Melville to Polk, October 26, 1844.

3. Two words illegible.

4. Reference is to Monroe County and Rochester , N.Y.

5. Sutherland probably intended to write the word "now."

6. St. Lawrence, home county of Silas Wright, Jr., did not adjoin Oswego County.

7. Word illegible.

FROM JAMES WHITCOMB

My Dear Sir Indianapolis Nov. 7th 1844

I have hitherto abstained from communicating to you the returns from Indiana, until I should feel a reasonable assurance of the result. I cannot adequately express the pleasure I feel in now being enabled to say that Indiana responds gloriously to the nomination of the Democratic convention. This gratification is greatly enhanced from the fact that the contest in this State, severe & excited as it has been beyond example with us, has been fought on the great principles contended for by our party. We have kept the issues of opposition to a National Bank, a Revenue as opposed to a Protective Tariff, opposition to the assumption of the State debts by the U. States & the distribution of the proceeds of the public lands, the re-annexation of Texas & the sole occupancy of Oregon constantly before the people in our public discussions.

We have had the wind in our faces from the commencement. We had Harrison's maj. of 13,698 to overcome. We had the Whig majority of the legislative members procured at the last August election by the fraudulent importation of votes as they were needed in certain counties, & the inference of their having the popular votes in their favor, to contend against. We had the discouraging effect of the election of Friday previous in Ohio, showing a Whig gain on Bartley's majority, & which was exaggerated & circulated at many precincts just on the eve of our election, to overcome. In addition to all which, the forged Birney letter[1] produced great effect in causing most of the abolitionists to merge with the Whigs.

In spite of all these difficulties, however, the Democracy of Indiana have achieved a victory. I say achieved a victory, because although we have not heard from the whole *ninety* counties, yet we have returns which are sufficiently correct from above *sixty* counties & embracing more than three fourths of the population of the State, & which shows that the Democratic Ticket wants but about 100 votes of equalling my vote in the same counties in 1843, when I was elected by a little over 2000 majority. These counties also, include all the strong Whig counties & nearly all the abolition portion of the State, & I confidently hope & believe that the remaining counties to be heard from will increase your vote 4 or 500 beyond my majority in 1843.

I enclose you a slip containing our latest returns, in which they are compared with our election in 1843.[2]

I cannot now suffer myself to doubt (as some returns from Pa. are just in) that the administration of our Government will be entrusted to your hands for the next four years, & exceedingly rejoice in the prospect of soon being able to congratulate you on the glorious result.

JAS. WHITCOMB

P.S. Your letter was duly rec'd[3] & was extremely satisfactory! You adopted a very proper course, in my judgment.

ALS. DLC–JKP. Addressed to Columbia.

1. See Gansevoort Melville to Polk, October 26, 1844.

2. Whitcomb enclosed Indiana's election results as reported in a broadside issued by *Indiana State Sentinel* on November 8, 1844.

3. Letter not found.

FROM CAMPBELL P. WHITE[1]

New York, N.Y. November 7, 1844

White relates that yesterday's initial returns from the interior were so unfavorable that he feared the loss of the whole state. Later returns indicate that although Polk's majority at present is but half of last year's twenty-two thousand victory margin, his lead will hold up in the final count. He encloses returns from forty of New York's fifty-eight counties showing a Democratic majority, but notes that three-fourths of the returns from the infected district have not come to hand.[2] White concludes that in many instances "the Abolition party have abandoned their separate organisation & gone for Clay."

ALS. DLC–JKP. Addressed to Columbia.

1. A New York City merchant, Campbell P. White emigrated from Ireland to the United States in 1816 and won election as a Democrat to the U.S. House, where he served from 1829 until his resignation and subsequent retirement in 1835.

2. See John T. Hudson to Polk, October 26, 1844.

TO GEORGE M. DALLAS

My Dear Sir: Columbia Ten. Nov. 8th 1844

We have returns from 18 Counties, which give a Democratic gain over the vote of 1843, of 1581 votes. We have to gain 2252 votes, in the Counties to be heard from, to overcome the majority against us, in 1843. This we will do unless there shall be a great falling off, from the estimates of our friends, in the *Eastern* and *Western* Divisions of the State. All the Counties heard from are in the *Middle division*, where we have done as well as we expected. The estimate before the election was, that the

Democratic majority in *Middle* Tennessee, would be 4000, that the Whig majority in *East* Tennessee would be 1500 to 2000, and in *West* Tennessee 1000 to 1200.

Twelve Counties in *Middle* Tennessee remain to be heard from, in which we must gain 753 votes to come up to the estimate in that Division. This I think we shall do, and perhaps exceed it by 200 or 300 votes. Our party in the *East* & *West*, were not so well organized as in the *Middle* Division, & I fear may not come up to our estimate. The result in the State will probably be decided by a majority not exceeding 1000, either way, and that in the largest poll ever given. I think our chances, to carry the State are best, but in so close a contest, there must still be doubt.

I have not heard a word from the Pennsylvania elections, but have great apprehensions that you may have been overwhelmed by the power of money and the corrupt means, which have been employed, by your unscrupulous adversaries. If we carry New York, we will succeed in the Union, whatever may be the result in Tennessee & Pennsylvania. That we will carry *Indiana, Louisiana* & *Georgia*, I have the strongest assurances from my friends in those States: & these with New York & our certain strength will make the election without Pennsylvania & Tennessee. But it is useless to indulge in speculations. The contest is settled, and whatever the result may be, you and I, will have the happy reflection, that neither ourselves or our party have resorted to any dishonorable means to attain success.

JAMES K. POLK

ALS. PT. Addressed to Philadelphia and marked "*Private*." An unidentified writer penned the following endorsement on the cover of the letter: "One other County heard from. Democrats gain 120."

FROM JOHN T. HUDSON

Erie County New York
Buffalo Novr. 8th 1844

Sir

I took the liberty a short time since to send you my estimate of the probable result of the Election in the Counties composing the 8th Senatorial District in this State[1] under the supposition that the opinion of an actual resident in this Whig stronghold might not be without interest to you. In that estimate I placed the probable loss of the Whigs in the Counties which compose this District on the majority which they gave for Harrison in 1840, at from 3500 to 4000 votes. The election has since taken place & the accuracy of my estimate can now be tested by the actual result, which I have now ascertained from accurate & undoubted returns received from all the Counties. I give them as follows:

Counties	*Maj for Harrison 1840*		*Maj for Clay 1844*
Chautauqua	2640		2200
Erie	3099		1850
Genessee	3248		1500
Wyoming			650
Niagara	745		516
Orleans	579		283
Monroe	1633		1279
Whig Maj. in 1840	11944	Whig maj 1844	8278
	8278		
Whig loss in 1844	3666		

The votes of 1844 as given above are as nearly accurate as unofficial returns can be. The official return may vary them a little, but the variation will be to our favor, as the first returns came from the Whig & are usually given in round numbers & as high as they actually are. I am of opinion that the actual Whig loss in the District will be as great as 3800. This reduction in this hitherto impregnable stronghold will be of great service, or rather I should say *has been* of great service in carrying the State for us, which has undoubtedly been done. To contend against such odds is an arduous matter & to preserve the integrity of our vote in these overwhelming Counties is difficult: but to not only retain that but to increase it as we have done at this election & to effect a reduction in the majority of our opponents required great energy resolution & enthusiasm. All these we had. Every man has done to the utmost of his ability, sparing neither time nor labor & the result has been the complete redemption of the state. We have returns from sufficient number of Counties including the City of New York to show conclusively that Democratic Electoral, Gubernatorial & Canal Commissioner ticket has been elected, that a majority of the Congressional delegation will be Democratic & that we have elected seven out of eight Senators & more than two thirds of the house of Assembly. We had to overcome in the state the Whig majority of 1840 which amounted to 13200. This we have overcome & the electoral ticket has, as far as heard from 1500 majority. The remaining Counties to be heard from voted in 1840 as follows: 5 Whig Counties gave collectively 2102 Whig majty & 7 Democratic Counties gave collectively 4196 Dem majty. If they vote as they did in 1840 the Democratic majty in them will be 2094 which added to the 1500 already obtained in the others heard from will make 3594 Dem majty in the state. But these Counties it is reasonable to suppose (judging from the manner in which those heard from have gone) will not vote as they did in 1840, but that the Democratic Counties will gain for us & that the Whig majorities in the Whig Counties will be diminished. Indeed we are sure that the latter will be the case; indeed one of the Counties which voted Whig in 1840 will this year give 100 Democrates. My opinion, after looking over the whole ground, is that the Democratic majority in this State will exceed 4000. This may be considered very small: indeed it was in a poll of full 500.000 votes which is without doubt the number which has been cast. But that majority is in fact equal to at least 17000, because we had first to overcome a Whig majority of 13200 which added to 4000 makes about 17000.

It is the greatest triumph since the first election of Mr Jefferson. We had especially in this State to contend against patronage, money, Commercial interest to say nothing about the frauds misrepresentations & deceit which were every where used to effect a Whig victory. After it became evident that Pennsylvania was Democratic this state was made the Battleground. On it rested the hopes of the opposition & to carry it every engine that unscrupulousness could use & every means that dispair could devise were put in requisition. But in vain. Democracy triumphed. New York gives its 36 votes to a Democrat, the Union is saved & a republican form of government & republican principles are preserved.

I would add that the County in which Mr Van Buren resides has doubled the Democratic majority it gave in 1840 & that in which Mr Wright resides which gave a Whig majority in 1840 gives this year a Democratic majority of 1400. We are now receiving returns from Michigan which indicate that the Democratic ticket will be elected there by at least 4000 majority.

The election of a Democratic President is in our opinion placed beyond all doubt. I gave it as my opinion at the Convention at Baltimore last May after the nomination had been made that the Democratic party would carry every state South of Maryland & West of it except Kentucky & Ohio. I may be mistaken perhaps in Indiana, but every other of the states referred to I doubt not will give a Democratic vote. Be that however as it may enough of them will be given with New York & Pennsylvania Maine & N. Hampshire to elect a Democrat. This was my ambition & that of every Democrat in this State. We promised not to be found lagging in the Contest & I think I can say that our pledge has been redeemed.

In the hope that you will not deem this an impertinent intrusion....

JOHN T. HUDSON

ALS. DLC–JKP. Addressed to Columbia.

1. Reference is to a seven-county area in the western part of New York. Recognized as a Whig stronghold, "the infected district," as Democrats called it, previously had supported the Anti-Mason movement and more recently had taken up the abolitionist cause. See John T. Hudson to Polk, October 26, 1844.

FROM JOHN McKEON

My Dear Sir New York Novr. 8. 1844

The die is cast. The struggle is over. The battle has been fought in the State and victory perched on the democratic banner. The returns brought by this mornings boat shew that Polk & Dallas have carried the State. The Courier & Enquirer gives us 5000. majority.[1] The Evening Journal at least 2000.[2] These are the leading Whig journals of the State. From all the returns I must advance on the majority I wrote yesterday we should receive. Instead of 2000 it will probably be almost 4000.

You may possibly hear that there is no certainty to the electoral ticket & that our majorities heard from are for Wright as Governor. There is *no doubt of our success in the electoral by thousands.* Wright will have 8 or 9 thousand majority. The cause of the difference is not Whig votes given to Wright but as I suspect some of Mr Van Burens friends who voted Wright & would not vote our electoral ticket. I am not disposed to say harsh things at such a time but I regret to see this difference between our tickets. We have gained back all the counties lost in 1840 by the Canadian excietment.[3]

The Whigs as usual cry out that fraud has defeated them. The truth is that the triumph is one in which the men of the country have defeated the money of the country. Immense sums I am satisfied were spent by the Whig party but in vain. The true Catalina part has been always evinced by them. *Profusus sui, alieni appetens.*[4] This splendid result accomplished by the democracy of the Union should teach the Whigs one lesson. At least to be more careful as to investing money in political questions.

The democracy of the City is in a blaze of excitement. Mutual congratulations are exchanged. Last night Tammany Hall was lighted up. The City resounded during the whole night with the huzzas of the exaulting democrats.

I have kept you advised almost daily since my return of the state of the war in this City & state. My task is finished. The New York election closes the campaign. Your troubles now begin. The responsibilities of the high office to which you have been called are I believe undertaken by you in a spirit which will shew the democracy how well their trust has been placed in you. I congratulate you on the magnificent triumph. I congratulate my fellow citizens on the prospect of a restoration of the general government to a democratic administration.

I pray you to present my regards to Mrs Polk and to remind her of the remark I made at Columbia when I parted with her that our next meeting would be in Washington.

JOHN MCKEON

ALS. DLC–JKP. Addressed to Columbia and marked "Private."

1. Reference is to the *Morning Courier and New York Enquirer*.

2. Reference probably is to the *Albany Evening Journal*.

3. For background on the *Caroline* affair, see Gansevoort Melville to Polk, October 26, 1844.

4. Quotation is a variant of "alieni appetens, sui profusus," which translates, "desiring others' wealth, squandering one's own." Reference is to the character of the Roman conspirator, Lucius Sergius Catilina. Sallust, *Catilina*, 5.

FROM ROBERT ARMSTRONG

Saturday night

Dr Govr. [Nashville, Tenn.] 9 Novr [18]44

The news to night from Pennsyl & Indiana is Most Cheering and has put our City in life & Spirits (the Democratic portion at least). You have carried Pennsyl sweepingly, 10 to 12 Thousand. The PM *Louisville*[1] writes that Indiana has gone by 2 to 3 Thousand. I have no doubt of it. The Whigs claim some little gain in the river Counties of Virginia. Tennessee is Close. Your majority in Middle Tennesse is 3800. *Not less*.

The Whig acct. from *Gibson Henderson* & *Madison* is not correctly given.[2] If East Tennessee has done her duty we are safe by a few hundred. I have requisitioned Harris & Humphreys to write and send you a full statement. Sunday nights Boat will bring all. You never saw such excitement and feeling such as rush to assertain the news. I am broke down.

I send Massleman[3] our old Watchman out with your letters & papers.

R. ARMSTRONG

[P.S.] We have not I hope lost Tennessee. The last vote must be in before we give her safe. I see Prentice[4] in his paper to night *gives up* Indiana. RA

ALS. DLC–JKP. Addressed to Columbia.

1. Reference is to Littleberry Mosby, who served as postmaster from 1841 until 1846.

2. The *Nashville Whig* of November 9, 1844, reported a total Whig gain of 297 votes for the counties of Carroll, Henderson, Madison, and Gibson.

3. Not identified further.

4. Formerly the editor of the Hartford *Connecticut Mirror* and author of an appreciative biography of Henry Clay (1830), George D. Prentice moved to Louisville, Ky., and established the *Louisville Journal*, which he edited from 1830 until 1868.

TO GEORGE M. DALLAS

My Dear Sir: Columbia Tenn. Nover. 9th 1844

I wrote to you on yesterday. Last night, we had returns from 25 out of the 30 counties in Middle Tennessee, which give a Democratic gain of 2198 votes over the vote of 1843. We have reported returns also from four of the Counties in the Western Division of the State, which give a Whig gain over the vote of 1843 of 88 votes. I fear our friends in the West have been mistaken in their estimates. The four Counties in that Division which have been heard from are all strong Whig Counties. As the account now stands there has been a gain in 29 Counties of 2110 votes, over the vote of 1843, which being deducted from 3833, the Whig majority in 1843, leaves 1723 votes to be overcome in the balance of the State. I am greatly disappointed in the vote of the 4 Counties heard from in the West, and if our friends are as much mistaken, in their estimates in the remaining Counties in the East & West, the contest in the State will be exceedingly close, and it is impossible to form a satisfactory opinion which party will carry the State. The returns from all the Strong Whig Counties in the East, will reach Nashville, a day earlier than they will this place and you will probably view them, by the mail which will convey you this letter.

The returns from the Counties heard from in Middle Tennessee, come fully up to our estimates, and I hope our friends have not been so much mistaken in their estimates in the East & West as I fear they have been.

We received returns to day from 5 Counties in Pennsylvania–viz Allegheny, Washington, Westmoreland, Green & Fayette, which give a gain of 717 votes over Mr Shunk's vote in your October election, which we think puts an end to all doubt about the vote of that State.

James K. Polk

ALS. PT. Addressed to Philadelphia and marked "*Private.*"

FROM J. GEORGE HARRIS

Saturday Eve 9 o'clock

My Dear Sir: Nashville [November 9, 1844][1]

We are in high spirits to-night. The intelligence from Pa. and Indiana, in the judgment of our friends, renders those States *certain*.

From the best calculations we can make our majority in all Middle Tennessee (Fentress excepted) is 3730. If there be a gain of 70 in Fentress, as we hope, it reaches 3800.

Hamilton, Marion, Knox, Grainger, Roane, Jefferson, Anderson and Bledsoe, of East Tennessee, show a *nett whig* gain of three, according to our figures.

Henry, Weakley, Benton, Hardeman Madison and Perry, give us 650 gain, while Carroll and Henderson give 57 the other way.

A gentleman at the Nashville Inn[2] tonight says he passed through McNairy on the evening of the election, and that our gain is great there—mere rumor.

A gentleman who voted in Shelby and left for this place immediately says our friends confidently expected to carry that county by a handsome majority.

The Whig published false reports for Madison Henderson, Gibson etc this morning which shook our confidence a little,[3] but we now believe if E. Tenn. does not *fall entirely through*, we have the State by a few hundreds.

In making our calculations for Middle Tenn. we have had access to official returns from some 20 counties.

I was most sadly disappointed in Ohio, after the full vote of Hamilton.[4] Therefore I will advance no opinion on the *exact* result of the State.

As I have always known since the nomination, we are to be *decidedly triumphant* in the Union. The all-absorbing solicitude of the present moment is for our own Tennessee. Gen. Armstrong thinks we have it.

J. GEO. HARRIS

[P.S.] *Indiana* Whig gain over vote of '43 in 18 counties—4 votes only. *Pa.* 21 counties Dem gain over Shunk's vote 1860. News from N. York cheering. Dem. portion of the natives have had a great & glorious meeting.[5]

ALS. DLC–JKP. Addressed to Columbia.

1. Date identified through content analysis.

2. A landmark hotel, the Nashville Inn was located on the north side of the public square.

3. See Robert Armstrong to Polk, November 9, 1844.

4. Returns from Cincinnati, seat of Hamilton County, gave Polk an early lead in the Ohio election count.

5. Democratic American Republicans held a meeting in front of City Hall on the evening of October 31, 1844, which was reported in the *New York Herald* of November 1, 1844.

FROM JOEL B. SUTHERLAND

6 oclock am
Philada Nov 9th 1844

My dear Sir.

Last night I met an immense mass of our Democratic friends overflowing with enthusiasm. Having promised, from my calculation, that the State of New York, would go for us & having explained my reasons for my belief, when they were over whelmed with misgivings, it was but natural that on the *receipt* of the news of our victory that they should call upon me most clamorously to address them. I accordingly ascended the platform & was recd as Democrats are capable of receiving their friends. After addressing them for sometime, & lamenting that we could not wait upon you personally, I proposed, that we should visit Mr Dallas, & congratulate him upon your, his, & our success. This proposition was recd with deafening applause. I then also proposed, that we should have a procession, to take place next Wednesday week when, the Democracy, will doubless turn out in its full might. The procession for the Evening was then formed, & Mr Dallas notified of the advance of the immense body of freemen to congratulate him. I then went to see Mr Dallas & explain the time of their *expected* arrival. A few minutes only elapsed, before we heard their approaching huzzas. At length they reachd the residence of the Vice Presidential candidate of the Democracy, who enchained the thousands present, with a most eloquent speech for about 1/2 an hour. The only, thing, that I desired was, that you & the Old Genl.[1] could have seen this *multitudinous* throng of freemen & had the chance of speaking to them. Many of them will however see & hear you at your Inauguration.

We have great hopes now of N.C. I have often in my speeches to the people here, *since* the Georgia election claimed NC. Yesterday afternoon the Hon. J. *Wentworth*,[2] met me in the street & told me, that he was just from Washington and that the *evening before*, they had celebrated at that place, our victory *anticipated* in N.C. They were all sure he said of N.C. I think we will have every slave holding state, except Maryland &

Kentucky. The Texas Question did a large business for us in the *border* counties of N.Y. lining Canada.[3]

Our cup of political joy is over flowing. Make my respects to Mrs Polk.

J. B. SUTHERLAND

ALS. DLC–JKP. Addressed to Columbia and franked by Andrew Jackson.

1. Andrew Jackson

2. Elected as a Democrat to five terms in the U.S. House, 1843–51 and 1853–55, John Wentworth of Illinois switched parties and in 1857 won election as a Republican to the mayorship of Chicago and served in that post until 1863; he won a sixth term in the U.S. House in 1865.

3. Reference probably is to strong anti-British feelings among New York citizens residing on the Niagara River border with Canada, where British troops had made incursions onto American soil while in pursuit of Canadian rebels in 1838. See details of the *Caroline* incident in Gansevoort Melville to Polk, October 26, 1844.

FROM ROBERT ARMSTRONG

Sunday night

D Sir [Nashville, Tenn. November 10, 1844][1]

I send you enclosed a list of Gains etc. for the State. Official in part and others Reported. I am fearfull we have lost The State by some 200 or 300. It is mortifying. Eastman is in and brings official from East Tennessee all but five Counties. Taking his report for them

East Tennessee has *gained*	1019
Middle Tennessee *placing* Fentress at 47 Gain gives	2100
The District Gives *but*	508
	3627

This leaves a small majority against us. Perhaps when reports are corrected we may Fare better.

The News from Pennsyl. is good. The Whigs crow and say they have carried Indiana. Ried[2] and Dawson say we have and Prentice *again* in his paper[3] received to night gives it up.

It is one oclk. Heiss has my letters or I would send them. We look to New York—every thing depends on her.

R. ARMSTRONG

ALS. DLC–JKP. Addressed to Columbia.

1. Date identified through content analysis.

2. An Indiana Democrat, James G. Read served in the state legislature for over twenty years. He ran as the Democratic candidate for governor in 1831 and 1834, but lost both races. He was a Polk presidential elector in 1844.

3. Reference is to the *Louisville Journal*.

FROM SAMUEL H. LAUGHLIN

My dear sir, McMinnville, Tenn. Nov. 10, 1844

The battle is over, and the smoke and clouds of dust raised by the rencontre have already sufficiently passed away to enable us to see, as I am well satisfied, that to providence and a virtuous people our cause is indebted for a crowning and glorious victory. To say that I feel proud and happy, although writing in a sick bed, would not express half the joy and exultation I feel on the occasion.

Here, returns come in slowly and irregularly. The enclosed[1] contains all we had here up to yesterday evening. Today, we have good news, showing upwards of 800 gain in East Tennessee, and many of our good counties, or rather several of our good counties to hear from. This news is on Whig authority, and when we get the truth, I expect it will be still better. You, however, I doubt, will have returns from all the counties before this reaches you.

Our friends here are still under excitement, and parading nightly with bands of music, lights, small arms and a small cannon—marching in successive nights, to the houses of prominent democrats in every direction for ten miles round. In this County the Whigs put forth all their powers from Nashville, and really believed they were going to gain 100 votes. Morford has hurried off to Nashville today, to *explain* I suppose how they were deceived, or rather to *hedge* off as they say in his *bettings*, for he and others hereabouts are in the way of losing enough to ruin them.

In attending a meeting on Monday before the Election, I got a thorough wetting, which has added both to the heat and cold of my ague, and which has kept me pretty nearly in bed ever since. Dr. Smartt, however, is patching me up with quinine pills, and I shall soon be well. I packed up on Thursday to start back to finish my few weeks of valedictory labors, but had to go to bed. The last of the copy I left at Nashville was exhausted in an article on Tennessee political statistics, and an appeal to go to the polls, quoting Humphrey's revolutionary poetical address[2] to Washington's Army; but Col. Harris will keep things going well. I shall conclude my labors with serious, candid appeals to the democracy of

Tennessee upon their *rights* and future *duties*, both in regard to their position and their principles, and as a means of security, their duty in sustaining an independent press. These valedictories, and all leading Editorials of the Union from now till after the Inauguration you being elected, should be *general* in their character, so as to avoid the appearance of committing you on any subject by implication as to the details of any measure. They, however, should be strong for the broad, general principles of democracy. This shall be the character of what I shall write, and in a few weeks I shall write a good deal.

The moment I can bear the stage, or buck my old gray, I will be at Nashville. Old Gen. Smartt[3] is here today at church. In his anticipations of final victory, he is a most happy man, and says that when I write I must convey you his respects and say, "may God bless you and yours."

I know how you are pressed with letters, and when I began to write, thought I would only write four lines uniting my congratulations with the tens of thousands which are daily reaching, and being sent to you.

Already, I have a favor, however, to ask, not, however, as of the future President, but as of an old friend. If our electoral ticket prevails, and it has I doubt not, please say to Mr. J. H. Thomas, or any Elector you see, that I shall be thankful for the respectable but humble appointment of Messenger to carry the vote. Last time I went to Washington, it was at my own expense.[4] Now, I want to go at Uncle Sam's. I believe the pay about covers the expense of the whole trip.

S. H. LAUGHLIN

P.S. Dr. Smartt having distributed the copy of Owen's Texas Speech which the envelope of this covered, and saved me the frank, I use it to avoid the post office tariff. I suppose it is no harm. I learnt the way of it of yankee Editors and their members of Congress. S.H.L.

ALS. DLC–JKP. Addressed to Columbia and franked by Julius W. Blackwell. Laughlin marked the letter "Private."

1. Enclosure not found.

2. Laughlin's references are to the *Nashville Union* editorials "Tennessee Election Statistics" and "To the Polls!"; they appeared respectively in the issues of November 2 and 4, 1844. A soldier, diplomat, and poet, David Humphreys rose to the rank of lieutenant colonel during the Revolutionary War and served as aide-de-camp to George Washington. Apart from poetry, he also published books on sheep breeding and agriculture and a biography of Israel Putnam. In the editorial "To the Polls!" Laughlin quoted two lines from Humphreys' poem, "On the Future Glory of the United States of America": "With God-like aim, in one firm union bind,/ the common good and interest of mankind."

3. A farmer in Warren County since 1806, William C. Smartt attained the rank of brigadier general in the militia following the War of 1812; he served one

term in the Tennessee House, 1817–19, and two terms in the Tennessee Senate, 1821–23 and 1825–27. He was the father of Thomas C. Smartt, Laughlin's son-in-law and physician.

4. Laughlin last visited Washington City in May and June while en route to and from the meeting of the Democratic National Convention, which met in Baltimore, Md., May 27–31, 1844.

FROM SAMUEL MEDARY

Dear Sir, Columbus, O. Nov. 10, 1844

It is with unusual gratification that I can call you *President elect*. I feel as though our country had been snatched as it were from the jaws of despotism just ready to swallow her up. Had Mr. Clay succeeded in fastening upon us his measures I should almost have dispaired of the republic.

The loss of Ohio cast us down beyond measure, our hopes of redeeming ourselves on the 1st of Nov. from the disgrace of defeat on the 8th of Oct. were too high. Fraud, forgery and the cursed abolitionists ruined us. They positively worked the women and children into the belief that if you were elected, their husbands and brothers should instantly be called to march as soldiers into Texas or Mexico to be butchered by Spaniards and Indians! I cannot think the country would suffer much, however, by such a catastrophy!

Your majority in Indiana will be from one to two thousand.

If our returns here from Kentucky are evidence of the State, Mr. Clay will be hard pushed at home.

Our friends are in the greatest possible glee. The Whigs declare that their party is dissolved.

S. MEDARY

[P.S.] The news from N. York to-night reduces our maj. from expectations last night, but all safe. I have sent a statement to Genl. Armstrong, which he will send you with this.[1]

ALS. DLC–JKP. Addressed to Columbia.

1. Medary wrote his postscript in the left margin of his letter. Reference is probably to Medary's letter to Robert Armstrong of November 9, 1844. ALS. DLC–JKP.

FROM ROBERT ARMSTRONG

Dr Sir [Nashville, Tenn. November 11, 1844][1]

I send you slips, Letters &c in another envelope. Virginia has done noblely, a fine increase in her vote upon Van Buren.

Indiana following handsomely, while the Old Key Stone comes up with her Ten thousands.

Federal Maryland has gone for Clay. The Signs from No Carolina look Improving. M[iss]ouri Miss & Georgia are all increasing and give the best Indications.

Tennessee has been the bloody Ground in this Contest. So Close that it is Impossible to determine how the State has voted untill the Official returns come in and the Reported Majorities are Corrected.

I place all the returns in Young's *Box* and have them opened here and take them down.[2] I will attend to this matter.

The New York news shall go out by express & more rapidly than the *last*. We cannot have it before Wednesday night unless it is sent out from N. Y. by Express to Connect with the *Mail* at Cumberland.

You never saw a people in so much confusion, so much at a loss, as Daring to get at and Determine this States Election. No business doing or attended to an nothing but a *Searching after* "The News."

My Impression is that we have carried the State. We surely have if our Reported Majorities are Correct, and Eastman says those of East Tennessee will *turn out* better when the Official reports are recvd.

The Majority cannot be more than 50 votes. I am fearful that we have a wrong Report from Tipton: 200 Demo Majr brought by Judge Miller.[3] We will have it all by Wednesday evening and forward on to you.

The Old Genl[4] sent me a Letter from Mr Van Buren of 3d in which he says "That all the combinations combined cannot defeat the Democratic party in New York. That your majority will be 1500 to 2000 in spite of every thing, let Whigs Natives &c do their utmost." Harris' Brother writes me from Buffalo that in that Quarter all is going on Swimingly and Safely that *no* combinations can or has been effected there. In haste....

R. ARMSTRONG

ALS. DLC–JKP. Addressed to Columbia.

1. Date identified through content analysis.

2. John S. Young, a native of Virginia, settled in Warren County, Tenn., about 1830 and later moved to Nashville, where he practiced medicine. The General Assembly elected him secretary of state in 1839, and he held that position until 1847.

3. Reference probably is to Austin Miller, a lawyer from Bolivar, Tenn. Judge of Tennessee's Eleventh Circuit Court from 1836 until 1838, Miller won election as a Democrat to three terms in the Tennessee House, 1843–47 and 1861–1863.
4. Andrew Jackson.

FROM CHARLES G. ATHERTON[1]

My dear Sir, Nashville N.H. November 11th 1844

I cannot refrain from congratulating you on the result of the Election in New York Pa & Virginia, which must render your Election to the Presidency & the glorious triumph of Democracy certain. Thanks–ten thousand thanks to our friends in those states who have conducted the contest with a zeal & energy worthy of the cause. The Empire State, Wright & Van Buren have behaved nobly.

I spoke at Worcester Mass. on thursday Evening last. On that day the Whigs there, & in Boston were claiming a triumph in New York. They got out handbills in Worcester for a Whig Meeting in the Evening claiming New York as sure for Clay. At half past four p.m. the democratic news came in by the Western Rail Road, & we had a Democratic gathering of two thousand in the Town Hall the enthusiasm of which defies description. The Whigs at Worcester, & Boston on friday were so completely chopfallen that they would have been really objects of compassion, did we not well know their overbearing insolence in times of success.

I trust we shall hear in a few days that Tennessee has done her duty.

Our good friends Col. & Mrs. Bell, it is to be feared, will not be highly gratified with the result of the Presidential campaign.

Mrs. Atherton sends her congratulations and regards to Mrs. Polk to which please add my own, and believe me ....

C. G. ATHERTON

ALS. DLC–JKP. Addressed to Columbia.

1. A Harvard graduate and lawyer in Dunstable (now Nashua), New Hampshire, Charles G. Atherton served three terms as a Democrat in the U.S. House, 1837–43, and one term in the U.S. Senate, 1843–49.

FROM JOHN F. H. CLAIBORNE[1]

My dear Sir, Natchez Nov 11th 1844

We are now sanguine of carrying this state by at least 5,000 majority & Louisiana by at least 1,000.

We have fought hard, & almost every man has done his duty.

I have edited the Free Trader & Vicksburg Sentinel during the canvass, gratuitously, and done a large portion of the writing for the N.O.

Herald & Jeffersonian, a strong democratic journal, which you will see I am going down to take charge of & hope to give it a tremendous circulation in La. this state & Arkansas.

J. F. H. CLAIBORNE

P.S. I recd. a letter from Silas Wright to day, but he speaks with much distrust of the result in N.Y., but still hopes strongly. My faith never wavers. There can be no doubt. We *cannot* be beaten more than once in a qr of a century.

ALS. DLC–JKP. Addressed to Columbia.

1. A lawyer, editor, and historian, Claiborne served two terms in the Mississippi House, 1830–34, before his election to the U.S. House in 1835. His bid for a second term failed when Sergeant S. Prentiss contested the 1837 election and the House voted to seat Prentiss. Claiborne moved to New Orleans, La., in 1844, where he edited the *Daily Herald and Weekly Jeffersonian*, the *Louisiana Statesman*, and later the *Louisiana Courier*. He also wrote several historical works including a history of Mississippi.

FROM ROBERT P. FLENNIKEN

My dear Sir Union Town 11 Nov [18]44

Although from the moment I first heard of your nomination I have never doubted your election, yet this is the earliest opertunity I have of conveying to you absolute certainty of the result, & my *most hearty* congratulations upon *your* success & that of democratic principles. Your election is now *certain*. Your triumph *noble*, & the issue of the contest *Glorious*. Principle has succeeded over the duplicity, the chicanery & the fraud of the Whig party. The power of their money & the power of their combinations have alike proved unavailing, and the single hearted, honest yeomanry of the country, firmly fixed upon their principles with unshaken attachment to the institutions of their country have eminently triumphed.

But my dear Sir, the moral effect of this achievement is perhaps its greatest beauty. Not only our political institutions in their simplicity & harmony are *safe*, but the veracity of the country of is *safe*. & Mr Clay with his many moral delinquencys, & the respectable & numerous party who sustained him are not only emphaticaly but I trust effectually *rebuked*. Again with heart felt Joy I congratulate you for your elevation to the "great office."

I have not time now nor has my feeling of anxiety sufficiently subsided since the result of N. York has been known, to render a letter interesting to you. My principle object in writing is to apprise you that Dr Kennedy[1] of this town one of the principle owners of the National Road Line of stages and a distinguished democrat has proposed, or rather has in process of building a coach to convey you upon your Journey to Washington from the city of Wheeling to Cumberland where you will take the cars. This coach although it will be a superb one, yet neither it nor any of our arrangements for conducting you from Wheeling to Cumberland on the N.R.[2] will have any thing of pageantry connected with them, but will conform to the true dignity of democratic style & deportment. This line of stages upon our road is owned mainly by democrats. The other entirely by Whigs. I hope you will therefore allow me to take charge of you as indicated from Wheeling to Cumberland.

Penna has gone *well*, N. York *nobly*. We have not as yet heard one word from Tennessee. I am extremely anxious that we carry that state although not necessary to your election. I will write to you again in a few days[3] embracing a few things within our political Horoscope.

I hope I may have the pleasure of an answer to this as early as your convenience will enable you.

R. P. FLENNIKEN

P.S. You will in a few days receive an invitation from Dr Kennedy[4] to take his coach at Wheeling. R.P.F.

ALS. DLC–JKP. Addressed to Columbia. Polk's AE on the cover reads, "Tenders a stage coach from Wheeling to Washington. Ans & left it to my friends Jany 20th 1845." Polk's reply has not been found.

1. Howard Kennedy served as the postmaster of Hagerstown, Md., during the 1830's; after working several years as a special agent in the Post Office department, he resigned from that post in 1844 and became a partner in the National Road Stage Company.

2. The National Road.

3. Flenniken's letter has not been found.

4. On November 12, 1844, Howard Kennedy wrote Robert Armstrong and warned him that members of the rival stage line, the Good Intent Company, were all "most decided Whigs." Kennedy added that since he and one of his partners were Democrats, they believed that they had "the right to the company of *President Polk*." ALS. DLC–JKP.

FROM JAMES S. McFARLANE[1]

Monday 10 O'clock A.M.
New Orleans 11th Nov 1844

Respected Sir

It affords me inexpressible pleasure to be able to assure you that a glorious triumph has just been achieved by the Democracy of Louisiana.

You have no doubt ere this received similar communications; but up to this period they have been merely conjectural.

The unexpected & alarming Whig majorities in what is termed "The Atakapas Country," created great apprehensions in the minds of the democracy of New Orleans until the returns *just received*, placed the result beyond a doubt.

The Atakapas country is an extensive prairie district and almost every inhabitant is engaged in the raising of stock, and dependant upon the grazing capacities of the soil.

Our unscrupulous & untiring opponents sprung a mine upon us for which we were entirely unprepared. They stated to the unsuspecting & primitive inhabitants, generally denominated "Acadiens," that Texas being a great Prairie country; its annexation would completely destroy the stock and grazing business of "Atakapas," and ruin all its inhabitants. You may judge sir of the untoward effects of their artful misrepresentations, when you learn that in the three counties of St. Landry St Martin and St Mary, in which three counties Gov Mouton[2] received Forty eight majority in 1842 (July). At the late election the Whig ticket received *eight hundred and eighty four*, majority. You may judge sir that our apprehensions up to this period were not without reasonable foundations.

So far as the returns are in, the Democratic ticket is seven votes ahead, and we have the following parishes to hear from viz. Vermillion, De Soto, & Sabine, Franklin, Caddo Calcasieu, Claiborne, Morehouse, Lafayette (Gov Moutons Dist) Natchitoches, Ouichita, Union & Bossier, all Democratic strongholds, (except Caddo, which has heretofore given a varying vote;) which will according to the most rational calculations, carry our majority up to from eight hundred to a thousand in the State.

With the most sincere wishes for your health and happiness Sir, and the most earnest prayers for the success of the holy cause of popular rights, and human liberty in which you are engaged....

JAMES S. MCFARLANE

ALS. DLC–JKP. Addressed to Columbia and enclosed in McFarlane's letter to Polk dated November 12, 1844.

1. A Louisiana physician, James S. McFarlane served as corresponding secretary of the Louisiana Democratic Association during the presidential campaign of 1844. In 1853 he published a pamphlet on yellow fever entitled, *A Review of the Yellow Fever, Its Causes, etc. With Some Remarks on Hygiene.*

2. Born in the Attakapas district, now Jefferson Parish, Alexander Mouton served several terms in the Louisiana House, 1826–32 and 1836–37. A Democratic presidential elector in 1828, 1832, and 1836, Mouton won election to the U.S. Senate in 1837, resigned his seat in 1842 to run for the Louisiana governorship, and served in that post from 1842 until 1846.

FROM JAMES M. PORTER[1]

Dear Sir Easton Pennsa. Nov. 11. 1844

Permit me to congratulate you on the result of the Election which makes you Chief Magistrate of this great Republic. A result in my judgment infinitely important to our County and its institutions, whilst it cannot but be a gratifying tribute to your talent, Character and public services. I regret to perceive however that there has been in New York some little evidence given of the disappointed feelings of some of the friends of Mr. Van Buren, as manifested by their giving the Electoral ticket a smaller vote than the Governor. I may be mistaken, and I hope to be forgiven if I do the man injustice, but I think the fact that Lancaster County in this State gave Mr. Clay 400 more majority than it did Markel,[2] furnishes some evidence that Mr. Buchanan had not his heart as much in this Contest as he ought. For I think such a result is not to be found in any Other County in our state, and could not have been brought about if he had and Excercised the influence which his friends claim that he once at least possessed.

I have no other interest in your administration than any other private Citizen, professing democratic principles. If I retain my present feelings I shall have no desire to quit my present retirement and the practise of my profession, and hence shall not be of the tribe of those who will be pestering you with applications either in behalf of myself or friends. I feel deeply solicitous that your administration should be such as to promote the best interests of the Country and by so doing redound to your own Credit and I may from these Considerations be induced occasionally to trouble you with my opinions both as to men and things. If I should I shall pledge myself to do so as disinterestedly as I would to my own Brother. It is not to be expected that any gentleman should personally know all the men who are either spoken of or who become aspirants for office and I know that on that subject it is very hard for a President to ascertain the exact truth. The most importunate are seldom the best qualified or the most deserving. And it is almost impossible to discover real and modest merit which is ever retiring and kept in the shade by the more prominent, though generally the less deserving applicant who presses his own Claims.

In the selection of your Cabinet You will of Course see to the selection of men of talents. You will find great comfort in having them men of industrious business habits. In some of the departments men of talents *for detail*, as well as for understanding principles are essentially necessary. I particularly refer to the departments of the Treasury, War, Navy,

& Post Office. I think they have never had the Equal of David Henshaw[3] in the Navy Department since the Government was organized And had he remained with that department he would have systematized it and saved the Government millions. I consider him, take him for all in all, the greatest man, at this day, in New England, and if ever again brought into public life his merits will be appreciated. He was rejected by the Whigs, because Danl Webster required it at their hands ere he would support Henry Clay, and the leading friends of Mr. Van Buren joined in endeavoring to Crush him because he honestly thought & expressed the opinion that the nomination of Mr. Van Buren would secure the election of Mr. Clay. But I find I am running into a long letter, which I certainly did not intend doing when I commenced. I therefore beg leave to Close assuring you that you have no more sincere friend than....

J. M. PORTER

ALS. DLC–JKP. Addressed to Columbia.

1. James M. Porter, a Pennsylvania lawyer, jurist, and brother of David R. Porter, served as ad interim secretary of war from March 8, 1843, until January 30, 1844.

2. Joseph Markle.

3. A prominent Democrat from Massachusetts, David Henshaw had previously served as collector of the port of Boston prior to his service as ad interim secretary of navy from July 23, 1843, to February 19, 1844. The Senate overwhelmingly rejected nomination to the permanent post on January 15, 1844. In a similar vote on January 30, 1844, the Senate rejected the nomination of James M. Porter as secretary of war.

FROM JOSEPH B. SOUTHALL

My Dear Sir — Nashville Nov. 11. 1844

You may be at a loss, as we all here, have been, and still are, to ascertain the result in Tenn. After the mail came in from E. Tenn last night I gave up the state as lost but I have been reassured to day, and I still cling to the *beleif* that all is well here, and that without the state of N. York. To night's news settles the matter in your favor. I have *carefully* examined the returns official, in the office of Secretary of State, and they are as above stated. The rest are as they have reached us by mail. The only points I fear are *Tipton* and *Campbell*. My report from [...][1] was brot by Judge Miller and was adopted by Whigs in an Extra until to night, when *they* claim 19 gain. Eastman says he obtained the report from *Sevier*,[2] from [...] the old & new sheriff of the County and may be relied on. If these reports be confirmed, we have then only 55. to overcome by *Fentress*, the only county to be heard from. These Tables may enable you to form an opinion of the result. I must & will believe that Tennessee is true. If we are beaten at all, God grant, my calculations all may be false and that it may be, by such a majority as will save us from the Mortifying reflection, that if we had done and worked a little more, we should have triumphed.

The news to night is cheering which you *will receive—1300* gain in 12 counties being Pennsylvania, 6 to 8000 majority. Prentiss of Louisville[3] says after a careful examination, the Whigs have gained only 186, as far as heard from, in *Indiana* and that the State is lost beyond a doubt. Tyack writes good news from N. York, that the State is safe, but says (Nov 3) that the Whigs have given up their tickets for congress and assembly, but that the Natives will vote as Whigs or Democrats. This looks too much like a coalition but yet the state must be safe. Maryland gone for the Whigs. If we lose Tenn, which I can't beleive, I trust to our Old Mother to supply her place.[4] If She is recreant, then to New York.

But I cannot surrender my strong and *abiding conviction*, until the last and I am compelled to it, by the result, that Heaven has ordained it in its wisdom, that Mr. Clay is not to rule over us.[5]

J. J. B. SOUTHALL

[P.S.] I omit for want of room the counties in West Tenn. that are reported officially, but you may rely on the aggregate, to wit—314 nett gain.[6]

ALS. DLC–JKP. Addressed to Columbia.

1. Manuscript torn here and below. Probably Austin Miller of Jackson, Tenn., brought the election reports from Tipton County.

2. Reference probably is to Elbridge Gerry Sevier, who served as a major in the Roane County militia and ran unsuccessfully in 1843 for a seat in the Tennessee Senate. Roane County was in the same senatorial district as Campbell County.

3. George D. Prentice.

4. Reference is to Tennessee's "mother state," North Carolina.

5. Southall enclosed in his letter an extensive county-by-county list of election returns for Tennessee.

6. Southall wrote his postscript at the top of the first page of his letter.

FROM ROBERT ARMSTRONG

Dr Sir Nashville Nov. 12 [18]44

We are still in doubt of the result in Tennessee. No additional returns recvd. Fentress holds the power and will decide the Case Should Our *reported* majority prove true. I am only fearful of that from Tipton. Campbell Polk & McMinn will *Improve*. We have a report from Gallatin, that Fentress has given 140.

The Sheriff of Warren corrected his returns by a second one to day by which we gain eight votes.[1]

I refer you to Dawsons Letter inclosed for the rumours of an Express to Cincinnati.[2] We have the same in the Baltimore Sun (*except the Democratic* Majty) That trio of the Natives *killed* and a Native (a leader) from Philadelphia badly wounded &c &c. There is something in Dawsons rumour for it is plain that he had not heard of any thing of the Kind by News papers &c.

Tomorrow night will settle all & I will be prepared to forward it rapidly. I will not wait for the East Tennessee mail to bring any returns if Tipton comes in right. I think we are safe. That mail comes in at 6 Oclk in the evening.

I send Dawson Letter & others in a separate envelope.

R. ARMSTRONG

ALS. DLC–JKP. Addressed to Columbia.

1. Not identified.

2. On November 10, 1844, Moses Dawson wrote Armstrong that the Whigs in Cincinnati, Ohio, had received word the previous day from an express rider that New York City reportedly had given the Democratic electoral ticket a three to four-thousand vote majority; rumors further prevailed that "there had been much blood shed by an attempt being made by the Native party to get possession of the Polls" in New York City. Dawson makes no reference to any newspaper reports of violence attending the elections in New York City. ALS. DLC–JKP.

FROM BENJAMIN F. BUTLER

My Dear Sir, New York, Nov. 12th 1844

Before receiving this letter, you will have heard from the public prints, and from other quarters, that this state has sustained, by a handsome majority, the nomination of yourself & Mr. Dallas. I cannot forbear congratulating you on this result, especially as it is now reasonably certain, that it ensures your election to the high office of President of the United States.

In any event, it would have given me great pleasure to fulfill the duty, which, as one of the Electors of this state, my fellow citizens have laid on me; it's discharge, with the prospects now before us, will be one of the most gratifying circumstances of my life. For not only shall I feel satisfied, that my country will be saved from the pernicious measures to which your opponents are so fatally wedded, and that her interests will be committed to safe & able hands; but I shall also feel that benefits higher & more lasting even than these, will have been gained by our success.

Your election brings to a fit end, the great Whig Party—a party which had its origin in the reckless efforts of the Bank of the United States, to overthrow, by its vast influence & power, the solemnly expressed will of the People and which has ever since been laboring, in opposition to that will, to fasten upon our institutions another excrescence of the like dangerous character. It settles and I hope forever, the question presented in 1833–4, and under various forms ever since pending, whether this Nation is to be ruled by *Men* or by *Money*, in other words, whether we are to retain the semblance and the semblance only, of a free Republic, or to remain such in fact as well as in form. It thus adds to the civic triumphs of President Jackson, and to the equally heroic efforts of his successor, all that was needed, to complete the victory of the Democracy of numbers, over the combined hosts of the Aristocracy of Wealth.

To be elevated to the chief magistracy of this great Republic, in connexion with a triumph in such issues, is, indeed, a very high honor, one which you doubtless will feel more intensely than any of your fellow citizens, and which, I am sure, will prompt you to the greatest exertions to discharge, in a proper manner, the heavy duties which will press upon you. That you may have the guidance & support, and may win the approbation & reward, of Him, "by whom kings reign & princes decree justice,"[1] and to whom every faithful public servant may confidently look for favor & direction, is my most earnest prayer.

You will at once, be exposed to those harassing applications for office, which within the last few years, have become so incessant & disgusting. From this city especially, you must expect to receive a large amount of this kind of trouble.

On a single point, I will take the liberty to make a few remarks.

Certain politicians in our ranks, who, prior to the Balto. Convention were clamorous against the nomination of Mr. Van Buren have already begun to disparage the efforts of his friends and to charge them with coldness in the support of the National nominations. Nothing can be more unfounded or unjust. Out of this city, the Democrats, to a man were united in desiring the nomination of Mr. Van Buren, and his opponents in this city were but a small fragment of the party. He & all his personal friends were earnest & honest in support of the Balt. nominations. Had they withheld their support, Mr. Clay would have carried the state by an overwhelming majority. Mr. Wright, in particular, was most active and laborious, in the canvass, until silenced by his nomination for Governor, an event, however, of the utmost importance to the cause. His increased vote was not owing to any defection of Democrats, but chiefly to the well known fact, that on his election depended the continuance of the debt-paying & debt-avoiding policy of the last three years.[2] This consideration, aided by his great personal popularity, induced many Whigs, Native Americans, & Abolitionists, who feared the consequences of a Whig triumph, on the financial interest & character of the state, to give him their votes.

I take this occasion to acknowledge my obligations for your friendly invitation of April last, which was forwarded to me after my departure from Nashville, by Gen. Armstrong.[3]

B. F. BUTLER

ALS. DLC–JKP. Addressed to Columbia. Polk's AE on the cover states that he answered this letter on November 25, 1844.

1. Paraphrase of the scriptural verse, "By me kings reign and princes decree justice." Proverbs 8:15.

2. Reference is to New York's "stop and tax" law. See Gansevoort Melville to Polk, October 26, 1844.

3. Letter not found.

FROM ALBERT G. JEWETT

Dear Sir Cincinnati Nov 12 [18]44

Immediately after my arrival in this City, there was an intense excitement as to the result in New York, but an examination of the returns satisfies me that you will receive the vote of that great State. Forty nine counties are heard from, having 628 of Harrison's majority to be overcome in the ten remaining counties, nearly all of which are in Mr Wrights neighborhood,[1] which counties gave over 4000 majority for Gov. Bouck in /42. I was in some of these counties several days, and our well advised friends expected to gain pretty largely in that section. The Tribune thinks St Lawrence County may gain for us 1500.[2] I think not so much. Our friends expected 1000. But the State is safe I feel well assured, but the majority will not exceed I think 2000 or 3000! The whole Whig portion of the Abolitionists has undoubtedly gone for Clay. In the City of New York there was a coalition between Whigs & Natives evidently to a certain extent, but not so fully as in Phila. In all the Eastern States the Abolitionists have voted for Clay, and I have no doubt, they will do so in Maine, but that cannot effect the result here. I have not heard from Tennessee & can but hope you have carried the State. Upon the general result, we have reason I think to rejoice, & to congratulate the country upon the fall of a *man* and a *party*, whose means have been worthy of their purposes. All kinds of stories have been put in circulation about Indiana, and two thousand Whigs claimed that state yesterday afternoon, upon the strength of a story that a passenger had come through Indianapolis, & was there informed, the Whigs have the state by 300, Maj. We have the state by about 2000, and the whipping which the Whigs have received they cannot rub off, let them twist & turn as much as they may.

Please remember me to Mrs. Polk....

A. G. JEWETT

P.S. When at Louisville I was informed that upon the reception of the news from Ohio, about 28 of the Clay glee club went 75 miles in omnibuses to *sing* to Mr. Clay, and that when they arrived at his house, Mr. Clay told them he had so much company he *could not admit them*, and they returned in the rain, having sung one song for Clay.

ALS. DLC–JKP. Addressed to Columbia.

1. Jewett's reference is to upstate New York. Silas Wright, Jr., a native of Vermont, moved to New York in 1819 and settled in Canton, a small town near the Canadian border.

2. Reference is to the *New York Tribune*. St. Lawrence was Silas Wright's home county.

FROM ELAM P. LANGDON[1]

Dr. Sir, Cincinnati, Ohio, Nov. 12. 1844

It gives me great pleasure to hand you the enclosed, Extra, from the "Ohio Statesman"[2] which contains the news that New York has cast her votes in favor of the Democracy, and which ensures its triumph through out the Union. I regret that Ohio did not retain her position, & share in this glorious result. I believe she is still a Democratic State, and will prove herself a loyal member of the National Family. The divisions growing out of the monied influences of the State, has tended to divide the Democrats. It has been with us somewhat as it was at the State elections in Missouri this fall, on the part of the *hard & softs*.[3] And although our leading men were united on the Presidential question, yet, the mass of the people, as the result shows, were not thus united.

I have sent the news daily, since the election returns commenced coming in, to our most worthy friend Genl. Armstrong P M at Nashville, & presume he has not failed to communicate the same to you. About 20 years Since I had the honor of reciving a letter from Genl. Jackson, in reply to one which I wrote to him conveying similar tidings as is contained in this, which gave me great pleasure, & which I have preserved. Shall I enjoy a similar favor from you?

ELAM P. LANGDON

ALS. DLC–JKP. Addressed to Columbia and franked by Robert Armstrong. Polk's AE on the cover reads, "to be answered"; Polk's reply has not been found.

1. A dedicated Democrat, Langdon served as assistant postmaster of Cincinnati for over twenty years.

2. Reference is to the Columbus *Ohio Statesman*; Langdon's enclosure has not been found.

3. Reference is to divisions within the Missouri Democracy over rechartering state banks that issued paper or "soft" notes inconvertible into specie or "hard" currency. See Gansevoort Melville to Polk, October 3, 1844.

FROM JOEL B. SUTHERLAND

My dear Sir Philada. Novr. 12th 1844

The Election is now over & of course your *troubles* will soon begin. Having been *tolerably near* President Tyler[1] I have had some experience of some of the difficulties that environ the *Presidential* Chair. I therefore use the word *troubles*.

I am not an advocate of a *single* term of 4 years. One of 6 might answer as was once suggested during Genl Jacksons Administration[2] & I would not care to see the Constitution so altered. But, I prefer 8 years to keep a *just share of quiet about an administration*. Upon a single term each of the Presidential candidates enter the field of contest instanter & Jealousy injures a thousand good propositions. Both Houses, in such cases necessarily feel the jaring effects of Presidential aspirations. Each will use his best endeavor to get the Executive to his side. It is for these and a host of other reasons, that I am opposed to a single Presidential term of 4 years.

Clubs & Societies are even starting in different states, *at this early day, with reference to the Presidential succession*. This is calculated to draw the attention of our friends away *from* the great object (which is the success of President Polks Administration) to *personal* politics. Nothing of this kind, ought to be allowed. For the *peace* & *quiet* of the Administration which is to commence on the 4th of March, it ought to be distinctly understood *in advance*, that every early movement as to the *succession* to say the least of it, would be considered *indelicate*, if not *absolutely offensive*. It is important, that the next Administration *should wear your own impress upon its face*. But if the Presidential candidates are to *break into the field now* & bring their bickerings in the several states into the ranks of the Democratic party at this time, the *spirit* of *faction* will become too *boisterous* for the *pacific career*, that you are so justly entitled to.

In electing you to the Presidency, the Democrats of the Union *had no eye upon the succession*. They voted for you, because you were just the kind of man they wished & it is their sincere desire that you may administer the govt, as you in your sound discretion may deem right. All they desire, is, that it may be a *Polk Administration* which it can *only be*, by keeping the *competitors* for the *succession* from *splitting up many of your friends into clans* & *exposing your friends whether they agree* or *refuse* to join the clans to the *hostility of Rival competitors*.

I have sent you this for as much as it is worth. Look over it, & I think you will see it has some points about it worthy of consideration. Nothing has been neglected on my part to secure your election, & I think it no more than right, as a proof of my anxiety about your future prosperity to send you this for your perusal. Present my kind regards to Mrs Polk and say to her, that I am desired to ask her first name, as a Farmers wife in Bucks County in this state wishes to call her daughter after her.

J. B. SUTHERLAND

ALS. DLC–JKP. Addressed to Columbia.

1. See John O. Bradford to Polk, October 5, 1844.

2. In several of his annual messages, Andrew Jackson had advocated the elimination of "intermediate" agencies in the election of president and the limitation of the president's tenure in office to a single term of either four or six years.

FROM AARON V. BROWN

Dear Sir Pulaski Novr. 13th 1844

I have no doubt like all the rest of us—you are in a painful suspense. In a few days you will *know* about it & if you ascertain the *final* result on a day when the stage does not come to Pulaski send *an express* to McLaurin[1] at Lynnville with directions to send it to me here, that *is, if favorable*—if not it will get here soon enough. I have given out my Mississippi trip, so I expect to be with you in a few days after the result is known however it may go. We heard here to day (in advance of the mail) that the majority *in the state is* only 70 against us. I suppose the mail of tonight will settle that. No matter we made a noble fight & I think we can do without her.

Do not allow yourself to feel too sensitively on the subject. If elected it is no very great thing to preside over a nation whose morals & princples have degenerated so much of late years & if defeated you have every right to be satisfied with the prompt united & zealous support given you by the Democracy—from the Aroostook[2] to Florida & from the shores of the Atlantic to the farthest mountains of the West.

Farewell but keep me not in ignorance a moment after you know the result. I shall not value a few dollars to an express.

A. V. BROWN

[P.S.] Take some thought of *where* you go & eat & drink, for a little while after your election—the suggestion was first made to me at Nashville.

There is propriety in it too—in the midst of the desperado spirit which now prevails. Throw this in the fire that Mrs. P. may not see this note.[3] A.V.B.

ALS. DLC–JKP. Addressed to Columbia.

1. Frank T. McLaurine served as postmaster of Lynnville, Tenn., from 1837 until the early 1850's.
2. Reference is to the Aroostook River in northern Maine.
3. Above his postscript Brown wrote the word "*confidential.*"

FROM WILLIAM E. CRAMER

Argus Office
Dear Sir Albany Novem 13th 1844

My congratulations are not needed on your elevation to the first office in the Nation. Deeds have shown better than words, the intense interest I felt in the canvass. I can say with truth, that I perilled my political existence on your carrying New York and Pennsylvania.

You probably heard of an "Appeal" to the Adopted Citizens in your behalf, which appeared in the Albany Argus[1] and which excited so much sensation, I might almost say, throughout the Union.

The Whigs had a hope of making political capital out of it. Their State Central Committee had *thirty thousand* copies struck off, which they circulated throughout this State and Pennsylvania.

At first, our friends were frightened for it excited a terrible storm. Mr Croswell himself was *so much scared* that he disclaimed it and threw the entire responsibility on me, though he had read it carefully *previous* to its insertion in the Argus. I did not shrink. I freely avowed myself the athor and was willing to suffer the consequences.

The election is now over, the returns are in and *the result has* so eminently confirmed *the political wisdom* of that Article, that now I have a shower of compliments from the very persons who quailed before the Storm and were anxious to throw me overboard.

When the returns came in, from the Eighth District, where the Germans are very strong, and where the Whig losses were so heavy, Comptroller *Flagg* remarked (as I was informed) "That Appeal in the Albany Argus has been one of the chief means of carrying this State for Gov Polk."

Since the election, I have heard this opinion repeatedly expressed by our most sagacious Politicians. While the Whig Press freely acknowledge their error in giving my Appeal so wide a circulation.

I relate these circumstances to you to show that *I had staked my political existence* on your election, for I have reason to know that had New

York or Pennsylvania went against you, it would have been my political death warrant. With such men, as Mr Croswell Mr Flagg &c success is *the only* criterion of Wisdom and since we have that in our favor, it will now be considered a most fortunate move on my part.

I write thus to you, because from what Mr Melville has told me of your character, I believe that you have the heart to appreciate self-sacrificing devotedness to friends.

In this State, though we have triumphed by a majority on the Electoral of about 5000, our grey heads all say that it was the most terrible as well as doubtful battle that they ever fought. The Whigs are now pretending that the Abolitionists have killed them. This is all nonsense. Nearly *every Whig* abolitionists voted for Clay. Of the Abolition vote in this State, three fourths of the number were originally Democrats. The truth is, the true-hearted Adopted Citizens abandoned the Whig Party almost *en-masse* and supported you with the same zeal and devotedness they did General Jackson. It was an avalanche they could not resist.

As I anticipated Mr Ellis[2] loses his election. He is a man of superior talents and I regret this very much, but such is the fortune of War. His district, however, has done its share in our great triumph. It gave 944 for Harrison and only 400 for Clay. My Father[3] is over-joyed at the general result. Since the election of Gen Jackson, he has never evinced so deep an interest in a Presidential canvass. His relations of friendship when you were at Washington together has made him feel not only a political but a personal pride in your elevation to the Presidency.

WM. E. CRAMER

P.S. The good news from Indiana and Georgia today, has crowned our joy.

ALS. DLC–JKP. Addressed to Columbia and marked "*Confidential.*"

1. On October 12, 1844, the *Albany Argus* ran an article attacking the coalition in Philadelphia between Whigs and Nativist "church-burners." Calling on the Irish, Swiss, and Germans to rally to the Democratic party, the article urged them to overthrow the Whigs in Ohio, New York, Indiana, and Maryland. See the *New York Herald*, October 14, 1844.

2. Chesselden Ellis served as the prosecuting attorney of Saratoga County, N.Y., from 1837 to 1843. He won election in 1843 as a Democrat to the U.S. House but lost his seat in the 1844 election.

3. John Cramer.

FROM MOSES DAWSON

Cincinnati, Ohio. November 13, 1844

Dawson congratulates Polk on his election to the presidency and observes that as the election now stands Polk has the "support of at least sixteen states of the twenty-six" and may yet win North Carolina, his native state. Dawson counts 183 Democratic electoral votes excluding North Carolina. In Cincinnati the Whigs believed that they had won New York, but news received this date by the mails "cooled them down and they sneaked off to their homes leaving a clear field of victory to the democracy who set to firing cannon till near midnight."

ALS. DLC–JKP. Addressed to Columbia.

FROM AMASA J. PARKER[1]

My Dr Sir, Albany. N.Y. Novr 13. 1844

Long before this reaches you, you will have learned the glorious result in our Empire State, a result the more satisfactory because we have succeeded over the influence of large sums of money employed against us & against the combined efforts of Nativeism, anti-rentism[2] & other local factions leagued against us. Your majority in this State will be about 5000. Wright's will probably be over 10.000. You may be surprised at this difference & it ought to be explained. It is not because any set of men belonging to us have been untrue—for all interests, Van Buren men, Cass men & Tyler men were true to our ticket. I do not learn of any leading politician, or any interest, who was not devotedly engaged in our cause, but it is because we have much more difficulty here on questions of National, than of State policy. In all the manufacturing counties we have lost heavily on the tariff question. On the lakes, the supposed hostility of our party to the improving of harbours etc has cost us many votes. On the other hand, on questions of State policy we have received more than a party vote: The prominent & distinguishing State policy adopted & pursued by the Democratic party here, of stopping the public works & of raising half a million a year by direct tax,[3] has met with great favor & inasmuch as it has enabled the State to restore its credit, which depreciated under Whig auspices, it has commanded the support of many of the Whig party & particularly of those interested in State Stocks. These are the true reasons of the difference in the vote & I say to you decidedly that I think your majority in this State quite as large as Mr Van Buren's would have been if he had been re-nominated for President.

We wait here in great anxiety to hear from Tennessee. Not enough returns have reached us from Georgia & Indiana to enable us to learn the result in these States. Yet we are already rejoicing in confidence that a great victory has been achieved & that the nation will be saved from Federal misrule for four years to come. But I will not trespass too long on your time, which is no doubt much pressed by your correspondents, but only add with my sincere congratulations that I am very....

A. J. PARKER

ALS. DLC–JKP. Addressed to Columbia.

1. A lawyer from Delhi, N.Y., Parker won election to one term in the New York House, 1833–34, and to one term in the U.S. House, 1837–39. He served as vice-chancellor and circuit judge, 1844–47, before going to the state supreme court in 1847. In both 1856 and 1858 Parker ran unsuccessfully for the governorship of New York.

2. See William E. Cramer to Polk, October 22, 1844.

3. Reference is to the "stop and tax" law of New York. See Gansevoort Melville to Polk, October 26, 1844.

FROM ROBERT ARMSTRONG

D Sir [Nashville, Tenn.] 14 November [18]44

The News from New York to Night gave us a chill. In the slips last night the *Majority* was given as *gains*.

I have no doubt we have carried the State but by a much less Majority than our friends expected. The slip sent you with your letter &c by Mr Thomas[1] is made up from one sent me by Medary. He is Confident and tells me he has written you. No Carolina is doing better than at her August Election but I *fear* will not come up to do us any good.

New Jersey has [gone] for the Whigs.

William Polk[2] will go out tomorrow night after the mail arrives and take the "Final from New York." I feel satisfied that she has cast her vote for you but Birney has deceived all our friends and come near giving the State to Clay.

R. Armstrong

ALS. DLC–JKP. Addressed to Columbia.

1. Reference is probably to James H. Thomas or Jonas E. Thomas.

2. William H. Polk

FROM GEORGE READ RIDDLE[1]

Dsir Wilmington Del. Nov 14th 1844

I anticipated the pleasure of giving you very different news from our little state of Delaware. Never was a party better organised, more united, or more enthusiastic than the Democratic Party here during the last campaign. To this morning we confidently expected success. We had run you on our ticket in 1840, and had every reason to expect a triumphant victory under your banner in 1844, but upon the very eve of the election, as the paper which accompany's this will show,[2] the Clay Clubs of New York, Philada, and Baltimore, being apprised of our prospects, inundated us with their gamblers, and literally wrested the state from us by means of their *gold*.

I promised, in the National Convention, to send your Tennessee friends good returns, from Delaware. I hope *they* will have a better account to give. I have been so taken up in endiavouring to carry the state, and secure my own election, that their names have escaped my memory. As it has happened the news will reach them soon enough. We have lost the state by about *two hundred* votes.

I beg the liberty congratulating you, that the vote of Delaware, however much we desired to give it, is not necessary to secure your Election....

GEO. READ RIDDLE

ALS. DLC–JKP. Addressed to Columbia and franked by William R. Sellars.

1. A civil engineer and lawyer, Riddle served as a delegate to the Democratic National Conventions of 1844, 1848, and 1856. He won election to two terms in the U.S. House, 1851–55, but failed in his bid for reelection. He was elected to a part term in the U.S. Senate and served from February 2, 1864, until his death on March 29, 1867.

2. Enclosure not found.

FROM ROBERT ARMSTRONG

6 Oclk

Dr Sir [Nashville, Tenn.] 15 Novr [18]44

Reid of Louisville[1] sends me an Express with the *Glorious* News that New York is Yours.

Sloan[2] will deliver you this with the *Extras*. I send enclosed Reid & Irwin letters.[3] This settles the matter and put Whiggery & Mr Clay to *rest*.

Our friends are *happy* and rejoicing, *after* a *Gloomy* night & *day*.

R. ARMSTRONG

ALS. DLC–JKP. Addressed to Columbia and delivered by courier.

1. A staunch Jacksonian Democrat, Thomas J. Read moved from Nashville to Louisville in 1835 and became a wealthy commission merchant.

2. George L. Sloan owned a livery stable and in partnership with F. Sloan manufactured carriages; their establishment was located on Lower Market Street in Nashville.

3. Armstrong enclosed two letter, both dated November 13th and received by express courier from Louisville. See Thomas J. Read to Armstrong and J. M. Irwin to Armstrong, November 13, 1844. ALsS. DLC–JKP. Irwin is not identified further.

FROM ROBERT ARMSTRONG

Dr Sir [Nashville, Tenn.] 15 Novmr [18]44

You receved the News by William & Sloan[1] brought from Louisville by *Reids Express*.

It is all *confirmed* by the mail of to night. What a Triumph—I am too much rejoiced to be reasonable in my Exultations.

Ewing has been addressing *Thousands* to night from the *Bank Steps* and the Cannon is roaring every *note* of which reaches the Old Chief[2] of the Hermitage who had the News in Two Hours after it arrived here.

We (The Democracy) are all *happy* all *rejoicing*.

R. ARMSTRONG

ALS. DLC–JKP. Addressed to Columbia.

1. William H. Polk and George L. Sloan. See Robert Armstrong to Polk, November 14 and 15, 1844.

2. Andrew Jackson.

FROM WILLIAM C. BOUCK

Dr Sir Albany Nov. 15th 1844

Allow me to congratulate you, on your election to the higest office in the gift of the people, and to express the hope that you may be guided by divine Providence, to a successful administration.

The majority in this State is not so large as I supposed it would be, six weeks before the Election. It was evident to me, as I mentioned to you in my last letter,[1] that we were losing strength. The Whigs have spent a large sum of money in this state, but they went into the field at least a fortnight too late. Your true friends regret that you have fallen behind the democratic ticket in this state, but this I think was to some extent unavoidable. It was not the popularity of Mr. Clay, but the Tariff and Texas question. These were the points urged by the Whig party, and I think with some success.

You are doubtless aware that a section of the party here had imbibed strong feelings against the annexation of Texas; and although as I think, they in general gave you an honest support, and wished your success, they were not unwilling that you Should fall behind Mr. Wright, who was considered by them to favor their views, on this question.

The New York Evening Post is the organ of this section of the party, and if you see this paper, you will perceive that they claim that Mr.

Wright has saved the state, and for the reason, that he was opposed to annexation.

The news we have from your state is flattering, and we hope to hear that you have the Electoral vote.

WM. C. BOUCK

ALS. DLC–JKP. Addressed to Columbia.

1. See William C. Bouck to Polk, October 17, 1844.

FROM J. GEORGE HARRIS

My Dear Sir, Nashville Nov. 15. 1844

Some of our friends were strucken a little "a back" last night by the intelligence from New York by the mails, but Medary's advices satisfied us that all was well.[1]

At 3 p.m. to-day, an express from Louisville corroborates and confirms all as you will perceive.

I send you two or three little extras which I prepared and had printed in haste at the Union office.[2]

We *believe* that it is not all impossible that we yet have Tennessee.

J. GEO. HARRIS

ALS. DLC–JKP. Addressed to Columbia.

1. See Samuel Medary to Polk, November 10, 1844.

2. Enclosures not found.

FROM ALLEN McLANE

Respected Sir Wilmington Del Novb. 15th 1844

It gives me real pleasure to address you as President elect of the U. States.

I should have rejoiced indeed, if little Delaware had have cast her votes for you, and it would have been the case if this County, or even this City had been true etc.

Up to Saturday before our election every thing appeared to be going on prosperously; but on that evening, our City was filled with the very worst kind of people from New York Phila. and Baltimore. Bela Badger & Wm B. Reed & Charles Gibbons,[1] of Philadelphia and others of the same kind from N.Y. & Balt. A compleate Union was formed with the Whigs and Native Americans. Money was used whereever it would tell, and the manufacturers compelled their workmen to vote as they dictated. After the Polls closed on the 12th Inst the Whigs, (those who were not in the secret) would have given us 120 maj. in the City; we had only about 30. We have lost our Governor[2] by only 45 maj. I remain....

ALLEN MCLANE

[P.S.] The Leaders of the Whigs, made their followers believe that the Election of President and the control of the U.S. Senate, depended upon Del. We had not fully heard from Georgia & N. Carolina had gone against us.[3]

ALS. DLC–JKP. Addressed to Columbia.

1. John Tyler nominated Bela Badger as naval officer for the district of Philadelphia on June 16, 1841. On July 22, 1841, the Senate postponed consideration of the nomination and in September formally rejected the appointment. Charles Gibbons headed the National Clay Club of Philadelphia and won election to one term in the Pennsylvania Senate, 1845–47.

2. In 1844 William Tharp lost his gubernatorial contest to Thomas Stockton but won election to the post two years later and served from 1847 until 1851.

3. McLane wrote his postscript in the left hand margin of his letter.

FROM WILSON LUMPKIN

My dear Sir — Athens Ga. Nov. 16th 1844

In the result of the late political contest, I am enjoying my full share of gratification, & gratitude to *almighty God*.

You will enter upon the discharge of the important duties which devolve upon you, under a deep sense of their magnitude, and with the kind feelings & best wishes, of the pure patriots, & unaspireing private citizens of our great & glorious confederacy. Your greatest difficulties & perplexities, will arise from *cliques & factions*, who have fought by our sides, in our own ranks. All parties in our country, must necessarily encounter such obstacles.

You are more peculiarly fortunate however in your present position, than most of your predecessors, *unsought, unexpected*, & uncommitted to faction, you are called by the voice of the people, to the cheif majestry of this great nation.

Your own *principles*, & views in regard to all the *important measures* which have divided parties & men, have been triumphantly sustained by the soverign people, *at the polls*. These principles are expounded & published by our friends, who composed the Baltimore Convention, will be adhered to by the great masses of the people who have called you to the presidency. Nothing less than a strict adherence to these principles will satisfy the Country.

It is peculiarly fortunate, that you are elected by the votes of the

Democracy, *dispersed over the whole Union*. You are not the chief magistrate of a section or faction, but of the whole people. Therefore it will be all important, to watch over & guard the interest of *all*. The stronger sections of the country, can never under our constitution, oppress the weaker, by mere majority measures, so long as our chief magistrate adheres to the constitution. May that wisdom which comes from above, guard you against the wiles & intrigues of all *factions*, *cliques*, and ambitious individuals, whose selfish objects are the greatest curse which now threatens our beloved Country. The great difficulty will be to harmonize jaring elements, & make the coming administration *a unit*. From this time till march, is the favorable season, for mature deliberation and wise conclusions. If his health be sufficient, your *best adviser* will be the *Sage* of the *Hermitage*[1]; his opinions have often approached a spirit of inspiration. I consider it very important to conciliate the kind feelings and cooperation of the expireing administration, as far as the interest of the Country will allow. By the liberty herein assumed, I fear I may have placed myself in the atitude of a vain old man, offering advise, or making suggestions for the consideration of the chief magistrate of the Country, but you will recive it, as I intend it—The humble tribute of a private Citizen, who neither holds or desires office, and of one whose youth & riper years, have been spent in the busy scenes of political life, and of one who feels, that the Country, wants more patriotism & less partyism. Let our motto be, *God & our Country*.

Yet no man, in all our wide land, has more ardently desired, to put down modern Whigery with all its abominations than myself, and to place the government in the hands & under the controul, of old fashioned Democratic Republicans. I abhor every measure tending to consolidation, or an infringement of State Rights.

I am enjoying a greene old age of good health, 61 years old, & few men can do more work. Content with my humble condition, and kind feelings for my fellow men.

WILSON LUMPKIN

ALS. DLC–JKP. Addressed to Columbia.

1. Andrew Jackson.

FROM JOHN Y. MASON

My dear Sir: Washington. Nov. 16th 1844

It is now ascertained that a great majority of the people of the United States have determined to devolve on you the arduous and responsible duties of President of the United States. To you it is the highest honor which could be conferred by mortal man, that your course during the canvass has been marked by the highest dignity, while the purity of a virtuous life, has protected you from a single charge of a personal character. Need I say that I congratulate you on the result? With my opinions of the poor moral character, temper and opinions of your opponent, I humbly thank God, that his good Providence has averted the calamity of Mr. Clay's election, from our Country.

We have been acquainted a long time; I flatter myself have always been friends, and I propose to communicate with you in a spirit of perfect candor and frankness, and hope that you will observe the same course in your reply. I do not doubt it.

I resigned my office as a Judge, to take on myself the duties of the Navy Department in obedience to a high sense of public duty. After the Baltimore Convention, I felt very unhappy at the position in which Mr. Tyler's being a candidate was likely to place the members of his Cabinet, who had no desire to separate from the Democratic party. I consulted Genl. Jackson, and he advised me to continue, that Mr. Tyler would withdraw & I have since had reason to know that Mr. Tyler's course had been long determined, and he only postponed it to carry his friends with him. I have continued here, and I believe, that I can render the Country some service in this Department. But on this subject I sincerely desire to relieve you from all embarrassment, and to say to you, that I desire the success of your administration far more anxiously than any personal gratification and if in your opinion, it will conduce in the slightest degree to that result, my resignation will be tendered on the 3d of March. It is however desireable that I should have some intimation of your wishes, and I beg that you will make them known to me, in the full confidence, that they will be my guide without hesitation or heart burning. My family is large, and my arrangements this winter will materially depend, on the answer on your part, that I trust, that you will excuse this communication.

Mrs. Mason[1] unites with me in the Kindest regards to Mrs. Polk. Tell her, that I have not forgotten how we parted when she was in the House of Representatives, but now that she is Mrs. President, I shall fear to be so bold, but that our esteem and affection for her are unabated.

I feel assured, that I do not mistake your feelings, in not doubting that you will fully appreciate my motives in making this communication. I should deeply regret it, if you shall consider it in the slightest degree indelicate or improper.

J. Y. Mason

ALS. DLC–JKP. Addressed to Columbia and marked "Private." Polk's AE on the cover states that he answered this letter on December 6, 1844.

1. Mary Anne Fort Mason.

FROM GEORGE M. DALLAS

No. 20

My Dear Sir, [Philadelphia, Penn.] 17 Nov. 1844

Your letters of the 8 & 9 instant reached me in succession yesterday and today. They contain no news as to your election which we had not received at least twenty four hours before, and I am happy in having known a week ago that the desponding tone of your feelings must be long ere you get this entirely relieved. When, in my last,[1] I announced the result in the City and River Counties of New-York, I was quite convinced, and remained immoveably so, that you were signally successful, even though portions of the South should prove recreant to their own peculiar cause. It is now ten days since I consented to regard the victory as certain, and to receive at my own door, and mainly as your mouthpiece, the congratulatory visit of some fifteen thousand democrats to whom I made an address and returned your thanks.[2] We shall continue a day longer in doubt whether you have carried Tennessee or not; but, however personally agreeable it may be to yourself, to the great cause it is ascertained to be unimportant.

The necessity of preparing to discharge the highest and most delicate public duties is now devolved upon you. That you are abundantly able, I not only know individually, but it is the recorded judgment of the country. You will realize all that your friends have promised, and you will do more. My confidence in this is entire, and cannot be shaken. When, therefore, in the frankness of conversational letter-writing, I put before you the ruminations of my own mind, do not, I beseech you, imagine for a moment that I think you can possibly require them; you do not; but I can't help, by such, voluntary contributions of thoughts and feelings, making an effort to retain unimpaired your esteem and good will. It has pleased our fellow citizens to write us in a remarkable manner, etc. to achieve, by that union, one of the proudest exploits of which the democratic annals can boast; my wish and purpose are to keep that union indissoluble, to make it the means it was intended to be of general and permanent good, and to do nothing, in word or thought, which will not strengthen it. Let me then know, in a single line, and with the candor inherent in your nature, whether this be not, as indeed I feel that it must be, reciprocated.

You will be looking about you, I suppose, at once, so that the 4th of March may find you prepared at all points. Your Inaugural address, your Cabinet, your leading foreign and domestic nominations to the Senate etc. will absorb your meditations, and I am afraid, you will have but little time for correspondence, especially with so unimportant a functionary as a Vice-President. Yet, I shall, of course, exceedingly desire to be initiated into the mysteries of your intentions; particularly if you harbour any in respect to this good State of mine Pennsylvania.

At what time will you leave Columbia on your way to Washington? Cannot you and Mrs. Polk determine to precede your occupation of the White-house by a visit to this City, and allow Mrs Dallas to be your hostess? This step would be very gratifying to the republicans here, who have really fought the battle with extraordinary enthusiasm and who, as the first to speak through the ballot-boxes claim for themselves the foremost honors. I need not say that Mrs. D. and her daughters[3] would be delighted to make Mrs. Polk pass her time comfortably and pleasantly.

G. M. DALLAS

ALS. DLC–JKP. Addressed to Columbia. Polk's AE on the cover states that he answered this letter on December 4, 1844; Polk's reply has not been found.

1. Letter not found.

2. See Joel B. Sutherland to Polk, November 9, 1844.

3. George M. Dallas married Sophia Chew Nicklin, the daughter of a prominent Philadelphia businessman, Philip Nicklin. Dallas and his wife had six daughters: Julia, Elizabeth, Sophia, Catherine, Susan, and Charlotte. Charlotte married Charles H. Morrell, a Cuban merchant; Catherine married a wealthy Bostonian, FitzEugene Dixon; and Elizabeth married David H. Tucker, a Richmond doctor. The other three daughters never married.

FROM ADAM HUNTSMAN

My Dear Sir [Jackson, Tenn. November 17, 1844][1]

A wise general not only knows how to fight, but how to secure the victory. We have taken the outworks, but the Citadel must be taken also. Julias Caesar after the battle of Pharsalia, did not finally conquer the enemy Untill he cut of their supplies of water.[2] We cannot cut down the *Tariff* Untill we cut down their *bread*. We must keep up our organization every where and fight this Bill of abominations[3] on any, & every occasion. If nothing else will bring the Tariff people to their senses, we must as the dernier resort, do as our Fathers did in the Revolution, refuse to use or wear their Northern Fabricks.[4] We must start this immediately on for the next summer election.[5] Moot it in the primary assemblies. Instruct our representatives, vote for no one, for the Legislature who will not aid us by Legislative Resolutions, and By his example in wearing nothing but our western home made stuffs.

If the democrats will adhere to this they will either compel the reduction of the Tariff, or the Whigs will bear the greatest part of the burthen (If the Democracy refuse to purchase). Secondly we must renew the combat for Texas, which will be a gaining business of itself, as the cause of Justice always ought to be. These two questions alone, will be irresistable in the south & west, and many parts of the north, For I have no sort of doubt, that many ten thousands, voted for Clay with great reluctance by reason of his objecting to Texas. As he is out of the way, we can use it with great success. We have a senator to elect at the next session, and have a certainty of gaining two members in the Legislature and an equal chance for success for another in the district. Let our friends throughout the state, begin the work early. With those two questions well managed, we can carry the Governor and both Branches of the Legislature and we must do it. The same degree of enthusiasm cannot be got if for any other man than Clay in the West. Therefore now is the acceptable hour for us to strike. If the Democracy has whipped him, with his opinions upon those subjects upon a full and thorough canvass of them What have we to fight but the capitalists of N England. That they will struggle hard is to be expected. They did so before. If you concur with me in these opinions, I shall be glad to hear from you, for this work must commence shortly. I am only waiting to hear the final result of your Election, to begin my operations. I am old *but chuck fu[ll]*[6] *of fight upon these two subjects* [...] believing from what I have h[eard] that the Democracy has succeeded. It is not impro[per] to consult our friends now [...] [sh]all start to Montgomery County on tomorrow. A letter if you write shortly will find me at *McCallisters Cross Roads*. I may remain there two weeks.

Please present me kindly to *Mrs President* and accept for yourself my hearty good wishes.

ADAM HUNTSMAN

ALS. DLC–JKP. Addressed to Columbia. Published in *THQ*, VI, pp. 363–64.

1. Date and place identified through content analysis.

2. Huntsman's reference is to the Battle of Pharsalus in 48 B.C. Defeated by the legions of Julius Caesar, the remnants of Pompey's forces withdrew and took up a position on one of the hills above the plain of Pharsalus. By cutting off access to a nearby stream, Caesar's legions forced Pompey's troops to surrender.

3. Huntsman probably refers to the 1842 tariff and its likeness to the 1828 "tariff of abominations."

4. Hoping to use economic pressure to overturn the Stamp Act and Townshend Acts, colonial merchants put together in the 1760's a number of nonimportation agreements; in late 1774 the First Continental Congress adopted a nonimportation, nonexportation, and nonconsumption agreement, "The Association," against trade of any kind with Great Britain, Ireland, and the West Indies.

5. Tennessee held elections for Congress, the state legislature, and governor on the first Thursday of August in odd-numbered years.
6. Manuscript torn here and below.

FROM IVESON L. BROOKES[1]

Dear Polk Penfield Greene County Georgia Nov. 18th 1844

I suppose you have occasionally thrown back thoughts to the scenes of Chapel Hill, and it may be, you have not forgotten all your Dialectic associates. Permit me to remind you of the disposition you made of your Euclid. When about taking leave of your friends you called at my room and extending to me that work of unexampled Genius, said "Brookes I present you this Book as a token of friendship." Now sir you may be surprized to learn that I have that book at this moment before me having carefully preserved it in remembrance of the Donor, and that I have never cast my eyes upon it without its having called up the recollection of James Knox Polk and the Debates of the Dialectic Hall. After mentioning this circumstance, which may, perhaps, give you a faint remembrance of an old school mate, I will say to you that I have been gratified, in seeing, through the public papers, from time to time, the onward progress of an esteemed friend on the road to fame; and it is now with feelings of special pleasure I congratulate you upon your elevation thro' the late electoral canvass to the highest seat in the gift of the American people. After leaving college I entered upon the profession of the Gospel ministry and have seldom intermeddled with the politics of the Country even so far as to exercise the elective franchise; yet I have found it difficult not to take sides with one or other of the great political parties of the Country. From N.C. I came to Georgia in 1822, went to S.C. in 1830, removed back to Georgia in 1841. In the old North State I was considered identified in opinion with the Jeffersonian Republicans, in Georgia with the States rights party, and in S.C. with the Nullifiers, having all the while been opposed to a high Tariff for protection, as its object, and in favor of a strict and litteral construction of the Constitution. Upon principle then I have felt constrained to go against the new system of Whiggery in which Clay Adams & Webster seem to be the leaders, combining those measures which would fix upon the Country Clays American System, drive Texas to an alliance with England, Render our great Southen Staple worthless and our slaves a burthen to us, all of which would be as Adams & the rest of the abolitionists wish. I have therefore in the late presidential canvass taken an unusual interest not merely on account of my personal friendship toward yourself but for the sake of the great principles involved in the Election. Mr Clay's partizan leaders in S.C. & Ga have manifested a zeal which has recoiled upon them by rendering it too evident that they are Mr Randolph's[2] men of five principles, going for the loaves & fishes of office. Instance those of them who in '32 went for Nullifying at the peril of the Union and now are the bold advocates of a Tariff even more odious to the South when taken in all its bearings. They have attempted to blind the minds of the people by exalting the talents & qualifications of Clay asserting yourself to be a very obscure individual and utterly incapacitated to honor the high office to which you had been nominated. It is on this point sir that I was perhaps enabled to render you a little service by giving my testimony in your favor (as living in the midst of a whig region under the influence of Dawson & Stephens).[3] I took the liberty to state to the Democratic candidate in Stephens' District[4] (which testimony he voiced) and I also stated the same facts to many others & wrote to some at a distance viz that I was personally acquainted with you during your collegiate course in which you took the first honor & characterized by a laudable ambition & high minded integrity which placed you above the suspicion of a mean action and left the impression upon the minds of your fellow students that you was destined to rise to future eminence; and that such anticipations had been fulfilling in the various instances of your promotion, as by your state to a seat in Congress, by that honorable body to be the Chairman of several important committees, and to their speaker's Chair, and again by your fellow citizens, to that gubernatorial Chair. All of which evinced the high testimony of those best calculated to judge of your talents to fill responsible offices, & which indicated that the helm of this great Republic would not suffer in your hands. May the Greater Ruler of Nations under whose Providence you have been promoted to the most responsible office enable you to make a wise selection of counsellors ("in the multitude of Counsellors there is safety")[5] and so administer the affairs of this great Nation as to baffle the gainsayings of your enemies & meet the expectations of your friends. While just here permit me to say that it would be a source of much gratification to me to have confirmed by your own pen a statement which has reached me affirming you to be a member of a Christian Church.

I have already I fear taxed your patience but it occurs to me that you perhaps may feel some curiosity to hear something of my personal condition after a lapse of a quarter of a century. As to my moral character so far as I know, my garments are thus far unstained and in reference to my transactions with men my conscience is, I trust, void of offence. I have passed some scenes of affliction & reverses of fortune. I have lost by death two wives & two children[6] and perhaps more than forty slaves within the last twenty years. Also by a foolish purchase on credit of a considerable amount of property on the heel of the change in times I have perhaps lost the nett income of my resources for the last ten years. Yet like Job I may under all these reverses be considered as attended by a favoring Providence. I am now blessed with a lovely wife[7] with whom I have lived for some 13 years. She has five daughters, by the second I have two daughters & by the first the youngest of three children survives, and the only son[8] I have had born to me. He is now 18, is in the Senior Class in College & is a promising boy. My daughters[9] with one exception (who has had feeble health from infancy) are healthy handsome and intellectual. In my marriages I have become connected with highly respectable families & have fallen into the hands of pretty women. I have under the divine Providence been enabled to contribute several thousand dollars for the promotion of Education & Religion and with my attention to the small patrimony derived from my parents[10] and the amounts received by my wives I am the owner of largely over a hundred slaves & more real estate than is sufficient for them to cultivate. I mention my condition not boastingly but that you may see I have not been idle, and that as a southern planter I am deeply interested in having the Tariff reduced to the revenue standard & so arranged as to bear equably upon all sections of the Country & thus to raise the price of cotton in Europe by the sale of their fabrics here being allowed a fair competition with American fabrics, and in having the Annexation of Texas effected & thereby the value of our slaves sustained by opening up that fertile region for the employment of their labor & by paving the way for a further outlet to their intrance into Mexico etc.

Finally as you will very likely have many applications for office I imagine you may be tempted to wonder which of Uncle Sams loaves in the gift of the President does my old schoolmate desire? Here sir to relieve this address from the suspicion of any other than motives of disinterested friendship permit me to assure you that all I ask is that you will shortly (before the press of business) find time to write me a line in reply to this letter....

IVESON L. BROOKES

ALS. DLC–JKP. Addressed to Columbia. Polk's AE on the cover states that he answered this letter on January 3, 1845; Polk's reply has not been found.

1. Brookes, an 1819 graduate of the University of North Carolina, was ordained a Baptist minister in 1820; he served as rector of an academy in Eatonton, Ga., before his first marriage. Through marriage he acquired a substantial fortune and became a wealthy planter. In 1835 he began to write letters and tracts defending slavery; his best known pamphlets, written in 1850 and 1851, were entitled respectively, *A Defence of the South against the Reproaches and Incroachments of the North* and *A Defence of Southern Slavery against the Attacks*

of Henry Clay and Alexander Campbell. Polk and Brookes were members of the same college debating club, the Dialectic Society.

2. John Randolph of Roanoke, a states' rights Democrat from Virginia, served in the U.S. House, 1799–1813, 1815–17, 1819–25, and 1827–29. He sat in the U.S. Senate, 1825–27, and served briefly as U.S. minister to Russia in 1830.

3. William C. Dawson and Alexander H. Stephens. Dawson represented Georgia in the U.S. House, 1836–41 and in the U.S. Senate, 1849–55. He lost his bid for the governorship of Georga in 1841 to Charles J. McDonald.

4. A cotton planter who had served in the lower house of the Georgia General Assembly, Absalom Janes opposed Stephens in the race for the U.S. House in 1844.

5. Probably a variant of the scriptural verse, "Where no counsel is the people fall: but in the multitude of counselors there is safety."

6. Brookes married Lucina Sarah Walker and after her death, Prudence E. Johnson. His two deceased children have not been identified.

7. In 1831, he married Sarah J. Myers.

8. Walker I. Brookes.

9. Not identified further.

10. Brookes' parents, Jonathan and Annie Lewis Brookes, resided in Caswell County, N.C.

FROM WILLIAM M. LOWRY

Dear Col. Greeneville Ten Nov 18 1844

I assure you it is with no little pleasure, I seat myself to congratulate you upon your recent triumphant elevation to the Presidency. Sorry I am that Tennessee has acted so inglorus a part in this grate contest. I have now no fears but that Tennessee will be found in August next right side up.[1] Had the 2nd Congressional Destrict, been better attended too than it was we would certainly have carried the state, for but few folks have any confidence in Our Elector for that Destrict (this is private).[2] Under all the circumstances East Tennessee has done well. The Whig Party seemd to make this theire battle ground & particularly this Congressional Destrict seemd to be theire grate reliance for gain which thanks to the noble Democracy of the 1st Destrict proved untrue. I am told that Genl Barrow on his return informd his Whig freinds that E Tenns was good for 6 thousand for Clay & Co. As before stated I am sorry that Tens has acted as he has tho we have runn them just close enough to Know what we can do in next August. This town as you are aware (I think I told you when here last) has the degradation of containing the malignant slanderer who invented, the story about your revolutionary Grand fathers being a tory[3] & which was made theire principal electionary Hobby in this & other parts of the Union. I would like much to get a peep at Mr Bell Foster Henry & Jones. If theire faces are propotionably long with the small whigs of this region It would be a sight worth seeing. These hard times I wonder what Jones now thinks of his pledge to Gibbon of Pens "that Tenns was as firm as the everlasting Hills that she would give Clay 5000 majority".[4] He has rendered him self completely infamous & contemptible amongst a number of his own party & the Democracy would hardly touch him with a ten foot pole. The Democracy of old Greene intend having a grand illumination on thursday night in Honor of your elevation to the Presidency. You will please remember me to Mrs Polk with whom I become acquainted partialy in the Spring of 1837....

WM. M. LOWRY

NB Since writeing the foregoing the thought of Mr Clays remarks made while you Were speaker & giving the casting vote on the Missippi contested Election crosses my mind.[5] I wonder what he now thinks of his ungenerous attack, "go home Gd dam you, where you belong" to reverse the parties names. It will fit his case exactly. At present in a speech made in our ct house by Wm H S[...]d[6] he solemnly declared that he did not think you would carry one state unless it was south carolina and that depended upon the will of J C Calhoun. Excuse the libertys I have taken, in mentioning these matters. WML

ALS. DLC–JKP. Addressed to Columbia.

1. Lowry's reference is to the Tennessee elections in August 1845.

2. An East Tennessee physician, Thomas Von Albade Anderson was a son of Joseph Anderson and brother of Alexander O., Pierce B., and Addison A. Anderson; he replaced William Wallace, who declined nomination for reasons of health, as Democratic elector for the Second Congressional District of Tennessee.

3. During the 1840 presidential campaign, William G. Brownlow publicized in his newspaper, the *Jonesborough Whig and Independent Journal*, rumors about Ezekiel Polk's Revolutionary War record. Lowry's reference to the Greeneville "slanderer" has not been identified further.

4. In October 1844 James C. Jones sent Charles Gibbons, the president of the National Clay Club of Philadelphia, materials on Polk's anti-tariff views. See John P. Heiss to Polk, November 3, 1844. Jones' pledge has not been identified further.

5. When a special session of Congress was called for September 1837, Mississippi had not held congressional elections. The Democrats John F. H. Claiborne and Samuel J. Gholson won decisive victories in the July election and served during the special session. Although the House of Representatives declared that the two men were elected for the full term, Mississippi held the usual November elections; and the Whig candidates Sergeant S. Prentiss and Thomas J. Word, won easily and on December 27, 1837, presented their credentials. In Febru-

ary 1838 the House rescinded its earlier decision and declared the seats vacant. Democrats then proposed a compromise denying the seats to the two Whigs and calling for a third election; Polk cast the tie-breaking vote on that proposition. Prentiss and Word won a second time and were seated on May 30, 1838.

6. Letters obscured by oil from sealing wax. Lowry's reference probably is to William H. Sneed. A Murfreesboro lawyer, he won election as a Whig to a single term in the Tennessee Senate, 1843–45. Sneed moved to Greeneville in 1844 and then to Knoxville the next year. He won election as a Know-Nothing to the U.S. House, 1855–57.

FROM ROBERT ARMSTRONG AND J. GEORGE HARRIS

Dear Sir, Nashville Nov. 19. 1844

The citizens of Davidson are desirous of receiving you at Nashville with popular honors when you shall pass through our city on your contemplated visit to Gen. Jackson. Supposing you may leave Columbia on Monday morning, stop at Williamson over night, and proceed to the Hermitage on Tuesday, they are disposed to make arrangements for meeting you (Thursday) on your return, some five or six miles distant, escorting you into our city with military and civic honors usual on such occasions.

The public anxiety thus to mark your arrival here is ardent and all-pervading. Will you be kind enough to say by return mail whether arrangements of this kind will meet your approbation?

R. Armstrong
J. Geo. Harris

LS. DLC–JKP. Addressed to Columbia.

FROM ROBERT ARMSTRONG

Dr Sir Nashville 19th Novemr [18]44

By direction of the Genl Jackson I hand you the inclosed, please notice the *Notes* ordered be made on it by the Genl.[1]

Hand it to Mr James Walker Thomas[2] or such of your friends as will make up a Suitable reply &c to Mr. Lawrence.

The Genl. says we will enclose it to Mr Prescott.[3] I fear he is not as well as usual. I will go up to *night* & see him.

R. Armstrong

ALS. DLC–JKP. Addressed to Columbia.

1. William Prescott, a physician from Lynn, Mass., wrote Andrew Jackson on November 7, 1844, and requested a refutation of Abbott Lawrence's recent attack on Polk's record as a slaveowner; at a local Whig meeting Lawrence had

described Polk as "an *ultra* slaveholder" and had claimed that Polk was "cruel, hardhearted, and tyrannical to his slaves." ALS. DLC–AJ.

2. Armstrong's references probably are to James Walker and James H. Thomas.

3. Jackson's AE on the cover of Prescott's November 7, 1844, letter indicates that on November 30, 1844, he forwarded to Prescott a defense of Polk by Gideon J. Pillow. Pillow's defense has not been found.

FROM JULIUS W. BLACKWELL

Dear Sir Athens Ten. Novr. 19th 1844

I hail you as President elect of the United States. Altho you are cheated out of Tennessee, you have New York. We have just recd. the intelligence that you have carried N.Y. but no doubt, you recd. it before we did. Our friend are now shouting and singing and shooting, and tomorrow night intend to illuminate. We did less for you in the way of gains than either of the Congressional destricts in E. Ten. but we did the best we could. Old McMinn gave you a majority of 185, a small gain over the vote of 1843. The Whigs here fought like desperadoes.

When I see the talent and money we had to contend against I wonder that we did as well as we have. But I will not trouble you any further now. Altho we grieve for the loss of Tennessee, we are nevertheless happy as the die is cast and you are elected.

The Coons have cheated you out of Tennessee, mark that.

J. W. BLACKWELL

P.S. I leave home for Washington City in a day or two. J.W.B.

ALS. DLC–JKP. Addressed to Columbia.

FROM SAMUEL P. CALDWELL

Dear Sir Memphis Tennessee November 19th 1844

I have concluded to settle my negroes upon a plantation, and consequently have given the proposition which you made to me last winter my attention more particularly of late.

My father[1] was here a few days since and told me to write to you that he and I would purchase half of your Mississippi plantation, and enter into a partnership with you down there, if it met with your approbation. I am willing to it, if you will take my Haywood land as you proposed. I suppose we could agree as to the price of your land, and mine also. We will furnish a force equal to yours. Write to me at Memphis, your price for your land, and whether or not the arrangement would suit you and such other particulars in regard to the matter (if it does) as you may think proper.

SAMUEL P. CALDWELL

P.S. Answer this letter[2] soon as the time to agree in is very limited. S.P.C.

ALS. DLC–JKP. Addressed to Columbia.

1. Silas M. Caldwell.
2. Polk's reply, if any, has not been found.

FROM RANSOM H. GILLET

My Dear Sir, Ogdensburgh Nov 19. 1844

Allow me to congratulate you upon the result of the Election. You are now the head of our nation & have its destinies in your hand to no limited extent. I feel that all is well for four years. Indeed this election settles the question of the policy of our goverment for many years. The whigs here tell me they suppose that the *Confession of faith* that I drew in Baltimore in 1840,[1] is to be adopted in our political Church. I tell them, doubtless it will, & that I feel prouder of those Baltimore resolutions than anything that I have ever done.

How well Genl Jackson must feel at the result. But poor Bell, his speeches have not killed, but elevated you. He must feel as bad as some of Milton's fallen devils.[2]

I wish you a most prosperous & happy administration. I cannot well come to see you inaugurated. It would not be paying you so high a compliment, as we have done at the polls. But I shall expect to see you here next summer on your tour to the north. Dont fail to take it & be sure that you see the St. Lawrence & your old friend in particular. Mrs. G.[3] is counting upon it already. It will do much to vanish the feeling that an election engenders.

Next week we bring out the Cannon & celebrate our victory, when you will be appropriately remembered by all.

You will have to use all your nerves to Cleanse the Augean stable.[4] If you follow Mr Van Buren & omit it, you like him may have enemies doing mischief to do you injury. In this he made a great mistake. Mr Wright soon leaves for his new home at Albany. When will you reach Washington? We do not hear from your state yet. I alone here have confidence that you will carry it. Nothing could give me more pleasure than to see your state in line again with the democracy.

Make my best respects to Mrs Polk & believe me....

R. H. GILLET

ALS. DLC–JKP. Addressed to Columbia.

1. Gillet served as chairman of the resolutions committee of the Democratic National Convention of 1840. His committee prepared a set of nine resolutions setting forth the party's basic principles, the text of which was published in the Washington *Globe* of May 7, 1840.

2. Reference is to John Milton's epic poem, *Paradise Lost.*

3. Eleanor C. Barhydt Gillet.

4. In classical mythology King Augeas housed 3000 oxen in stables but failed to clean the stables for thirty years. Hercules finally cleaned them by diverting the river Alpheus through them.

FROM JOEL B. SUTHERLAND

My dear Sir — Washington Nov. 20th 1844

I think it probable, that you will receive letters from Philada suggesting what had better be done, as soon as you enter upon your Presidential duties. With reference to such a state of things, before you take any steps in relation to Philada it may not be improper to say to you, that a large majority of the *office holders here*, *voted the Democratic Ticket*. Propositions for *turning out*, no doubt will be made. Some will *want changes* to suit *ulterior views* & some for the sake of *personal* advantage. But it appears to me, that where the officers are competent & are of the *right faith*, no changes ought to be made, unless the incumbents have been *in sufficiently* long to require a change. The *Body* of the party here as I informed you in my last,[1] wish to see a *Polk administration* & certainly at this *early* day, do not wish to be disturbed by the *rivalry* of candidates for the *succession*.

I may be mistaken, but I think *I see the path*, that ought to be taken, to keep the party *united* in Penna. Men *write*, & think their advice ought to be taken although they know but little about the *state of Penna at large*. To meet the wishes of your friends in Penna. I have made an arrangement to have a suit of American cloth presented to you by a *Democratic* Manufacturer, to be worn on the day of your Inauguration.

Tennessee has gone for the Whigs I fear. But *such* a victory carried its *death blow* with it.

Present my kind regards to Mrs. Polk & believe me....

J. B. SUTHERLAND

ALS. DLC–JKP. Addressed to Columbia.

1. See Joel B. Sutherland to Polk, November 12, 1844.

FROM ROGER B. TANEY[1]

My Dear Sir Baltimore, Nov. 20. 1844

I feel so truly rejoiced at your election as President of the U. States, that I must indulge myself in the pleasure of offering you my cordial congratulations. We have passed through no contest for the Presidency more important than the one just over; nor have I seen any one before in which so many dangerous influences were combined together as were united in support of Mr. Clay. Your triumphant success gives me increased confidence in the intelligence firmness & virtue of the American people; and in the safety and stability of the principles upon which our institutions are founded. I need not say with what pleasure I shall again meet you in Washington, & see you entering upon the high station to which you have been so honorably called.

R. B. Taney

ALS. DLC–JKP. Addressed to Columbia.

1. A 1795 graduate of Dickinson College and member of the Maryland House for one term, 1799–1800, Taney broke with the Federalist party over its opposition to the War of 1812; he subsequently served in Andrew Jackson's cabinet as attorney general and later as secretary of the Treasury. Whig opposition in the U.S. Senate denied him an associate's seat on the U.S. Supreme Court in 1835; however, the following year he went to the Court as its chief justice and served in that post until his death in 1864.

FROM SAMUEL P. WALKER

Dear Sir. Memphis Nov. 20th 1844

The battle is over & the victory complete with but one thing to regret, *we ought to have had the vote of Tennessee.* The gallant Middle division did nobly (and old Maury I am proud of her). If the the wings had done *half* duty the State would have been safe. However, the vote is *so close* it is almost equal to a victory. In this county[1] there is an increased vote of near 700, nearly 500 of them in the City of Memphis; this increase was very *largely* in favor of the Whigs. Out of 260 merchants & clerks we have but 15 or 20, & but few of them *worth a cent* in an election—in fact some of them deserted us on the day of the election and voted the Whig ticket. The Banks and Insurance Offices with all their *money* and officers were against us. This influence extended all over the District. I doubt whether we could do as well in this county if the battle had to be fought over again. At all events I know but *few men* who have not done their whole duty.

But my object in writing to you is on other business. I am *almost* satisfied with a *drawn battle* in Ten. and a victory in the Union. There is great interest felt here in relation to the Naval depo. Many applications have already been made for Offices in that establishment, almost altogether by Whigs. I dont wish to assume the priviledge of advising but have thought that it might be important to let you know the state of things here. Mr. Tyler will probably have the appointments to make. He would probably be advised by Cave Johnson & other democrats from Ten. The applicants, so far, are all Whigs. This ought not to be. We have heavy odds against us any how, and there is no good reason for placing our enemies in a position to fight with more *effect* against us. There *will* be applicants among the democrats and my object in writing to you is to suggest that it is not at all important that the officers should be appointed immediately, except the superintendant of public buildings & there is I think but one applicant for that office (Col Morrison)[2] a very competent democrat. Gains, Judge Dunlap, Geo W. Smith[3] and others are very desirous that the appointments should not be made in a hurry. They dont know that I have written you.

You will probably receive letters and applications in abundance. What we want is a little time to consult and endeavor to reccommend such persons, among our friends, as will make good officers. Within the last day or two this subject has attracted a great deal of attention. I have heard several persons spoken of. Among the number Mr. Harris[4] has been spoken of for one of the offices. You know his qualifications as well as I do. If he can get the reccommendation of our democratic friends here I would be glad to see him get something. He needs it and would make a good officer. He voted with us & was very decided firm for some time before the election & may be able to do this. If he cannot I will advise him not to apply.

There is another important suggestion. I think we can carry this county next August with proper efforts & it may be important in the election of a Senator. If the work could begun by the 1st Feby—a few additional voters would be of service as the labouring men are generally democrats. You will be the best judge as to the propriety of advising with Johnson on the subjects mentioned above.

SAML. P. WALKER

ALS. DLC–JKP. Addressed to Columbia.

1. Shelby County.

2. Probably David Morison, an assistant civil engineer at the Memphis Navy Yard from 1845 until 1849.

3. Pendleton G. Gaines, William C. Dunlap, and George W. Smith. Gaines, a lawyer and editor of the Memphis *Gazette* from 1834 until 1838, served a sin-

gle term as a Democrat in the Tennessee House, 1839–41. A young Shelby County lawyer, Smith lost his bid for a seat in the Tennessee House to Adam R. Alexander in 1841. Smith was confirmed by the U.S. Senate for the post of navy agent at the Memphis Navy Yard on July 8, 1848.

4. Adlai O. Harris, widower of Polk's sister, Naomi, had engaged formerly in business with James Walker in Columbia, Tenn.; in the 1830's he formed a New Orleans cotton brokerage firm with Madison Caruthers; after Naomi's death in 1836 Harris moved to Memphis and engaged in sundry mercantile pursuits.

FROM WILLIAM WALTERS[1]

Respected Sir: Terre Haute, (Ind.) Nov. 20, 1844

I congratulate you most sincerely on the glorious result which has placed you in the Presidential Chair; and feel, myself, the deepest sensations of joy, in remembering that I gave you my vote in the Baltimore Convention, and my whole influence with the Illinois delegation, of which I was a member. But my object in addressing you now, is not, merely to congratulate you on your election; but to speak of the next U.S. Senate. The late news from Delaware shows that that body will stand 26 Whig; 25 Dem. and Indiana to hear from. Thos. Dowling, Esq. of this place,[2] who is in favor of the Annexation of Texas, who is aginst a U.S. Bank, and who is friendly to you, can command 6 Whig votes in the Legislature of Indiana, and with the Democratic party in the Legislature, *could be elected*. I have today, written to Gov. Whitcomb, with whom I am personally acquainted, on this subject.

I know that all this is out of rule; and is liable to a construction of meddling in affairs beyond my jurisdiction; but when we reflect that the next U.S. Senate may thwart every measure of your administration, placing a barren sceptre in your grasp, it is worth the risk of such an accusation. Dowling was a Tyler man; and is at heart against Clay. Your friend, Cave Johnson knows him, I think; and a word from him to Gov Whitcomb, or any other influential friend in Indiana, would aid in accomplishing the object, if he should think it desirable.

In Illinois, I think we shall elect Col. E. D. Taylor[3] to the next Senate, in place of Gen. Semple.[4]

WM. WALTERS

ALS. DLC–JKP. Addressed to Columbia.

1. A former editor of the *Wilmingtonian and Delaware Advertiser*, William Walters held the state printing contract in Illinois; and in partnership with George R. Weber he published a Democratic newspaper, the Springfield *Illinois State Register*.

2. Before settling in Terre Haute, Ind., in 1832, Thomas Dowling had worked

for the Washington *National Intelligencer*. He served several terms in the Indiana legislature and in the early 1840's published the *Wabash Express*, a Whig newspaper.

3. One of the early settlers of Springfield, Ill., E. D. Taylor served in the state legislature during the 1830's. In 1835 he was appointed receiver of public monies at Chicago; he subsequently joined in promoting construction of the Galena & Chicago Union railroad and the Illinois & Michigan canal.

4. A lawyer and state legislator, James Semple served as attorney general for the state and as Speaker of the Illinois House. Appointed in 1843 to fill the unexpired Senate term of Samuel McRoberts, he subsequently won election as a Democrat and served until March 1847.

FROM ROBERT ARMSTRONG

Dr Sir Nashville Nov. 21. [18]44

To pass Monday night at Mr Childress's[1] & reach the Hermitage on Tuesday, spend two nights and a day with the Genl and arrive at Nashville on Thursday forenoon would be a proper arrangement, I think.

Your visit to the Hermitage will not be generally known *here* before Thursday. So many would *follow* you that you would have no *peace* or *quiet*.

I send you a letter from Mr. Kennedy.[2] He will be well prepared to convey you over the mountains.

Our friend Thomas J. Read came in the Louisville stage this evening and will visit you on Saturday. One of the truest and best men of our Democracy.

No news further from Lousn. Delre & Masst have gone Whig. Maine Democratic by increased majority.

R. Armstrong

ALS. DLC–JKP. Addressed to Columbia.

1. A resident of Williamson County and a cousin to Sarah Childress Polk, William G. Childress served one term as a Democratic member of the Tennessee House, 1835–37, and ran unsuccessfully for the U.S. House in 1839. In 1844 he attended the Democratic National Convention as a delegate from Tennessee.

2. See Robert P. Flenniken to Polk, November 11, 1844.

FROM ALEXANDER JONES

241 8th Avenue
Dear Sir *New York Nov. 21st 1844*

I again congratulate you and the country on your election to the highest office in the gift of a free people.

Take the result all in all, and it is one of the most important political triumphs which has occurred in the United States, since the period, when Mr. Jefferson defeated the elder Adams.

I discover the closeness of the contest in Tennessee is without a parallel! And whether the Democrats have carried the state or not, they have nevertheless fought a noble battle and covered themselves with glory. Had I foreseen the closeness of the vote, I would have tried hard to have reached the State sooner & to have exercised my humble powers on the stump more widely and actively.

However, let Tennessee go as she may, we have abundant and heartfelt cause of congratulation.

I see our old native State of North Carolina has gone against us. Your native county, Mecklinburg, adheres to Democracy, while Rowan, my native country, sticks to federalism, as of old. I should be pleased to see the "Old North State" once more return to the ranks of Democracy.

In no part of the Union probably, had the whigs felt more keenly their defeat than in this city and state. Never was there a party more confident of success. The whigs of New York boasted, bet and swaggered to an extent unequalled by their party elsewhere, or at any previous election. The daily and confident tone of triumph put forth by their partizan papers in this city caused many members of their party to bet in the most daring and wreckless manner, on the final result. During the whole campaign, they have been urging the Democrats to bet, "to back their judgement," as they called it; offering double and treble odds. The consequence has been that large sums of money have changed hands and many whigs have become utterly ruined. On my return from the west, I was appealed to for the purpose of obtaining my opinion as to how certain states in the west would vote, as it was known, I had travelled through the western states, as far south as New Orleans and as far west and north, as St. Louis, Mo. and Galena in Illinois; during two months of summer & two months, in the present autumn, making four months since the beginning of the campaign. While, I uniformly felt great gratification in being able from personal experience and observation among the people, to state my *firm* and *candid belief*, in your triumphant election; I at the same time, done all I could to dissuade our friends from betting, holding the practice, nothing more or less than gambling.

Being, all my life through, *on principle*, opposed to betting on anything, I endeavoured to pursuade others to the adoption of a similar course. I fear, however my advice had little, or no weight with many of the friends thus advised. Immense sums were bet in this city and lost by the whigs. In many instances the most disastrous consequences have resulted.

One whig gentleman, after betting all his other available means, staked his household furniture! He has lost all. His family being left destitute! This man was formerly a whig sheriff in New York. Another whig, the owner of a well conducted and lucrative *Tavern*, bet his all, including, money, Tavern and furniture. He has of course lost all. His wife was a most laborious, worthy and respectable woman, aiding him by years of hard toil to accumulate the property, her husband, has thus wickedly gambled away. She has since gone mad and is now a maniac in the Lunatic Asylum!

Another whig, a carpet merchant, I am creditably informed, bet his whole stock in trade, valued at 38.000 Dollars and has lost the whole! Another has lost 40.000 dollars in cash, and others various sums from 5, 10, to 20,000 dollars! No wonder, such whig merchants, are depressed, and unite in trying to create an imaginary panic! It is high time, some severe laws were passed against betting on elections.

For the evil consequences resulting from betting, on the exciting election, which has just terminated, the whigs have no one to blame; but the Editors of their own wreckless, arrogant, and over confident journals. These inflammatory concerns, were continually filled with heavy banters to bet, accompanied with confident predictions of success to persons staking their money on Mr. Clays election.

In some instances, I have understood, the whigs bet, with a view of creating a kind of capital to electioneer on. For instance, if they had staked 500, or 1000 Dollars on the result, they would go out among the people and appeal to persons of more or less influence, telling them, that, they had bet such and such sums, on Clay; and hence, they were willing, if successful to divide out their winings with them, giving them from 10, 20, to 30 dollars for every vote they could carry to the polls for the whigs, seduced from the Democratic ranks.

This election has shown more than any other, that, the *great mass of the American people, are not only not for sale; but incapable of being purchased. Long may they remain, so.*

Since the result of the canvass became certain, the whigs, and especially many of the manufacturing capitalist at the north, have been endeavouring to create an alarm, or panic, among business men. Owing to the recent somewhat increased shipment of spicie[1] to Europe, to settle differences of trade, foreign Exchange having advanced to a point to justify it (a thing not at all unusual), the city Banks have become more stringent, have advanced, slightly, their rate of interest and curtailed their loans.

They had previously made considerable loans on pledges of State and other stocks, the calling in of which, has had the effect, to throw a large amount of stock upon the market, with a corresponding depreciation in value; especially, among that description of securities, in Wall Street, *parlance*, called "*fancy stocks*." This decline in the price of stocks, is gravely put forth by the whigs and whig papers, as the result of your election![2] Their attempt to get up an imaginery panic will prove a failure. Their efforts will result in nothing more than injury to many of their devoted and timid followers and their poorer dependents or operatives; while their influence will only operate locally.

I have travelled much over the United States within the last few months, as well as in former years, and I can safely declare, that, according to my observation, the country in general, was never in a sounder or safer condition. The people by their industry and economy are in a measure freed from debt. They have generally made large crops and although produce is low, yet they find no difficulty in obtaining all reasonable comforts without going in debt. While the people continue thus industrious and prudent, relying upon their own labour, and enterprize, rather than upon the Legislative action of the Government for prosperity; we will defy all the whigs, whig newspapers and panic manufacturers, in Christendom to inflict any general distress upon them; or to sustain for any length of time, any panic local, or general.

Your prediction with regard to the whigs changing their name, if defeated, and assuming, that of "Native Americans," you will have perceived, is already to a great extent consumated. Their change would, probably, at once be general; but it seems they cannot agree among themselves with regard to the plan of operations. You will discover many of their papers, have already openly declared in favour of the new name, while others, such as the Albany Evening Journal, and New York Tribune, are for delay and caution.[3] They wisely consider the question in the light of a two edged sword and that it may cut both ways.

To the Democracy of the United States, it is a matter of indifference, what new name the whigs may adopt. We can defeat them under any and every name they can possibly give themselves. They can never steal or take a name, better calculated to deceived the people, than that of "*whig*." That name, alone, there can be no doubt, duped thousands, and induced thousands of ignorant men to vote with them, under the delusion, impressed upon their minds by disingenuous whig orators, such as Webster &c that they were the real and enclusive descendants of our *whig ancestors* of the *Revolutionary war*! Having defeated them, most gloriously, under their strongest and best name, I have not question; bet we can hereafter beat them, under the disguise of "*Nativism*," or under any other "*ism*" they can possibly assume.

I with all my heart, wish you a long life, health and happiness; hoping and beleiving as I do, that, your Administration, will be crowned with the highest degree of success and usefulness to the country, and with enduring and distinguished honor to yourself. Be pleased to present my highest....

ALEXR. JONES

N.B. I shall be pleased to hear from you, at any time it may suit your convenience. A.J.

ALS. DLC–JKP. Addressed to Columbia.

1. Misspelling of the word "specie."

2. The *New York Herald* of November 16, 17, 19, and 20, 1844, reported Whig efforts to create a panic on Wall Street, blaming falling stock prices on Polk's election. Prices of "fancy stocks" fluctuated between two and fifteen percentage points during that period.

3. In an article that was published in two parts on November 11, and 12, 1844, the *New York Tribune* cautioned restraint with regard to Whigs joining with Native Americans. On November 13, 1844, the *Tribune* published the same sentiment in an article reprinted from the *Albany Evening Journal*.

FROM NATHANIEL JONES[1]

State of New York
Surveyor Generals' Office
Albany Nov. 21. 1844

Dear Sir,

Now that all is safe by reason of the greatest political and moral triumph which has ever been achieved by the advocates of equal rights in this or any other country, Allow me, honored sir, to salute you with my most hearty congratulations as the victorious Standard Bearer in our recent, noble contest. Your own elevation to the highest position among men, though highly gratifying to us all, is but a part of the acquisition which the great result secures. In this canvass, the chief and principal issues have been boldly promulged on the part of the democracy and cavalierly accepted by the common foe and upon those issues the battle has been hotly waged and most gloriously won. It remains for the future to determine whether federalism will again, under a new cognomen, attempt to galvanize the defunct issues of National Bank, Distribution of the Land revenues and Class Protection. The probabilities seem to be opposed to such hypothesis and that modern whiggery, with the great "Embodiment,"[2] is to be supersceded by a compound of Nativism and Abolitionism, duly christened "American Republican." The simultaneous announcement of their New Name by the federal Journals in the Northern, Middle, and a few of the Southern states, certainly indicates an abandonment of some of their long cherished measures. But whatever new principles they may choose to affirm as the basis of their party ethics, the old federal leaven must be their pervading and quickening element and should be, and probably will be represented by their pontifical Head or High Priest, Daniel Webster.

You will have seen ere this reaches you, that your majority in this state is larger than the estimate I sent you on the 7th instant,[3] and varies but little from 5000. This is indeed close work in a Poll of some 500,000 votes. The state ticket leads that of the Electoral about 3 to 5000 and is accounted for, in part, by a most silly but pernicious report circulated in many counties of this state, that soon after the Baltimore Nomination of the Dem. Candidates, Gov. Polk addressed each of the Heads of the Departments at Washington, pledging himself to them, that in the event of his election they should retain their present places in his Cabinet should they desire to do so. Coming as it did from persons in the employ of the general govt, and who claimed to be in the confidence of President Tyler, the report, in portions of our state, received undeserved credence and consequently, to the extent of such credence and belief diminished our electoral vote. Our firm friends and public speakers boldly denied that such was the case, as the whole life, public and private of James K. Polk proved him incapable of making such an overture even should his election seem dependent upon it. These same individuals now have the baseness to charge Mr. Van Buren's friends, or so many of them as would make up the disparity between the electoral and state Tickets, with having withheld their votes from Polk and Dallas. Of a piece with the above allegations, are the proceedings of a meeting of the same school as published in Bennett's Herald of the 14th instant,[4] a majority of whom are well known to have favored a more southern candidate[5] and who came if at all, to the support of our Nominees at the eleventh hour. These persons now claim to have been essentially instrumental in carrying this state and therefore, entitled to all the glory in securing the grand & crowning result. I should not be surprised to see a published manifesto of these gentlemen asserting their great conservative service to the party and modestly demanding full pay therefore immediately after the 4th of March next.

Among the most unscrupulous of the class are the following—viz Lewis Eaton of Black Rock,[6] for some time past and at the present a special Agent for this state, of the Post Office Department. This individual was never known to be other than a federalist of the true blue stamp or ever to have supported the Democratic ticket except on one occasion. Mordecai Ogden another Special Agent in the employ of the gen. government, Parmenter of Buffalo[7] another of the same type; last but not least, John Lorimer Graham, Postmaster in the City of New York.[8] These men will arrogate the right to all the places under the general government within this state, and I now predict that they will besiege the President Elect, cormorant like, ere he leaves Tennessee for the White House.

I have written the above in a hurried manner, and with entire frankness that you may be early advised of the character of a class of men in this state who will be as eager and forward in their claims upon you for place as they are believed here to be deceitful and untrustworthy.

NATH. JONES

[P.S.] Our last advises from Tenn. gives us great concern. We fear the state has gone for Clay by a trifling majority. N.J.

ALS. DLC–JKP. Addressed to Columbia.

1. Nathaniel Jones won two terms as a Democrat to the U.S. House, 1837–41, and served as surveyor general of New York, 1842–44, and as state canal commissioner, 1844–47.

2. Henry Clay.

3. In his letter of November 7, 1844, Jones related that Polk had won the state of New York by a majority of between 3,000 and 5,000 votes. ALS. DLC–JKP.

4. James Gordon Bennett established the *New York Herald* in 1835. One of the first of the penny presses, the *Herald* opposed the renomination of Martin Van Buren in 1840 and supported the election of Polk in 1844. Although it was considered non-partisan, the *Herald* generally sided with the Democratic party until the election of 1856. Reference to the meeting of John Tyler's friends has not been identified further.

5. Jones' reference probably is to John Tyler.

6. Lewis Eaton has not been identified further.

7. Mordecai Ogden and Parmenter have not been identified further.

8. John L. Graham, a lawyer, held the office of postmaster of New York City from 1842 to 1845 and served as one of John Tyler's chief patronage dispensers in the city.

FROM GOUVERNEUR KEMBLE[1]

My dear Sir — Cold Spring 21 Nov. 1844

Your letter came to hand, and I have now to congratulate you on being President-elect, which I do with all my heart. Of the event of the election in this State I have never entertained a doubt since the nomination of Mr. Wright for Governor, and the enthusiasm with which it was received by the Democratic party. It was a great, but necessary sacrafice, and no man regretted it more than[2] himself, but without it, I believe that we should have been defeated.

I look with some anxiety on the position of your administration between the friends of Mr Calhoun and the Democratic party north of Virginia, and I have been led to think of it more in consequence of a letter from a strong friend in Columbia S.C. who says, that Mr. Calhoun had written to his friends in that State, I give the words, "to wait and watch the first movements of the successful party before they committed themselves."

Presuming that you are fully advised of the state of public opinion there, I shall not occupy your time with it. My district will send you a friend in Congress, but coming from the adjacent county which is strongly Tariff, I presume him to be so inclined, as was his predecessor.[3] For my own party, amid these dissensions, and difficulty of choice, I have had more trouble to be permitted to remain at home than most men take to get to Congress, but I have had the honors of the House and know what they are worth....

GOUV KEMBLE

ALS. DLC–JKP. Addressed to Columbia.

1. A New York cannon manufacturer, Gouverneur Kemble sat in the U.S. House from 1837 to 1841; he served as a delegate to the state constitutional convention of 1846 and to the Democratic National conventions of 1844 and 1860.

2. Here Kemble cancelled the word "myself."

3. William B. Maclay and Aaron Ward. A New York City lawyer and member of the state assembly from 1840 until 1842, Maclay served five terms in the U.S. House as a Democrat, 1843–49, 1857–61. Formerly district attorney of Westchester County, New York, Ward won election to the U.S. House as a Democrat and served six terms, 1825–29, 1831–37, and 1841–43.

FROM HENRY SIMPSON[1]

Dear Sir, Philadelphia, November 21st 1844

Allow me to congratulate you on your election to the Presidency of these United States, and I think after four years toil, I have a right to the high satisfaction of this joy, for after our overthrow in *1840*, the Federal Whigs *craped* the door of my sisters dwelling two nights in succession from the bell to the steps of the front door.[2] If ever any circumstance created an incentive to action, this did; from the first knowledge of our defeat in Novr. of that year, I began a correspondence with our political friends throughout the United States, and continued it until our late glorious and lasting victory over the vilest and most vicious of political opponents. I was at the National Convention and united with our friends in the nomination of yourself and Mr. Dallas. I was acting chairman of the Democratic Hickory club of the city and county of Philadelphia's committee of Correspondence—of which club, our friend the Honorable Henry Horn is President, and we have the honor of numbering among our correspondents the first men of the nation and your warm supporters.

The Tyler men in office at a meeting the night before last Resolved to address you a letter, on the ground that they ought to be kept in office.[3] Nearly all true Democrats refused office under President Tyler, and those who accepted, never came out openly and warmly to your support until within a few months of the election day. What claims they can have, rests with your Excellency to determine. Dr. Sutherland, who left our party at the memorable time of the re-chartering of the Bank U. States by Penna. proposed the other day, that our Democratic friends who want office should apply to Mr. Tyler, remove the Clay men in office, and so arrange matters as to make no changes necessary on or after the 4th March next. I take the liberty of giving you this information, knowing that you will at the proper time take such measures as you may deem wise and prudent. Mr. Dallas is fully acquainted with the whole plan of the Tyler men, and their daring efforts to retain office. 'To the victors belong the spoils'[4] was truly carried out by our opponents in 1840, and Mr. Clay himself, in the United States Senate boldly espoused the doctrine that no Democrat should be kept in office under the administration of Harrison & Tyler. I, for one, refused to take office under Mr. Tyler. Others accepted and have been reaping the spoils for *three* years at least. Mr. Thomas Cooper,[5] the player has just been appointed Surveyor of this port, in place of Jno. G. Watmough,[6] a *Clay* man, removed.

Wishing you every happiness....

HENRY SIMPSON

ALS. DLC–JKP. Addressed to Columbia.

1. Henry Simpson, brother of the noted Philadelphia editor and author, Stephen Simpson, served as alderman of Philadelphia and member of the state legislature. In the late 1830's, he was an appraiser for the port of Philadelphia but lost his post in 1841.

2. Simpson's sister has not been identified further.

3. For the activities of the Tylerites in Philadelphia, see Joel B. Sutherland to Polk, November 20 and December 12, 1844.

4. Simpson's reference is to William L. Marcy's remark, "to the victor belong the spoils of the enemy," made in Senate debate on Martin Van Buren's nomination as minister to Great Britain in 1832. See *Register of Debates in Congress*, 22nd Congress, 1st Session, Vol. VIII, p. 1325.

5. An adopted son of the English free thinker and reformer, William Godwin, Thomas A. Cooper was a well-known actor and theatrical manager. He was related to the family of John Tyler through the marriage of his daughter, Priscilla

Cooper, to Robert Tyler. After his retirement from the stage, Cooper secured through executive patronage a series of government positions. In 1845 he failed to receive Senate confirmation for the office of surveyor of the Port of Philadelphia; Polk subsequently appointed him to an inspectorship in the New York Customs House, where he remained until 1846.

6. John G. Watmough won election as a Whig to two terms in the U.S. House, 1831–35, and served as the surveyor of the Port of Philadelphia, 1841–44.

FROM CHARLES DOUGLAS[1]

Sir, New London, Connecticut Nov. 22, 1844

I take leave to tender you my congratulations on the favourable result of the contest which has elevated you to the highest station in the gift of a free people. The battle was a hard fought one, and consequently the victory is the more glorious. In most of the New England States, the power of capital over labor was fearfully and successfully demonstrated. In this State, Massachusetts, and unfortunate little Rhode Island, the *lords of the spindles* compelled the degraded operatives to vote their will, and thus obtained large majorities for your opponent, and the English system of protecting labor by taxing it.

Aside from the controlling power of the manufacturing aristocracy over labor, I am well convinced that the result, in the above named states, would have been different, as a majority of their inhabitants are as soundly democratic as their bretheren in other parts of this Union. But this aristocracy, little better than the feudal aristocracy of olden time, not only controlled the volitions of their immediate dependents, but also subjected to their bad influences not a few of the farmers and mechanics and thus obtained their local and useless victories. Yet, I trust, the time will soon come when legislators will cease to bestow their special favors on interests adverse to equal rights, equal laws, equal justice, equal burdens, equal protection. Then, and not until then, will the democracy of the manufacturing states regain and maintain their rightful power and consequence.

My high regards to your excellent Lady.

CHARLES DOUGLAS

ALS. DLC–JKP. Addressed to Columbia.

1. An outspoken critic of the factory system, the physician Charles Douglas had been one of the leaders of the Working Men's movement in New England. In the early 1830's he established the *New England Artisan* and the New London *Political Observer and Working Man's Friend*. In 1832 he served as the president of the New England Association of Farmers, Mechanics, and other Workingmen and also ran as the Democratic nominee for state senator from Connecticut's

Seventh District. In 1845 Douglas declined Polk's offer of a consulate in Brazil but accepted in 1847 a position as commissioner of public buildings in Washington.

FROM AUGUSTUS B. LONGSTREET[1]

[Dear Sir:] Oxford Georgia 22 Nov 1844

You are accustomed, my dear sir, to receive letters from hundreds of whom you know nothing, and therefore you will readily excuse me for making myself one of that number. Surely you will, when the writer informs you that he will readily excuse you for throwing his epistle in the fire at sight of the unknown signature. "Why then" you will naturally ask "put yourself to the trouble of writing a letter upon which you yourself place so low an estimate?" I answer, upon the principle that a man takes a ticket in a lottery, that it may perchance be productive of good. Let me promise by way of bespeaking your indulgence, at least so far as to hear what I have to say that I am entirely beyond the reach of Executive patronage. I ask for nothing, I desire nothing, within the gift of any public functionary in the Union. To be a worthy disciple of the great Head of the Church, is the utmost reach of my ambition. But I have a deep interest in the government under which I live. I believe its destiny for weal or for woe is in your hands; and it is in the forlorn hope of doing it some little service through you, that I venture to obtrude myself upon notice. If you were asked what is the uppermost wish of your heart at this time, you would doubtless endevor, "to bring back the government to its original principles, and to establish those principles upon an immovable basis." This I believe it is your power to do, and it is what no other President could have done since the days of Madison. The times are peculiarly propitious to this end, though alarmingly critical. Federalism is not dead. As it sank in 1800 under that name, and rose again in 1840 under the name of Whig, so it sinks now to rise again in 1845 under the name of *Native American*. It is to have for a time, but one political principle: "our hands and hearts to foreigners; but no suffrage to them until they become identified with us in interest!" Under this ensign it will gain recruits rapidly especially from the churches, a powerful interest. As soon as it shall have gained strength enough to make battle, it will begin to resume its old principles, and if its movements cannot be anticipated and counteracted, it will at last triumph, and maintain its victory until it is lost in revolution. How did it gain its late gigantic triumph? I answer entirely from private & local interests, which have grown up from a partial compromise with it, on the part of Republicanism. The republican party yielded their ground to serve the times, in 1816; and they have been growing weaker ever since; for it is a property of Federalism, that it makes the power that sustains it.[2] The Bank favored northern capitalists and the Tariff, Yankee labor, and both combined to strengthen each other. It became the interest of both to fill the public coffers with useless treasure; and to stimulate the government to extravagance in proportion to its income. The consequences were inevitable. Ten thousand collateral interests sprung up out of the extravagance of the government; labor and capital were turned from their natural channels, the agricultural & manufacturing interests were arrayed against each other, the north was arrayed against the south, and all the politics of the country settled upon these two measures. They have produced a state of things, that are mischievous in the extreme but which cannot be altered without great care, prudence, and circumspection; and yet they must be altered, or there is no security for republicanism, no hopes for the country. You will not consider me as laying claim to these attributes even in an equal degree with yourself, much less as calling in question your claims to them, when I venture to suggest how I think this can be done. No sir, the case calls for the united wisdom of the whole Democratic party, and I present myself before you only to contribute my mite. Deal with it as you please.

If I were in your place then thus would I reason, and thus would I act: I come into office with a Senate opposed to me, whose aim it will be to embarrass my administration as much as possible. Our appeal must be to the people. At present the majority is on my side, but that majority is made up of very discordant materials which it will be extremely difficult to keep united. On the other hand the Whig party is made up of elements, manifestly differing in interests if not in principle. Among those are a vast multitude of honest well meaning men who are disposed to do right irrespective of party. Those Whigs whose real interests lie on the side of republicanism, and those who mean to do right, are not irreclaimable. Is it possible to strike out any measure that will win them over, and yet drive none from our ranks? It is possible if there be any measure that all parties approve of. Is there such an one? There is; it is *retrenchment*, the very thing that no man dare oppose; and the very thing to make easy all the reforms that republicanism demands. But to *propose* retrenchment is to do nothing; I must set an *example* of it if possible, and no matter how unimportant the instance it will do much. I will look through all the avenues of the Executive Department, and cut off every useless officer and every useless expenditure from that, and I will recommend to Congress to do the like. I will furnish the President's house myself in neat, handsome, but not extravagant style, and request that no appropriations might be made for this purpose, or only enough to cover the cost. "This could be known for I would lay in my furniture before the fourth of March." I will look through all the other departments of the governments, and wherever retrenchment can be made in them without weakening my force I will recommend it. In those states which are hopelessly federal, if it can be done without partiality or injustice, I will retrench boldly. Not as a vindictive measure, but as a wholesome one, which may be pushed rapidly here without defeating itself as it should be everywhere under like circumstances. In my Message I will concede that these are things in themselves of no great moment, but that it ill becomes the people's agents to recommend economy and republican simplicity without practicing it themselves, at least as far as they can. That the policy is adopted rather to prevent the *growth* of extravagance and luxury at the seat of government, for the time to come, than to correct existing evils, and that after all, nothing should be considered as unworthy of notice, which relieves the people from taxation in any degree. Such conduct and such a message, would in my opinion give you a popularity at once, that no Senate can undermine, and that any President might be proud to possess. I have much more to say but that I may not entirely defeat my object by overtaxing your patience with my first letter I reserve it for another....[3]

A. B. LONGSTREET

P.S. Please let it not be known that you have received a letter from me, for though you know nothing and care nothing who I am, or what I write; it is a matter of consequence to me not to be known as yr correspondent.[4]

ALS. DLC–JKP. Addressed to Columbia. Polk's AE on the cover reads "Some good suggestions."

1. A friend of John C. Calhoun and George McDuffie, Longstreet fervently advocated nullification during the 1830's and published the Augusta *State Right's Sentinel*, 1834–36. In 1838 he became a Methodist minister and presided over Emory College, 1839–48, in Oxford, Ga.; he later served as president of the University of Mississippi and the University of South Carolina. He wrote the popular *Georgia Scenes* and also penned a series of short works on slavery, the Know Nothing party, and various political subjects.

2. Longstreet's reference probably is to the founding of the Second Bank of the United States in 1816.

3. On November 28, 1844, Longstreet wrote Polk a second lengthy letter of advice.

4. Longstreet wrote his postscript in the left-hand margin of the third page of his letter.

FROM JOHN M. McCALLA[1]

Dear Sir. Lexington Novr. 22 1844

After presenting my sincere congratulations on your success in the late canvass, permit me to inform you of various hints and threats which we have heard here. I know that similar ones were made in 1828 when General Jackson was elected, and that no overt attempt was made on his person until his arrival in Washington.[2] But circumstances are somewhat different now from what they were at that time. I need not suggest them to you, as you will percieve them at once.

Two gentlemen arrived here last night, one of whom came from Memphis and the other from Mississippi. I came in the car with them from Frankfort, and heard their statements. They are democrats and were at first of opinion that the language used was not sufficient to create alarm but hearing other declarations on the steamboats, and at taverns, made by whigs and addressed to small circles with apparent earnestness and sincerity, they told me their apprehensions, and I at once said that I would write to you on the subject.

There *may be* no imminent danger. But if there is *any* danger, it would be well to be on your guard. I would not expose myself near a window, particularly after night, and in general would observe a caution in that particular, which although it may be a little irksome at first, will at last become a habit, and not troublesome.

As many of your friends too should be near you as convenient.

Excuse my suggestions, if they shall be deemed unnecessary; although I confess that my own mind has become infected to some extent by the fears which others around me exibit.

The whigs here are savage, and exibit great agony on their defeat. Their confidence of success, from Mr. Clay down to his lowest subaltern, amounted to fanaticism, and they suffer in proportion at their disappointment.

I saw Judge Catron yesterday. He is well.

JOHN M. McCALLA

ALS. DLC–JKP. Addressed to Columbia and marked "Private."

1. McCalla served as U.S. marshal for Kentucky during the Jackson and Van Buren administrations; in 1844 he ran on the Democratic electoral ticket in Kentucky; and in 1845 Polk appointed him second auditor of the U.S. Treasury.

2. Several threats upon Andrew Jackson's life were made prior to his first inaugural, but no overt attempts after his arrival in Washington have been identified.

FROM ROBERT MITCHELL[1]

Zanesville, Ohio. November 22, 1844

After congratulating Polk on his victory, Mitchell attributes the loss of Ohio to the power of certain "influences" in the state and points in particular to "the Mammoth Stage Company" of Neil, Moore, and Company.[2] The company controls almost every stage route in the state and places "agents who are efficient politicians" on every road. He claims that these agents threw the whole influence of the company behind the Whigs and made possible their victory in Ohio. Mitchell urges Polk to appoint a postmaster general who will hold a tight rein on the company.

ALS. DLC–JKP. Addressed to Columbia.

1. Robert Mitchell, a physician, won election as a Democrat to one term in the U.S. House, 1833–35, but lost his bid for reelection; he returned to Zanesville and resumed the practice of medicine.

2. In the 1840's the firm of Neil, Moore, and Company carried mail and ran stages over all of the main roads of Ohio; its stage lines also extended as far east as Buffalo and Erie and as far west as Indianapolis and ran north to Detroit. William Neil, the key figure in the firm, owned an inn near the statehouse in Columbus, Ohio, a popular lodging place for politicians and businessmen. His daughter Ann Neil was married to William Dennison, a leading Ohio Whig and later Republican.

FROM HENDERSON K. YOAKUM

Dear Sir, Murfreesboro' Tenn Nov 22. 1844

So many have doubless written you letters of congratulation that you are tired of them. I did not intend to add another to the troublesome list of letters you have to read: but Col Benton's late St. Louis speech[1] has in it some allusions so extraordinary, and uncalled for, that I must call your attention at least to one part of it. It is in the semiweekly Globe of 7 inst.[2] "Its very author would incur less odium by dropping the pretext, and avowing the motive, which induced them, at the price of foreign war and domestic disunion to bring the Texas question to a head on the 12th day of April 1844; and explode it upon the country precisely forty days before the Baltimore Convention! just time enough for candidates to be interrogated, and for the *novices* to amend their answers!"

I have no doubt but Col Benton has injured us 100.000 votes, with no other object on earth that I can see, than to wound Mr Calhoun & promote himself. If you have time to read that St Louis speech you will see that Mr B. is fully determined to effect a breach between the democracy of the north and south. Another object of his speech seems to be to misconstrue the Baltimore resolution on Texas question,[3] so as to avoid your letters on that subject.[4] The latter we mean to adhere to, and we mean that Messrs Foster & Jarnigan shall do the same, or fail before the ordeal of the next Legislature.[5] It is quite surprising after Mr Wright has substantially abandoned his objections to immediate annexation, and Messrs Tappan and Allen have fallen in Ohio[6] that Mr Benton should still wage that eternal war between Texas & Mexico, which Gov Houston has thrown into such perfect ridicule.

H. YOAKUM

ALS. DLC–JKP. Addressed to Columbia.

1. Reference is to a speech made by Thomas H. Benton in St. Louis on October 19, 1844.

2. Washington *Globe*.

3. The Democratic platform of 1844 included the following resolution: "Resolved, That our title to the whole of the Territory of Oregon is clear and unquestionable; that no portion of the same ought to be ceded to England or any other power, and that the reoccupation of Oregon and the reannexation of Texas at the earliest practicable period are great American measures, which this convention recommends to the cordial support of the Democracy of the Union."

4. See Polk to Salmon P. Chase et al., April 23, 1844.

5. Yoakum's reference is to possible instructions from the Tennessee General Assembly to its two U.S. senators, Ephraim H. Foster and Spencer Jarnigan, regarding their votes on the admission of Texas to the Union.

6. Yoakum's reference is to the possible loss of two Democratic seats in the U.S. Senate; Ohio Whigs had won control of the legislature in 1844.

FROM JOHN CATRON

Dr Sir. Frankfort Ky. Nov. 23d 1844

On my way here I heard the result of the Presdl. Election & have heard in the last ten days, much speculation, from both sides in regard to your position, and probable course, in organizing the new Administration. The Whigs here believe confidently, you are under pledges to Mr. Calhoun. Gov. Letcher[1] is my authority: of course, this is confidential amongst ourselves. They think the consequence will be a split in the outset, between the friends of Col. Benton, Mr. Van Buren, &c, and those of Mr. Calhoun. I took pains to assure Gov. L. that the report had not the Slightest foundation; that no man ever went into the Presidency less pledged to any wing of party friends. Col. Benton has been in this neighbourhood for some days, and passed down yesterday on his way to Washington & left his respects for me; I did not see him, being at the Court room. His feelings are not abated, I should think, towards Mr Tyler, and Mr. Calhoun, from what he is reported to have said here. The conclusion also is that the northern and southern Democracy, cannot be satisfied in the formation of a Cabinet; and that discord will prevail in the outset, and disaster follow. The Smoke of the Contest has pretty well passed off here & these are sensible ideas resting on facts, of which such conclusions may well be predicated. That they present the difficulties attributed to them by your opponents, is true to a great extent. I have thought much and anxiously of the matter; and come to this conclusion: That you ought to go to Washington *entirely* unpledged, down to a post office; that you should view all solicitations, in advance, as out of place and too early for conclusion or action on them, if words could be so deemed. The solicitous; and especially those extremely so, are usually, almost uniformly, from persons the *least* meritorious, of applicants. From the approaches to me already made, I see you are to be cruelly harrassed; and that firm resistance to all pledges will be indespensible on your part: If the cold shoulder gives offence for the time, be it so; it will soon wear off, and if it does not, in my judgment no man ever elected Presdt. was in a position better to bear it. You was made the candidate because of your strength in the west, and south: Because your character as a man of talent, industry, and gentlemanship, squared itself to the ideas of worth that forms the Standard of men of simalar characters. All this the Democrats admit, and the Whigs admit, *now*, openly and broadly. I mean the leaders of course. After the vote on the Texas treaty, you was the only man that could have beaten Mr. Clay: Such is the opinion expressed by both sides. I think Wright might have done so—no matter—you are under no pressure of obligation to your party, other than to administer the Government through the agency of men of undoubted strength and worth of Character, *from head to foot*. The Whigs calculate largely on the chance, that in the ardour of friendship, and burst of gratitude, consequent on what they suppose unlooked[2] success by you; and because of the warmth of your friendships and temperament, discrimination will be made bounded on *decided* qualifications and merit; but that every grade will be let in, as reward for party service, and that the administration can be rapped on this ground. It is as I think, their 2d. hope—the Jars of the Cabinet, the first: and that by the one or other cause, your small majorities in various states may be over-come. The ideas may be of use, & I give them, for what they are worth—as I do the balance of this hasty sketch, of pretty well matured thoughts. I leave tomorrow for Washington.

J. CATRON

ALS. DLC–JKP. Addressed to Columbia.

1. A lawyer, Robert P. Letcher served several terms in the Kentucky legisla-

ture before winning election as a Clay Democrat and later as a Whig to the U.S. House, 1823–33 and 1834–35. He was a presidential elector on the Whig ticket of William H. Harrison and Francis Granger in 1836 and was governor of Kentucky from 1840 until 1844.

2. Catron probably intended to write "unlooked for."

FROM LEVIN H. COE

Dear Sir Somerville Nov. 23 1844

The designing part of the Whig party here are setting their pegs for a new game & I fear the same movement is on foot in every county in the state, perhaps in all the United States. Native Americanism becomes American Republicanism. The name of Whig merges into it. Thru this region they are now secretly circulating subscriptions, taking indentures & when they have got the peoples bond then their papers will unmuzzle and the organizations be made public. "You've beat us in the election but you cant take the Bible from us" is in the mouth of every little scamp of a whipper in among them.

Is not delay dangerous? Our people the Democrats must be warned. The leaders in this movement unmasked & scored. At the same time I am satisfied there are many of the rank & file of the Whigs who voted against us at the late election but now intend to support us next summer. Their feelings must not be touched. Whilst we meet & by a firm bearing nip this new movement in the bud, we may do so in a way not to rasp the feelings of such as lately against us are now inclined to go with us. At least it seems such a thing might be done, but my genius runs more in the crab-apple than the sugar vein and I have deemed it more prudent to draw your attention to the matter. We look with anxiety to see the tone of our Columbia & Nashville papers on this question.

Since we are safe without their help the Democrats of this region seem to be pretty well satisfied that old Rip & her slut of a daughter[1] have the shame of standing alone in the south.

Our Methodist conference is in session here. No opposition. All zealously support Bishop Andrew & vote to separate from the North.[2]

L. H. Coe

P.S. You sir, will pardon an humble individual, who is both personally & politically your friend, while I inform you that yourself and the illustrious Heroe of New Orleans, were this Evening Constituted *life Members* of *Our Missionary Society*. This was provoked by the Disappointed friends of *Harry* the *fallen* who first constituted him a life member. To you Sir, that the pride of political parties has at least in this instance

been turned to good account. Accept assurances of my Sincere regard.
G. W. D. Harris[3]

ALS. DLC–JKP. Addressed to Columbia.

1. Coe's points of reference are North Carolina, the "Rip Van Winkle" state, and Tennessee.

2. The son of the first native Georgian to enter the itinerant ministry of the Methodist Episcopal Church, James O. Andrew served in Georgia and North Carolina during the first twenty years of his ministry; at the 1832 General Conference of the church he won election to the Methodist episcopacy. Through marriage Andrew became a major slaveholder in 1844; and in May of that year at the church's General Conference in New York City his status as a slaveholder touched off a debate on the issue of slavery that ultimately led to a North-South division of the denomination. See John P. Gordon to Polk, September 4, 1844.

3. A Methodist minister, George W. D. Harris was a leading figure in the Memphis Annual Conference from its creation in 1840 until his death in 1872; he was the brother of Isham G. Harris and William R. Harris.

FROM GEORGE R. RIDDLE ET AL.[1]

Sir Pittsburgh, Nov. 24, 1844

The undersigned, who are among your most ardent supporters in this county, and have always been active and somewhat prominent in the Democratic ranks, beg leave, most respectfully, to address you a few words upon the state of the Democratic party, its wishes and its prospects, in the State of Pennsylvania. Let us premise, sir, that we are no factionists—nor are we applicants to you for any office.

Great pains have, and will no doubt, be taken to impress you with the idea that Geo. M. Dallas and William Wilkins[2] have great influence, and are much beloved by the Democracy of Penns. Permit us to inform you that their fame is out of the State, and that they do not enjoy the confidence of the party at home. But you will ask, how have they obtained prominence and place? We will answer. They are both gentlemen of affable manners and are brothers-in-laws, and being the centre of a large family connection with branches over the State and Union (Hon. R. J. Walker forms a part of it) they have, by laboring for each other, without reference, as we believe, to the good of the party, been able to keep before the people. But so notorious has their conduct been in advancing each other, that it is a saying in Pennsylvania that no man can hope for preferment unless he belongs to "the family." It would astonish you to learn the number of this large "family" who may be found in the service of every Department of the Government. Messrs. D. & W. were both Senators from Pa. at one time, and both, as you may remember, supported the old Bank against the veto. They were, by turns, Ministers to Russia, and they were rival candidates for the nomination of Penna for Vice President, when, by their own efforts, the party in this State refused to sustain Mr. Van Buren, the regular nominee for that office. This inveterate greed of office, which hesitates not to violate the integrity of the party, has rendered them unpopular here. Mr. Dallas's nomination for V.P. was received with wide-spread and profound mortification in Penna: for proof of his want of influence, look at the disasters of the Democracy in Philadelphia City and county. Mr. Wilkins was a candidate for the Governor's nomination last March. Not one, of the 64 delegates who composed the Convention in this county were instructed for him, in this county where he has lived all his life. Mr. Shunk, a comparative stranger here, (having been but 2 years in the county) got every vote. Mr. W. declined just before the vote was taken, his friends seeing how it would result. As a candidate for Speaker, he got but 10 votes in Caucus. Yet, low as he and Mr. Dallas stand in the estimation of the Democracy of the State, the few who are attached to them, are already boasting of the influence they will have with President Polk, and *offering to bet* that certain applicants for the offices in this city (who are the relatives of Mesr. D & W.) will succeed through their influence. When Mr. W. took office under Mr. Tyler, his intimate friends here declared for Mr. T. for the Presidency. D. Lynch late postmaster,[3] and a defaulter, who now has, through Mr. W. a share in the great Choctaw contract, was a Vice President of the Tyler convention. These facts, and the others we have mentioned, have cast much distrust on Mr. Wilkins's democracy, and the suggestion that he would be kept in the Cabinet has given much dissatisfaction here.

We have mentioned the name of Mr. Walker. We do not wish to impugn that gentlemen's democracy, nor take one jot from the fame he has obtained by his devotion to the cause. All we wish to say is that he is a member of that great "family" whose overshadowing influence Pennsylvania Democrats dread so much.

Far be it from us to say that any man should be proscribed *merely* because he belongs to "the family." All we desire is that you may know that Messrs. W. & D. have not the confidence of our Democracy, and that you will not place too much confidence in their suggestions. We are sure that you find abundant corroborative evidence of what we have written; and in the confidence that this evidence will at once be an apology for intruding this letter upon you, and prevent Messrs. D & W. from having more influence than they should have, We remain....

GEO. R. RIDDLE

[Addendum]
(Note by S. Snowden)[4] Col Trovillo[5] is now the Sheriff of Allegheny County. Geo. R. Riddle is now the Prothonotary of Alleghy C. and Thos. Farley is Clerk of the Court of Q. Sess. Messrs Trovillo & Riddle were elected last year. Mr. R. was elected by a majority of 1200 votes over the united vote of two Whig competitors. Mr. Farley was elected in 1842 by about 600 thus showing that they are men who have the confidence of the people & the party in our County.

LS. DLC–JKP. Addressed to Columbia.

1. A Pittsburgh conveyancer and later a lawyer, Riddle served as the clerk of council for the borough of Allegheny, 1834–38, and as prothonotary of the district court of Allegheny County in 1844. Besides Riddle, six others signed this letter, including Samuel Snowden and those identified in the addendum to Riddle's letter.

2. Originally from Carlisle, Penn., Wilkins served in the Pennsylvania House in 1820 and in the Pennsylvania Senate, 1855–57. He was presiding judge of the Fifth Judicial District of Pennsylvania, 1821–24, and judge of the U.S. District Court for Western Pennsylvania, 1824–31. Elected as a Democrat and Anti-Mason to the U.S. Senate in 1830, he resigned on June 30, 1834, to assume his duties as minister to Russia. He won election to the U.S. House as a Democrat and served from March 4, 1843, until February 14, 1844, when he resigned to become John Tyler's secretary of war. He served in that post until March 6, 1845.

3. David Lynch served as postmaster at Pittsburgh from 1833 until 1840 and as a delegate to the Pennsylvania State Democratic Convention of 1843.

4. Samuel Snowden, secretary of the Pittsburgh Fire Association in 1839, wrote his note on the verso of Riddle's second sheet.

5. Reference is to Elijah Trovillo.

FROM ARCHIBALD YELL

Dear Polk Little Rock 24th Nov 1844

The great battle has been fought and we of Arkansas are now in the midst of our rejoicing & reveling. Such a display of fire works and Glorification has not been witnessed in brave Ark. and we are the more gratified from the fact that we are the *Banner* State; and will give you a majority of from 4 to 5000. You can not concieve the exticacys of your old friends in Ark such as old Jimy McKisick Whinry Macline Armstrong (Bill) Harris, Sivier Judge Oldham Genl Saml. Mitchell E. Rector[1] and a thousand others. Many of your old friends are anxious to have *Genl. Maclin* appointed Messenger that he may be at Washington and attend to the interest of our friends. Our new Senator *Col Ashly*,[2] got in by accident, having no prominent man to run against him at this time. He will go for Democracy so long as it serves him & his particular friends. This hint is enough for you to keep an eye out & scan his movements.

There are many changes desired, demanded by our party in this state. I hope Sevier & myself & I believe we will agree who should be promoted. Ashly I fear will have his own pecular views & friends. His term expires in two years & he may desire to be reelected, which may cause him to differ with Sivier & myself. Upon his success with you in a great degree depends the prospect of his reelection. He has pledged himself to my friends not to run two years hince but I know the man, & believe it will depend upon his chances of success. All this is for your own eye.

I could have beaten him now but I could not consistently and prudently resign my present station without again endangering our cause, and besides I was content to remain in the Ho of Reps where I can be of more service to you than in the Senate.

I need not say to you that I have the success of your Admtn much at heart. I have also, great solicitude that Arkansas shall be kept "right side up" and no disunion and decensions created among friends at home.

At the same time you may well emagine the pleasure it would afford me to see such men as McKisick Maclin Whinry & Rector provided for. In due time I will fully apprise you of the manner which I hope all can be served. I will write more fully by Maclin. If Sevier & myself can agree about the different office & men, I shall not go to Washington. If not, then I must in Justice to my friends have their claims fairly & fully laid before you and I will meet you the 4th March at Washington.

I have no Idea who will form your Cabinet but I am sure of one fact. They will be able and patriotic and such men as will rally around you in the presovation of ourt republican Institutions. I hope Mr Calhoun will be ritained as Prime Minister until the Annexation of Texas is effected. In your Judgement & prudence I have full and abiding confidence. I have twelve months rest & in that time I can in some degree prepare myself for the support of your leading measures if you will but inform me & perhaps I ask too much. If so let it pass.

I wrote you a few lines soon after the Octr elections.[3] I presume you have had not leasure to reply. Should you find a leasure moment, a letter will find me a Fayetteville Ark where I shall spend the winter; many of my firends here are anxious that [I] visit Washington next spring but it will be an expensive trip for no purpose and I am now pressed to pay up my "election Bills."

I desire you to present me kindly to Madam Polk & say I am still a *Young Widdower* and that I hold her still to her promise. Her opportunities are now better than they were 6 months ago. I feel myself advanced in the same ratio. What has become of her Giles Widdow? Is she still in market—but enough upon the subject of Widdows!

I hope I do not ask too much when I say I shall be pleased to have a line from you when ever your time will permit.

I have sent you the Ark Banner[4] which will give you all our local news.

A. YELL

ALS. DLC–JKP. Addressed to Columbia, marked "Private," and franked by "A. H. Sevier."

1. James McKisick, Abraham Whinnery, Sackfield Maclin, William Armstrong, Arnold S. Harris, Ambrose H. Sevier, Williamson S. Oldham, Samuel Mitchell, and Elias Rector. Armstrong, a brother of Robert Armstrong of Nashville, served as Indian agent for the southern agency of the Western Territory, 1836–39, and subsequently as agent for the Choctaws west of the Mississippi River. Sevier represented Arkansas Territory from 1828 to 1836 in the U.S. House and won election as a Democrat to two terms in the U.S. Senate, 1836–48. Oldham served in the Arkansas legislature in 1838 and again in 1842; sat on the Arkansas Supreme Court for three years, 1845–48; resigned to run for Congress; and moved to Texas after losing his congressional race. Rector served as U.S. marshal for Arkansas from 1831 until 1841 and again from 1846 until 1849.

2. Chester Ashley.

3. See Yell to Polk, October 20, 1844.

4. Little Rock *Arkansas Democratic Banner*.

TO BENJAMIN F. BUTLER

My Dear Sir: Columbia Tenn. Nov. 25th 1844

I have received your very acceptable and friendly letter of the 12th Instant. I thank you for your congratulations upon the result of the late political contest. The vote of New York was indispensible to our success. With her vote we could have lost several of the smaller States and still have carried the election, but without her vote, we must have been defeated.

I was fully advised of the true causes, which, produced the difference between the vote given to Mr Wright, and that given to the electoral ticket, before I received your letter, and I asure you I had given not the slightest attention, to what I saw in some of the newspapers, attributing it to other causes. Both Mr Van Buren and his friends, I am fully satisfied have acted a magnanimous and noble part. I fully concur with you in opinion that if they had withheld their zealous and cordial support, the Democratic party in New York must have been defeated by a large majority.

When you shall next see Mr Van Buren make my respectfully regards to him, and be assured that I remain....

JAMES K. POLK

ALS, draft. Polk Memorial Association. Addressed to New York City and marked "*Private*" and "*Copy*."

FROM HENRY HUBBARD[1]

My Dear Sir Charlestown Nov 25th 1844

I mailed you a short communication a few days since,[2] in which I took occasion to congratulate you on the result of the late election and I want again express to you the same gladness of heart. Our true democracy have achieved a great and glorious victory over the enemies of their principles and over the enemies of our free government. In a letter to me,[3] you were pleased to make known your grateful feelings for the part I acted in the Baltimore Convention, in bringing you before the American people as our candidate for the Presidency. I claim no merit for that effort. I acted under the responsibilities then resting upon me, and in obedience to my sense of public duty. And the result of the late contest has shown most conclusively that the people were ready to approve and confirm the then suggestions of my best judgment. It is well known that I repaired to that convention with strong preferences for Mr Van Buren for the Presidency, and for yourself for the Vice Presidency. And it is equally well known that those preferences were in accordance with the views and feelings of a great Majority of the radical democracy of New Hampshire. But I soon perceived that it would be useless to press Mr. Van Buren, that he must be withdrawn. Strongly attached as I was personally and politically to him, and firmly convinced as I then was that the opposition to him was not only ungenerous but anti democratic, I could not persevere in my continued support of him to the death of our Party. I reluctantly yielded him from considerations of pure patriotism, from a deep conviction of public duty. At the close of the seventh balloting I made up my mind that we ought no longer to give support to Mr. Van Buren, and I thought that like considerations would induce the friends of the other candidates to look beyond the list of competitors for this high office, and to unite with us in selecting from among the people one (up to that time not mentioned) and to present him as the democratic candidate for the Presidency. But I deeply regretted to find how pertinacious and unyielding were most of those who had from the beginning supported for their candidates men in opposition to Mr Van Buren. I said all I could say. I urged every consideration I could urge to induce the friends of the other candidates to cooperate with us in bringing before the people a new man, *one* who would be worthy of the confidence, and justly meriting the support of the Democracy of our land, But to very little purpose. I said over and again to the friends of Genl. Cass that it would be entirely unavailing to present him in nomination. That he could not be elected. That I firmly believed defeat would be our fate if we should be compelled to fight under his banner. And in my opinion the continued and prolonged support of Mr Van Buren by his friends proceeded not so much from a conviction that he would ultimately obtain the nomination as to induce the friends of the other candidates to unite with them in yielding their respective candidates and to agree on a new man.

The delegation from your own State, from Alabama, from Louisiana, on the eighth balloting withdrew their support from Genl. Cass and united with the New Hampshire delegation and with a portion of the Massachusetts delegation in the support of yourself. Had they not have so done, Cass might have been nominated and in that event we should in my judgement have been defeated. At the close of the eighth balloting I made a short speech stating the reasons which had induced the delegation from New Hampshire to bring you forward and it seemed to produce a happy effect upon the temper and disposition of the convention. I verily believe that we could not have made a different nomination with any fair prospect of success. I thought so at the time the nomination was made and the events which have taken place since have confirmed me in that belief. I have thus in a brief manner stated the part our delegation took in the convention. And with one heart & with one united will have we used our best exertions to carry into full effect our purpose. All is well and most sincerely do we rejoice at a result so glorious to the Republic and so honourable to yourself. I desire, as one of your old and true friends at this time to make a few additional remarks. In all New England, particularly in New Hampshire previous to the Baltimore Convention, there was an open and active opposition to Mr Van Buren. In my own state, that party had for its leaders, men who had been for the last three years the most untiring opponents of radical Democracy. Hills New Hampshire Patriot and the New Hampshire Gazette[4] were among the papers which sustained their views. I presume you are not ignorant of these facts. During my Administration of the Government of this State and during the administration thus far of our present excellent Chief Magistrate,[5] those papers, (once well known for their democratic character), were found united with the Whig press in making all the opposition in their power and even after the return of the New Hampshire Delegation from the Baltimore Convention these very papers openly and pointedly condemned us for not supporting Lewis Cass for the Presidency.

These very papers have not hesitated after all to sustain your nomination. Many have joined our party, who were our most virulent opponents before and after your nomination, and until they discovered that the tide of popular opinion was setting so strong in your favour that it could not be resisted. I feel called upon, from the friendly relations which have subsisted between us, from the great respect I entertain personally and politically for yourself, to mention these things because I know them to be true, and because I know further that these very men before the close of the campaign were your most clamorous advocates, and because they will be among the very first to seek favours at your hands. Those who were the active friends of Cass in my own State were the avowed enemies of Mr Van Buren and of yourself. I do not design to be officious or intrusive but presuming that you would wish to know your substantial friends who are invariably the true friends of our democracy, I have ventured to write thus much, and I will add, that if your shall at any time desire information about men in this or in the neighboring states I shall communicate the same unerring truth and with the strictest honor. You can at all times rely with entire confidence on Messrs Burke, Reding & Norris, three of our Delegation in Congress for advice.[6] Permit me to add that no course could be more unpopular as far as my native state in concerned in these matters, than to reward politicians with favours who have been openly arrayed against us for the last three years notwithstanding these very men have been found among your active supporters. Many of these men who are ready

"To crook the pliant hinges of the knee
That thrift might follow fawning"[7]

have been read [out] of our Party and publicly denounced as unworthy the confidence of our democracy. We have men as fine as steel. We have some as brittle as glass, in their principles. I will not hesitate, if desired, to mark the true man and expose the hypocrite. Excuse, My dear sir, this long letter. Mrs. Hubbard is near and asks me to say to whom I am writing such an unconscionable discourse, and when I named you she wished me to request you to present her love to Mrs Polk and be pleased to add my kind remembrances for her.[8]

HENRY HUBBARD

ALS. DLC–JKP. Addressed to Columbia.

1. A New Hampshire lawyer, Hubbard was elected several times to the state legislature and sat both in the U.S. House 1829–35, and in the U.S. Senate 1835–41. He served as governor of New Hampshire, 1841–43 and as U.S. subtreasurer at Boston, 1846–49.

2. Letter not found.

3. Letter not found.

4. Concord *Hill's New Hampshire Patriot* and Portsmouth *New Hampshire Gazette*. An ardent Democrat and newspaper editor, Isaac Hill served as a member in both houses of the New Hampshire legislature; as second comptroller of the U.S. Treasury and member of Jackson's "Kitchen Cabinet," 1829–30; as U.S. senator, 1831–36; as governor of New Hampshire, 1836–39; and as U.S. subtreasurer at Boston, 1840–41. In 1842 the New Hampshire Democratic party divided over state economic policies, and radical Democratic newspapers accused Hill of uniting with the Whigs in representing their banking and manufacturing interests. *Hill's New Hampshire Patriot* was published in Concord from 1840 until 1847.

5. John H. Steele, a mill owner, served as the Democratic governor of New Hampshire from 1844 until 1846.

6. Edmund Burke, John R. Reding, and Moses Norris, Jr. Burke practiced law until 1833, when he became editor of the *New Hampshire Argus*. When the *Argus* united with the Newport *Spectator* in 1834, Burke continued as editor. He was elected as a Democrat to three terms in the U.S. House, 1839–44, and was appointed commissioner of patents by Polk, 1846–50. A Democrat, Reding sat for two terms in the U.S. House, 1841–45, and later served as mayor of Portsmouth, N.H. Norris represented New Hampshire in the U.S. House as a Democrat from 1843 until 1847 and in the U.S. Senate from 1849 until 1855.

7. Corruption of William Shakespeare's phrase, "And crook the pregnant hinges of the knee/ where thrift may follow fawning." *Hamlet*, Act 3, scene 2, lines 66–67.

8. Sally Walker Hubbard.

FROM NATHAN CLIFFORD[1]

[Dear Sir] Newfield Nov 26 1844

It is not too late I hope to congratulate you upon your triumphant election to the chief magistracy of the United States. For once at least the democracy have triumphed upon the field of principle & have shown to the world that the yeoman of America are not only capable of self government but that they are able to assert and maintain their right to equal laws against the combined influences of the aristocracy and the corporate & associated wealth of the country. The struggle has been a fearful one & on the part of the aristocracy desperate & unprincipled without a parallel. The triumph is great & glorious as it will be valuable & enduring if our party are firm & united. Your thoughts are doubtless employed as to the selections to be made for your cabinet advisers. I am aware that this matter peculiarly belongs to yourself & it is not my wish or intention to do more than make such suggestions as I think may be servicaable to you in forming your own conclusions. There is a strong feeling in this state that our democracy have been neglected by the Federal government. That Maine has never had either her just share of influence or a suitable portion of the offices at Washington. That she has too long been placed in the rear by her sister state N.H. That she has uniformly been put off with a meager share of clerkships. The past has furnished some ground for these complaints & yet you will do us the justice to say that we fought a gallant battle in Sept[2] which to say the least had its share of influence in bringing about the glorious result. Gov. Fairfield & myself traversed most of the state making speeches at every point. For myself I ask nothing & shall not during your administration & yet it would afford me the same pleasure to render every aid in my power (if any there be) to sustain & render prosperous your administration. My friend Gov Fairfield is much talked of in this state as a suitable person for Secretary of the Navy & his pretentions I think he will be generally urged upon your notice by our democracy. He is capable & honest as free from guile as any man in New England. I most sincerely hope it may be consistent with your views to give the place to him & in expressing this wish I know I speak the general wish of the democracy of the state. Maine has never had a cabinet officer & her democracy will feel highly honored in any favor which you may see fit to confer on Mr Fairfield.

Allow me to suggest even at the hazard of being regarded as selfish that should Mr Fairfield be selected it is quite desirable that he should be early notified of your intentions, as it may have some influence upon his deliberations whether he will be a candidate for reelection.[3] It is quite important to us that our senator questions should be finally settled for six years by the present Legislature which is already elected & *made up of the right material*. The contingencies of another election immediately following a Presidential contest when party discipline is usually lax & where some must necessarily be disappointed in their anticipations of place ought not to fall upon a place so important as that of U S Senator & it will be particularly dangerous in Maine the succeeding year judging from present appearances. I know that I am addressing a frank man & it is my purpose to speak in the language of frankness & therefore say while it is not my wish to press the matter beyond the proprieties of the occasion still it would be peculiarly gratifying to me as an individual to have the place confered upon Mr. Fairfield, provided the solution would meet the public expectation & in my judgement no better can be made in New England.

NATHAN CLIFFORD

ALS. DLC–JKP. Probably addressed to Columbia and marked "Confidential."

1. A lawyer and two-term member of the Maine House, 1830–34, Nathan Clifford won election as a Democrat to the U.S. House in 1839 and 1841; he served as U.S. attorney general under Polk, 1846–48, and sat as associate justice on the bench of the Supreme Court from 1858 until 1881.

2. Clifford's reference is to state elections held in Maine in September 1844.

3. In 1843 John Fairfield resigned as governor of Maine and entered the U.S. Senate to fill the unexpired term of Reuel Williams.

FROM WILLIAM WALLACE[1]

Maryville, Tenn. November 26, 1844

Wallace regrets that he was unable to be more active during the presidential campaign and tells Polk that after a lengthy confinement his wife died a few days after the election.[2] Concerned with consolidating election gains made in Tennessee, Wallace favors running Aaron V. Brown for governor in the August election and A. O. P. Nicholson for the U.S. Senate. He further informs Polk that he is fearful of losing the Democratic newspaper at Knoxville[3] which would be particularly misfortunate at this crucial time before the August elections.

ALS. DLC–JKP. Addressed to Columbia.

1. An active railroad promoter, Wallace served as sheriff of Blount County, 1820–42, and sat one term in the Tennessee House, 1853–55. Nominated as Democratic elector for the Second Congressional District of Tennessee in 1844, he declined for reasons of health.

2. Margaret Chamberlain Wallace died on November 8, 1844.

3. Reference is to the Knoxville *Argus*.

FROM ROBERT ARMSTRONG

Sir. Nashville Nov. 28. 1844

The line of reception[1] will be formed on the Common opposite Fairfield[2] this day at half past eleven o'clock.

Will you be kind enough to come on in your own carriage as far as the turnpike gate in that vicinity where I will, about 12 o'clock, have all things in readiness for your reception in the State Carriage which our fellow citizens have prepared for the occasion.

The weather is fine; and every thing favors the prospect of a great and glorious day.

With sentiments of the highest consideration.

R. ARMSTRONG

LS. DLC–JKP. Addressed to the Hermitage.

1. The *Nashville Union* of November 28, 1844, detailed arrangements for the reception of the president elect at Nashville. Robert Armstrong served as chief marshal of the event and was assisted by J. George Harris, Joseph B. Southall, Cornelius Connor, George W. Campbell, Lewis Craig, and Granville P. Smith.

2. Reference probably is to Fairfield Landing on the banks of the Cumberland River.

FROM BLACKSMITH HARRY[1]

My Dear Master Carrollton Miss 28th Novr 1844

Suffer your faithful survant Harry to say a fuw words to you by letter written by one of your best frinds in this Country to inform you that I am doing the best I can. I have been so over Joyed at the newse of your Elevation that I have hardly Known what I was and some of the whigs call me President to Plage me and to ridicule you but this I know that I have hardly Eate drank slep or worked any since I heared the Glorous newse. You may be assured my dear Master Jimmy that I have done all in my Power for you though an humble negro. I made some votes for I have ben betting and lousing on you for the last several years but I have made it all up now. I must tell you whate I have won on your Election & I have got near all in hand cash $25 and 11 Par Boots 40 Gallons Whiskey 1 Barrel flower & Lotts of tobacco but you must not think that I will drink the whiskey my self. No sir for I have Treated it all out in Electionaring for you through my friends who stood by me in Electionaring troble. I tell you Master Jimmy that I made some big speaches for you and though an humble negro I made some votes for you. I am in hopes that you will come to this State befoure you go to the white house & let me see you once more before I die for I am in fear that I will never injoy that Pleasure. If you do come down to your Plantation & dont come to Carrollton Please write to me or to Mr Kimbrough[2] the man that has me hired and I will come up & see you. I am getting ould & my Eye sight getting so bad and I am so badly afflicted with the rheumattis Pain that I cant do as well as I would like to do and I do not Know whose hands I may fall into the next year as Mr Kimbrough sayes that he cant hire me any more if he has to give near the Price that he has had to give heretofore. I would like to live with him if the Price is so as to Jestify him in hiring me but let that be as it may my dear master I axspect to serve you faithfull as long as I live let my condition be what it may. I have nothing more but remain your faithfull & loving survant during life. Give my best love to my old mi[ ].[3] When you write Please let me know how she is also Mr Walkers family.[4] I have 12 Children all living. Give my love to all the rest of my frinds & relations.

BLACKSMITH HARRY

L, written and signed in unknown hand. DLC–JKP. Addressed to Columbia.

1. One of Polk's duties as executor of Samuel W. Polk's estate was the oversight of the slave, Harry, who was hired out as a blacksmith in Carrollton, Mis-

sissippi. Polk's youngest brother, Samuel W., died of tuberculosis on February 24, 1839, at twenty-one years of age.

2. Not identified further.

3. Part of the word "mistress" has been obliterated by sealing wax oil; reference is to Polk's mother, Jane Knox Polk, who resided in Columbia.

4. Reference is to James Walker, a prosperous Columbia businessman and husband of Polk's sister, Jane Maria.

FROM MARY AND ROBERT ATHERTON[1]

Dear and honored sir Village Green Nov 29th 1844

I now imbrace the present oportunity of informing you that I am under the Impression from family register that you are A relation of mine. I would be highly gratified if you would let me know or give an account of your family. I never have had the pleasure of knowing any of my fathers relations. I can give you an account of my father. James Polk was born Feb. 27th 1757 in Pennsylvania London Derry township and At the age of nineteen went out with the first Mellissia that went out of pennsylvania under Col Allen Cunningham.[2] How long he Served I know not but he was in the battle of brandywine And Germantown and Trenton and was at the takeing of the heissions At Shades fords.[3] My father settled in Maryland near Elkton Cecil County and Married At the age of forty and their resided untill 1831 always Teaching School and then my Mother died and then he removed to Pa Delaware County with me and lived with my Family untill 1838 and died Aged 82 years. My father never drew a pension untill one year and half before his Death he drew A state pension of forty dollars A year. I was Married in 1827 and now we are in possession of five Children 2 daughters and 3 Sons. My husband has always been employed in the Cotton Manfactureing as A Maneger. He is A geting tired of it. His friends and your friends has been adviseing him to apply to you for An Office and we hope that you will grant it. We live 5 Mile from Marcus Hook. The people in the District thinks that Robert L Atherton My husband would be a suitable man for Custom house Oficer at that place. I forgot to tell you that my father Always voted the Democrat ticket and my husband likewise. He has had A hard time contending for that ticket for all the Cotton Bosses are Strong Whig's that we ever knew. If he had not been A good hand At his buisness they would have taken his work from him on account of his politics many A time. If you want any better recommendation than I Can give you can have it with the Greatest of Pleasure. He is a Sober Industrous hard working Man Age'd forty years of age. We have had the pleasure of purchising your likeness and we have it framed and hung in our parlor.

Some account of my Ancestors wrote in the year 1804: The farthest back I have any knowledge of is my great grandfather Robert Pollock a Native of Scotland who removed to the North of Ireland with his family shortly after the Wars of 1641. Of his Children I have no account of any but James Pogue who caried on the weaving of Diaper and other Draught work extensively in the North of Ireland and lastly at Lisnefiffy in the County of Down from which place he removed to South Carolina near Charleston in September 1738. My father did not go with them but staid in Ireland teaching A Small School sometime untill September 1748 And then my father came to America in the Ship Happy Recovery and my Mother came Likewise and were Married in this Country.

This is an account written by my father which I have Coppyed of and if you are A Relation of mine I intind on going to the Big white house to see you next Summer If I live.

Please excuse me for takeing the liberty of writing to you. Please to Answer this letter soon. Direct for Village Green Post Office Deleware County Pennsylvania.

ROBERT AND MARY ATHERTON

ALS. DLC–JKP. Addressed to Winchester, Tenn. Polk's AE on the cover reads, "History of the Polk family: she is no doubt a relation."

1. Not identified further. Compare the Polk family migration to America discussed in Nathaniel Ewing to Polk, September 3, 1844.

2. James Polk and Allen Cunningham have not been identified further.

3. Atherton's points of reference are the Battle of Brandywine (September 11, 1777); the Battle of Germantown (October 4, 1777); and the Battle of Trenton (December 26, 1776). The last reference probably is to the assault of the British and Hessian troops on the American forces at Chad's Ford during the Battle of Brandywine.

FROM JAMES HAMILTON, JR.

My Dear Sir. Rice Hope Savannah River Nov 29th 1844

I received in the midst of our Struggle in this part of Georgia, your kind favor which I should have answered before, but for my unceasing occupations, both agricultural & political.[1]

I now desire to tender to you my sincere congratulations for being made the victorious subject of one of most glorious triumphs which graces the History of our Country. God grant that you may improve it in every particular calculated to promote your own repute & the welfare & renown of our Country.

You are aware of the relations which I have borne to So. Carolina on that public Question, on which her people have been and now are to a certain extent deeply agitated. Since the authentic declaration of the Baltimore Convention, combined with your nomination, I have employed every effort to soothe the irritation of the public feeling in So. Ca. on the ground, that we had much to hope from your election and were bound in good faith to the party with which we were acting (the Democracy of the North & West) to forbear from every expression of violence which might endanger your success. I am happy to know that my Counsels were not without their effect with my old Confederates in the Struggle of 1831 & 32. I sent you a published letter to my former Constituents of Beaufort District entirely illustrative of my course on this subject.[2] I have to add that this course met with the concurrence of Mr. Calhoun, and indeed was the result of our joint consultations in July last, in Washington. I believe now with the exception of a few cases of *ultra inflammation*, which will exist in all parties, the great body of the old Nullifiers are quiet, under a sincere disposition to support your Standard and an equally sincere confidence that you will do all in your power to procure such a modification of the Tariff as ought to satisfy all reasonable Men.[3]

I now approach a subject of extreme delicacy. It is in relation to the Individual who in your Cabinet shall represent the interests of the South. I believe taking into account the whole Democracy from the Potomac to Louisiana, they would in reference to Numbers as well as character and intelligence, prefer that Mr. Calhoun should occupy this position to any other individual. Whether he will consent to remain in his present post is a question I can not answer. But I should think in the midst of the Oregon & annexation Questions, as a matter of just & honourable ambition, he would desire to bring these most important affairs to a successful issue. To say nothing of the possibility at an early period of your administration, of his being instrumental under your direction by the fit employment of a suitable plenipotentiary at the Court of St. James, of forming a reciprocity Treaty with England, on a new Commercial basis, which by procuring a modification of her Corn Laws in our favor, would in effect operate reciprocally, a reduction of the duties, to a strictly Revenue Standard on our import of her Staple articles of manufacture, viz of Iron Woolens & Cottons. The result of such a negtiation would be this. If the manufacturers in the Senate, or those representing their interest were sufficiently powerful in that body to defeat the Treaty, the Grain Growing States, New-York Ohio, Indiana, Illinois & Michigan, would cordially unite with the South in doing by Legislation what your administration could not do under the Treaty making power. And thus set this vexing Question entirely at rest by the adoption of a Tariff, equivalent to the concessions under the Compromise Act, which in point of fact would give the Manufacturers a protection of 30 p cent, including freight & insurance & other charges—as much as in reason they ought to ask.

I was in Europe four years in the diplomatic Service of Texas. Two years as Minister plenipotentiary to G.B. My intercourse was most intimate & friendly with both Lord Melbourne's administration and subsequently that of Sir Robert Peel. With Lord Palmerston, a free Trade Man, and really now the Leader of the opposition in the House of Commons, and afterwards with Lord Aberdeen; I was as intimate, as a plain Republican could be with two of the first Peers of the Realm. The subject of a reciprocity Treaty with the United States, was often broached between us, and I think they entertained with much favor the proposition.[4]

Their only doubt seemed to be *first* the difficulty of getting a Treaty thro' our Senate, in which they seem to regard the power of the manufacturing interests as altogether predominant, whilst on my part I invariably *predicated* the impossibility of getting the landed aristocracy of England to consent to any relaxation of the Corn Laws. To this their reply was, that the power of the Crown was absolute under the Treaty making power, not qualified as with us. And that it would at last resolve itself into a question whether England received an *equivalent* for the immense boon of allowing the people of the U. States to feed a part of her overgrown population. The progress which the Anti-Corn League (with some of whose members I am now in correspondence) has made bears a just proportion to the progress of the principles of Free Trade in the U States as indicated by the large majority which has signalized your Election. I believe the period most propitious for attempting such a Treaty, arranged and defined by your conjoint instructions, with those of Mr. Calhoun, given to a Minister at St. James on the part of this Country, who should be *out & out a free Trade Man.*[5]

My own experience at that Court has taught me what perseverance thro' the almost insensible approaches of social intercourse may accomplish in bringing about the consummation of affairs of apparently great difficulty & complication. After two years siege of Lord Melbourne's administration I carried the recognition of the Independence of Texas against the whole power of the Abolitionists of Great Britain, perhaps the most potent confederation existing in that Kingdom, excepting the Repeal Associations in Ireland. I had moreover to encounter the active & hostile opposition of the Liberator himself.[6] I believe with Mr. Calhoun as Secretary of State in your hands, & both of you giving an impulse to the negotiations on the other side of the water, the most valuable & most momentous results might be accomplished. Besides from the Department of State animating and invigorating your Minister at St. James, must come the tone of both wisdom & moral courage to disabuse the public mind of Great Britain as well as that of its government, of their ignorance prejudice and fanaticism on the Slave Question. I fear with all his talent & moral worth Mr. Everett's language has not been higher in its tone than merely *apolegetic* on a subject which if to meet at all must be met with unaltering firmness.[7] I think it must be admitted that there is not in the U. States a Man better calculated to give direction to these great public Questions than Mr. Calhoun, and I thank God that the destinies of the Country have fallen into your hands—hands that I believe are not afraid to meet them, whatever aspect they may bear.

I desire My Dear Sir however that you should not misapprehend me. I do not ask you to appoint Mr Calhoun your Secy. of State because *first*, I know that he would repudiate my authority if he supposed I was engaged in such a mission. If the position which he occupies in one of the great Sections of the Union (the greatest in Moral power beyond all Question) if his stupendous Talent, great experience in public affairs, spotless private character, & incorruptible integrity are not calculated to invite him into the public service, in any Station, worthy of his distinguished ability, I am quite sure nothing I can say will have this power.

I write this letter without his knowledge privity or connivance whatsoever, simply for the purpose of informing you of what I know to be the feeling of the people of the South and because I like wise know that every influence which deep cunning and sleepless malice can devise, will be employed to prejudice you against him and induce you to *distrust his friends*.

As to South Carolina she stands forth the Banner State in this great Democratic Victory. You will receive her electoral vote next Monday by an entire unanimity in both branches of her Legislature. A vote which will reflect the suffrages of a majority of Fifty thousand freemen in your favor. Every member of her Delegation in both branches of Congress will be the warm supporters of your administration, with a confidence even in advance of its existence. *Whilst at home we have not one Whig Member in either branch of our Legislature*. What State in the whole Union can say as much? Yet every corrupt an envious villain will at first attempt to denounce and then to proscribe us. You see my Dear Sir altho' I have become a citizen of another State yet I can not refrain from feeling and speaking as a South Carolinian, a cherished illusion which I shall carry with me to my grave—*die* where and *how* I may.

To be frank with you I have given up all idea of seeing Mr. Calhoun President of the U. States. Like all strong currents he has too many eddies against him every to succeed. Without he could be nominated as you were by the unanimous vote of the Democratic Party, I should advise him as one of his friends who always ventures to tell him the truth, to withdraw at an early period in the ensuing Canvass (a measure I fear which will be essential to the harmony of the Democratic Party) and rest content with the monument he has already built to his own fame. It rests on a solid foundation & will be sufficiently enduring.

My Dear Sir this comes from a man who neither *asks* or *expects* anythin at your hands beyond the privilege, which he feels assured your ability & public virtue will accord to him—The gratification of supporting in his retirement, conscientiously and fearlessly your administration however limited may be the sphere of his influence.

Indeed my Dear Sir what have you to do but to consult the best interests of the country and your own renown? By a self-denying ordinance highly to your honor you are no Candidate for a second Term (the pestilent Root of one half of the public evils of our Country). By this determination you are placed in a situation which enables you divorce yourself from all *cliques* & factions either existing or to be formed, and to go for the glories of an administration around which you may call the highest genius & public virtue of the Land. To be at once tributary to its blessings & to the fame which you will establish and consolidate for yourself.

After participating this night in the enthusiastic celebration in the City of Savannah, of that Victory which gives you the first Office in the civilized world, I shall return to my cotton fields in Alabama where I hope to find at present that happiness and ultimately that independence, which public Station can never give.

I beg you to be assured my Dear Sir of the esteem with which I am....

J. HAMILTON

P.S. Should you find either leisure or inclination to write me, be so kind as to direct to me at New Orleans to the care of Dick & Hill[8] as private business next week will take me to Texas, where with my friends (among the most respectable & influential People in that Country) I shall be quite happy to aid Major Donaldson[9] all in my power

N.B. My own scrawl is so wretchedly illegible that I have had to employ the pen of my wife which in no degree destroys the confidential character of this communication.[10]

LS. DLC–JKP. Addressed to Columbia and marked "Private." A copy, written in an unidentified hand, is in ScCleU–JCC.

1. See James K. Polk to James Hamilton, Jr., October 31, 1844.

2. See James Hamilton, Jr., to Polk, September 8, 1844.

3. Opposition to the Tariff Act of 1842 gained strength among South Carolinians during the spring of 1844. In July at a public dinner in Bluffton, S.C., Robert

Barnwell Rhett called for a state convention to nullify the tariff or secede from the Union. John C. Calhoun, secretary of state, counseled patience and argued that the annexation of Texas was of more immediate importance and that South Carolinians should unite behind Polk's election campaign. Wishing to bolster his position, Calhoun dispatched Francis Pickens to Nashville to attend a mass rally of the Democratic party scheduled for August 15 and to extract a pledge from Polk regarding the tariff.

4. William Lamb, Lord Melbourne; Sir Robert Peel; Henry John Temple, Lord Palmerston; and George Hamilton-Gordon, Earl of Aberdeen. Melbourne served four years as home secretary before forming his first right-wing Liberal party ministry, which governed only from July until November 1834; in 1835 he again rose to the position of prime minister and served four years; his third ministry lasted from 1839 until 1841. Peel, the son of a self-made industrialist, began his service in Parliament in 1809 and became a leader of the House of Commons in 1828; he served as home secretary and chancellor of the Exchecquer before becoming prime minister in 1841; his ministry lasted five years. Having served both as foreign secretary and as home secretary, Palmerston attained the position of prime minister in 1855; his first ministry lasted three years; and his second extended from 1859 to 1865. Aberdeen, a native of Scotland, was raised to the peerage of the United Kingdom in 1814; he served as chancellor of the Duchy of Lancaster, twice as foreign secretary, and as secretary for war and colonies; after 1846 Aberdeen became the Peelite leader in the House of Lords and formed a coalition government of Whigs and Peelites that lasted from 1852 until 1855.

5. The Anti-Corn Law League sought repeal of the Corn laws, which prohibited the importation of cheap foreign grain. The League found its strongest base of support in the industrial middle class of Lancashire and Yorkshire, and its strongest opponents among Tory land owners. Peel's support for repeal fractured the Conservative party.

6. Daniel O'Connell was an Irish nationalist and member of the House of Commons.

7. Edward Everett. In 1834, following a long abolition campaign led by William Wilberforce, the British government abolished slavery throughout the empire. Southern slaveholders found the action particularly disturbing and anticipated an increase in abolitionist pressure in the United States. Everett, a Unitarian clergyman, served as an Independent in the U.S. House, 1825–35; won election as governor of Massachusetts in 1835 with the backing of Whigs and Anti-Masons; went to the Court of St. James in 1841 as U.S. minister and remained in that post until 1845; returned to the United States to serve as president of Harvard College; served as secretary of state under Millard Fillmore, 1852–53; won election to the U.S. Senate in 1853; and ran as the vice-presidential candidate with John Bell on the Constitutional-Union ticket in 1860.

8. Probably a reference to Dicks and Hill, a New Orleans cotton brokerage firm.

9. Andrew J. Donelson.

10. Elizabeth Heyward Hamilton.

FROM ETHER SHEPLEY[1]

Dear Sir Portland. Me. November. 29. 1844

While a throng seeking for place and power are breaking in upon your time and exhausting your patience, one who does not wish to be numbered among them, desires to congratulate you and the country upon the result of the election.

Withdrawn as I have been, since I had the pleasure of seeing you, from all active participation in political contests by a judicial office, I may not fully understand the present aspect of political affairs. Yet it has seemed to me to be possible, that such a position may enable me to look more calmly upon the surrounding scene than some of those, who have been active and agitated in the contest. The place of power will not be found for you more than for others to be the place of ease or comfort. And recent events have taught us anew, that it may not be the place to acquire lasting reputation or honor. Having obtained the highest place ambition is satisfied. It remains only to prove, that you were worthy of it. The declaration, which I perceive with regret that you have made, that you should not be a candidate for reelection, leaves you nothing further to expect but a good name to be increased and perpetuated by good deeds performed for the benefit of the country. You will not be disturbed by a friendly allusion to some of the dangers, that may be expected to arise out of that declaration during your administration of the government. I believe it to be suited to produce a comparatively inefficient and unsuccessful administration. It will be more difficult to secure an efficient and useful performance of duty by your assistants and subordinates. They will very soon be more anxiously proposing to obtain favor from the succeeding, than earnest to promote the efficiency and credit of the existing administration. If you should be surrounded by advisers, whose hearts and hopes are strongly fixed upon different persons as your successor, and who will therefore be jealous of each other's movements, counsels, and reputations, what can be expected but distracted counsels, weakness, and loss of character? And as time should pass away, there would be an increasing indifference to the present and a more interested earnestness for the future. Is there reason to believe, that such men could be heartily united in the exertion of all their powers to promote the usefulness, efficiency, and credit, of your administration? If not, how is this danger to be avoided? But two modes of avoiding it occur to me.

One is by excluding from your cabinet every aspirant for the succession; and all those, who are very decided and strong partisans for any particular person as your successor. I am aware, that this would deprive you of the aid of some of the best powers of mind in the country. And there may be danger, that a cabinet so formed would have too little capacity and weight of character to bring to your administration the influence required to enable you to accomplish any great or desirable object. Is there not however reason to hope, that you could find men of sufficient mental power and weight of character to make your administration more powerful, useful, and creditable, than the separate interests and distracted counsels of men of higher powers possibly could do? And that you could find them without attachments so strong to any person as your successor that if distinctly informed before admitted to your counsels, that their whole hearts and heads must be exclusively devoted to exalt and maintain the character of your administration, they would not violate the pledge? Such a selection might relieve you from another danger, that of forming your cabinet in such a manner as to give a balance favorable to the succession of a particular person thereby producing opposition and hostility from the friends of those less favored. If this course should be considered expedient, it would be necessary to take a firm and decided stand in the selection; and to be careful, that each member should be fully informed, that you are aware of the danger, and are determined to avoid the weakness and distraction of counsels, which would be introduced by a struggle for the succession among those, who are to assist you. And anyone, who should violate his pledge and use his influence to assist an expected successor instead of the President should be instantly displaced.

The other mode of avoiding the danger is, I think, to be preferred, if your own mind has come to a settled conclusion as to the person who would be most useful to the country as your successor. The proposal then would be, to invite that person to accept a place in your cabinet, and that all the other members should be so selected as to act unitedly and cordially with him. The effect would be to induce the expected successor to exert every possible power to acquire strength and character for your administration hoping to reap the fruits of well doing and well deserving. And the other members partaking of the same spirit there would be an united, energetic, and watchful, cabinet impelled by the strongest motives to make your administration worthy of the confidence and approbation of the country. The danger attending such a selection would consist in the offence taken by other expectants and their friends. Such a cabinet would however be fully sensible of the expediency of avoiding all just cause of offence and of conciliating all the opposing elements. And if it should not succeed in accomplishing this, and should even fail to reap the expected fruits, it would not fail to be united and efficient for the purposes of your administration. I would not be understood to propose in such case any agreement or arrangement with the man of your choice or with any member of your cabinet. That would be inadmissible. It would bind you to him, and deprive you of that freedom of action, which you should preserve. Your purpose need not be disclosed. The whole object could be accomplished by obtaining the assistance of that man, and by consulting him in the selection of such other persons as might be relied on to act unitedly with him.

I must trust to your kindness to pardon these suggestions.

You will not be surprised at my alluding to another subject interesting to me, and I hope also to you. You will desire and need rest from the anxieties of a ruler, the toils of office, and the entertainment of visisters.[2] The Lords day will afford you that rest. You can on that day exclude all visiters and persons on business, and spend the time in public worship and in the enjoyment of domestic peace and comfort with your Lady. Such a course will commend itself to all classes, and to persons of all varieties of religous opinion. It can be adopted without giving offence; and a very great majority of the people of the country will feel its appropriateness and commend you for it. You will be enabled by it to recruit your exhausted strength and spirits for the trials of the coming week. And while you are thus setting a good example and promoting the public morals, you will increase your personal comforts and secure to yourself an opportunity to look forward to and be prepared for, that account, which rulers and people must alike render to the final Judge.

That your administration may prove to be a blessing to the country, and to highly exalt your character; and that you and your Lady may be prepared for an endless life of happiness is my earnest prayer.

Please remember me gratefully to your Lady, and accept assurances of my highest regard.

ETHER SHEPLEY

P.S. I wish to say a few words respecting my own State, which I have taken the liberty to do in a separate note.[3]

ALS. DLC–JKP. Addressed to Columbia.

1. A Maine lawyer, Ether Shepley served as a member of the Massachusetts House in 1819; as a delegate to the Maine constitutional convention in 1820; as U.S. attorney for the district of Maine, 1821–33; as a Democrat in the U.S. Senate, 1833–36; and as a judge of the Maine Supreme Court, 1836–55.

2. Shepley probably intended to write the word "visitors."

3. Shepley wrote to Polk again on November 30, 1844, recommending John Fairfield of Maine for the cabinet post of secretary of the navy. ALS. DLC–JKP.

FROM EDWIN CROSWELL

My dear Sir, Albany, Nov. 30, 1844

Allow me to congratulate you, as I do most cordially, upon the result of the great contest thro which we have passed, with honor & victory. The victory, altho one of the highest importance to yourself, & grateful as a manifestation of the popular partiality & favor, is yet of higher moment as an emphatic reassertion of the democratic principle, & its reestablishment in the administration of the Government. This great Election must be regarded as scarcely less material in its consequences upon the future destinies of the republic than the Declaration of '98,[1] & the Election of 1800: and yr. elevation will be regarded in the history of the country, by all who look to the democratic tendencies of our government & the durable interests of the people, as the counterpart of that of Mr. Jefferson. I feel that we have passed a crisis of momentous importance in our political history; and I do not doubt that the American Democracy will ascribe it, under 'Providence' to the wise decision of the Baltimore Convention.

Of Course no great good is without its alloy. The smoke of the conflict will scarcely have passed before this will be sufficiently obvious. Questions of difference among friends, & applications for office, will present themselves in many forms. But I do not apprehend that altho' annoying, they will be found insurmountable.

Upon the two great questions, which will probably, above others, first present themselves, the Texas & Tariff questions, your positions are, fortunately, clearly defined, & the popular expression has been quite unequivocal. In my judgment, Annexation is truly "a great American Measure," the accomplishment of which the American people desire, if they do not demand "at the earliest practicable moment."[2] Even Col. Benton, in his St. Louis speech,[3] plants himself upon the Baltimore Declaration; while his construction of our relations with Mexico, under such a consummation, is calculated to continue the alarm among the sensitive & interested portion of our population, who erroneously imagine that war must follow Annexation. In conceding to that portion of our citizens so much as to make even sacrifices to Mexico, to obtain annexation with her concurrence, no more it appears to me ought to be required in that Question, and then, if it cannot be consummated, because that power impotent to enforce her belligerent attitude towards Texas, continues to persist in denying the independence of that republic, & insists in maintaining an offensive attitude towards such nations as may treat with it as such, it will be thought, I suspect, a dictate of sound policy, that annexation, within a reasonable time, ought not to be defeated.

In this state, the prevalent democratic feeling is in favor of annexation. So far from suffering a loss of votes by the question, it was an element in our favor especially in all the frontier counties. The "circular" gentlemen, (the principal organ of which is the Eve. Post,)[4] most of whom profess ultraism in all respects, are the only portion of the democratic party who approach the whig positions upon this subject; but they constitute a very inconsiderable body of persons. Their objections lie deep; for they are directed against the supposed addition to the power of the South, & the alleged extension of Slavery, neither of which can be obviated by any amicable arrangement with Mexico.

Mere party (whig) hostility to the measure, at the north, growing out of the first of these considerations, cannot be formidable, & the opposition of the mercantile & manufacturing classes, will yield to the obvious advantages it will ultimately & soon bring to both. With an adjustment of the question with Mexico, & the avoidance of the unfortunate ground assumed by Mr Calhoun, it c'd not fail to be a popular measure, *in all sections*, & w'd bear down all opposition.

The tariff Question it is to be hoped may be satisfactorily disposed of at the approaching session. It is not to be disguised that in this state, & in most of the northern and middle states, the idea of free trade is not a favorite one; and if the whigs c'd have inculcated that belief extensively as applicable to yr. own views, we scarely c'd have been successful here. Happily, the admirable letter to Mr Kane[5] put to flight any such impression, & deprived the enemy of a weapon that might otherwise have been wielded with potency. Its positions were in perfect accordance with the sentiments of our people, & will be fully sustained by the country. Modifications of the inequalities and excesses of the present tariff, are clearly demanded by the general interests; and if the principle of incidental equal protection to all the great American interests is maintained, no one interest, where all are promoted, can complain with justice or with effect: tho of course all modifications sh'd be made with care, & in a reasonable & liberal spirit.

I have not the presumption to proffer an interference with the Cabinet arrangements. These will be such, yr friends here feel assured, as will comport with the best interests of the nation, & the dignity of yr position. It will not be an easy task, to meet the expectations of all sections, or the wishes of all aspirants. But as our State may be thought of for one of the Cabinet appointments, you will pardon me for a suggestion or two, of local application. Mr Wright will be naturally be thought of for the State Department: and certainly no one presents higher qualifications for its duties, & no one c'd go into it with the more universal concurrence of the American Democracy. But we have reason to believe that he conceives an acceptance of it incompatible with his new relations here, and if tendered him, he will no doubt feel compelled to decline it. Beyond Mr Wright no one in this state has been seriously named for that station, except Mr. Butler. He also possesses eminent qualities & a high position. But he has said to me since the election that he c'd not, in justice to himself & his family, accept a public station, either under the national or state government. This determination may possibly be modified by circumstances, & by strong appeals to his patriotism & disinterestedness, but the probabilities are against it. Under such a state of things, perhaps the selection best adapted to the central & commercial position of this state & most in accordance with the expectations of the people, is the Treasury Department. For that place, in canvassing the candidates believed to be qualified for it, Gov. Marcy has been very generally brought into view. The public mind has taken this direction undoubtedly from an appreciation of his successful & unassailable public career of 20 years, & particularly from his six year administration of the finances of this state, & his six [year] administration of the Executive department of the government, in which he displayed not only financial skill, but high administrative power. It w'd certainly be a very acceptable appointment, with all parties, and with few exceptions, w'd have the approval of both sections (for, altho considerably mollified, we have yet sections among us) of the democratic party. Upon all the great questions of the day, his views & yr. own are congenial.

Gov. Bouck this afternoon commissioned Henry A. Foster and Daniel S. Dickinson for the vacancies in the U.S. Senate occasioned by the resignations of Mr Wright & Mr Tallmadge.[6] One of the places was tendered to Gov. Marcy, & declined by him. Mr Foster formerly represented his district in Congress, & has served two terms in our State Senate, & is now president of that body. Mr Dickinson has served in our State Senate, was twice a candidate for & is now, Lt. Gov. of the state, was a prominent member of the Balt. Convention, and is now a State Elector of our Electoral College. They were both prominent & most efficient in the recent Canvass. They are men of undoubted abilities, and sh'd they be confirmed by the legislature, they can be relied upon to give yr. adm. an efficient support. There are many candidates in the field, and it is possible that the legislature may make other selections for one or both the places, but the probabilities, according to the present aspects, are in their favor. We shall strive at least to prevent collission or bad feelings in the progress of the legislative canvass.

We are on the threshhold of a most important legislative year. As yet the harmony which characterized the recent Contest has been only partially & slightly disturbed. Mr. Wright will undoubtedly endeavor to consolidate & strengthen the democratic party; & in all such efforts he will be cordially seconded by all except the extremes of old sections.

I pray yr. indulgence for this long letter, & for the freedom with which I have thrown out views which I fear you may think obtrusive.

E. CROSWELL

ALS. DLC–JKP. Addressed to Columbia and marked "Private."

1. Croswell's reference probably is to the Virginia Resolutions of 1798 and the Kentucky Resolutions of 1798–99.

2. Croswell paraphrases here a passage from the platform statement of the 1844 Democratic National Convention. The text reads: "The re-occupation of Oregon and the re-annexation of Texas at the earliest practicable period are great American measures, which this Convention recommends to the cordial support of the democracy of the Union." See *Niles' National Register*, June 8, 1844.

3. See Samuel H. Laughlin to Polk, October 28, 1844.

4. See William C. Bouck to Polk, September 7, 1844.

5. See Polk to John K. Kane, June 19, 1844.

6. William C. Bouck, Henry A. Foster, Daniel S. Dickinson, Silas Wright, Jr., and Nathaniel P. Tallmadge. Foster won election as a Democrat to one term in the U.S. House, 1837–39; however, he broke with the party over the Independent Treasury Bill and supported efforts to depose Francis Blair and William C. Rives as printers of the House. He served as U.S. senator from November 30, 1844, until January 27, 1845, when he was replaced by a Van Burenite, John A. Dix. Although the Van Burenites disliked Dickinson's support of deficit spending on internal improvements, they regarded him, unlike Foster, as a strict party man. Dickinson previously was a member of the state senate, lieutentant governor, and president of the Court of Errors of New York; he served as U.S. senator for New York from 1844 to 1851. Nathaniel P. Tallmadge served as U.S. senator from March 1833 to June 1844, when he resigned to become governor of the Wisconsin Territory; formerly a Democrat, he moved into the Whig ranks over the national bank question.

DECEMBER

FROM CAVE JOHNSON

Dear Sir, Washington 1st Dec. 1844

I reached the city on Friday evening but have had no opportunity of seeing many of our distinguished friends. There is much feeling as well as apprehension as to the effect of your first movement. It is understood that *Mr. Cn.*[1] as well as the other members of the cabinet desire to retain their present situation. In the event of retaining Mr C then it is apprehended that T.H.B.[2] will at once break ground agt. the Admin. If he is not retained, then it is apprehended that opposition will arise in the South. It is the old difficulty between the northern & southern democracy—the *Constitution* & *Mr. C's friends* are using every effort to have the control of the cabinet and appointments &c whilst the Northern democracy think they are entitled to it, & will maintain the Globe.[3] Great efforts are said to be making to rally around the former standard, the South & West, Texas & Oregon. The *proper men*, it is said have been invited *by letters*, to stop at the U.S. Hotel, (where Mr. C. now has rooms) lately erected on the Avenue, near Elliott's building, where an astonishing number of the S. & Western members have stopped & it is probable messes will be formed, with a view to a western & southern combination.

The Southern men as far as I can learn desire Mr. Calhoun to remain at the head of the Cabinet whilst the northern men desire S.W. Jr.[4] if he can be obtained—whilst not a small number think that all presidential aspirants should be thrown aside & new men brought in. It is said here that *the Capt.*[5] will aspire to the succession and considers your election a ratification by the people of all the acts of his administration. A recommendation of annexation of Texas by law is expected. Would it not be better, simply to pass a resolution that we will defend her & maintain her independence and leave annexation for your Admn? I make these suggestions for your reflection & of course not expecting you to answer—knowing that you will be overwhelmed with letters. I write now principally to enquire when & what way you expect to take in coming on to Washington. There is great anxiety among your friends here & elsewhere as to your rout & the time. You are expected thro. Georgia, thro. Va. thro. Pennsylvania—at Philadelphia & N.Y. Dallas is here but I have not seen him.

I am located with Cobb & Lumpkin, Hannegan & Stone[6] & their ladies at Dowson's No 2.[7]

C. JOHNSON

ALS. DLC–JKP. Addressed to Columbia and marked "*Private*." Polk's AE on the cover states that he answered this letter on December 21, 1844.

1. John C. Calhoun.
2. Thomas H. Benton.
3. Washington *Globe*.
4. Silas Wright, Jr.
5. John Tyler.
6. Howell Cobb, John Lumpkin, Edward A. Hannegan, and James W. Stone. A Kentucky lawyer, and former member of the Kentucky House, Stone won election as a Democrat to two terms in the U.S. House, 1843–45 and 1851–53.
7. A popular boarding house on Capitol Hill.

FROM ALFRED BALCH

Dear Sir, Nashville 2d Decr 1844

I had intended to visit you at Columbia and may do so before you go to Rutherford: But I know that the eyes of eighteen millions of people are fixed upon *you*. Here I have already seen that many are looking to you with ardent hopes and that those who may happen to enjoy your intimate association are regarded with envy and jealousy. I would not disturb for an instant the envies of these sordid selfish creatures. Before many months have passed away you will know much more of our race than you now do altho your knowledge is already very extensive. Since my return from the District I have received many letters and personal applications for my interfence with you in the behalf of the writers and the applicants which I have unhesitatingly refused.

The whole Whig party humbled as it is by our late glorious victory is ground into the dust. But it will rise to its feet again to seek its revenge upon you by whom it has been beaten. You will have enough of thorns in the path along which you must tread your way. But unflinching firmness and an honest conscience will take you through your journey in triumph. The sincere wish of my heart is that you may in the execution of your great trust promote the national prosperity and happiness and secure an enduring fame for yourself. You will always remember that you will sit in the seat once occupied by the Father of our beloved country and by the noble Patriarch of the Hermitage.[1] Their examples will aid and animate you in the discharge of your onerous and multiplied duties. The first great act of your career as our President will carry with it great and lasting consequences. I mean of course the formation of your Cabinet. The number of aspirants you will find to be great and the vanity and selfishness of the disappointed will be deeply mortified.

In April 1837 I reached Washington to discharge my duties as a Commissioner under the Creek treaty.[2] Mr. Van Buren had then been in office 60 days. He was kind enough to invite me to dine with him and his Cabinet which I accepted. With these gentlemen I had no personal acquaintance and I sat by a looker on in Venice.[3] Very soon I saw that Van Buren had made a bad beginning. Forsyth his secretary of state was too selfish to love any man and Woodbury of the Treasury ditto. Old Dickinson[4] was an imbecile. Kendalls vanity and self consequence had already begun to act fatally upon that vast and powerful mass of individuals attached to and affiliated with his department. The fatal secret was at once disclosed that these men did not *love* Van Buren and that they only regarded themselves as "loci tenentes" who were entitled to their pay.[5] When I became intimate with Mr. Butler I admonished him of these difficulties which he said he saw felt and deplored but the error had been committed and could not be corrected. Kendall did Van Buren more injury than 10 thousand of his bitterest enemies and all the whole body of contractors and all their stipendiaries against the new administration. No man's popularity could have withstood the consequences of his follies but that of the invulnerable Jackson. I remember that he established an Express mail to N.O.[6] whilst I was in the Indian country, that one of the little riders was drowned in a bayou whilst getting forward and that the contractor was fined 100 dollars for this failure. The decision of Kendall was spoken of throughout the south with a shuddering horror!! He refused to remit the fine and the contractor appealed to the sympathies of the public along his whole line and cursed Kendall every where. So true it is that men of sphrightly talents often want judgt the great and commanding faculty of the mind.

In forming your cabinet you will be beset by many cliques at the bottom of whose movements you will find that monstrous principle of selfishness which depraves the character of so many of our acts. Associations will be formed because associations will be more powerful than individuals and a promise of mutual help and benefits will be the cement of all such Unions.

It will become your duty to consider whether in selecting your high confidential advisers, you can safely connect yourself with any of the appendages of Mr. Van Buren or Mr Tylers administrations. The disastrous defalcations of the former and the open shocking use of the Executive patronage by the latter at least for a time, in order to create a *new party* affected poor Van Buren deeply and have covered with mud and mire the present unfortunate incumbent. Whether your administration should not be distinct from and independent of the past can be decided by you alone. In all those arrangments which must precede your decisive action in the selection of your constitutional advisers you will of course fortify yourself against impertinent and importunate intrusion by the agency of a friend of immaculate purity, of [...][7] who will understand perfectly your position as well as his own.

The selection of a competent secretary is a matter of far greater consequence than many suppose. Such a man domiciliated as he will be in your house should be capable of keeping a set of books, of seeing to the economical disbursement of your funds, on a matured system the object of which will be to make an annual saving which I have no doubt can be effected and still a sufficient display made to satisfy the public. A fit person to fill this post and sign the patents in addition has been named to me but I do not know whether he would accept the appt if offered.

I am in correspondence with Ritchie and have been for many years. His solicitude that your administration should be entirely successful is as great and sincere as my own. He has his views as to *men* and measures but I do not feel authorized to communicate them at present. It is possible that you may find in the foregoing hints and suggestions nothing worthy of grave consideration. I claim for them only one merit that of disinterestedness and sincerity.

ALFRED BALCH

P.S. I have just received a letter from Gov. Branch[8] who begs me to offer you "his heartfelt congratulations on your glorious triumph. He looks for justice to Florida from a distinguished son of his native Carolina."[9]

ALS. DLC–JKP. Addressed to Columbia.

1. George Washington and Andrew Jackson.
2. Balch's reference probably is to the Creek treaty of 1832, which opened

approximately five million acres of eastern Alabama to white settlement and led in 1836 to the removal of the remaining Creeks. From 1836 to 1838 Balch served as special Indian commissioner to investigate alleged frauds in the sale of Creek reservation lands.

3. Paraphrase of a quotation from William Shakespeare, *Measure for Measure*, act 5, scene 1, line 315.

4. John Forsyth, Levi Woodbury, and Mahlon Dickerson. Forsyth served as a member of the U.S. House, 1813–18, 1823–27; as a U.S. senator for Georgia, 1818–19, 1829–34; and as governor of Georgia, 1827–29. He held the post of secretary of state under Andrew Jackson and Martin Van Buren, 1834–41. Dickerson won election as governor of New Jersey in 1815; represented New Jersey in the U.S. Senate from 1817 until 1833; and served as secretary of the navy in the cabinets of Jackson and Van Buren from 1834 until 1838.

5. The medieval Latin phrase "locum tenens" literally means "one holding a place." The plural form of the phrase is "locum tenentes."

6. New Orleans.

7. Sealing wax oil has rendered illegible one or more words on this line.

8. John Branch won election as governor of North Carolina, 1817–20, and as U.S. senator, 1823–29; he served as secretary of the navy from 1829 until his election to the U.S. House in 1831. Branch was appointed governor of Florida by Tyler in 1844.

9. Balch wrote his postscript on the verso of his second sheet.

FROM JOHN BLAIR

Dr sir: Jonesborough Decr. 2d 1844

As the fog of the late unparralled canvass has somewhat subsided, and we are enabled to see the ground which we occupy in Tennessee, I have thus early been looking into the future & much very much depends upon being *started aright*. I would regard our November victory as being a partial defeat were it possible for our wiley opponents to chain Tennessee to the *Northern Feds*. To avert this calamity, & give the requisite aid to your administration we must elect our Governor & legislature in August next, to do which we must have the proper candidate for Governor, & see to it that he shall be sustained throughout the state by Judiciously selected candidates for Congress & both branches of the Legislature, & that but one Democrat run even in our strongest election Districts & Counties. I have been feeling the public pulse as to our Gubernatorial candidate, & Nicholdson,[1] would combine more strength than any other of our friends. I am aware that it would be an unpleasant as well as unprofitable situation for him, but a remedy could be applied, & I without disguise suggest it. He ought not if elected (as he certainly would be) to remain in that office but the Senate (if of the proper complexion) could select for its Speaker a suitable substitute, & Mr. N. be transferred to the US Senate, where he certainly would be willing to go. I know he will be opposed to this arrangement but we can give him great relief in the canvass by so arranging matters as that he will not be driven with the velocity of a race horse through the extent of the state as you were.

Had I the planning of the campaign, I would keep our candidates from active operations as long as possible, & when entered into run it to the day of election with life & spirit, & whenever & wherever Nicholdson could not leisurely meet the Whig appointments (of 100 thick for his constitution & health) select the proper points for him & then meet the others with our most efficient speakers least occupied. We will have Johnston, Haynes, Campbell[2] & others who will have time & to spare in this District, as I fell confident we can make another rise of 100 votes in this County with Nicholdson at the head.

The Whigs are to have a glorification here on next wednesday for holding Tennee. *by the skin of the teeth*, but the true object is to rally for August next, instead of rejoice over the past. We certainly have here to contend with, the most incorrigible of the whole Tribe, and if a gain can be made, our friends elsewhere by proper exertions surely can. In this town we had 4 Methodist preachers, one Presbyterian & one Baptist being the whole of the ministry, The Circuit Judge, the Attorney-General, the three magistrates, constables, Teachers of both Academies, all the Lawyers & Doctors save one, & still we made a gain of nearly 100 & feel confident of being able to go up to 100 more. I did not mention the scurvy Editor of the Whig[3] for I believe his operations have favoured us. I wish to know as early as possible, whom we may expect to be our candidate for Governor. I have made my suggestions as to the individual with whom the public so far as I can learn, would be best pleased.

Again, you have it in your power to dissipate much of the cloud of opposition during the first of your administration. You will have but one *dangerous rock* & that is the *Tariff*. Human wisdom could not chalk out a course calculated to please all, but you must think before you act on this subject with as much wisdom as you did in your Penna. letter.[4] That was as it should have been for the then occasion, but in your inaugural you will be compelled to define your exact position, & for your reflection may I suggest that in my opinion, the nomination convention at Balt. gave the Index—a Revenue Tariff with incidental protection to all the great interests of the Country. I know the South dislike the *term protection* but under a revenue tariff it is due to certain leading interests to give protection. Hence the act of 1842 should be modified & all the excess above the revenue point lopped off.

You should not forget the course adopted by Jefferson & Madison.

They acted upon the principle that the South should be satisfied with the establishment of *Southern principles* to a certain extent & the *patronage of the Government* be conferred upon *the North.* I mean to the greatest extent. Penna. is to be the most difficult state to hold in the Democratic ring because she is such strongly manufacturing & consequently in favour of *protection.* Her stern Democracy will hold her on against what she might think injurious, to her pecuniary interests. Yet, in the selection of your cabinet she should be represented. North of Mason & Dicksons line should be *plied* with *patronage* as principles more congenial to the south must of necessity be established & carried out whatever may be your personal predelictions. Ought not Va & N.Y. to be looked to with Penna. in the formation of your cabinet? Silas Wright bids fairest to be your successor & such course ought to be adopted in reference to him as would most tend to his preservation; a place in your cabinet might lay him *on the shelf.* Should you look to the far south, Calhoun if he wished to have a place would be most acceptable to Southerners, but enough on this, as I know you will see to your advisers being of a true stamp & from the proper divisions.

You will see I think as I do, that under Providence it has been ordered that you are to be the instrument by which *new bonds of Union* are to be formed between the North South East & West. Yes I may say strange *bonds* as I trust Texas will be embraced, and that it will devolve upon you as the head of the great Republic to recommend mutual harmony, union & forbearance & put to flight every vagrant thought of dissension & secession in every quarter. Proper attention should be given to our erring mother N Carolina. She presents a strange picture in the test of Southern States, & must be redeemed from the Federal imbrace of Massachusetts.

This brings me to the subject upon which I set out to write you, & which, in the license given to my pen, I had almost edged out. It was to press upon you at this critical stage of the political game to urge it upon you to set out for Washington in advance of your allotted time & pass thro this state to the N Carolina line & then NC to the Raleigh Railroad taking old Guilford in your route. I do sincerely believe that such travel in the unostentatious manner in which you would make it & seeing *as tho you did not aim at it,* so, many of our Citizens would in Tennessee be worth half the Summers labour. I do not mean to partake of dinners & banquets, but on the annunciation of your travelling this route & leisurely passing thro, much good could be done both in Tennee. & NC. If I am correct in saying that the cause would be benefitted thereby, I know the difficulties of a winter travel would not cause you to forego the advantage. Of all the evils conceivable I know of none so appalling in prospect as the remote idea of Tennee. being held in league with your enemies, & warring to pull down your Administration.

I write you freely, because I can say that in none of my *personal conflicts for place* had I the same desire for success that I felt *for yours*, not on your account alone but the Country. Yes the cause of rational liberty which I believed in dangered by Clays latitudinarian principles. And again because I want no office which you have to confer & stand in a situation from disinterested feelings & motives to desire to see you enter upon prosecute & complete your arduous labours for the lasting good of the present, as well as unborn generations. Write me in reference to such things mentioned *as are tangible*, & believe what you wish private shall be so kept. My respects to Mrs. Polk.

JOHN BLAIR

PS Since writing the within I learn that the Whig leaders have discovered that to rejoice at defeat would not go down with the County Whigs & they have pulled down their dinner notices & abandoned the idea of rejoicing.

ALS. DLC–JKP. Addressed to Columbia. Polk's AE on the cover states that he answered this letter on January 3, 1845; Polk's reply has not been found.

1. A. O. P. Nicholson.

2. Landon C. Haynes, Brookins Campbell, and Andrew Johnson. A lawyer from Washington County, Campbell served five terms as a Democrat in the Tennessee House, 1835–39, 1841–43, 1845–47, and 1851–53; he won election to the U.S. House in 1853 and served until his death in December of that year.

3. Blair's points of reference are William G. Brownlow and the *Jonesborough Whig and Independent Journal*.

4. See Polk to John K. Kane, June 19, 1844.

FROM JOHN B. JONES[1]

Madisonian Office
Washington, Dec. 2d 1844

Dear Sir,

Accompanying this I send you an early copy of Mr. Tyler's Message,[2] which I think you will find to be a good old-fashioned Republican Document. I hope and trust so, at all events. And I am quite sure the prosperity of this country, under your auspices, will know no diminution during the next four years.

J. B. JONES

P.S. Of course, your Excellency will not permit this message to fall into any printer's hand, until it is ascertained that it has been delivered to Congress.

ALS. DLC–JKP. Addressed to Columbia.

1. In late 1841, John B. Jones succeeded Thomas Allen as editor of the Washington *Madisonian*. A prolific author, he wrote a number of popular books and poems during the 1840's and 1850's and later published an account of his experiences in the Confederate War Department, *A Rebel War Clerk's Diary*.

2. On December 3, 1844, Tyler's annual message was received in the U.S. House and Senate.

FROM JOHN STAATS

Dr Sir Geneva, Ontario Co. N.Y. Dec. 2, 1844

On the 4th Sept. last,[1] I addressed you a letter, requesting you to state (with a view to publication,) "under what circumstances, and upon what conditions you are (were) in favor of the *immediate* re-annexation of Texas." Through inadvertence, the letter was directed to Nashville. It is possible that you may have received it, though too late to admit a reply, before election, for the purpose contemplated.

I regard the practice of questioning Candidates for Office, as of doubtful propriety; yet as it has been sanctioned of late years, I took the liberty, as a citizen, to ask you on a point, which, as your declaration in your Cincinnati letter of April 28th,[2] stood, I was fearful might endanger your success at the North and West.

In the main, there could hardly be a doubt of the favorable result in this State, but as there was no *absolute certainty* of it, a doubt would still, occasionally, cast its shadow over the future and excite alarm.

There was reason for apprehension when it was seen with what effect the Whigs were using your declaration, but especially the faultering it produced in some of our firmest Democrats. In their public addresses they carefully avoided the "Texas question"; in private, some denounced it, and you, on its account.

It is highly probably that it is owing to the perverse construction put on your letter, that your majority in this State, is about Four thousand less than that of Mr Wright. Had every Democrat who voted for him, likewise voted for you, your majority, of course, must have been equal. It is preposterous to suppose that any considerable number of Whigs voted for him.

The evil which I could not avoid anticipating at times, must be my apology for what, under other circumstances, might justly have been considered an impertinence. I hesitated and delayed a long time, in the hope that some one else would write to you on the subject, but as nothing appeared befor the public, I took the liberty to do so.

I do not wish to be understood as endeavoring to make the impression that I was more zealous, and did more, for your election than others. I performed what believed to be my duty, they, no doubt, did the same.

Allow me to congratulate you on the general result, and accept my wishes that a benign and all-wise Providence may guide and direct you in the discharge of the arduous duties devolving upon you, in the high station to which you have been elected.

It would afford me great gratification to make your personal acquaintance, but, in all probability, I shall never enjoy that pleasure.

JOHN STAATS

ALS. DLC–JKP. Addressed to Columbia.

1. See John Staats to Polk, September 4, 1844.
2. See Polk to Salmon P. Chase et al., April 23, 1844.

FROM WILLIAM TYACK

New York, N.Y. December 2, 1844

After congratulating Polk on his victory, Tyack gives an account of the situation in New York and describes the struggle over patronage in New York City. He notes that they will soon appoint from each ward three members to the General Committee of Tammany Hall. The Custom House officers hope to exert influence in and through the committee and intend to secure the committee's endorsement of certain men for office in the event of C. P. Van Ness' confirmation by the U.S. Senate.[1] While the men who support the Tyler interest try to move heaven and earth for influence, the old Democracy of "the Jackson & Van Buren & Polk school" are entirely still. These men are Polk's warmest friends; they have worked hard and have spent their money freely in the cause.

ALS. DLC–JKP. Forwarded to Columbia by Robert Armstrong.

1. Born in Kinderhook, N.Y., Cornelius P. Van Ness moved to Vermont where he served in the state legislature, 1818–20, and presided as chief justice over the state supreme court, 1821–22, prior to his tenure as governor, 1823–26. He served as minister to Spain during Andrew Jackson's administration. In mid-1844 John Tyler appointed him collector of the Port of New York. After the presidential election, Van Ness took advantage of the growing rift within the New York Democracy and came to an understanding with the Hunkers; in return for their support, he agreed to remove the Barnburners in the Custom House. Insisting that Polk replace Van Ness immediately, Martin Van Buren and his friends backed Jonathan I. Coddington for the post. In June 1845 Polk removed Van Ness and replaced him with Cornelius Lawrence.

FROM J. GEORGE HARRIS

Dear Sir, Nashville, Tenn. Wednes. Dec. 4, 1844

I came into town this morning to witness the whig parade over "the whig electors." Supposing a brief description might not be uninteresting to you I have taken notes as follows:

The H. Guards and the Mill Boys of the slashes[1] appeared in uniform at an early hour, drumming and firing with a view to *get up enthusiasm*, but were signally unsuccessful. At length a train of carriages was formed on Broad street. The military marched to the spot and escorted it through the same streets in which our procession moved on Thursday.[2] I stood near the P.O. corner as it passed down Cherry street and viewed it from a window as it passed from right to left. There was not enthusiasm. Scarcely a smile was to be seen in the procession. It looked to me more like a funeral train than aught else I have ever witnessed.

Mrs. Bell with Mrs. Barrow[3] in her carriage in *front* of course. Now and then the military essayed to cheer, but the citizens refused to join. In a word, it was truly a ludicrous affair. Most of the leading whig citizens declined taking any part—indeed several of them informed that it was, in their judgment, a foolish parade; that it was an expedient of Mr. Bell and a few others to hold the party together which was almost shaken to pieces on Thursday last.

Well, they marched round the square and up into the Hall of the Ho. of Rep., where the electors formally voted for their Pres. candidates. Then there was speaking, and *such* speaking. All the rancor and bitterness of feeling which characterised whiggery in the most excited moments of the late campaign were manifested by Henry, Nelson, Brown, Haskell, et. al.[4] Their personal allusions to the Pres. Elect were dishonorable to themselves, disgraceful to their party, and elicited no applause. Mr. Bell who called them to order, and organized the meeting suggested that as there were crowds out-of-doors who were unable to press their way into the Hall, it would be well to have the remainder of the speaking in the Court-Ho. Yard. Accordingly they descended, when lo and behold! There were no such crowds out there! Indeed, the Hall of the Ho of Rep. had not been more than two-thirds filled; and about one half of these were boys who had been taken up by their seniors expressly to scream.

From beginning to end it is one of the most decided failures I have ever witnessed. Every man in the procession looked as though he were following his father to the grave. It cannot fail to have a beneficial effect upon our common cause. The contrast between this and our great day of last week, is indescribable. *That* was incomparably magnificent—this incomparably meagre.

Gov. Jones was in one of the carriages for Electors; and I noticed that whenever he received a nod from a person on the pave he rose and bowed with a most wonderful air of self-sufficiency, as though *he* were the hero of the day. But I also noticed that those "nods" were "like angels visits, few and far between."[5]

Make my best respects to your lady, and believe me....

J. GEO. HARRIS

ALS. DLC–JKP. Addressed to Columbia. Polk's AE on the cover states that he answered this letter on December 7, 1844; Polk's reply has not been found.

1. Harris' references are to two of Nashville's Whig militia companies, the Harrison Guards and the Mill Boys of the Slashes. Admirers of Henry Clay had dubbed him "the Mill Boy of the Slashes," a person of humble origins.

2. On November 28, 1844, Nashville Democrats organized a grand reception and procession in Polk's honor. See Robert Armstrong to Polk, November 28, 1844.

3. Harris' references are to Jane Erwin Yeatman Bell, the wife of John Bell, and to Ann Shelby Barrow, the wife of Washington Barrow.

4. Gustavus A. Henry, Thomas A. R. Nelson, Neill S. Brown, and William T. Haskell. A well-known lawyer and two-term attorney general of the First Judicial Circuit of Tennessee, Nelson was a presidential elector on the Whig ticket in 1844 and 1848; he served one term as a Unionist in the U.S. House, 1859–61; reelected in 1861, he was arrested en route to Washington by the Confederates and thus was prevented from serving a second term.

5. Paraphrase of a line from Thomas Campbell's poem "The Pleasures of Hope."

FROM ANDREW T. JUDSON

Dear Sir Canterbury Ct. December 4. 1844

The scenes of rejoicing in which our friends have indulged since the great question of the Presidency has been settled, can neither be described nor imagined. The conflict has been a mighty one, and the result will be felt and seen for many years to come. The influences upon our democratic institutions will be most happy, and the constitution and the union will be preserved. "Rome will not be sacked nor the people plundered."[1] To guard our sacred rights, the people have placed upon the watch towers, one who is faithfull, and one who will prove true to the constitution. Many of our friends feared for the result, and looking back to 1840, those fears were not wonderfull. However, I was not of that number. The moment the Baltimore convention broke up, light sprang up every where, confidence restored, and as I wrote you some weeks ago,[2] the nomination of Mr. Wright in the Empire State made all things sure, and completely settled the whole matter.

In Connecticut we have passed through the warmest contest ever witnessed by our sober people. Our loss of the State was not unexpected. We knew the powers we had to contend against. The abolition party had drawn off some of our men, and as those could not be influenced by Whigs, they remained and continued in the support of their own candidate, but not so with those who were originally in the Whig ranks. But little was required to gain them back to the support of the Clay ticket.

C. M. Clay spent several weeks here and made a visible impression in favor of his friend Henry. A still more potent reason for our defeat, came from the manufacturing districts. There, the incessant cry was "the tariff, the tariff will be destroyed." "No bread for the laborers." Our friends, with all their might, scouted this cry. Our candidate had as much regard for the working man as theirs–was as good a protectionist as theirs. Our candidate had voted for as many tariff laws as theirs. They said their candidate voted for the tariff of 1832; we replied, so did ours. They said their candidate voted for the compromise act. We replied, so did ours. Coming to more recent opinions, we hesitated not to believe and say that now there was no difference in reality between the two candidates.

Both were now in favor of a tariff for revenue with incidental protection to manufactures, agriculture and commerce. The democrats at the North claim an *equal* protection to the three great interests of the country, agriculture, commerce and manufactures, and that a *discrimination* should be made for their protection so far as the harmony of the states and the Union will permit. Beyond this the democracy do not wish to go. The peace and harmony of the Union are above all price. As heretofore, so there should now be a mutual conceeding to each other, and in the regulation of the tax laws, the people should not be unwilling to aid each and every other portion of the Union. Make war upon one State, and all the rest volunteer to fight her battles. When the energies of one State are depressed and her prosperity retarded, it may be the duty of the other states in generosity to tender their assistance and timely suckor.

So it should be in the matter of taxation. At the north there should be no disposition to avoid all necessary burthens to promote the sugar interest of the south. So also with the south when their aid is required to promote or sustain this great manufacturing interest of the north, or the wool growing, or iron interests of the middle states. But all this must be reasonable and *judicious*. Your far sighted predecessor, Genl. Jackson used the term *judicious* which, when properly *explained* and *understood*, was the identical term suited to this matter. Any tariff, other than this, would be *unjust* and oppressive. This should never be. To oppress one portion for the exclusive benefit of another is not, cannot be required. A reasonable amount, judiciously applied will never become oppressive. These suggestions are not new to you, because no man has been over the whole ground more than yourself, or can understand the condition of the country better. I make them, not because I have the remotest personal interest, but only to show you the true cause of our late defeat in Connecticut. Our contest will be renewed again on the 1st Monday of April,[3] just after your Inauguration. Upon that message to the people, will much depend our success or defeat then. For one, I should rejoice to see my native State arranged at so early a period, in the support of your administration, with her democratic sisters. I trust it will be so.

Suffer me, in conclusion, to congratulate You in your success; & the country in her hopes.

ANDREW T. JUDSON

ALS. DLC–JKP. Addressed to Columbia.

1. Quotation has not been identified further.

2. See Andrew T. Judson to Polk, September 14, 1844.

3. Judson's reference is to congressional and state elections in Connecticut in 1845.

FROM AARON V. BROWN

Dear Sir Washington City Decr. 5th 1844

I made my journey in seven days, travelling from Cincinnati with Robt. J. Walker, Mississippi's favorite Senator. He is a very great favorite here with the District Democracy who bear testimony to the amazing industry with which he sent off & prepared documents through the Summer. He entertains the same opinion with us as to the importance of getting for Ritchie half the Globe (Blairs interest) & I talked today with Cave Johnson about *his* going over in a day or two to sound the old gentleman at Richmond on the subject. He did not promise to go, but I shall be at him again tomorrow. The more I think on it, the more I am convinced that *such* would be the very best thing that could be done. It is useless to sound Blair at all until Ritchie's views are known. If that dont take, then B. & Rives must sink into mere *propriators* with *an able & competent* Editor having *absolute* control of the political character of the paper. The best directed & most judicious movements must be made on this point.[1] Much is saying here of course in relation to your Cabinet—nothing however in the wrong spirit. All anticipate your difficulties but most of your friends think you can successfully overcome them. I have seen the President but not under circumstances admitting any *confidential* conversation. In a day or so I shall seek such an interview. I met with Mr. Dallas here who talked very freely with me making divers suggestions which I assured him he might freely make to you without giving rise to any suspicion on his part that you ment to dictate to him. You will find that he would not favor the idea of Mr. Buchannon[2] being Secretary of State. There are probably various reasons for this. It might have a tendency to *exclude* his Brother in Law Wilkins,[3] or it might in some other respect cross his own *future* purposes.[4] I understand that he properly belongs to the Buchannon & *not* to the Van Buren & Henry Horn concern of Pennsylvania which makes it a little singular that he should not go on for Buchannon. But on the suppositions alone, I have taken & shall continue to do so, the most prudent steps to ascertain if Mr. Calhoun would not be content with the mission to England *there* to finish off the Oregon negotiation supposing the Texas question to be settled this session or to take on the form of *Congressional annexation*. If the Ritchie arrangement could be made I rather think he would. If that he ascertained, then how would Buchannon do for the State & Mr. Wright to be *offered* the Treasury department or vice versa, & if Mr. Wright would not accept (supposing that previous ascertained) let the state department be offer to him, *then* to Mr. Buchannon, Genl Cass offered the War department, Mr. Woodbury the Treasury[5] (if Mr. Wright would not have it). By the bye, Mr. Woodbury would make the best Post Master Genl in America & its peculiar patronage might tempt him to take it & in my opinion, the Treasury or the Post office would be well filled by him. But it would be best for you & him both, that he should take charge of the latter, for reasons which I have not time to give. The Navy could be retained by Mason[6] But I hear some strange things about his *incredulity* about your success etc. which I will trace up & ascertain in time for your consideration. Wickliffe went the *whole hog*, spent his money largely & freely franked by cart loads & illuminated brightly on the result. So if excluded from the cabinet he must be liberally provided for.[7]

I saw Mr. Kendall to day who meets our Wishes promply on the subject we last conversed on & I think will do it elegantly.[8] He says he does not seek any position for its *honor* & some position *below* the cabinet but nearest to it in its emoluments would keep him at home with his family & relieve his necessities. He spoke of the City Post office or the Marshall of the District etc. In the way of suggestion, so that our notions in relation to *him* are likely to be met. Dont bring yourself under any obligations as to the Comr. of the Genl Land office, as I want to furnish you with a good one & if not other can be found that I like better I may take it myself.

The carrier is waiting & you must take this as one of those random sheets that I may often send you.

A. V. BROWN

ALS. DLC–JKP. Addressed to Columbia and marked "*Confidential.*"

1. Thomas Ritchie, Francis P. Blair, and John C. Rives. The Washington *Globe*, owned by Blair and Rives, had long served as the official organ of Jacksonian Democracy; however, in 1844 its publishers angered the southern wing of the party by denouncing those who had defeated Martin Van Buren's bid for the presidential nomination and by continuing to attack John Tyler's efforts to annex Texas. After extended negotiations, Thomas Ritchie and John P. Heiss purchased the *Globe* on April 12, 1845; subsequently the administration newspaper took the name Washington *Union*.

2. James Buchanan.

3. William Wilkins, a lawyer, businessman, banker, and federal judge from Pennsylvania, won election as a Democrat to the U.S. Senate and served from 1831 until 1834, when he resigned to become U.S. minister to Russia; he served one year in the U.S. House and in 1844 resigned to accept the post of secretary of war in John Tyler's cabinet. Wilkins married George M. Dallas' sister, Mathilda, in 1818.

4. George M. Dallas, a prominent member of the "Family" party in Pennsylvania, was identified for many years as a staunch Van Burenite; his revival of the "Old Hickory Club" in 1843 helped remove James Buchanan's name from the list of potential presidential nominees. Early in 1844 Dallas followed the lead of Robert J. Walker in advocating the annexation of Texas. Dallas' niece, Mary Blechynden Bache, married Robert J. Walker in 1825; she was the daughter of Richard and Sophia Dallas Bache and the great-grand-daughter of Benjamin and Deborah Read Franklin.

5. Leader of the New Hampshire Democracy, Levi Woodbury served as judge of the Superior Court, 1816; governor, 1823–24; U.S. senator, 1825–31 and 1841–45; secretary of the navy, 1831–34; secretary of the Treasury, 1834–41; and associate justice of the U.S. Supreme Court, 1845–51.

6. John Y. Mason.

7. Charles A. Wickliffe served several terms in the Kentucky legislature before winning election to the U.S. House, where he served five terms beginning in 1823; he won the lieutenant governorship in 1836 and succeeded James Clark as governor upon the latter's death in 1839; and he served as U.S. postmaster general from 1841 until 1845.

8. Reference is to securing Amos Kendall's services in writing Polk's inaugural address.

FROM FRANCIS W. PICKENS

Senate Chamber
My dear Sir [Columbia, S.C. December 5, 1844][1]

I wrote you some time since and I hope you recd. it.[2] I found great excitement when I met the Legislature here. You will see *my resolutions*.[3] They were absolutely necessary to prevent excesses and mischief. They passed this body unanimously by yeas & nays, and will pass the House. There are a few here who are very bitter agst me because I will not go their length. Mr Calhoun is agst. all ultra or rash moves, but for waiting events with confidence in the Republican party and the President Elect. "We have no reason to fear results—it is due to them to the country & to good faith."[4]

I thank God you are in power. I know your feelings & principles & have full reliance.

We voted unanimously for you yesterday.[5] There is *not a Whig in the whole Legislature*.

You will recollect that I requested you and Mrs Polk to come through Georgia & So. Ca. on your way to Washington. If you could do so with convenience and propriety you would be received with great cordiality, and I would meet you in Augusta and go with you to Charleston. And if you had time, it would afford me very great pleasure to take you to my house about 20 miles from Augusta where you could rest yourselves for a day or two. I need not say to you and Mrs. Polk that such an arrangement would afford me the very highest gratification.

I have recd. several important letters from New York and one from Judge Fine[6] the particular friend of Mr. Wright, in which he says that Mr. Wright will not expect any appointment as he is under obligation to Administer the Office of Gov: &c. But of course you have more information than I have on this point.

The main point will be a distinct and clear avowal of your principles in favor of a Revenue Tariff. This will give peace, dignity & power to your position immediately and I think you will have an easy time.

In haste....

F. W. PICKENS

P.S. If you should come through So. Ca. & Geo., let me know the exact time we can expect you in Augusta. FWP

ALS. DLC–JKP. Addressed to Columbia.

1. Place and date identified through content analysis.
2. See Francis W. Pickens to Polk, October 11, 1844.

3. On November 26, 1844, James Hammond sent the legislature his annual governor's message, at the conclusion of which he attacked Congress for its failure to lower the tariff and ratify the Texas annexation treaty. Hammond transmitted resolutions of the Massachusetts legislature urging disunion if Texas were annexed; he concluded his message with a reciprocal call for disunion. When a motion was introduced in the South Carolina Senate to publish Hammond's message, Pickens objected and then proposed a set of resolutions affirming the annexation of Texas, pointing out the determination of abolitionists in Great Britain to influence the future of slavery in Texas, looking to the next administration of the general government for protection of southern rights, protesting the injustice of the Tariff of 1842, and asserting the argument that any present delays in implementing South Carolina's rights need not prejudice subsequent calls for action on those questions. The South Carolina Senate unanimously approved Pickens' resolutions on November 28, 1844. South Carolina, Senate, *Journal* 1844 Sess. pp. 20, 25, and 26.

4. Quotation not identified further.

5. On December 3, 1844, the South Carolina General Assembly met in joint session to choose the state's presidential electors; Pickens was one of those chosen. On the following day the electors cast South Carolina's nine votes for Polk.

6. A New York lawyer, John Fine served as judge of the Court of Common Pleas for St. Lawrence County, 1824–39 and 1843–47, and as a Democrat for one term in the U.S. House, 1839–41.

FROM DAVID T. DISNEY

Senate Chamber
Columbus Ohio 6 Dec. 1844

Dr Sir

Among the first fruits of our unfortunate defeat in Ohio as you will see by the Ohio Statesman which I send you by this same mail[1] is the loss of a democratic senator. On yesterday Thos. Corwin was elected by a vote of 60 to 46 over me to fill the place now occupied by Judge Tappan in the Senate of the U. States.

There was one matter however of *peculiar* gratification to us all notwithstanding the result. *Every democratic* member of the General Assembly was at his post and they cast an *unanimous* vote in my behalf. I confess that I allude to this with considerable pride as a party man because unfortunately for us during the last few years our own peculiar dissensions have almost invariably shown some scattering votes.

It was these dissensions and these dissensions alone as I advised you this fall which caused us to lose the state legislature.[2] The vote for senator and judge of our supreme court[3] which you will notice in the Statesman seem to show that our defeat in this state has led to good results in making us once more an united party.

Our general assembly commenced its sessions on Monday last 2d prox and the whigs having both branches are absolutely running riot in their accidental power. They are determined to make us feel it in its fullest extent. No considerations restrain them and if chastening can benefit a political party us poor democrats in Ohio ought to become the best of men.

You probably remember Judge Kennon[4] as I think that he was in Congress with you. You see by the Statesman that he also received with the exception of one vote the entire support of our party. These votes augur well for the democracy of Ohio and I sadly mistake the indication if the whig party do not find to their cost what it points to.

So far as Ohio is concerned under your coming administration her vote will of course be divided Allen democrat Corwin Whig. By the bye Tom. Ewings[5] friends struggled hard but Corwin ultimately proved too much for him.

The whigs are every where sounding the note of preparation and seem determined to obstruct your path with all means under their control.

D. T. DISNEY

ALS. DLC–JKP. Addressed to Columbia.

1. Copy of the Columbus *Ohio Statesman* not found.

2. On October 17, 1844, Disney wrote Polk that the Ohio Democrats had lost the state legislature "through the divisions among our own people on the subject of local banks." ALS. DLC–JKP. For the struggle within the Ohio Democracy between "hard" and "soft" money Democrats, see Gansevoort Melville to Polk, October 3, 1844, and Elam P. Langdon to Polk, November 12, 1844.

3. In early December 1844, the Ohio General Assembly reelected Ebenezer Lane to a third term on the Ohio Supreme Court; Lane defeated William Kennon, Sr., by the vote of 62 to 45.

4. William Kennon, Sr., won election as a Democrat to the U.S. House, 1829–33 and 1835–37, and served as president judge of the Ohio Court of Common Pleas, 1840–47.

5. Thomas Ewing, an Ohio lawyer, twice won election as a Whig to the U.S. Senate, 1831–36 and 1850–51. He served as secretary of the Treasury in 1841 but resigned in protest to Tyler's opposition to a national bank. Ewing later held the office of secretary of the interior, 1849–50, during the administration of Zachary Taylor.

FROM JOHN C. EDWARDS[1]

My Dear Gov: Jefferson. Mo. Dec. 6, 1844

If I am later in congratulating you, on your triumphant election, than many other friends have been, still I am sure you will not with-hold from me, full credit for sincerity in my rejoicings at your success, especially when I tell you that I delayed, first, because I was too unwell to write; next because I have had an incessant crowd since the opening of our Legislature; and, last, because my congratulations would have annoyed you, if they had been tendered when so many friends were overwhelming you with their rejoicings.

Truly we have gained a glorious victory. I never doubted our success. That our own state has gone against us, is a matter to be regretted; but that we reduced her majority to nothing, & then succeeded without her, is some consolation. In this state, our official returns are all in, & our Secretary of State[2] informs me, that your majority is 10.125 over Mr. Clay. I believe I wrote to you last summer,[3] that our majority would be about ten thousand. It was a guess, but happened to be nearly right.

Our majority ought to have been twelve thousand; but I suppose that some of the leaders of the "softs"[4] carried a few votes with them. The "soft" candidate for governor[5] was openly and bitterly against you, and warmly and actively for Mr Clay. Indeed I so considered him during all the canvass last summer; but at that time my proof against him was not so clear and unequivocal. Since our August elections, he has been open in his eulogies of Mr. Clay, and bitter in his denunciations against you. Simms,[6] who is from my own county in Tennessee, is a warm friend of yours, and will act with the democratic party, although he was a leader with the "softs" &, I think an unsound man. I have no doubt but there was a perfect understanding between the leaders of the "softs" and the leaders of the whigs throughout the state canvass.

Our loss in consequence of the defection of the "softs" has been about a thousand. The leaders will generally go to the whigs, and, from the best calculation I can make, four fifths of the rank and file will return to their old friends. Their presses will go down, unless the whigs sustain them to anoy us in the election of delegates to a convention next summer, called to amend our constitution.

You will perceive by this, that I am still full of local politics. I am anxious to let you into our household, and to reveal to you our family secrets. As we have become one of your daughters, and have put ourselves under your care and protection, it is right for you to examine & understand our condition. You must look into it as far as you can. I am anxious to see matters go right here, if we can make them do so; & I shall exert myself for that purpose. We have made a good fight, and our victory has been a glorious victory; but I am afraid all our difficulties are not over. But for one, as far as your cabinet is concerned, I am confident you will select men who will satisfy me.

Our delegation in Congress will be instructed on the subject of Texas.[7] Such at least seems to be the general impression now. We are all Texas men here, except the whigs, and many of them will soon join us on this subject. We go for Texas at the earliest practicable period, & without the consent of Mexico, & we are against being the first to propose to divide the Country into slave holding & nonslaveholding territory. But there seems to be every disposition to make the instructions as emolient as possible, &, to drive neither of our senators[8] from his seat. We are in earnest in wanting them there, and we are equally in earnest in wanting Texas. I wish you had time to write to me on this subject. I hope you have.

I have a favor to ask of Mrs Polk but I believe I will ask the madam herself, instead of asking through you. If I take this liberty, I am sure the madam wil pardon me, when I tell her that we were once school-mates together; and that to her I am indebted for the first permanent rule of conduct I ever adopted towards my fellow students. If she does not, then I must suffer the penalty she may inflict.

Here, we hope yet, that Tennessee may have gone with us. It is true, the count of Gov. Jones is against us; but I have a letter from one friend, S. H. Laughlin Esq. which induces us to believe that the rejection of some irregular votes, may have changed the scale.

I fear I have written too much to get any reply. If you have time, I shall be glad to hear from you.

JOHN C. EDWARDS

ALS. DLC–JKP. Addressed to Columbia and marked "*Confidential*."

1. Born in Kentucky, John C. Edwards moved to Rutherford County; passed the Tennessee bar examination in 1825; practiced law in Murfreesboro for several years before moving to Missouri; served one term in the U.S. House as a Democrat, 1841–43; and in 1844 won election to the governorship of Missouri and served until 1848.

2. James Lawrence Minor served as secretary of state for Missouri from 1839 until 1845.

3. Reference is to his letter of August 4, 1844.

4. The terms "hards" and "softs" referred to contrasting positions on currency and banking: "hards" favored an all metallic currency and sought strict specie convertibility on bank-note issues; "softs" preferred generous issues of bank paper and easy credit practices during periods of business contractions.

5. Charles A. Allen.

6. Leonard H. Sims.

7. The Missouri legislature met on November 18, 1844, and subsequently passed a series of eight resolutions calling for the reannexation of Texas "at the earliest practicable period," leaving the boundary line between Texas and Mexico to be determined in future negotiations and admitting Texas to the Union without a prior division of the territory into free and slave states. *Nile's National Register*, January 4, 1845.

8. Thomas Hart Benton and David R. Atchison. Atchison, a Whig, served in the Missouri House and as a judge on the Platte County Circuit Court prior to his election to the U.S. Senate in 1841 to fill the vacancy caused by the death of Lewis F. Linn; he served in the Senate until 1855 and was chosen president pro tempore on several occasions during his service in that body.

FROM CAVE JOHNSON

Dear Sir. Washington Saturday 6th Dec. 1844

I suppose a statement of occurrences here, management &c may not be uninteresting to you at this time & therefore take it upon myself to give you such facts as I suppose may interest you as is probable many others will do and allow me to say without any expectation of an answer as I know you will have enough of that to do.

Every body here considers a disruption in our ranks inevitable at the commencement of your Admn—first, upon the formation of the cabinet second upon the public printer.

The northern democracy are averse to the continuation of C—n or any member of the present cabinet–so is Mr. THB.[1] Rumor has been long in repeating his declarations, that *if you pursued such a course*, you would make for yourself a better bed than Tyler ever lay on, that if a "*rotten egg*" was left he would fire at it &c. The repetition of these things every where induced Genl. McKay[2] & myself to call on him last night. I have never met him in a better humor, more mild, in every way conciliatory, both of *consulting our friends* before he made any movement on Texas. Your excellent friend Genl McK. will have a full interview with him on Monday. I do not believe half that I hear as to him. The northern democracy would prefer Silas Wright in the Treasury but they think it hardly probable that he will accept & in that event, they speak of Flagg or Marcy or Butler. There is no truth as his Rep. (King)[3] says in the Report, published in the Whig paper, that he said in Albany that he would not go into the cabinet. They also speak of Gov Hubbard or Fairfield for the War or Navy and Jones or Dromgoole[4] for the State department. Another set thinks of Cass for the State, SW[5] or Flagg for the Treasury & Hubbard for PM Genl. without specifying for the South. The great object is among them to exclude C—n.

In the South the great object is to retain him. He wishes it & it is said that a movement will be soon made in Va. to present his name for the succession unless Ritchie can suppress it. Genl. Saunders is sd to be looking to the P.O. Dep. If Calhoun is excluded, then many say that King of Geo.[6] should go into the Treasury, giving most of the others to the north and that J. Y. Mason should be retained. This I think is the opinion of Genl McK. Buckhanon I think will go on the Supreme Bench & efforts are making in Va. to place J.Y.M.[7] in the Senate. There is no chance for Rives.[8]

From what his friends say I am inclined to believe that Mr. C—n would be willing to go to England. There will be some difficulty I fear in disposing of Wilkins & Walker, Bibb & Wickliffe[9] satisfactorily. The general opinion among our friends here seems to be, that Van Burens cabinet & the present one should be passed & make selections to suit yourself including aspirants as the Baltimore Convention did in your nomination. Our friends Bagby & Judge Wayne[10] have acted badly if all is true that is told of them.

As to the printing, the same feeling prevails. The South fears that the Globe will be the organ of T.H.B. & the northern democrats & opposed to C—n. The Southern I think irreconcilably opposed to it. I see no chance of a reconciliation with them if F. P. Blair is retained. The Constitution designs & is intended to supersede him, & will probably amalgamate with the Madisonian.[11] The *only* difficulty I understand between them is this—that the Madisonian insists as a condition that the Capt. T. shall be supported as the Candidate of 1848 whilst the other intends to support J.C.C.[12] Brown made a suggestion to me on yesterday, which he intimated met your approbation, that I should see T. Ritchie & try & get him at the head of the Globe in the best way possible. I like the idea well & suggested it to Genl McK on my own on yesterday. He approved highly of it & urged me to go to Richmond this morning. I was not well enough but am so much pleased with the idea that I shall visit Richmond during the week. Looking at every thing I think it practicable & the best that can be done.

The northern democrats seem to have entire confidence in me whilst the Southern have the same in Brown. I am sometimes uneasy lest they should think our Course a concerted one under your direction. The N.Y. Senators pro. tem (Dickenson and Foster) from the former I shall be able to learn fully & reliably the feelings & wishes of N.Y.

Many are exceedingly anxious to know the time you will be here. Brown tells them the last of Feby.

There is a strong feeling among our friends in the House, that your trip should be as far as practicable just the opposite of Genl Harrison's, that the simplicity of a republican should as far as practicable be maintained, avoiding all ostentation & show.

I mention these little things, the chit chat of the House which may not be uninteresting.

C. JOHNSON

[P.S.] I forgot to say it is very generally understood that Mr Clay & Mr Webster will return to the Senate & if Mr C—n is not retained that he will do so likewise. It is expected also that Cass will come from Michigan & if so, so should Van Buren & Butler.

ALS. DLC–JKP. Addressed to Columbia and marked "*Private.*"

1. John C. Calhoun and Thomas Hart Benton.

2. James I. McKay, a lawyer and Democrat from North Carolina, served in the U.S. House from 1831 to 1849; earlier he had won election to several terms in the state senate and had served as U.S. attorney for the district of North Carolina.

3. A lawyer in Ogdensburg, N.Y., Preston King sat in the New York Assembly, 1835–38; won four terms in the U.S. House, 1843–47 and 1849–53; and served one term as a Republican in the U.S. Senate, 1857–63.

4. Henry Hubbard, John Fairfield, John W. Jones, and George C. Dromgoole. Jones, a Virginia lawyer, served five consecutive terms in the U.S. House, 1835–45, and won election as Speaker in 1843; he held the office for one term.

5. Silas Wright, Jr.

6. John P. King served as a Democrat in the U.S. Senate, 1833–37, and as president of the Georgia Railroad & Banking Co., 1841–78.

7. John Y. Mason.

8. A Virginia lawyer and planter, William C. Rives served several terms in the U.S. House and Senate. Originally a Democrat, he subsequently became a Whig. He twice served as U.S. minister to France, 1829–32 and 1849–53.

9. William Wilkins, Robert J. Walker, George M. Bibb, and Charles A. Wickliffe. Bibb, a Kentucky lawyer and judge, served in the U.S. Senate, 1811–14 and 1829–35. An early admirer of Andrew Jackson, he broke with Jackson over the bank question. Bibb served as secretary of the Treasury in the Tyler cabinet from July 1844 until March 1845.

10. Johnson probably refers to Arthur P. Bagby and James M. Wayne. A Democrat and an ally of Thomas Hart Benton, Bagby served as governor of Alabama, 1837–41; U.S. senator, 1841–48; and minister to Russia, 1848–49. On November 26, 1844, Hampton C. Williams, a party operative, wrote Andrew Jackson that during the summer Bagby, who had remained in Washington, had contributed little to the party's campaign efforts and had publicly ridiculed Polk's nomination. ALS. DLC–JKP. Wayne, a Georgian, served in the U.S. House, 1829–35, and sat on the U.S. Supreme Court, 1835–67.

11. Baltimore *Constitution* and Washington *Madisonian.*

12. John Tyler and John C. Calhoun.

TO JOHN Y. MASON

My Dear Sir. Columbia Tenn Dec 6. 1844

I have received your letter of the 16th ultimo.[1] I thank you for the congratulations which you convey to me upon the result of the late political contest.

As you truly remark we have been acquainted a long time and I am happy to know that no circumstance has ever occurred to impair in the slightest degree that intimate personal friendship, early formed, which has for so many years existed between us. I am happy also to know that in political sentiment, we have generally perhaps always agreed.

I was apprised of the delicacy & embarrassment of your situation some months ago, and of your letter to Genl Jackson. I received the nomination at Baltimore as you know without seeking or expecting it. During the canvass I made no pledges or commitments of any kind except to adhere to my political principles. Since the result has been known I have made none. I am therefore perfectly free to consult with my friends, to receive their opinions & advice & finally to act upon my own judgment in the discharge of the high duties which must soon devolve upon me. I have deemed it the prudent course to remain uncommitted in regard to all matters connected with my duties, on & after the 4th of March, until I reach Washington, which I expect will be about the 20th of February. At that time it will give me pleasure to see and confer with you. I know you will properly appreciate the reason & motives for this course.

With the kind salutations of Mrs. Polk & myself to Mrs Mason ....[2]

JAMES K. POLK

L, copied, signed, and certified by J. Knox Walker. DLC–JKP. Addressed to Washington City and marked "*Confidential.*"

1. See John Y. Mason to Polk, November 16, 1844.
2. Mary Anne Fort Mason.

FROM SAMUEL P. WALKER

Memphis, Tenn. December 6, 1844

Walker writes Polk about the competition for contracts and offices at the naval yard in Memphis; he discusses in particular the office of naval agent and stresses that it is "as important as any office in Tennessee." Walker points out that "the political complexion of this Congressional and Senatorial district" depends upon the vote of the city, and the arrangement of offices at the Naval Depot will exercise great influence. Concerned that only Whigs have applied thus far for the position, he emphasizes the need to appoint a sound Democrat and recommends George W. Smith.

ALS. DNA–RG 45. Addressed to Columbia.

TO SILAS WRIGHT, JR.

My Dear Sir: Columbia Tenn. Dec. 7th, 1844

I received in due season your letter of the 1st of November.[1] I congratulate you upon your election as Governor of New York, and upon the success of our common principles, in the late political struggle through which the country has passed.

The electors of President and Vice President have now cast their votes, and I suppose there can no longer be a doubt of my election. In preparing to discharge the high duties which must soon devolve upon me, I feel most sensibly the great importance of calling to my aid a proper Cabinet. They should be able men, of sound Democratic principles, of public reputation, known to the country, and with whom my personal as well as political relations are such, as to permit the freest and most unreserved confidential intercourse. Such relations I am happy to know have long existed between you and myself, and to come directly to my object, I desire that you will accept a place in my Cabinet. The Treasury has in my judgment become the most important of the Executive Departments. Your long experience in public life, and extensive knowledge of our financial system, induce me to invite you to take charge of that Department on the 4th of March next. If you are at the head of the Treasury Department the whole country will feel and know that it is in able and safe hands. You are the first and only person to whom I have given an intimation of my wishes on the subject of the Cabinet. You are the only one whom I have invited to take a place in it. In regard to the other Departments and indeed all other offices which it may be my duty to fill, I am wholly uncommitted. I received the nomination at Baltimore, as you know without seeking or expecting it. During the canvass I made no pledges. Since the result has been known I have made none. I am therefore perfectly free to consult with my friends, and select the best men to fill the other Executive Departments. I desire to have the benefit of the advice of my friends, and of none more than yourself. Any communication which you make to me will be regarded as *sacredly and inviolably confidential*, as I desire you to consider this letter, and any other which I may address to you on the same subject. Under this *injunction of confidence* I request that you will give me your opinion freely and unreservedly, and especially of the persons whom it would in your judgment be proper to call to my aid in the administration. In the hope that you will accept the invitation which I tender, and thus give your valuable service to the Country in the administration of the Federal Government, I shall await your answer before I take any step with a view to fill the other Executive Departments.

Will you be pleased to favour me with an answer, at your earliest convenience?

JAMES K. POLK

ALS. ICHi. Addressed to Canton, N.Y., and marked "*Strictly Confidential.*" In his draft of this letter Polk wrote and then cancelled the following postscript: "Should you be willing, to accept a place in the Cabinet, and should prefer the State or some other than the Treasury Department, I hope you will feel no delicacy in signifying said preference in your answer. Yours &c. J.K.P." DLC–JKP.

1. See Silas Wright, Jr., to Polk, October 31, 1844.

FROM JOHN O. BRADFORD

Dear Sir Washington Dec 9th 1844

I arrived in this city a few days since, and have busied myself in looking around me. I have been well aware of the conflicting interests (personal) in the Dem: party, but was not aware until my arrival here that the feeling was so intense. Our glorious triumph is the result of our harmonious action, I trust we are not now to be robbed of the fruits by dissensions among ourselves. Your own personal comfort; the future harmony of our party, and the prosperity and glory of your administration, eminently depend upon your arrangement of cabinet officers. This being the case I feel that I need make no apology for giving you a statement of what is talked about and of what is really transpiring here. I have purposely thrown myself into positions where I might obtain a fair impression of general and sectional sentiment and as such I give it to you. The particular friends of Col Benton are determined to have Mr Calhoun superceded in the state dept, and in order to effect their purpose have assumed the ground that no one who is at all prominent as a candidate for the presidency must be allowed a seat in the cabinet. Of the force of this objection you must be the judge; for my own part I cannot see the justice or sound policy of ostracising a man from all participation in the administration merely because his abilities and worth have indicated him as a probable candidate for the chief magistracy. This opinion is favored by few, very few. The great majority of your friends entertain no such views; on the contrary would be glad to see you gather around you such men as Calhoun, Buchanan, Wright, Cass &c—men who would eminently adorn their several stations, be serviceable to you and useful to the country. Whether these several gentlemen would be willing to accept the responsibilities and duties of cabinet appointments I do not know. Mr Wright I am sure would not. And Mr Buchanan will be influenced altogether by the Judgement of friends. As to whether should he be invited to a seat in the cabinet he should accept, or remain in his present honorable position in the Senate where he will necessarily be the leader of the administrative party. Still it would gratifying to Mr Buchanan to be tendered an appointment, and if there is one man in the Union who more than another deserve the honor I firmly belive it is James Buchanan. It is said that New York achieved our Victory; the truth is the battle was fought and the victory won in Pennsylvania; we all knew, that if defeated in Penn: we would be defeated in New York. The New Yorkers themselves said so, and still say so—every man in Penn felt so, and worked according. Mr Buchanan took the stump in the iron counties and by reference to their votes you will find that they saved us the state. The Whigs calculated upon large gains in those counties, on account of the tariff excitement, and I am sure that they have been disappointed only by the indefatigable exertions of our distinguished senator. I repeat I know of no one who has stronger claims upon your notice than Mr Buchanan; he eminently deserves the compliment of a tender of a seat in the cabinet; and the compliment is alike due to the iron hearted democracy of his state, who have through their electoral College unanimously recommended him for the post of secretary of state.[1] As it is probable that Dept will not be vacated I believe Mr Buchanan would under the circumstances be equally gratified with the tender of the Treasury. I am sure no appointment could be made that would give so much general satisfaction. He enjoys in an eminent degree the respect and confidence of the several sections of interests of the party; and while his appointment would be hailed with pleasure by the great majority, it would be really exceptionable to none. I write now what I know—the sentiment of the North, South, East and West, alike favour him.

Will you excuse the liberty I have taken in thus writing to you. I do so not from a disposition to give myself prominence; I write from a pure motive, and with the best feelings. I have no particular interest to gratify. Should I receive any appointment under your administration I will attribute it solely to whatever interest you may feel in my welfare, and your disposition [to] serve me. There is much speculation here as to who will compose your cabinet; among others common consent seems to indicate your old friend and fellow soldier Cave Johnson for the Post Office dept. Your speech at Nashville[2] has been received here. It has won for you golden opinions.

JOHN O. BRADFORD

[P.S.] Dec 10: I have opened this letter to say that this morning Mr McDuffie offered in his place in the senate a resolution to annex Texas to the U.S. conformable to the treaty already made. Immediately Mr Benton rose and gave notice that he would tomorrow introduce a resolution providing for the annexation of Texas.[3]

With this I send you the Demo Union, our organ in P.[4]

ALS. DLC–JKP. Addressed to Columbia.

1. Having cast their votes for Polk and Dallas, Wilson McCandless and his fellow Pennsylvania electors wrote Polk on December 5, 1844, and urged him to appoint James Buchanan secretary of state. LS. DLC–JKP. Accounts of their support for Buchanan appeared in newspapers throughout the country.

2. On November 28, 1844, Nashville Democrats organized a grand reception in honor of Polk. In reply to a congratulatory address by A. O. P. Nicholson, Polk reminded his listeners of the political rights of the defeated Whigs and declared himself the representative of all the people and not that of his party only. *Nashville Union*, November 30, 1844.

3. Bradford wrote his postscript above the date line on the first page of his letter. On December 10, 1844, George McDuffie introduced a joint resolution calling for the immediate annexation of Texas; his joint resolution included the first eight articles of the Tyler administration's treaty, which the U.S. Senate had rejected during the previous session. In response to McDuffie's move, Benton reintroduced on December 11, 1844, his annexation bill authorizing negotiations with Mexico and Texas and providing for a future division of Texas into free and slave states.

4. Bradford's reference is to the Harrisburg *Democratic Union*. Bradford wrote the second paragraph of his postscript in the lower left margin of the first page of his letter.

FROM ORVILLE T. BRADLEY

Dear Sir. Rogersville Ten. Decr 9th. 1844

I saw Mr Gifford of the "Sentinel",[1] some ten days ago, and he informed that when in your town, some two months ago, you expressed a desire to hear from me by letter; to this wish, & to a desire that you may so execute the high trust to which you are called, as to reflect honor on the choices of your friends, by conferring a safe & judicious admininistration upon the country, you will owe the trouble of this communication. And I hope you will pardon the presumption of this address for the sake of the good wishes which have prompted it. I know the difficulties of your position & the impossibility for a man who does not see all the ground to appreciate it properly. Yet I feel tempted to offer for your reflection some suggestions. Do you not owe to your own security & to the future strength of the democratic party to strengthen as far as possible your own position in the nation? In the event Pennsylvania should be dissatisfied with such a reduction of duties as you may deem just to the whole nation, is it not desirable to secure some additional strength to fall back on? And cannot that strength be secured in Tennessee & N. Carolina? And to affect Ten & N. Ca can any thing better be done than for *you* to pass to Washington thro E Tennessee & N Carolina by Mecklenberg Chapel Hill & Raligh on your way to Washington? Such a trip, well managed, will give your friends great advantages in the next elections. We can doubtless carry Tennessee next Aug 1; but it is necessary, if we can, to carry it by such a majority as to preclude the hope of its recapture by the Whigs. For a real vigorous administration, we must not only have a majority, but a strong & reliable one. If you should conclude to pass thro E. Ten & N. Ca. your friends ought to know it early to prepare for it. The party that have brot. you into power, it seems to me are like to be divided in their wishes for a successor, into three great sections, the friends of Calhoun, Wright & Cass. Will not the policy of Mr Monroe be the best in your situation, to bring the heads of each of these sections into your Cabinet? Will it not prevent jealousy & distrust & secure the support of all to your administration? Will not such a union of the aspirants in the Cabinet, secure a submission on the part of the friends of each to the decision of a convention? To secure the permanent ascendency of the principles of republicanism or southern democracy will it not become necessary for you to adopt the principles upon which it is understood Jefferson & Madison acted in the use of the patronage of the Federal government, to let the South not satisfied with the ascendency of its principles, the possesion of the Presidency & the actual control of the government, and let all its patronage, but the purely local, be used to the North of Mason's & Dixon's line? You will come into power under circumstance very similar to Mr Jefferson, and in his management of domestic parties you will find many useful lessons. In that part of the art of government, he has never been excelled. I am happy to say that I find all your frinds here concurring in approving the tone & manner of your reply to the Nashville address.[2] It is conceived in the spirit of Jeffersons inaugural address "We are all federalists we are all republicans." The Nation is wearied by the long contests of the Whig & democratic parties, & naturally, at present thirsts for repose; and in spite of leaders, will now support any administration that has vigor & ability enough to secure its respect, & moderation & discretion enough not to affront its prejudices or shock its sympathies. If I understand the present temper of the nation it is opposed to all ultraisms & new experiments. Whenever we are "well enough," there is the wish to be "let alone." Will it be safe or prudent in regard to this feeling, as also, the business of the country to meddle with the currency, at least for the ensuing two years? A large portion of the whig party has opposed your election from honest apprehension of the spirit of Dorrism & agrarianism that pervades a portion of the democratic party; will it not be wise to allay such apprehensions, by discountenancing these & all other ultraisms?

I see our friends in Sumner County have requested a call of a convention at Nashville to nominate a candidate for governor, on the 8th of Jany. Is not this premature? Is it not the true policy of the democratic party to postpone the commencement of the next canvass as late as possible? To let the whig army in Tennessee cool & disband as much as possible? If we commence the fight now, shall we not enable the leaders to keep nearly all their present powers arrayed against us? Ought we not to wait till the new administration is organized & our members of Congress get home? Say till the first monday in April? In the next canvass the democracy ought to bring forward their ablest men upon the stump every where, for every office for the next race will depend more upon the strength of the issues and the ability of discussion & less upon the popular strength of the men run, than any that has ever taken place in Tennessee.

If there is a necessity for any removals that may be odious cannot it not be arranged to have them made by Tyler? So of some other things? Will it not be your just policy for yourself & party to avoid every thing calculated to hazard your strength, till you are firmly seated in the confidence of the nation? I do not mean any thing more than prudence, moderation, & conciliation; for boldness & decision when proper occasions arise as Jackson proved are essential elements of strength & popularity.

Ought not the democratic party at Nashville to hold a meeting & pass a set of resolutions on national & state issues for the next canvass, & thus give our friends the cue? By so doing we can, in some degree, particularly for the state, choose our own issues, instead of having them selected for us by our opponents. Ought we not to go, in relation to state affairs, for a reduction of salaries & pay when they may be in the power of the legislature, to correspond with the increased value of money since they were settled, instead of increased taxes to meet the liabilities of the state?

The democratic candidates in this district are, I think, like to be Brookins Campbell & Critz for senators, Haynes for Washington, Greene & Hawkins, Hord for Hawkins, Milligan for Greene & Dr Martin probably for Washington.[3] For Governor, it is important to have the best man upon the stump, that we can command in the state. Will this be Nicholson, C. Johnson, or A. Johnson?

ORVILLE BRADLEY

ALS. DLC–JKP. Addressed to Columbia. Polk's AE on the cover states that he answered this letter on January 3, 1845; Polk's reply has not been found.

1. Jonesboro *Tennessee Sentinel*.

2. See John O. Bradford to Polk, December 9, 1844.

3. Brookins Campbell, Phillip Critz, Landon Carter Haynes, James Madison Hord, Sam Milligan, and Alfred Martin. Critz represented Hawkins County two terms in the Tennessee House, 1841–43 and 1859–61, and two terms in the Tennessee Senate, 1843–47. Haynes of Washington County won election to two terms in the Tennessee House, 1845–47 and 1849–51, and to one term in the Tennessee Senate, 1847–49. Hord of Hawkins County served one term in the Tennessee House, 1843–45. Milligan represented Greene and Washington counties in the Tennessee House from 1841 until 1847. Martin of Washington County sat for two terms in the Tennessee House, 1837–41, and for one term in the Tennessee Senate, 1845–47.

FROM AARON V. BROWN

Dear Sir. Washington City Decr. 9th 1844

The speculations still continue, but have taken on no malignant aspect. Our friends have all been notified not to put any reliance on rumors which they may find afloat. Your address at Nashville is well received—evinced, as they all agree, of the right tone of feeling. I disclaim truly any knowledge of your purposes & assure every one who approaches me that no settled purposes were matured in your own mind in relation to your Cabinet. I called on Mr Calhoun this morning in the course of Civility. He spoke right off of the circumstances by which you were surrounded & expressd his opinions of the best mode of action under them but gave the conversation no direction in relation to himself. Your administration he thinks must be essentially southern in its measures but so temperd with moderation & justice as to create no northern aversions. He concurs in your own opinions that you need not be here much in advance of the period for inauguration; especially as it is not the case of one party triumphing over another party holding the offices of government. This he thinks gives you a great advantage in the way of leisure to look around you & to effect *gradually* those changes in the instruments of your administrations which you may intend. If great crowds of office seekers shall assemble here & you should attempt *forth with* to pass on removals & appointments, more he thinks would be disappointed than could be gratified & being here the sparks of dissatisfaction could catch from one to another untill they kindled up to a great flame. Whereas if the work of removal & appointment were to go on slowly & gradually, most of them would return home during deliberations & when disappointment did come, the spirit of revolt would not spread so rapidly nor extend so far. He stated that it might be well to give out some declaration of this sort in your inaugural preparatory to such thinning out & despersion of the crowd of applicants. His suggestions seemed to me to be worthy of communication to you. This was the great error & crisis in Harrisons time & you well remember if it was not in Genl Jacksons & Mr Van Burens time. Mr Fernando Wood called this evening & talked a great deal about the state of things in N. York. He thinks a cabinet position should be *offd* to Mr Wright althogh he says there is no earthly probability of its acceptance. He thinks it would be taken well by him & his friends. When declined, then New York would expect a place in your Cabinet to be offd. to some other Citizen of that State. He mentiond the following as much spoken of: Cambrelling[1] not much identified with either of the divisions of the N. York democracy. His recent employments have kept him out of close contact with either & hence he thinks he might be acceptable to both as Sec of the Treasury. Mr. Flagg[2] is the great financier of N. York & the protogee of Mr. Wright & he thinks would make a good Sec of the Treasury—clear headed & laborious but modest in his bearing. Of Marcy & Dick[3] he also spoke in terms of commendation. It occured to me during his conversation that Flagg on account of his having managed the finances of that state so well for several years back & his extensive reputation for integrity & business capacity might make you a first rate *collector* of the customs, if some one else was taken for the Treasury.

You will notice the recommendation of Mr Buchanan for the state Department by the college of electors. Some here think that was very indelicately done toward you & if followd by others might lead to bad consequences. I do not think there is much in this, althogh it would have been better to have avoided it. I hear nothing further as to Genl Cass' expectations.

I think Johnson & Hubbard of Va. will go over to Richmond in a few days.[4]

The Texas question will be up in a few days, Mr McDuffy having given notice to day that he would introduce joint resolutions on that subject.

Hannigan[5] said at table, that Benton soon after this notice was given, said to McDuffie that he had nothing to fear from his opposition at this session. This I fear is too good to be true, but we shall soon see. I assured Mr Calhoun this morning that you & your friends so far from being opposed most heartily desired that question to be settled this session.

On tomorrow I shall visit the President on the subject mentiond by your Brother.[6]

There is talk here that Genl Saunders would be glad to get position in the Cabinet, but many have turned the ear of incredulity to it. He is you know an inveterate office seeker & has thereby weakend himself considerably as I apprehend in his own state. There seems to be quite a general expectation here that you would have some one bosom & confidential friend with you & conjectures are a float in relation to Johnson & myself, to all which I answer that you will bring with you certainly, *one bosom* & confidential friend. But I apprehend not of the *Cabinet*. A very dear & particular friend of your acquaintance will understand *that* I guess.

Jones[7] mentiond to night that he heard it said that you intended to bring on Genl. Armstrong for the post office Department. Could he finally make any money by that? Could he acquire any increase of reputation? & finally can any one be found to supply his place at Nashville? Who else could escape the daily attacks of the Whig press & the Whig orators for making his office Democratic head quarters? Think of all these things. There is quite a rivalry here as to what house you will come to. All are Whig houses. Your old friend Dr. Haws is here (at Browns)[8] a good democrat of great activity anxious on the subject & I doubt whether you could do any better than to come here, where I shall hang out for the Winter. Another random sheet you see.

A. V. Brown

ALS. DLC–JKP. Probably addressed to Columbia; marked "*Confidential.*"

1. Churchill C. Cambreleng.
2. Azariah C. Flagg.
3. William L. Marcy and John A. Dix.
4. Cave Johnson and Edmund W. Hubard. A graduate of the University of Virginia and a planter from Buckingham County, Va., Edmund W. Hubard served as Democrat in the U.S. House from 1841 until 1847, when he declined to run for a fourth term and retired to his agricultural pursuits. Brown wanted Johnson and Hubard to travel to Richmond and persuade Thomas Ritchie to purchase Francis P. Blair's interest in the Washington *Globe*.
5. Edward A. Hannegan.
6. William H. Polk wanted Brown to speak to John Tyler about a position in the general government. On January 13, 1845, Tyler nominated William to be the chargé d'affaires in Naples; the Senate declined to act on the nomination. On March 12 Polk resubmitted his brother's name for that post; and the Senate consented the following day.
7. George W. Jones.
8. Henry Haw is not identified further.

FROM ANDREW JACKSON

[Dear Sir] [Hermitage, Tenn.][1] December 10, 1844

I enclose you letters[2] from my friend N. P. Trist, who married the Grand daughter of Mr. Jefferson,[3] and the only true representative that great & good man has left, and who has been most cruelly treated by Mr. Tyler, in being dismissed from the consulate at the Havanna. I know Trist well, he is a man of first rate talents, a man of unimpeacheable moral character, of high honorable feelings & bearing, & not one drop of aristocratic blood in his vains. He is worthy of your attention & there is safety to the executive in having such men near him. Mr. Trist was of much use to me—every confidence in him may be reposed, & let me assure you, in Washington where is so much intrigue going on such a man near you is beyond price.

ANDREW JACKSON

ALS. DNA–RG 59. Probably addressed to Columbia.

1. Place identified through content analysis.

2. Letters not found.

3. Nicholas P. Trist, husband of Virginia Jefferson Randolph, studied law under Thomas Jefferson and began his career in public service in 1827 as a clerk in the State Department; Jackson appointed Trist consul in the port of Havana, Cuba, in 1833; John Tyler recalled him in July 1841 following a congressional investigation of U.S. affairs in Havana; and Polk appointed Trist chief clerk of the State Department in 1845 and then in 1847 special agent to negotiate a peace treaty with Mexico.

FROM JOHN M. BASS[1]

Union Bk of Ten

Dr Sir Nashville Decr 11 [18]44

In reply to your verbal application when last in this city I have to inform you that this Bank will discount a bill or bills drawn on yourself at Washington for the amt you mentioned say $8000, or $10.000 so as to fall due about the 1 July next or about the close of the 1st quarter after the 4 March, with the understanding that you may at that time renew or extend for 90 days or six months such portion of the above amt as it may not be convenient then to pay.

JNO. M. BASS

ALS. DLC–JKP. Addressed to Columbia.

1. John M. Bass married Malvina Grundy, daughter of Felix Grundy; Bass served as mayor of Nashville in 1833 and subsequently headed the Union Bank of Tennessee in the late 1830's and early 1840's.

FROM LEONARD P. CHEATHAM

Dr Sir: Nashville December 11th 1844

As we scarsely ever have time for conversation even when we meet, & as no answer will be expected: permit me to make a few suggestions in addition to the few words we had.

As to the questions of the Tariff, Texas & Oregon, the positions you have assumed are so clearly defined & so well approved of by your friends, that we can not apprehend any injuries to your administration from either source notwithstanding the restless disposition of the Whig papers on the first subject. Whig bitterness is daily displayed in our streets: I think it is the result more from desperation for the future than the unexpectedness of defeat. The most frequent charge now made is the same the Federalists made against Jefferson, the want of *skill* & *firmness* to guide the reins of government: and I have no fear that the charge will turn out equally untrue.

Under Whig rule, State debts have been created in many of the States & the National debt greatly enlarged: for the reduction of the latter, much will depend on *you* & the Secretary of the Treasury, with the joint aid of Congress; & if successful, the glory will be principally yours & the reward will be gathered by the Democracy. The States being so much in debt the people are a little alarmed at the prospects of taxes & therefore more sensitive with regard to the nation's debt. Perhapse I attempted a more minute explanation of this matter than all the joint efforts of our speakers & as Coe & others thought with much effect: it is a rod we will continue to wield over the head of Whiggery: & in my opinion your successful exertions in lessening the *National* debt will not only give giant strength to the Democracy throughout the *Union*, but will be one of the most prominent measures to fill up the *cup* of *fame*.

So far as I have learned the public sentiment of this State of Kentucky, it is almost of one accord that there should be a pretty general sweep of the Whigs from office. Upon this subject knowing your prudence & that you will have the means of judging correctly at the time of action on each & every case, I will merely make the following suggestions: Harrison went into office pledged against proscription or removals, & most he found in office were placed there not with a view of making political capital: *You* not only go in unpledged, but will find many *verry* many selected with a view to *Whig* organization: with a view to this latter idea perhaps stronger pruning will be expected from your hands than was from Mr Jefferson's: & he you know not only acted promptly on most of the important Offices such as Attorney's Marshalls etc, but in making his appointments in States where Legislatures had acted with intolerance used the same intolerance in filling all the places with Republicans: in the two States above however I suppose there are but few places *our* friends would press for. But I am saying more than I intended, but you know my anxiety that the Whigs shall never regain power in the Union or in this State: I know them *too* well & have fought them without breastworks, *too long* & prize my countries interest *too* much to take any pleasure in the resurrection of Whiggery: & I write with the greater freedom, because of our general uniformity of thinking on public policy.

And if we look back but for a short space we see on what a slender thread *large* matter hang: success in the Cass movement would have ruined us either for the 2nd or 1st point: & again you know at the final State convention *we* at first were almost alone in resisting the wishes of Donelson & others to have V.B. placed in front; if that had have been done you would not have gained your present position, *or if you had*, not with the same unanimity & fervour: but this should only teach us [...][1] prudense, & we will not boast of the past.[2] Bell gave a dinner to the Electors on Thursday; on Monday Madam Foster[3] gave one; it is thought that the old jealousy is still at work. You get a true account of the procession in the Union,[4] & such speeches![5] They were just such as ought to have lost them the State. *Jones* I learn was peculiarly bitter: but why this shift? I will close with something more amusing. Two little boys lately born in my neighborhood have been dubbed J.K.P. On yesterday a *Doll* was sent out to my youngest & she promptly called it Sarah P. So the Madam can learn *she* is dividing honors with *you*: You may say to *her* Sallie the Texian flag bearer is this day to be married to Doct. Chapman a cotton Planter on lake Washington.[6] That will lessen expenses some, but there are still six youngens, but all pretty fair looking.

L. P. CHEATHAM

P.S. I thought I had said enough, but as I have just received some news that may take me to Mississippi, & perhaps will not see you until about the 4th of March & knowing, as *you* know I do, some about the public sentiment: permit me to *suggest* further that it is true we can gain strenght by throwing guards around the public fund as it now rests: but in any future modification, I would shun the name of *Sub Treasury: Independent might do*. This latter idea, the keeping of the public funds in the best possible manner, *& the gradual* extinguishment of the public debt, will be the two *main Levers* for the continuation of *democratic* ascendensy.[7] L.P.C.

ALS. DLC–JKP. Addressed to Columbia.

1. Word or words obliterated by sealing wax oil.

2. For an account of the State Democratic Convention, which was held in Nashville on November 23, 1843, see Polk to Martin Van Buren, November 30, 1843.

3. Jane Mebane Lytle Dickinson Foster married Ephraim H. Foster following the death of her first husband, John Dickinson, under whom Ephraim Foster had studied law.

4. *Nashville Union*, December 5, 1844.

5. See J. George Harris to Polk, December 4, 1844.

6. Cheatham's daughter, Sarah, presented a banner to the Texas Volunteer militia companies "on behalf of the democratic ladies of Nashville," during ceremonies on Capitol Hill, August 3, 1844. Chapman is not further identified.

7. Cheatham wrote his postscript on the inside folds of his cover sheet.

FROM CAVE JOHNSON

Dear Sir, Washington December 12h 1844

The great battle between Mr. THB & Mr C.[1] has commenced. You will see in the papers McDuffies proposition for annexation. B's notice of his bill. Ingersol from Com. of Foreign affairs introduced McDuffies Bill this evening.[2] This is the admn. project. The friends of T.H.B. [and] Silas Wright who took ground before the people for annexation but against the Treaty are to be forced to take that Treaty or appear before the people as hostile to Texas. Mr. C. thinks apparently that he has got the advantage of T.H.B. on this issue & intends to drive him home upon it. The N.Y. democrats will go en masse agt the treaty & I have no idea, that the friends of C. will take anything but the Treaty. Mr B. is outrageous upon the subject. Our friend Genl. McKay is doing all he can to quiet him and induce him to give up his Bill, which will get but few votes. He has before him for consideration, the proposition I suggested to you in my last—that we pass a joint resolution declaring the independence of Texas and that we will defend her as an independent nation agt any & all assaults; leaving the proposition for annexation to your administration. This [is] all that can be done, if even that can. In connection with this subject is the formation of your cabinet as far at least as Mr C. is concerned. His friends will not yield him willingly; indeed they are producing much excitement about Richmond & urging vehemently his retention. The entire democracy of the North (except the friends of L. W—y[3]) are opposed to it, headed of course by T.H.B. who will make war upon *him* and the admn instantly & I am somewhat fearful that he will make war upon it whatever may happen. The northern gentlemen do not seem to have settled upon any one but seem willing to abide by your choice. Judge Fine (of St. Lawrence) suggested Genl. Drumgoole.[4]

The Sec. of State or Sec. of the Treasury is expected to come from N. York & I think their preference is for the Treasury & for Flag[5] if Silas Wright will not accept. Gov. Marcy & Cambreling are often spoken of. They are both said to be ready, particularly the latter, who is said lately to have been deeply engaged in speculation. Flag is represented by them as one of the purest men, as well as great financial talent, "of the Silas Wright order" as they often express it. I have heard no other suggestion for the Treasury except Geo P. King of Georgia.[6] The Dem. of Maine seem exceedingly anxious to have Gov. Fairfield in the War or Navy department as they never have had one. The Pen. seem anxious for Buckhanon[7] in the State & occasionally mention his name in connexion with the Treasury. Ritchie & his friends I understand are anxious for Stephenson[8] to fill that place, which involves the retirement of Mason and as such greatly displease his friends. The North West occasionally mention Genl. Cass for the State but most generally doubt the propriety of his acceptance, as they intend to run him next time. Genl. Saunders & Medare[9] are mentioned in connection with P.O. Dep. & also Henry Hubbard & Saunders occasionally mentioned for the War or Navy. He called to see me the other evening & commenced immediately on the difference between us as to men before your nomination, & professed that he had no hopes in future of electing C—n[10] & should go in thoroughly & decidedly for your admn., of course, as I supposed, expecting me to write it to you. The names of Pickens & Elmore[11] are occasionally mentioned for the War or Navy. In connexion with these difficulties comes the public printer. The Globe is regarded as Bentons organ by the friends of C. & will oppose him to the uttermost & will in connection with the Whigs defeat him, & therefore B[12] & myself have been sounding to have the prospect of getting Ritchie. We fear there is no chance but I shall perhaps go to Richmond on Saturday to learn if any arrangement can be made. I should have gone earlier but it has by some means got into so many hands that I have been fearful that it might get out & become the subject of news papers comment. I might escape notice if the House shall adjourn over tomorrow. T.H.B. has a great dislike to Ritchie & I expect will be greatly provoked, if he learns any such movement. Webster will come into the Senate & I think Clay will & if united with B.[13] in assaults upon the admn. would make your position very unpleasant. I see Man from N.Y.[14] the other day. He thinks that Van Buren & Admiral Hoffman[15] will be tendered seats in the Senate & that it is probable they both will accept. I think so too, because Van will feel great interest in superintending the future fortunes of S.W. Jr[16] as well as in sustaining your Admn. Genl. Cass, it is said has written here for the advice of his friends as to the propriety of his taking a seat in the Senate from Michigan. I do not know the advice that has been returned to him. I think, probably he is advised agt it. Mr. Woodbury sd. this evening in my presence that you would probably be in the neighborhood when the electoral votes were counted, as a Committee would have to wait on you to announce the fact & it would be too near the close of the session to perform a trip to Tennessee.[17] There is much anxiety here as to the time of your arrival as well as the manner of travelling and the greatest anxiety expressed, that you should avoid going to N.Y. or Philadelphia, as it is announced in the papers that you will do. It is supposed that these pressing invitations to those cities, which are filled with trading politicians, are designed to have an influence upon the distribution of the patronage & that no purity could shield you from imputations &c.

My health is not very good. I have a slight return of the neuralgia.

C. JOHNSON

ALS. DLC–JKP. Addressed to Columbia. Polk's AE on the cover states that he answered this letter on December 21, 1844.

1. Thomas H. Benton and John C. Calhoun.
2. See John O. Bradford to Polk, December 9, 1844. On December 12, 1844, Charles J. Ingersoll, chairman of the House Committee on Foreign Affairs, reported a joint resolution providing for the annexation of the Republic of Texas.
3. Levi Woodbury.
4. George C. Dromgoole.
5. Azariah C. Flagg.
6. Johnson's reference probably is to John P. King.
7. James Buchanan.
8. Andrew Stevenson, a lawyer, served several terms in the Virginia House of Delegates before winning election to the U.S. House, where he served from 1821 to 1834. He presided as Speaker of that body during his last four terms. Stevenson served as minister to Great Britain from 1836 until 1841.
9. Romulus M. Saunders and Samuel Medary.
10. John C. Calhoun.
11. Franklin Harper Elmore, a South Carolina lawyer and Calhoun supporter, sat in the U.S. House, 1836–39; presided over the Bank of the State of South Carolina, 1839–50; and served briefly in the U.S. Senate in 1850.
12. Aaron V. Brown.
13. Thomas H. Benton.
14. A New York merchant, Abijah Mann, Jr., served two terms in the U.S. House as a Jackson Democrat, 1833–37.
15. Johnson's reference probably is to Michael Hoffman. An ardent Van Burenite, Hoffman won election as a Democrat to four terms in the U.S. House, 1825–33. He also served as canal commissioner of New York, 1833–35; as chairman of the New York Ways and Means Committee in the early 1840's; and as naval officer of the port of New York from 1845 until his death in 1848.
16. Silas Wright, Jr.
17. On February 12, 1845, the two houses of Congress assembled in the Representatives' Chamber to count the electoral votes. The president of the Senate, the presiding officer of the joint meeting, opened the sealed certificates and delivered to the tellers the votes of the electors of each state. Afterwards the House passed a resolution calling for the appointment of a joint committee to wait upon Polk and Dallas and to inform them of the results. On February 14, 1845, the day after Polk's arrival in Washington, a committee of the two houses of Congress visited Polk and officially notified him of his election.

FROM ANDREW JACKSON

My dear Sir, Hermitage Decbr 13th 1844

Having received from my friend Blair, a letter disclosing the movements at the city of Washington writing with a view that I might put you on your guard—first All the offices are filling up by Tyler, so that all his partizans must remain in office or you be compelled to remove them. I have said to my friend Blair that you have sufficient energy to give yourself elbow room whenever it becomes necessary. That the people have selected you to administer the Gov. on the broad democratic principles you have made known to the people and constantly acted on through your whole public life. That you will, as I believe from your wisdom on all occasions displayed keep from your cabinet all aspirants to the presidency, or *vice*, & that you will endeavour, for your four years, to administer the Government for the benefit of the whole Union &c.

There is much intrigue going on at washington, and one that may divide the democratic party & destroy you, and some of our imprudent political friends are at the bottom of it, viz, to substitute the Madisonian for the Globe,[1] others to get Richie concerned with the Globe and Editor of it. As far as you are concerned put your force against all these Maneuvres. The first would blow you sky high & destroy the Republican party. The second would be an insult to the Editor of the Globe & seperate him from you, whose administration he is determined to support. Keep Blairs Globe the administration paper, and William B. Lewis,[2] to ferret out & make known to you, all the plotts & intrigues Hatching against your administration and you are safe. The Major will be faithfull & I pledge myself for Blair & you will be shielded, & if attacked well defended by the Globe. Richie is a good Editor but a very unsafe one. He goes off at half bent, & does great injury before he can be set right—remember his course on my removal of the deposits & how much injury he did us before he got back into the right track—again did he not go with Rives a conservative upon the special deposit system,[3] when every reflecting man knew there were no more safety in a special deposit, where the directors were corrupt, than in a general deposit. But enough for the present, as I request as your real friend to have, as far as you have influence, this dangerous movement by a few politicians put down, or great injury will be done to the democratic party & yourself.

Whilst I am writing, & uncertain from my situation, how long I may be here or able to write, I cannot close without bring our trusty & worthy friend again to your view.[4] You know he is a military man. Should our affairs with Mexico & England add a new Regiment to the U. States army he is the very man to command it. Should this not happen, you have seen from Mr Trists letters I enclosed you[5] that he will not accept again the consulate at Cuba. The Genl being a merchant would fill this or the consulate at Liverpool *well*, and to these offices I wish to rivet your attention for the Genl. He cannot where he is lay up any thing and he has two charming children to educate & he deserves anything that you can bestow.

I have just received from Mr Kendall a concise note indicating his wish to be sent to Spain, in such modest & retiring words, & of gratitude that *delights me*—if this cannot be done consistently then any other that will free him from Washington and from poverty that can be properly bestowed. There can be no delicacy in recalling Erwin[6] —he is only fit to write a Book & scarcely that, and has become a good Whigg. In hase with usual good wishes yr friend. I will when I see you, have a good deal to communicate of scenes at Washington. Beware of the Tyler *leven* in Tennessee.

ANDREW JACKSON

ALS. DLC–JKP. Addressed to Columbia. Published in Basset, ed., *Correspondence of Andrew Jackson*, VI, pp. 339–40.

1. Washington *Madisonian* and Washington *Globe*.

2. Lewis, a neighbor and longtime friend of Andrew Jackson, resided in the White House during Jackson's presidency and served as second auditor of the Treasury from 1829 until 1845.

3. Conservative or "soft money" Democrats supported Jackson's removal of government funds from the Second Bank of the United States to specie-paying state banks. Henry Clay's Distribution Bill, subsequently adopted and titled the Deposit Act of 1836, required the secretary of the Treasury to designate at least one bank in each state as a place of public deposit and provided for the distribution among the states any Treasury surplus in excess of $5 million. By rewarding the state banks with special deposits, Clay's bill induced Conservative Democrats to support distribution and to moderate their demands for lowering the tariff, which had produced sufficient revenues to pay off the general government's debt and promised to generate large surpluses in the Treasury.

4. Robert Armstrong.

5. See Jackson to Polk, December 10, 1844.

6. Washington Irving spent much of his adulthood living and writing in Europe. In 1842 he went to Spain as U.S. minister and served in that post until 1846, when he returned to his home in New York.

FROM AARON V. BROWN

Sunday night
Dear Sir Washington City Decr. 14th 1844

I received yours of the 7th Inst.[1] *Our friend* called yesterday & informed me that he would be ready in a few days & I shall lose no time after examination to forward it to you.[2] Mr Tyler shews the utmost willingness to mind the wishes of your Brother[3] & we are *casting about* to find some place that will suit him. I refer you to a letter to him written a day or two ago.[4] There is no necessity for him to be here that I know of unless it be to exert some influence on Foster about confirmation, & perhaps he could do that by letters from his friends (enclosed to me).

I have had a long talk with the President since I saw you resulting in nothing important to be communicated to you. He tenders you rooms in the white house if you reach here before your time & desired them, for which I thankd him but supposd you would hardly desire such a position. There are no developments yet as to Colo. Bentons bearing toward the new Administration. Nor is it known whether he will relax his course on the Texas question—hopes are entertained that the measure may be effected this session although I have my doubts. I have persons engaged to sound Benton as to what he means to do & the New York democrats as to their course & on their report during the week I can form a pretty good opinion.

I have talked very freely with Mason since I saw you. By the bye I have heard nothing additional about his incredulity of your success. He I have no doubt is anxious to retain his position but expresses the most earnest opinion that you shall not be at all trameld with him. I ventured to advance the general opinion that if you should choose to employ any of the present cabinet you ought to left at liberty to make any new cast of position that you might think proper.

Judge Catron called to see me last night & insists that *Wright would* accept the office of Sec. of the Treasury. I found however he had no *specific* information although he says he will [be] home in a week or two. He thinks Buchannon[5] should be Sec of State, Wright Treasury & Cass of War. Good say I—very good if you could get it so, but I doubt about Wrights acceptance & if not then Who? Those three would work together in harmony & would like each other pretty well. Ritchie may want something for Stephenson,[6] but several Virginians deny that Stephenson has any very strong hold on the feelings of the people of that State & you will consider of course whether any thing could be gained by pretermitting Mason & taking up Stephenson. I can say nothing as yet to you about the Ritchie & the Globe arrangement. You shall know it at the first moment of ascertainment. If *that* dont take, then something else must be done. The rumor here is that Blair breaks ground forthwith against Benton's Bill & goes out & out with us for Texas, but I have been so often disappointed that I doubt it. Mr. Woodberry occupies a room opposite (Brown's)[7] & has just said that he expects Cass to be here about the 4th March as Senator. He has some information from Michigan to this effect, that Cass had informed a gentleman who enquired "that if it was tenderd to him he would accept" & we know he can be elected if he chooses. This would enable you to notify any one you desired after your arrival here.

I have not ascertained yet any thing satisfactory as to Mr. Calhoun's notions about going abroad. If circumstances should induce any doubts as to your retaining him I think he will express himself favorable to such an idea & several of his friends are occasionally advancing the opinions to him, that such would be his most desirable position. He would thereby cease to be the focus of general opposition by all rival pretenders, who would give him no rest day nor night, whilst he continued in the Cabinet. The main danger as to him is this—If the impression becomes general that from his inflamable nature there would be danger of a blow up of the Cabinet, others that you might desire would not be apt to come into it—you can see now the signs of concentration against him on account of his recent French & Mexican correspondence.[8]

I notice with pleasure still that none of the rumors of letter writers or others from here, gain any credence or excite apprehensions of any sort unfavorable to you or your course when you get here.

A. V. BROWN

ALS. DLC–JKP. Addressed to Columbia and marked "*Confidential*."

1. Letter not found.

2. Reference is to Amos Kendall, who was in the process of drafting Polk's inaugural address.

3. William H. Polk.

4. Letter not found.

5. James Buchanan.

6. Andrew Stevenson.

7. Reference is to Brown's Hotel.

8. Reference probably is to John C. Calhoun's dispatch of August 12, 1844, to William Rufus Devane King, U.S. minister to France, noting with pleasure King's report that France would not join Great Britain militarily in opposing U.S. annexation of Texas. On September 10, 1844, Calhoun informed Wilson Shannon, U.S. minister to Mexico, of the administration's determination to defend Texas' borders. The texts of these and other documents accompanying John Tyler's Annual Message to Congress of December 3, 1844, were reprinted in newspapers throughout the Union.

FROM CAVE JOHNSON

(Saturday night)
Washington Dec 14h 1844

Dear Sir,

Since I last wrote you I recd yours of the 8th.[1] I have not been to Richmond & say to our friends generally that I have declined having any thing to do with the matter. A.V.B.[2] after mentioning the subject to me, mentioned it to Hubbard, for the purpose of getting him with me. He mentioned it to Judge Baily who he supposed had more influence at Richmond, as his substitute to accompany me.[3] He mentioned it to Genl R.M.S.[4] who came & talked to me on the subject. I mentioned it to Genl. McK.[5] Among hands it has become very public. Even old J.Q.A.[6] asked when we were going to Richmond & many others. The movement is looked to among the Whigs with great interest as likely to make wider the break between Calhoun & Bentons friends by exciting the Globe agt us. I thought it best for me, as I was regarded generally as particularly intimate with you & suspected to some extent of acting under your direction, to make no move for the present & to say to those, who had been in some way let into the secret, that I should have nothing to do with any such movement & that I had declined going to Richmond but intend taking the first opportunity, after all surmises & talk shall cease, to slip off & see T.R.[7] letting *no body* know any thing about it until I learn what can be done. Genl McK. approves this course upon a full view. I was surprised to learn that T.H.B.[8] felt displeased at me in consequence of some remarks he saw in a newspaper denouncing him which were attributed to me. I called to see him this morning with Genl. McK. & made the proper explanation which seemed satisfactory. He talked mildly & reasonably tho it is evident he has much feeling on subject of Texas and I am fearful that we shall be able to do nothing to reconcile him and the friends of Mr. C.[9] He persists in the propriety of consulting Mexico & that the object of Mr. C. is to involve us in a war with Mexico & that the North will refuse to take part & so dissolve the Union. Nor will he yield to the idea of defending Texas agt. Mexico, if she chooses to attack her but will defend Texas agt. any *European* nation. Nor can he be kept silent. Mr C. and his friends seem determined to *press the Treaty & nothing but the Treaty*, so that annexation *at present is dead* unless indeed the Southern Whigs change their course or we can hit upon some happy idea that may reconcile of which I have little hope. The impression at present is that we shall not touch the Tariff, because it is probable, there will be a blow up in the manufacturing establishments before this time next year & that of itself works the destruction of the Tariff & this had better take place under the Tariff of 1842 than be saddled upon any Bill we might pass. And again, the South (the extremes) think we can get a better Bill under the new Admn. than the one of last session & will not now probably vote for it. The manufacturers begin to be alarmed at the same idea. In the next Congress we may have both Houses & reinstate the Compromise & therefore many of them urge the passage of McK. Bill[10] now, thinking the next Congress may then take no further action upon the subject. Rhett has intimated that he will not now vote McKays Bill. It is not yet settled what we shall do. The chances are that it will not be touched tho I am satisfied we could pass it. Certainly, if the South goes with us. This would be a great relief to your Admn if done & yet might damage the party materially, if an explosion should take place among the manufacturers.

I have heard but little more as to the Cabinet. Judge Catron is anxious for Mr. Buckhanon[11] to go into the State, Silas Wright into the Treasury & Genl Cass to War. The Whig Senators, will reject the nomination of King[12] if Buckhanon can be placed upon the bench, so as to get rid of his influence in Penna.

Your friends here are extremely solicitous that you should avoid Philadelphia & N.Y. Mr. Dallas has been writing members here to urge you to visit Philadelphia. It is generally believed that S.W. Jr.[13] would decline an invitation to go into the Cabinet tho anxious to avoid the dispensation of this patronage in N.Y., which may break him down there. Would it not be well to invite him? All here expect it except those who think that all aspirants to the Presidency should be excluded. Many think, if Wright, Buckhanon & Cass were in the Cabinet & all aspirants they would move on harmoniously & deal fairly & justly by the Admn.

One of your distant relations in Geo. by your name,[14] upon your election, went to Cobb,[15] to get his influence in procuring an appointment & inquired about the duties of the PM Genl. Thought he could perform them &c. He is a plain good man.

C. JOHNSON

[P.S.] Burke[16] can now be got to Nashville. I have said so to Genl Armstrong.

ALS. DLC–JKP. Addressed to Columbia and marked "Private."

1. Letter not found.

2. Aaron V. Brown.

3. Edmund W. Hubard and Thomas H. Bayly. A lawyer and judge from Accomac County, Va., Bayly served several terms in the Virginia House of Delegates, 1835–45. Elected to the U.S. House as a States' Rights Democrat in 1844, he served in that body until 1856.

4. Romulus M. Saunders.

5. James I. McKay.
6. John Quincy Adams.
7. Thomas Ritchie.
8. Thomas Hart Benton.
9. John C. Calhoun.
10. Reference is to James I. McKay's tariff bill, which proposed to reduce duties imposed by the Tariff of 1842. Introduced in the Senate on March 8, 1844, McKay's proposal was debated several times before being tabled on May 10, 1844.
11. James Buchanan.
12. Edward King of Philadelphia, Pa., entered politics as a Federalist but switched to the Democratic party in the 1820's; he served on the bench of the Pennsylvania Court of Common Pleas from 1825 until 1852. John Tyler nominated King to be associate justice of the U.S. Supreme Court on June 5, 1844, but withdrew the nomination on February 7, 1845.
13. Silas Wright, Jr.
14. Johnson's reference probably is to Charles Clark Polk or Ezekiel Polk, both distant cousins and residents of Georgia in 1844.
15. Howell Cobb.
16. In a subsequent letter to Polk of December 26, 1844, Johnson clarifies this reference to "Burke," noting that the former newspaper editor "is a very able and efficient writer" and could prove useful to the *Nashville Union*.

FROM GEORGE M. DALLAS

My Dear Sir [Philadelphia, Penn.][1] 15 Dec. 1844

Yours of the 4th instant[2] reached me on the 12th. I was anxious to hear your intention as to visiting this city, to be able to answer the many daily enquiries upon the subject; but I shall still abstain from giving any information, because I hope you may reconsider your decision. It is impossible for you to reach Washington without travelling many hundreds of miles in constant popular triumph, and this, tho' both you and Mrs. Polk may dislike it, and whether you come to Philadelphia or not, will furnish political opponents all the basis they want for an imputation of a fondness and a pursuit of public display. Your friends Know you better than to dream such a motive; and those of your fellow-citizens whom you enable to see you by so short an extension of the journey will, I am quite sure, be much more apt to regard it as a manifestation of reciprocal and courteous kindness. The short time you spent with us would, I confess, be much occupied in the sort of congratulation and exhibition which, for a season, cannot be separated from your position, and to which you must submit with as little shew of weariness and as good a grace as possible; but then the days consumed in Philadelphia and at the house of a friend will be days deducted from the roaring public city and central éclat of Washington; they would be days of comparative seclusion and quiet. It does not appear to me that you need be in Washington before the 12. or 15. of February; if you got to this place on the 8th or 10th, you can stay 4 or 5 days, and, without the slightest trouble or fatigue, quitting in the rail-road cars at 8 a.m. you pass through Baltimore and arrive at the Capital at about 8 p.m., conveniently *after* dark.

I am impressed with the conviction that every hour you can, with decorum, abstain from spending at Washington, before your inauguration, will be so much saved in political perplexity and gained in personal comfort. You will not have the excuse of national business to attend to, and you will be beset by shoals of exulting and devoted friends, of anxious advisers, of indefatigable and forecasting office-seekers, and of penny-paper spies and letter-writers. It is enough to endure this process for the inauguration week; to live it through for a month is beyond the powers of most men. It is certainly the most trying and impracticable season of Presidential duty. I invoke the persuasive aid of Mrs. Polk to save you from as much of it as possible by a brief sojourn with Mrs. Dallas.

In the frank and confidential spirit which marks your last letter, I propose sending you, whenever I can, my views as well of men as of measures, and all that I hear apparently worthy of being submitted to your consideration and judgment. If I shall thus assist in the smallest degree, in the wise, safe, and honorable performance of the exalted and arduous task to which you have been called, at a most interesting period of American History, I shall feel a secret and unalloyed pleasure.

Your short address at Nashville, published in the "Union,"[3] was effective and happy. It has given universal satisfaction; and is regarded, as the first kindling streak of a new and auspicious dawn. It combines a just allegiance to the democratic party with the loftier spirit of constitutional patriotism. The Sentiment is of fine moral tendency, and will bear repetition on a more imposing occasion.

You will be severely exercized in the construction of your Cabinet. The Departments are all well filled; the incumbents are unexceptionable as men and as officers, and almost so as politicians; and there are obviously some points of private feeling in relation to several of them not easy to controul. To me, however, it appears, harsh as it may at first seem, that the country expects an entire and undiscriminating change. It wants a cabinet at the hands of James K. Polk, of his original and exclusive choosing. This, too, is not only the general wish; it is the safest, and fairest, and gentlest principle of action, for, where a recognized rule is applied to all, no one is found fault with or has cause of complaint. To retain some implies censure upon those dismissed, inflicts unavoidably even tho' unintentionally a wound and its pain, and lays the groundwork of reproach and discontent.

I have presumed that you might be reluctant to accept the resignations of Mr. Calhoun, Mr. Mason, and Mr. Wilkins: The *first* as an eminent southern republican statesman, of great ability and experience, who went *unanimously* into the cabinet of Pres. Tyler, solely to adjust, if possible, the Texas and Oregon questions; the *second* as an early and long esteemed associate, of unblemished fame, sound practical talent, and of the best political school of Virginia; and the *third*, as one whom you would wish to treat with every delicacy owing to his connexion with my family. My opinion (to be expressed to none but yourself) is, that averse as you may be to give pain to him or his friends, you cannot retain Mr. Calhoun as Secretary of State without hazarding endless mischiefs, and as this opinion governs the cases of the War and the Navy departments, you must be patient with me while I explain its reasons.

1. Mr. C. looks, and has cause and right to look, and his admirers insist upon his looking, to the Presidency. He is thus the head of a certain sect and system, which sect and system are not *your's*, which have their peculiar enemies, whose numbers are great and already organized. To keep him where he is would, so to speak, be a merger into that sect and system in the estimation of the people at large, and could not fail to involve your administration in all the partialities and oppositions of that sect and system. Much of that sect and system is undoubtedly admirable, but there are parts very doubtful and debateable, to say the least, and with these the people have not identified you for a moment. These remarks apply, directly or remotely, to every aspirant for the chief magistracy, any one of whom, introduced into the cabinet, would necessarily introduce along with him the attachments and hostilities peculiar to his pretensions.

2. Mr. C. is universally regarded as the apostle of *Free Trade*, and his retention would, at once, be a heavy blow upon the republicans in Pennsylvania, who cheerfully adopted your wise and constitutional doctrine,[4] and rallied their majority upon assurances that the government would be administered upon *that*, and not upon *free trade*. I will not say that even this State may not gradually, in the progress of time, be weaned from it's existing opinions and apparent interests, but at present our condition is such that a sudden and unexpected stroke of this character might throw us all aback.

3. Mr. C. has made some *signal*, if not fatal, mistakes in his treatment of our foreign relations, and has thus created an apprehension that, notwithstanding his extraordinary powers of mind and unquestionable elevation of purpose, he is unfit for a post which requires profound caution, an habitual spirit of conciliation, and a total absence of what

may be termed sectarian and sectional, in contradiction to universal and national politics.

As I wish before concluding, (which I must do speedily) to mention the person whom, after the most careful reflection, I should say might most properly and most popularly be selected by you for the department of State, you will have to pardon my brevity and abruptness. Mr. Walker, of Mississippi, is obnoxious to none of the objections that might be raised against others, and his merits are conceded by every section of the republican party. His letter on Texas[5] flew like wildfire through the whole country, and created for him a solid national reputation. Perhaps no one of our statesmen and politicians is entitled to a larger share of merit & honor, as connected with the moving impulse or the active progress of the past canvass. There is no organized party averse to him; each and all would regard his appointment as the natural result of events, of your discriminating sense of his peculiar position, and of his own fitness to manage the subjects foremost in interest.

Anxious to say more, and to send you my notions as to the other departments, I find that I have exhausted my time, and probably your patience, on the State alone. I will tax your indulgence again in a few days.

G. M. DALLAS

ALS. DLC–JKP. Addressed to Columbia. Polk's AE on the cover states that he answered this letter on January 22, 1845; Polk's reply has not been found. Published in Roy F. Nichols, "The Mystery of the Dallas Papers," *The Pennsylvania Magazine of History and Biography*, LXXIII (July, 1949), pp. 355–59.

1. Place identified through content analysis.
2. Polk's letter has not been found.
3. See John O. Bradford to Polk, December 9, 1844.
4. See Polk to John K. Kane, June 19, 1844.
5. Walker's letter, dated January 8, 1844, was published as a separate in pamphlet form under the title, *Letter of Mr. Walker of Mississippi in Reply to the Call of the People of Carroll County, Kentucky* (Philadelphia: Mifflin and Parry, 1844). A staunch advocate of Texas annexation, Walker argued that Texas was a part of the Louisiana Purchase and should not have been relinquished in the Adams-Onís Treaty of 1819; that the sovereign people of Texas had established their freedom and had indicated their desire to enter the union of American states; and that such an annexation could be accomplished legally by treaty, by an act of Congress, or by the power of any one of the states to extend its boundaries, provided Congress so consented to the annexation. According to Walker, Texas annexation would remove British influence in Texas, provide fertile lands and home markets for the American people, and open an escape zone into and through which slavery might recede until it disappeared entirely into northern Mexico.

FROM AMOS DAVID[1]

Dear Sir, Wolf River, Fayette County Tennessee, Dec. 15th 1844

You are probably verry much annoyed at this time with congratulatory epistles; and perchance an Occasional indirect application for an office, appointment, or some favour, pertaining to the high station you are about to occupy; and it may be, some of the More wise & highly Gifted, condesend to favour you with advice, concerning the duty which will devolve on you, the formation of your Cabinet &c &c.

Amid all this confusion, I beg leave to tender you my warm and sincere congratulations, personally, & Politically; on the result of the late highly excited canvass. It is true, I received the account of the Nomination, with doubt & Missgivings,[2] as to the result; which I believe was the case with a large portion of the Democratic Party; but as the canvass progressed, confidence increased, until the Party become enveloped in a blaze of enthusiasm. It is to be regretted we could not carry Tennessee, but she will be right next August. I witnessed the closeing scene of our *external* rejoicing, in La Grange, on last thursday night; A hickory tree, planted where the Whig pole had stood, surmounted with a flag, & illuminated with 34 Transparancies; a Balloon raised in fine style, Democratic Houses illuminated, a procession with Music, &c. &c. All passed off in harmony & Glee; it was a brilliant affair.

It is many years since I was in the lobby of the Senate chamber of the Tennessee legislature; when the Clerk (who appeared but little more than a boy)[3] read a petition for a Divorce, in which the petitioner (the wife) complained "that her husband did not embrace her as a Husband should embrace his wife; that when he made the attempt, it was but a dry abortive effort." The reading of the Petition braught a deep blush, on the face of the Clerk, & caused Great laughter in the Senate. If my Memory serves me, the Petition was drawn up by a young Lawyer who I suppose to be the present Editor of the Nashville Union.[4] Have weightier matters errased the subject from your Memory?

AMOS DAVID

ALS. DLC–JKP. Addressed to Columbia.

1. One of the first residents of Fayette County, Tenn., Amos David settled in the county during the mid-1820's and practiced medicine there for many years; during the late 1830's and 1840's, he served as postmaster at Wolf River, Tenn.

2. On June 23, 1844, David wrote Polk and urged him to decline the presidential nomination; David argued that only Lewis Cass could defeat Henry Clay.

3. Polk served four years as chief clerk of the Tennessee Senate, 1819–22.

4. Samuel H. Laughlin.

FROM J. GEORGE HARRIS

My Dear Sir, Nashville Dec 15. 1844

According to your suggestion I conferred with General Armstrong respecting arrangements for a steamboat passage down the Cumberland and up the Ohio when you shall be ready to start for Washington.

Capt. Irwin's new boat is too large for the Louisville canal.[1] Capt. Jo. Miller's boat passes it, and the General informs me that it will be tendered you in a few days.[2]

I received a couple of letters last night from the north and east, one from Boston, the other from Albany,[3] which I have requested Gen. A. to enclose to you next mail. They may be worth reading as indicative of some of the *currents* in their respective places of date.

Mr. Blair's son[4] is here from St. Louis, and from all I can learn is saying as many good words as he can for Mr. Benton & *his father* at and near the Hermitage. I understand he talks about the importance of conciliating Mr. Benton &c &c, as "the mountain" were coming "to Mahomet."[5] Such "vicarious" indirection is contemptible.

I understand there are more committees here on their way to Columbia, one of which is from Louisiana.

If, at any moment I can be of any service to you at Columbia, just drop me a line and I will take a corner of stage by night and be with you before morn. Make my best respects to Mrs. Polk....

J. Geo. Harris

ALS. DLC–JKP. Addressed to Columbia.

1. Irwin is not identified further.

2. Joseph Miller was captain of the steamboat *Nashville*.

3. Reference probably is to letters written to Harris by Albert Gallup and Lenis Joselyn on December 4, 1844. ALS. DLC–JKP.

4. Montgomery Blair, eldest son of Francis P. Blair, argued the Dred Scott case before the U.S. Supreme Court and later served as postmaster general under Abraham Lincoln.

5. Paraphrase of Francis Bacon's quotation, "If the hill will not come to Mahomet, Mahomet will go to the hill." *Of Boldness* (1612).

FROM ROBERT ARMSTRONG

Dr Sir Nashville 16 Decmr [18]44

I find that I cannot leave by the Stage to night but will, tomorrow night.

Montgomery Blair is here. Speaks of the support his Father[1] will give you, and what Col. Benton will do *after* this Session &c &c. He has been at the Hermitage making a short visit.

We have no news but what you see in the papers; the affairs of Mexico are Important. I will see you on Wednesday.

R. ARMSTRONG

ALS. DLC–JKP. Addressed to Columbia.

1. Francis P. Blair.

TO CLEMENT C. CLAY

My Dear Sir: Columbia Tenn. Decr. 16th 1844

I should have answered your letter of the 22nd ultimo earlier, but that I was absent from home when it arrived, and have been since that time, so overwhelmed with company and business, that I have had scarcely a moment to devote to my correspondence.

Nothing would afford Mrs. Polk and myself more sincere pleasure, than to accept, the kind invitation of Mrs. Clay[1] and yourself to visit you before we leave for Washington, but I find it will be impossible, for us to do so. The only visit which Mrs. P. can possibly make will be a very short one to her mother's[2] in Rutherford. I beg you to make our kind regards to Mrs. Clay, and to assure her of how much pleasure it would afford us to pay her a visit if it was possibly in our power.

JAMES K. POLK

ALS. NcD. Addressed to Huntsville, Ala.

1. Susanna Claiborne Withers Clay.
2. Elizabeth Whitsitt Childress.

FROM ANDREW JACKSON

at night

My dear Sir, Hermitage Decbr 16th 1844

I intended today to have writen you a long letter, but company crowded on me, so that I had not time, and have to take the night for it, whilst my family entertain the company who remain. This with my debility will confine this to a few hints, rather to put you on your guard than any thing else. I have many letters from office seekers, that at present, I will not trouble you with, nor will I, entermeddle with that subject only in special cases, that personally I may make suggestions.

I have recd. from my friends at Washington many letters. You will see from the papers that great speculation is made as it regards your

Cabinet. I would suggest, that if you have not written your confidential letter to Mr Wright,[1] that you pospone it for the present, as it might be thought, as some has already pointed to him as your successor, that it was done to exclude him from being a canddate, to succeed you. You will, I know, weigh well this suggestion. From all I can learn, all the offices are filling with men not agreable to the great democratic party and with the view of causing you to meet the oblyque[2] of turning them out, or to keep them in office to annoy you & serve Mr. Calhoun or Mr Tylers views in becoming your successor. I have been enquired of by several who I think will compose your Cabinet. My answer is allways I cannot conjecture, nor do I suppose you have yet begun to think upon that subject. But there is one thing I believe you have energy & wisdom enough to select a good one, *a unit*, that will go hand and hand with you in carrying out those great principles on which you have allways acted, and will continue to act, and to have no one in your cabinett that is looking to the presidency, who, to promote their own views, might attempt to athwart your great principles of policy made known by you to the american people. Every confidential communication I receive, holds forth that it will not do for Calhoun to be in your cabinett. This view I have no doubt is correct. You could not get on with him. England is the place for him there to combat with my Lord Aberdeen, the abolition question.

I have recd. a long interesting letter from our friend Blare. He is prepared to go the whole in your support. But is of the opinion, that the whole cabinet must go or it may be a heartburning to the friends of those who are left out. He speaks in the highest terms of our friend Mason, but says the democracy will not approve of his being retained and the others turned out. But suggests, as Major Lewis did to me, (Major Lewis has suggested to Mr. Richie the election of Mason to the Senate) that a senatorial appointment by virginia or a Foreign Mission would be gratefull to him. Therefore, England, Rusia, prusia & austria, will give you room for *all* and Spain for poor Kendall whose modest letter I enclose you.[3] There will be no dificulty in recalling all these *good Whiggs*. Our mutual friend Major Claibourne called up to see me today on the subject of his son John at New Orleans,[4] who solicits the place, *there*, of the attorney of the United States. He, I have no doubt, will be sustained as well as any other democrat, and it is believed our quondam friend *Bailey Payton*[5] will not be retained.

My dear Col. I know your prudence that you will be silent on appointments until you act, and I have said to hundreds that you have energy to carry out yr great principle, and make your cabinet of strong men who will go hand in hand with you in their execution. That you cannot, nay will not be swayed by clekes, or factions. I have much to say to you when I see you. Davazac returns with increased respect for you. I hope to see you & your lady soon. But I must close. I am greatly afflicted by shortness of breathing, cough, & pain in my side.

ANDREW JACKSON

ALS. DLC–JKP. Addressed to Columbia and marked "*Confidential.*" Published in Bassett, ed., *Correspondence of Andrew Jackson*, VI, pp. 342–43.

1. See Polk to Silas Wright, Jr., December 7, 1844.
2. Probably a misspelling of the word "obloquy."
3. On December 2, 1844, Amos Kendall wrote Jackson and expressed his interest in the mission to Spain. ALS. DLC–JKP.
4. Jackson's reference is to Thomas Claiborne's son John, a New Orleans lawyer.
5. Balie Peyton, a lawyer from Gallatin, Tenn., sat as a Whig in the U.S. House, 1833–37; declined appointment as secretary of war under Tyler; became U.S. district attorney for eastern Louisiana in 1841; went to Chile as U.S. minister, 1849–53; and sat one term in the Tennessee Senate, 1869–70.

FROM GANSEVOORT MELVILLE

Tuesday
New York December 17th 1844

My dear Sir

Being well aware that the favorable result of the Presidential canvass would cause you to be for a time fairly overwhelmed with letters of congratulation and business from all parts of the country, I have purposely abstained until the present moment from tendering my warm political and personal congratulations. My letters of the 26th of October and 1st of November were I presume duly received. In them it was my aim to present a faithful picture of the then-condition of things here, and if I remember rightly the opinion arrived at as to the probable result in this state was corroborated by the event. Your speech at Nashville has been read by all parties and given universal satisfaction. High approbation of its tone and spirit was expressed in my hearing by several leading Whig merchants and citizens who seldom find anything satisfactory emanating from a Democratic source. It was admirable in its adaptation to the occasion and has done much to allay the acerbity of feeling among the Whigs caused by their defeat.

Gov Bouck was for some time in a state of great uncertainty as to the proper persons for executive appointment to fill the vacancies in the United States Senate occasioned by the resignation of Messrs Wright & Tallmadge, but finally fixed upon Lt Gov Dickinson and Mr Foster. They are both candidates before the Legislature and have some eight or ten active competitors. On this question of Senators there will be a severe struggle the result of which is attended with greater uncertainty than usual owing to the fact that of the democratic majority in the House of Assembly only one has been a member before. The rest are all in legislation at least, novi homines,[1] hence their views and preferences are in a great degree unascertained.

The calm which exists with us in politics is only broken by three things. The Texas question. Office seeking, ie. procuring letters, signatures, making interest &c for appointments in the gift of the State or National Executives for one's self or somebody else. And idle speculations as to the Cabinet. In none of these have I indulged save an attentive observation of the varying aspects of the Texas question. The Evening Post, the peculiar organ of the secret-circular set[2] is actively engaged in multiplying doubts in relation to and entangling the Texas matter. The Courier & Enquirer Col Webb's paper[3] has broken ground in favor of Annexation.

Gov Wright is expected in Albany on the 21st or 23d inst. He will be sworn in on the 1st prox and immediately assume the difficult duties of his new position.

Be pleased to present my respectful regards and warm congratulations to Mrs Polk as also to your mother. With kind remembrances to Mr Walker, Gen Pillow, Mr Thomas and Mr W. H. Polk and the expression of the firm belief which I entertain that the coming administration will redound to the prosperity and honor of the country and that the pilot who will assume the helm on the 4th day of March next will prove himself eminently worthy of his high responsibilities and exalted station....

GANSEVOORT MELVILLE

ALS. DLC–JKP. Addressed to Columbia and marked "Confidential."

1. Latin phrase meaning "new men."
2. See William C. Bouck to Polk, September 7, 1844.
3. Reference is to the *Morning Courier and New York Enquirer*, edited by James Watson Webb.

FROM CAVE JOHNSON

Dear Sir. Washington Dec 18th 1844

It is perhaps proper that I should send you the enclosed letter,[1] tho. I know you must worried with such documents.[2] If you knew the number I receive you would excuse me for the number I send.

I do not see much hope of harmony upon the several questions to which I have heretofore alluded. The *manner of presenting* the question of annexation is regarded as an attack upon S.W. Jr. & T.H.B.[3] & will be resisted by their friends. An effort is making to reconcile. The effort to supersede the Globe, I fear will be regarded in the same point of view by them and on that account my omission to visit Richmond will operate favorably in keeping down any suspicion, that you are inclined to favor the Southern democracy at the expense of the northern, for what I say or do seems to be regarded as some evidence of your wishes, notwithstanding my protestations to the contrary. If we had succeeded in getting T.R's[4] consent, then some arrangement with the Globe must follow, which probably could not be effected. Then what is to be done? They would have expected me to unite in substituting another paper in place of the Globe. I will find some means of getting T.R's views in the course of 8 or 10 days without any further commitment. The north fears that you may lean too much to the South, whilst similar feelings are felt at the South. I heard on yesterday that Buckhanon[5] complained of the Tennessee delegation on not being more attentive to him &c. I called on him today, made proper explanations & am to visit him tomorrow.

The chances are now that we shall loose annexation at the present session. Mr Woodbury said to me today, that if you should take an opportunity in some of your speeches soon to express an opinion favorable to "immediate annexation" it would help us here when this question was decided, but I need not remind you that the friends of S.W. Jr. took ground agt. the treaty but in favor of annexation as stated in the Baltimore resolution[6] & generally think it should be delayed until your administration commences.

You will have a delicate game to play between the North & South. Most that speak to me say, that you should avoid the cabinet of Van B.,[7] the present cabinet, the supposed candidates for the presidency & *get Polk men* who will stand by your admn. & will act without any regard to the succession.

I shall write you again in a few days.

C. JOHNSON

[P.S.] Leigh of Dresden is with me.[8]

ALS. DLC–JKP. Addressed to Columbia.

1. Reference probably is to a letter addressed to Johnson from Beverly Leonidas Clarke and L. Finn and dated December 12, 1844. LS. DLC–JKP.

2. Syntax garbled.

3. Silas Wright, Jr., and Thomas Hart Benton.

4. Thomas Ritchie.

5. James Buchanan.

6. Reference is to the platform statement on Texas annexation by the 1844 Democratic National Convention. See Edwin Croswell to Polk, November 30, 1844.

7. Martin Van Buren.

8. Jesse Leigh edited the Dresden *Tennessee Patriot*, the first issue of which appeared December 21, 1838.

FROM ADAM HUNTSMAN

Dear Sir Jackson Ten Dec 20th 1844

I have not written to you since the election under the belief that, *what money you had is exhausted in the payment of postage*. However there is a little difficulty ahead, I wish to suggest but do not in so doing wish to draw more upon your Confidence than you feel justified in Communicating. I see that the people in your County has suggested the 4th of March for a meeting of the democratic delegates at Nashville for the purpose of nominating our Candidate for Governor etc.[1] It having been nearly a uniform rule for the president to select some one Confidential friend from his State, in the making of his Cabinet. If that rule prevails with you it may disconcert us in this way. We might select the same man as it is to be done on the same day that you would select. The people of the District will be satisfied with Cave Johnson A V Brown Coe[2] or any good democrat. Johnson I think would be the strongest, with us but if any one from this State is to go into the Cabinet he deserves it most. His talents is perhaps suited to the Treasury. I think the Convention at Nashville should have [been] set about the 20th of March when we could have known the Cabinet from the public papers. But if it Assembles on that day Will it not be proper for you to intimate to some one in whom you have Confidence, the person (if any) who may be selected by you from this State, so that in our selection for Governor we may steer clear of difficulties. We intend to make a powerful effort in the District for Governor, and want no bets. We will gain two more members in the next Legislature *certain*. I would be glad to hear from you.

A. HUNTSMAN

ALS. DLC–JKP. Addressed to Columbia.

1. On December 2, 1844, Maury County Democrats held a public meeting and adopted resolutions calling for a state convention to be held in Nashville on March 4, 1845, for purposes of selecting a gubernatorial nominee for state elections scheduled for the first Thursday in August next. Columbia *Tennessee Democrat*, December 6, 1844.

2. Cave Johnson, Aaron V. Brown, and Levin H. Coe.

FROM CAVE JOHNSON

Dear Sir, Washington Dec 20h 1844

I enclose you the within at the request of the writer.[1] You will probably not decide on it until you come here. I seize the opportunity however to say that there is much feeling among the members as to the principle which is strongly urged by some, of *a restoration* of those who were improperly ejected. The idea, that if Van was nominated & elected, it would be a mere restoration, operated greatly agt. him. I make the suggestion generally & not in relation to Danl. G.[2] who is a very worthy man. There is much feeling *in the city* as to *removals & appointments*. The young Hickory club & the democratic association are now but *cliques to serve themselves*. They all acted nobly in their situation & will all be for *proscription* up to the hub & will then quarrel among themselves for the loaves & fishes.

We have some hope of reconciling dissentions upon Wellers proposition for annexation.[3] From the quarter it comes from, we hope it will meet the views of THB[4] & extremes on the other side. There is however such jealousy growing up agt S.W. Jr.[5] that is doubtful whether we can do any thing. No arrangement of your Cabinet can be made that will give satisfaction to the North & South—at least I see none. Great efforts will be made & are making to identify you with one or the other.

I suggested to some of our friends the propriety of addressing you a letter inviting you to come on, without waiting on Com. of Congress. They said you would of course do so, as there was not time to send a Com. after the votes were counted and for you to reach this place before the 4h of March.

There is so strong a feeling to get rid of the Globe. It is so intimately connected with the succession, that a movement by your particular friends here at present, might give great dissatisfaction. Genl McK.[6] this evening expressed himself much gratified that I had not gone to Richmond. Yet if we could succeed in getting T.R.[7] at the head of the Globe, it would be of essential service to the incoming admr. Yet I have no hope of that at present.

Dutee J. Pearce!!! is exceedingly anxious to know how & what way "our excellent friend" will travel. There is much feling at Wheeling to know when you will be there & Complaints at your omitting to answer as Steenrod[8] told me today.

C. JOHNSON

ALS. DLC–JKP. Addressed to Columbia.

1. Enclosure not found.
2. Daniel Gold.
3. Although John B. Weller previously had supported Martin Van Buren's counsel to delay the annexation of Texas, he introduced on December 19th a joint resolution providing for the immediate incorporation of Texas into the Union as a federal territory and subsequently its admission as a state "as soon as may be consistent with the principles of the federal constitution." *Niles' National Register*, December 28, 1844.
4. Thomas Hart Benton.
5. Silas Wright, Jr.
6. James I. McKay.
7. Thomas Ritchie.
8. Lewis Steenrod, a lawyer from Wheeling, Va., won election as a Democrat to three terms in the U.S. House, 1839–45.

FROM JESSE MILLER

My Dear Sir Harrisburg Decr. 20. 1844

Ever since the election I have had some intention to trouble you with a letter, but knowing that you would be over run with congratulations many from real friends and some from the very worst members of the party and being myself much engaged preparatory to the annual report of our Board[1] I have delay'd it till now. I am sincerely gratified at the success of our party because I believe its success and the best interests of our Country are identified and I am the more pleased because I know that in you the democracy of the Country has a representative that coincides with them in their principles and participates in their feelings. Two things not always united. You will as a matter of course be harrassed on all sides wherever you move and importuned beyond reasonable endurance for places and as a general rule the least deserving will be most troublesome. But I know you will appoint none to office who are not honest & deserving unless you are deceived, which will some times happen. My dear Sr on this point you cannot be too careful. In my own State I know you will have a full share of your trouble, and I know that you are liable to be deceived by some of our public men. I trust that miserable hangers on who are always trimming their sails to suit the political breeze will have to give place to the honest democrats of the Country who nobly buffetted the storm in the late unparalelled contest. Mr Tyler has done some acts which have resulted in great good to the Country but he has suffered himself to be deceived by a very unprincipled set of hangers on for office. I saw them congregated at Baltimore in May last and a most disgusting exhibition they presented.

Mr Buchanan's name has been suggested for Secry of State. On this subject I have but little to say. Of his abilities and fitness you are more competent to Judge than I am but I take it for granted they are not doubted by any one & whatever representations may be made to the contrary from any quarter I can *assure you* he is the strong man with the democracy of this State especially in the interior where the reliable democracy is found. He may have some opponents in the City who are jealous of his promotion, but I can assure you that if the Counsels in that quarter had prevaild the democracy would now be in a state of defeat and Henry Clay Prest elect of the U States.

We in Penna. think it was the battle ground on which the late contest was decided as we believe if we had been defeated New York would have given way. But all did their duty nobly. Should you in making your Cabinets arrangement think of giving a member to Penna. as I think you ought Mr Buchanan is the man *beyond doubt* to whom it should be offerred.

Whethr he would accept I know not. This however I do know that many of his friends who would be gratified to see the place tendered would not like to see him leave the Senate. We have a U S Senator elect at the coming session and we are not without apprehensions of some trouble. The Prest. Gov D R Porter I have long since regarded as one of the most corrupt politicians of any Country or age and who is a consumate intriguer & manager is as *I know* now trying to form a Combination with the whigs and a portion of the Democratic members whom he hopes to be able to delude and lead off from the body of the party. I trust he will be defeated but it will require some tact and energy to do it. It is all important in the present state of parties in Senate that we elect a sound man. You my dear sir nor no other man who does not know this man Porter well, can form any idea of the extent, of his schemes & how well he practices on the motto "that the end justifies the means."[2] I know not when I shall have the pleasure of seeing you. The Ceremonies of the Inauguration are not new to me and as there will be such a crowd in Washington about the 4th March, I think I will not be there, but perhaps may have the pleasure of seeing you some time thereafter. There are many things connected with the success of the Democracy in this State and its permanency to which I would like to refer but have not time now. To maintain the Democracy of this State in the ascendant requires much Judgt & prudence. If you can snatch a moment I would like to hear from you. My respects to Mrs Polk.

J. MILLER

ALS. DLC–JKP. Addressed to Columbia.

1. Miller served as Pennsylvania Commissioner of Canals in 1844 and 1845.

2. English translation of a Latin phrase from *Medulla Theologiae Moralis* (1650) by Hermann Busenbaum.

FROM BENJAMIN PATTON[1]

Pittsburgh, Penn. December 20, 1844

Patton asks Polk for an appointment as chargé d'affaires to one of the European capitals and comments on the "political map of Penn." Noting that the election of George M. Dallas as vice-president has created "a rival interest to the 'House of Lancaster' (Mr Buchanan)," he warns Polk to expect a great deal of jealousy and competition between the friends of the two men and adds that the great body of the Democracy supports Buchanan. On the subject of government patronage, Patton cautions Polk that any additional favors to the Dallas family will offend the great mass of the people.

ALS. DLC–JKP. Addressed to Columbia.

1. Benjamin Patton, a lawyer and Jacksonian Democrat, considered establishing his practice in Nashville, Tenn., but chose to settle in his native state of Pennsylvania. He served as U.S. district attorney for the Western District of Pennsylvania, 1837–39, and as judge on the Court of Common Pleas during the 1840's. He moved to Ohio in the 1870's and sat in the state legislature from 1880 until 1883.

FROM SILAS WRIGHT, JR.

My Dear Sir, Canton 20 December 1844

Your favor of the 7th Int. came to me yesterday.[1] For the favorable opinion it conveys, and the honorable and friendly confidence you repose in me, I most sincerely thank you. It is fully reciprocated, and I regret that my condition forbids that I should yield to your request, and thus denies to me the opportunity of manifesting by acts, as I should have an opportunity to do if thus related to you, the truth of what I express in words.

Still I am consoled by the reflection that a simple statement of that condition to you, will satisfy you that I am not at liberty, either as a matter of public duty, of party obligation, or of personal justice, to accept of your offer. That statement I will proceed to give to you in as direct and simple a form as possible, and in the *confidence* you invite.

It may not have escaped your notice that our party in this state has not been perfectly united, upon questions of State policy, for the last two years.[2] Our State Debt and public expenditures have constituted the grounds for the difference, so far as it has been one of principle; and the friends to a continuance of our borrowing policy, and to a continuance of our works of improvement, almost irrespective of the consideration of debt, made themselves the especial and peculiar advocates of the nomination of our present very honest and worthy Governor, in 1842, and as markedly the friends of his person and administration, after his election. There was then really no difference in our party as to our Candidate for the office of Governor, although Governor Bouck was unfortunately made to believe there was a serious one, and that the great exertions of these men had made him the successful competitor for it. Hence, as an almost necessary consequence, after his election, his confidence was given to that class of men, and although the sound policy adopted by our Legislature, at the session before his election, has been maintained, it has been done against the exertions of those most in his confidence, and as many honestly believe against his private wishes and feelings. This naturally produced want of confidence in him, on the part of those who sustained the debt paying policy. This state of things soon gave rise to the distinctions, within our own party, of Bouck men and anti-Bouck men, and the appointments of the governor, strongly influenced by such as imaginary line, soon widened the breach, and the foundation for a dangerous feud was rapidly being laid.

Mr. Van Buren was notoriously in favor of the sound, debt-paying, financial policy of the Legislature in 1842, and yet he openly, upon all proper occasions, defended the Governor from the suspicions indulged to his prejudice, and especially insisted upon the purity of his motives and intentions. Still those who were the strongest in their want of confidence were among our strongest men, most unbending democrats, and his most marked friends. This caused some of the indiscreet friends of the Governor, who considered the nomination of Mr. Van Buren for the Presidency a settled question, to threaten that he would be held responsible for the course of these friends of his, and that if the Governor should not be renominated, he must look for his support where he could find it. I do not feel authorized to say that the Governor countenanced this course on the part of his friends, but he was unwise enough, upon some occasions, to presuppose that such a feeling might be excited.

All these things, as you will readily see, were calculated to strengthen the distrust entertained toward him, and to increase the unwillingness that he should continue at the head of the state government. Still the fear of exciting division in reference to the presidency restrained the expression of discontent within very narrow limits, until after the meeting of the Baltimore Convention.

The proceedings of that Convention, and the influences exerted upon it, were, at the time, and have been since, looked upon by our democracy with the deepest concern, but happily for the country, and for us in this state, the results of its labours and deliberations were greeted as cordially, and hailed as sincerely and heartily, by the democracy of New York as by any portion of their political brethren of any section of the Union, not even excepting Tennessee or Pennsylvania. They looked upon the nomination made as a complete triumph over the intriguers, and a triumph of principle and integrity over unregulated ambition. The resolution was instantaneous and universally felt, throughout the whole party, that its utmost energies, aided by every collateral support, and unitedly directed, could alone secure that result.

Under this feeling, the state nominations began at once to excite universal attention and profound interest, and the absolute necessity of avoiding the dangers which might attend the re-nomination of Gov. Bouck seemed to become more and more sensibly realized by those who had taken no part in the scism in respect to him, or who had been his honest and disinterested friends.

I saw the danger that I might be forced into the position which I was finally made to occupy, and did every thing which I dare do to avert it. I was unsuccessful however, and recieved the nomination under circumstances which left me no alternative but to accept it.

Instantly the report was started that this was all a trick; that it was known I would not accept the nomination to hold the office, and that it was not designed I should, but that, if elected, I would either continue in my place in the Senate, and not enter upon the duties at all, or that I would look to you to call me from the office and the State, in any event, leaving the administration of the government upon the hands of the Lieutenant Governor.[3] In the then excited state of the public mind and feeling, this story produced a shock, and absolutely threatened a pause in the enthusiastic, onward march of our democracy. The mass, as was most natural, feared that a fraud was to be practiced upon them, and that they were to be made *really* to elect, as Governor *de facto*, a man they had not selected for the office. The honest and undesigning friends of Gov. Bouck thought they saw in it a trick to get rid of him, and *practically* substitute a man whom they did not believe the party would have prefered before him. And the opponents of Gov. Bouck, and ardent friends of a sound financial policy, did not know the views of the Lieutenant Governor upon these questions, considered him as selected rather as favorable to those who did not like my rigid notions upon those points, and therefore felt that they were to be defrauded of their great and vital object, by such a transfer. All around, therefore, the tendency of the report was decidedly unfavorable and dangerous, and the duty upon me was imperious to authorize its prompt and unequivocal contradiction.

Every step which led to my nomination, as well as the circumstances under which it was made, showed to me, and to all who marked the progress of events and their causes as a statesman should, that, if placed in nomination, it was not for the purpose of paying a compliment to me, or with any reference to any other disposition of my services, but with the earnest and determinate intention that I should discharge the responsible duties of the office of Governor, and be responsible, so far as our chief Executive office constitutionally is, for the administration of our State Government, and especially for our State financial policy, for the official term. It was not, therefore, to my disappointment that I was forced, by the reports I have mentioned, to declare my determination, if elected, to devote myself to the duties of the place for which I was a candidate; nor was the necessity for that *conclusion* produced by the reports. It existed in the causes which forced the nomination upon me, and the necessity for the early and wide *declaration* of it only was the consequence of the reports.

Yet you will not fail to see that those declarations, made at such a time and under such circumstances, preclude, if the original circumstances did not as I think they did, any idea of a reconsideration of the conclusion pronounced.

The case of Mr. Van Buren, in 1828–9, was precisely different. He was nominated with the Confident expectation that, if we were successful, he would be called into the cabinet of Genl. Jackson. The Lieutenant Governor[4] placed upon the ticket with him was selected under the expectation that the administration of the State Government would devolve upon him. The mind of our party was prepared for this transfer and desired it. Now, as I have told you, the desire and expectation are both different, and taken in connection with my declared determination, made under the circumstance I have detailed, must and should be conclusive upon my action.

I have been thus particular, and perhaps tedious, in giving you this history, because it is due to the subject, to yourself, and to me, that you should know the true grounds upon which my declination of your request is made, and because I have reason to apprehend that efforts may be made to fasten the impression upon your mind that this act of mine, and my declination of the nomination as Vice President upon the ticket with you, should be looked upon as evidence of a disinclination on my part to be connected with your administration. Rely upon it, you should not abuse either yourself, or me, by any such suspicion, nor would it have a shadow of foundation in fact. If I was ever your friend, I was never more sincerely so than at this moment; and if I ever anxiously wished you success in the discharge of any public duty, and felt willing to do every thing in my power and consistent with my position to support and sustain you, that anxiety and that feeling were never more strongly experienced than at this moment. But for the confident belief of our friend that it was essential to the success of the presidential ticket in this state, I certainly never should have yielded my consent to be a candidate for the office of Governor, and I could not give that consent and remain subject to the call you now make, because the very grounds upon which it was asked were inconsistent with such a transfer on my part.

In connection with these facts relating to our condition in New York, and in the same spirit of frankness and *confidence*, I feel bound to mention to you another subject, which has been, and perhaps continues to be, one of considerable speculative remarks and I do so because I am extremely anxious that your mind should not be led into error about it. I refer to the difference between the vote given to yourself, and that which I received, in this State. Some affect to see in it a want of fidelity on the part of our democracy to the National ticket, and especially towards yourself and of course impute the disaffection to the more peculiar friends of Mr. Van Buren. This is wholly without foundation. You had not, according to his position, a more anxious, or earnest supporter in this State than Mr. Van Buren himself, and not a true friend of his in the State failed to support you to the utmost of his power. When you see that the electoral ticket polled more than 485,000 votes in the State, and that the difference between it and the State ticket was but about 5000, a very trifle more than 1 per cent, I am satisfied you will not be able to believe, for a moment, that the friends of Mr. Van Buren, as a body, could have been unfaithful to you. If they have not the power to make a greater impression than this upon such a vote, they must be a mere faction too inconsiderable to deserve grave consideration, and that you know they are not, in his own state, or in any other. The truth is that I have never known the whole democratic party work more unitedly, or more cordially, or so energentically, as they did in support of the electoral ticket, during the late canvass, from the hour the nominations were announced, up to the hour of closing our polls; and any charge of unfaithfulness, against any portion of them, of whatever cast of opinion as to state questions and the men of our state, would be unfounded and unjust. It was this knowledge which induced me to say to you in my letter of the 1st. Nov.[5] that I believed you would get more votes in the State than I should. I spoke with reference to the democratic party, not believing that either of us would get a vote from any other source; and I am now satisfied that, as applicable to that party, my opinion was a sound one. I do not now doubt that you received more votes from those who recognize themselves, and are recognized, as members of that party, than I did, because some of our canal counties cut me off to some extent, though less than I expected. The true explanation of my increased vote, to the principal extent, is found in the fact that many of the most wealthy members of the whig party, and especially those whose interests are opposed to a repetition of the speculating period, desire that the policy established in 1842 should continue to govern the financial affairs of our state,[6] and consequently do not wish the re-ascendency of their own party here, for the present. This feeling was known to prevail extensively among the capitalists and heavy merchants of the City of New York, as many of them avowed it; but I thought the excitement had risen so high that they would vote their whole party ticket. The returns, however, prove that they did not, and the difference between your vote and mine, in that City, being from 1200 to 1500 votes, is accounted for almost exclusively in this way. The abolition candidate for Gov.[7] received some 700 less votes than Birney, and the returns authorize the presumption that the most of these were given to me; being doubtless the votes of such members of that party as were originally democrats, and that excitement has, of late, extended broadly among our Wesleyan methodists and Baptist churches, thus taking hold of many democrats.[8] The remaining votes were, with few exceptions where personal considerations may have had influence, those of members of the whig party, scattered over the state, who desire a sound and safe financial policy on the part of the State government.

I ask your pardon for the long explanations, and feel sure you will justly appreciate the motives which have induced them. The democracy of this state are as ready and determined, as that of your own, to support your administration, and look forward to it with as strong hope and confidence; and it could not but be productive of unpleasant and unfortunate results, if any of these misrepresentations, or misapprehensions, should clothe your mind with distrust upon this point. Your generous letter has appeared to me to authorize me to say what I have, without exciting in your mind a suspicion of improper motive, while the compulsion I am under to decline your request seemed to call for so frank a statement of the grounds, as to prevent that act from giving strength to these not very friendly speculations.

If my time and space permitted, as they do not, I should scarcely feel at liberty, after declining the place you tender, to enter upon the suggestions you invite as to the formation of your cabinet. Did I propose to myself to be a member of it, I should cheerfully speak to you without restraint upon that whole subject, as well in reference to men as to measure; but as I cannot take a place in it, I think it would be improper for me to offer my speculations. And, to tell you the truth, as to men I have formed no impressions, which I could communicate, with any promise to myself that, upon careful reflection, they would be acceptable to myself, much less that they could be useful to you; and as to measures I feel sure there can be no material differences in our respective views.

My position, during the second term of General Jackson, and the whole of Mr. Van Buren's time, has enabled me to appreciate, to some extent, the difficulty of the task of forming a good and harmonious cabinet, and one that shall feel and observe that subordination and fidelity to the constitutional head, which I consider indispensable to a safe and successful administration, without enabling me to do the thing myself, or tell another how it is to be done.

If, however, any thing, in the course of your inquiries and examinations, should induce you to suppose that any information in my possession, or within my reach, will be of service to you, I beg you to feel perfectly free to call upon me in the unreserved *confidence* of this correspondence, and you shall command my thoughts.

SILAS WRIGHT

ALS. DLC–JKP. Addressed to Columbia.

1. Polk to Silas Wright, Jr., December 7, 1844.

2. For divisions within the New York Democracy over the "stop and tax" bill of 1842, see Gansevoort Melville to Polk, October 26, 1844.

3. Addison Gardiner.

4. A lawyer, Congressman, and governor of New York, Enos T. Throop was admitted to the New York bar in 1806; was elected to Congress for one term in 1814; was appointed circuit judge, 1823–28; was elected lieutenant governor of New York on Martin Van Buren's ticket in 1828; was advanced to the post of acting governor upon Van Buren's resignation to become secretary of state; was appointed by Andrew Jackson to the post of naval officer at the port of New York in 1833; and was sent as chargé d'affaires to the Kingdom of the Two Sicilies in 1838.

5. Silas Wright, Jr., to Polk, dated October 31, 1844, and postmarked November 1, 1844.

6. Wright's reference probably is to the Stop and Tax Law of 1842. Opposed to the increase of public debt for the completion of various canal projects, radical Democrats gained control of the principle state offices in New York in 1842 and successfully sponsored a bill known as the "Stop and Tax Law of 1842." The law suspended work on the canals, imposed a direct tax, and established a sinking fund to repay the existing debt.

7. A lawyer and abolitionist, Alvan Stewart was widely known for his shrewdness as a legal adversary. Beginning in 1835, he served as president of the New York Anti-Slavery Society and presided at the 1840 convention that founded the Liberty Party. Though defeated in the gubernatorial election of 1844, Stewart's party held the balance of power in the New York General Assembly.

8. Led by the abolitionist minister, Orange Scott, some Methodist advocates of

anti-slavery withdrew from the Methodist Episcopal Church in 1842 and formed a new church, the Wesleyan Methodist Connection of America. The organization's second convention met in Utica, New York, the home of Alvan Stewart, on May 31, 1843. Thus Wesleyan Methodism emerged two years before the divisive general conference of the Methodist Episcopal Church in which the question of slavery was openly debated and the sectional fracture was recognized and institutionalized. In 1844 Baptists remained loosely united under the Board of Foreign Missions and the American Baptist Home Mission Society. The denomination barely survived dissolution when the Board of Foreign Missions met in its triennial convention in Philadelphia in April of 1844. However, continuing dissatisfaction with the anti-slavery sentiments of northern Baptists led the Virginia Foreign Mission Society to issue a call for a convention of southern Baptists to be held in May, 1845.

ALFRED BALCH

Dear Sir, Nashville 21st December 1844

All the politicians from Maine to Florida and from the Atlantic to the Rocky Mountains are enquiring what the President elect will do and who he will set up and who he will put down by his mere "sic volo," "sic Iubeo."[1] But, you have one precious consolation. You can satisfy your own conscience by doing what you beleive to be just to your self and to the nation whose trustee you are.

I am grieved to see so many rushing after the spoils of our victory with such indecent haste. The recommendation by Prest Tyler of all the members of his Cabinet, in his annual message,[2] under the circumstances, is in my judgment in the worst taste. Equally bad is the certificate of the Electors of the "Key Stone" in favor of Buchannan.[3] It seems to me that they might as well have recommended some fat ugly cock eyed old maid to be your wife had you been a single gentleman! My humble opinion is that a President should select as members of his Cabinet, his own political family, men whom he can like for their personal qualities as well as their talents attainments industry, energy and spotless moral characters. Mr Madison it is well known extended his enquiries to the qualities of the wives and daughters of those whom he proposed to call into intimate political and personal association with him in the managment of the great affairs of the country. He had a wife who might be endangered by the gossip and folly and vulgarity of a foolish woman. The calm which prevails here at present is exceedingly [so]. The Whigs are mourning over their political defeat and their pecuniary losses. Some of them say that they must wait patiently until November 48.

Our Govr has stated that he will not be a candidate for re-election. His position with regard to Brownlows story about the widow and the Hermitage Church would be painful enough to any man but such a wholly *unscrupulous* one as he is. His defence just published[4] is disrespectful to the General cringing to that Miscreant Brownlow and mortifying to those of his adherents who have any regard for truth and honor. The feelings of some of them are revolted at the whole affair.

It seems that the Honorable Wilson Shannon is no great Diplomatist.[5] The contrast between his official notes and the chaste elevated dispatches of Marshall and Madison is striking enough.[6] The news from Washington is that he will be rejected by the Senate. It is certain that his abilities are not equal to his new position. Mr Tyler I fear will make another nomination for he appears to be determined to block the game up on you. But, I trust that the senate will resist.

Ritchie in one of his last papers comes out like a gentleman in regard to the new Cabinet. He says let Mr Polk take whomsoever he pleases as the members of his Cabinet. Let him please *himself*. This is liberal and it is right in itself.

You have much trouble before you. But, if you can make a good start you will get forward triumphantly. The old adage is as true as trite that a good beginning makes a good ending. You have my most ardent wishes for your success.

The President of the U States must always remember that every word which he utters and every act which he does is of consequence: and it is so even with his immediate family. His wife is of the greatest importance to him & In this particular you are most happily situated. A *Christian* woman however elevated by the elevation of her husband whose distinctions she reflects can never be at a loss what character to assume, above all others, before the matrons of the Land.

ALFRED BALCH

ALS. DLC–JKP. Addressed to Columbia.

1. Latin phrase meaning "thus I will, thus I command." Balch is probably paraphrasing Juvenal, *Satires*, VI, line 223.

2. Near the end of his annual message, John Tyler praised "the zeal and untiring industry" of his cabinet.

3. See John O. Bradford to Polk, December 9, 1844.

4. On December 16, 1844, James C. Jones wrote Caleb C. Norvell, editor of the *Nashville Whig*, a letter in which Jones defended his conduct during the controversy over an alleged attempt by Andrew Jackson to expel a widow from the Hermitage Presbyterian Church. Jones' letter appeared in the *Nashville Whig* on December 19, 1844.

5. Balch's reference probably is to a letter from Wilson Shannon, the U.S. minister to Mexico, to Manuel Crescencio Rejón, Mexico's minister of foreign relations; written on October 14, 1844, Shannon's letter was one of the documents accompanying Tyler's annual message. In his letter Shannon attacks the

Mexican government for its proposed invasion of Texas and denounces in particular "the barbarous mode in which the government of Mexico has proclaimed to the world it is her intention to conduct the war." For a copy of this letter, see the Washington *Globe*, December 6, 1844. Shannon's charges initiated a heated exchange of letters with Rejón; their correspondence appeared in newspapers throughout the country.

6. John Marshall and James Madison. Chief justice of the U.S. Supreme Court from 1801 until 1835, Marshall served briefly as secretary of state under John Adams, 1800–01.

TO CAVE JOHNSON

[Dear Sir,] [Columbia, Tenn.] December 21, 1844

I have received your several letters of the 1st, 6th, and 12th Instant, for which I thank you. I should have written you more frequently but that every moment of my spare time has been occupied by company or other indispensable engagements, and even now I seized a moment to write you very hastily. I will leave here between the 1st and 10th of February, it being my intention to reach Washington about the 20th. I prefer to stop at *Coleman's* (formerly Gadsby's) to any other place. On yesterday I wrote to *Brown* and *Judge Catron*[1] to engage apartments at *Coleman's* for me, provided they could make a bargain in advance that I might know precisely what I had to pay. You know I have no money to spend unnecessarily, and to avoid being subjected to an extravagant or enormous charge, it is necessary that a *distinct bargain* shall be made in advance. A gentleman called on me on yesterday who left Washington ten days ago. He informed me that *Coleman*[2] showed him rooms which he had reserved for me, that he asked him what he charged for them, and that Coleman replied *just what I pleased*. Now I will not take them upon such terms. I must know before-hand, distinctly what his terms are. I greatly prefer to go to Coleman's and will do so, if his charges are not exorbitant and beyond all reason. Will you see *Brown* and tell him so. As to the route which I will travel I take the same view that you do.[3] I shall take a boat at Nashville, and travel the usual route by the River to Wheeling, and then direct to Washington. I have already declined numerous invitations to depart from the main route and visit various places. I shall travel with as little ostentation or parade as possible, stopping only a few hours, as I shall be compelled to do, at the principal towns on the route. Such an idea as visiting Phila. and New York never entered my mind.

All the speculations at Washington and in the newspapers about my Cabinet, you may rely upon it, are *mere speculations*. I would write you freely upon this subject, but for the danger that my letter might possibly fall into other hands before it reached you and because I expect to see you in full time (20th Feby.) to confer freely and unreservedly with you. In the meantime I will thank you to keep me advised of all the speculation, opinions, and wishes which you may have on the subject. One thing I can say to you, and that is, that I am under no pledges or commitments to any of the cliques (if such exist) mentioned by the newspapers. My object will be to do my duty to the country, and I do not intend if I can avoid it, that my counsels shall be distracted by the supposed or not conflicting intents of those cliques. Another thing I will say, that I will if I can have a united and harmonious set of cabinet counsellors, who will have the existing administration and the good of the country more at heart than the question who shall succeed me, and that in any event I intend to be *myself* President of the U.S. I shall rely much on you for the information which you may give me, which I hope may be free and unreserved. As to the *press* which may be regarded as the Government organ, one thing is settled in my mind. It must have no connection with, nor be under the influence or control of any clique or portion of the party which is making war upon any other portion of the party, with a view to the succession and not with a view to the success of my administration. I think the view you take of it proper and of the proposed arrangement the best that can be made.[4] I hope it may be effected.

[JAMES K. POLK]

P.S. May I ask you to see Brown and Judge Catron, and if necessary confer with them about engaging apartments at *Coleman's*. I prefer that to any other house, if the terms are at all reasonable.

PL. Published in *THM*, I, pp. 253–55. Addressed to Washington, D.C., and marked "*Private and Confidential.*"

1. Letters not found.
2. Samuel S. Coleman was the proprietor of the National Hotel, which was also known as Coleman's Hotel.
3. See Cave Johnson to Polk, December 6, 1844.
4. Polk's reference is to Johnson's proposed Richmond trip to sound out Thomas Ritchie about becoming the editorial spokesman of Polk's administration. See Cave Johnson to Polk, December 6 and 12, 1844.

FROM AARON V. BROWN

(at night)

Dear Sir — Washington City Decr 23rd 1844

You must not be impatient. Our friend[1] has been sick a few days—has sent me for examination about *half* to be returned with my comments

& then the whole to be finishd & polishd, say all by the first January or sooner. So far it is a happy conception for instance in allusion to the Union:

"If this be not enough, if that freedom of thought word and action given by his Creator to fallen man & left by human institutions as free as they were given, are not sufficient to lead him into the paths of liberty & peace, whither shall he turn? Has the *sword* proved to be a safer and surer instrument of reform than enlighten'd reason? Does he expect to find among the ruins of this Union a happier abode for our swarming millions, than they now have under its lofty arch & among its beautiful columns?[2] No, my countrymen never, untill like the blind Israelite[3] in the Temple of the Philistines we find ourselves in chains and dispair, shall we be justified in thrusting those pillars from their base; For whenere we do, we shall like him be crushed by their fall."

It will be surely ready in time & finishd with a polish suitable to the occasion. I shall enclose it to you under an envelope to Our friend J. H. Thomas but securely sealed so that he shall be aware of contents.

Mr Burk[4] called last night & seemed desirous to know if I thought New England would have a Cabinet officer. He seemed disposed to communicate the views of Govr Hubbard to be such as not to embarrass you if you found you could not well do it & had no thought of offering him a position then through Burk he could get an intimation & by his previous declarations place himself right in anticipation of such result. I dont suppose there is much in this for Burk admitted that if an appointment was intended for N Hampshire or New England, that of Mr. Woodberry[5] would be much more acceptable—that old *federal* blood would be thrown up against Hubbard pretty strong. Moreover if you found it difficult to give a Cabenet office to New England, there are several of the minor ones (3d Assistant P. Master, Patent office, Pension agent, Auditor &c) that would do well for that region where salaries are low &c. Some such position as one of these would be well bestowed on Burk quite a favorite in that quarter & a man of quiet but decided ability.

The Ritchie affair is getting along slowly. Johnson did not & would not go. He feared some new paper squibs at him & *I feared* he was rather indifferent about any matter that was against the Globe Benton & Co. but perhaps I was wrong. Judge Bayly his confidential friend has written to him & after all this may do as well as visit. Ritchie is afraid to come here & we rather so to go there to see him. But there is time enough yet. If my road is blocked there I shall then go for sinking Blair & Rives into *Proprietors* only & putting the political controul (absolute) into the hands of a new Editor & that man Burk would not be a bad one, but more of this when things take that turn.

Blair will hardly be much opposed if at all to this course if he sees that Benton means to be antagonistical to your administration as many of his *Western* friends think likely enough. He shews no *mitigation* of his opposition & nothing but instructions plain & powerful can subdue him. Many of his expressions are current in the City which lead me to think he will be troublesome & disaffected, if he is not allowed to sway & direct every think at his pleasure & possibly may go clean off, but be assured he will take none with him. Both of the New York Senators[6] go with us on Texas & I think that I & Judge Douglas last night, at my room, have fixd up a proposition of annexation which will be satisfactory to the New York democrats & which will succeed. I invite your attention to it, it will be in the Globe of the morning[7] & I take some pride in presenting it as a document of some merit. On the whole I expect annexation at this session. If we pass it in the house & the *Wright* interest goes with us, Benton rather than be solitary & alone, will ease off & let it go in the Senate. Wo! Wo! be it to any one or 2 or 3 Democrats of the Senate who might defeat it, after its passage in the house! Applications for office to me "the President elect ad interim" are numerous. I *sign* for none promise all, *when I am elected*, but note the important cases *in a book of remembrance*. So must you. Fold up & file such letters to themselves where practicable & by keeping a blank Book you can make a short entry that will help your memory & simplify matters very much. I assure every one not to be impatient nor in a hurry to *send on* but wait—that you *will not do things in a hurry* but to do it well you will do it slowly. My time is incessantly occupied. My committee[8] this session is the great laboratory of business for the house. The Oregon & Nebrask Territories & the admission of Iowa & Florida, are all great matters under my charge: & then the Texas question calling for much very much of my time & best powers of negotiation & conciliation, gives me full employment. Not to say any thing of my Defence of you & Genl Jackson against "Old Malignant."[9] By the bye I question if you are aware of the extent of his abuse throughout Massachusetts against all of us. It is Known here, & my reply is heartily received by all our friends & hailed as conclusive in every quarter of the country. I hope it has been acceptible *to the culprits* whose object it was to defend.

Present my best respects to Mrs. Polk with the full right & privelege of inspecting any of the letters I write to you: & with the further request that if she or any of her female friends being in Nashville can enquire after my Dear little girls[10] & see them with a few words of interest & advice it will be very gratifying to me. Indeed I scarcely can think or write of them but with emotions which I cannot express.

A. V. BROWN

[P.S.] Tell the Major[11] to be patient & assured that Johnson & myself will do every think that can be done to meet his wishes.

ALS. DLC–JKP. Probably addressed to Columbia.

1. Amos Kendall.

2. A revised version of this sentence and the preceding one appeared in Polk's inaugural address.

3. Kendall's allusion is the Old Testament account of Samson's death. *Judges* 16:25–30.

4. Edmund Burke.

5. Levi Woodbury.

6. Daniel S. Dickinson and Henry A. Foster.

7. On December 23, 1844, the Washington *Globe* reported that Stephen Douglas had introduced a joint resolution for the annexation of Texas "in conformity with the treaty of 1803 for the purchase of Louisiana."

8. Brown was the chairman of the U.S. House Committee on the Territories.

9. On December 14, 1844, the Washington *Globe* published Aaron V. Brown's address "To the Public at Large, and to the Constituents of the Hon. John Quincy Adams in Particular." In the address Brown responded to speeches of "the old man malignant" at Boston, Weymouth Landing, and Bridgewater in which Adams had bitterly attacked Andrew Jackson, Polk, and those who supported Texas annexation.

10. Brown's reference is to his daughters Laura Louise and Myra M. Brown.

11. Brown's reference probably is to William H. Polk's quest for a government position. See Aaron V. Brown to Polk, December 14, 1844.

FROM ANDREW JACKSON

My dear Col, Hermitage Decbr. 23rd 1844

By some fatality, in sending you letters, the one for president Tyler in pursuance of your request, and agreable to the recommendation of Doctor Hays, & Mr Lantry,[1] was omitted altho written long since. Major Lewis having wrote me, which was received on saturday night, which drew my attention to this subject and I found the letter now enclosed to you,[2] amonghst those letters recd, & for your perusal, which I have retained for your perusal when you come to see me. I am worn down with letters for you & I am determined not to interfere with appointments further than to give you my friendly opinion on the subject. My whole Houshold salute you & yours. Expect to see you soon at the Hermitage.

ANDREW JACKSON

ALS. DLC–JKP. Addressed to Columbia.

1. John B. Hays and Hillary Langtry. Hays, a Columbia physician, was the husband of Polk's youngest sister, Ophelia Clarissa Polk.

2. Enclosure not found.

FROM FERNANDO WOOD

My dear Sir New York Decr. 23 1844

If it is deemed advisable to select one gentleman from this state for The Cabinet, as I am confident it will be, it is the duty of competent persons to offer their opinion as to the selection. I shall now offer my own with the utmost deference and respect, and it is done with an intimate knowledge of the wishes of our people, our younger democracy more particularly with whom I am identified. Were it possible to take the sense of the democracy of this state I am confident that eight tenths would name Hon C C Cambreling as the man of their choice.

For twenty years this gentleman has held the unshaken confidence of our people. They have tried him through the most difficult periods, and he was never known to falter. Of irreproachable private integrity, great sincerity of manners and sterling democracy we all feel that he is the man. Of his capacity and peculiar fitness for executive duties it is unnecessary to write. His associations with you in the House of Representatives makes your own knowledge on this point better than mine. An additional reason why he is preferable to any gentleman named for your cabinet from this state is that he is in no way identified with the local difficulties which have so long divided us. His absence from the country during the most exciting disscusions left him entirely out of it and without loss of confidence of either of the contending factions. Each of the persons named for your selection, except him, have been fully identified with this contest. Govr Marcy was the head of the anti sub-treasury, conservative democratic party and has been known as the leader of the antiliberals ever since. Besides his pecuniary embarrassments entirely unfit him. He is much in debt; hopelessly so! Mr. Flagg is a sterling democrat and true man, but unfortunately the leader of the other branch of the party. He is an ultra "Barn Burner," and however unexceptionable he is as a man the appointment could not fail to give great dissatisfaction to a very large and reputable part of the party. Besides these, Mr. Tracy of Buffalo[1] is the only gentleman named. He is only known to us as a reputable lawyer who in 1840 was an active Whig and strongly tinctured with *abolitionism*.

Now my dear Sir I hope you will receive this letter in the spirit in which it is written—to give the true feelings of the great party of the Empire state. No man has done more here to produce the result than he. Continually active and vigilant he has contributed in every way as much as any other man in this section of country.

FERNANDO WOOD

ALS. DLC–JKP. Addressed to Columbia.

1. Albert Haller Tracy of Buffalo, N.Y., was elected as a Democrat to three terms in the U.S. House, 1819–25. He refused a cabinet appointment in the administration of John Q. Adams; served in the New York State Senate from 1830 until 1837; ran unsuccessfully as a Whig for the U.S. Senate in 1839; and declined a place in the cabinet of John Tyler.

FROM ANDREW J. DONELSON

Dr. Sir, New Orleans Decr 24: 1844

I am here for a few days for the purpose of communicating a little more freely and frequently with the Government on the Texan subject.

As far as Texas is concerned the question of annexation is safe. Her people have taken your election as evidence of a sincere sympathy on the part of the U States, with their cause, and as reparation for the injury they have sustained by the long postponement of their wishes.

It remains for our Government to do their duty now and pass the resolution of Mr McDuffie.[1] The sooner it is done the better.

I have sent a dispatch to the Government calculated to enforce the necessity of early action, having obtained an assurance from Texas that nothing would be done by her Government to change her position on the subject.

I have a letter from Mr. Butler of New York since the election, adverting to the noble part performed by that state in the election. You will have a difficult task in adjusting the conflicting expectations of what is already termed in the papers the New York and So. Carolina influence. Much is due to Mr Van Buren as the first choice of a majority of the Baltimore convention, and as a victim to the Humbuggeries of 1840. I would therefore consult him. My belief is that a full interchange of sentiment between him & Mr Calhoun would leave you unembarrassed, as neither of them can desire any thing but to secure you the most efficient support of the principles and measures of the Republican party.

You are the President of the nation, elevated by the voice of a party whose prominent objects have been defined by severe trials and many hard fought battles. As the instrument of this party acting for the whole country you are entitled of course to all the aid its most experienced members can give. And I trust that when your administration closes you will have the satisfaction of feeling that the American people will find in your conduct additional proofs of the efficacy of Republican principles, and new motives for sustaining and perpetuating them.

I would be glad to visit my home before I return to Texas, but do not feel at liberty to do so without further advices from Washington.

With my kind regards to Mrs Polk....

A. J. DONELSON

ALS. DLC–JKP. Addressed to Nashville care of Robert Armstrong and marked "*Private.*"

1. See Cave Johnson to Polk, December 12, 1844.

FROM J. GEORGE HARRIS

My Dear Sir Nashville Dec. 24. 1844

The Louisiana Committee[1] appear very desirous that a publication should be made of the interview between them and yourself at the Nashville Inn this morning; and Dr DeShields and Judge Bosworth[2] have requested me to attend to it, giving me the "notes" of the Dr's speech, and requesting that I will give a summary of your reply as pronounced in my hearing.

The object of this present writing is to make the private inquiry whether you would prefer *the substance of your speech* given, or *merely* some running remarks upon its fitness for the occasion?

As they seem to regret very much the necessity which compels you to decline their invitation to New Orleans, perhaps their sorrow would be somewhat alleviated by a publication of the cordial and kind sentiments with which you received them. If you think so, and are disposed to gratify them, please drop a little abstract of your reply (especially that portion referring to the purchase of La & the annexation of Texas) into the P.O. addressed to Genl Armstrong, and I will see that it is attended to according to such directions as you may please to give.[3]

Or, if the running editorial will suffice, give the subject no thought, for I will see to it.

J. GEO. HARRIS

[P.S.] A right happy and merry Christmas to yourself, your lady, relatives, & friends. J.G.H.

ALS. DLC–JKP. Addressed to Murfreesboro, Tenn., in care of the postmaster, Greenville T. Henderson.

1. A committee of Democrats, including Felix Bosworth, Jeremiah Y. Dashiell, J. S. Crockett, James S. McFarlane, J. M. P. Richardson, and A. D. Green, from New Orleans, La., arrived in Nashville on December 22, 1844, to deliver an invitation to Polk and Andrew Jackson to attend the anniversary celebration of the Battle of New Orleans to be held in that city on January 8, 1845.

2. Jeremiah Y. Dashiell and Felix Bosworth. A physician from Maryland, Dashiell helped to establish the Louisville Medical College; he practiced medicine in Mississippi and Louisiana before removing to Texas in 1849; there he served

for a time as editor of the *San Antonio Herald*. Felix Bosworth, a native of Tennessee, resided in Carroll Parish, La.

3. See Polk to Felix Bosworth et al., December 31, 1844. Harris subsequently advised Polk that his reply to the Louisiana invitation would be published in the *Nashville Union* on January 7, 1845. Harris to Polk, January 4, 1845. ALS. DLC–JKP.

FROM JOHN POPE

Dr Sir Little Rock Arkansas Dec 25th [1844][1]

I presume that you are elected to the Presidency of the United States and I must be permitted to say that few men in the union felt a more sincere solicitude for your success than myself. Nor was any actor in the contest influenced more by public considerations. I belived that Texas would [be][2] annexed and that the difficult and agitating subject the Tariff would be settled in a manner which ought to be satisfactory to all parties. The bank question has become almost an obselete idea and few men of impartial & sober reflection can desire to see it agitated again until public opinion under the influence of the most obvious necessity shall force the subject on the attention of Congress. The land distribution hobby is nearly worn out and will not shortly disturb the nation or the public Councils. Genl Jackson advanced the most statesman-like sentiment on the land subject ever uttered by any public man: That after the payment of the public debt the lands should not be looked to as a source of revenue but as an asylum for settlement of the poorer classes from all the states collecting only enough from them to defray expences.[3] As I have identified my name and exertions with your cause and the cause of the democratic party and policy I feel a deep interest in the success of your administration and if good I desire its continuance for eight instead of four years.[4] A good administration in eight years may give some stability to the course of public affairs, a thing much to be desired and essential to the lasting welfare of this great and rising nation.

To secure the approbation of the Country and the purity and perpetuity to our republican institutions it is indispensible to have the most competent and faithful officers and agents who may be charged with the management and disbursment of the public money. No partyzan feeling should tolerate for a moment a friend or enemy in plundering the Treasury at the expence of the tax paying people. For vigilance and integrity in this branch of the public service no administration of this or any other government had higher claims to the thanks and approbation of the people, than that of Mr Jefferson. I was chosen an elector and voted for him for the Presidency in 1800 and was a member of the Senate during a part of the second term of his administration and an eye witness to the course of public business at that time. We must get back to the honest and oeconomical system of that period if we desire to perpetuate our free government. Your Postmaster general should be from the West of the highest character for integrity & honor and your personal & political friend. He should be incapable of using the power and patronage of that department to promote his own aspirations or advance the views of any aspirant to the Presidency. The Atto genl ought not only to be a man of talents but of inflexible integrity as a vast amount of claims on the public depend on the opinion of that officer. Felix Grundy if not the most learned lawyer was firm in his opinions & had fine common hard sense with sound judgment and was a most excellent officer. Mr Legare[5] was learned and above reproach as a man of integrity and honor. In Atto genl Butler of New York I had not much confidence with all his learning in the law for reasons not necessary to assign now. The offices of State and the Treasury should be filled by men of the first order for weight of Character and inspire general confidence. If Mr Calhoun and his southern friends desire it you cannot well decline to renew his appointment to the State depart. He was unamously approved by the Senate and can bring much support to your administration. Governor Silas Wright should be pressed with great earnestness to take the Treasury department for which he is eminently qualified & could do much good at the present moment in adjusting the Tariff. Such men as Governor Marcy [and] Saunders of North Carolina &c &c however meritorious will not answer. They are not the great lights with which you should surround yourself at this critical juncture of public affairs, with a determined & talented opposition to contend with.

The people have placed you at the head of the government. The responsibility of the administration rests essentially on you and your own fame and the good of the Country require you to select the best & soundest materials to aid in the great works before you. I have it much at heart that Governor Wright should go into the Treasury department, he is a profound man & will bring you much support. I beg you to take counsel of our good sense as doubtless you will for many of your friends in giving advice are too much actuated by concealed selfish ends, as it was under Mr Madison and the first term of Genl Jackson's administration some men desired to have the cabinet filled for their benefit rather than for the support of the President. On this point you cannot be too cautious. Appoint no man for a cabinet minister who is to be under the control of another member of your administration. Mr Monroe's plan was the best and it would be well for you and all others to profit by it. Adams

Crawford and Calhoun[6] were political rivals without control over each other and each identified with & interested in the success of the administration.

I do not know that the Tyler men and especially the members of his cabinet have any superior claim on you. They held office and stuck to Tyler until he released them from their allegiance and then they arrayed themselves on your side. All this was well enough but because they have been in office I cant perceive on that gound along their better right or claim to any honors within your gift. The members of the Tyler Cabinet will of course resign and you will stand unembarassed by their pretensions & you will be free to select regardless of their official positions. The cabinet will be clear and you will owe it to yourself & the Country to form the best cabinet regardless of individual feeling. I am not acquainted with Mr Mason of Virginia Secretary of the Navy but if a man of worth & capacity & your Virginia friends wish it reappoint him. You owe much to the great states of Virginia New York & Pensylvania. The secretary of War should be from the west & although Benton has done the party much harm it may be policy to offer him the War department which he will no doubt decline, or reappoint Wilkins a sort of Western man if your friends in Pensylvania request it, but in the event of Mr Buchanan's appointment to a seat in the Cabinet for which he is well qualified, then take the War secretary from the far west, Colo Sevier [or] Walker[7] or some other very fit man. Sevier is a talented & honorable man & would bring you some support. Walker is a man of talent & worthy your confidence but his constitution is too feeble I fear for the confinement & severe duties of the department. He would do better for the bench & a vacancy will probably occur in this quarter before long. Buchanan and Woodbury are able men for the supreme bench or the cabinet but neither you nor your friends should forget that many of your able men should be retained in the senate to meet the Whig forces there. Webster will return to the Senate & Rives will be superseded by Governor McDowell[8] & then there will be a tie in the Senate. In such a state of things it would seem to me unwise to weaken your number or talents in that body. Add to the character & talents of the Supreme Court and inspire general confidence in and respect for that branch of the Government. Our character as a nation with the high and important duties assigned to the supreme Court demand this course. I beg you to select for the State and Treasury department men of the first order for character & Talent.

The success of your administration, be assured, essentially depends on the judicious choice of the wisest and best men in the land for your cabinet counsellors. From the President and leading members of his administration a high moral tone, should be diffused through the nation, the only real sterling capital upon which our republican system rests. Since I commenced this letter the documents in relation to Mexico & Texas reached here in the National Intelligencer,[9] which I have perused with some care & on which there is neither time nor room for commentary in this letter except to remark that the tone of our ministers is hardly strong and decisive enough on the subject and for the occasion. Something in the spirit and tone of old Jackson when he says By the eternal such a thing shall be or not be, would have pleased me better. The Mexican and all other governments should be given to understand in a decisive & lofty tone that this government will not permit their weaker and free neighbour to be sacrificed.

I shall leave here in a few days for Kentucky and shall take Nashville in my way if the Cumberland river should be up. I desire to see Genl Jackson before he leaves us and to have an interview with you previous to your departure for Washington. You will I know pardon the freedom with which I address you, because you must believe that it proceeds from a deep solicitude for your good & the good of the Country. Please to present my respects to Genl Jackson and your lady and accept for yourself assurances of my respect & regard....

JOHN POPE

ALS. DLC–JKP. Addressed to Nashville.

1. Date identified through content analysis.

2. An ink blot has obliterated this word.

3. Pope's reference probably is to a passage from Andrew Jackson's fourth annual message. The passage reads: "It seems to me to be our true policy that the public lands shall cease as soon as practicable to be a source of revenue, and that they be sold to settlers in limited parcels at a price barely sufficient to reimburse the United States the expense of the present system and the cost arising under our Indian compacts." James D. Richardson, ed., *A Compilation of the Messages and Papers of the Presidents, 1789–1902* (10 vols.; Washington, D.C.: Bureau of National Literature and Art, 1903), II, p. 601.

4. Pope's reference is to Polk's single-term pledge.

5. Hugh Swint Legaré, founding editor of the *Southern Review*, 1828–32, served as attorney general of South Carolina, 1830–32; went to Belgium as U.S. chargé d'affaires, 1832–36; and sat one term in Congress as a Union Democrat, 1837–39. Appointed to John Tyler's cabinet in 1841, Legaré served as attorney general until his death in 1843.

6. John Q. Adams, William H. Crawford, and John C. Calhoun. Crawford, a Georgia lawyer, served as U.S. Senator, 1807–13; U.S. minister to France, 1813–15; and secretary of the Treasury, 1816–25. He was an unsuccessful candidate for the presidency in 1824.

7. Ambrose H. Sevier and Robert J. Walker.

8. James McDowell served as governor of Virginia, 1842–46, and won election as a Democrat to the U.S. House, 1846–51. Thomas H. Benton married McDowell's sister, Elizabeth McDowell.

9. In a special message, dated December 18, 1844, Tyler described the tense state of relations between the United States and Mexico; he also submitted to Congress copies of recent diplomatic correspondence, which consisted primarily of an exchange of letters between Wilson Shannon and Mexico's minister of Foreign Relations, Rejón. On December 20, 1844, the Washington *National Intelligencer* published that correspondence.

FROM CAVE JOHNSON

Dear Sir, Washington Dec 26h 1844

I am inclined to think the feelings of hostility between the nothern & southern democrats is gradually widening and that a war between them is inevitable. I hear many things as coming from T.H.B.[1] that I suspect is a good deal exaggerated though I am seriously apprehensive that he will eventually go off from us. Some southern men exagerate & use all that comes from him as designed to dictate & control your action on behalf of the nothern wing agt. the southern, or to drive you from the retention of Calhoun, if you have any inclinations in that way. I find there has been so much said in an under tone *as to your course*, that many of the nothern democrats have become very uneasy lest southern influence should prevail over nothern with you & hence I have been privately asked of late by very many from the North, as to the reliance to be placed on these things. I have uniformely said to them, expressly telling them that I have heard nothing from you on the subject that I thought the North had nothing to fear from your Administration that I was sure you would endeavor to do justice & act liberally to every section. I believe most of them would be satisfied with almost any arrangement of the Cabinet, if Mr. C[2] is not retained whilst I think the South will not be satisfied with any other disposition of him. The foolish article I seen published in the Banner[3] purporting to be a letter from this place to the Charleston Mercury I suppose to be from Rhett. They seem to fear that you will endeavor to satisfy both by retaining Calhoun & surrounding him with men who will lean to nothern influence. The fate of Texas this session in any form is still doubtful. The *manner* in which it was brought forward & the supposed *object* of Calhoun has excited nothern men a good deal & it is doubtful whether they will take either Wellers or Douglas' proposition. No meeting has yet been holden among nothern democrats but will be probably this week. If we do annex, it would give you more quiet than I expect you will enjoy. The Tariff too I think might be adjusted. We can pass McKays Bill[4] if the South goes for it. Many think it is *designedly* left open for *ulterior objects*, so that if the southern friends should by any means be thrown with the opposition, any attempt at adjustment other than the 20 pct would be an additional weapon. In the Treasury Report you will have noticed, that at the conclusion, a paragraph is thrown in recomending *no action* at present: this paragraph is wholy disconnected from the subject in the Report, seems to have been *an after thought* and probably the result of *a cabinet consultation*.[5] The nothern men seem inclined to keep Texas open for *your action* whilst the south wish to have the Tariff left open for your adjustment. It is not impossible that Gov Steeles (NH) message[6] stating the dangers of an explosion among the manufacturers in the next year and it might be attributed to any modification of the Tariff we might make & be made to tell agt. us hereafter, might have been designed to prevent any action at the present session of Congress. This reason induced me to think so at first but I should now like to see it out of your way, if practicable, by a fair & proper adjustment at this Session & I now think the chance better to do it then will be probably in the next Congress. A curious story is circulated among a few, very secretly & *which is no doubt true*, that the Treasury Report has been taken, a great part of it, *verbatim et litteratim*,[7] from Hamiltons treatise on the British debt, funding system etc published about 30 years ago, *without any acknowledgement what ever*.[8]

I have not yet been to Richmond. I may learn from McKay or Baily[9] upon their return whether any thing can be done in that quarter & besides the nothern democracy, as the Globe is considered favorable to them, might suspect me of being secretly hostile to them, which would not be true & prevent them from confiding in me as much as they do at present. I wish therefore the idea among some to be entirely given up before I make any move. I cannot but think that if *he can be had*, that it is of the greatest importance. Mr. A.V.B.[10] yesterday mentioned Mr Burke to me. He was a year since more identified with Mr C than any man in the north. He is a very able & efficient writer. We should get him at Nashville if possible. There has been a rumor in the North that you would bring a Ten. editor, probably started by Eastman who has gone North & I learn has been talking of some such movement.

I called to the see the Pres. three times last week to converse with him on the application of W. H. Polk. I could only see him once & then so surrounded with company that I had no opportunity of speaking a word. I shall see him in a day or two & will write Wm. He will grant if he can. He considers your admn. to be a mere continuance of his own.

I have a great number of letters asking me to name them as applicants for office & among them Jas Garland's[11] friends are very pressing. I will not trouble you with them until you come on.

In the course of ten days we shall probably be able to tell the fate of Texas the Tariff &c.

C. JOHNSON

ALS. DLC–JKP. Addressed to Columbia. Polk's AE on the cover states that he answered this letter on January 3, 1845; Polk's reply has not been found.

1. Thomas Hart Benton.
2. John C. Calhoun.
3. The Nashville *Republican Banner* of December 18, 1844, reprinted a letter previously published in the *Charleston Mercury* in which it was alleged that the composition of Polk's cabinet would be determined by the wishes of Andrew Jackson. Under the circumstances, the letterwriter assumed John C. Calhoun would be eliminated from the cabinet, or his views would be thwarted by the presence of staunch Jacksonians such as Benjamin F. Butler, Cave Johnson, and George Bancroft.
4. See Cave Johnson to Polk, January 21 and May 12, 1844.
5. In the concluding paragraph of his report to Congress on December 16, 1844, George M. Bibb noted that the Treasury department "deems it proper to remark that the proposed review and modification of the act of 1842, for imposing duties on imports, are presented, not so much with a view to the action of the Congress during their present session, but to awaken attention and inquiry, and to lead the way towards eliciting all the information necessary for such matured legislation as the important principles and interests involved seem to require." Senate Document No. 6, 28 Congress, 2 Session, p. 25.
6. Governor of New Hampshire from 1844 until 1846, John H. Steele set up the first power loom in his state in 1817; built a cotton mill in 1824 and managed it until 1845; favored low tariffs; and supported the annexation of Texas. In his legislative message of November 30, 1844, Steele warned that current tariff schedules would destroy those very manufacturing interests thought to require the greatest measure of protection, for artificially high prices and profits stimulate speculation and overproduction. When supply outruns demand, prices fall and manufacturers dump their products in foreign markets at ruinous prices. Steele noted that manufacturing establishments were being "erected or enlarged with such haste that time is not given for the damp walls of the building or the paint on the machinery to dry." Only fair competition would check excessive speculation and prevent unwanted revulsions, the burden of which fall most heavily upon the workers. *Niles National Register*, December 7, 1844.
7. Latin phrase meaning *word for word and a literal translation*.
8. Comparison's between George M. Bibb's report and Alexander Hamilton's Report on the Public Credit, dated January 14, 1790, reveal a close similarity of language and syntax between the two documents. Occasionally Bibb's report

duplicates whole sentences verbatim; more often the report lifts key phrases and rearranges their order in the sentence. As Johnson indicated, however, no acknowledgment of Hamilton's contribution was made. House Document No. 6, 1 Cong., 2 Sess., published in *American State Papers* (38 vols.; Washington: Gales & Seaton, 1832–61): *Finance*, I, pp. 15–37.

9. Thomas H. Bayly.

10. Aaron V. Brown.

11. A lawyer, James Garland practiced at Lovingston, Va. Having served one term in the Virginia House, 1829–31, he was elected as a Democrat to the U.S. House and served from 1835 until 1841. An unsuccessful candidate for reelection in 1840, Garland moved the following year to Lynchburg where he was elected judge of the corporation court and served from 1841 until 1882; he was also commonwealth attorney for Lynchburg, 1849–72.

FROM RICHARD RUSH

Dear Sir, Lyndenham, near Philadelphia December 27. 1844

It is with the greatest deference, and not until overcoming many scruples, that I bring myself to write this letter, hoping to be shielded by its motive.

No one can have stronger objections than I have to intimations concerning appointments proceeding from private citizens, to one now clothed with your high responsibilities, which all ought to suppose will be met with a single eye to the public good; nor am I now about to presume to bring any name before you for an appointment, but simply taking the liberty to say a few words respecting a name prominently presented by others. I allude to Mr Buchanans.

Without meaning to detract in the least from that gentlemans merits, I may safely say, that the presentation of his name as secretary of state, by the persons composing the electoral college of Pennsylvania,[1] was without warrant by the constituency who chose them; and who chose them for the discharge of quite a different duty, which the law prescribed.

And I am of those in this state who think that the step they took, would not be sanctioned by a majority of those constituents, could a door be opened for bringing it to any proper test.

The gentleman thus held up extra oficiously by the electors as well as unexpectedly, stands in such a position towards the distinguished Pennsylvanian just elected Vice President,[2] that his selection for the primary post in your cabinet, it is to be feared might be open to misconstruction by the many friends of Mr Dallas in this state, when nothing would be farther from your intentions than to prejudice the latter.

It is foreign to my purpose to go into any, the least, detail, as to the relative history and merits of these two gentlemen. Such a course would be wholly out of place in this letter, and not respectful to you. The utmost that I propose to myself is, that it may have whatever consideration your better judgment may deem it worth, whilst weighing the recommendation of of the electors of Pennsylvania.

It is proper I should add, that Mr Dallas is entirely ignorant of my writing it; and however it may seem to me dictated by a right motive, (the consciousness of which could alone excuse me to myself for writing it,) it may be that he would disapprove it, such is his dignity and delicacy on all occasions that involve him personally.

Hoping that the letter may find excuse in your eyes, through its motive, and joining your friends every where in ardent wishes for the success of your administration, of the wisdom of which your answer to the Nashville adress on the 27th of November has already given such happy augury....

RICHARD RUSH

ALS. DLC–JKP. Addressed to Columbia.

1. Reference is to a recommendation from Wilson McCandless et al. to Polk, December 5, 1844.

2. George M. Dallas.

FROM CHARLES J. INGERSOLL

Dear Sir Washington Decr. 28. [18]44

On the nomination last May I took leave to send you I think two letters, and afterwards during the canvass one more,[1] venturing to suggest a course concerning the tariff—a plain, national and perfectly just course for any candidate, which proved vitally available to us in Pennsylvania, a state hard to keep right for many more reasons than you need now be informed of.

At the same time I made bold to suggest further that except on that one subject, having spoken on Texas recently,[2] and being known on all the other issues, I presumed to advise that you should remain inflexibly silent. Let me say that in nothing was your canvass more superior to your formidable opponent than in your observance and his reiterated impingement of this rule of action.

Deluged as you no doubt are now with letters suggestions, counsel, and recommendations, and relying on seeing you soon, I do not mean by this letter to violate my own principle. I expect no answer to it, but there is an object I have for many years been laboring to impress on our Executives which I have so much at heart that you must excuse my planting it if I may and can in your thoughts before you come to the turmoil of this metropolis. It is this:

During the last sixteen years our government has been so beset by questions of banks and tariffs that it has lost sight in some measure of its primary purpose—foreign commerce for which the present union was organised.

General Jackson had fought the English, his character was supposed to be naturally inimical to them. To counteract this impression his administration treated them with partial amity.

Mr. Van Buren was essentially their admirer, tho' he did not think so.

The consequence was that our connexions with England became more intimate, complicated and detrimental than ever. Much of our present trouble pecuniary, local, altogether, is the result.

There is no need of our quarrelling with Great Britain. She will not come to a rupture with the US but in the last necessity.

By why are our merchants—three fourths of them foreigners, our manufacturers, lawyers, people who go abroad, and others, all opposed to us in party politics, sufferred to keep our commerce, manufactures, products of the earth, currency, all, in colonial dependence on England? Suppose british exports to be 1000, this country takes 181 of them which is 80 more than Germany, next on the list of her customers, takes, and greatly more than any other country takes: and this to be the manifest disadvantage of our foreign commerce.

In cotton alone we have the talisman to change the whole scene. Tobacco has been for several years the object of great attention on our part. Several agencies, and two foreign missions, the Austrian and Prussian, have been directed to tobacco & with some success. While for cotton nothing has been done, nothing even attempted. France, Germany, Belgium, other countries can employ three times as much of our cotton as they now buy, not only raw cotton, but cotton twist, that is in its first stage of fabrication. Indeed even coarse cotton cloth might be introduced in Germany, to sixty millions of consumers. Moreover, coal, stone coal may be sent from this country to France, iron in its raw state to Germany, flesh, bacon & beef, rice, timber, in short the exports of the US vastly increased to countries which have no adequate colonies to make them compete with our productions, but once customers would be so forever. The Zollverein treaty lately accomplished with the German League of States is only the first step in this immense development of our foreign commerce.

Yet the blind supporters of the Boston tariff we have in force[3] opposed this treaty, laid it on the Senate table till it expired.

But it is by extending foreign commerce that the Tariff is to be both regulated and established.

A president has in his own hands the peacable, prompt—that is as soon as absurd prejudice at home and abroad can be overcome—and complete reform of this matter.

But hitherto what have our foreign missions been? chapels of ease for party favorites, doing less than those of any other government for their employers.

Hence colonial habits and british supremacy have kept us colonised to England. Nine tenths of our cotton &c go to Liverpool, as tho' Antwerp, the key by railroads to all Germany, and Havre, and Trieste, France, Germany and all continental Europe did not exist.

I read with great satisfaction that part especially of what you said in public since the election which intimated that Tariffs and the like will be left by you to Congress, as certainly they should have been long ago.[4]

But the great reform and development I desire to see in our foreign commerce and relations belays to Executive action. If begun forthwith with your administration, it will be achieved before it closes, and a glorious consummation will it be of prosperity and of peace.

We have got, without any ill will, to transfer a part of our dealings in cotton, tobacco, coal, iron, flesh, timbers, rice, lead, and flour to the continent of Europe, and our exports may soon be two instead of one hundred millions of dollars.

I have thus very summarily and most imperfectly indicated a view of what I consider the primary duty of the federal Executive, and I am sure that I need do no more than indicate to carry it home to your consideration, whether favorable or otherwise.

I regard it as the great policy of the day in wh[. . .][5] I am anxious to perform any honorable part.

Texas is doubtful this congress: so many party and personal commitments in the way. Still I think we shall carry it in some form or other, and substantially that of the rejected treaty tho' that will never be voted in the form it presents itself.

The intimacy it has been my happiness for some years to enjoy with the Judge and Mrs. Catron brings you and Mrs. Polk into frequent conversation and authorises, I trust, my offering her the compliments of this season, with assurances of the respect and regard in which I remain . . . .

C. J. INGERSOLL

[P.S.] I sent you and General Jackson about a fortnight since a copy in the Globe which I hope reached you of an answer I felt constrained to publish to Mr. Adams illnatured and unprovoked assault on him, you, me and others.[6]

More than twenty years intimacy with Joseph Bonaparte gives me a talisman to touch whenever the memory of his immense brother[7] is invoked, and I have often talked the cotton operation over with him.

ALS. DLC–JKP. Addressed to Columbia.

1. On June 8, 1844, Polk acknowledged receipt of Ingersoll's May 30th letter (not found) relating to the decision of the Baltimore Convention; no second letter from Ingersoll to Polk on the occasion of the nomination has been identified. On June 18, 1844, Ingersoll wrote Polk advising him on the tariff question.

2. Reference probably is to Polk's letter on Texas to Salmon P. Chase et al., April 23, 1844.

3. Reference is to the Tariff Act of 1842.

4. For Polk's remarks in Nashville on November 28, 1844, see John O. Bradford, December 9, 1844.

5. Word obliterated by an ink splotch.

6. Ingersoll published his rejoinder in the Washington *Globe* on December 10, 1844. See Aaron V. Brown to Polk, December 23, 1844.

7. Napoleon Bonaparte.

FROM AARON V. BROWN

Sunday
Dear Sir [Washington City] Decr. 29th 1844

Judge Catron & myself are negotiating about your quarters as you desired. Fine rooms can be had at Colemans & the only question is as to terms. We do not let him know *your* selection of his house as that might lead to too extravagant charges: and rather than submit to extortion we will go somewhere else. I think you will know the result by tomorrow.

All the elements are at work here to induce you not to retain Mr Calhoun & if you were not to do that but place Genl. Cass in the first office of your cabinet I have no doubt that the same opposition of feeling would manifest itself against him, from the same quarter (N. York & Missouri). Mr. Buchannons[1] appointment would not be *so much* opposed but still it would encounter more opposition by far than I lately supposed & from the same quarter (Wright & Benton) but not from the same motive. They do not fear him *in future* but they *want revenge for the past* on account of his favoring the 2/3 rule of the convention.[2] The feeling is bitter on *this point* in N. York. In Pennsylvania a fierce war is breaking out between him & Dallas for the succession, aye the succession, to which Dallas is now looking with no concealment of purpose. This materially effect the question of appointing Buchannon because if it will displease *all* N. York & *half* Pennsylvania & give no special satisfaction elsewhere, where is the inducement for his appointment. I learn that Buchannon will soon be assailed strongly on His *Old federal* associations & sayings which may materially affect him.[3] There are evidently strong determinations to punish all you[4] come under the description of the *Baltimore conspirators* who will never be forgiven by Mr. Van Buren's & Mr Benton's friends. They will be supported by none but those who think that Van Burenism & Bentonism are synonomous terms. The young Democracy who care more for the country than for their leaders will not go an inch with them. With the *subsidence* of Buchannons claims (now rather on the decline) those of Robt J Walker seem evidently to increase. Calhoun would give place more willingly to him. The Dallas party would be delighted & the Van Buren or Benton interest could not "cut such high capers"[5] against it. Genl Cass would feel no reluctance to it, whilst all accord to him talents equal to the station. In the event of *his* appointment & Buchannons nomination to the Bench of sup ct. all would go pretty well in Pennsylvania & in most other other places. Dr. Gwin[6] is here & thinks he can find out Mr Calhoun's willingness to go to England. I am very much inclined to think that in the exasperated state of feeling it would hardly do to retain him in his present position. Of one thing I am certain that it is not *his* interest to become such a focus of concentrated attack from all quarters. No one seems to take any *preeminent* stand among the N. York aspirants Marcy Cambrelling & Flagg.[7] One other suggestion I will make in Relation to Walker; that his professional attainments are such that all admit he would make a Good *Attorney Genl.* I hear nothing special from Virginia but expect something from Mr Ritchie soon after the Christmas holidays.

On the Texas question we held our first caucus last night, nothing was finally concluded on nor any developements more unfavorable than I expected against its final success. *Our whole* difficulty is with the N. York Democrats. They shew a strong leaning against us & will go for Texas or against it just as they think it will help or harm Mr Wrights prospects. But for this wing of our party Mr Benton would stand solitary & alone. The Douglass resolutions[8] are the strongest & are getting to be known here as embodying Genl. Jackson's views as expressed in letters to Blair.[9]

In a few days now I shall hear from our Friend K.[10] again & be ready to meet your wishes. The Major[11] is here. On yesterday we went up to see the President. He is acting very prudently but I shall encourage the idea of his remaining here but a short time or the letter writers will be speculating on the purposes of his visit &c.

A. V. BROWN

NB. I drop the "confidential" because all I write now a days is of that description, & is to be taken more as a description of the scene around me than as containing any opinions of my own. A.V.B.

ALS. DLC–JKP. Probably addressed to Columbia.

1. James Buchanan.
2. Following the publication of Martin Van Buren's Texas letter of April 20, 1844, many of James Buchanan's friends urged the Pennsylvania delegation to vote for Buchanan. Nominally pledged to support Van Buren, the Pennsylvania delegates supported the two-thirds rule and thus aided in forcing the convention to select a compromise candidate.
3. An opponent of the War of 1812, Buchanan served as a Federalist in the state legislature, 1814–15, and won election in 1820 to the U.S. House as a Federalist.
4. Brown probably miswrote "you" for "who."
5. Quotation not identified.
6. Brown's reference probably is to William S. Gwin. A native Tennessean, physician, and staunch supporter of Andrew Jackson, Gwin served as U.S. marshal for Mississippi, 1833–41, and sat in the U.S. House, 1841–43. During his term in the U.S. House, he became an admirer of John C. Calhoun and supported his candidacy for the nomination in 1844. In 1849 Gwin moved from Mississippi to California and represented that state for portions of two terms in the U.S. Senate, 1850–55 and 1857–61.
7. William L. Marcy, Churchill C. Cambreleng, and Azariah C. Flagg.
8. See Aaron V. Brown to Polk, December 23, 1844.
9. In 1844 Andrew Jackson discussed the question of Texas annexation in several published letters. He argued in favor of immediate annexation and emphasized the United States' claim to Texas under provisions of the Louisiana Purchase. For the texts of two such letters, see the Washington *Globe*, March 20 and November 2, 1844.
10. Reference is to Amos Kendall, who was drafting Polk's inaugural address.
11. William H. Polk.

FROM AARON V. BROWN

Dear Sir — Washington City Decr. 30th 1844

I had another interview with the President today. I think in a day or two he will recal Bulwer from Naples (who is to come home by request in April) & nominate your Brother in his stead.[1] He thinks Bulwer will have no objection to the shortning the time especially when the matter is explained to him. So that matter will run in the current we desire. What will you do for a private Secretary. Graham[2] would make one of the best in the world. The Salary would about support him—hardly do it—but pretty nearly or quite. A chamber & parlor at some elegant boarding house close by. He might after a while take one of the Auditorships when you had made a satisfactory arrangement for another Secretary. Six or 12 months spent here might be gratifying to him & Mrs. Graham[3] even if they did not desire to remain any longer. Will Maj Lewis be retained? If not, Graham would make a very good successor. These are all impromptu notions of my own, founded on the knowledge of how gracefully & properly he would deliver your messages & with what good sense & prudence he would bear himself on all occasions. I wish the salary were double what it is that he might accept of it. He is a very sensible man whose opinions would often be worthy of your attention.

We can get the four rooms for you at Colemans & the terms we now understood to be $140 for the 1st week & $100 per week afterwards. Gwin & Catron both say it is cheap enough & I suppose the Judge will have articles signed tomorrow & enclose you a copy. The rooms are very elegant in deed & very conveniently arranged to each other. At Brown's they seem quite mortified at being pretermitted, *but you must divide your company* (western friends) *& cause a goodly number of them to come to Brown's*, which you can easily do. I think Mr. Dallas will take rooms also at Coleman's. Gwin (The Dr) is here & is evidently making a smart push for Walker to be in the Cabinet. He talks of adjusting the pretensions of Buchannon[4] & Walker to the State department & I think will propose to have Buchannon *for that* but press Walker for the *Treasury* & in truth he is finely qualified for it. He is great in statistics & tables & calculations & I do not dout would make a most unexceptionable officer of finance. But you may ask in that event what shall be done with N York? Great in fact & great in her *demands* at the present moment. Well, I answer. Walworth will not be confirmed they say.[5] If that be so then give the *Van Buren clique* a judge in the person of Mr. Butler. That will be *a good sop*, rather undeserving I think, but satisfactory. Then give the opposite clique the War office or the atto Genl ship or the post office. Wont that do them? If not & they seem I think a little inordinate then put Mr. Flagg Mr. Wrights protogee in the custom house & I fancy all would be pretty quiet.

Gwin says he has been sounding Mr Calhoun about England & he thinks he would be very willing to go, if he could get at this session *secret instructions* from the Senate on the subject being laid before them by the Prest in secret session as to the ultimatum of the U. States.[6] If those instructions should be of a character rendering it probable that the negotiation could be brought to a successful close, then he would take charge of it at St. Jame's. But there *is so much* in all this that I cant make much out of it. But yet it may mean *something* & so I give it to you.

One suggestion I will make if in casting about you should determine to call *a present Senator* to your cabinet it will create a vacancy after the 4th March in all cases where the Senator was from a distance. Say Buchannons vacancy could be provided for *after your* arrival here—it takes but few days to fill it. Walkers could not under 20 or 30 days & so of Genl Cass if he were thought of. If any distant case like these existed, you ought to notify them of the fact early so that they might write home to their Executive tendering their resignations to take effect 4th March & by that time a successor could have been appointed & be here in time to vote on your nominations & nothing be known to the public untill you made known your general determenation. I suggest these things as they might not otherwise be thought of.

I sent the document of our friend last night rather than retain it for any inspection & examination of mine.[7] He read it to me. You will have to adjust *the Tariff* paragraphs a little differently. He represents you as comeing out for protection in the abstract. You know how to *prefix* the term incidental, & let whatever you have to say come in under the idea of *discrimination* for the benefit of *all* the great interests of the country. All that is said on Texas will depend somewhat & chiefly on what is the fate of that question at the present session & must be framed accordingly. Nothing has occured yet shewing with *certainty* its fate at this session.

The latter part of the address is intended for Europe. You see what vile stuff is in their newspapers about you. Now I desire your first address to be such as will strike quite a different sort of feeling amongst them. Hence the introduction of the topic of state debts. *That* topic is not so well handled in the paper as some others, but from what is said you can fix up something that will make a fine impression on the European powers. Perhaps you ought to have a few other striking passages as to your course in relation to them, but not having the paper before me I cannot say. It was sent under cover to Mr. Jas H. Thomas & if he is from home you must send down for it.

I am greatly distressd at what I see going on at home in relation to my nomination in the spring for governor. I think it all wrong. Somebody else can run as strong or stronger than I can. Next to yourself I have been fighting longer & harder than any other man in the state for remember I antedate several years in the Legislature before Cave Johnson & the old battles of 1821, 23, 25 were full of annoyance to me in the days of old Colo. Erwin.[8] But no matter about all that, it is past & I do not regret it. Now that my Dear children have need daily of my presence with them, at the most important period to two of them, I know not how to think of further neglect & seperation from them as such a canvass would necessarily produce. Yet I acknowledge if any body who has been with me in Congress is to be the Whig candidate I should like to give him battle. Such one has *some points* to get at home on, but such a man as Jones or Henry are invincible because of their not having done any thing of a public nature. To ascertain *who* is to be their nag & to abridge the campaign to some endurable period I think the 1 April soon enough to have the convention. That too would enable this congress to be over & to shew who of us can come out of it undisgraced. Pardon me for writing so much about myself, but not a day passes over me which is not concluded by the wish & sometimes the vow that nothing shall postpone my assembling around me at the earliest moment, my little children, whose neglect now, can never be compensated by any success in political life.

So soon as Tyler determines exactly *what* & *when* he will act in reference to your Brother, I shall advise him to return, as there are many speculations here as to the object of his visit. Excuse such *scrawls* as I send you for I have no time even to look over them.

A. V. Brown

ALS. DLC–JKP. Addressed to Columbia. Polk's AE on the cover states that he answered this letter on January 8, 1845; Polk's reply has not been found.

1. William Boulware and William H. Polk. Boulware, a native of Virginia, was appointed chargé d'affaires to the Kingdom of the Two Sicilies in 1841 and held that post until 1845.

2. Daniel Graham, a resident of Murfreesboro, became Tennessee's secretary of state in 1818 and served until 1830; in 1836 he moved to the post of state comptroller and served seven years.

3. Maria M'Iver Graham.

4. James Buchanan.

5. Reuben Hyde Walworth served as a circuit judge of the New York Supreme Court and as chancellor from 1828 until 1848. On March 13, 1844, John Tyler submitted Walworth's name to the Senate for a place on the U.S. Supreme Court; Tyler withdrew the nomination on February 4, 1845.

6. John C. Calhoun's reported reservation probably related to the settlement of the Oregon boundary dispute with Great Britain. Brown's language suggests that Calhoun wanted the Senate's prior consent to threaten unilateral termination of the joint-occupation agreements of 1818 and 1827 if a satisfactory division of the territory could not be negotiated.

7. Brown's reference is to a draft of Polk's inaugural address, which was prepared by Amos Kendall and forwarded to Polk. Kendall's draft has not been found.

8. Brown's reference is to the factionalized politics of Tennessee state government in the early 1820's, which coalesced around William Blount and Andrew Erwin. Their rivalry had centered on the state's response to the Panic of 1819. The Erwin faction gained the governorship in 1821, and their success led the Blount faction to court popular favor the following year by nominating Andrew Jackson for a presidential bid in 1824. Andrew Erwin, a native of Virginia, speculated in early land sales in middle Tennessee; he settled first in Davidson County and then moved to Bedford County, which he represented for one term in the Tennessee House, 1821–23.

FROM AARON V. BROWN

Dear Sir — Washington city Decr. 30th 1844

I forgot to say in the letter now sealed up,[1] that our friend Kendall desires the *City Post office* as most convenient to him & more suitable to his other purposes of which I promised to apprise you. I can think of no special reason why he should not be gratified in that respect.

A. V. BROWN

ALS. DLC–JKP. Addressed to Columbia.

1. See Aaron V. Brown to Polk, December 30, 1844.

FROM ROBERT P. DUNLAP[1]

Sir, — Washington Dec 30. 1844

As a friend of Gov Fairfield he has shown me a letter from Hon George Bancroft of Boston, & believing that it contains views, that I think it of importance that you should be made acquainted with, I have taken the liberty to make a few extracts for *your own eye*. Mr Bancroft in his letter to Gov Fairfield says, "Some persons are suggesting my name for consideration in making up the Cabinet. This is done by some personal friends with the kindest motives: by some with a view to counteract your wishes: by some for ulterior purposes. I cannot directly take notice of this myself in the present aspect of things: but I have written to several whose friendship I cherish and avowed to them my views with the same frankness, with which I opened myself to you. I am convinced that a position like that at Berlin would be considered as better suited to my purposes of life than a seat in the Cabinet: and I write this letter, of which you will make none but a discreet use, that you may be able, if opportunity offers, to interpret my feelings without risque of mistake."

R. P. DUNLAP

ALS. DLC–JKP. Addressed to Columbia.

1. Robert Pinckney Dunlap served in both houses of the Maine legislature, 1821–33; won election to the governorship in 1834 and 1836; and sat in the U.S. House from 1843 until 1847. Polk appointed him collector of customs in Portland in 1848, and Franklin Pierce named him postmaster of Brunswick in 1853.

TO FELIX BOSWORTH ET AL.

Gentlemen: Columbia Tenn. Decr. 31st, 1844

I regret that necessary engagements which must occupy my time prepatory, to my removal to the seat of Government, place it out of my power, to accept the invitation which you have conveyed to me, from a large "meeting of the Democracy of Louisiana, called by the Electoral College of that State," to visit New Orleans in Company with Genl. Jackson, on the 8th of January next.[1] These engagements will probably detain me in Tennessee until the early part of February, when I must proceed to Washington by the most direct route. If the Venerable patriot, with whom, the meeting of citizens, whom you represent, have done me the honor in their proceedings, to associate my name, had found it convenient or possible to have revisited the scene of one of the greatest achievements, of his useful and eventful life, an achievement which has made the 8th of January, one of the proudest of our National anniversaries, I would at any sacrifice of personal convenience, have done myself the honour of accompanying him. His feeble state of health precludes the possibility of such a visit on his part. I hope at some future time to have the gratification of visiting your great and growing City.

I am deeply grateful to the Democracy of Louisiana, whom you represent, for the favourable and kind feelings of confidence and regard which they have been pleased to express, personally towards myself. I beg Gentlemen: that you will present to them my sincere acknowledgements, for the honor done me by their invitation, and that you will accept for yourselves, my thanks for the kind measure in which you have communicated it to me.

James K. Polk

Note: Duplicate copies of the above were fowarded to New Orleans & for publication in the Nashville Union, on Jany 2nd, 1845.

ALS, draft. DLC–JKP. Addressed to New Orleans and marked "Copy."

1. See J. George Harris to Polk, December 24, 1844.

FROM JOHN CATRON

dear sir. Washington, Decr 31, 1844

I had the pleasure to receive yours on the subject of procuring rooms.[1] I have done so at Coleman's. A Copy follows of the agreement.

"The Presdt elect will reach Washington about the 20th of February next—wanted for him:

1 Public parlour. 1 Dining room. 1 Chamber. 1 office room.

All to be selected by Judge Catron. Company Gov. and Mrs Polk (2) private Secretary (1) one other person (1). These to dine at his table only. Four in all.[2] And two Servants to be kept.[3] The rooms to be retained as long as Gov. Polk sees proper; and if he stays a fraction of a week, he is to be charged for the time he stays only. He is to pay no Corkage for any wines of his own he sees proper to drink. The price per week to be subscribed here for transmission to Gov. Polk.

28th Decr 1844.
J. Catron

For the accommodations on the otherside Gov. Polk is to pay for the first week one hundred and forty dollars; and after the rate of one hundred dollars for each succeeding week, or part of week, and if he should need another small room for private conference it is to be furnished on the terms usual in the House. The rooms selected by Judge Catron are the S. West four at the Corner of the National Hotel, Nos. 72. 73. 78. 79.

Decr. 30th 1844.
Saml. S Colemans
Prop."

I keep the original. The rooms are the old parlour, its adjoining smaller parlor, adjoining chamber, very good, & the Old ordinary dining room. The way to them is narrow, & crooked. I dont like it as well as I might. There is a good Parlour in the House, but the two adjoining here—one for an office, is the best, than can be done. Say to Mrs. Polk the *women* will find her, & as for you, it is also likely. The House is very well kept.

I have ordered your Ice House to be filled by Gnl Hunter.[4] If some small lot of wine is needed, 3 or 4 dozen say so to me. I know all about this.

In your inaugural, say as to Mr Kane on the Tariff,[5] and 2, that the Presdt. has little to do with it. This is expected in Penn. Of other matters A. V. Brown will do the writing. I am too much hurried. There is nothing worth telling, save come here *President*, disregarding grumblers, &

clicks. This is indispensible to a great extent; it is indispensible to make a fair beginning.

J. CATRON

ALS. DLC–JKP. Probably addressed to Columbia.

1. Letter not found.

2. Polk was accompanied by his wife, Sarah, his nephew and personal secretary, J. Knox Walker, and his thirteen-year-old nephew and ward, Marshall T. Polk, Jr.

3. The two servants probably were William Goff, a black freedman, and his mulatto wife, Dilsey. In November a committee of Polk's friends had strongly recommended that he hire the couple to act as his servants during his presidency. Felix Robertson et al. to Polk, November 28, 1844. LS. DLC–JKP.

4. Reference probably is to Alexander Hunter, who served as U.S. marshal for the District of Columbia from 1834 until 1848.

5. See Polk to John K. Kane, June 19, 1844.

FROM CHARLES G. GREENE[1]

Sir, Boston, 31st Dec. 1844

My friend Colonel Hall,[2] having informed me of his intention to visit Tennessee, I avail myself of his kind offer to convey any message I might desire to to communicate to you, to make him the bearer of my respectful congratulations to the President elect upon the fortunate issue of the great national contest which has just terminated.

Mr. Hall as you know from personal observation, is an old fashioned Jeffersonian democrat, and the deep interest he took in the recent canvass, and the active exertions he made during the contest to secure the triumph won for our principles in the election of the democratic candidate for the Presidency, will enable him to give you full and accurate information in relation to all of the political nature here that your curiosity, or desire for correct information, may require. Yet, I cannot refrain from briefly alluding to the peculiarity of the circumstances which encompass the democracy of the East, and claiming for them a meed of praise which a hasty view of their action would hardly accord to them. In Massachusetts, particularly, the hand of the enemy is heavy. The whigs control all our monied instutions; possess nearly all the incorporated capital, and nine-tenths of the individual wealth of the state. Hence, if a young man desires money to enter the world with, to attain his object, he must be a whig; if the man of established and extensive business needs large pecuniary facilities, he must be a whig, and even if the day laborer would obtain employment, he too must be a whig. Indeed, it does not stop here, but political prejudice enters into social influences with harsh rigour, and the unyielding democrat is made to experience attempted mortifications which his own independence and integrity may scorn, but the stings of which his family cannot always escape. These facts, among others more obvious, will at once convince a reflecting mind that nothing but an honest love of Republican Liberty, and the sternest Party Fidelity, could induce fifty-three thousand members of *such a community* to stand firmly by the Standard of Democracy in defiance of all persuasion, all threats, and all persecution.

But I will not dwell upon this subject—the whole country has proved itself worthy of the Institutions which bless it, and which, under the favor of heaven, I pray may endure forever.

Hoping, sir, that the lofty position to which the voluntary suffrages of your countrymen have assigned you will prove as pleasing to you as I am confident your administration will prove honorable to the nation, I beg leave to apologise for this trespass upon your attention, and to subscribe myself....

CHARLES G. GREENE

ALS. DLC–JKP. Addressed to Columbia and delivered "By Col. Hall."

1. Greene founded the *Boston Morning Post* in 1831; under his leadership the *Morning Post*, a staunchly Democratic newspaper, prospered for some forty-eight years.

2. Joseph Hall of Maine won election to two terms in the U.S. House, 1833–37; served as measurer in the Boston customhouse from 1838 to 1846; held the naval agency at Boston from 1846 to 1849; and ran unsuccessfully in 1849 for the mayorship of Boston.

CALENDAR

N.B. Items entered in *italic* type have been published or briefed in the Correspondence Series.

1844

1 Sept	From George C. Dodge. ALS. DLC–JKP. Encloses a letter (letter not identified) from an "uncompromising federal Whig," who deposited it in the Cleveland, Ohio, post office with the intention of practicing a fraud on Polk; signs his cover letter as assistant post master and writes in "the spirit of political friendship."
1 Sept	From Cave Johnson. ALS. DLC–JKP. Requests that a copy of his campaign appointments be sent to his home in Clarksville; expects to have a large meeting in Clarksville on October 17; urges a large attendance by friends from Columbia.
1 Sept	From Maria Sigafoose. ALS. DLC–JKP. Relates that she has quit her job as a domestic servant because her Whig master forbid her to support Polk's election; states that she participated in a large procession of twenty thousand people in Winchester, Va., on August 27.
2 Sept	From James K. Gibson. ALS. DLC–JKP. Assures Polk that he will carry Virginia, including the Abingdon district.
2 Sept	From Robert Halsey. ALS. DLC–JKP. Introduces Augustus H. Pease.
2 Sept	*From Andrew Jackson.*
2 Sept	*From John K. Kane.*
2 Sept	From William J. Lieper. ALS. DLC–JKP. Reports that Pennsylvania Democrats have chosen Francis R. Shunk as their candidate for governor.

2 Sept	From William Parker. ALS. DLC–JKP. Requests that Polk state his views on "the Veto Power" of the United States Bank.
2 Sept	From Lewis H. Turner. ALS. DLC–JKP. Asks Polk's views on the tariff question; anticipates that voters in the vicinity of Chemung County, N.Y., will support Polk's candidacy.
3 Sept	*From George M. Dallas.*
3 Sept	*From Nathaniel Ewing.*
3 Sept	From George W. Harris et al. LS. DLC–JKP. Inquire on behalf of Democrats of Oneida County, N.Y., if Polk favors Texas annexation "independent of forms or consequences," as claimed by their Whig opponents.
3 Sept	*From J. G. M. Ramsey.*
3 Sept	From William Wallace. ALS. DLC–JKP. Expects that Blount County, Tenn., will reduce the Whig majority by one hundred votes; regrets that the illness of his wife compels him to decline serving as the party's nominee for elector in Tennessee's Second Congressional District.
4 Sept	From Leonard P. Cheatham. ALS. DLC–JKP. Gives a detailed account of the debate between Levin H. Coe and Robert L. Caruthers at Springfield, Tenn., on September 2; notes that Caruthers charged Polk with having opposed all of the House pension bills proposed in 1832; adds that Coe defended Polk's voting record by explaining that his candidate had voted for the Senate version of the pension bill.
4 Sept	*From John P. Gordon.*
4 Sept	From Charles J. Ingersoll. ALS. DLC–JKP. Requests that Polk state whether or not he is or ever has been a Freemason and whether or not as a member of the Tennessee General Assembly he ever voted for land bounties to encourage building or improving iron factories and forges.
4 Sept	*From Cave Johnson.*
4 Sept	*From J. G. M. Ramsey.*
4 Sept	From J. G. Read. ALS. DLC–JKP. Reports that Indiana is "safe for Democracy"; denies that the Whig majority in the legislature is a true measure of popular opinion in the state; points to the fact that the Whig majority in the legislature had attached nearly all of the nine floating members of the lower house to strong Whig counties and thus enlarged their majority.
4 Sept	*From John Staats.*
4 Sept	From James A. Tulloss. ALS. DLC–JKP. Wishes to have Polk's projection of the presidential vote in Tennessee; states that Democrats in Bledsoe County, Tenn., will make a small gain.
4 Sept	From Thomas Ward. ALS. DLC–JKP. States that he is an Episcopal clergyman in Wood County, Va., and a brother of

	"Extra Billy" William Smith of Virginia; solicits donation for his missionary work in western Virginia.
5 Sept	*From Patrick Collins.*
5 Sept	*From Albert Gallup.*
5 Sept	From Cave Johnson. ALS. DLC–JKP. Requests information on Polk's voting record in Congress with respect to Revolutionary War pensions.
5 Sept	From George Richardson et al. LS. DLC–JKP. Solicit Polk's views on the Tariff Act of 1842.
6 Sept	From Edwin Croswell. ALS. DLC–JKP. Reports that harmony prevailed at the New York Democratic State Convention, which has nominated Silas Wright, Jr., for governor.
6 Sept	*From Robert P. Flenniken.*
6 Sept	From Thomas Goin. ALS. DLC–JKP. Encloses a draft of "Hickory Ship" float to be built and displayed in New York City.
6 Sept	From Henry Hicks. ALS. DLC–JKP. Advises that three young Whigs of Wilmington, Del., have addressed a letter to Polk requesting his views on the Tariff Act of 1842; states that Delaware Democrats are better organized than in recent years; expects the state to vote for Polk in the presidential election.
6 Sept	*From Allen McLane.*
7 Sept	*From William C. Bouck.*
7 Sept	From John Fairfield. ALS. DLC–JKP. Reports that prospects are good for a Democratic win in Maine's state elections, scheduled for September 9.
7 Sept	From Joseph C. Hornblower et al. C. DLC–JKP. Solicit Polk's aid in support of the New Jersey State Colonization Society.
7 Sept	From Solomon J. H. Snyder. ALS. DLC–JKP. On behalf of friends in Tuscarawas County, Ohio, requests clarification of Polk's views on an Independent Treasury system.
7 Sept	*From William Tyack.*
8 Sept	*From James Hamilton, Jr.*
8 Sept	From A. H. Langston. ALS. DLC–JKP. States that although he is a "humble farmer" from Leake County, Miss., he is entitled to know Polk's position on Texas annexation, a national bank, and protective tariffs; requests Polk's written answers to these interrogatories.
9 Sept	From Anonymous. L. DLC–JKP. Asks for Polk's opinions on amalgamations, rats, and Henry Clay.
9 Sept	From A. Billings. ALS. DLC–JKP. Writes from McMinnville, Tenn., that Polk is gaining strength and will win Tennessee in November.
9 Sept	From Daniel M. Brodhead. ALS. DLC–JKP. Informs Polk that he has been elected to membership in the Democratic

	Association of Forestburg recently organized in Sullivan County, N.Y.
[9 Sept 1844]	*From Levin H. Coe.*
9 Sept	*From John M. Davis.*
9 Sept	To Andrew Jackson. ALS. NjP–BLL. Introduces an acquaintance from Alabama, Lewis B. McCarty.
9 Sept	From Daniel T. Jenks. ALS. DLC–JKP. States that although Bucks County, Penn., has never been carried by a Democratic presidential nominee, not even Andrew Jackson, Polk may do so; requests a copy of one of Polk's speeches containing his tariff views; expresses satisfaction with Polk's letter to John K. Kane on the tariff.
9 Sept	From Richard F. Richmond et al. C. DLC–JKP. Invite Polk to attend a mass Democratic meeting to be held in Hannibal, Mo., on October 1, 1844.
9 Sept	From Williamson Smith. ALS. DLC–JKP. Solicits position as marshal of the southern district of Mississippi, should Polk be elected to the presidency.
9 Sept	From W. P. Wisehart. ALS. DLC–JKP. Requests Polk's views on the tariff, a national bank, distribution of public land-sale revenues to the states, and a single-term presidency; wishes to read Polk's reply to a mass meeting of the Democracy in Delaware, Ohio.
10 Sept	From Henry Allen. ALS. DLC–JKP. Inquires whether or not Henry Clay ever said of Polk, "Go home, G—d d—n you, where you belong"; thinks that Whigs in Madison County, N.Y., would not vote for Clay if convinced that he had used such profane language.
10 Sept	From Leonard Jarvis. ALS. DLC–JKP. Reports that partial election returns in Maine's state elections indicate a large Democratic victory by some nine thousand votes.
10 Sept	From Ely Moore. ALS. DLC–JKP. Advises that Vermont will vote Whig, as expected; thinks that New York, Pennsylvania, and New Jersey will go Democratic.
10 Sept	*From Hopkins L. Turney.*
11 Sept	*From John Anderson.*
11 Sept	*From Jonathan I. Coddington.*
11 Sept	From George H. Franklin. ALS. DLC–JKP. Asks on behalf of a number of Polk's political friends in New York City what his views might be on the subject of dueling.
11 Sept	*From William H. Haywood, Jr.*
11 Sept	*From William C. Hazen.*
11 Sept	From John P. Heiss. ALS. DLC–JKP. Estimates that a sixteen-page pamphlet, containing the "Vindication" article in this day's *Nashville Union,* would cost $160 for ten thousand copies or $85 for five thousand copies.
11 Sept	*From William L. Marcy.*

11 Sept	From William G. Sanders. ALS. DLC–JKP. Writes from Dudleyville, Ala., and inquires about Polk's views on the tariff and Texas annexation questions.
11 Sept	*From James M. Williamson.*
12 Sept	From Auguste D'Avezac. ALS. DLC–JKP. Details stops on his campaign speaking tour, including mass meetings at Baltimore, Trenton, and Wheeling.
12 Sept	*From Edwin F. Polk.*
12 Sept	*From J. G. M. Ramsey.*
12 Sept	From Job W. Ray. ALS. DLC–JKP. States that the citizens of Alleghany County, Md., would appreciate having Polk's tariff views communicated directly in writing to them, as the partisan newspapers of that area cannot be relied upon to convey the facts accurately.
12 Sept	From Aaron Wagar. L, copy in the hand of and certified by E. Dibrell. DLC–JKP. Claims that Polk owes him $2.25 payable on the account of William E. Woodruff of Little Rock, Ark.
13 Sept	*From Robert Armstrong.*
13 Sept	*From George Bancroft.*
13 Sept	From A. Ettinger. ALS. DLC–JKP. Writes on behalf of a Protestant congregation in New Berlin, Penn., and solicits Polk's views on "the impending danger of our Government falling into the hands of Roman power."
13 Sept	From Jehiel H. Halsey. ALS. DLC–JKP. Introduces Augustus H. Pease.
13 Sept	*To John P. Heiss.*
13 Sept	From George R. Hughes. ALS. DLC–JKP. Proposes that Polk answer five questions relating to a new national bank, an Independent Treasury system, distribution of land revenues, tariff protection on household commodities, and the general ticket method of electing U.S. House members.
13 Sept	From Frederick P. Stanton. ALS. DLC–JKP. Regrets that illness prevents his going to Middle Tennessee to campaign.
13 Sept	From V. M. Swayze. ALS. DLC–JKP. Renews his unanswered interrogatories of August 26th respecting Polk's tariff views.
13 Sept	*From William E. Venable.*
14 Sept	From Anonymous. L, signed "A Democrat." DLC–JKP. Traces William C. Bouck's political career and maintains that the nomination of Silas Wright, Jr., for governor will diminish Polk's chances of carrying New York.
14 Sept	From William Henry Brisbane. ALS. DLC–JKP. States that as Polk's opponent is often charged with "obliquities of character," questions about the candidates' moral views must be asked; wishes to know if Polk would ever fight a duel, gamble, or use profane language.

14 Sept	From William A. Coleman. ALS. DLC–JKP. Invites Polk to honorary membership in the Philomathesian Society of Wake Forest College.
14 Sept	*From John Galbraith.*
14 Sept	From Edward Harden. ALS. DLC–JKP. Affirms his private support for Polk but explains that as the collector of customs at Savannah, he can take no public part in the election contest.
14 Sept	*From J. George Harris.*
14 Sept	*From John P. Heiss.*
14 Sept	*From Andrew T. Judson.*
14 Sept	*From Bromfield L. Ridley.*
14 Sept	From C. Smith. ALS. DLC–JKP. Queries Polk's views on topics of public concern in Clarke County, Ohio; desires written statements on proposals for a new national bank, tariff protection, assumption of state debts, Texas annexation, occupation of Oregon, and continuation of the Cumberland Road.
14 Sept	*From James M. Williamson.*
15 Sept	From R. H. Hammond. ALS. DLC–JKP. Reports that James Buchanan spoke the previous day at Milton, Penn., to one of the largest meetings ever assembled in that part of the state.
15 Sept	*From James McKisick.*
15 Sept	From Robert J. Nelson. ALS. DLC–JKP. States that in Memphis the Whigs are boasting about the large number of Polks in Maury County who are publicly supporting Henry Clay for president.
15 Sept	From Edward Southwick. ALS. DLC–JKP. Urges an amalgamation of political parties on republican principles; anticipates that the southern states will eventually move toward a system of free labor.
15 Sept	From William J. Whitthorne. ALS. DLC–JKP. Encloses a list of appointments for William T. Ross and Barkly Martin in Bedford, Coffee, and Rutherford counties of Middle Tennessee.
16 Sept	From James Allen. ALS. DLC–JKP. States that although he is of the Whig persuasion, he has defended Polk against false charges circulating in Bates County, Mo.
16 Sept	*From John T. Andrews.*
16 Sept	*From Robert Armstrong.*
16 Sept	*To Robert Armstrong.*
16 Sept	From William G. Austin. ALS. DLC–JKP. Requests Polk's assistance in arranging an exchange between the *Nashville Union* and the *Ledger* of West Feliciana Parish, La.
16 Sept	From John O. Bradford. ALS. DLC–JKP. Compares state election results thus far in 1844 with those in 1840; pre-

	dicts large gains for the Democratic ticket for president in November; attributes prospects for success to party unity.
16 Sept	*From Leonard P. Cheatham.*
16 Sept	From John Cramer. ALS. DLC–JKP. Reports that there is strong support for Polk and Dallas throughout the western counties of New York.
16 Sept	From William Emmons. ALS. DLC–JKP. Reports on meetings in the Philadelphia area where he has spoken in behalf of the Democratic ticket.
16 Sept	*To John P. Heiss.*
16 Sept	*From Herschel V. Johnson.*
16 Sept	*From John K. Kane.*
16 Sept	From Isaac S. Ketcham. ALS. DLC–JKP. Encloses a letter of introduction from John C. Calhoun and explains his decision not to visit Tennessee as originally planned; states that he has campaigned for Polk from Maryland to Missouri; predicts that his home state of Michigan will vote Democratic.
16 Sept	From Warren Lincoln. ALS. DLC–JKP. Predicts that Polk will carry Chemung County, N.Y.; asks that Polk communicate his views on the annexation of Texas, the acquisition of Oregon, the distribution of surplus federal revenues, his private investments in slaves, and his personal religious principles.
16 Sept	From Thomas Martin. ALS. DLC–JKP. Advises Polk not to attend personally to the distribution of documents, for such actions might be used against him in the campaign.
16 Sept	*From J. G. M. Ramsey.*
17 Sept	*From Robert Armstrong.*
17 Sept	*From John Blair.*
17 Sept	From John A. Bryan. ALS. DLC–JKP. States that for eight years he headed the Ohio Democratic Central Committee and that he does not inflate his election estimates; having just toured Maryland, Virginia, Pennsylvania, and New York, he reports that he has never before seen Democrats so excited as in the present contest.
17 Sept	From William Conner. ALS. DLC–JKP. Relates the political outlook in several cities recently visited, including Philadelphia and Baltimore; notes that the Virginia Whigs are dispirited.
17 Sept	*From William E. Cramer.*
17 Sept	From Stephen H. Crane et al. LS. DLC–JKP. Write on behalf of loyal Democrats in Union, N.J., and solicit Polk's views on tariff protection.
17 Sept	From E. S. Davis. ALS. DLC–JKP. States that on his current trip to Boston he has observed the Whigs' great disappointment over the Maine elections; notes that James Hall, formerly a congressman from Maine, wishes to be remembered

to Polk; states that all seemed well as he passed through Pennsylvania and New York.

17 Sept *From J. George Harris.*

17 Sept *From William Hendricks.*

[17 Sept 1844] *From Andrew Jackson.*

17 Sept From Lawrence Taliaferro. ALS. DLC–JKP. Expresses his strong hopes for Polk's election and mentions that he attended the Baltimore Convention "at the instance of the working classes" in the Bedford area of Pennsylvania.

17 Sept From Robert J. Ward. ALS. DLC–JKP. Requests reliable information as to the course Tennessee will take in the presidential election; recalls that he served as a Jackson elector for Kentucky in 1828.

18 Sept *From Robert Armstrong.*

18 Sept *From John P. Heiss.*

18 Sept *From Daniel Kenney.*

18 Sept From Thomas Martin. ALS. DLC–JKP. States that Aaron V. Brown is still at his plantation in Lowndes County, Miss., and is not expected back in Pulaski until the end of next week.

18 Sept *From Robert Weakley.*

19 Sept *From Alfred Balch.*

19 Sept From William T. Brown. ALS. DLC–JKP. Urges Polk to send new speakers from Middle Tennessee to campaign in the Western District.

19 Sept From Jesse B. Clements. ALS. DLC–JKP. Informs Polk that Hopkins L. Turney has canceled his plans to go to the Western District and has gone to Giles and Marshall counties to debate Spencer Jarnagin and Robertson Topp.

19 Sept *From John I. DeGraff.*

19 Sept From David Files. ALS. DLC–JKP. Introduces Joseph H. Young, a Mobile, Ala., cotton factor.

[19 Sept 1844] *From Arnold S. Harris.*

19 Sept *From Samuel H. Laughlin.*

19 Sept From A. P. Stinson. ALS. DLC–JKP. Reports from St. Joseph, Mich., that his home state and Indiana are both safe for Polk and Dallas.

19 Sept From Hampton C. Williams. ALS. DLC–JKP. States that he presently serves as acting chief clerk in the Navy Department's Bureau of Construction and complains that for the fifth time he has been passed over for the permanent position in favor of a Whig.

20 Sept *From Robert Armstrong.*

20 Sept From William Bobbitt. ALS. DLC–JKP. Writes from Coffeeville, Miss., and inquires what disposition should be made of funds to be collected next month.

[20 Sept 1844] *From George M. Dallas.*

20 Sept	*From David T. Disney.*
20 Sept	*From John Fairfield.*
20 Sept	From George Given. ALS. DLC–JKP. Assures Polk that Pennsylvania will vote Democratic; bases his prediction on his recent campaign tour of eleven counties in the eastern part of the state. Given's letter posted without seal to Andrew Jackson for his prior perusal and mailed to Polk from Nashville on October 4, 1844.
20 Sept	*From J. George Harris.*
20 Sept	*To John P. Heiss.*
20 Sept	From Adam Huntsman. ALS. DLC–JKP. Reviews Democratic appointments for various speakers in the Western District of Tennessee.
20 Sept	From Samuel H. Laughlin. ALS. DLC–JKP. Expresses great delight in the Democratic victory in Maine's state elections; asks for directions about mailing the Nashville *Vindication* pamphlet to the Democratic members of Congress.
20 Sept	From William Stoms. ALS. DLC–JKP. Requests that Polk state in writing his views on the Tariff Act of 1842.
20 Sept	From Fernando Wood. ALS. DLC–JKP. Reports that he has just completed a tour of the southern counties of New York and that the Democratic majorities in that section of the state will be unprecedented.
21 Sept	*From Barnabas Bates.*
21 Sept	From James G. Bryce. ALS. DLC–JKP. States that on his return home to Louisiana he has observed favorable indications from Columbia to his present stop in St. Louis; mentions that he must attend a Democratic mass meeting in Baton Rouge on September 30th.
21 Sept	From Joseph Commander et al. LS. DLC–JKP. Solicit on behalf of the citizens of Greensboro, N.C., Polk's views on the tariff.
21 Sept	From Ezekiel H. Gage. ALS. DLC–JKP. States that local Democrats favor a "Judicial Tariff" and Texas annexation; complains that the Whigs are telling the Irish voters of Susquehanna County, Penn., that Polk opposes all tariffs.
21 Sept	*From John W. Goode et al.*
21 Sept	From Joseph Hall. ALS. DLC–JKP. Warns Polk against using the speaking services of Robert Rantoul, Jr., a former Democrat who supported John Tyler and thereby obtained the customs collectorship of Boston; recalls that he was the only northern Democrat to support the gag rule; mentions that E. S. Davis of Tennessee has offered to aid him in bettering his situation should Polk win the presidency.
21 Sept	From Samuel Hazlett. ALS. DLC–JKP. Desires Polk to state unequivocally whether he favors or opposes the Tariff Act of 1842.

21 Sept — From Hiram Hill. ALS. DLC–JKP. Wishes Polk well in the forthcoming election and says that in Virginia the Democratic ticket will win by at least five thousand votes.

21 Sept — From George W. Hopkins. ALS. DLC–JKP. Writes from Abingdon, Va., that his congressional district will give Polk a majority of some five hundred to a thousand votes; predicts that if the Democrats carry New York, Polk's election is certain.

21 Sept — From George S. Houston.

21 Sept — From Edward J. Mallett.

22 Sept — From Josiah Baldwin. ALS. DLC–JKP. Recalls serving as a page in the U.S. House during Polk's speakership; states that Democrats in Elmira, N.Y., received Polk's nomination "with Joy and Acclamation."

22 Sept — From Levin H. Coe. ALS. DLC–JKP. Relates that the Democrats have managed the campaign in Benton, Weakley, and Obion counties as well as the Whigs; however, the opposition has not been answered properly in Carroll, Gibson, Dyer, Madison, and Henderson counties.

22 Sept — From William Fitzgerald. ALS. DLC–JKP. Urges Polk to send outside speakers to the Western District; notes that the Whigs are going "to throw all their forces for the coming month on the District."

22 Sept — From John Gately. ALS. DLC–JKP. Encloses a political essay that he has written for publication in the newspaper of Polk's choice.

23 Sept — From James Buchanan.

[23 Sept 1844] — From David M. Currin.

23 Sept — From Levi S. D'Lyon. ALS. DLC–JKP. Encloses a pamphlet in defence of Ezekiel Polk's character; states that he has circulated the pamphlet throughout Georgia in advance of state elections; predicts that Polk will carry Georgia in November. (Enclosure not found.)

23 Sept — From Augustus R. Elwood et al. LS. DLC–JKP. Request on behalf of the citizens of Otsego County, N.Y., Polk's views on whether or not wool should be imported duty free.

23 Sept — From Ransom H. Gillet.

23 Sept — From Elbert Herring. ALS. DLC–JKP. Encloses a copy of a political article written by his brother for publication at Nashville. (Enclosure not found.)

23 Sept — From Wilson Lumpkin.

23 Sept — From William Moore.

23 Sept — From Franklin Pierce.

23 Sept — From John Reed. ALS. DLC–JKP. Inquires if Polk's family was formerly from the Eastern Shore of Maryland or from Delaware; states that his mother was a Polk and that when she was young some of her family moved to North Carolina.

23 Sept	From Edmund D. Taylor and William Walters. LS. DLC–JKP. Request Polk's support for the appointment of William L. D. Ewing of Illinois to be U.S. chargé d'affaires to the Republic of Texas.
23 Sept	From J. Thompson. ALS. DLC–JKP. Writes from the office of *Thompson's Reporter* of New York City and solicits Polk's views on postal reform.
23 Sept	From J. M. Thompson. ALS. DLC–JKP. Wants a loan of money for purposes of betting on the presidential election; requests that the money be sent to him at Clarksburg, Va.
24 Sept	From Robert Armstrong. ALS. DLC–JKP. Briefs Polk on latest campaign arrangements in Tennessee.
24 Sept	To Robert Armstrong. ALS. ICHi. Requests that Armstrong review the enclosed (probably copies of John W. Goode et al. to Polk, September 21, 1844, and its accompanying Giles County Whig Interrogatories); asks that he reply by the next day's mail after consulting with J. George Harris.
24 Sept	From John Bigler. ALS. DLC–JKP. Inquires whether or not Polk has written and published since his nomination any letters on the tariff issue other than that to Kane of Philadelphia.
24 Sept	From David Campbell. ALS. DLC–JKP. Asks on behalf of the Democracy of Pittsburgh, Penn., whether or not Polk favors the Tariff Act of 1842 without modification.
24 Sept	From D. B. Groat. ALS. DLC–JKP. Warns Polk that the Whigs of Richfield Springs, N.Y., plan to solicit his views under the guise of a nonpartisan inquiry.
24 Sept	*From J. George Harris.*
24 Sept	From John P. Heiss. ALS. DLC–JKP. States that he has completed the distribution of the Nashville *Vindication* pamphlet.
24 Sept	From Gansevoort Melville. ALS. DLC–JKP. Relates details of a mass meeting of Democrats in Columbus, Ohio.
24 Sept	*From Benjamin Rawls.*
24 Sept	From Richard Spurling. ALS. DLC–JKP. Asks Polk's views on creating an Independent Treasury system.
25 Sept	From Joseph B. Anthony. ALS. DLC–JKP. Predicts that Pennsylvania will vote Democratic in November; states that he is proud to be able to answer from personal knowledge the Whig inquiry, "Who is James K. Polk?"
25 Sept	*From Robert Armstrong.*
25 Sept	From W. Franklin Barr. ALS. DLC–JKP. Propounds interrogatories regarding Polk's views on an Independent Treasury system, free trade, direct taxation, limited veto power, and a one-term presidency.
25 Sept	From John M. Daniel. ALS. DLC–JKP. Requests assistance

	in documenting his repayment of a loan for which he had served as surety.
25 Sept	*To John W. Goode et al.*
25 Sept	*To John W. Goode et al.*
25 Sept	To John P. Heiss. ALS. T–JPH. Requests that Heiss send him the balance of the one thousand copies of the Nashville *Vindication* pamphlet reserved for his personal distribution.
25 Sept	From W. Y. Huston. ALS. DLC–JKP. Asks for a written statement of Polk's political principles.
25 Sept	From Asher A. Selover. ALS. DLC–JKP. Requests Polk's autograph.
26 Sept	*From Robert Armstrong.*
26 Sept	*From John Catron.*
26 Sept	*From J. George Harris.*
26 Sept	*From William H. Haywood, Jr.*
26 Sept	From John P. Heiss. ALS. DLC–JKP. Reports that he has sent the Nashville *Vindication* pamphlet "to every part of the United States" and to every Democratic member of Congress.
26 Sept	*From Andrew Jackson.*
26 Sept	*From John Law.*
26 Sept	From James B. Smith. ALS. DLC–JKP. Asks if Polk favors reducing the duties imposed by the 1842 Tariff Act; states that he is the son of James N. Smith and a former resident of Maury County.
27 Sept	*From Robert Armstrong.*
27 Sept	From Auguste D'Avezac. ALS. DLC–JKP. States that he has campaigned from the Ohio to the James rivers and has met large crowds every two days for the past two weeks; indicates that he will speak in Norfolk, Portsmouth, Philadelphia, and other towns on his return trip to New York.
27 Sept	*From John W. Goode et al.*
27 Sept	*From John W. P. McGimsey.*
28 Sept	*From Julius W. Blackwell.*
28 Sept	From Alexander I. McKnight and William J. Cooper. LS. DLC–JKP. Invite Polk to membership in the Eumenean Society of Davidson College.
28 Sept	From John B. Macy. ALS. DLC–JKP. Discusses D. B. Tallmadge's speech of September 23, 1844, which gave a full exposition of Polk's views on the tariff and which made a favorable impression on the citizens of Cincinnati, Ohio.
28 Sept	From William H. Noble. ALS. DLC–JKP. Notes strong support for Polk in Cayuga County, N.Y.
28 Sept	From Christopher S. Shnick. ALS. DLC–JKP. States that he and a number of his neighbors in Union Town, Penn., wish to know Polk's views on tariff protection.

28 Sept — From James T. Worthington. ALS. DLC–JKP. Offers Polk honorary membership in the Dialectic Society of Cincinnati College.

29 Sept — *From Robert Armstrong.*

29 Sept — *From Leonard P. Cheatham.*

30 Sept — From Robert Armstrong. ALS. DLC–JKP. States that he will attend to Polk's request tomorrow morning as soon as J. George Harris arrives at the office.

30 Sept — From J. Edward Baines. ALS. DLC–JKP. Encloses newspaper clipping of a letter purporting to be Polk's letter to the People of Tennessee, May 29, 1843; asks if the letter is genuine.

30 Sept — From George M. Dallas. ALS. DLC–JKP. Encloses letter from William E. Read of Baltimore to John M. Read of Philadelphia; this letter tells what may be expected from Maryland's state elections on Wednesday next.

30 Sept — *To John P. Heiss.*

30 Sept — From James R. Paynter et al. LS. DLC–JKP. Request that Polk reply to the charge that he favors "a dissolution of the Union in case Texas is not immediately annexed to the U. States."

30 Sept — *From J. G. M. Ramsey.*

30 Sept — From James G. Read. ALS. DLC–JKP. Assures Polk that Indiana is safe for the Democratic presidential ticket; acknowledges receipt of "a bundle of pamphlets" relative to charges against Ezekiel Polk.

30 Sept — From John S. Reed. ALS. DLC–JKP. Requests $30 for election expenses in Tioga County, Penn.

30 Sept — From Henry Simons, Jr. ALS. DLC–JKP. Notes that in some newspapers Polk is for tariff protection and in some, for free trade; asks Polk to state his position on this issue.

30 Sept — From James H. Thomas. ALS. DLC–JKP. States that in his haste to leave he neglected to obtain the will of George Barker and deliver it to the chancery court hearing the case of *McCullough v. Barker.*

30 Sept — From Richard A. L. Wilkes. ALS. DLC–JKP. Recommends that his brother-in-law, Mark Prewett, be appointed postmaster of Aberdeen, Miss., and that John W. Duke be named to the post of U.S. marshal for the northern district of Mississippi.

30 Sept — From Archibald Wright. ALS. DLC–JKP. States that Thomas M. Jones has indicated his willingness to accept speaking appointments for the party any time after October 14; Aaron V. Brown is not yet home.

[1 Oct 1844] — From Robert Armstrong. ALS. DLC–JKP. Encloses copy of the *Nashville Union* wherein is reprinted the *Cincinnati Gazette's* retraction of the Roorback stories; states that

	Moses Dawson had "put the matter right" in the *Cincinnati Advertiser.*
1 Oct	From Robert Armstrong. ALS. DLC–JKP. Explains that he could get nothing inserted in the *Nashville Union* today; will run the material in Thursday's issue.
1 Oct	From John M. Bass. ALS. DLC–JKP. Acknowledges receipt of Polk's check for $500 and encloses Polk's canceled note for that sum held formerly by the Union Bank of Nashville.
1 Oct	From Levin H. Coe. ALS. DLC–JKP. Reports that he debated John Bell last Saturday at Portersville, but that subsequently the Whigs have been unwilling to permit his continuing the debate with Bell at their mass meetings.
1 Oct	From Cyrus C. Crafts. ALS. DLC–JKP. Requests that Polk give a "full & clear exposition" of his views on slavery and direct his reply to Poland, Me.
1 Oct	From John P. Heiss. ALS. DLC–JKP. Urges Polk to send copy for the *Nashville Union* through Robert Armstrong rather than J. George Harris, as Harris arrives in town late in the morning and "puts off everything to the last hour, and then it is all bustle and confusion."
1 Oct	From John K. Kane. ALS. DLC–JKP. Reports the formation of an "absolute alliance of the Natives with the Whigs, the former engaging for Markle, in exchange for aid on the Congressional and Legislative tickets."
1 Oct	*From John H. Lumpkin.*
[1 Oct 1844]	From Thomas Martin. ALS. DLC–JKP. Details schedule of speaking engagements for Democratic meetings in Lawrence, Wayne, and Hardin counties; expects Aaron V. Brown to return soon to his home in Pulaski, Tenn.
1 Oct	From Franklin Pierce. ALS. DLC–JKP. Introduces the bearer, J. Shackford Kimball, formerly of Concord, N.H., but currently of Boston, Mass.
1 Oct	From J. G. M. Ramsey. ALS. DLC–JKP. Relates that a correspondent of his from Charleston has visited New York City and reported Polk's prospects to be very positive there.
1 Oct	From Joseph L. White. ALS. DLC–JKP. Encloses letter to Polk from citizens of Otsego County, N.Y. (Augustus R. Elwood et al. to Polk, September 23, 1844.)
2 Oct	From Alexander O. Anderson. ALS. DLC–JKP. Reports that in Maryland state elections Baltimore has gone Democratic by at least six hundred votes and that Baltimore County will give the Democrats a similar margin of victory.
2 Oct	From Alexander O. Anderson. ALS. DLC–JKP. States that since writing earlier this date he has learned of additional returns in the Maryland state elections; reports that the Democracy has triumphed in Baltimore by a majority of 1,301 and in the county by about 700 votes.

2 Oct	From Alfred Balch. ALS. DLC–JKP. Reviews election prospects in East Tennessee as related by travelers from Knox and Roane counties; tells of campaign plans for meetings in Nashville.
2 Oct	From William Elsey, Sr. ALS. DLC–JKP. Requests information about the current amount of his Revolutionary War pension and to what back pay, if any, he may be entitled under the Pension Act of 1828.
2 Oct	From J. George Harris. ALS. DLC–JKP. Indicates that campaign activities in Nashville are going according to Polk's wishes and directions; thinks that the Roorback stories will not harm Polk's election chances; discusses the impact, if any, of the Giles County Whig interrogatories.
2 Oct	From John V. Hoagland. ALS. DLC–JKP. Solicits the position of measurer at the Customs House in New York City.
2 Oct	From Holeman Rice. ALS. DLC–JKP. Asks if Polk supported legislation providing for Revolutionary War pensions.
2 Oct	From John Sheakley. ALS. DLC–JKP. Informs Polk that his township of Sandycreek won the prize banner at a large Democratic mass meeting held in Mercer, Penn., on September 25th.
2 Oct	From C. Spencer et al. LS. DLC–JKP. Request that Polk communicate his views on the tariff question and so assist his Democratic friends in Bloomington, Ind., and the state's Tenth Judicial District.
2 Oct	From Nathaniel Terry. ALS. DLC–JKP. Relates Whig allegations by Robert Desha of Mobile, Ala., asserting that Polk had played cards for money some years previously; offers to refute these falsehoods if Polk so wishes.
3 Oct	From Robert Armstrong. ALS. DLC–JKP. Urges Polk to send Clement C. Clay and James W. McClung to East Tennessee.
3 Oct	From Robert Armstrong. ALS. DLC–JKP. Relates plans for sending the Democratic military companies to a campaign meeting in Sumner County.
3 Oct	*To James Buchanan.*
3 Oct	From Arnold S. Harris. ALS. DLC–JKP. Reports on Democratic barbecue in Wilson County; notes that nine companies of Democratic militia will attend the Sumner County meeting on October 4th.
3 Oct	*From J. George Harris.*
3 Oct	From William M. Lowry. ALS. DLC–JKP. Predicts that East Tennessee will give Polk a larger vote than he received from that division of the state in the last gubernatorial election.
3 Oct	From Barkly Martin. ALS. DLC–JKP. Explains that four days previously he went to bed with chills and fever and that

	Polk must find someone to take his appointment at Palestine, Tenn.
3 Oct	*From Gansevoort Melville.*
3 Oct	From Amasa J. Parker. ALS. DLC–JKP. Thinks that Silas Wright's nomination for governor has brought unity to the New York Democracy and estimates that some seventy thousand attended yesterday's mass meeting here in Albany.
3 Oct	From Silas Reed. ALS. DLC–JKP. Observes that the friends of John Tyler hold the balance in Ohio's presidential contest and that he has assured his fellow Tylerites that Polk will not follow Martin Van Buren's policy of proscription against them.
3 Oct	From George W. Rice. ALS. DLC–JKP. Estimates that the Whig majority in Marion County, Tenn., will be held to fifty votes; encloses James Morgan's certificate defending Ezekiel Polk's loyalty to the patriot cause during the American Revolution.
3 Oct	From N. Wadsworth. ALS. DLC–JKP. Outlines his objections to the nature and extent of southern influence in the nation's governance.
4 Oct	From Hugh J. Anderson. ALS. DLC–JKP. Reports that in his gubernatorial race in Maine he has gained a five thousand vote majority over the combined votes of both the Whig and abolitionist tickets; notes that their common friend, John Fairfield, has performed excellently, despite poor health, in bringing about the victory in Maine.
4 Oct	*From Lewis Cass.*
4 Oct	*From William E. Cramer.*
4 Oct	From Auguste D'Avezac. ALS. DLC–JKP. Relates accounts of his speaking engagements in Norfolk, Va., and New York City.
4 Oct	From Auguste D'Avezac. ALS. DLC–JKP. Explains how his earlier letter of this date was sent enclosed in a letter written by his host, Albert G. Southall.
4 Oct	From E. S. Davis. ALS. DLC–JKP. Discusses state elections in Maryland and expects the margin of Whig victory to be only two or three hundred votes.
4 Oct	From William L. S. Dearing. ALS. DLC–JKP. States that he has learned from Samuel Morse's telegraph office that the Whigs have carried the Maryland state elections and thinks that the Democrats have done well there considering the large amounts of money provided to the Whigs by office holders wishing to be reappointed.
4 Oct	From Hudson S. Garland. ALS. DLC–JKP. Urges that Polk send everyone to the mass meeting in Clarksville, Tenn.; asks that Robert Armstrong be directed to make Edwin W.

	Hickman withdraw from the brigadier general's election in Dickson and Davidson counties; argues that Hickman's defeat "is certain as matters are," for the Dickson militia will be in Clarksville en masse in any case.
4 Oct	From David Henshaw. ALS. DLC–JKP. Complains that the Whigs followed a policy of total proscription against all office holders not of their political persuasion, even down to the lowliest lighthouse keeper; recommends that Polk reject the Whig approach and in its place take up reforms in those departments receiving and disbursing government funds.
4 Oct	*To Charles J. Ingersoll.*
4 Oct	From Andrew Jackson. ANS. DLC–JKP. Sends letter from John B. Macy, whose letter to Jackson of September 28, 1844, requests assistance in forwarding his letter to Polk of September 28, 1844.
4 Oct	From Cave Johnson. ALS. DLC–JKP. Reports on his campaign tour of the Western District; relates that informed friends do not think that the Whig majority in that part of Tennessee will exceed five hundred votes; states his personal belief that Polk will carry West Tennessee.
4 Oct	*To John K. Kane.*
4 Oct	From Albert G. Southall. ALS. DLC–JKP. States that although a loyal friend of John Tyler, he supports Polk's presidential bid fully and predicts victory in Virginia by some five thousand votes.
4 Oct	From James H. Thomas. ALS. DLC–JKP. Details his campaign efforts in Lawrence County, Tenn.; notes that in the last couple of days he has brought three Whigs "into the good old Democratic church, & clothed them in the *uniform* of the military companies."
5 Oct	*From John O. Bradford.*
5 Oct	From Robert J. Lackey. ALS. DLC–JKP. Requests a letter from Polk's hand stating his position on the tariff question.
[5 Oct 1844]	From Barkly Martin. ALS. DLC–JKP. Inquires by messenger if there is any news of election results in New Jersey, Pennsylvania, or Georgia; adds that he is still very feeble, but hopes "to make another fight or two before 5th Nov."
5 Oct	From Will M. Shipp. ALS. DLC–JKP. Reviews election news from Hopkinsville, Ky., and estimates that four hundred Democrats from Christian County will attend the mass meeting in Clarksville, Tenn.
6 Oct	From Arabia J. Brown. ALS. DLC–JKP. Reports that Democrats in Garrard County, Ky., are "on fire" for Polk, even though Garrard is the Whig stronghold for Robert P. Letcher, William Owsley, and George Robertson.
6 Oct	From Auguste D'Avezac. ALS. DLC–JKP. Tells of efforts to

	organize the Democrats of James City County, Va.
6 Oct	From Hugh W. Dunlap. ALS. DLC–JKP. Predicts that Louisiana will vote Democratic in the presidential election; maintains that New Orleans will support Polk now that the "Elliott" voters have been legalized.
6 Oct	From William Emmons. ALS. DLC–JKP. Praises James Buchanan's campaign speech yesterday in Salem, N.J.
6 Oct	From Boling Gordon. ALS. DLC–JKP. Agrees to canvass the western counties of Tennessee with appointments in Hardin, McNairy, Henderson, Perry, Carroll, Benton, and Humphries.
6 Oct	*From J. George Harris.*
6 Oct	*From Timothy Kezer.*
6 Oct	*From Samuel H. Laughlin.*
6 Oct	From Thomas K. Price. ALS. DLC–JKP. Expresses confidence that Polk will carry Louisiana, even though the Whigs have won the New Orleans city elections by a margin of some four hundred votes.
7 Oct	From Anonymous. L. DLC–JKP. Relates that the Whigs have raised a higher pole than the Locofocos.
7 Oct	*To Robert Armstrong.*
7 Oct	From Adam Fergusson. ALS. DLC–JKP. Admits that the Whigs outnumber the Democrats in Smith County, but claims that "no part of your friends in Tennessee can be more devoted" than the Smith County Democrats.
7 Oct	*From John A. Gardner.*
7 Oct	From Carter Gazlan and Hiram H. Hicks. LS. DLC–JKP. Allege that half a million dollars have been contributed from British sources to aid in Polk's election; request that Polk state his views on tariff protection and on creation of a national bank.
[7 Oct 1844]	*From Lawson Gifford.*
7 Oct	*To Boling Gordon.*
7 Oct	From John C. Hamilton. ALS. DLC–JKP. Worries that Polk will lose thousands of votes in Maine because of Whig assertions that he opposed bills for the relief of the Revolutionary War veterans.
7 Oct	*From Adam Huntsman.*
7 Oct	From Marie Leleatia Persis. ALS. DLC–JKP. Seeks gift of money with which to pay for travel from her home in Henry County, Tenn., to Louisville, where she will receive free medical assistance from a sympathetic physician.
7 Oct	From Richard H. Stanton. ALS. DLC–JKP. Assures Polk that election prospects are favorable and that if Ohio and Pennsylvania vote Democratic, Kentucky may yet be won.
8 Oct	From Robert Armstrong. ALS. DLC–JKP. Details distribution of campaign literature; discusses newspaper articles on

	the occupant question.
8 Oct	From Levin H. Coe. ALS. DLC–JKP. Estimates that the Whigs will carry the Western District by one thousand votes; details events at the highly successful meeting at Wesley, Tenn.; complains that Frederick P. Stanton has spent too much time campaigning in Memphis.
8 Oct	*From George M. Dallas.*
8 Oct	From Robert E. Finnell. ALS. DLC–JKP. Requests appointment to the place held by John W. Russell, a Whig in Franklin County, Ky.
8 Oct	From Boling Gordon. ALS. DLC–JKP. Replies to Polk's "letter by Capt Jones of yesterday" and lists his speaking engagements in Wayne and Hardin counties for the period of October 11th through October 22nd.
8 Oct	From J. George Harris. ALS. DLC–JKP. Explains financial difficulties in getting out a pamphlet on the occupant question; thinks that this material might better be "re-inserted into the Daily Union, and the type being up a few thousands of Extra Unions containing a *contrast* of your opinions with those of Mr. Clay might be made for $40 or $50."
8 Oct	From Edward B. Hubley. ALS. DLC–JKP. Reports Pennsylvania state election returns from Schuylkill County; expresses surprise that the Whigs of Philadelphia "had been so extensively engaged in *pipe laying*" as to win the city and county by a majority of seven thousand votes.
8 Oct	*From Edwin F. Polk.*
8 Oct	From Henry E. Riell. ALS. DLC–JKP. States that a coalition of Whigs and Nativists have carried Philadelphia by five thousand votes; maintains that in the presidential election that majority will be reduced by half.
9 Oct	From Anonymous. L. DLC–JKP. Sends a few stanzas of a campaign song "the mountain boys" of Bedford County, Va., are singing; predicts that Polk will carry the Electoral College with a total of 171 votes.
9 Oct	From Robert Armstrong. ALS. DLC–JKP. Relates that he has sent Polk's letter to Armstrong of October 7, 1844, and Aaron Wagar's letter to Polk of September 12, 1844, to Jean Baptiste Plauché to be used in New Orleans should Wagar's charges be made public there; discusses campaign appointments in Middle Tennessee.
9 Oct	From William Bobbitt. ALS. DLC–JKP. Reports that $250 of Polk's money is now available at Coffeeville, Miss., and that the balance will be ready by the first of next week.
9 Oct	*From George M. Dallas.*
9 Oct	From Moses Dawson. ALS. DLC–JKP. Takes pleasure in reporting that in Ohio's state elections the Democrats have carried Cincinnati by a majority of two thousand votes.

9 Oct — From David T. Disney. ALS. DLC–JKP. Thinks that Ohio is safe for the Democrats, who have gained a majority of eighteen hundred votes in Hamilton County.

9 Oct — From B. Dwinell. ALS. DLC–JKP. Explains that the Whig arrangement with the Native Americans has resulted in a swing of some six thousand votes against the Democracy of Pennsylvania.

9 Oct — From James H. Ewing. ALS. DLC–JKP. Relates that Polk's political friends have achieved a "splendid victory" in Cincinnati and Hamilton County; notes that "a gang of Whig bully's and loafers led on by a few desperate *Whig nativists*" drove off a large number of German voters from the polls in the ninth ward.

9 Oct — From Albert Gallup.

9 Oct — From H. L. Jeffers. ALS. DLC–JKP. Inquires of Polk's views on slavery and asks that same be sent to him in writing (at Nashville, Ohio).

9 Oct — To Cave Johnson.

9 Oct — From John K. Kane. ALS. DLC–JKP. States that the Democrats are "awfully whipped" in Philadelphia and surrounding counties "by a combination of nativism & Whiggery" operating in their state elections.

9 Oct — From J. G. M. Ramsey.

9 Oct — From Joel B. Sutherland. ALS. DLC–JKP. Indicates that the Democrats have lost their hold on the Southwark and Kensington districts of Philadelphia County, Penn.; maintains that the "late disturbances" in those districts have aided the Nativists in winning control over them.

9 Oct — From Hendrick B. Wright. ALS. DLC–JKP. States that the election returns in Northern Pennsylvania are "truly cheering" and that if Democrats in other parts of the state do as well, they will carry the gubernatorial election by twenty thousand votes.

10 Oct — From Robert Armstrong. ALS. DLC–JKP. Learns from Moses Dawson, James G. Read, and others that Maryland has voted Democratic in state elections.

10 Oct — From George M. Dallas.

10 Oct — From David T. Disney. ALS. DLC–JKP. Returns from fifteen counties indicate that the Ohio governor's race is "extremely close"; still adheres to his earlier prediction of a Democratic victory in Ohio's state elections.

10 Oct — From Powhatan Ellis. ALS. DLC–JKP. Reports on Democratic meetings held in Ripley, Tenn., and Jackson, Miss.

10 Oct — From William Emmons. ALS. DLC–JKP. Asserts that the coalition of Whigs and Native Americans is the work of Anglophiles and that "this last movement of the British party in this Country will tend to rouse up every true friend to

Republican Liberty through out the land."

10 Oct — From William Fitzgerald. ALS. DLC–JKP. Advises that he has relieved A. O. P. Nicholson of his pending engagements in the Western District, excepting that of the Paris meeting on October 21st; observes this arrangement will free Nicholson to go where there is greater need, for John Bell is making no gains on his present tour.

10 Oct — From Cave Johnson. ALS. DLC–JKP. Fears that he cannot fill his appointments of October 21st and following, as he expects an addition to his family on October 25th; recommends that A. O. P. Nicholson substitute for his engagements.

10 Oct — From Chauncey P. E. Johnson. ALS. DLC–JKP. Solicits appointment to the U.S. Military Academy at West Point.

10 Oct — From Daniel Newnan. ALS. DLC–JKP. Projects that the Democratic majority in Georgia's state election will be some 1,262 votes over that of the previous year; bases his estimate on returns from nine counties.

10 Oct — From E. Rucker et al. LS. DLC–JKP. Invite Polk to attend a mass meeting of Democrats from Wilson and surrounding counties on October 20th at Lebanon, Tenn.

10 Oct — From Richard H. Stanton. ALS. DLC–JKP. Communicates Ohio state election returns received to date in Maysville, Ky.; notes that the Quakers have voted for Mordecai Bartley for governor.

10 Oct — From Vernon K. Stevenson. ALS. DLC–JKP. Encloses five one hundred dollar bills of the Union Bank of Tennessee; explains that John Catron could not attend to Polk's loan request personally and asked that he forward Polk the advance.

10 Oct — From Joel B. Sutherland. ALS. DLC–JKP. Estimates on the basis of partial returns that Pennsylvania Democrats have elected Francis R. Shunk their next governor by a margin of some five to eight thousand votes; adds that New Jersey has gone Whig in the state elections.

10 Oct — From C. P. Young. ALS. DLC–JKP. Reviews Polk's election prospects in Louisiana, Kentucky, and Mississippi.

11 Oct — From Richard Brodhead. ALS. DLC–JKP. Reports that in the Pennsylvania state elections the Democrats have carried his congressional district by more than the three thousand votes that he promised to Aaron V. Brown at the close of the last session of Congress.

11 Oct — From George M. Dallas. ALS. DLC–JKP. Analyzes Pennsylvania state election returns and concludes that Francis R. Shunk has been elected governor by some five thousand votes; estimates that Polk's majority in the presidential voting should be double that number; adds that Charles J. In-

	gersoll has been returned to the U.S. House by a narrow majority.
11 Oct	From J. George Harris. ALS. DLC–JKP. Thinks that James Carroll may yet have won the Maryland gubernatorial election, despite unfavorable reports from Whig newspapers in Louisville and Baltimore.
11 Oct	From David Hubbard. ALS. DLC–JKP. Relates that Georgia Democrats reportedly have won five and probably six of that state's congressional elections.
11 Oct	From John K. Kane. ALS. DLC–JKP. Calculates that Francis R. Shunk's majority cannot be less than thirty-five hundred votes; asserts that "the Anti-Catholic libels have had effect enough to place Mr. Shunk considerably below the County tickets almost every where."
11 Oct	*From Francis W. Pickens.*
11 Oct	From William H. Stiles. ALS. DLC–JKP. Takes pleasure in reporting the Democratic victory in Georgia's state elections; expects the majority to run between three and five thousand votes.
11 Oct	From Daniel Sturgeon. ALS. DLC–JKP. Regrets that Democratic majorities in Pennsylvania's state election were not larger; maintains that a "nefarious coalition" between Native Americans and Whigs led to opposition gains, but only in the City and County of Philadelphia.
12 Oct	*From Alfred Balch.*
12 Oct	From Joel Branham. ALS. DLC–JKP. States that Georgia Democrats have elected four candidates to the U.S. House; notes that the Whigs had gerrymandered the state with a view of limiting the Democrats to but two seats; adds that the popular vote gave the Democracy a margin of about three thousand votes.
12 Oct	*From David T. Disney.*
12 Oct	From Edward Harden. ALS. DLC–JKP. Estimates that Georgia Democrats have carried the state elections by three thousand votes; attributes Whig victories in four congressional races to gerrymandering.
12 Oct	*From Samuel H. Laughlin.*
[12 Oct 1844]	*From Jesse Miller.*
12 Oct	From B. E. Patrick. ALS. DLC–JKP. Inquires of Polk's views on the protective tariff issue.
12 Oct	From William H. Polk. ALS. DLC–JKP. Relates that in addition to "the news contained, in the letter of Dawson to you," friends in Nashville have received confirmation from the Whig *Louisville Journal* that Ohio is going Democrat; observes that he has never before seen such a joyous celebration as that in Nashville, where the city is "in a blaze—Torches, Transparences, and every kind of *fire light* that

	can be conceived."
12 Oct	From James M. Porter. ALS. DLC–JKP. Acknowledges receipt of the Nashville *Vindication* pamphlet; maintains that the Whig slanders against Polk's grandfather "has signally recoiled upon them"; states that Francis R. Shunk's margin of victory in the Pennsylvania gubernatorial election would have been five thousand greater had he not written "a very inconsiderate letter" in answer to Whig charges that he was sympathetic to the Roman Catholic Church's opposition to the use of the Bible in the common schools.
13 Oct	From Jonas J. Bell. ALS. DLC–JKP. Promises to forward the latest news received in Tuscumbia, Ala., which is Polk's most convenient point from which to receive the earliest informations from the eastern seaboard; explains that Tuscumbia's position on "the great Central Mail Route" from Charleston, S.C., to Memphis, Tenn., has placed it within seven days of New York City; reports on Georgia's state elections; asks to be remembered to Sarah C. Polk, whom he knew when he clerked for her father, Joel Childress.
13 Oct	From John C. Edwards. ALS. DLC–JKP. Discusses Missouri state politics and Thomas H. Benton's prospects for reelection to the U.S. Senate.
13 Oct	*From James Hamilton, Jr.*
13 Oct	*From John K. Kane.*
13 Oct	From James H. Thomas. ALS. DLC–JKP. Predicts that Tennessee's Western District will give Polk more support than presently calculated; lists his appointments in the District from October 21st through November 1st.
13 Oct	From Henderson K. Yoakum. ALS. DLC–JKP. Reports that Democrats in Cannon, Warren, and DeKalb counties of Tennessee are very enthusiastic; notes that Democrats in Smith County are less active.
14 Oct	From Robert Armstrong. ALS. DLC–JKP. Details distribution of campaign literature; complains that Robert J. Walker's sheet, "The South In Danger," may have done injury in Pennsylvania and New York.
14 Oct	From John B. Butler. ALS. DLC–JKP. Congratulates Polk on the Democratic victory in Pennsylvania's recent state elections.
14 Oct	From John P. Chester. ALS. DLC–JKP. Relates that Andrew Johnson divided time with Washington Barrow at a Whig meeting this date at Jonesboro, Tenn.; asserts that "there never was a Coon so completely skinned at any time or place."
14 Oct	*To Cave Johnson.*
14 Oct	*To Cave Johnson.*
14 Oct	From Seaborn Jones. ALS. DLC–JKP. Encloses a clipping

	from the Columbus *Times* detailing results in the recent Georgia state elections; predicts that Georgia will return to the Democrat column in November.
14 Oct	*From John K. Kane.*
14 Oct	From Micajah G. Lewis. ALS. DLC–JKP. Gives latest election returns from Ohio and Georgia as supplied by the post office in Nashville; advises that Alexander Jones of New York will call upon Polk bearing a letter from Robert W. Powell.
14 Oct	From John McKeon. ALS. DLC–JKP. Explains that the Whig victory in Ohio's gubernatorial election suggests that the abolitionists voted for the Whig candidate, Mordecai Bartley; predicts that if the abolitionists vote for James G. Birney in November, Polk will carry Ohio.
14 Oct	From George W. Mayo. ALS. DLC–JKP. Believes that Clay's majority in East Tennessee will not be much greater than a thousand votes; states that returns in Georgia's state elections are most encouraging.
14 Oct	From Robert W. Powell. ALS. DLC–JKP. Introduces Alexander Jones, a physician from New York.
14 Oct	*From J. G. M. Ramsey.*
14 Oct	*From Francis R. Shunk.*
14 Oct	From James H. Thomas. ALS. DLC–JKP. Urges that his speaking schedule in Perry and Hickman counties be revised; states that another engagement at Palestine, Tenn., is useless.
14 Oct	From Joel Turrill. ALS. DLC–JKP. Praises the *Vindication* pamphlet recently received from Columbia, Tenn.; expects that if Democrats succeed in the current struggle, the Whigs will not mount another such campaign in the next ten or fifteen years.
14 Oct	From David D. Wagener. ALS. DLC–JKP. Maintains that the recent state elections in Pennsylvania may be considered as a fair test of the forthcoming presidential vote; expects that Polk will do at least as well as Shunk did in the Pennsylvania gubernatorial election.
14 Oct	*From Samuel P. Walker.*
14 Oct	From Hampton C. Williams. ALS. DLC–JKP. Observes that in New York the Democrats must oppose all of the extremist parties and notes that Horace Greeley is courting the Irish vote while other Whigs are recruiting the Native Americans.
14 Oct	From William T. Willis. ALS. DLC–JKP. Reviews vote returns from state elections in Pennsylvania, Ohio, New Jersey, Maryland, and Delaware; makes no promise of carrying Kentucky; but claims that they at least deserve to do so.
15 Oct	*From Robert Armstrong.*

15 Oct — From Charles G. Atherton. ALS. DLC–JKP. Reports that in Maine the Whigs have not campaigned much since their defeat in the recent state elections.

15 Oct — To Clement C. Clay.

15 Oct — To J. George Harris.

15 Oct — From Charles J. Ingersoll. ALS. DLC–JKP. Encloses a printed letter "To the Friends of American Industry" signed by nineteen Democratic leaders in Pennsylvania under date of October 14th; explains that he prepared this publication from material sent by Polk on October 2nd and 4th; thinks that distribution of the publication in the iron producing counties will enhance Polk's vote in the coming election.

15 Oct — From William M. Lowry. ALS. DLC–JKP. Recommends that Polk avoid Henry Clay's mistake of writing public position letters; maintains that East Tennessee Democrats have fought their best political campaign in years.

15 Oct — From John McKeon. ALS. DLC–JKP. Worries that New York will follow Pennsylvania in forming a Whig-Native American arrangement; rejects notion that the "democratic natives" will vote for Clay; indicates that he will hasten home from Cincinnati to New York City.

15 Oct — To A. O. P. Nicholson.

15 Oct — From Job Pierson.

15 Oct — From J. G. M. Ramsey. ALS. DLC–JKP. Reviews in detail East Tennessee campaign arrangements, including speaking engagements, newspaper publications, and distribution of printed election tickets.

15 Oct — To Richard H. Stanton.

16 Oct — To Thomas H. Bradley. ALS. NcU. States that he has sent William G. Childress a letter this date addressed to Franklin, Tenn.; requests that Bradley take the letter out of the post office and send it to Childress this evening.

16 Oct — From George M. Dallas.

16 Oct — From N. Holland. ALS. DLC–JKP. Relates political findings gathered while en route home through Giles and McNairy counties to Holly Springs, Miss.

16 Oct — From George W. Owens. ALS. DLC–JKP. Concludes that Polk will carry Georgia but may lose Tennessee; comes to such determinations on the basis of his travels through Tennessee and north Georgia to Savannah.

16 Oct — From A. Williams. ALS. DLC–JKP. Solicits post of surveyor general of Arkansas.

16 Oct — From Fernando Wood. ALS. DLC–JKP. Asserts that New York is as safe for Polk as Alabama; bases his estimates on district canvasses in every county; praises Polk for making no mistakes in the campaign; maintains that Polk is the only electable public figure in the country "whose public life

	is irreproachable and against whom inconsistencies could not have been charged."
17 Oct	From Robert Armstrong. ALS. DLC–JKP. Reviews speaking appointments in Middle Tennessee and notes that local Whigs are rejoicing at the news of their carrying Philadelphia in Pennsylvania's state elections.
17 Oct	From Jonas J. Bell. ALS. DLC–JKP. Communicates latest state election reports from Pennsylvania, New Jersey, and Georgia, as received to date in Tuscumbia, Ala.
17 Oct	*From William C. Bouck.*
17 Oct	From David T. Disney. ALS. DLC–JKP. Advises that Ohio is "yet a battle field"; but puts the state in the doubtful column because of Whig successes in their recent state elections.
17 Oct	From Robert P. Flenniken. ALS. DLC–JKP. Calculates that in the Pennsylvania state election the coalition between Whigs and Native Americans reduced the Democratic majority by at least seven thousand votes; maintains that the coalition systematically lied about Shunk being a Roman Catholic and thus an enemy of the Protestant religion.
17 Oct	From Julian Frazier. ALS. DLC–JKP. Reports that the Democrats have "made a clean sweep of new-born Whiggery" in the western counties of Arkansas; notes that the Whigs have not elected a single member to the legislature from that section of the state.
17 Oct	From James K. Gibson. Encloses an account of a Whig meeting in Abingdon, Va.; comments that the opposition rally was "a complete failure"; states that he is related on his mother's side to Polk's family.
17 Oct	*From J. George Harris.*
17 Oct	*To John K. Kane.*
17 Oct	From William M. Lowry. ALS. DLC–JKP. Encloses a report from Augusta telling of Democratic successes in Georgia's recent state elections.
17 Oct	*From Gansevoort Melville.*
17 Oct	From J. G. M. Ramsey. ALS. DLC–JKP. Reviews Democratic campaign plans in East Tennessee.
17 Oct	*From William Taylor.*
18 Oct	*To William Allen.*
18 Oct	From Robert Armstrong. ALS. DLC–JKP. Reviews state elections in Pennsylvania, New Jersey, and Georgia; thinks that the Democracy has done well in state elections and may do better in November in New Jersey and Ohio.
18 Oct	From Simon Cameron. ALS. DLC–JKP. Assures Polk that he will carry Pennsylvania; offers his calculations of the electoral vote.
18 Oct	From Robert M. Echols. ALS. DLC–JKP. Anticipates that

	Polk will carry Georgia by five thousand votes; claims that the Whigs had gerrymandered the state so as to carry six of the eight congressional districts; thinks that the Democracy has won five seats in the late election.
18 Oct	From George S. Houston. ALS. DLC–JKP. Agrees to speak at Lawrenceburg on October 25th and then elsewhere in Tennessee for ten days or so; regrets that he could not return to the Western District as requested; explains that he was ill for ten days following his last tour of service there.
18 Oct	From Wilson C. Newsum. ALS. DLC–JKP. Wishes Polk well in the coming election; projects that Polk's majority in Mississippi will be from four to six thousand votes.
18 Oct	From Thomas A. Norment. ALS. DLC–JKP. Recalls his former acquaintanceship with Polk's brother, Marshall; regrets that Thomas G. Polk has retained his Whig affiliation and has supported Henry Clay in the presidential contest.
18 Oct	From Samuel T. Wilson. ALS. DLC–JKP. Notifies Polk that he has been elected to honorary membership in the Philalethic Society of Greensburg, Ky.
19 Oct	From Benjamin H. Brewster. ALS. DLC–JKP. Attributes the poor showing of the Democrats in Philadelphia to the Whig alliance with the Native Americans; asserts that the leaders of the Native American party are "corrupt vicious men who have heretofore been Whigs" and that their followers are "animated with a spirit of social or rather political and religious intolerance, that knows no bounds, and will stay at nothing to secure success."
19 Oct	From Charles C. Cargill. ALS. DLC–JKP. Anticipates visiting Polk in Columbia in November and discussing "some scientific discoveries in the manufacturing of crude Iron"; congratulates Polk on his "brightening prospects" in Georgia.
19 Oct	From Charles A. Frensley. ALS. DLC–JKP. Solicits Polk's assistance in securing the release of his brother, William H. Frensley, from Perote Castle in Mexico; reminds Polk of their associations in Rutherford County prior to his brother's joining the Mier Expedition in 1842; notes that his brother's plight is very desperate, as revealed in a letter from him written on August 25th.
19 Oct	*From Edwin A. Keeble.*
19 Oct	From John M. McCalla. ALS. DLC–JKP. Reports that Kentucky Whigs have renewed their expectations of Henry Clay's election; claims that their hopes have been raised by an influx of new money from London.
[19 Oct 1844]	From Edwin F. Polk. ALS. DLC–JKP. Reviews controversies arising from George Alexander's testimony about Ezekiel Polk's participation in the Revolutionary War; states that

	he has survey returns from every civil district in the county and that Hardeman will give a majority of 450 votes in Polk's favor.
19 Oct	From James Webster. ALS. DLC–JKP. Sends estimates of the New York vote in each congressional district; explains that the numbers are based upon "a careful survey of every county in the State, giving the doubtful on the poll list to the Whigs"; projects a Polk victory of from five to seven thousand votes.
[20 Oct 1844]	From Robert Armstrong. ALS. DLC–JKP. Urges Polk to come to Nashville on the Tuesday stage.
20 Oct	From John A. Donohoo. ALS. DLC–JKP. Interprets the results of the recent state elections as evidence that Polk will win the presidential election.
20 Oct	From Arnold S. Harris. ALS. DLC–JKP. Calculates that the Whig combination with Native Americans in Philadelphia was only for the state election; notes that the Whigs acted "in bad faith towards their allies by electing their own ticket in the city and have besides thrown off *their own friends* in the county producing much dissatisfaction both among Whigs and Natives."
20 Oct	From J. B. Thomas. ALS. DLC–JKP. Attributes David Tod's defeat in the Ohio gubernatorial election to Democratic divisions in Stark and Wayne counties.
20 Oct	*From Isaac Toucey.*
20 Oct	*From Archibald Yell.*
21 Oct	From Robert Armstrong. ALS. DLC–JKP. Sends Polk a sack of miscellaneous campaign literature purchased from the *Nashville Union* office.
21 Oct	*From Alfred Balch.*
21 Oct	*From David Craighead.*
21 Oct	*To George M. Dallas.*
21 Oct	From John I. DeGraff. ALS. DLC–JKP. Reports that Polk's prospects in New York look "auspicious" except in the City of New York, where the Whigs and Native Americans are likely to play the same game as that in Philadelphia; notes that the opposition is as vigorous as in 1840 but that the Democrats are "much more active than they were then."
21 Oct	*From David T. Disney.*
21 Oct	From Wilson Lumpkin. ALS. DLC–JKP. Assures Polk that he may consider the favorable results in the Georgia state elections to be "a test vote of the Presidential election."
21 Oct	From Sherman Page. ALS. DLC–JKP. Reports "that the interior of New York was never fighting more manfully in the cause of Democracy than at this time"; thinks that the state is safe regardless of what the Native Americans do in New York City.

21 Oct	From Robert F. Stockton. Asserts that they have had "a bitter conflict" in New Jersey's recent state elections and that the Democrats lost through "the *treachery* of some of *our own men.*"
22 Oct	From Aaron V. Brown. ALS. DLC–JKP. Reports on his numerous speaking engagements in East Tennessee.
22 Oct	From Clement C. Clay, Jr. ALS. DLC–JKP. Answers for his father, Clement C. Clay, Sr., Polk's letter of October 21st; states that his father has already left for Tennessee and will attend the Lawrenceburg meeting of October 25th, as requested by Polk.
22 Oct	*From William E. Cramer.*
22 Oct	From William Fitzgerald. ALS. DLC–JKP. Suggests that on the first Monday in November every county in Tennessee will hold a meeting of their county court and that the Democrats should have two speakers assigned to meet the people at every county seat in the state on court day.
22 Oct	*From J. G. M. Ramsey.*
22 Oct	From James Ross Snowden. ALS. DLC–JKP. Denounces Pennsylvania's Native Americans for their "narrow minded and illiberal views"; expresses pride in the fact that there "is nothing congenial between them and Democracy."
22 Oct	*To Aaron Vanderpoel.*
23 Oct	From John Adams. ALS. DLC–JKP. Expects Polk to carry New York state, even if the Natives and abolitionists vote with the opposition.
23 Oct	From Elias J. Armstrong. ALS. DLC–JKP. Advises that he leaves Pleasant Exchange for the South tomorrow.
23 Oct	*From Andrew Beaumont.*
23 Oct	*From John Carr.*
23 Oct	From John W. Childress. ALS. DLC–JKP. Relates that in Rutherford County, Tenn., the Democrats are "straining every nerve," sparing "neither money nor labor,"and holding "large night meetings in various parts of the county 2 or 3 times a week where there is speaking, singing, exhibition of lights &c."
23 Oct	From Clement C. Clay and George S. Houston. L, fragment. DLC–JKP. Describe mass meetings at Winchester and Lynchburg, Tenn.
23 Oct	From James Conner. LS. DLC–JKP. Encloses projected majority in the presidential contest for each county in New York; includes name and place of each county contact solicited for a vote estimate.
23 Oct.	From David Craighead. AL. DLC–JKP. Relates accounts of campaign appointments in Jackson, Brownsville, Porterville, Raleigh, and Memphis.
23 Oct	From Wallace Estill. ALS. DLC–JKP. Expects that Polk will

	carry Franklin County, Tenn.; maintains that "if the other Counties in the state only do half as well, we shall give Federalism a death blow in Tennessee."
23 Oct	From Thomas L. Hamer. ALS. DLC–JKP. Anticipates victories for Polk in Ohio and Indiana.
23 Oct	From Micajah G. Lewis. ALS. DLC–JKP. Hastens to tell Polk that "all things are right" in Perry and surrounding counties.
23 Oct	*From John McKeon.*
23 Oct	From Thomas Martin. ALS. DLC–JKP. Thinks that Clement C. Clay gave a "well tempered and argumentative" address at yesterday's meeting in Pulaski; suspects that the speech made few converts since "arguments, truth, and facts are of but little consequence, in the present turgid state of the public mind."
23 Oct	From Arnold Plumer. ALS. DLC–JKP. Argues that Francis R. Shunk would have won a larger majority in the Pennsylvania gubernatorial election had he not published letters on the Bible's use in the schools; adds that in western Pennsylvania many farmers did not vote because the weather was "remarkably favourable" for gathering their crops.
24 Oct	From John Blair. ALS. DLC–JKP. Assures Polk that all precautionary measures have been taken to prevent pipelaying in the East Tennessee border counties; thinks that if North Carolina Democrats had worked half as hard as those in Tennessee, Carolina would be redeemed; places his hopes for victory in Tennessee on getting every Democrat to vote, not on converting Whigs, for Tennesseans are "harder to move than any other people."
24 Oct	From Catherine Crockett. ALS. DLC–JKP. Fears that Polk "will think it extremely indelicate for a young lady to write to a gentleman with whom she is not personally acquainted"; explains that she takes this liberty to secure the vote of a Whig gentleman who promised to vote Democratic if she would dare to write Polk a letter such as this.
24 Oct	From J. George Harris. ALS. DLC–JKP. Advises that Alexander Duncan arrived in Nashville about an hour after Polk's departure; says that Duncan will join Polk tomorrow morning at the residence of William G. Childress in Williamson County.
24 Oct	*From John K. Kane.*
24 Oct	From George M. Martin. ALS. DLC–JKP. Reports on a brief visit to Polk's plantation in Mississippi; relates that all are well and that the crop may yield 130 or 140 bales of cotton.
24 Oct	From J. G. M. Ramsey. ALS. DLC–JKP. Discusses appointments announced for James W. McClung and Aaron V. Brown in East Tennessee.

24 Oct	From Charles P. Young. ALS. DLC–JKP. Estimates that the Whig majority in New Orleans will not exceed four hundred and that Louisiana is safe; mentions that he is on his way to the residence of Alfred M. Young, where he votes.
25 Oct	From Anonymous. C, signed "Simon Snooks." DLC–JKP. Announces the last Whig rally for Henry Clay in Philadelphia.
25 Oct	From Tippeo Brownlow. ALS. DLC–JKP. Solicits a clerkship in the offices of the general government; names several prominent North Carolinians as references.
25 Oct	From Jeptha Fowlkes. ALS. DLC–JKP. Requests that Polk support his application to be navy agent at Memphis, Tenn.
25 Oct	From Thomas Martin. ALS. DLC–JKP. Encloses a communication sent to Polk under cover addressed to Aaron V. Brown, who is away from home. (Enclosure not identified.)
25 Oct	From David Morison. ALS. DLC–JKP. Applies for superintendency of buildings to be built at the Memphis navy yard.
26 Oct	*From John T. Hudson.*
26 Oct	From Arthur T. Isom. ALS. DLC–JKP. Projects that Polk will carry Mississippi by four thousand votes; expects that Hinds County, formerly a "hot bed of whiggery," will reduce its Whig majority from eight hundred to two thousand votes.
26 Oct	From Leonard Jones. ALS. DLC–JKP. Urges Polk to fast and pray until the election results are known.
26 Oct	From John K. Kane. ALS. DLC–JKP. Discusses election prospects in Pennsylvania and New York; claims that Whig campaign leaders work for hire, as "they dress better, make parade of more money, live more recklessly, and give us everything but the absolute proof that they are bought."
26 Oct	*From Gansevoort Melville.*
[26 Oct 1844]	From Gideon J. Pillow. ALS. DLC–JKP. Suggests that he host the visit with "Gov Clay, Genl Houston & Col Terry"; thinks that their coming into town to Polk's residence would attract too much attention. (Formerly calendared under date of August 10, 1839.)
26 Oct	From Edwin F. Polk. ALS. DLC–JKP. Expects to send a check in the amount of $160 in the next three days; explains that he, Charles Perry Polk, and William H. Wood are providing the money, not having heard from their brother, William Wilson Polk.
26 Oct	*From Collin S. Tarpley.*
26 Oct	From Hopkins L. Turney. ALS. DLC–JKP. Agrees to continue campaigning through the final week before the election, noting that he has already devoted the whole of his summer to the cause.

26 Oct	*To Fernando Wood.*
27 Oct	From Robert Armstrong. ALS. DLC–JKP. Urges publication, without attribution, of an extract from Dallas' letter; thinks that the piece would help carry North Carolina, Indiana, Georgia, and Louisiana.
27 Oct	*From J. George Harris.*
27 Oct	From Alfred M. Young. ALS. DLC–JKP. States that he returned to Madison Parish, La., from New York just two weeks previously and that a straw pool of passengers on board the lake steamer *Nile* gave Polk 315 votes to Clay's 191.
[28 Oct 1844]	From Aaron V. Brown. ALS. DLC–JKP. Reports that he arrived home last night; notes that he spoke to large crowds on his recent campaign tour, and that gains in East Tennessee will run upward of fifteen hundred votes; adds that he wishes to come to Columbia the day following the election.
28 Oct	*From Samuel P. Caldwell.*
28 Oct	From H.L. Clay. ALS. DLC–JKP. Solicits Polk's voting record on pensions for soldiers as well as officers of the Revolutionary War; thinks that the Democratic majority in the Huntsville area of Alabama will be increased by assurances of Polk's past support for that class of pensioners.
28 Oct	*From David T. Disney.*
28 Oct	*From J. George Harris.*
28 Oct	*From Samuel H. Laughlin.*
28 Oct	From Samuel Medary. ALS. DLC–JKP. Assures Polk that Ohio Democrats are working hard and still hopeful of carrying the state.
28 Oct	*From J. G. M. Ramsey.*
28 Oct	From William Tyack. ALS. DLC–JKP. Reports that the Native Americans and Whigs in New York City say they will run separate tickets; thinks that if they do, the Democrats will have a large majority; discounts the credibility of both Natives and Whigs.
29 Oct	*From Julius W. Blackwell.*
29 Oct	*To Clement C. Clay.*
29 Oct	*From John McKeon.*
29 Oct	From James Page. ALS. DLC–JKP. Observes that the combination of Whigs and Nativists in Pennsylvania had reduced the Democratic majority in their recent gubernatorial election; expects that the same coalition will produce a majority of four thousand for Henry Clay in Philadelphia County and City.
29 Oct	From Zadock Pratt. ALS. DLC–JKP. Reports that Democrats in Prattsville and Albany, N.Y., are both united and confident about carrying the state for Polk.

29 Oct	*From Sylvester S. Southworth.*
29 Oct	From William B. Whitecar. ALS. DLC–JKP. Denounces the recent bargain between the Philadelphia Whigs and Nativists, the terms of which included "*a free pardon*" for their friends who had been or might be convicted "for participating in the late riots."
30 Oct	From Joseph B. Anthony. ALS. DLC–JKP. States that in the rural part of Pennsylvania neither the abolitionists nor the Nativists are very numerous.
30 Oct	From Robert Armstrong. ALS. DLC–JKP. Recounts special arrangements put in place to have the election news from southern Ohio delivered in Nashville by Monday night and distributed in Middle Tennessee early morning of the next day.
30 Oct	From David B. Grant. ALS. DLC–JKP. Requests that Polk send the Tennessee election returns to him in Otsego County, N.Y.
30 Oct	*To Cave Johnson.*
30 Oct	From Alexander Jones. ALS. DLC–JKP. Calculates election prospects in states through which he passed recently in traveling from Indiana to New York; notes that in New York City the Whigs have "raised a hue and cry against the Catholics," have alleged that the Democrats are tied to "that sect in the local public school question," and so have tried to gain "as many votes from the Protestant churches as possible."
30 Oct	*From Kenedy Lonergan.*
31 Oct	From William J. Alexander. ALS. DLC–JKP. Writes on behalf of Sarah F. Davidson of Mecklenburg County, N.C.; explains that she wishes information about lands sold by Polk as agent for her father, William Davidson.
31 Oct	From Robert Armstrong. ALS. DLC–JKP. Reviews recent meetings in Middle Tennessee; predicts success both in Tennessee and the Union.
31 Oct	From Henry L. Ellsworth. ALS. DLC–JKP. Extols the unity that Polk's nomination has brought to the party; thinks that Ohio, North Carolina, Maryland, Delaware, and New Jersey are doubtful.
31 Oct	From William Emmons. ALS. DLC–JKP. Asserts that the Whigs have circulated false tickets in "Old Democratic Berks County"; interprets such frauds as a sign of Whig desperation in Pennsylvania.
31 Oct	From John D. Goss. ALS. DLC–JKP. Denounces John Catron as a dishonest and "impure" judge.
31 Oct	*To James Hamilton, Jr.*
31 Oct	From Andrew Jackson. AN. DLC–JKP. Encloses mail under his cover and frank.

31 Oct	From John K. Kane. ALS. DLC–JKP. Assures Polk that Pennsylvania is safe; relates that news from New York is "most cheering."
31 Oct	From William H. Wood. ALS. DLC–JKP. Encloses check for $120 to pay for printing the pamphlet vindicating the honor of Ezekiel Polk; explains that the money is provided equally by himself, Charles Perry Polk, and John H. Bills.
31 Oct	*From Silas Wright, Jr.*
[Nov 1844]	From Andrew Jackson. ALS. DLC–JKP. Forwards Henry Horn's letter of October 31, 1844.
[Nov 1844]	From Thomas M. Jones. ALS. DLC–JKP. Predicts that the Democrats will carry Giles County, Tenn., by a margin of seventy-five or eighty votes.
1 Nov	From Robert Armstrong. ALS. DLC–JKP. Predicts a tremendous majority in New York and so discounts effects of a Whig-Native American combination; encloses a letter from Samuel Medary, who sends news about the election in Ohio.
1 Nov	From A. Billings. ALS. DLC–JKP. Describes the Democratic mass meeting held this day in Gallatin, Tenn.; states that he is a member of Nashville's Hickory Cavalry, which has been out five days attending earlier meetings in Lebanon and Hartsville.
1 Nov	*From George M. Dallas.*
1 Nov	From Lewis Eaton. ALS. DLC–JKP. Predicts that the Democrats will carry New York for Polk by over eight thousand votes; adds that Native Americans will elect their candidates in legislative and congressional races in New York City.
1 Nov	From A. C. Gillespie. ALS. DLC–JKP. Expresses confidence that Polk will carry Mississippi by a six to eight thousand vote majority; anticipates that Madison County, Miss., will increase its Democratic majority.
1 Nov	From Edward B. Hubley. ALS. DLC–JKP. Gives the latest election returns from Schuylkill County, Penn.; notes that although the coal districts give increased majorities for Clay, the country districts strongly support the Polk and Dallas ticket.
1 Nov	From John K. Kane. ALS. DLC–JKP. Predicts that the Democrats will reduce the Whig majority in Philadelphia by more than two thousand votes.
1 Nov	*From John W. P. McGimsey.*
1 Nov	*From Gansevoort Melville.*
2 Nov	*From Alexander Best.*
2 Nov	From James Buchanan. ALS. DLC–JKP. Estimates on the basis of partial returns that Polk has carried Pennsylvania.
2 Nov	From Moses W. Coolbaugh. ALS. DLC–JKP. Gives the election return for Monroe County, Penn.

2 Nov — From George M. Dallas. ALS. DLC–JKP. Communicates the latest county election returns from Pennsylvania.

2 Nov — From David T. Disney. ALS. DLC–JKP. Believes that the Democrats have lost Ohio; notes that the abolitionists have abandoned the Liberty party and have voted for Clay.

2 Nov — From Daniel Gold. ALS. DLC–JKP. Predicts that Polk will carry New York and Pennsylvania; states that his father-in-law, Amos Kendall, has supported Polk's candidacy with "hearty good will."

2 Nov — From Henry Horn. ALS. DLC–JKP. Assures Polk that he has carried Pennsylvania, even though the Whigs have "rung the changes upon the tariff question."

2 Nov — From James Hoyt, Jr. ALS. DLC–JKP. Sends the latest county election returns from Pennsylvania.

2 Nov — *From Cave Johnson.*

2 Nov — *From Alexander Jones.*

2 Nov — From John K. Kane. ALS. DLC–JKP. Congratulates Polk on his victory in Pennsylvania; encloses newspaper accounts of the election returns.

2 Nov — From Joseph P. LeClerc. ALS. DLC–JKP. Sends the latest election returns from Pennsylvania. (Enclosure not found.)

2 Nov — *From John McKeon.*

2 Nov — From Charles McVean. ALS. DLC–JKP. Predicts that Polk will carry New York by a majority of ten thousand.

2 Nov — From Benjamin Patton. ALS. DLC–JKP. Sends county election returns from southwest Pennsylvania; notes that even in this area, the Whigs' "great strong-hold," Clay's majority exceeds Markle's majority only by one hundred votes.

2 Nov — From John L. Rightmyer. ALS. DLC–JKP. Reports that Berks County, Penn., has voted Democratic, as it has for many years past.

2 Nov — *From Sylvester S. Southworth.*

2 Nov — From Joel B. Sutherland. ALS. DLC–JKP. Gives the latest election returns from Pennsylvania; adds that "our glorious news" has been sent to New York by express mail.

3 Nov — From Alvin W. Bills. ALS. DLC–JKP. Predicts "a close *hunt*" in Kentucky and waits in suspense for the election returns from Ohio and Tennessee.

3 Nov — From George W. Bowman. ALS. DLC–JKP. Congratulates Polk on his victory in Pennsylvania.

3 Nov — From D. Casey. ALS. DLC–JKP. Reports on the state of the campaign in western New York and New York City; predicts that the Democrats will carry the state.

3 Nov — From George M. Dallas. ALS. DLC–JKP. States that the Pennsylvania Whigs "have hauled down their flags and given up the contest"; estimates that the Democrats will carry the state by a majority of seven thousand.

3 Nov *From David T. Disney.*

3 Nov From Josephus C. Guild. ALS. DLC–JKP. Predicts that Polk will carry Tennessee; notes that over the last forty days Democratic support has grown in numbers and enthusiasm.

3 Nov From J. B. Guthrie. ALS. DLC–JKP. Sends election returns from the counties of western Pennsylvania; assures Polk that he has carried Pennsylvania.

3 Nov *From John P. Heiss.*

3 Nov From Marshall S. Howe. ALS. DLC–JKP. Recommends John Fairfield for the office of secretary of war.

3 Nov From Edward B. Hubley. ALS. DLC–JKP. Notes that in Schuylkill County, Penn., Polk's majority has exceeded that of Francis R. Shunk.

3 Nov From Harriet A. Johnston. ALS. DLC–JKP. Inquires if Polk has any ancestors named Witherow; states that her maternal great grandfather, John Witherow, had a sister who married a Polk and resided in Pennsylvania.

3 Nov From John K. Kane. ALS. DLC–JKP. Encloses the latest election returns from Pennsylvania. (Enclosure not found.)

3 Nov From James G. Read. ALS. DLC–JKP. Predicts that Polk will receive increased majorities in the northern counties of Indiana and will carry the state.

3 Nov From Sylvester S. Southworth. ALS. DLC–JKP. States that Polk has carried Pennsylvania; assures Polk that he will also carry New York and New Jersey.

3 Nov From Joel B. Sutherland. ALS. DLC–JKP. Reports that in the City and County of Philadelphia the Democrats have reduced the Whig majority by about thirteen hundred votes; believes that the Democrats of the state's interior will increase the gubernatorial majorities of last month.

3 Nov From John Tomlin. ALS. DLC–JKP. Relates that last night the Democrats of Jackson, Tenn., held the last "revelry" and "illumination" of the campaign and that they have done their duty.

3 Nov From William Tyack. ALS. DLC–JKP. Stresses the unanimity and enthusiasm of New York Democrats and predicts that Polk will carry the state by a majority of twenty thousand votes.

4 Nov From John M. Bell. ALS. DLC–JKP. Reports that the Whigs have carried New Orleans by only 402 votes and that Democrats consider Louisiana safe.

4 Nov *From James Buchanan.*

4 Nov From George M. Dallas. ALS. Polk Memorial Association, Columbia, Tenn. States that Polk will carry Pennsylvania by a majority of seventy-five hundred to eight thousand votes.

[4 Nov 1844] From J. George Harris. ALS. DLC–JKP. Notes Democratic gains in Ohio; believes that Polk will carry the state, although Samuel Medary "gives us no encouragement."

4 Nov — From Charles J. Ingersoll. ALS. DLC–JKP. Estimates that Polk has carried Pennsylvania by at least seven thousand votes; argues that Henry Clay received the support of the leaders of the Native American party, but that enough of the followers returned to the Democratic ranks to decrease his expected majority in Philadelphia.

4 Nov — *From Alexander Jones.*

4 Nov — From S. Jones. ALS. DLC–JKP. Sends the latest county election returns from Pennsylvania; predicts that Polk has carried the state.

4 Nov — *From John K. Kane.*

4 Nov — *From John McKeon.*

4 Nov — From Ezekiel P. McNeal. ALS. DLC–JKP. Discusses his unsuccessful efforts to sell Polk's land near Bolivar, Tenn., and offers to loan Polk a thousand dollars; assures Polk that in the Western District "every democrat that can sit up will be hauled to the polls."

4 Nov — *From J. G. M. Ramsey.*

4 Nov — *From John M. Read.*

4 Nov — From Sylvester S. Southworth. ALS. DLC–JKP. Assures Polk that he will carry the state of New York.

4 Nov — *From Joel B. Sutherland.*

4 Nov — From A. H. Waddle. ALS. DLC–JKP. Solicits position as overseer.

4 Nov — From Fernando Wood. ALS. DLC–JKP. Predicts that tomorrow New York will cast its vote for Polk and Dallas.

5 Nov — From Robert Armstrong. ALS. DLC–JKP. Estimates that the Whig majority in Davidson County, Tenn., will be about six hundred; predicts that Polk will carry Tennessee by a majority ranging from fourteen to thirty-two hundred votes.

5 Nov — From John S. Beall. ALS. DLC–JKP. Reports that the Whigs of Murray County, Ga., now know who James K. Polk is; puts Democratic majority for the county at 396.

[5 Nov 1844] — From Aaron V. Brown. ALS. DLC–JKP. Assures Polk that he has carried Giles County, Tenn.

5 Nov — From Jonathan I. Coddington. ALS. DLC–JKP. Gives latest election returns from New York City; states that Polk has carried both the city and the state.

5 Nov — *From David T. Disney.*

5 Nov — From William Emmons. ALS. DLC–JKP. Writes from Philadelphia that Joseph Hall and others have gone to New York to watch the movements of the Whigs and Native Americans at the polls; mentions that a friend has seen a private letter of Henry Clay's in support of nativism.

5 Nov	From Edward Harden. ALS. DLC–JKP. Assures Polk that he will carry Georgia by at least five thousand; reports that John M. Berrien circulated rumors alleging a combination between Polk's friends and northern abolitionists.
5 Nov	From Hugh Hearkins. ALS. DLC–JKP. Places Polk's majority in Hardeman County, Tenn., at not less than four hundred.
[5 Nov 1844]	*From Andrew Jackson.*
[5 Nov 1844]	From William J. Leiper. ALS. DLC–JKP. Reports that the Democrats have carried New York City by two thousand votes and probably have won the state as well.
5 Nov	From Henry A. Lyons. ALS. DLC–JKP. Writes from New Orleans and congratulates Polk on his victory over "Federalism, Nativism, Abolitionism, & Clayism."
5 Nov	From John McKeon. ALS. DLC–JKP. States that a gentleman who has visited most of New York City's wards has told a Tammany Hall meeting that the Democrats have carried the city.
5 Nov	From George M. Martin. ALS. DLC–JKP. Predicts that the freemen of the republic will cast their votes for Polk and Dallas and "the Constitution of our dear & revolutionary fathers."
5 Nov	From Edward K. Miles. ALS. DLC–JKP. Communicates the latest election returns from Maryland; believes that Clay has won the state in yesterday's voting; solicits a government office.
5 Nov	From Elijah F. Purdy. ALS. DLC–JKP. States that the election in New York City is "now quietly going on" and that the Democrat electoral ticket will carry the city by some two or three thousand votes; observes that the state is also safe for Polk and Dallas.
5 Nov	From Wyndham Robertson, Jr. ALS. DLC–JKP. Predicts that Polk has carried Virginia; notes that in New York and Pennsylvania efforts to form alliances between Whigs and abolitionists have failed.
5 Nov	From William P. Rowles. ALS. DLC–JKP. States that Polk has carried Lawrence County, Tenn., after "a most unprecedented scrutiny & challenging" of voters.
5 Nov	From Sylvester S. Southworth. ALS. DLC–JKP. Notes that in New York City the Whigs have supported the Nativists' local and congressional tickets; assures Polk that he will carry the city and the state.
5 Nov	From William G. Stevens. ALS. DLC–JKP. Sends the latest election returns from the "Tenth Legion" of Virginia.
5 Nov	From Fitzgerald Tasistro. ALS. DLC–JKP. Writes from New York to congratulate Polk on his victory in Pennsylvania.
[5 Nov 1844]	From John Tomlin. ALS. DLC–JKP. Sends the latest elec-

	tion returns from Madison County, Tenn.
[5 Nov 1844]	From William Tyack. ALS. DLC–JKP. States that in New York City Polk's majority is about two thousand votes.
5 Nov	From William J. Whitthorne. ALS. DLC–JKP. Relates that Polk has won Bedford County, Tenn., by a majority of seventy-two votes.
5 Nov	*From Fernando Wood.*
6 Nov	From John Adams. ALS. DLC–JKP. Sends latest election returns from Greene and Columbia counties, N.Y.
6 Nov	From Robert Armstrong. ALS. DLC–JKP. Reports that the Whigs have carried Ohio; gives county election returns for Middle Tennessee; believes that Tennessee is redeemed.
[6 Nov 1844]	From John Blair. ALS. DLC–JKP. Sends election returns from Washington, Sullivan, Carter, Greene, and Johnson counties, Tenn.
6 Nov	From Felix Bosworth. LS. DLC–JKP. Congratulates Polk on his victory in Carroll Parish, La.; notes that the Whigs "imported" fifty voters from an adjoining parish.
6 Nov	From William J. Brown. ALS. DLC–JKP. Assures Polk that he will carry Indiana by a majority of about two thousand votes.
6 Nov	From B. W. D. Carty. ALS. DLC–JKP. Sends latest election return from Lincoln County, Tenn.
6 Nov	*From George M. Dallas.*
6 Nov	*To George M. Dallas.*
6 Nov	From John W. Davis. ALS. DLC–JKP. Sends election returns from Sullivan County, Ind.
[6 Nov 1844]	From William L. S. Dearing. ALS. DLC–JKP. Communicates election returns from Warren County, Tenn.
6 Nov	From James A. Deery et al. LS. DLC–JKP. Send county election returns from East Tennessee; note that during the last month the Sullivan County Democracy delivered speeches and formed associations at schoolhouses throughout the county.
6 Nov	*From Andrew J. Donelson.*
[6 Nov 1844]	From Thomas B. Eastland. ALS. DLC–JKP. States that the Whig majority in New Orleans has been reduced to 414 votes and predicts that Polk will carry Louisiana.
6 Nov	From Nicholas Fain. ALS. DLC–JKP. Relates that the Democratic gain in Hawkins County, Tenn., is 49 votes; notes that their majority of 215 votes is some 75 less than expected; explains that they have had "a tremendous struggle against the most desperate and unscrupulous faction that ever existed in any County in the State."
6 Nov	From Albert Gallup. ALS. DLC–JKP. Assures Polk that he has carried New York; notes that certain "enemies within" the New York Democracy voted for the state ticket but re-

	fused to support Polk and Dallas.
6 Nov	From Ransom H. Gillet. ALS. DLC–JKP. Believes that Polk has carried New York by a large majority; mentions the Whigs' use of "fraud & tricks" during the campaign.
6 Nov	From Kemp S. Holland. ALS. DLC–JKP. Predicts that Polk will carry Mississippi by a majority of five to six thousand votes.
6 Nov	*From Alexander Jones.*
6 Nov	From John T. Kiger. ALS. DLC–JKP. Congratulates Polk on his victory in Pennsylvania; notes that the Democrats have carried New York City by a two thousand majority.
6 Nov	From Amos Lane. ALS. DLC–JKP. Notes that the contest in Indiana has been "a hard fight"; claims that the Democrats have carried the state by some 2,329 votes.
6 Nov	From Wilson McCandless. ALS. DLC–JKP. Assures Polk that he has carried Pennsylvania by a majority of seven to ten thousand votes; expresses pleasure that he will be casting an electoral vote for Polk come the first Wednesday in December.
6 Nov	From Abraham McClellan. ALS. DLC–JKP. Sends word that Polk has carried Sullivan County, Tenn., by a majority of 1,183.
6 Nov	*From John McKeon.*
6 Nov	From Augustus Maher. ALS. DLC–JKP. Congratulates Polk on his victory in New York City, which assures his election as president.
6 Nov	From William Moore. ALS. DLC–JKP. Communicates that Lincoln County, Tenn., has given Polk a majority of 1,836 votes, a gain of 211 over the previous year's gubernatorial election.
6 Nov	From John Norvell. ALS. DLC–JKP. Reports that Polk has carried Michigan by a majority of at least three thousand votes.
6 Nov	From George R. Powell. ALS. DLC–JKP. Sends Hawkins County returns showing Polk the victor by a majority of 215 votes; notes that the Whigs have used "all kinds of tricks" and bribery to carry East Tennessee.
6 Nov	*From J. G. M. Ramsey.*
6 Nov	From Henry Simpson. ALS. DLC–JKP. Notes that the express mail brings news of Polk's victory in New York City; encloses a printed list of county election returns from Pennsylvania.
6 Nov	From John Simpson. ALS. DLC–JKP. Forwards by special express at 4 a.m. a slip from the *New York Morning News*. (Enclosure not found.)
6 Nov	From John Simpson. ALS. DLC–JKP. Writes from New Brunswick, N.J., about the election; hopes that the Democ-

	racy has carried the state for Polk and Dallas.
6 Nov	From Sylvester S. Southworth. ALS. DLC–JKP. Predicts that Polk has carried New York by a majority of five to ten thousand votes.
6 Nov	From John A. Stemmler. ALS. DLC–JKP. Introduces the Bavarian consul for New York, George H. Siemon.
6 Nov	*From Joel B. Sutherland.*
6 Nov	*From James D. Wasson.*
6 Nov	From Campbell P. White. ALS. DLC–JKP. Assures Polk that the Democracy has triumphed over the Whigs and Natives "after a most desperate conflict" and has carried New York City by a majority of around two thousand votes.
6 Nov	From William B. Whitecar. ALS. DLC–JKP. Reports that in Philadelphia news from New York City has dispelled all forebodings; notes that the Pennsylvania Whigs relied heavily on "forgery, fraud and the powerfull, and corrupting influence of gold."
6 Nov	From Charles A. Wickliffe. ALS. DLC–JKP. Writes from New York and states that Thurlow Weed has given up the state.
6 Nov	From Archibald Yell. ALS. DLC–JKP. Assures Polk that he has carried Arkansas; remarks that he has declined to stand for election to the U.S. Senate.
6 Nov	*From Henderson K. Yoakum.*
7 Nov	From John Adams. ALS. DLC–JKP. Explains that the steamboat has just arrived in Catskill, N.Y., and believes that there is no longer any reasonable doubt of Polk's having carried New York, although full returns are not at hand.
7 Nov	*From Robert Armstrong.*
7 Nov	From Jonas J. Bell. ALS. DLC–JKP. Sends Mississippi election returns received this date in Tuscumbia, Ala.
[7 Nov 1844]	*From John P. Chester.*
7 Nov	From John Claiborne. ALS. DLC–JKP. Assures Polk that he has carried Louisiana; mentions that in New Orleans the Whigs have accused the Democrats of "fraud, pipe laying &c."
7 Nov	*From Jonathan I. Coddington.*
7 Nov	From Isaac B. Dunn. ALS. DLC–JKP. Sends county election returns from southwest Virginia; notes that in Maryland the strong reaction of the Irish and Catholics to news of the alliance between the Whigs and the Nativists in Philadelphia ensures Polk's victory.
7 Nov	From Lewis Eaton. ALS. DLC–JKP. Believes that Polk has carried New York by a majority of twenty-five hundred to three thousand votes.
7 Nov	From Henry A. Foster. ALS. DLC–JKP. States that in New York the Whigs have suffered a complete defeat, despite

their free and unscrupulous use of money during the campaign.

7 Nov — From John L. Graham. AL. DLC–JKP. Sends a list of county election returns from New York; assures Polk that he has carried the state.

7 Nov — From William R. Hallett. ALS. DLC–JKP. Notes that earlier in the evening Tammany Hall proclaimed Polk victorious; remarks that Martin Van Buren and his sons took a great interest in Polk's election; relates that many Whigs voted for Silas Wright for governor and thus gave him a larger majority than that for the electoral ticket.

7 Nov — From Alexander Jones.

7 Nov — From Nathaniel Jones. ALS. DLC–JKP. Assures Polk that in New York he has defeated the party of "Distribution, Assumption, Bank of U. States & Class Protection" by a majority of three to five thousand votes.

7 Nov — From Henry G. Lamar. ALS. DLC–JKP. Congratulates Polk on the Democratic victory in Georgia.

7 Nov — From William M. Lowry. ALS. DLC–JKP. Reports that Polk has carried Greene County, Tenn., even though the Whigs have fought "with perfect desperation."

7 Nov — From John McKeon. ALS. DLC–JKP. Notes that last night the Whigs claimed New York, but now they are in doubt; believes that Polk has carried the state by a very small majority.

7 Nov — From John Peirce. ALS. DLC–JKP. Estimates that the Whigs have spent five-hundred thousand dollars on their election campaign in New York; notes that the upstate Whig counties have reported insufficient majorities for a statewide victory; adds that the Democratic counties on the Canadian border have given unexpectedly large majorities for Polk.

7 Nov — From Robert W. Powell. ALS. DLC–JKP. Regrets that there were "but two or three efficient men" in Johnson County, Tenn., to guard the polls; states that the Whigs there resorted to "Frauds villainies and physical force."

7 Nov — From Sylvester S. Southworth. ALS. DLC–JKP. Estimates on the basis of partial returns that Polk has carried New York by a small majority; hopes to receive additional returns within the next four hours.

7 Nov — From Sylvester S. Southworth. ALS. DLC–JKP. Notes the arrival of additional returns; congratulates Polk on his victory in New York.

7 Nov — From Joel B. Sutherland.

7 Nov — From Anthony Ten Eyck. ALS. DLC–JKP. States that Polk has carried Michigan by a majority of four to six thousand votes.

7 Nov	From Aaron Ward. ALS. DLC–JKP. Sends county election returns from New York; congratulates Polk on his election.
7 Nov	From Horace Warren. ALS. DLC–JKP. Communicates parish election returns from Louisiana; observes that unlike the sugar producing parishes, the cotton region "will all be Polk"; estimates that the Democrats will carry the state by a majority of twelve to sixteen hundred votes.
7 Nov	*From James Whitcomb.*
7 Nov	*From Campbell P. White.*
[8 Nov 1844]	From Robert Armstrong. ALS. DLC–JKP. Discusses county election returns for East and Middle Tennessee; emphasizes that the vote in the state is "very *Close* and doubtful."
8 Nov	From William A. Benjamin. ALS. DLC–JKP. Assures Polk that the Democrats of Trenton, N.J., are "perfectly on fire" for his success.
8 Nov	From W. H. Bruyn et al. LS. DLC–JKP. Send on behalf of the Young Hickory Glee Club of Ithaca, N.Y., a copy of its collection of campaign songs.
8 Nov	From George W. Clinton. ALS. DLC–JKP. Reports that in Erie County, N.Y., the Whig majority has been reduced from thirty-one hundred to eighteen hundred and that the Democrats have carried Buffalo by sixty votes; predicts that the election victory has fixed New York's political course for at least twenty years.
8 Nov	From James Conner. ALS. DLC–JKP. Encloses a corrected copy of his printed list of the projected majority in the presidential contest for each county in New York.
8 Nov	*To George M. Dallas.*
8 Nov	From John W. Davis. ALS. DLC–JKP. Communicates the county election returns from Indiana.
8 Nov	From David T. Disney. ALS. DLC–JKP. Sends county election returns for northwest Virginia; believes that Polk has carried Virginia and Indiana but has lost Maryland.
8 Nov	From Thomas Goodson. ALS. DLC–JKP. Reports that Henry Clay has carried New York by five hundred votes. Polk's AE reads, "A Hoax."
8 Nov	From John L. Graham. N. DLC–JKP. Sends election returns for New York; congratulates Polk on his victory.
8 Nov	From William R. Hallett. ALS. DLC–JKP. Notes that New York Democrats have lost two members of Congress but have retained control of the state legislature.
[8 Nov 1844]	From William H. Haywood, Jr. ALS. DLC–JKP. Estimates on the basis of partial returns that Henry Clay has carried North Carolina.
8 Nov	From Elbert Herring. ALS. DLC–JKP. Congratulates Polk on his victory in New York.
8 Nov	From Henry Horn. ALS. DLC–JKP. Reports that news of

	Polk's victory in New York has just arrived in Philadelphia; congratulates Polk on his election as president.
8 Nov	*From John T. Hudson.*
8 Nov	From Peter V. Husted. ALS. DLC–JKP. Offers to make a suit of clothes for Polk's inauguration.
8 Nov	From Jonas R. McClintock. ALS. DLC–JKP. Writes from Philadelphia to congratulate Polk on his victory in New York.
8 Nov	*From John McKeon.*
8 Nov	From Thomas Maxwell. ALS. DLC–JKP. Estimates that Polk has carried New York by a majority of twelve to fifteen thousand votes.
8 Nov	From James Osborn. ALS. DLC–JKP. Reports that Indiana Democrats have won a narrow two thousand vote victory over the "Combined elements of Federalism."
8 Nov	From N. W. Rowley. ALS. DLC–JKP. Estimates on the basis of early news reports in Philadelphia that Polk has carried New York.
8 Nov	From Sylvester S. Southworth. ALS. DLC–JKP. Predicts that Polk has carried New York.
8 Nov	From Joel B. Sutherland. ALS. DLC–JKP. Discusses the effects of the Texas annexation and abolition questions on the New York election.
8 Nov	From Joel B. Sutherland. ALS. DLC–JKP. Confirms his report of earlier in the day that Polk has triumphed in New York; regrets rumors that Silas Wright has run ahead of the electoral ticket; hopes that Polk will carry North Carolina and Delaware.
[8 Nov 1844]	From John Tomlin. ALS. DLC–JKP. Sends county election returns for West Tennessee.
8 Nov	From Campbell P. White. ALS. DLC–JKP. Criticizes the defection in New York of "the whole Corps of Office Holders" under Martin Van Buren's administration; points to the larger vote of Silas Wright for governor as evidence of their revenge for Van Buren's not receiving the presidential nomination.
8 Nov	From Marcus B. Winchester. ALS. DLC–JKP. Reports that the latest "arrival" from Louisville in Memphis confirms Polk's victory in New York and thus his election as president.
8 Nov	From Fernando Wood. ALS. DLC–JKP. States that "after three days of intense excitement" Polk's victory in New York is secure and beyond question.
9 Nov	From William Anderson. ALS. DLC–JKP. Notes that in New York and Michigan, "Birney's forces" have kept together and have dashed Whig hopes; offers his calculations of the electoral vote.

9 Nov — *From Robert Armstrong.*

9 Nov — From William A. Booth. ALS. DLC–JKP. Requests that Polk state his views on the projected split in the Methodist Episcopal Church; thinks that "dissention on the delicate subject of Slavery" may speed the dissolution of the Union.

9 Nov — From Walter T. Brooke. ALS. DLC–JKP. Congratulates Polk on his election as president.

9 Nov — *To George M. Dallas.*

9 Nov — From David T. Disney. ALS. DLC–JKP. Reports that news of the New York election has not yet reached Cincinnati; assures Polk that he has carried Michigan, Virginia, and Indiana.

9 Nov — From R. P. Dowden. ALS. DLC–JKP. Predicts that Polk has won the election; sends the congratulations of the Democratic Association of Bladensburg, Md.

9 Nov — From Henry L. Ellsworth. ALS. DLC–JKP. Congratulates Polk on his election as president.

9 Nov — From William Emmons. ALS. DLC–JKP. Praises "the noble tillers of the soil" for their role in Polk's victory over "the opponants of Republican principles."

9 Nov — From James Garland. ALS. DLC–JKP. Assures Polk that he has carried Virginia.

9 Nov — From James Harris, Jr. ALS. DLC–JKP. Rejoices at Polk's victory; expresses fear that he will be turned out of his sales job in Baltimore because of the "*bitter*" feelings of his Whig employers.

[9 Nov 1844] — *From J. George Harris.*

9 Nov — From John D. Jackson. ALS. DLC–JKP. Reports that the tariff issue caused many Democrats in New Jersey, "a Tariff State," to vote for Clay.

9 Nov — From Cave Johnson. ALS. DLC–JKP. Believes that Polk has carried Tennessee as well as the Union; notes that the Democracy has lost votes in Stewart County, Tenn., because of Whig "trickery."

9 Nov — From Charles R. Kay. ALS. DLC–JKP. Solicits a position in the federal government.

9 Nov — From John Law. ALS. DLC–JKP. Reports that after "a desperate Struggle" the Democracy has carried Indiana by a small majority.

9 Nov — From Moses G. Leonard. ALS. DLC–JKP. Celebrates Polk's victory in New York; attributes his failure to win his congressional race to a combination of Whigs and Nativists; counts his defeat as of little consequence.

9 Nov — From Wilson Lumpkin. ALS. DLC–JKP. Assures Polk that he has carried Georgia; anxiously awaits news of Tennessee and New York.

9 Nov — From Richard Rush. ALS. DLC–JKP. Congratulates Polk

	on his election; asserts that the Whigs spent an "incredible" amount of money to win the election in Pennsylvania and New York.
9 Nov	From Sylvester S. Southworth. ALS. DLC–JKP. Reports that he has sent news of Polk's election to newspapers in London and Paris.
9 Nov	*From Joel B. Sutherland.*
10 Nov	From Anonymous. L, signed "A Staunch Whig." DLC–JKP. Claims that Polk's opposition to the tariff has led to his defeat in Mississippi; criticizes Polk's inconsistency on the tariff issue.
[10 Nov 1844]	*From Robert Armstrong.*
10 Nov	From Jerome Bayon. ALS. DLC–JKP. Estimates that Polk will carry Louisiana by a majority of four thousand votes.
10 Nov	From Jonas J. Bell. ALS. DLC–JKP. Predicts that Polk has carried Mississippi and Georgia.
10 Nov	From William Burke. ALS. DLC–JKP. Reports from Cincinnati that the eastern mail brings news of Polk's victory in New York.
10 Nov	From George W. Clutter. ALS. DLC–JKP. Congratulates Polk on the Democratic victories in New York, Virginia, and Pennsylvania.
10 Nov	From Owen Conway. LS. DLC–JKP. Claims that at the naval yard in Norfolk, Va., the Whigs have tried to influence the votes of the journeymen.
10 Nov	From David T. Disney. ALS. DLC–JKP. Congratulates Polk on his election as president; encloses "a slip" of the Columbus *Ohio Statesman*. (Enclosure not found.)
10 Nov	From Joseph Favor. ALS. DLC–JKP. States that Washington Hunt, a Whig who represents Niagara County, N.Y., in Congress, has frequently asked in public the taunt, "Who is James K. Polk?"; suggests that Polk invite Hunt to the White House that he may answer his question for the Whigs back home.
10 Nov	From Albert G. Jewett. ALS. DLC–JKP. Claims that William S. Archer offered Philadelphia's Native Americans control of customs appointments in return for supporting Henry Clay; blames the loss of Ohio on the defection of Thomas Morris and on the forged letter in which James G. Birney supposedly claimed to be a Democrat.
10 Nov	*From Samuel H. Laughlin.*
10 Nov	*From Samuel Medary.*
10 Nov	From E. J. Purse. ALS. DLC–JKP. Congratulates Polk on the Democratic victory in New York and his election as president.
10 Nov	From Richard H. Stanton. ALS. DLC–JKP. Reports from Maysville, Ky., that the latest election returns from New

	York and Tennessee dispel all doubts about Polk's election.
10 Nov	From J. D. Swan. ALS. DLC–JKP. Points to his work on Polk's behalf during the canvass in Jefferson County, Va.; emphasizes his vulnerable position as "a pore mecnic" in a Whig county.
[10 Nov 1844]	From John Tomlin. ALS. DLC–JKP. Reports that in West Tennessee the Democrats have reduced the Whig majority to about seventeen hundred votes.
10 Nov	From James Whitcomb. ALS. DLC–JKP. Assures Polk that he has carried Indiana by a majority of twenty-five hundred votes.
[11 Nov 1844]	*From Robert Armstrong.*
11 Nov	*From Charles G. Atherton.*
[11 Nov 1844]	From Aaron V. Brown. ALS. DLC–JKP. Waits in suspense to hear news about the outcome of the election in Tennessee; asks Polk to send the news by express mail, if the returns are favorable.
11 Nov	*From John F. H. Claiborne.*
11 Nov	From Auguste D'Avezac. ALS. DLC–JKP. Reviews his part in the recent campaign and notes that he addressed the Democracy of five states on some fifty-seven occasions; rejoices in the "moral sublimity" of Polk's election.
11 Nov	*From Robert P. Flenniken.*
11 Nov	From Jesse T. Harrison. LS. DLC–JKP. Urges Polk to keep the present level of tariff protection.
11 Nov	From James W. Jeffreys. ALS. DLC–JKP. Predicts that Polk has carried New York and Virginia; expresses his disappointment at the vote of Polk's native state, North Carolina; dates an addendum November 13, 1844.
11 Nov	From Phineas M. Kent. ALS. DLC–JKP. Assures Polk that he has carried New York, Michigan, Indiana, and Virginia.
11 Nov	From Wilson McCandless. ALS. DLC–JKP. Congratulates Polk on his election as president.
11 Nov	*From James S. McFarlane.*
11 Nov	From William S. Pickett. ALS. DLC–JKP. Predicts that Polk will carry Louisiana; reports on the state of the cotton market in New Orleans.
11 Nov	*From James M. Porter.*
11 Nov	*From Joseph B. Southall.*
11 Nov	From Sylvester S. Southworth. ALS. DLC–JKP. Estimates that Polk has carried Georgia, Michigan, and Maine.
12 Nov	From Anonymous. L, signed "Henry Horn." DLC–JKP. Warns Polk about possible difficulties in several Pennsylvania counties in relation to the gubernatorial and electoral votes.
12 Nov	*From Robert Armstrong.*
12 Nov	From Joel Branham. ALS. DLC–JKP. Describes Polk's elec-

	tion as a glorious victory over "the combined forces of Federalism and Fanaticism."
12 Nov	*From Benjamin F. Butler.*
12 Nov	From Henry A. Cargill. ALS. DLC–JKP. Sends county election returns from Mississippi.
12 Nov	From John Catron. ALS. DLC–JKP. Reports from Nashville that Polk's prospects "look fair"; notes that Chester Harding wishes to paint Polk's portrait.
12 Nov	From W. W. Dallas. ALS. DLC–JKP. Encloses a newspaper containing material on the controversy between Andrew Jackson and John Q. Adams. (Enclosure not found.)
12 Nov	From David T. Disney. ALS. DLC–JKP. Estimates on the basis of partial returns that Polk has carried New York by "a small, very small majority."
12 Nov	From David T. Disney. ALS. DLC–JKP. Reports that news of the final result in New York has arrived in Cincinnati; congratulates Polk on his election as president.
12 Nov	From Robert E. Finnell. ALS. DLC–JKP. Warns Polk to guard against possible assassination attempts by the Whigs.
12 Nov	From Ira R. Foster. ALS. DLC–JKP. Assures Polk that he has carried Georgia.
12 Nov	From A. Haines et al. LS. DLC–JKP. Congratulate Polk on his election as president.
12 Nov	*From Albert G. Jewett.*
12 Nov	*From Elam P. Langdon.*
12 Nov	From Thomas C. McDowell. ALS. DLC–JKP. Congratulates Polk on his victory in the presidential election.
12 Nov	From James S. McFarlane. ALS. DLC–JKP. Sends news of the latest parish election returns in Louisiana.
12 Nov	From Sylvester S. Southworth. ALS. DLC–JKP. Notes that according to a rumor circulating in New York City, Massachusetts has failed to elect presidential electors and will send the decision to the state legislature.
12 Nov	From Richard H. Stanton. ALS. DLC–JKP. Reports from Maysville, Ky., that the latest returns from New York confirm Polk's victory.
12 Nov	*From Joel B. Sutherland.*
13 Nov	*From Aaron V. Brown.*
13 Nov	From John A. Bryan. ALS. DLC–JKP. Describes Polk's victory as "a *perfect Waterloo*" for the "federal dynasty."
13 Nov	*From William E. Cramer.*
13 Nov	*From Moses Dawson.*
13 Nov	From William A. Elmore. ALS. DLC–JKP. Estimates that Polk has carried Louisiana by a majority of eight hundred votes.
13 Nov	From J. George Harris. ALS. DLC–JKP. Predicts on the basis of the recent news that "the question is settled."

13 Nov	From Thomas M. Hicks. ALS. DLC–JKP. Writes from Louisville at 10 p.m. that New York is Polk's without a doubt; adds that the mail boat will be down at midnight, and that the present letter will leave about two hours later; relates that Louisville is "in a blaze of rejoicing this Night—100 guns for our triumph."
13 Nov	From Sackfield Maclin. ALS. DLC–JKP. Regrets that Arkansas was not canvassed "with as much energy as it should have been"; explains that there the election was not in doubt; predicts that Polk has carried the state by a majority of five thousand votes; anxiously awaits news of Tennessee.
13 Nov	From John B. Macy. ALS. DLC–JKP. Claims that the Democrats lost in Ohio because the abolitionists voted for Clay.
13 Nov	*From Amasa J. Parker.*
13 Nov	From Lawrence Taliaferro. ALS. DLC–JKP. Congratulates Polk on his victory over "Abolitionism, Nativeism, Antimasonry, drunkeness, and profligacy."
14 Nov	*From Robert Armstrong.*
14 Nov	From Arthur Crichfield. ALS. DLC–JKP. Solicits the position of postmaster of Covington, Ky.
14 Nov	From Rufus Dolbear. ALS. DLC–JKP. Reports that Polk has carried Louisiana.
14 Nov	From Hugh W. Dunlap. ALS. DLC–JKP. Predicts that Polk has carried Mississippi and Louisiana.
14 Nov	From William Griffith. ALS. DLC–JKP. Requests that Polk send a summary of his voting record on revolutionary soldiers' pensions.
14 Nov	From Edward Harden. ALS. DLC–JKP. Congratulates Polk on his election as president.
14 Nov	From Thomas Irwin. ALS. DLC–JKP. Invites Polk to visit Pittsburgh en route to his inauguration.
[14 Nov 1844]	From Andrew Jackson. ALI. DLC–JKP. Encloses Azariah Flagg's letter dated November 7, 1844.
[14 Nov 1844]	From Andrew Jackson. ALI. DLC–JKP. Encloses Joel B. Sutherland's letter dated November 8, 1844.
14 Nov	From James W. McClung. ALS. DLC–JKP. Predicts that Polk has carried Georgia, North Carolina, and Virginia.
14 Nov	From James G. Read. ALS. DLC–JKP. Inquires about the route of Polk's inaugural trip.
14 Nov	From Thomas J. Read. ALS. DLC–JKP. Congratulates Polk on his election as president.
14 Nov	*From George Read Riddle.*
14 Nov	From Moses M. Russell. ALS. DLC–JKP. Congratulates Polk on his victory over "the combined forces of the Federal Whigs and their new allies, self styled Native Americans."
14 Nov	From Will M. Shipp. ALS. DLC–JKP. Wishes to give his

	newborn daughter the name of Mrs. Polk; requests that Polk send his wife's first name.
14 Nov	From Sylvester S. Southworth. ALS. DLC–JKP. Reports from New York City that the arrival of the latest news from Tennessee has renewed hopes of a Democratic victory there; notes that he has bet heavily on the outcome.
15 Nov	From Anonymous. L, signed "Henry Clay Foreever." DLC–JKP. Attacks Polk as a "*dam Son of a Bitch*" who will ruin the country through his policies on Texas and free trade.
15 Nov	*From Robert Armstrong.*
15 Nov	*From Robert Armstrong.*
15 Nov	*From William C. Bouck.*
15 Nov	From James G. Bryce. ALS. DLC–JKP. Predicts that Polk has carried Louisiana by a small majority, even though the Whigs have "practised their accustomed frauds."
15 Nov	From Miles N. Carpenter. ALS. DLC–JKP. Congratulates Polk on his election as president.
15 Nov	*From J. George Harris.*
15 Nov	From Charles P. Harrison. ALS. DLC–JKP. Offers his services as a historical painter and engraver. Harrison's letter was enclosed in the letter of John Tyler, Jr., to Polk, November 18, 1844.
15 Nov	From Henry Hicks. ALS. DLC–JKP. Attributes the narrow Whig victory in Delaware to Native Americanism, "the strong influence of the manufacturers," and the importation of voters from New York City, Philadelphia, and Baltimore.
15 Nov	From William Hopkins et al. LS. DLC–JKP. Inquire about the route of Polk's inaugural trip; offer to build a coach for his use should he travel the National Road.
15 Nov	From Kenedy Lonergan. ALS. DLC–JKP. Congratulates Polk on his victory in the presidential election.
15 Nov	*From Allen McLane.*
15 Nov	From C. C. Seely et al. C. DLC–JKP. Invite Polk to attend a celebration at Warren, Ohio, in honor of his victory.
15 Nov	From Aaron Sergeant. ALS. DLC–JKP. Suggests that Polk appoint Henry Clay as minister to Great Britain.
15 Nov	From Sylvester S. Southworth. ALS. DLC–JKP. Describes the procession of the Native Americans in New York City on November 15, 1844; predicts on the basis of the latest election returns that Polk has carried Tennessee.
15 Nov	From John A. Thomas. ALS. DLC–JKP. Congratulates Polk on his election to the "highest of all earthly stations."
15 Nov	From John Tomlin. ALS. DLC–JKP. Believes that Tennessee is lost; assures Polk that he has carried New York, Virginia, and Pennsylvania.
15 Nov	From Hendrick B. Wright. ALS. DLC–JKP. States that the

	nation has ratified the decision of the Baltimore Convention and has silenced those in Pennsylvania who continued to clamor against the supposed injustice to Martin Van Buren.
16 Nov	From Anonymous. L. DLC–JKP. Urges Polk to take the Bible as "the guide of your life."
16 Nov	From Anonymous. L, signed "G." DLC–JKP. Claims that the Democrats resorted to bribery of "the poorer class" to elect Polk; notes that in Hartford, Conn., the Whigs are "the richest and most influential men we have."
16 Nov	From Anonymous. L, signed "Henry Horn." DLC–JKP. Advises Polk to pursue a moderate course on the tariff and Texas annexation.
16 Nov	From William R. Hallett. ALS. DLC–JKP. Reports that in New York City the Whigs "are trying hard to get up a panic" on Wall Street.
16 Nov	From Andrew Jackson. ALS. DLC–AJ. Congratulates Polk on his victory in New York and his election as president; encloses Moses Dawson's letter of November 13, 1844.
16 Nov	From Cave Johnson. ALS. DLC–JKP. Encloses Henry Simpson's letter of November 6, 1844; congratulates Polk on his victory in the presidential election.
16 Nov	*From Wilson Lumpkin.*
16 Nov	*From John Y. Mason.*
16 Nov	From Gayton P. Osgood. ALS. DNA–RG 45. Recommends Joseph Hall for the position of surveyor of the port of Boston.
16 Nov	From William Steed. ALS. DLC–JKP. Reports that Polk has carried Louisiana by a majority of one thousand votes; offers his calculations of the electoral vote.
16 Nov	From A. P. Stinson. ALS. DLC–JKP. Congratulates Polk on his election as president; predicts that the Whig party will disband or will amalgamate with either the Native Americans or the abolitionists.
16 Nov	From C. B. Wilson. ALS. DLC–JKP. Wishes to return home to Maury County, Tenn.; asks Polk to send the necessary funds.
17 Nov	From Robert Armstrong. ALS. DLC–JKP. Reports that last night he was unable to find any trustworthy person to deliver Polk's mail; notes that Felix Robertson leaves this morning to deliver the mail.
17 Nov	From Jonas J. Bell. ALS. DLC–JKP. Congratulates Polk on his election as president.
[17 Nov 1844]	From David Craighead. ALS. DLC–JKP. Congratulates Polk on his victory at this critical point in the history of free government.
17 Nov	*From George M. Dallas.*
17 Nov	From Charles Glasier. ALS. DLC–JKP. Wishes to dedicate

	a grand waltz to Polk.
[17 Nov 1844]	*From Adam Huntsman.*
17 Nov	From William D. Mason. ALS. DLC–JKP. Congratulates Polk on his victory in the presidential election.
17 Nov	From Robert D. Maupin. ALS. DLC–JKP. Congratulates Polk on the "brilliant triumph" of the Democracy.
18 Nov	From Anonymous. L. DLC–JKP. Solicits a position in the federal government.
18 Nov	*From Iveson L. Brookes.*
18 Nov	From Churchill C. Cambreleng et al. LS. DLC–JKP. Recommend Joseph Cowdin for a position in the federal government.
18 Nov	From Isaiah Cooper et al. LS. DLC–JKP. Invite Polk to visit Wheeling, Va., en route to his inauguration.
18 Nov	From John A. Donohoo. ALS. DLC–JKP. Reports that the Whigs of Washington City have made threats "to bury" Polk; warns Polk to guard against possible attempts on his life.
18 Nov	From Thomas Fletcher. ALS. DLC–JKP. Notes that the Mississippi Democracy has won "a signal victory"; congratulates Polk on his election as president.
18 Nov	From Joseph Hall. ALS. DLC–JKP. Recommends David Henshaw as a man "who is qualified to fill any station in the country."
18 Nov	From K. L. Haralson. ALS. DLC–JKP. Recalls that he attended a debate between Polk and James C. Jones during the 1843 campaign; congratulates Polk on his victory in the presidential election.
18 Nov	From Vincent Haralson. ALS. DLC–JKP. Invites Polk to visit Holly Springs, Miss., during his next trip to his Mississippi plantation.
18 Nov	From George S. Houston. ALS. DLC–JKP. Congratulates Polk on his election as president.
18 Nov	From Russell Houston. ALS. DLC–JKP. Inquires about renting Polk's house in Columbia, Tenn.
18 Nov	From Philip Barton Key. ALS. DLC–JKP. Notes that his father Francis Scott Key, a loyal Democrat, lost the position of U.S. attorney for the District of Columbia after the 1840 election; requests that Polk consider his application for the same post.
18 Nov	From W. H. Lamberton. ALS. DLC–JKP. Writes on behalf of the Young Hickory Club of Franklin, Penn.; congratulates Polk on his election as president.
18 Nov	*From William M. Lowry.*
18 Nov	From Josiah F. Polk. ALS. DLC–JKP. Writes on behalf of his sister, Sarah; invites Polk and family to stay at his sister's boarding house in Washington City; adds that the landlord

of "Polk House," John A. Donohoo, "has gone to the expense of procuring a Parisian artist to paint the parlour etc, in the most elegant style."

18 Nov — From Levi Reynolds. ALS. DLC–JKP. Offers general advice on cabinet selection and federal appointments in Pennsylvania; emphasizes that Lewis Cass zealously campaigned on Polk's behalf.

18 Nov — From Walter A. Smith. ALS. DLC–JKP. Urges Polk to help Thomas W. Dorr and to keep down "the scarlet whore of Babylon the united states Bank"; offers advice on cabinet appointments.

18 Nov — From Sylvester S. Southworth. ALS. DLC–JKP. Notes that in New York they still await reliable news of the result in Tennessee; hopes that the report of a narrow Whig victory is incorrect.

18 Nov — From John Tyler, Jr. ALS. DLC–JKP. Congratulates Polk on his election as president; encloses "lithographic likenesses" of George M. Dallas and accompanying letters from Charles P. Harrison.

18 Nov — From John Wynne et al. LS. DLC–JKP. Write on behalf of an association of journeymen tailors; congratulate Polk upon his victory over the "stock jobers, bank monyers and speculators, who prey upon the verry vitals of society"; invite Polk to visit Pittsburgh, Penn., en route to his inauguration.

19 Nov — *From Robert Armstrong and J. George Harris.*

19 Nov — *From Robert Armstrong.*

19 Nov — From J. Barnard. ALS. DLC–JKP. Asks for a statement attesting to the accuracy of his portraits of Polk.

19 Nov — *From Julius W. Blackwell.*

19 Nov — *From Samuel P. Caldwell.*

19 Nov — From Henry A. Cargill. ALS. DLC–JKP. Congratulates Polk on the Democratic victory in New York; sends the latest returns from Mississippi.

19 Nov — From John W. Chapman. ALS. DLC–JKP. Requests Polk's autograph.

19 Nov — *From Ransom H. Gillet.*

19 Nov — From William H. Haywood, Jr. ALS. DLC–JKP. Inquires about the route of Polk's inaugural trip; would meet him in Raleigh, where Democrat members of the North Carolina legislature would like to pay him their respects.

19 Nov — From J. G. McWhorter et al. LS. DLC–JKP. Invite Polk to visit Augusta, Ga., en route to his inauguration.

19 Nov — From J. G. McWhorter. ALS. DLC–JKP. Offers to act as host during Polk's proposed visit to Augusta, Ga.

19 Nov — From Moses G. Reeves. ALS. DLC–JKP. Invites Polk to Murfreesboro, Tenn., for a visit with the Democracy of

	Rutherford County.
19 Nov	From Jesse Speight. ALS. DLC–JKP. Congratulates Polk on the "happy result" of the election; declares his intention to attend any special session of the U.S. Senate that may be called to advise and consent to Polk's cabinet nominations.
19 Nov	From Joseph R. A. Tomkins. ALS. DLC–JKP. Introduces Mr. Champion of New York City.
20 Nov	From Anonymous. L, signed "A Bostonian." DLC–JKP. Offers advice on Texas, the tariff, and the Independent Treasury system; warns Polk to avoid "ultra politicians" and "party names."
20 Nov	From John O. Bradford et al. LS. DLC–JKP. Discuss the political platform on which the Democratic Invincible Legion of Philadelphia conducted its campaign in support of Polk.
20 Nov	From Thomas Brown. ALS. DLC–JKP. Invites Polk to visit Kingston, Tenn.
20 Nov	From John H. Cook. ALS. DLC–JKP. Notes that the presidential campaign in Indiana had been a "desperate" contest; adds that many of the Democratic speakers had been compelled "to go constantly armed" during the campaign.
20 Nov	From Thomas Davis. ALS. DLC–JKP. Relates that some of the Lincoln County boys joined their celebration in Shelbyville, Tenn., last night; expresses relief that the Whigs will not have the power to turn him out of office.
20 Nov	From Josephus C. Guild. ALS. DLC–JKP. Invites Polk to visit Gallatin, Tenn., and to give the citizens and "particularly the women the opportunity of being taken by the hand by you."
20 Nov	From Henry Horn. ALS. DLC–JKP. Notes that the contest for "spoils" has begun; urges Polk to avoid "any committal or premature action" in regards to appointments.
20 Nov	From John Jones, Jr. ALS. DLC–JKP. Warns Polk to decline any invitation to visit Augusta, Ga., because a visit might result in attempts on his life.
20 Nov	From William W. Lea. ALS. DLC–JKP. Congratulates Polk on his election as president.
20 Nov	From Lemuel Long. ALS. DLC–JKP. Encloses a newspaper from John H. Hill of Philadelphia, Penn. (Enclosure not found.)
20 Nov	From Rody Patterson et al. LS. DLC–JKP. Invite Polk to visit Pittsburgh, Penn., en route to his inauguration.
20 Nov	From J. G. M. Ramsey. ALS. DLC–JKP. Congratulates Polk on his victory in the presidential election.
20 Nov	From Thomas Ritchie. ALS. DLC–JKP. Recommends Andrew Stevenson for a position in the cabinet.
20 Nov	*From Joel B. Sutherland.*
20 Nov	*From Roger B. Taney.*

20 Nov	*From Samuel P. Walker.*
20 Nov	*From William Walters.*
21 Nov	*From Robert Armstrong.*
21 Nov	From George M. Dallas. ALS. DLC–JKP. Introduces Auguste D'Avezac.
21 Nov	*From Alexander Jones.*
21 Nov	*From Nathaniel Jones.*
21 Nov	From Lewis R. Justice. ALS. DLC–JKP. Attributes the Whigs' narrow victory in New Jersey to the influence of money and "frauds of the grossest description."
21 Nov	*From Gouverneur Kemble.*
21 Nov	From Lavenia Kerr. ALS. DLC–JKP. Inquires about renting Polk's house in Columbia, Tenn.
21 Nov	From Samuel Rhea. ALS. DLC–JKP. Congratulates Polk on the "glorious triumph of democracy"; hopes that Polk will pass through East Tennessee en route to his inauguration.
21 Nov	From William R. Rucker. ALS. DLC–JKP. Attributes the loss of Tennessee to the Whigs' resort to "the most extraordinary and corrupt appliances."
21 Nov	*From Henry Simpson.*
21 Nov	From Ebenezer Tucker. ALS. DLC–JKP. Congratulates Polk on his election as president.
22 Nov	From Felix Bosworth. LS. DLC–JKP. Congratulates Polk on his victory over Henry Clay; inquires about the route of Polk's inaugural trip.
[22 Nov 1844]	From Isaac Bradley. ALS. DLC–JKP. States that Polk's election represents the triumph of "the republican partty" over "Ignorent Whigism."
22 Nov	From D. C. Campbell. ALS. DLC–JKP. Invites Polk to visit Macon, Ga., en route to his inauguration; observes that the "facilities now afforded by Rail Roads through our State and by Rail Roads and Steam-boats hence to the City of Washington, may perhaps constitute this as agreeable and expeditious a route as any other."
22 Nov	From John McMahon Clancie. ALS. DLC–JKP. Solicits a position in the federal government.
22 Nov	From Clement C. Clay. ALS. DLC–JKP. Congratulates Polk on his election as president; invites the Polks to visit Huntsville, Ala.
22 Nov	*From Charles Douglas.*
[22 Nov 1844]	From Jesse W. Griffiths et al. LS. DLC–JKP. Recommend on behalf of the Johnson Democratic National Club of Philadelphia the appointment of Richard M. Johnson to the cabinet; discuss "the Anti-Van Buren feeling" within the Pennsylvania delegation to the 1844 Democratic National Convention.
22 Nov	From William Hemingway. ALS. DLC–JKP. Predicts that

	Polk has carried Mississippi by a majority of six thousand votes.
22 Nov	From Edward M. Holden. ALS. DLC–JKP. Believes that Polk's victory represents the triumph of "the peoples will" over "the intrigues and corruptions" of the Whigs.
22 Nov	From Russell Houston. ALS. DLC–JKP. Postpones his meeting of this date to discuss the rental or purchase of Polk's residence in Columbia.
22 Nov	From Richard M. Johnson. ALS. DLC–JKP. Introduces George Taylor, "a young gentleman of great promise in his profession of politics" who made himself "dear to the hearts of your Democratic friends, in Indiana, Ohio, Michigan, & Kentucky by his able & eloquent support of the Democratic cause in the late presidential canvass."
22 Nov	*From Augustus B. Longstreet.*
22 Nov	*From John M. McCalla.*
22 Nov	*From Robert Mitchell.*
22 Nov	From James C. Record. ALS. DLC–JKP. Notes that sometime next week the Polk Dragoons and some of the "Democratic Ladies" of Marshall County, Tenn., will visit Polk.
22 Nov	*From Henderson K. Yoakum.*
23 Nov	From James C. Alderson. ALS. DLC–JKP. Invites Polk to visit Holly Springs, Miss.
23 Nov	From Anonymous. L, signed "Henry Horn." DLC–JKP. Advises Polk "to use Tyler in any practicable manner" to advance the great measures of the tariff, Texas, and the Independent Treasury.
23 Nov	*From John Catron.*
23 Nov	*From Levin H. Coe.*
23 Nov	From Moses Dawson. ALS. DLC–JKP. Relays to Polk the offer of Messrs. Strader and Gorman, mail boat contractors, to place their steamboat at Polk's disposal for his inaugural trip.
23 Nov	From H. L. Holbrook. ALS. DLC–JKP. Intends to name his newborn daughter after Polk's wife; wishes to know her given name.
23 Nov	From Medicus A. Long. ALS. DLC–JKP. Urges Polk to avoid "northern and southern ultraism" and to protect the Union from both abolition and nullification.
23 Nov	From Rufus McIntire. ALS. DLC–JKP. Warns Polk about divisions within the Maine Democracy; offers advice about patronage and appointments.
23 Nov	From John M. Niles. ALS. DLC–JKP. Urges Polk to keep his administration free of "discordant elements" within the Democratic party.
23 Nov	From Gorham Parks et al. LS. DLC–JKP. Write Polk on the behalf of the citizens of Bangor, Me.; congratulate Polk on

	his election as president.
23 Nov	To Jack Shackleford. ALS, copy. DLC–JKP. Declines invitation to attend a public dinner to be given in his honor at Courtland, Ala.
23 Nov	From James Tennison. ALS. DLC–JKP. Claims that his shift of party allegiance to the Democrats has outraged his Whig creditors, who have called in his notes; asks Polk for financial assistance.
23 Nov	From George W. Thompson. ALS. DLC–JKP. Invites Polk to visit Wheeling, Va., en route to his inauguration.
24 Nov	From Anonymous. L. DLC–JKP. Criticizes Polk's views on the tariff and Texas annexation.
24 Nov	From William Emmons. ALS. DLC–JKP. Notes that the struggle for public office has begun in Pennsylvania and Philadelphia; praises Calvin Blythe, Joel B. Sutherland, and Joseph Hall for their work during the campaign.
24 Nov	From John B. Helm. ALS. DLC–JKP. Advises Polk to appoint Martin Van Buren and John Tyler to foreign missions; recommends James Guthrie for a cabinet position.
[24 Nov 1844]	From Robert Ball Hughes. ALS. DLC–JKP. Offers his services as a sculptor; requests that Polk forward a daguerreotype.
24 Nov	From A. S. Pratt. ALS. DLC–JKP. Urges Polk to appoint only "new men" to his cabinet.
24 Nov	*From George R. Riddle et al.*
24 Nov	*From Archibald Yell.*
25 Nov	From Anonymous. L, signed "Henry Horn." DLC–JKP. Warns Polk to beware of "interlopers into our party" and attacks in particular Charles J. Ingersoll and the Tyler appointees in Philadelphia's Custom House and post office.
25 Nov	From Samuel Beardsley. ALS. DLC–JKP. Introduces Chesselden Ellis.
25 Nov	*To Benjamin F. Butler.*
25 Nov	From Joseph W. Chalmers. ALS. DLC–JKP. Urges Polk to appoint to the U.S. Supreme Court only those who will make "that bench *Republican* & *Anti Bank* on *constitutional grounds*."
25 Nov	From George W. Clutter. ALS. DLC–JKP. Congratulates Polk on his election as president.
25 Nov	From Mark N. Cooper. ALS. DLC–JKP. Invites Polk to visit northwest Georgia en route to his inauguration.
25 Nov	From E. B. Cox et al. LS. DLC–JKP. Inform Polk that the members of the literary society of Sunfish, Ohio, have named their society the Polk Literary Institute.
25 Nov	From George M. Dallas. ALS. DLC–JKP. Introduces Thomas Sully, Jr.
25 Nov	From W. Freeman. ALS. DLC–JKP. Solicits Polk's support

	for relief from a court-martial sentence.
25 Nov	From Horace Hawes. ALS. DLC–JKP. Congratulates Polk on his election as president.
25 Nov	*From Henry Hubbard.*
25 Nov	From Charles J. Ingersoll. ALS. DLC–JKP. Introduces Thomas Sully, Jr.
25 Nov	From James W. Jeffreys. ALS. DLC–JKP. Notes with regret the vote of North Carolina; believes that the state will return to the Democratic fold in 1846.
25 Nov	From John K. Kane. ALS. DLC–JKP. Reports that several of Polk's friends in Philadelphia wish to acquire an accurate portrait to act as a corrective to "the strange pictures which have been paraded as your representative during the canvas"; introduces Thomas Sully, Jr.
25 Nov	From Thomas F. Scott. ALS. DLC–JKP. Suggests that Polk take the "Southern route" to Washington City; invites Polk to visit Marietta, Ga., en route to his inauguration.
25 Nov	From Henry L. Sims et al. LS. DLC–JKP. Invite Polk to visit Cumming, Ga., en route to his inauguration.
25 Nov	From James T. Worthington. ALS. DLC–JKP. Informs Polk of his election to honorary membership in the Dialectic Society of Cincinnati College.
26 Nov	From Thomas W. Bartley. ALS. DLC–JKP. Assures Polk that the Ohio Democracy holds him in high regard; attributes defeat in Ohio to "peculiar local circumstances."
26 Nov	*From Nathan Clifford.*
26 Nov	From David Darnall. ALS. DLC–JKP. Congratulates Polk on the outcome of the election; recalls memories of the years that he spent in Samuel Polk's household.
26 Nov	From William Daveiss. ALS. DLC–JKP. Recommends John M. McCalla for a cabinet position.
26 Nov	From Edward Devlin. ALS. DLC–JKP. Congratulates Polk on his victory in the presidential election.
26 Nov	From G. W. Garrett et al. LS. DLC–JKP. Invite Polk to attend a public dinner in his honor in Tishemingo County, Miss., on January 8, 1845.
26 Nov	From Harmon Kingsbury. ALS. DLC–JKP. Urges Polk to put an end to Sunday mails.
26 Nov	*From William Wallace.*
26 Nov	From Thomas White. ALS. DLC–JKP. Invites Polk to visit Blountsville, Tenn., en route to his inauguration; notes that news of the final vote of Tennessee has not yet reached Sullivan County.
26 Nov	From Joel Yowell. ALS. DLC–JKP. Congratulates Polk on his election as president.
27 Nov	From William A. Elmore. ALS. DLC–JKP. Encloses a copy of the official return of the vote in Louisiana.

27 Nov	From Abraham Fulkerson. ALS. DLC–JKP. Reports that Polk has carried Missouri by ten thousand votes.
27 Nov	From Theodore Ingalls. ALS. DLC–JKP. Writes on behalf of the Executive Council of Maine; encloses a note of this date recommending the appointment of John Fairfield to Polk's cabinet.
27 Nov	From Theodore Ingalls et al. NS. DLC–JKP. Recommend John Fairfield for a position in Polk's cabinet either as secretary of the navy or as secretary of war.
27 Nov	From Thomas J. McLain. ALS. DLC–JKP. Notes that the election settles the Texas question; claims that he was the only man in Warren, Ohio, to defend Texas annexation against the attacks of Whigs and abolitionists.
27 Nov	From Rody Patterson et al. C. DLC–JKP. Invite Polk to attend a public dinner at Pittsburgh, Penn., on December 4, 1844.
27 Nov	From James Robertson. ALS. DLC–JKP. Advises Polk to avoid all cliques and factions.
28 Nov	*From Robert Armstrong.*
28 Nov	From J. D'Autel. ALS. DLC–JKP. Intends to name his newborn daughter after Mrs. Polk; wishes to know Mrs. Polk's name.
28 Nov	From Jacob M. Guerry et al. LS. DLC–JKP. Invite Polk to visit Columbus, Ga., en route to his inauguration.
28 Nov	*From Blacksmith Harry.*
28 Nov	From Oscar T. Keeler. ALS. DLC–JKP. Asks for Polk's autograph.
28 Nov	From Augustus B. Longstreet. ALS. DLC–JKP. Offers Polk advice on Sunday mails, extension of the presidential term of office, the tariff, Texas annexation, banking, naturalization laws, and cabinet appointments.
28 Nov	From Louis McLane. ALS. DLC–JKP. Congratulates Polk on his election as president.
28 Nov	From Felix Robertson et al. NS. DLC–JKP. Recommend a free man, William Goff, and his wife, Dilsey, for positions on Polk's domestic staff at the White House.
28 Nov	From Robert Smith. ALS. DLC–JKP. Solicits position in the federal government either as steward of the White House or as an Indian agent.
28 Nov	From Shepherd Spencer. ALS. DLC–JKP. Urges Polk to retain John C. Calhoun as secretary of state.
28 Nov	From John F. Wills. ALS. DLC–JKP. Congratulates Polk on his victory in the presidential election.
29 Nov	*From Mary and Robert Atherton.*
29 Nov	From Daniel W. Dryden and John Baines. LS. DLC–JKP. Invite Polk to visit Xenia, Ohio, en route to his inauguration.
29 Nov	*From James Hamilton, Jr.*

29 Nov	From Charles Jarvis. ALS. DLC–JKP. Recommends Leonard Jarvis to be secretary of the navy.
[29 Nov 1844]	From Ezekiel P. McNeal. ALS. DLC–JKP. Sends Polk a check for $1000; discusses the narrow Whig victory in Tennessee.
29 Nov	From William L. Mitchell et al. L. DLC–JKP. Invite Polk to visit Athens, Ga., en route to his inauguration.
29 Nov	*From Ether Shepley.*
29 Nov	From John Tomlin. ALS. DLC–JKP. Writes on behalf of Israel K. Tefft, corresponding secretary of the Georgia Historical Society; asks for Polk's autograph.
[30 Nov 1844]	From Alvin W. Bills. ALS. DLC–JKP. Offers general advice on cabinet appointments; invites Polk to pass through Kentucky en route to his inauguration.
30 Nov	*From Edwin Croswell.*
30 Nov	From Wiley Daniel. ALS. DLC–JKP. Reports that the Democrats have skinned "the Coons" about Shelbyville, Tenn., and "have made their fur fly"; urges Polk to work for the release of Thomas W. Dorr.
30 Nov	From Patrick Davidson et al. LS. DLC–JKP. Invite Polk to visit Carlisle, Penn., en route to his inauguration.
30 Nov	From Francis Duffy. ALS. DLC–JKP. Requests that Polk support the application of Patrick Duffy for tobacco inspector.
30 Nov	From Thomas P. Moore. ALS. DLC–JKP. Discusses how he tried during the campaign to undermine the alliance between the Whigs and abolitionists in Ohio and elsewhere; notes that he sent William Allen evidence of Henry Clay's partnership with James Erwin in the slave trade.
30 Nov	From Palmer R. Phillips. ALS. DLC–JKP. Solicits a position in the federal government.
30 Nov	From Ether Shepley. ALS. DLC–JKP. Recommends John Fairfield for the cabinet position of secretary of the navy.
[Dec 1844]	From John McNeil. ALS. DLC–JKP. Praises Polk's election as a deathblow to "the many projects and schemes of Federalism."
[Dec 1844]	From John McNeil. ALS. DLC–JKP. Recommends Henry Hubbard for a position in Polk's cabinet.
[Dec 1844]	From Tilghman M. Tucker et al. NS. DLC–JKP. Recommend Romulus M. Saunders for the cabinet position of postmaster general.
1 Dec	From Nicholas D. Coleman. ALS. DLC–JKP. Inquires about the route of Polk's inaugural trip.
1 Dec	*From Cave Johnson.*
1 Dec	From Ebenezer Mayle. ALS. DLC–JKP. Describes his campaign experiences in Kentucky as a peddler of "Polk Songs, Clay Songs & Novels."

1 Dec	From Leonard H. Sims. ALS. DLC–JKP. Notes with concern rumors about Polk's intention to appoint Thomas H. Benton to the cabinet; points out that Benton has differed with Polk on the issue of Texas annexation.
2 Dec	From William J. Alexander et al. LS. DLC–JKP. Write on behalf of the Democratic Association of Mecklenburg County, N.C.; invite him to attend a public dinner in his honor.
2 Dec	*From Alfred Balch.*
2 Dec	*From John Blair.*
2 Dec	From Matthias J. Bovee. ALS. DLC–JKP. Congratulates Polk on the outcome of the election; recounts their years in Congress together; discusses Wisconsin Territory patronage questions.
2 Dec	From W. F. Boyakin. ALS. DLC–JKP. Recalls that in his 1827 congressional race Polk was dubbed "the Black Pony" by the Crockett Campbell boys because he "used to boast of his speed 'over a quarter track.'"
2 Dec	From James Connor et al. LS. DLC–JKP. Invite Polk to attend the annual ball of the Tammany Society on January 8, 1845.
2 Dec	From Samuel Hobson. ALS. DLC–JKP. Hopes that Polk will take the principles of 1798 as his textbook; predicts that Polk's great challenge will be the conflict between North and South over the tariff.
2 Dec	*From John B. Jones.*
2 Dec	From Alexander Mouton et al. LS. DLC–JKP. Invite Polk to visit New Orleans, La., en route to his inauguration.
2 Dec	From Benton Van Buren Reynolds. ALS. DLC–JKP. Asks Polk for a small donation to allow him to complete his education.
2 Dec	From William L. Rodgers. ALS. DLC–JKP. States that Lawrence Kearney, a captain in the navy, has sent him "a piece of *rich Mandarin Silk*, obtained by him in China, on his late visit there" and that Kearney wishes Sarah Polk to have the piece of goods for making her inaugural gown; inquires when he may see Polk in Philadelphia to present the gift in person.
2 Dec	*From John Staats.*
2 Dec	From J. S. Strickler. ALS. DLC–JKP. Manufactures iron chests and vault doors in "the Whig City of Pittsburgh" but is a sound Democrat; asks Polk to "throw in our Way" contracts for supplying vaults and locks to public buildings.
2 Dec	From John C. P. Tolleson. ALS. DLC–JKP. Congratulates Polk on the triumph of "the principles of Democracy"; notes that he retires this week as editor of the Helena *Arkansas Journal*.
2 Dec	*From William Tyack.*

2 Dec	From R. H. Tyler. ALS. DLC–JKP. Asks for Polk's autograph.
2 Dec	From John Williamson. ALS. DLC–JKP. Requests that Polk help him to collect his Revolutionary War pension.
3 Dec	From John Bruce et al. LS. DLC–JKP. Invite Polk to visit Winchester, Va., en route to his inauguration.
3 Dec	From A. C. Nimrod. ALS. DLC–JKP. Discusses a recent proposal to purchase 250 acres of Polk's land in Gibson County, Tenn.
3 Dec	From James B. Shepard et al. NS. DLC–JKP. Recommend Romulus M. Saunders for a cabinet position.
3 Dec	From James Webster. ALS. DLC–JKP. Encloses a copy of his *The People's Democratic Guide* and the December 2, 1844, issue of the New York *Evening Post*. (Enclosures not found.)
4 Dec	From John T. Andrews. ALS. DLC–JKP. Introduces Robert Campbell, Jr., a delegate to the Democratic National Convention at Baltimore and a fellow Democrat from Steuben County, N.Y.
4 Dec	From John M. Bell. ALS. DLC–JKP. Reports that James W. Breedlove intends to visit Polk and to pass on the congratulations of Polk's many "personal and political friends" in New Orleans, La.
4 Dec	From James W. Bradbury et al. NS. DLC–JKP. Recommend John Fairfield of Maine to be secretary of the navy.
4 Dec	From Alfred W. Cavarly et al. LS. DLC–JKP. Inform Polk that they have this day cast Illinois' electoral votes for him and congratulate him upon his election as president.
4 Dec	From Jeremiah Y. Dashiell. ALS. DLC–JKP. Looks to Sarah Polk "for a revival of the days of Mrs. Madison, in dispensing the courtesies and hospitalities of the Presidential Mansion"; states that Louisiana "wishes to be represented in your escort to the Metropolis of the Nation."
4 Dec	From John G. Getz. ALS. DLC–JKP. Wishes to present Polk with "*The Inauguration Hat*" when he arrives in Philadelphia; requests that Polk send his hat size.
4 Dec	*From J. George Harris.*
4 Dec	*From Andrew T. Judson.*
4 Dec	From Samuel H. Laughlin. ALS. Polk Memorial Association, Columbia, Tenn. Asks Polk to appoint him to "some respectable office" in one of the departments in Washington City; prefers an office with an annual income of about $2500 to $3000.
4 Dec	From James G. Read et al. NS. DLC–JKP. State that the undersigned presidential electors for Indiana have discharged their duty; urge their state's claims to furnishing one member of Polk's cabinet.
4 Dec	From Seth Salisbury et al. LS. DLC–JKP. Send Polk a copy

	of the proceedings of a Democratic mass meeting at Athens, Penn., on November 20, 1844.
4 Dec	From Samuel N. White. ALS. DLC–JKP. Recommends Isaac T. Preston for a diplomatic position.
4 Dec	From Henderson K. Yoakum et al. L. DLC–JKP. Inquire about the date of Polk's next visit to Murfreesboro, Tenn.
5 Dec	From William Anderson. AL. DLC–JKP. Encloses an article from the Washington *Madisonian*; appends a copy of John B. Jones' certificate on his behalf. (Enclosure not found.)
5 Dec	*From Aaron V. Brown.*
5 Dec	From F. Cioffi. ANS. DLC–JKP. Dedicates his "Presidents' March" to Polk and encloses a copy. (Enclosure not found.)
5 Dec	From David T. Disney et al. LS. DLC–JKP. Invite Polk to visit Columbus, Ohio, en route to his inauguration.
5 Dec	From Preston Frazer. ALS. DLC–JKP. Offers to loan Polk his copy of the laws of Texas.
5 Dec	From Timothy Gilbert. ALS. DLC–JKP. Proposes to place an Aeolian Patent Piano in the "Presidents house at Washington" on a trial basis.
[5 Dec 1844]	From Thomas E. Higgins. ALS. DLC–JKP. Describes his efforts on the behalf of the New York Democracy and the poor health of his "afflicted family"; asks Polk for a donation.
5 Dec	From George W. Jones. ALS. DLC–JKP. Advises Polk to avoid "old political hacks" and "Cliques" in his cabinet appointments; recommends James Fulton of Lincoln County, Tenn., for a cabinet position.
5 Dec	From Wilson McCandless. ALS. DLC–JKP. Encloses the Pennsylvania electors' testimonial recommending James Buchanan for secretary of state.
5 Dec	From Wilson McCandless et al. LS. DLC–JKP. Recommend James Buchanan for the cabinet post of secretary of state.
5 Dec	From Joseph Merrick et al. L. DLC–JKP. Invite Polk to visit Hagerstown, Md., en route to his inauguration.
5 Dec	From Mahlon Nailor. ALS. DLC–JKP. Claims that after he won election bets with two New Jersey Whigs, they set fire to his barn; appeals to Polk for financial assistance.
5 Dec	From John M. Niles. ALS. DLC–JKP. Recommends John Fairfield for a cabinet position.
[5 Dec 1844]	*From Francis W. Pickens.*
5 Dec	From Levi Tyler et al. NS. DLC–JKP. Invite Polk to visit Louisville, Ky., en route to his inauguration.
[6 Dec 1844]	From Anonymous. L, signed "A Looker On." DLC–JKP. Sends from New York "the enclosed remarks." (Enclosure not found.)
[6 Dec 1844]	From Robert Armstrong. ALS. DLC–JKP. Alludes to the recent Nashville procession in honor of the Whig electors and to the Boston Whigs' efforts to persuade the South Carolina

	electors to vote for John C. Calhoun.
6 Dec	From James Bailey and Samuel Bush. LS. DLC–JKP. Inform Polk of his election to honorary membership in the Union Society of Hamilton College.
6 Dec	From Levin H. Coe. AL, fragment. DNA–RG 45. Recommends Joseph S. Watkins for the position of naval agent at Memphis, Tenn.
6 Dec	*From David T. Disney.*
6 Dec	*From John C. Edwards.*
6 Dec	From Hannibal Hamlin. ALS. DLC–JKP. Encloses a letter from Nathan Clifford.
6 Dec	*From Cave Johnson.*
6 Dec	*From John Y. Mason.*
6 Dec	From Arnold Plumer. ALS. DLC–JKP. Claims that during the campaign Pennsylvania Whigs and Democrats held meetings in nearly every town, "a new mode of warfare" in the northern states; recommends James Buchanan for secretary of state.
6 Dec	From Nathan Ranney. ALS. DLC–JKP. Believes that Polk's views on the tariff and annexation ensure the popularity of his administration; sees "the extention of the area of Freedom" as a great blessing for all mankind.
6 Dec	From George W. Smith. ALS. DNA–RG 45. Requests that Polk support his application for naval agent at Memphis, Tenn.
6 Dec	*From Samuel P. Walker.*
6 Dec	From Charles A. Wickliffe. ALS. DLC–JKP. Wishes to leave Polk a free hand in the selection of his cabinet; offers his resignation as postmaster general.
7 Dec	From John Brough. ALS. DLC–JKP. Encloses a letter inviting Polk to visit Columbus, Ohio, en route to his inauguration.
7 Dec	From John F. H. Claiborne. ALS. DLC–JKP. Introduces James S. McFarlane, a physician and fellow citizen of New Orleans.
7 Dec	From Emily R. Lewis. ALS. DLC–JKP. Asks for Polk's autograph.
7 Dec	From Cullen Sawtelle. ALS. DLC–JKP. Recommends Nathan Weston for a cabinet position.
7 Dec	From Robert Wickliffe. ALS. DLC–JKP. Invites Polk to visit Lexington, Ky., en route to his inauguration; discusses the condition of the roads from Louisville to Lexington and from there through Kentucky and Ohio.
7 Dec	From Reuel Williams. ALS. DLC–JKP. Recommends Nathan Weston for the cabinet position of U.S. attorney general.
7 Dec	*To Silas Wright, Jr.*

8 Dec	From Judah Dana. ALS. DLC–JKP. Offers advice on New England candidates for a position in Polk's cabinet; recommends John Fairfield for secretary of war and Nathan Weston for U.S. attorney general.
8 Dec	From Andrew Jackson. ALS. DNA–RG 59. Introduces Jerome Bayon; encloses letters of reference regarding his application for federal office. (Enclosures not found.)
9 Dec	From Samuel Baker. ALS. DLC–JKP. Recommends Richard M. Johnson for a cabinet position; inquires about Polk's religious beliefs and his record as a slaveholder.
9 Dec	*From John O. Bradford.*
9 Dec	*From Orville T. Bradley.*
9 Dec	*From Aaron V. Brown.*
9 Dec	From Ezekiel Brown. ALS. DLC–JKP. Congratulates Polk on his election as president.
9 Dec	From William Kennon, Sr. ALS. DLC–JKP. Recommends Hugh J. Jewett for the position of solicitor of the Treasury.
9 Dec	From Wyman B. S. Moor. ALS. DLC–JKP. Recommends Nathan Weston for U.S. attorney general.
9 Dec	From William T. Willis. ALS. DLC–JKP. Inquires about the route of Polk's inaugural trip.
[10 Dec 1844]	From S. S. Austin. L. DLC–JKP. Asks on behalf of the Empire Club of New York City if Polk ever substituted for Richard M. Johnson as presiding officer of the U.S. Senate; Polk's endorsement reads, "Believed to be a Hoax or a forgery."
10 Dec	From Lewis Cass. ALS. DLC–JKP. Introduces Edward Brooks, customs collector at Detroit, Mich.
10 Dec	From Robert P. Dunlap et al. LS. DLC–JKP. Recommend John Fairfield to be secretary of the navy.
10 Dec	*From Andrew Jackson.*
10 Dec	From Andrew Jackson. ALS. DNA–RG 59. Recommends Auguste D'Avezac for a foreign mission.
10 Dec	From Howard Kennedy and Moor A. Falls. L. DLC–JKP. On behalf of the National Road Stage Company offer Polk the use of a coach to convey him and his party from Wheeling to Cumberland.
10 Dec	From Amos Lane et al. LS. DLC–JKP. Recommend Lewis Cass for secretary of state.
10 Dec	From H. H. Phelps et al. LS. DLC–JKP. Invite Polk to visit Parkersburg, Va., en route to his inauguration.
10 Dec	From Alfred Redington. ALS. DLC–JKP. Recommends Nathan Weston for the cabinet position of U.S. attorney general.
10 Dec	From Daniel Williams. ALS. DLC–JKP. Urges Polk to appoint a Maine Democrat to the cabinet; recommends Nathan Weston for U.S. attorney general.

[11 Dec 1844]	From Anonymous. L, signed "John McCalla." Recounts vignettes of the settlement of New England and curses Polk's election.
11 Dec	*From John M. Bass.*
11 Dec	From Otis L. Bridges. ALS. DLC–JKP. Recommends Nathan Weston for a position in Polk's cabinet.
11 Dec	From Miles N. Carpenter et al. LS. DLC–JKP. Invite Polk to attend a public meeting in Philadelphia, Penn., to commemorate the Battle of New Orleans.
11 Dec	From Anson G. Chandler. ALS. DLC–JKP. Recommends Nathan Weston for U.S. attorney general.
11 Dec	*From Leonard P. Cheatham.*
11 Dec	From Thomas B. Eastland. ALS. DLC–JKP. Introduces James S. McFarlane of New Orleans.
11 Dec	From Andrew Jackson. ALS. DNA–RG 59. Encloses a letter of November 14, 1844, from Martin Van Buren urging Jackson's cooperation in securing preferment for Auguste D'Avezac.
11 Dec	From Leonard Jarvis. ALS. DLC–JKP. Advises Polk to appoint David Henshaw, not John Fairfield, as secretary of the navy.
11 Dec	From Alfred Marshall. ALS. DLC–JKP. Urges Polk to appoint a Maine Democrat to the cabinet; recommends Nathan Weston for U.S. attorney general.
11 Dec	From Alexander Mouton. ALS. DLC–JKP. Introduces Felix Bosworth of Carroll Parish, La.
11 Dec	From David Tod. LS. DLC–JKP. Recommends Samuel Medary for the cabinet position of postmaster general.
[11 Dec 1844]	From Horace Warren. ALS. DLC–JKP. Introduces James S. McFarlane, a member of the committee appointed to attend Polk and invite him to visit New Orleans; notes that McFarlane will tell Polk about the Creoles' policy of political proscription in their city.
12 Dec	From John Anderson. ALS. DLC–JKP. Recommends John Fairfield to be secretary of the navy.
12 Dec	From John W. Childress. ALS. DLC–JKP. Inquires about the date of Polk's proposed visit to Murfreesboro, Tenn.
12 Dec	From George S. Hampton et al. L. DLC–JKP. Write on behalf of a Democratic mass meeting which was held in Iowa City, Iowa Territory, on December 2, 1844; congratulate Polk on his election as president.
12 Dec	*From Cave Johnson.*
12 Dec	From William Murrey. ALS. DLC–JKP. Solicits a position as porter in the Customs House of New York City.
12 Dec	From Abel C. Pepper. ALS. DLC–JKP. Encloses a letter from Indiana Democrats recommending Lewis Cass for secretary of state. (Enclosure not found.)

12 Dec	From Jacob W. Piatt. ALS. DLC–JKP. Congratulates Polk on his election as president; assures Polk that Ohio favors Texas annexation.
12 Dec	From Joel B. Sutherland. ALS. DLC–JKP. Offers advice on cabinet appointments and patronage.
12 Dec	From David D. Wagener. ALS. DLC–JKP. Advises Polk on cabinet appointments and the tariff; notes the divisions within "the Democracy of the North and Middle States" over the Texas question; warns Polk to beware of "certain Politicians in Pa."
12 Dec	From Reuben M. Whitney. ALS. DLC–JKP. Solicits a position in the federal government.
12 Dec	From Reuben M. Whitney. ALS. DLC–JKP. Recommends David Henshaw for the cabinet position of secretary of the navy.
12 Dec	From William H. Wood. ALS. DLC–JKP. Sends Polk a draft for $911.11 and sets forth terms for its repayment.
[13 Dec 1844]	From Anonymous. L, signed "Asaph." DLC–JKP. Writes from Milford, N.H., and urges Polk to emancipate his slaves on inauguration day.
13 Dec	From Madison Caruthers. ALS. DLC–JKP. Introduces James S. McFarlane.
13 Dec	From J. W. and S. T. Crenshaw. L. DLC–JKP. Offer to provide Polk with one of their best cotton gins.
13 Dec	*From Andrew Jackson.*
13 Dec	From Andrew Jackson. ALS. DNA–RG 59. Recommends Anderson Bean for the office of U.S. marshal for north Mississippi.
13 Dec	From S. B. Kingston et al. LS. DLC–JKP. Write on behalf of the Democracy of the Third Congressional District of Pennsylvania; invite Polk to attend a public festival to commemorate the Battle of New Orleans.
13 Dec	From M. B. D. Lane. ALS. DLC–JKP. Invites Polk to visit Jonesville, Va., en route to his inauguration.
13 Dec	From T. P. Minor. ALS. DLC–JKP. Hopes that Polk will accept the committee's invitation to visit New Orleans; invites Polk to stay at his house.
13 Dec	From Thomas J. Read. ALS. DLC–JKP. Recommends Joseph Cowdin of New York for a position in the federal government.
13 Dec	From William A. Scott. ALS. DLC–JKP. Congratulates Polk on his election as president; encloses a copy of "a discourse 'on the duty of Christians to pray for their Rulers."' (Enclosure not found.)
13 Dec	From Thomas Sherlock et al. LS. DLC–JKP. Invite Polk to visit Cincinnati, Ohio, en route to his inauguration.
13 Dec	From Will M. Shipp. ALS. DLC–JKP. Repeats his earlier

	request to know the first name of Polk's wife, after whom he wishes to name his infant daughter.
13 Dec	From Alden S. Stevens. ALS. DLC–JKP. Believes that since the country's safety depends upon "the intelligence of the people," education should be one of the primary concerns of government; encloses a copy of the "common school law" of Attica, N.Y. (Enclosure not found.)
13 Dec	From the Young Hickory Club of New Orleans. L, fragment. DLC–JKP. Invites Polk and Andrew Jackson to visit New Orleans en route to Polk's inauguration.
14 Dec	From Anonymous. N. DLC–JKP. Sends Polk a series of extracts commenting on free trade and tariffs; notes that the extracts are taken from a book in his possession.
14 Dec	From Hugh J. Anderson. ALS. DLC–JKP. Recommends John Fairfield to be secretary of the navy.
14 Dec	From James Bates. ALS. DLC–JKP. Congratulates Polk on his victory in the presidential election.
14 Dec	*From Aaron V. Brown.*
14 Dec	From David England et al. LS. DLC–JKP. Invite Polk to visit Steubenville, Ohio, en route to his inauguration.
14 Dec	From Thomas L. Hamer. ALS. DLC–JKP. Attributes the Whig victory in Ohio to the forged Birney letter, which "drove many Abolitionists to Mr Clay."
14 Dec	From James K. Hill. ALS. DLC–JKP. Inquires if his brother, William A. Hill, has left Columbia and gone to Texas.
14 Dec	*From Cave Johnson.*
14 Dec	From Seth W. Jones. ALS. DLC–JKP. Wishes to purchase Polk's plantation in Yalobusha County, Miss.; proposes to pay for the land in cotton.
14 Dec	From Guston Kearney. ALS. DLC–JKP. Offers general advice on appointments to federal office.
14 Dec	From William W. Lea. ALS. DLC–JKP. Discusses the proposed establishment of the *True American*, a Democratic weekly newspaper to be published by Thomas Claiborne, Jr., in Trenton, Tenn.
14 Dec	From Charles J. McDonald et al. LS. DLC–JKP. Invite Polk to visit Marietta, Ga., en route to his inauguration.
[14 Dec 1844]	From John Stapleton. ALS. DLC–JKP. Writes from Berks County, Penn.; remarks that he once knew a resident of the county who was named James Polk.
15 Dec	From Robert Armstrong. ALS. DLC–JKP. Encloses a letter from Polk's friends in New Orleans, La., in which they invite Polk to visit the city en route to his inauguration.
15 Dec	*From George M. Dallas.*
15 Dec	*From Amos David.*
15 Dec	*From J. George Harris.*
16 Dec	*From Robert Armstrong.*

16 Dec	From Julius W. Blackwell. ALS. DLC–JKP. Writes on behalf of some Georgia Democrats; urges Polk to visit the state en route to his inauguration.
16 Dec	From Shepard Cary. ALS. DLC–JKP. Encloses recommendations for the appointment of Nathan Weston to be attorney general; identifies the author of each letter, including Alfred Marshall, Wyman B. S. Moor, and Daniel Williams.
16 Dec	*To Clement C. Clay.*
16 Dec	From Stephen Emery. ALS. DLC–JKP. Recommends John Fairfield to be secretary of the navy.
16 Dec	From Robert E. Finnell. ALS. DLC–JKP. Solicits a position in the general government.
16 Dec	*From Andrew Jackson.*
16 Dec	From Rufus McIntire. ALS. DLC–JKP. Believes that of the Maine candidates for a cabinet position, John Fairfield is the one most likely to inspire confidence in Polk's administration.
17 Dec	From Daniel F. Carter. ALS. DLC–JKP. Proposes to provide Polk with a coach for his inaugural trip and to convey him and his party from Nashville, Tenn., to Louisville, Ky.
17 Dec	*From Gansevoort Melville.*
17 Dec	From James Walker. ALS. DLC–JKP. Discusses the terms on which William Wilson Polk will loan Polk $9,000.
18 Dec	From Thomas Dunn English et al. LS. DLC–JKP. Write on behalf of the White Eagle Club; invite Polk to attend a public dinner on January 8, 1845, at the Mercer House, New York City.
18 Dec	From Elijah Hise. ALS. DLC–JKP. Introduces Thomas Strange of Warren County, Ky.
18 Dec	*From Cave Johnson.*
18 Dec	From Joseph A. Linscott. ALS. DLC–JKP. Recommends Nathan Weston to be U.S. attorney general.
18 Dec	From John M. Niles. ALS. DLC–JKP. Details background of Gideon Welles, whom he recommends to be postmaster general.
18 Dec	From Samuel P. Walker. ALS. DLC–JKP. Recommends his business partner, William S. Pickett, for the office of U.S. consul at Liverpool.
[19 Dec 1844]	From Thomas Clark. ALS. DLC–JKP. Relates that Polk's slave, Blacksmith Harry of Carrollton, Miss., wishes Polk to write him by William Bobbitt; states that Harry does not wish to live with Kimbrough, who is a Whig and will not let him hear from Polk.
19 Dec	From Thomas Goin. ALS. DLC–JKP. Intends to publish a pamphlet on "Naval Schools"; asks Polk to write a letter in support of these schools.
19 Dec	From James X. McLanahan et al. LS. DLC–JKP. Invite Polk

	to visit Chambersburg, Penn., en route to his inauguration.
19 Dec	From David Myerle. ALS. DLC–JKP. Claims that at the urging of James K. Paulding, secretary of the navy in 1840, he invested $45,000 in the experimental cultivation of water-rotted hemp; believes that the general government should reimburse him for his losses.
19 Dec	From Thomas M. Ward. ALS. DLC–JKP. Introduces himself and congratulates Polk on his election as president.
20 Dec	From Michael G. Bright. ALS. DLC–JKP. Recommends James Whitcomb for a cabinet position; notes that neither Indiana nor Illinois has had a representative in the cabinet and that both states reversed huge Whig majorities in the presidential contest.
20 Dec	From Joseph W. Chalmers. ALS. DLC–JKP. Advises Polk on the appointment of the marshal of north Mississippi.
20 Dec	From W. L. Crandal. ALS. DLC–JKP. Writes on behalf of the Democracy of Onondaga County, N.Y.; urges Polk to remember in the selection of his cabinet members that he owes his nomination and election to the people, not the old "circle of personal influence."
20 Dec	From William Foster. ALS. DLC–JKP. Claims that in Massachusetts "bad appointments" by Andrew Jackson and Martin Van Buren have hurt the reputation of the Democratic party; emphasizes the need to appoint only "virtuous and enlightened men."
20 Dec	From John Hamm et al. LS. DLC–JKP. Invite Polk to visit Zanesville, Ohio, en route to his inauguration.
20 Dec	*From Adam Huntsman.*
20 Dec	*From Cave Johnson.*
20 Dec	From Samuel M. Leiper. ALS. DLC–JKP. Claims that during the campaign in Pennsylvania "the clergy almost to a man" opposed the Democrats; urges Polk to give "a decided Christian spirit" to his inaugural address.
20 Dec	*From Jesse Miller.*
20 Dec	*From Benjamin Patton.*
20 Dec	From John S. Smith. ALS. DLC–JKP. Advises Polk to replace all the Democratic officeholders in New York with "an entire new set of democrats."
20 Dec	*From Silas Wright, Jr.*
21 Dec	*From Alfred Balch.*
21 Dec	From James Bradford. ALS. DLC–JKP. Invites Polk to visit Columbus, Ohio, en route to his inauguration.
21 Dec	*To Cave Johnson.*
21 Dec	From Marcus Morton. ALS. DLC–JKP. Attributes the Whigs' domination of Massachusetts to the immorality and corruption of the Democratic officeholders there; warns Polk to beware of the "clique" of office seekers.

21 Dec	From Henry Nixdorff and William B. McLanahan. LS. DLC–JKP. Invite Polk to visit Frederick County, Md., en route to his inauguration.
22 Dec	From Richard M. Johnson. ALS. DLC–AJ. Recommends John G. Scroggin of Kentucky for the position of agent for procuring hemp for the U.S. navy.
23 Dec	From James W. Bradbury. ALS. DLC–JKP. Recommends John Fairfield for a position in Polk's cabinet; recalls the evening before the Baltimore Convention gave Polk its nomination; states that he was one of those delegates from Maine, New York, and Ohio who "determined upon concentrating the *unbroken* strength for Mr Van Buren in the Convention, upon the tried and constant friend of the venerable Jackson."
23 Dec	*From Aaron V. Brown.*
23 Dec	*From Andrew Jackson.*
23 Dec	From George F. Lehman et al. LS. DLC–JKP. Invite Polk to attend a public dinner in Philadelphia, Penn., on January 8, 1845.
23 Dec	From Peter Rawls et al. L. DLC–JKP. Write on behalf of the Democracy of the Fourth Congressional District of Penn.; invite Polk to attend a dinner to commemorate the Battle of New Orleans.
23 Dec	From J. T. Shane. ALS. DLC–JKP. Solicits a position in the general government.
23 Dec	*From Fernando Wood.*
24 Dec	From Calvin Blythe and John O. Bradford. LS. DLC–JKP. Write on behalf of the Democratic Invincible Legion of Philadelphia, Penn.; invite Polk to attend a public dinner to commemorate the Battle of New Orleans.
24 Dec	*From Andrew J. Donelson.*
24 Dec	*From J. George Harris.*
24 Dec	From John Law. ALS. DLC–JKP. Wishes to accompany Polk on his inaugural trip.
25 Dec	From Anonymous. L, signed "A true democrat." DLC–JKP. Recommends Alexander Hale of Rogersville, Tenn., for an office in the federal government.
25 Dec	From R. W. Morrison. L. DLC–JKP. Claims that he lost his position as overseer because he voted for Polk; appeals to Polk for financial assistance.
[25 Dec 1844]	*From John Pope.*
26 Dec	From James H. Cox et al. LS. DLC–JKP. Ask Polk to retain John Y. Mason as secretary of navy.
26 Dec	*From Cave Johnson.*
26 Dec	From Franklin Pierce. ALS. DLC–FP. Recommends John McNeil for an office in the federal government
27 Dec	From William Anderson. ALS. DLC–JKP. Encloses the De-

	cember 26th issue of the Washington *Madisonian*; points to his article refuting Whig charges that the English favored Polk's election. (Enclosure not found.)
27 Dec	From John D. McCrate. ALS. DLC–JKP. Recommends Joseph Hall for a federal office.
27 Dec	*From Richard Rush.*
28 Dec	From Reuben Burlingame. ALS. DLC–JKP. Congratulates Polk on his election as president.
28 Dec	From A. N. Clark et al. LS. DLC–JKP. Write on behalf of the Kensington Democracy of Philadelphia, Penn.; invite Polk to attend a public dinner to commemorate the Battle of New Orleans.
28 Dec	From R. E. Denton. ALS. DLC–JKP. Promises to become a good Democrat if Polk will give him a federal office.
28 Dec	From Robert P. Dunlap. ALS. DLC–JKP. Encloses a personal letter from James W. Bradbury.
28 Dec	From Robert P. Dunlap. ALS. DLC–JKP. Encloses a letter from James W. Bradbury and other members of the Electoral College of Maine, who recommend John Fairfield to be secretary of the navy.
28 Dec	*From Charles J. Ingersoll.*
28 Dec	From Simon P. Jordan. ALS. DLC–JKP. Asks Polk to write a letter of recommendation for William G. Canders, a Presbyterian minister in Mt. Pleasant, Tenn.
28 Dec	From John Schnierle. ALS. DLC–JKP. Invites Polk to visit Charleston, S.C., en route to his inauguration.
29 Dec	*From Aaron V. Brown.*
29 Dec	From John H. Steele and Harry Hibbard. L. DLC–JKP. Recommend Henry Hubbard for a position in Polk's cabinet.
30 Dec	*From Aaron V. Brown.*
30 Dec	*From Aaron V. Brown.*
30 Dec	From James Cone. ALS. DLC–JKP. Agrees to the proposed arrangement for settling his debts with Polk.
30 Dec	*From Robert P. Dunlap.*
30 Dec	From Gordius A. Hall et al. LS. DLC–JKP. Invite Polk to visit Zanesville, Ohio, en route to his inauguration.
30 Dec	From Gayton P. Osgood. ALS. DLC–JKP. Notes that Joseph Hall will visit Tennessee and will ask for an interview to discuss his prospects for an appointment; assures Polk that Hall's advice on appointments represents the views of a majority of Massachusetts Democrats.
30 Dec	From James Tennison. ALS. DLC–JKP. Repeats his plea for financial assistance.
31 Dec	*To Felix Bosworth et al.*
31 Dec	*From John Catron.*
[31 Dec 1844]	From A. A. Foley. ALS. DLC–JKP. Congratulates Polk on his election as president.

31 Dec	*From Charles G. Greene.*
31 Dec	From Howard Kennedy et al. LS. DLC–JKP. Invite Polk to visit Uniontown, Penn., en route to his inauguration.
31 Dec	From E. M. Patterson. ALS. DLC–JKP. Recommends William A. Murray for a clerkship in the Post Office department.
31 Dec	From William S. Pickett. LS. DLC–JKP. Reports from New Orleans that he is holding Polk's 101 bales of cotton off the market until prices steady following receipt of "the most disastrous news for the Cotton market" from Liverpool, where manufacturers are now buying on their own terms.
31 Dec	From James Robertson. ALS. DLC–JKP. Offers advice on cabinet appointments; recommends Silas Wright, Jr., for secretary of state.

INDEX